Chronology

OF WOMEN WORLDWIDE

HIGHLIGHTS

The Chronology of Women Worldwide is a reference source designed for users seeking information on important people, places, and events in the history of women from ancient times to the present. Chronologically arranged entries cover all fields of endeavor, including:

- Activism
- Administration
- Arts
- Aviation
- Business
- Cultures
- Education
- Exploration
- Government
- Health Care
- Labor
- Law
- Literature
- Medicine
- Performing Arts
- Politics
- Religion
- Sports
- Suffrage
- Science

The Chronology of Women Worldwide provides an abundance of information, and its orderly format makes it easy to use. Special features include:

- Over 30 outstanding contributors
- Foreword by JoAnne Hanley of the Women's Rights National Historical Park
- Historical Timeline
- Excerpts from significant speeches and documents
- Index by woman's name
- Index by day of the month
- Keyword index listing important events, issues, and locations
- Over 160 illustrations

Chronology

OF WOMEN WORLDWIDE

PEOPLE, PLACES
& EVENTS
THAT SHAPED
WOMEN'S HISTORY

LYNNE BRAKEMAN, EDITOR

SUSAN GALL, MANAGING EDITOR

GALE

DETROIT · NEW YORK · TORONTO · LONDON

Chronology of Women Worldwide was produced by
Eastword Publications Development, Inc., Cleveland, Ohio.

Gale Research Staff

Marie Ellavich, Rebecca Nelson, and Jessica Proctor, Project Editors; **Karen Uchic,** Assistant Editor; **Stephanie Samulski,** Editorial Assistant; **Leah Knight,** Acquisitions Editor; **Lawrence W. Baker,** Managing Editor; **Mary Beth Trimper,** Production Director; **Evi Seoud,** Assistant Production Manager; **Shanna P. Heilveil,** Production Assistant; **Cynthia Baldwin,** Production Design Manager; **Barbara J. Yarrow,** Graphic Services Manager; **Pamela A. E. Galbreath,** Cover and Page Designer.

Cover Illustrations (clockwise from left): Maria Mitchell and her class, c.1878, Special Collections, Vassar College Libraries; New York suffrage parade, 1912, Cleveland Public Library; Wilma Rudolf, 1960, UPI/Bettman.
Back Cover Illustration: Egyptian woman, Cleveland Antiquarian Books.

Library of Congress Cataloging-in-Publication Data

Chronology of women worldwide : people, places & events that shaped
 women's history / Lynne Brakeman, editor.
  p. cm.
Includes bibliographical references and index.
ISBN 0-7876-0154-3
  1. Women—History—Chronology. I. Brakeman, Lynne.
HQ1121.C617 1996
305.4'09—dc20   96-23915
   CIP

ISBN 0-7876-0154-3
Printed in the United States of America
10 9 8 7 6 5 4 3 2

EDITORIAL TEAM

Editor

Lynne Brakeman

Contributors

Anne Barker, Rochester Institute of Technology
Cynthia Bily, Adrian College
Jennifer Brantley, University of Nebraska, Lincoln
Thomas Cardoza, University of California, Santa Barbara
JoAnn Castagna, University of Iowa
Dianne Daeg de Mott
Virginia Elwood-Akers, California State University, Northridge
Susan Gall
Gala Gates, Cleveland State University
Joan Hac, University of Kentucky
Helga Harriman, Oklahoma State University
Mary Hess, Michigan State University
Kirk Hutson, Iowa State University
Linda Johnson, Concordia College
Mary Ellen Kelm, University of Northern British Columbia
Megan McClintock, University of Washington, Tacoma
Jennifer McDaid, Library of Virginia, Archives Division
Diane Menghetti, James Cook University, Townsville, Queensland, Australia
Debra Meyers
Brian Pavlac, Kings College
Ariana Ranson
Connie Reeves
Charlene Regester, Univeristy of North Carolina, Chapel Hill
Vivien Rose, Women's Rights National Historical Park
Susan Shifrin, Bryn Mawr College
Hugh Stewart
Mila Su, Pennsylvania State University, Altoona
Julie Taddeo, University of Rochester
Margaret Tennant, Massey University, Palmerston, New Zealand
Kay Vandergrift, Rutgers University
Connie Vivrett, Iowa State University
Ann Waltner, University of Minnesota
Kris Wright

ILLUSTRATION CREDITS

Many of the illustrations appearing in *Chronology of Women Worldwide* are in the public domain. Sources of other illustrations are:

Photo by Lillian Kemp, American Academy of Arts and Letters: page 416-left; AARP: page 407; © American Heart Association: pages 420, 460; APF/Bettman: page 457; AP/Wide World: pages 186, 189, 194, 218, 226, 234, 278, 290, 332, 353, 363, 369, 377-right, 391, 401, 406-left, 409, 414, 422, 423, 439, 442, 450; Architect of the U.S. Capitol: pages 166, 183, 242, 286, 341, 455; Estate of Mary Beard: page 393; The Bettmann Archive: pages 205, 206, 211, 232, 249, 323, 330, 378, 392; Camp Fire, Inc.: page 305; Photo by Sammy Still, Cherokee Nation: page 456; The Church of Jesus Christ of Latter-Day Saints: page 209; Courtesy of Cleveland Antiquarian Books: pages 23, 29, 43, 238; Photograph Collection, Cleveland Public Library: pages 289, 384, 385; Corbis-Bettmann: page 230; Corel Corporation: page 7; Courtesy Dwight D. Eisenhower Library: pages 388, 403; Courtesy Gerald R. Ford Library: page 428; Girl Scouts of the U.S.A.: pages 311, 314; International Swimming Hall of Fame: page 313; John Carroll University Archives: page 394; John F. Kennedy Library: page 413; League of Women Voters: pages 318, 325, 336; Courtesy of Lukens Steel: page 168; Yoichi R. Okamoto, LBJ Library Collection: pages 424, 425; Courtesy of the Archives and Special Collections on Women in Medicine, Medical College of Pennsylvania and Hahnemann University (MCPHU): page 198; National 4-H Council: pages 283, 324; National Library of Medicine: page 236; National Organization for Women: page 461; Courtesy of Irene Natividad: page 462; Pepperidge Farm: page 375; Ronald Reagan Library: page 449; Susan D. Rock: page 110; The Salvation Army National Archives: page 292; The Seeing Eye: page 362; State Historical Society of North Dakota: page 143; Archives of the History of American Psychology, University of Akron: page 215; UPI/Corbis-Bettmann: pages 287, 418; UPI/Bettmann: pages 204, 231, 270, 285, 291, 365, 366, 372, 377-left, 379, 383, 400, 406-right, 408, 410, 416-right, 429, 441, 443, 444; Archives, U.S. Military Institute at West Point: page 447; Special Collections, Vassar College Libraries: page 235; Women in Military Service for America Memorial Foundation, Inc.: pages 134, 386, 438, 445, 454.

TABLE OF CONTENTS

FOREWORD

WHY STUDY WOMEN'S HISTORY?

Elizabeth Cady Stanton, one of the five organizers of the first Women's Rights Convention, held in Seneca Falls, New York, knew very well the importance of understanding the past to effect change for the future. In the Declaration of Sentiments, drafted and ratified by the convention, the organizers paraphrased the Declaration of Independence and wrote "The history of mankind is a history of repeated injuries and usurpations on the part of man towards woman, having in direct object the establishment of a direct tyranny over her...." This point of view carried Stanton through a lifetime of activism for women's rights and human rights. Much of what we enjoy in the United States today is a direct result of her work.

The history we all learn in school is the story of wars and conquests, discoveries, and inventions. This can be thought of as the history of public life. There is also another history that needs to be told: the history of workers, slaves, minorities, serfs, domestic servants, and, crucially, the history of women.

The history of women is unique in one way. Women do appear throughout the narrative of the history of public life. There are great women in all areas of endeavor—queens, writers, warriors, martyrs, scientists, industrialists, land owners—whose names have become part of the permanent historical record. It is also important to mention that the history of "women" varies greatly across cultures and classes around the world. The story of aristocratic women in 18th century China is different than the story of mill workers in 18th century New England.

It behooves us to consider what core values shape the creation of historical understanding worldwide. If a *truer* story is to be told (and who can claim to be uninterested in truth), a fuller story needs to be told.

Studying the contributions of women throughout history, as this book intends to do, is an important endeavor for several reasons. It is fun to look at the past with new eyes. Including women in history gives one an entirely new perspective on what was important about the past. It shines a new light on what was presumed known. When one uses a different angle of vision, the questions and the patterns one sees in the past change. Mental barriers give way, and significant events take on new meaning. Reexamining the past can tell us new things even about what we thought we knew.

In order to make good decisions for the present and the future, we need to understand the diverse histories that are essential tools in shaping our choices today. For example, if we do not know that women have consistently worked for world peace, we may assume that war is the only option in conflict resolution, because it plays such a large role in the history we teach our children. In short, not knowing women's history hinders us as we move into the future.

THE HISTORY OF WOMEN'S HISTORY

The study of women's history has gone through roughly four stages in the last several decades. As described by Gerda Lerner in her studies of the history of western civilization, and by Linda Kerber, who advises us to assume that women have always been important players in history, they are:

1) *Behind every great man there's a great woman.*

In this stage, women are attached to great men and are considered important only as they assisted or enhanced the power of these "great men," no matter what their contributions were. Examples from U.S. history are Martha Washington, Abigail Adams, and Eleanor Roosevelt.

2) *Some women are just like men.*

On occasion, women achieve similar status to men by accomplishing extraordinary feats that mimic accomplishments of the type that normally make it into history text books. Such women are generally treated as curiosities in history books with their gender mentioned alongside their accomplishments; so that Charles Lindbergh is a "great aviator" but Amelia Earhart is a "great female aviator."

3) *Women were there but their experience was different from men's.*

This can be called "sidebar history," because women's experience is described in a little sidebar to the main text of a history book. A typical example of this type of history, would be the inclusion of a small essay about women's work in war production during World War II. Such a "sidebar" would feature a picture of women on an assembly line and mention (perhaps) that their work was crucial to the Allied victory. The length of the essay would pale, however, in comparison to the detailed battlefield and geopolitical analysis.

4) *Women's experiences are an integral part of human history.*

This stage assumes that human experience includes women, and that women's experience is equally important to men's. When this assumption is made, the research questions change and women's and men's experiences are integrated into a new history showing that women have made substantial contributions in every historical era and in every culture around the world.

Understanding women's history is essential to understanding the landscape of the past. If one thinks of history as a road through a landscape, the view is always changing. Sometimes one sees mountains, sometimes hills, sometimes rivers. Is the landscape the mountains? the rivers? the hills? No, it is all of them. Is history the story of men? of women? of children? of workers? slaves? merchants? explorers? intellectuals? No, it is the story of them all. And although no history can ever be complete, all stories need to be told as fully as they can.

Joanne M. Hanley, Superintendent
Women's Rights National Historical Park
National Park Service
U.S. Department of the Interior
Seneca Falls, New York
U.S.A

PREFACE

The Chronology of Women Worldwide presents a comprehensive account of historical and cultural events involving women from all cultures throughout history. Over thirty scholars, each with a particular focus in women's history, have contributed to the hundreds of entries that comprise the work. Notable are the entries on Asian and Australian women, providing insight about women's lives in cultures that are relatively uncharted in widely available reference works.

Divided into 25 chapters, *The Chronology of Women Worldwide* proceeds from ancient times to 1996. Illustrations and expanded biographical information accompany selected entries throughout. The first section of the backmatter, "Myths and Legends," presents stories about women from a range of world cultures. Although not designed to be comprehensive, it provides the reader with a perspective on the status of women in legends around the world. In "Documents of History," readers can view excerpts from the historical record of women's struggle for rights, access, and recognition.

Special indexes—by woman's name, and by day of the month—enable users to access the material presented from two different vantage points. The general subject index covers issues, locations, and events of significance, from abortion to Zimbabwe.

In this first edition, omissions and oversights are inevitable; we invite readers' suggestions for additions and amplifications to be included in future editions.

We express our deepest gratitude to all those who stepped forward to share their knowledge or to provide their support. The staff at Gale Research—beginning with Christine Nasso and Leah Knight; progressing with Larry Baker, Rebecca Nelson, Marie Ellavich, Jessica Proctor, and Pamela Galbreath; and culminating with Shanna Heilveil and Evi Seoud—managed the project with competence and diligence. The advisors and contributors gave the book its heart and soul. And the staff at Eastword Publications Development—notably Debby Baron, Brian Rajewski, and Deb Rutti—pulled all the elements together to produce the final volume.

SUGGESTIONS ARE WELCOME

A work the size of *The Chronology of Women Worldwide* may contain oversights and errors, and we appreciate any suggestions for correction of factual material or additions that will enhance future editions. Please send comments to:

Editor
The Chronology of Women Worldwide
Gale Research
835 Penobscot Bldg.
Detroit, MI 48226
(313) 961-2242

Lynne Brakeman
Susan Gall
July 1996

Historical Timeline

40,000 B.C. Modern *Homo Sapiens* well-established in Europe.

25,000 B.C. Earliest known oil lamps in France.

24,000 B.C. Sculptured clay figurines in Europe.

11,000 B.C. Small bands of hunters make their way across the Bering Sea Land Bridge from Siberia.

10,000 B.C. Bow and arrow in use in Europe (earliest known use).

9000 B.C. Jericho established; among earliest known towns.

9000 B.C. Earliest fired pottery in Japan (Jomon period).

8500 B.C. Sheep are domesticated in Near East.

8350 B.C. Cold-hammered copper in use in Turkey.

7000 B.C. Copper-casting in Near East.

3000 B.C. Oldest pottery in New World, Colombia.

3000 B.C. First bronze artifacts in Middle East.

2570 B.C. Queen Nefertari rules in Egypt, calling herself "God's wife."

2500 B.C. Pyramid construction begins in Egypt.

2500 B.C. Beginnings of Indus River civilization in India.

1490 B.C. Queen Hatsheput rules in Egypt, claiming rights of pharaoh.

1360 B.C. Queen Nefertiti rules in Egypt.

40,000 B.C. Modern *Homo sapiens* well established in Europe.	24,000 B.C. Sculptured clay figurines in Europe.	9000 B.C. Jericho established; among earliest known towns.

| 50,000 B.C. | 30,000 | 10,000 | 5,000 |

1200 B.C. Fu Hao, woman warrior in China, leads military expeditions.

1180 B.C. Spartan Queen Helen kidnapped by Paris.

1150 B.C. Deborah leads Israel in victory over the invading Canaanites.

C. 1000 B.C. First extensive use of wool clothing (Scandinavia).

1000 B.C. Earliest rotary hand mills for grain in Middle East.

776 B.C. First recorded Olympiad in Greece.

750 B.C. Assyrian Empire establishes world's first highway system.

C. 625 B.C. Spartan woman are the most independent of all in the ancient world; Sappho, Greek poetess, flourishes on the island of Lesbos.

563 B.C. Beginning of Buddhism in India.

C. 400 B.C. Peak of classical Greece.

C. 400 B.C. Democritus introduces concept of atom.

250 B.C. Cultivation of locally domesticated plants begins in present-day northeastern United States.

C. 240 B.C. Initial phases of construction of Great Wall of China.

226 B.C. Colossus of Rhodes destroyed by earthquake.

51 B.C. Cleopatra VII is queen of Egypt.

C. 30 A.D. Crucifixion of Jesus of Nazareth; Christian faith established.

64 A.D. Burning of Rome.

267 A.D. Queen Zenobia leads independence movement for Palmyra (present-day Syria).

330 A.D. Constantinople founded at Byzantium.

C. 400 A.D. Invention of stern post rudder in northern Europe.

C. 570 A.D. Muhammad, founder of Islam, is born.

592 A.D. Empress Gemmei orders the writing of the *Kojiki*, first national history of Japan.

700 A.D. *Beowulf* written in northern Europe.

700 A.D. Polynesian Triangle (Hawaii, Easter Island, New Zealand) now settled.

725 A.D. Earliest known mechanical clock.

C. 800 A.D. First porcelain produced in China.

800 A.D. Charlemagne, king of Franks, proclaimed Holy Roman Emperor by pope.

900 A.D. Agriculture is commonly practiced in most areas. Maize becomes a major crop.

910 A.D. First paper currency (China).

969 A.D. Cairo, Egypt, founded.

1000 B.C.
First extensive
use of wool
clothing.

30 A.D.
Crucifixion of Jesus
of Nazareth;
Christian faith
established.

800 A.D.
Charlemagne, king
of Franks,
proclaimed Holy
Roman Emperor
by pope.

3,000   1,000   100 A.D.   1000

C. 1000 A.D. Arabic numerals begin to replace Roman numerals in Europe.

C. 1000 A.D. Japanese author Murasaki Shikibu writes *The Tale of Genji*, generally considered the world's first novel.

1138 Byzantine princess Anna Comnena, early woman historian, writes the *Alexiad*, a 15-volume historical work.

1157 Hojo Masako is influential woman in medieval Japan.

1174 Eleanor of Aquitaine is influential woman in twelfth century Europe.

1215 Magna Carta limits royal power in England.

C. 1250 Earliest development of cannons in Europe.

C. 1300 Invention of spinning wheel.

C. 1300 Beginning of Renaissance in Italy.

1342 Chinese Empress Ma is born.

C. 1350 Cast-metal type developed in Korea.

1431 Joan of Arc burned at the stake.

1470 Queen Isabella creates unified Spain with her husband Ferdinand.

1492 Queen Isabella approves the expedition to America led by Christopher Columbus; they touch ground in the Bahamas.

1497 Vasco da Gama rounds the Cape of Good Hope.

C. 1500 Beginnings of empirical science in Europe.

C. 1503 Leonardo da Vinci paints the *Mona Lisa*.

1507 German mapmaker Martin Waldseemüller, after reading Amerigo Vespucci's descriptions of the New World, names it America after him.

1512 Michelangelo completes painting of the Sistine chapel ceiling.

1513 Juan Ponce de León discovers Florida. Vasco Nuñez de Balboa crosses Panama and sights the Pacific Ocean.

1517 Protestant Reformation begins when Martin Luther posts his "Ninety-Five Theses" on Nurenberg, Germany, church door.

1519 Hernán Cortéz lands in Mexico.

1520 First circumnavigation of globe by Ferdinand Magellan's crew.

1521 Maria von Habsburg becomes queen of Hungary and Bohemia.

1525 Martin Luther translates Bible into German; Luther marries former nun Katherine von Bora.

1536 John Calvin publishes the *Institutes of the Christian Religion*.

1215
Magna Carta
limits royal power
in England.

c. 1300
Beginning of
Renaissance
in Italy.

1100	1200	1300	1400

1541   Coronado discovers Mississippi River.

1542   Portuguese traders reach Japan.

1542   Copernicus formulates theory of sun-centered solar system.

1553   Queen Mary I tries to reestablish Roman Catholicism in England.

1584   Sir Walter Raleigh discovers Roanoke Island and names land Virginia, after Queen Elizabeth.

1587   Mary, Queen of Scots is executed.

1597   Shakespeare's *Romeo and Juliet*.

1605   Cervantes' *Don Quixote*.

1607   Jamestown, Virginia, the first English colony in the New World, is founded.

1609   Galileo builds first effective telescope.

1618   Thirty Years' War.

1620   Pilgrims and others arrive in Plymouth, Massachusetts, aboard the *Mayflower*.

1630   Taj Mahal is constructed in Agra, India, as a memorial to emperor Shah Jahan's favorite wife, Mumataz Mahal.

1642   Pascal builds early mechanical calculating device.

c. 1648   Margaret Brent of Maryland is first American woman to demand right to vote.

1654   Antoni van Leeuwenhoek invents microscope.

1655   Lady Deborah Moody of Long Island becomes first American woman to vote.

1665   Great plague in London kills 68,000 people.

1665   First microscope-based description of living cells (Hooks).

1670   Newton develops the principles of calculus.

1687   Newton formulates law of gravity.

1688   Aphra Behn's novel *Oroonoko* published.

1700   Rise of modern national states in Europe.

1702   Queen Anne's War.

1717   Halley shows that solar system moves through space.

1729   J. S. Bach's *St. Matthew Passion*.

c. 1738   Eliza Lucas Pinckney, first woman agriculturist in America, develops cultivation of indigo in South Carolina.

c. 1750   Beginning of the Industrial Revolution.

1752   Benjamin Franklin proves lightning is electrical; develops lightning rod.

1762   Catherine the Great becomes empress of Russia.

1542
Copernicus
formulates theory
of sun-centered
solar system.

1620
Pilgrims and others
arrive in Plymouth,
Massachusetts,
aboard the
Mayflower.

c. 1750
Beginning of the
Industrial
Revolution.

| 1500 | 1600 | 1700 | 1750 |

1765 Scottish inventor James Watt develops first efficient steam engine.

1769 Spinning machine patented.

1774 Marie Antoinette becomes queen of France.

1776 The American Revolution.

1781 Immanuel Kant's *Critique of Pure Reason* published.

1782 England recognizes United States independence.

1787 Convention in Philadelphia writes United States Constitution.

1787 Mozart's *Don Giovanni*.

1788 United States Constitution ratified and takes effect.

1789 French Revolution begins.

1789 First United States presidential election results in victory for George Washington.

1792 Mary Wollstonecraft's *A Vindication of the Rights of Woman* is published.

1793 Eli Whitney invents cotton gin.

1804 Napoleon crowns himself emperor.

1808 Beethoven's *Fifth* and *Sixth Symphonies* performed.

1813 Jane Austen's novel *Pride and Prejudice* is published.

1833 Oberlin College (Ohio) becomes first coed college in U.S.

1835 Morse invents the telegraph.

1840s Dorothea Dix lobbies for reform in treatment of mental illness in the United States.

1842 Edgar Allan Poe writes his poem, "The Raven."

1846 Potato famine in Ireland.

1848 California Gold Rush.

1848 *Communist Manifesto* (Marx and Engels) published.

1848 Women's Rights Convention in Seneca Falls, New York. It produces the Declaration of Sentiments, patterned after the Declaration of Independence, calling for equal rights for women.

1849 Elizabeth Blackwell becomes first American woman to receive medical degree.

1850 World population reaches one billion.

1850 Elizabeth Barrett Browning's *Sonnets from the Portuguese* published.

1851 Taipei Revolution in China.

1852 Harriet Beecher Stowe's *Uncle Tom's Cabin* is published.

1854–60 Susan B. Anthony crusades for women's rights.

1789
French Revolution
begins.

1835
Morse invents
the telegraph.

1850
World population
reaches
one billion.

| 1775 | 1800 | 1825 | 1850 |

1856 Sewing machine invented.

1859 *On the Origin of Species* published by Charles Darwin.

1860 Charles Dickens publishes *Great Expectations*.

1860 Florence Nightingale publishes *Notes on Nursing*, the first textbook for nurses.

1861 First transcontinental telegraph line.

1861–65 American Civil War.

1865 The first volume of Tolstoy's *War and Peace* is published.

1869 Transcontinental railroad completed in United States.

1869 National Woman Suffrage Association and American Woman Suffrage Association formed in the United States.

1869 John Stuart Mill publishes *The Subjection of Women*.

1874 Sophia Jex-Blake establishes the London School of Medicine for Women.

1874 Women's Christian Temperance Union founded to fight alcohol abuse in the United States.

1876 Alexander Graham Bell invents the telephone.

1879 Belva Ann Lockwood becomes the first woman lawyer to practice before the U.S. Supreme Court.

1882 American Red Cross is founded by Clara Barton.

1883 Cosima Wagner, wife of composer Richard Wagner and daughter of Franz Liszt, becomes director of Bayreuth (Music) Festival in Germany.

1885 Friedrich Nietzsche publishes *Beyond Good and Evil*.

1890 Wounded Knee massacre.

1893 New Zealand becomes the first nation to grant women the right to vote.

1893 Mary Cassatt paints *The Boating Party*.

1895 Discovery of X-rays by Abraham Roentgen.

1898 Spanish-American War.

1900 Sigmund Freud publishes *The Interpretation of Dreams*.

1901 First trans-Atlantic radio transmission.

1902 Australian women get the right to vote in all federal elections. Vida Goldstein runs for the senate there, becoming the first woman in the British Empire to run for a national office.

1903 Orville and Wilbur Wright brothers fly first successful heavier-than-air aircraft.

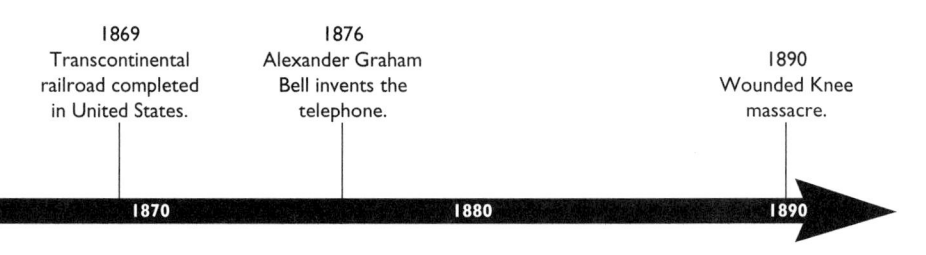

1869
Transcontinental railroad completed in United States.

1876
Alexander Graham Bell invents the telephone.

1890
Wounded Knee massacre.

1860   1870   1880   1890

1903 Marie Curie is awarded Nobel Prize for Physics for discovery of radioactivity.

1907 Chinese feminist and radical Qiu Jin is assassinated.

1909 North Pole reached by Peary and Henson.

1910 First Mother's Day celebrated in West Virginia.

1911 First transcontinental flight.

1911 Marie Curie is awarded second Nobel Prize for Chemistry for her discovery and isolation of pure radium.

1913 Willa Cather publishes *O Pioneers*.

1913 Stravinsky's *The Rite of Spring*.

1915 Liner *Lusitania* is sunk by German U-boat.

1915 Albert Einstein's *General Theory of Relativity*.

1916 Margaret Sanger opens first birth control clinic.

1917 Russian Revolution; Soviet women get the vote.

1918 Canadian women get the vote.

1919 Treaty of Versailles ends WWI.

1920 League of Nations is established.

1920 With the passage of the Nineteenth Amendment to the U. S. Constitution, American women get the vote.

1921 Chinese Communist Party founded. Jinhyu Xiang, Chinese feminist revolutionary, is cofounder.

1922 U.S.S.R. is established.

1922 James Joyce's *Ulysses* published.

1924 Stalin seizes power in Soviet Union.

1924 Ichikawa Fusae organizes *Fusen Kakutoku Domei* (Women's Suffrage League) in Japan.

1925 Nellie Tayloe Ross is elected first woman governor in U.S. (Wyoming).

1927 Virginia Woolf publishes *To the Lighthouse*.

1928 Margaret Mead publishes *Coming of Age in Samoa*.

1928 Age of suffrage is lowered from 30 to 21 in Great Britain.

1929 Collapse of stock market in the United States triggers world depression.

1930 World population reaches two billion.

1930 Kubushiro Ochimi organizes *Zen Nihon Fusen Taikai* (All-Japan Women's Suffrage Conference).

1931 Margaret Sanger publishes *My Fight for Birth Control*.

	1911 First transcontinental flight.	1917 Russian Revolution; Soviet women get the vote.	1929 Collapse of stock market in the United States triggers world depression.	
1900	1910	1920		1930

1932 Amelia Earhart becomes the first woman to fly across the Atlantic alone.

1933 Frances Perkins becomes Secretary of Labor, first woman cabinet member in U.S. history.

1934 Hitler assumes power in Germany.

1939 World War II begins in Europe.

1942 Atomic age begins with first controlled atomic chain reaction.

1945 World War II ends.

1946 Winston Churchill's "Iron Curtain" speech.

1947 Radiocarbon (carbon-14) dating developed by Willard Libby.

1947 British India partitioned into independent nations of India and Pakistan.

1948 United Nations establishes State of Israel.

1949 Communists establish People's Republic of China; women get the vote.

1949 Simone de Beauvoir publishes *The Second Sex*.

1950 In India, women over 21 get to vote.

1950 North Korean Communist forces invade South Korea.

1953 Mexican women get the vote.

1954 *Brown* v. *Board of Education*.

1957 Soviet satellite *Sputnik* is launched.

1962 Rachel Carson publishes *Silent Spring*.

1962 John Glenn is first American to orbit Earth.

1963 Valentina Vladimirovna Nikolayeva Tereshkova becomes first woman in space.

1963 Betty Friedan publishes *The Feminine Mystique*.

1966 National Organization for Women (NOW) is founded in the United States.

1966 Indira Gandhi becomes prime minister of India.

1967 The Beatles release *Sgt. Pepper's Lonely Hearts Club Band*.

1967 World's first successful human heart transplant.

1968 Dr. Martin Luther King, Jr., is assassinated.

1969 American astronaut Neil Armstrong becomes first person to set foot on the moon.

1969 Golda Meir becomes prime minister of Israel.

1969 Maya Angelou publishes *I Know Why the Caged Bird Sings*.

1970 First "Earth Day."

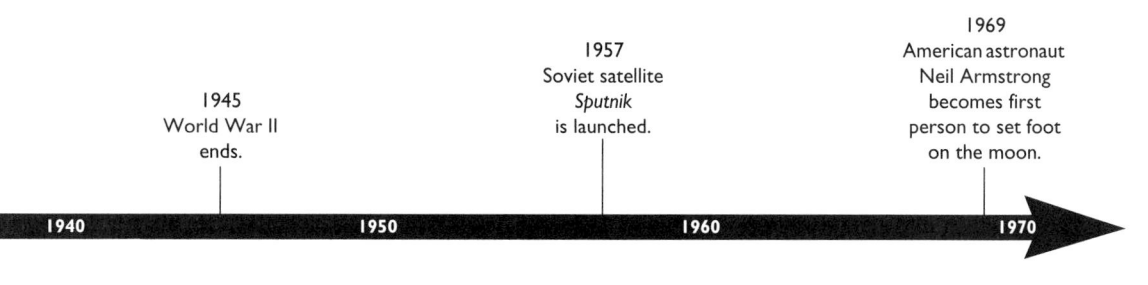

1945
World War II
ends.

1957
Soviet satellite
Sputnik
is launched.

1969
American astronaut
Neil Armstrong
becomes first
person to set foot
on the moon.

1940   1950   1960   1970

1973 *Roe* v. *Wade*

1976 World population reaches four billion.

1977 Smallpox eradicated.

1979 Margaret Thatcher elected first woman prime minister of Great Britain.

1979 Nuclear power plant accident at Three Mile Island in Pennsylvania.

1980 Mount St. Helens erupts in Washington state.

1981 Sandra Day O'Connor appointed first woman U.S. Supreme Court justice.

1983 Sally Ride becomes the first American woman in space.

1984 Geraldine Ferraro becomes first woman vice-presidential nominee of a major U.S. political party.

1984 Kathryn Sullivan is first U.S. woman astronaut to walk in space.

1986 Major nuclear power plant accident at Chernobyl in the Soviet Union.

1986 Corazon Aquino elected president of Philippines.

1988 Benazir Bhutto sworn in as prime minister of Pakistan

1989 Exxon supertanker *Valdez* runs aground in Alaska.

1989 Opening of Berlin Wall signifies end to the Cold War.

1989 Tiannanmen Square massacre in Beijing.

1989 Victoria Murden and Shirley Metz (American) become the first women to reach the South Pole overland.

1993 Janet Reno named first U.S. attorney general.

1994 United Nations Fourth World Conference on Women is held in Beijing, China.

1989
Opening of Berlin
Wall signifies end to
the Cold War.

1976
World population
reaches four billion.

| 1975 | 1980 | 1985 | 1990 | 1995 |

Part 1

THE ANCIENT WORLD
3500 B.C. – 499 A.D.

Chapter 1

3500 B.C. TO 14 B.C.

3500–2000 B.C.

C. 3500 B.C. Pelasgians Reach Greece and Believe Eurynome Created the Universe. The most ancient inhabitants of Greece, the Pelasgians, are thought to have reached Greece from the area of Israel around 3500 B.C. They believe that the world was created by a goddess, Eurynome, the Goddess of All Things, who rose from the waters of Chaos but couldn't find any substantial place to set her feet. She divided Chaos into sky and sea and danced upon its waves. The north wind created by her dance turned into the great serpent, Ophion, which coiled about her limbs while she danced and impregnated her. Eurynome assumed the form of a dove and laid the Universal Egg upon the waves. Ophion coiled seven times around the egg until it hatched in two. Out of the egg tumbled all the multitude of things of the universe: sun, moon, planets, stars, the earth, mountains, rivers, trees, and living creatures. The divine couple made their home on Mount Olympus. Eventually, Ophion claimed to be the author of the Universe, whereupon Eurynome beat him and banished him to dark caves in the earth below.

Eurynome created a Titan and Titaness for each of the seven planetary powers: sun, moon, and the planets now called Mars, Mercury, Jupiter, Venus, and Saturn. The first human, Pelasgus, sprang from the soil of Arcadia (a region of Greece). He taught the other humans who also were born of the soil to make huts and collect acorns for food.

The ancient Greek epic poet, Homer, recounts a version of this same myth, calling the goddess who ruled the seas Tethys and her spouse who encircled the Universe, Oceanus.

C. 3100 B.C. A Stable Society. During the Archaic Period of ancient Egypt (c.3100 to 2680 B.C.), advances in shipbuilding allow the Egyptians to trade with people as far away as Phoenecia in what is called the Middle East today. During this period, the basic mythologies of the Egyptian people and the structure of their society are solidified and will vary little in their essence for nearly 3,000 years. In the Third Dynasty, the ruler Djoser builds the first of the great Egyptian stone monuments, the Step Pyramid at Saqqara. The ruler Sneferu constructs a pyramid at Maidum.

C. 3000 B.C. Fertility Deities Worshipped in China. The most striking images available of Chinese women in the Neolithic period are clay statues unearthed in the Liaoning province in north China, dating from about 3000 B.C. Some of them are large breasted, and one particularly striking life-size clay image has eyes of inlaid jade. These images are probably fertility deities, worshipped by the ancient Chinese to guarantee the fertility of both the people and the land.

C. 3000 B.C.   Lower and Upper Egypt Before Recorded History. In the time before recorded history begins, Lower Egypt is essentially the region of the Nile delta and immediately to the south. Upper Egypt is the region along the Nile south to about the first cataract (present day Aswan). These two countries are united around 3000 B.C. by the Pharaoh Menes, who governs the country from Memphis (near present-day Cairo). For nearly 500 years, the Pharaohs of the Early Dynastic Period lay the foundation for a culture, a religion, and a way of life that is to endure nearly 3,500 years.

C. 2680–1000 B.C.   Style of Clothing in Egypt. From the Fourth to the Eighteenth Dynasty in Egypt (c.2680 to 1305 B.C.), both peasant women and princesses wear the same kind of garment. It is a narrow sheath of linen without folds that falls to the ankles. It is held in place by two braces which pass over the shoulders. Pictures in the tombs show this garment to be either white, yellow, or red. Noble women may have merely some fine embroidery at the upper hem. A few statues show women wearing a dress with long sleeves and a deep v-neck.

During the Middle Kingdom (c.2000 to 1786 B.C.), women wear a narrow dress which covers the breasts and leaves the right shoulder free. This is further covered by a cloak clasped in front of the breast. Both garments are of very fine, transparent linen.

By the Eighteenth Dynasty (c.1570 to 1305 B.C.), the cloak may sometimes be let loose to fall over the arms, and a short sleeve is added for the left arm only. The right arm remains free. By the close of the Twentieth Dynasty (c.1085 B.C.), a thick undergarment appears under the two transparent overgarments.

Women of the lower classes wear garments very similar to their mistresses. However, the tight sheath dress does not allow them to move freely. For active work, women servants wear the same costume as men, a short skirt that leaves the upper body and legs free. In the New Kingdom (c.1570 to 1085 B.C.), young slaves serving lords and ladies at a feast wear only an embroidered belt with a leather thong that passes between their legs.

Men and women of the upper classes wear elaborate, heavy wigs while the lower classes let their hair grow long. Fashions in wigs vary widely over the centuries, unlike fashion for women's clothes.

Under the Old and Middle Empires, women always go barefoot. Men probably wear sandals only when going out of the house. Men and women of all periods wear embroidered necklets and bracelets on their wrists and upper arms. Women also wear anklets. Earrings appear under the New Empire, probably introduced by foreign influences.

Only the queen appears to wear a special vulture headdress. Ordinary women wear only a wreath or colored ribbon in their hair on special occasions.

Women are never seen carrying the various symbols of office bestowed on men, such as walking sticks and staffs.

Cosmetics and makeup are a very important part of Egyptian life (and death). In fact, part of the art of medicine involves prescriptions for cosmetics and perfume. The dark lines around the eyes are drawn with the mascara-like *kohl*. Kohl is still widely in use in the Middle East and India. Rouge, bodypainting, and tattoos are also used to beautify the body. Oil is an important luxury item. Anointing the head with cooling oil is a way to honor guests at a feast. Oil is a symbolic emblem of joy. When the king's procession passes the common people on festival day, they pour sweet oil on their heads.

C. 2680 B.C. Women Musicians and Dancers Common. Illustrations in tombs and monuments make it clear that women dancers and musicians are common in Ancient Egypt. One Old Kingdom (c.2680–2258 B.C.) tomb shows

Sistrum

that the women of a wealthy household entertain their husbands and fathers with music. In fact, some women are named as overseers of musical troupes during the Old Kingdom. By the Middle Kingdom (c.2000–1786 B.C.), overseeing is done by men only. However, men and women perform together.

Illustrations of religious processions show women musicians carrying the loop sistrum, a rattle sacred to the goddess Hathor. A shrine erected by Queen Hatshepsut shows a male harpist singing a hymn, while acrobatic men and women dancers do back-bends or energetically dance. In the same scene, other women shake their sistra and sing.

C. 2680 B.C. Priestesses Important in Religious and Political Life. The title "priestess of Hathor" is common among high-class women of the Old Kingdom (c.2680–2258 B.C.) and the Middle Kingdom (c.2000–1786 B.C.) in Egypt. Occasionally there is reference to priestesses of the goddess Neith. There are rarely references to a priestess of a male god.

However, even in the temples of Hathor, only male priests read out loud from scriptures. It is not known if this is because all women of ancient Egypt are illiterate, or because it is considered improper for a woman to read aloud in public.

In the Eighteenth Dynasty (c.1570–1305 B.C.), another priestly title for women is "divine adoratrice." This title is held by the daughter of the Chief Priest of the Theban god Amun during the reign of Queen Hatshepsut. Later, it becomes associated with the king's principal wife, who is also called "god's wife of Amun." This becomes a powerful position in Thebes in Late Dynastic Egypt, both religiously and politically. Eventually, the "god's wife of Amun" will be a celibate daughter of the reigning king. By the Twenty-third Dynasty, this priestess will adopt the daughter of another king and thereby peacefully transfer the allegiance of Thebes to the new king. The priestess' position comes with much wealth, property, and land. However, her property is administered by male stewards.

Scenes depicting the god's wife are typical of kingly iconography. She is shown adoring the god and performing the same rituals a king might perform. In addition, deities are shown purifying her, crowning her and embracing her. One of her functions is to play her sistrum before the god to appease his anger. This act also ensures the continuing fertility of the universe.

Depictions of the "god's wife of Amun" are found only in Thebes. Such powerful female figures do not occur anywhere else in ancient Egypt.

C. 2680 B.C. Women Have Legal Rights. Legal documents from the Old Kingdom (c.2680–2258 B.C.) show that male officials of the upper class can inherit property from their mothers. Similarly, wives can inherit property from their husbands. In a Middle Kingdom (c.2000–1786 B.C.) document, a man and his daughter are having a legal dispute about the ownership of some property. This particular record indicates that a woman can initiate a lawsuit on her own behalf. Other records reveal that women can make wills and decide for themselves how their property will be distributed after their death.

Records also show that women can own slaves, rent property, and sell goods (often textiles that they may have woven). Although there is no money by modern definition, barter and the time-sharing of slave labor are common forms of exchange. One inscription reveals that a woman owns rights to the work of ten slaves for a certain number of days. Another record indicates that a woman has purchased some items for a down payment of garments and vegetables, but owes the rest. This woman obviously is considered creditworthy.

C. 2680 B.C. Grinding Wheat into Flour. According to archaeological evidence, homes in the communities of Amarna and Deir el-Medina are equipped with mortars where wheat is ground into flour. Water and other ingredients are added and the bread is kneaded. Then it is baked in special ovens at the back of the house or on the roof.

These cities are state-supported communities of workers who are employed building the great monuments for the Pharaohs. The workers are government employees whose special status means that they are allotted female slaves, apparently with the sole purpose of grinding grain and making bread for them. Each household is allotted so many days' work from one of these slaves.

In models and tomb scenes from wealthy owners, men are usually depicted brewing beer, which is the staple beverage of ancient Egypt. However, a story called the *Eloquent Peasant* has a peasant telling his wife to measure out barley and brew beer. In households that do not have many servants, making beer probably falls to the women of the household.

C. 2680 B.C. Hieroglyphs Feature Girls. Various stone reliefs and hieroglyphs dated to the Old Kingdom of Egypt (c.2680 to 2258 B.C.) are identified as girls swimming, playing games, and dancing.

C. 2680 B.C. Conception, Contraception, and Childbirth in Egypt. Although some myths and folktales of ancient Egypt give biologically impossible accounts about conception, according to inscriptions in Old Kingdom (c.2680 to 2258 B.C.) Pyramid texts, the Egyptians understand that sexual coitus leads to pregnancy. One inscription describes the conception of the god Horus: "Your sister Isis comes to you [Osiris] rejoicing for love of you. You have placed her on your phallus and your seed issues forth into her..."

Sterility is a source of shame and remedies include placing dates in the vagina, massaging the thighs and stomach with menstrual blood, and praying to the gods.

Various magico-medical tests to determine pregnancy also exist. In one pregnancy test, a woman urinates on grains of barley and wheat every day. If the barley sprouts first, she is supposed to have a boy, but if the wheat sprouts, the baby will be a girl.

Some medical texts deal with contraception. Some methods appear superstitious today, but others deal with inserting medications into the vagina, so they may have been effective. Induced abortions are illegal in the Old Kingdom.

The one female deity ever shown pregnant is the hippopotamus goddess, Taweret, the protector of pregnant women. She has the limbs of a lion, the tail of a crocodile, and human breasts.

One type of vessel that has been found is made in the shape of a pregnant woman. The figure stands or squats and has her hands placed on her abdomen, as if rubbing it. The vessels may have contained oil to massage the skin of pregnant women.

Egyptian women bear their first child usually between the ages of 12 and 15. Over her life, an Egyptian woman may have as many as five children, perhaps more. Birth takes place in a special bower with the assistance of midwives. The new mother gives birth squatting on two bricks.

Upper-class women have access to wet nurses, who can become extremely influential at court. A nurse's name or portrait often

The Great Pyramids

appears on a child's tomb, alongside those of parents and spouses.

2680 B.C. The Great Pyramids of Egypt at Giza Are Built. During the Old Kingdom (c.2680 to 2258 B.C.), the "Great Pyramids" of Egypt are built at Giza. Monumental Obelisk temples to the sun and the Pyramid of Unis are built at Saqqara. These are possible due to a system of conscripted labor by which common people come to work part of the year for the state. The Egyptians have tools and weapons of copper. There is no money. Instead, people barter services and goods for the things they need. The royal solar cult becomes predominant, and the pharaoh becomes identified with the god of the sun.

C. 2600 B.C. Pharaohs and Queens in Egypt. An Egyptian pharaoh ascends to his throne with one of his half-sisters as his queen. Only rarely does he take two wives. Very little is known about a queen's life, since all the inscriptions that have come down describe her in her formal role. She is of equal birth with the pharaoh and is given a share in all honors. In the Old Kingdom (c.2680 to 2258 B.C.) the queen is called: "She who sees the gods Horus and Set," "the most pleasant, the highly praised, the friend of Horus, the beloved of him who wears the two diadems." Under the New Kingdom (c.1570 to 1085 B.C.) she is called: "The Consort of the god, the mother of the god, the great consort of the King."

After the death of her husband, the queen continues to play an official role as royal mother of his successor. She has her own property and is sometimes the recipient of divine honors.

Besides the queen, the pharaohs maintain a harem of women who are called "the secluded." They are not allowed to interact with the outside world and are supervised by a matron, a governor, and a scribe, all high court positions. The secluded are sometimes Egyptian, sometimes foreign slaves, and sometimes gifts from the royal families of other potentates. King Amenhotep III received a gift of one royal princess and 317 maidens ("the choicest of the secluded") from a prince of Naharina. Although not much is known about their lives, it is known that their purpose is to give the pharaoh pleasure and that some of them are musicians.

The harem is not the sole province of the pharaoh. Rich officials of the court have left pictures in their tombs showing the women of their harems singing and dancing before their masters. The tomb of a priest of the Eighteenth Dynasty (c.1570 to 1305 B.C.) called 'Ey contains a diagram of his home, including two back-to-back buildings separated by a small garden. These are the women's apartments, where the women and children live. The pictures show women eating, dancing, playing music, or dressing each other's hair. The storerooms to the rear seem to be full of musical instruments, mirrors, and boxes for clothes.

Both men and women dancers are always present at funerary feasts, both wearing only the traditional short skirt or a fringed girdle. Balls are often used by women in these dances which are, at first, quiet and measured. In later centuries, the dance evolves in a direction more like the middle eastern dancing that comes to mind today. Girls dressed in transparent clothes carry tambourines or castanets and bend their bodies seductively. Dancers from the early dynasties perform stately unison dances.

Under the Old Empire, only men play instruments and sing. Women dance, or sing without accompaniment. Under the New Kingdom, illustrations of women and men singing together with instruments like the harp, lute, and flute are seen.

During these entertainments, it is customary for the noblewomen to amuse themselves by adorning and anointing each other's wigs. They pass each other lotus flowers to smell and admire each other's jewelry.

C. 2400 B.C. Mothers Figure Prominently. To marry in ancient Egypt is known as "to found for oneself a house." In later times, it is customary to call the first year of marriage "the year of eating," a kind of probation after which a marriage can be annulled along with a certain monetary payment. The common people may have laxer forms of union. Scholars have identified legal complaints presented by five women laborers, of whom only one is said to be a wife. The others are said to "live with" a certain workman. Records show that rape is common among the lower classes but is considered a crime.

Children are considered a great treasure in Egypt, and scenes from the tomb depict a warm relationship between children and parents.

Descent is traced from the mother's side, not the father's. In the Middle Kingdom (c.2000 to 1786 B.C.) men secure a fortune for their sons by marrying an heiress; i.e., inheritance passes to the son of a rich man's daughter, not to the deceased's son. It is the maternal grandfather who takes the greatest interest in promoting the welfare of his daughter's children. Egyptian daughters are sometimes called a name that translates as "Ruler of her father," or "Beautiful as her father." Other names for women include "Beautiful of Face," "She is Healthy," "First Favorite," or "Beauty Comes." By contrast, a son may be called "Riches Come," "Beautiful Morning," or "Beautiful Day" (the last two recalling the joy of the parents on the day a son is born).

Egyptian women carry their children for three months after birth. While they are young, girls and boys are naked, boys taking up clothes when they begin to attend school. Children of people from the upper class are often sent away from home to be educated.

2258 B.C. Invasions and Disorder in Egypt. The First Intermediate Period (c.2258 to 2000 B.C.) is a time of foreign invasions and civil disorder in ancient Egypt. The pharaohs become feudal lords, and provincial governors exploit religious cults to gain power. The country is torn in half between the southern region (Upper Egypt) and the Nile delta region (Lower Egypt). At the end of the era, the rulers of Thebes conquer and reunite the whole country and establish its capital at Thebes.

C. 2134 B.C. Athletes Represented in Tombs. Females are depicted in several tombs at the Egyptian site of Beni Hassen (2134 to 1668 B.C.) playing various ball games, doing acrobatics and gymnastic-like activities, and dancing. Most likely these activities are part of ceremonial games or rituals.

C. 2000 B.C. Men Warned Against Adultery. The Instructions of Ptahhotep, from the

Middle Kingdom in Egypt (c.2000 to 1786 B.C.), warn Egyptian men about the dangers of dallying with another man's wife:

"If you want to make friendship last in a house you enter, whether as lord, or brother, or friend, in any place you enter, beware of approaching the women! The place where this is done cannot be good; there can be no cleverness in revealing this. A thousand men are turned away from their good: a little moment, the likeness of a dream, and death is reached by knowing them. It is a vile thing, conceived by an enemy; one emerges from doing it with a heart (already) rejecting it. As for him who ails through lusting after them, no plan of his can (ever) succeed."

A text from the Eighteenth Dynasty (c.1570 to 1305 B.C.) also warns against fraternizing with strange women from other towns:

"Beware of a woman who is a stranger, one not known in her town; don't stare at her when she goes by, do not know her carnally. A deep water whose course is unknown, such is a woman away from her husband. 'I am pretty' she tells you daily, when she has no witnesses; she is ready to ensnare you, a great deadly crime when it is heard."

2000 B.C. **Women Spinners and Weavers in Egypt.** Evidence from Old Kingdom tombs shows women delivering cloth and receiving payment. The hieroglyph for "weaving" uses a female figure. There are also records of women with the title "overseer of weavers" or "overseer of the house of weavers." Since women are never depicted supervising men, it seems logical that these women supervise teams of women spinners and weavers.

Settlements dating from the Middle Kingdom (c.2000 to 1786 B.C.) show women engaged in spinning and weaving. The women depicted are part of a large household and are probably servants or slaves. One list of household servants from the era shows that 20 out of the 29 female servants are occupied with

making textiles. In less wealthy households, it is probable that women family members are responsible for making cloth.

Looms in the Middle Kingdom are horizontal. By the Eighteenth Dynasty (c.1570 to 1305 B.C.), tomb scenes show vertical looms being worked; however, by male servants. Vertical looms and evidence of spinning are discovered in worker's homes, and it seems reasonable to suppose that the lower-class women weave cloth while their worker husbands are out working during the day.

Although women spin and weave, it appears that washing clothing is not their job.

Both representations on tomb walls and lists of professions for men make it clear that washing clothing is a male occupation. In fact, men carry out almost all other occupations including herding cattle, working the fields, butchering, cooking, and making sweets. Jewelry makers, metal workers, sculptors, leather workers, vineyard workers, scribes, and government bureaucrats are all exclusively male.

Another occupation for women is that of professional mourner. This involves taking up residence in the house of a deceased and grieving openly during the process of mummification, which takes 70 days. Gestures of mourning include sprinkling dust on the head, wailing, tearing one's clothes, and scratching one's cheeks.

2000 B.C. **The Middle Kingdom in Egypt.** The Middle Kingdom (c.2000 to 1786 B.C.) of ancient Egypt sees the reestablishment of Egyptian wealth and the beginning of the Great Temple of Karnak at Thebes. It will take more than 1,000 years to complete. The capital is established near Memphis, in the north of the country. Local governors still remain powerful, and international trade becomes more important. Irrigation and drainage of the fertile farmland next to the Nile is developed. Amon, the god of Thebes, emerges as Amon-Ra, and an entire complex

EVOLUTION OF THE ROLE OF THE PHARAOH'S WIFE IN EGYPT.

C. 1600 B.C. A pharaoh's wife was usually both his wife and sister or half-sister (a daughter of his father), although he might have other wives who were princesses from foreign countries. Early scholars speculated that the pharaoh inherited his very right to rule through this marriage with his father's daughter, although others believe this has not been proven.

It appears that, until the Middle Kingdom (c. 2000 to 1786 B.C.), kings may have had only one wife (referred to as "king's wife"). In the Thirteenth Dynasty (c.1786 to 1650 B.C.), references are seen to "king's principal wife." During the Eighteenth Dynasty (c.1570 to 1305 B.C.), even the principal wives were divided up to distinguish those of royal and non-royal birth.

Important queens had their own households and estates, which were administered by male officials. Other royal women were housed in harems, which were administered separately. Some texts indicate that the women of these harems spent time weaving cloth.

The symbol of queenship was the vulture headdress. The close-fitting cap represented the body of the vulture-headed goddess, Nekhbet, protectress of Upper Egypt. Nekhbet's wings spread downward on either side of the headdress. As time went on, the vulture's head was sometimes replaced by the uraeus (cobra head), a symbol that also referred to a cobra goddess of Lower Egypt, Wadjyt. The pairing of the vulture and cobra symbolized the unification of the two countries under the divine king and queen.

By the Eighteenth Dynasty (C. 1570 TO 1305 B.C.), two uraeus appeared side by side on the queen's headdress. Sometimes one wore the red crown of Lower Egypt while the other wore the white crown of Upper Egypt. In other cases, the twin snakes represented the two eyes of the sun god Ra.

Queens were sometimes shown carrying the ankh symbol, more usually held by deities and kings. In these cases, she would usually be associated or identified with a goddess.

Queens were most often depicted following their husband in some ritual action. Since, according to Egyptian mythology, the king was born of the union of his mother and the god Amun-Ra (who was said to have taken the form of her mortal husband), the "king's mother" was also frequently depicted. Since she had been the consort of a god, she was a person of great importance. Sometimes a new pharaoh was not the son of his father's "principal wife." In this case, the son, after acceding to the throne, gave this title to his mother along with the title "king's mother."

of temples devoted to his cult become the seat for a powerful priesthood.

2000 B.C.   Women Take Part in Bull Vaulting. Between 2000 and 1600 B.C., girls are active participants in bull vaulting (also called bull jumping or bull leaping) events. Many of the activities incorporate acrobatics and gymnastics. Women and men are shown on frescoes, vaulting over the bull, poised to catch the vaulter, dancing, and somersaulting.

1999 – 1500 B.C.

C. 1786–1085 B.C.   Curved Wands Serve as Protection. Curved wands, usually made from the tusk of a hippopotamus, are associated with mothers and children in the Second Intermediate Period and the New Kingdom (c.1786 to 1085 B.C.). The wands are flat on one side and curved on the other. They are decorated with mythological animals and gods, including the hippopotamus goddess Tawaret. Inscriptions on some wands name the woman and her child and state their protective nature. Besides being used in nurseries or women's bedchambers, the wands also serve a purpose in funereal tombs. They are apparently placed there to protect the tomb owner during his rebirth into the next life.

1786 B.C. Second Intermediate Period in Egypt. During the Second Intermediate Period (c.1786 to 1570 B.C.) Upper and Lower Egypt are again separated, and foreign invaders wielding bronze age weapons in chariots invade the country. Rulers known as the Hyksos (Shepherd Kings), from what is now Syria, control all of Egypt. They adopt Egyptian customs and favor the warlike god, Set. In 1570, the Theban pharaoh Ahmose I expels the Hyksos rulers and reunites the country.

1570 B.C. Queen Nefertari of Egypt Calls Herself God's Wife. Queen Ahmose Nefertari is the sister and principal wife of King Ahmose during the Eighteenth Dynasty, the beginning of what is called the "New Kingdom" (c.1570 to 1305 B.C.). During their reign, Ahmose enacts a law creating the position of "god's wife of Ahmun" for Nefertari and her heirs. The act endows the office with goods and land. Nefertari prefers to be memorialized with the title "god's wife" instead of the more usual "king's wife." She participates in temple rituals along with male priests. She also advises her husband on various building projects, including the construction of a cenotaph (a monument erected in honor of a person whose remains are buried elsewhere) at Abydos.

Nerfertari outlives her husband and her son, surviving into the reign of Thutmose I,

during which she is still highly honored. She is deified and worshipped throughout the New Kingdom, overshadowing her son's principal wife, Meritamun.

1570 B.C. New Kingdom in Egypt. During the New Kingdom (c.1570 to 1085 B.C.), the pharaoh Ahmose I founds the glorious Eighteenth Dynasty, during which many of the monumental temples and tombs of ancient Egypt are built that will last until the present day. In the Valley of the Kings, tombs are tunneled into the high rock face above the west bank of the Nile. The fabulous tombs of Amenhotep II, Thutmosis III, Tutankhamon, Rameses II, and the Great Sphinx are built. The Queen Hatshepsut's temple is constructed in what is now Deir el-Bahri. The rebel pharaoh Akhenaten builds an entire monumental city in the desert and cuts tombs in the rock at Tell el-Amarna.

The pharaohs of this period reduce the local governors to administrators. Thutmosis III establishes the Egyptian empire all the way into Asia, past the Euphrates River. Akhenaten will lose all this territory during his short, disastrous reign. The "Sea People," nomads armed with Iron Age weapons, invade the country and are barely beaten back by the pharaoh Rameses III. Egypt declines as a world power, and the people turn inward, copying the art and fashions of the already mythical Old Kingdom.

1570 B.C. Queen Ahhotep Helps Rule. During the rule of King Ahmose an Asiatic people called "Hyksos" invade northern Egypt and control Nubia, an area south of Egypt. Ahmose succeeds in repelling the Hyksos from both northern and southern territories. His eulogy to his mother, Queen Ahhotep, suggests that she may have served as coregent. In a passage that is a distinct break with stereotypic phrases, the inscription says the queen has been "One who cares for Egypt. She has looked after Egypt's soldiers. She has guarded her. She has brought back her fugitives and collected together her deserters. She has pacified Upper Egypt and expelled her rebels."

1570 B.C.   Instructions to Take Care of Mothers. During the New Kingdom (c.1570 to 1085 B.C.), the scribe called Any leaves an *Instruction* that admonishes young scribes to take loving care of their mothers:

> *Double the food your mother gave you,*
> *Support her as she supported you;*
> *She had a heavy load in you,*
> *But she did not abandon you.*
> *When you were born after your months,*
> *She was yet yoked to you,*
> *Her breast in your mouth for three years.*
> *As you grew and your excrement disgusted,*
> *She was not disgusted, saying "What shall I do?"*
> *When she sent you to school*
> *And you were taught to write,*
> *She kept watch over you daily,*
> *With bread and beer in her house.*

1500 B.C.   Hathor, Primordial Mother of the Gods and Queen of Heaven. Worship of the Egyptian goddess Hathor, Mother of the Gods and Queen of Heaven, may go back as far as 5700 B.C. as the Sinai Tablets show. Hebrew miners in Sinai worship her in 1500 B.C. Existing before time itself, Hathor is said to have given birth to all other gods and goddesses. Her name is a part of all royal Egyptian names in the early dynasties, suggesting a matrilineal queenship based on the continuing incarnation of her spirit. In her Destroyer aspect, Hathor is known as the lion-headed huntress, or Sphinx.

1 4 9 9 - 1 0 0 0   B . C .

C. 1490 B.C.   Queen Hatshepsut Crowns Herself King. Queen Hatshepsut, daughter of Thutmose I, is the half-sister and wife of Thutmose II, with whom she begins ruling in 1488

B.C. She holds the important title "god's wife" and sometimes is seen referred to as "mistress of the Two Lands," a title normally given only to kings, i.e., "lord of the Two Lands."

When Thutmose II dies in 1490 B.C., Hatshepsut acts as regent for her half-brother, Thutmose III, who is still a child and the son of a minor wife of Thutmose II. After serving as regent for approximately seven years, Hatshepsut gives up the titles and insignia of a queen and adopts the five-fold title of a king. On her monuments she appears in the male costume of a king. She also disseminates texts stating that she has been designated by her father as his successor. When Thutmose III becomes old enough to rule independently, Hatshepsut invokes the institution of coregency, in which two kings may rule at the same time. She has herself crowned king with full royal titles and is pictured wearing king's clothing. Scribes even refer to her using male pronouns. Although the two regents are then pictured together, she is clearly the dominant partner.

During her reign, Hatshepsut expands foreign commerce and builds an extensive temple, Der-el-Bahri, in western Thebes. She approves the construction of new monuments, several of which still stand. The record also shows that she sends a trading mission to the Red Sea port city of Punt to obtain panthers, panther skins, ostrich feathers and eggs, ivory, gold, and incense. Her favorite, Senmut, an official in the temple of Amon, leaves an inscription boasting that Hatshepsut has made him "great in both countries" and "chief of chiefs" in the whole of Egypt. After her death, the name and figure of Hatshepsut as king are obliterated from monuments. However, her name and figure as queen are left intact.

1405 B.C.   Queen Tiy and the Cult of the Sun. Amenhotep III (1405 to 1367 B.C.), rules at the apogee of the Egyptian civilization's power and prosperity. His wife, Queen Tiy, is not, however, of royal parentage. Even so, she appears in ritual scenes with the king and is shown on an equal scale with the king in a colossal, seated statue. She is depicted in one private tomb scene sitting on a throne, on the arm of a sphinx that also resembles her, trampling enemies (a kingly icon). She is apparently the first queen to also adopt the horns of the goddess Hathor and the sun disk of the god Ra as part of her insignia, further identifying herself with the cult of the sun.

At this time, the Egyptian kingdom spreads from Nubia to Mitanni, or from Meroe (near the sixth cataract of the Nile) all the way north into what is now called the Middle East.

C. 1360 B.C.   Queen Nefertiti. Queen Nefertiti is the wife of the pharaoh Akhenaten, who rejects the ancient religion of Egypt and attempts to found his own religion based on the god "Aten," who is represented by the solar disk.

Akhenaten writes a hymn that proclaims himself to be the sole intermediary of Aten and equal in divinity. Both Akhenaten and Nefertiti are closely identified with the divinity, and both their figures appear on monuments, temples, and tombs. In 1359 B.C., Akhenaten begins construction of a new capital called Akhetaten ("horizon of the Aten"), located in a barren spot between Thebes and Memphis. The location is now called Amarna. Bas-reliefs later found there depict Nefertiti and her husband, daughters, and her husband's parents (Pharaoh Amenhotep II and Queen Tiy) doing homage to Aten. Stelae found in domestic residences at Amarna show that private people worship the royal couple and Aten in their homes. Prayers can also be addressed directly to Nefertiti.

The new religion proclaims that Aten, a symbol of the noon-day sun depicted as a red disk with rays stretching down to earth, is the supreme and only god worthy of worship. The new religion breaks sharply with the prevailing religions by conceiving of a very abstract god, unrelated to the polytheistic cults that have grown up in Egypt over the eons. An entirely new, more realistic, style of art is created and human sacrifice is abolished. However, eternal life in the hereafter is now the province only of the pharaoh, excluding the common people. Besides this, the older cults are violently repressed, setting the stage for revolt. After Akhenaten's death, his city and temples are destroyed and the names of himself, his queen, and his god are chipped off of monuments wherever they appear.

In 1912, a German expedition discovers a miraculously preserved and hauntingly beautiful bust of Nefertiti while excavating the workshop of a sculptor in Amarna. Records of Akhenaten's father, Amunhotep III, indicate that around 1366 B.C., he concludes a treaty with the Asiatic King Tushratta of Mitanni that includes a marriage with Tushratta's daughter, the princess Tadukhipa. The princess is 15 years old, her husband-to-be in his 50s. When she arrives in her new home, her name is changed to Nefertiti, meaning "the beautiful one who has come." The old pharaoh passes away about two years later. His son, Amenhotep IV, soon to become Akhenaten, marries Nefertiti, who will bear him seven daughters.

There are indications that Akhenaten suffers from some form of physical and mental illness. By around 1351 B.C., the pharaoh is depicted with a coregent, one Smenkhkare. Around that time, Nefertiti's name is obliterated from public monuments and replaced with the name of her oldest daughter, Meritaten. Nefertiti apparently lives in exile in a separate palace a few miles away from the court of her husband and Smenkhkare. For five years no monuments are constructed that bear her image or name.

After a 17-year reign, Akhenaten dies. Nefertiti is about 34 years old. Akhenaten has left no son to inherit the throne, so Tutankhaten, the husband of Nefertiti's third oldest daughter, accedes to the throne for a brief period. Around 1346 B.C., Tutankhaten changes his name to Tutankhamun. He restores the cult of the old god Amun and moves his capital back to Memphis, abandoning the city Akhetaten. Although it is not clear when Nefertiti dies, some Egyptologists believe she remains in the abandoned city until her death.

C. 1200 B.C.   Fu Hao, Esteemed Warrior. Fu Hao is a consort of the emperor Wu Ding, who reigns from about 1200 to 1180 B.C. during the Shang dynasty. She leads military expeditions, and it is known from the splendor of her tomb (which contains sacrificial victims, thousands of cowry shells, and hundreds of bronze and jade objects) something of the esteem in which she is held.

1180 B.C.   Spartan Queen Helen Kidnapped. According to the classic Greek myth, the Spartan queen Helen is kidnapped sometime around 1180 B.C. by the Trojan prince Paris, after which Helen's husband, King Menelaus, amasses his troops and comes to take her back, thus beginning the Trojan War. In other versions, however, Helen is a goddess who chooses her own king (Menelaus) but then later goes off with another lover (Paris). Because Menelaus cannot be king—or immortal—without Helen's backing, he wages the war to regain his throne and his immortality. The Trojan War can also be seen as a battle between the patriarchal Greeks and the matriarchal Trojans, which the Greeks won.

1150 B.C.   Deborah Leads Israel to Defeat Canaanite King Jabin. Deborah rallies the northern tribes—Issachar, Zebulon, and Naphtali—and the southern tribes—Ephraim, Benjamin, and Machir-Mannasseh—of Israel to defeat the invading Canaanite king Jabin. This results in several decades of peace. Deborah's story is recounted in chapter five of Judges in the Old Testament of the Bible. The *Song of Deborah* found there is considered to be one of the oldest surviving pieces of Biblical writing.

C. 1085 B.C.   Egypt in the Late Dynastic Period. During the Late Dynastic Period (c.1085 to 30 B.C.), Egypt becomes divided between the priest-kings of Amon-Ra at Thebes and the pharaohs in the north at Tanis. Libyans seize the government and move the capital to Bubastis, adopting the cat goddess Bast as their state deity. Nubians, then Assyrians, conquer Thebes. Iron comes into general use in Egypt as the government of Egypt continues to be passed from one nationality to another. Egyptians, the Medes, and Babylonians overthrow Assyria, only to be swallowed up themselves by the Persian Cambyses II. After years of struggle to overthrow the Persians, the Egyptians are conquered again, this time by Alexander the Great, who establishes a new city, Alexandria, to be the capital. He appoints his general, Ptolemy, as ruler of Egypt. In 405 B.C., Ptolemy becomes the first of a line of Ptolemaic pharaohs of Egypt that will end with the death of Cleopatra VII in 30 B.C.

999-500 B.C.

C. 945 B.C.   Bast, the Cat-headed Goddess. The cat-headed goddess Bast represents the beneficent, fertilizing warmth of the sun. Located in the Nile delta, her city, Bubastis, becomes capital of the kingdom during the Twenty-second Dynasty (945 to c.750 B.C.). Bast comes to be considered a daughter/spouse and protectress of Ra. She is a kindly goddess. Like Hathor, she is known as a goddess of joy, music, and dancing, whose orgiastic rituals are celebrated in processions of barges. In honor of Bast, cats are held to be sacred. Bubastis is the site of an enormous cemetery of mummified cats, known throughout the ancient world.

C. 800 B.C.   Vestal Virgins. The six Vestal Virgins hold a very special place in Roman society. They are chosen before they have entered puberty and take a vow to remain chaste for 30 years. They tend the sacred fire in the Temple of Vesta (Greek: Hestia) and are allowed to appear in public. However, if anyone touches their chair as they are being carried on the street, that person is put to death.

Once a year, in a special ceremony, the vestals sacrifice and burn a pregnant heifer. They use the ashes to wash and purify the temple. During this time, it is considered unlucky to enter into marriage.

The vestals can only be punished by the chief priest, who may be required to whip an offender. If a vestal is discovered to have broken the vow of chastity, the punishment is to be buried alive. In 90 A.D., the Emperor Domitian pronounces this punishment on the chief vestal, Cornelia, despite her pleas of innocence. Other vestals are also convicted of adultery and executed.

Although men are not allowed in the Temple of Vesta, the Emperor Augustus successfully transfers control of the vestals to himself by having himself named chief priest, and creating an altar to Vesta in his own residence. Succeeding emperors retain his title of *pontifus maximus*, or chief priest.

Legend records that Tarpeia is a Vestal Virgin in the ancient city of Rome at the time of the rape of the Sabine women. When the fathers of the women decide to attack Rome to try to liberate their daughters, Tarpeia shows them a secret path to the city's fortress. As a reward, she asks for "What you wear on your arms," meaning their gold bracelets. Instead, they treacherously kill her using the shields that they carry on their arms.

C. 800 B.C. Etruscan Women Play Greater Role. It is difficult to reconstruct the lives of Etruscan women, since they leave no literature. But evidence from ancient burial sites and contemporary accounts suggests that these women live a life very different from Roman or Greek women. Funerary art depicts husbands and wives in gestures of affection. The aristocratic women are buried with an elegance equal to that of men. Instead of taking their husband's name (as Roman and Greek women do), Etruscan women have their own names and even pass their titles on to their children. In art, women are depicted wearing mantles and shoes (unlike Greek women), which indicates that they can be found outdoors as much as men.

The evidence of Roman and Greek commentators usually paints the Etruscans in a very bad light. These commentators condemn Etruscan society for its luxury and are shocked by husbands and wives attending banquets in public together. Tomb paintings show women and men attending public games together, something unthinkable to other ancient societies. Unlike ancient Greece and Rome, the ancient Etruscans depict the naked female body. They also leave many statues of women holding their children, something uncommon in Greece and Rome, where children are considered to be the property of the father. Etruscan monuments make it clear that the married couple, not the *paterfamilias* alone, is the important feature of their society.

Although the Romans condemn the morals of the Etruscans and celebrate the downfall of the Etruscan Tarquin dynasty, their culture is deeply influenced by Etruscan customs and art. Roman women adopt the Etruscan rounded cloaks and their purple and bordered articles of clothing for ritual garments.

C. 800 B.C. Worship of Asherah, the Canaanite Great Mother Goddess. The worship of Asherah, the Canaanite Great Mother Goddess, becomes the official state religion of Israel and Judah during the reigns of queens Jezebel and Athaliah in the first half of the ninth century B.C. The Yahwists, supporters of the male god who eventually becomes the One God of monotheistic Judaism, Christianity, and Islam, wages a long and violent war against Asherah, as noted in passages throughout the Hebrew Bible (e.g., Exodus 34:13, Deuteronomy 16:21, Judges 6:25ff, 1

Kings 15:13, 2 Kings 18:4, and 2 Chronicles 34:3-7, among others).

C. 800 B.C. **"Second" Creation Story of the Hebrew Bible Written.** The "second" creation story of the Hebrew Bible, Genesis 2:46-3:24, is composed sometime during the ninth century B.C.—500 years before the "first" creation story of Genesis 1 is written. In it, Eve is depicted as a subordinate—and an insubordinate—being who brings sin and death to all creation through her disobedience, thus dooming all women, as "daughters of Eve," to be seen as inferior and evil for the millennia to follow. Once again the patriarchal Hebrews demote and demonize a Great Mother goddess whose name proves her status as a supreme deity: Eve, or Hawwah in Hebrew, means "life," and "mother of all living." The patriarchal Hebrew god, Yahweh, is himself a declaration of the Great Mother—the letters of his name, YHWH, mean "I am Eve" (Y=I; HWH=Hawwah, or Eve), "I am the mother of all living."

C. 750 B.C. **Pandora, Created by Zeus.** Hesiod, the poet who lives about 700 B.C., writes in Theogony that Pandora is created by Zeus to punish Prometheus and burden mankind. Originally Pandora is the "all-giver" goddess who pours out blessings from her honey-vase. Zeus, who wants to eradicate mankind, is enraged when the titan Prometheus, who has created human beings in the first place, gives men the gift of fire. In revenge, Zeus orders Hephaestus to make a clay woman and has the four Winds breathe life into her. She is called "Pandora" ("all-giving"). All the goddesses of Olympus adorn her so that she is the most beautiful woman ever created. Zeus then makes her as foolish, mischievous, and idle as she is beautiful and sends her to Prometheus' brother Epimetheus to marry.

Prometheus warns his brother to accept no gift from Zeus, and Epimetheus cautiously declines. Zeus is so angry at this that he chains

Prometheus to a mountain and dooms him to undergo eternal torture.

Epimetheus decides it will be safer to marry Pandora after all. However, he lives to regret it. In his possession he has a box that Prometheus has warned him never to open. Pandora's curiosity drives her to open it, and out fly all the Spites that plague human beings: Old Age, Labor, Sickness, Insanity, Vice, and Passion. They fly out of the box and sting Epimetheus and Pandora all over their bodies, then attack the human race, which may have committed mass suicide except for the last evil to escape from the box: Delusive Hope.

Contemporary poet and novelist Robert Graves conjectures that Hesiod's anti-feminist fable is based on the story of Demophon and Phyllis, told in Homer's much earlier Odyssey. Demophon, who wishes to desert Phyllis, tells her he is going on a short trip and will return. Phyllis, suspecting he is lying, gives him a box which she tells him never to open unless he is sure he will not be able to return to her. Demophon waits for years until his curiosity gets the better of him. He opens the box and is driven mad by what he sees. No one knows what is in the box, but Demophon is driven to commit suicide.

Another version of the story is that Zeus actually sends Pandora to men with good intentions. She is given a box into which each god has placed a blessing, as her marriage presents to mankind. However, Pandora opens the box too soon, and all the blessings fly out, except one. Hope remains in the box and has been a solace to mankind ever since.

Pandora is actually a name of the Earth goddess, Rhea, and is worshipped at Athens and elsewhere.

C. 712 B.C. **Japan's *Kojiki (Chronicle of Ancient Things)*.** The *Kojiki (Chronicle of Ancient Things)* records that the goddess Amaterasu o Mikami (Grand Divinity Illuminating Heaven) is the principal Shinto deity, identified with the sun as ruler of the heavens, progenitrix of the Japanese imperial line, and enshrined in the Grand Shrine of Ise. Accounts depict her as the most positive of the three deities born to the creator deities, Izanami and Izanagi. She is said to have taught her subjects to plant rice and weave cloth. Shamanesses derive their authority in the Shinto religion from the sun goddess. It has been speculated that matriarchal practices in early Japan (before the eighth century) are associated with the prominence of Amaterasu. Nobility in ancient Japan derive political power by listing their lineage to the sun goddess. Following the seventeenth century, thousands of Japanese participate in pilgrimages to Ise Shrine to worship Amaterasu. In the twentieth century, the writings of Japanese feminists refer to Amaterasu as a symbol of female power.

C. 712 B.C.   Amenouzume no Mikoto and the Origin of Music and Dance. The origins of music and dance in Japan are linked with the goddess Amenouzume no Mikoto in an account recorded in the Kojiki. According to the account, Amaterasu o Mikami, the sun goddess, having been insulted by her brother, who was the guardian of hell, retreats into a cave, leaving the world in darkness. In order to coax the sun goddess to return, Amenouzume no Mikoto dances a lewd and humorous dance before the assembled deities. The music, dancing, and raucous laughter arouses the sun goddess' curiosity and lures her out of the cave, thus returning light to the world.

C. 712 B.C.   Creation of Japan. The Kojiki records that the male deity, Izanagi no Mikoto, and the female deity, Izanami no Mikoto, create Japan and its deities. The pair is said to have descended from the heavens, after which Izanami gives birth to the Japanese islands, with their deities of mountains, rivers, trees, and crops. In giving birth to the fire deity, she burns and dies.

C. 700 B.C.   Marriage and Divorce in Egypt. Egyptian women marry shortly after beginning

to menstruate. Marriage is not a religious or legal institution. Two people are married if one of them takes up residence in the other one's home. Among the elite, men have the option of taking more than one wife, but most remain at least officially monogamous.

Beginning in the seventh century B.C., a husband gives his wife a gift, called a shep en sehemet, translated as "price or compensation for marrying a woman." In addition, the man signs a contract specifying the disposition of property and the economic rights of the spouses. In this contract, the man promises that, should he divorce his wife, he promises to give her a sum of money and a third of their joint property. Divorce is called "expulsion" or "departure." The man may also be required to pay a "divorce forfeit," which may be as much as a third of his own property.

If a woman is unfaithful, she receives no compensation in a divorce. Women who initiate a divorce are entitled only to their portion of the joint property.

Married men are permitted to have sexual relations with women other than their own wives. However, married women are forbidden to have affairs with other men. This is to ensure that a woman's children belong to the man who will support them, and to ensure that the children can inherit his property when he dies. Men who have affairs with someone else's wife are criticized and sometimes hauled into court.

700 B.C.   Scribe Produces Patriarchal Version of The Gilgamesh Epic. In the seventh century B.C., a royal Assyrian scribe at Nineveh copies The Gilgamesh Epic, written sometime between 1800 and 1600 B.C., onto 12 tablets now referred to as the Standard Version. This "standard" version converts the Babylonian Great Goddess, Ishtar, into a fickle and argumentative "goddess of love" who is rejected, with a volley of insulting criticism, by the hero Gilgamesh. Ishtar can then not even wreak vengeance on Gilgamesh herself but has to go running to the "great god" Anu for help. When Anu sends a bull from heaven to kill Gilgamesh, Gilgamesh and his side-kick Enkidu instead kill the bull and use the occasion to further insult Ishtar, who is left to cry helplessly. This later patriarchal portrayal of Ishtar is greatly at odds with her earlier revered status as Queen of Heaven, Goddess of Goddesses, Lawgiver, and Bestower of Strength.

C. 650 B.C. Korai Statues in Greece. Korai statues—life-size, standing statues of young women—are placed near Greek temples. They are often dressed in brightly painted garments. Some are funerary markers, others are dedicated to a divinity.

C. 650 B.C. Life in Sparta. All Spartan citizens are forbidden to engage in money-making occupations. The lower classes support the society by working plots of land that are distributed to Spartan citizens at birth, but revert to the state when they die. The principal task of women is to give birth to warriors. Their great lawgiver, Lycurgus, organizes a society based on eugenics, with the goal of producing the best children. Motherhood is therefore a most important function, and physical training is required in the belief that strong mothers give birth to strong children.

Men and women live apart in communal quarters. Once married, Spartan men can only visit their wives furtively, under cover of darkness. This is thought to increase desire, which will also increase fertility.

By the fourth century B.C. and in the Hellenistic period, the greater freedom they enjoy allows Spartan women to become wealthy and conspicuous consumers. Whereas Athenian women cannot own wealth, Spartan women own racehorses that are victorious at the Panhellenic festivals. They also own land and manage their own property. Athenian commentators will ascribe Sparta's decline to the greater influence of their women in their society.

C. 616 B.C. Tanaquil and Tarquin Found Etruscan Dynasty. Tanaquil interprets omens to mean that her husband, Tarquin, will become king of Rome. They found an Etruscan dynasty that rules Rome for 100 years, until, under Tarquin the Proud, it is overthrown by the Republic.

C. 600 B.C. The Poet Alcman. Alcman, like Sappho, writes poetry that illustrates the close bond of older women to younger women. Alcman's *Partheneia* or *Maiden Songs* emphasize the beauty and desirability of women. Two other Spartan poets are mentioned by contemporary writers, but none of their works have come down to modern times. Their names are Megalostrata (a contemporary of Alcman) and Cleitagora.

C. 600 B.C. Mourning Practices in Greece. In Homeric times, funerary vases depict both male and female mourners. In the late seventh century B.C., mourning falls increasingly to women. The Athenian lawgiver, Solon, drafts laws regulating mourning. The historian Plutarch suggests that Solon is concerned with stamping out "disorder and license." Mourners can only wear three garments, and lacerations of the flesh are forbidden. Women are also forbidden to mourn for someone who is not a blood relative, apparently in an attempt to suppress the practice of paying mourners.

Contemporary works of theater show women defying restrictions on burial rites and mourning, like Antigone and Elektra. Excessive mourning for the dead is often thought to threaten the courage of warriors waiting for battle.

C. 600 B.C. Guardians Take Care of Athenian Women. A woman in classical Athens (c.sixth century B.C.) is not considered an independent person in the eyes of the law. Throughout childhood she is part of a household (*oikos*). The head of that household (usually her father), is her *kyrios* or guardian. Upon marriage, she will pass to the *oikos* of her new husband, who will then be her *kyrios*. If her husband dies or she is divorced before she has a son, she can return to her father's guardianship.

The guardian carries out any business transactions that involve a woman's property and apparently is able to dispose of it even without her consent. The guardian represents the woman at any legal proceedings.

C. 600 B.C. **Spartan Women Are Most Independent in Ancient World.** Girls and women in Sparta, the powerful city-state of ancient Greece, are the freest and most independent of all women in the ancient world. Girls are required to complete a course of education, just as boys do. They participate in athletics, notably races dedicated to the goddess Hera. For sports activities, girls wear short chitons like those worn by the legendary Amazons. The names of the victors are inscribed on statues of themselves, in contrast to the Athenian custom of only naming a woman obliquely (i.e., "the wife of Socrates," "the sister of Plato"). Alcmen's poems clearly indicate that Spartan girls sing and recite poetry. Aristotle reports that girls and boys dance in processions in the nude, with no prudery or embarrassment. He also records that two-thirds of the land in Sparta is owned by women.

600 B.C. **Ishtar, Goddess of Love.** Ishtar is the goddess of love in the Assyrian empire, in the region surrounding the Tigris River in the Middle East. Ishtar is believed to be so powerful in the Assyrian city of Ninevah that her statue is sent to Egypt to help cure an ailing king there.

600 B.C. **Sappho, Renowned Greek Poet.** Sappho (c.600 B.C.) lives at Mitylene (present-day Mitilini) on the island of Lesbos, Greece. Only fragments of her poetry have come down, and yet these fragments alone show why Sappho is so influential in Greek and Roman literature. Later poets will imitate her stanza-form and meter to convey instantly the idea of the pain of lost love. The sixth-century poet and legislator, Solon, is reported to want to learn one of Sappho's songs, "So that having learned it, I may die." By the third and second centuries B.C., commentators are debating her sexual proclivities, suggesting that even people who have access to complete poems are speculating about the real meaning of her poems. By the second century A.D., the early Christian fathers are condemning Sappho for what they perceive as nymphomania and debauchery.

Sappho's poems are in the form of an address from an older to a younger woman. They illuminate a world never seen by men. She probably maintains a school for young women or is a priestess of Aphrodite who trains young initiates in the cult of the goddess.

C. 590 B.C. **Prostitution in Athens.** Since there is virtually no other legal form of employment for women in classical Athens, former slaves and women from poor families are often forced into prostitution to survive. They may be foreigners or Athenian-born women. The lowest rung of prostitutes are the pornai, who reside in brothels. Their fees are within the reach of most men and they pay a tax to the state on their activities. The sixth-century lawgiver, Solon, is said to have purchased slave women and put them to work in brothels at reasonable prices as part of his democratic reforms.

Female entertainers who provide dancing and singing at the male-only parties or *symposia* are also expected to provide sexual services. Their prices, as skilled artists, are higher than those of pornai.

At the top of the ladder are hetaerae or courtesans. These are very beautiful women, mostly foreigners, who can charge a very high price for an evening's companionship.

A favorite prostitute may manage to buy her freedom, or even become a man's legally-recognized concubine.

550 B.C. **Greek Females Participate in Physical Activities.** In general, females are allowed to participate in physical activities such as running and dancing in the context of religious and initiation ceremonies and festivals. The city-state of Sparta is well known for training both boys and girls in a variety of physical activities. It is part of the Spartan philosophy to have strong and healthy females, in order to bear strong and healthy children. On the island of Chios, it is reputed that girls wrestle boys.

C. 534 B.C. **Wife of Tarquin the Proud and the Roman Street of Crime.** The Roman historian Livy relates that the wife of Tarquin the Proud (rules 534–510 B.C.) urges her husband to make himself king by killing her own father. Afterwards, she drives in an open carriage to the Senate and loudly proclaims her husband king. When the driver stops the carriage because he recognizes her father's bloody body on the street, she grabs the reins and runs over it. The street comes to be named The Street of Crime. The evil deeds of this royal family (culminating with their son's rape of the chaste Roman matron Lucretia) are said to be the cause of the overthrow of the dynasty and the founding of the Republic.

C. 510 B.C. **Rape of Lucretia Leads to Revolution in Rome.** Lucretia, a chaste Roman matron, is raped by the wicked son of the hated King Tarquin. Rather than live with such shame, she summons her family and kills herself in their presence. Popular outrage at her death sparks a revolution that leads to the expulsion of the Tarquin dynasty and the creation of the Republic. Lucretia's husband, Collatinus, and her uncle, Lucius Junius Brutus, not only help lead the revolution, but are among the early leaders of the new government.

C. 508 B.C. **Cloelia and Friends Escape Abductors.** The ancient Romans leave very few representations of mortal women, whether on coins, statues, or paintings. However, from ancient sources, it is known that the Roman girl Cloelia earns the honor of being depicted in a statue. Legend says that Cloelia and other noble Roman girls are abducted by Etruscans. Cloelia persuades some of her companions to slip away from their captors with her. They swim across the Tiber River to safety, while their guards throw stones and spears at them. They all return safely to Rome and their families.

---

499 - 1 B . C .

C. 491 B.C. **Coriolanus' Mother Shames Son, Prevents Bloodshed.** In Livy's history, he records that when the renegade Roman general Coriolanus marches on Rome at the head of an enemy army, the women of Rome go to the house of his mother, Vetruria. They prevail upon her to go out to the front lines and speak to her son. There, the proud Roman matron reproaches her son for his evil deeds, evoking the image of the land as his mother. He retires to exile in shame. Thereafter, the Senate consecrates a temple to honor women.

C. 480 B.C. **Maenads, the Mad Women.** The Maenads (mad women) worship the god Dionysus in violent, ecstatic dancing rituals. Although not practiced everywhere in Greece, their festival entails women leaving their homes to wander mountains dressed in animal hides and wreaths of twigs and leaves, holding sacred wands (*thyrsoi*) with which they will beat others. The playwright Euripides reports in his play *The Bacchae* that they fall upon animals and tear them to pieces with their bare hands, and that they even attack and loot villages. These observances are not part of the official state religions and seem to involve only small numbers of women.

Athenian women play an important role in the Lenaia festival for Dionysus. Lenai is a synonym for maenad. Offerings of wine, meat, and bread are made to the god. Literature and vase paintings make it clear that drunkenness and release from ordinary life are a focus of the Dionysian festivals. Female worshippers of Dionysus are depicted wearing fawnskins, with their hair wreathed with ivy and snakes.

C. 480 B.C.   Polias, Priestess of Athena. The Priestess of Athena, Polias, presides at the Great Panathenaea festival held every four years at Athens. She is the only respectable woman whose name can be mentioned in public without disgrace. The priestesses all come from the aristocratic Eteobutadae family, which claims descent from the original royal family of Athens. In 480 B.C., on the eve of a major battle with the Persians, the priestess reports that the sacred snake that guards the sanctuary of Athena has refused the ritual honey cake offering. This bad omen moves the city fathers to evacuate the city.

C. 475 B.C. Marriage: Betrothal and Dowry in Ancient Greece.   An Athenian woman's natural and approved role is that of wife. Since women cannot participate in trade or become craftsmen, unmarried and infertile women are dependent on their nearest male relative: a brother, or perhaps an uncle. If those relatives are extremely poor, an unmarriageable woman may be sold as a concubine or forced into prostitution.

The marriage ritual in Athens resembles in its parts other sacred rituals related to death and other sacrifices. An Athenian girl will be betrothed at an early age. An Athenian woman's father provides her with a dowry that is usually given to the family of her intended husband at the formal betrothal. A large dowry attracts desirable suitors. Although the dowry remains the property of the woman, she cannot independently make decisions on how to dispose of it. The husband, who knows that he may be called upon to return the dowry if his wife's father decides to dissolve the marriage, is motivated to guard and invest it prop-

erly. The bride's family may decide to dissolve a marriage if, for instance, the couple remains childless too long.

The marriage will be celebrated when the young woman is between the ages of 14 and 18. First, her father will conduct a sacrifice. Then, the bride will cut her hair and remove a girdle (a kind of sash or belt) that she has worn since puberty. This will be dedicated to either Artemis or Athena. She then has a ritual bath. Before the public part of the ceremony begins, she will be partly veiled. At nightfall, the groom and his best friend carry the bride to her new home in a torchlight procession, where they will be greeted by the groom's mother. The bride will be conducted to her new home's *hestia* or sacred hearth, where bride and groom will be showered with nuts and dried fruits. At the end of the evening, the groom will lead the bride upstairs to the marriage chamber while the assembled friends and family sing a marriage hymn.

The equation of marriage with death is present in this marriage ritual. The carriage of the bride to the groom's home imitates the myth of Persephone's abduction by Hades, lord of the Underworld. This abrupt transition from the security of her childhood home to her husband's home, where she will be at the beck and call of his mother, and her impending loss of virginity to a man who is usually a total stranger, may have made the day of marriage a less than joyous occasion for the bride.

Individual choice and certainly romantic love are not considerations in Athenian society, although contemporary plays do attest to men and women having love affairs. In later Greek society, called the Hellenistic era, the Greek poet Menander begins to write popular comedies about young lovers who overcome all kinds of obstacles to their own marriage. This new theme in Greek literature seems to indicate the growing acceptability of individual aspirations.

After marriage, a respectable married woman will never be seen associating with men. If someone says she talks to men or even opens the front door herself, it will be a terrible insult. The husband or a slave will take care of shopping at the public market. The wives of poor men probably are not constrained in this manner.

If the wife dies, her husband retains control of her dowry until her sons are old enough to inherit. Daughters apparently do not receive an inheritance from their mother's dowry.

C. 475 B.C. Divorce in Ancient Greece. Divorce can be easily achieved by common agreement or by the wish of either party. In addition, a woman's father has the right to terminate her marriage. The usual reasons for this are maltreatment, childlessness, or the impoverishment of the husband. In such cases, the husband has to return the wife's dowry.

The husband is required by law to divorce his wife if she has committed adultery. From the fourth century B.C. onwards, he is required to divorce her if he discovers that she is not an Athenian citizen. If a woman becomes the sole heir of her father, another member of the father's family has the right to marry her to keep the father's property within his family. If such a woman is already married, the law nevertheless compels her to divorce her first husband and marry her relative, regardless of her wishes.

C. 460 B.C. Schooling of Athenian Children. While boys in the city-state of Athens, Greece, begin attending public school at around the age of six, Athenian girls are kept cloistered in their homes, practicing important household skills like spinning and weaving. However, evidence from contemporary illustrations and plays indicates that at least some women are able to read and write. Some Athenian girls may also have received instruction (presumably from their mothers) in music and dance.

C. 455 B.C. Thesmorphoria Festival, Female Religious Festival. The three-day Thesmorphoria Festival is an exclusively female religious celebration. In Athens, all the women gather together before the time of seed planting on a hill near the Assembly. During this time, if the men of the city need to convene the Assembly, they have to do so at the Theater, for men are strictly forbidden to observe the rites. On the first day, a procession of women climb the hill to the festival site carrying sacred objects. The women sleep in makeshift huts, utter obscene ritual words, and fast. Piglets and cakes in the shape of phalluses are thrown into the bottom of caves. After three days, certain women are lowered on ropes to bring back the rotting remains which are mixed with the seed-corn and used in planting. The final day is a time of joy when women celebrate Demeter's promise of renewed fertility with sacrifices and feasts.

C. 451 B.C. Athenian Citizenship. Before 450 B.C., the benefits of Athenian citizenship are open to all sons of Athenian males. Thereafter, Pericles decrees that only sons of an Athenian mother and father can be citizens. It is thought this law may have been meant to discourage aristocratic families from forming alliances with other city-states. Or it may have been intended to limit the numbers of citizens who have many special privileges under Athenian democracy.

Although the law may have fallen into disuse, it is reinstated around the year 403 B.C. In the next century, it becomes actually illegal for an Athenian citizen to marry a non-citizen.

C. 450 B.C. Women's Lives in Classical Greece. Women in the Archaic period of Greek history can be praised and blamed in public. But in classical Greece, respectable women have to be silent in public. It is considered improper to even mention their names in public; men are expected to name women only obliquely as some man's sister or wife. It is not considered respectable for women to leave the house for any reason other than family gatherings or religious festivals. Only slaves, the poor, and very elderly women are expected to be seen going to market.

Athenian women have legal and financial protection in the case of divorce, which is rather easy for a man to obtain. The woman has to become the guardian of another male relative and her dowry has to be returned. The Archon oversees the welfare of orphans and widows.

Men can legally have concubines, but if the concubines are not native Athenians, their children cannot be Athenian citizens.

Around 451 B.C., the ruler Pericles decrees a citizenship law that says only the children of two native Athenians can be citizens. Thereafter, the citizenship of women is carefully distinguished. However, this does not mean they have any part in the government. Outside the private sphere, women only have significant influence in religious rituals.

Although women aren't allowed to own or control property, due to accidents of birth and death, they may become heiresses. In this case, Athenian law decrees that they must marry a close relative in order to keep the wealth in the family.

In the realm of religious festivals, women are allowed to participate and their contributions are significant. The Athenian state religion has many festivals and rituals and is integrated into everyday life. Women of all positions, including foreigners, worship together. Girls weave, grind grain, carry offerings, and dance in public rituals. In processions, women carry offering trays and incense-burners to be used in the sacrifice.

Besides rituals to Dionysus, by the late fifth century, Athens' large foreign population has brought the worship of the Asiatic vegetation god Adonis. He may be especially popular with hetaerae (courtesans) and non-aristocratic women. In late July, groups of women

Queen Esther

lament the dead god on their roof tops and set out miniature "gardens for Adonis" in terracotta pots. These will spout quickly and then wither in the rooftop heat.

C. 440 B.C. Esther Chosen to Wed Ahasuerus of Persia. The Old Testament of the Bible, in the "Book of Esther," tells of the early life of Esther, an orphan who is raised by her cousin, Mordecai. Esther is chosen by the Persian king Ahasuerus (Xerxes) to replace his wife, Queen Vashti, who is banished for disobeying Ahasuerus. (In some accounts, Vashti is reportedly executed.) Ahasuerus conquers the Egyptians and attempts to overtake the Greeks, extending his empire from modern-day India to northern Africa. Mordecai advises Esther to conceal her Jewish origin from Ahasuerus.

Haman, one of Ahasuerus's advisors, asks for and receives an edict that all the palace servants must bow down to him. When Esther's cousin, Mordecai, refuses, Haman seeks revenge, ordering that all Jews—men, women, and children—be murdered during Adar, the last month of the Hebrew year. Esther reveals her Jewish identity to Ahasuerus, and reveals Haman's plot to hang Mordecai and kill all Jews. Upon learning of Haman's plan, Ahasuerus orders him executed and appoints Mordecai to replace Haman as advisor. Esther's action in saving her people is commemorated by modern-day Jews in the festival of Purim.

C. 430 B.C.   Aspasia, Influential Athenian. Aspasia, a foreign-born hetaera or courtesan, becomes famous and influential in classical Athens. She is the mistress of the ruler Pericles and is widely resented among Athenians for her supposed influence in Athenian politics. Aspasia becomes wealthy and independent by controlling other hetaerae. According to Plutarch, Aspasia is so renowned for her conversation and learning that she is often visited by Socrates and his students. Aspasia is prosecuted for impiety and procuring, but Pericles successfully defends her at her trial. After the death of his wife, Pericles lives openly with Aspasia. References in literature indicate that some people blame her for some of Pericles' political decisions that lead to the disastrous Peloponnesian Wars (431–404 B.C.).

C. 430 B.C.   Hippocrates and the Physiology of Women. The collection of writings ascribed to Hippocrates (c.460–370 B.C.) contains theories about women's physiology and diseases that are important in medicine until the advent of modern scientific method after the Enlightenment in the eighteenth century. Hippocrates' methods are still used to defend medical practices in Victorian England.

Hippocrates' writings may record his observations of ancient female traditions of women healers or his theories may be his own invention. Hippocrates postulates that people are born hot and wet and become drier and colder as they age. Women in particular are considered to be hot and wet in nature. Their softer flesh is considered to be "spongier" than men's, indicating that women absorb more moisture from their food. Women can become drier by vigorous exercise, becoming more like men and losing their ability to menstruate (having dried up their excess moisture). Therefore, women are meant to stay at home and partake of sedentary activities.

According to Hippocrates, women, being moister than men, produce excess moisture that has to be evacuated from the womb every month during menstruation. Women's illnesses are often ascribed to an errant womb, which has become dislodged and is moving throughout the body searching for moisture. If the opening of the womb becomes blocked, the blood can rise up through tubes and appear as a nosebleed or as vomit.

The absence of regular and heavy menstruation is a symptom of serious disease, and the Hippocratics have methods aimed at inducing menstruation. Marriage, in particular, is prescribed, because sex will open up the opening to the womb. However, the pregnant woman does not menstruate because the excess blood being produced by her body goes to form and nourish the fetus. Menopause is explained by the fact that people naturally dry out as they age.

The Hippocratic texts indicate that the doctor himself often does not physically examine women, but gets his information from the patient herself or a female assistant.

C. 425 B.C.   Classes of Women in Athens. An Athenian lawsuit, whose records have survived to the present, records the prosecutor's description of the various classes of Athenian women: "We have courtesans (*hetaerae*) for pleasure, concubines to take care of our day-to-day bodily needs, and wives to bear us legitimate children and to be the loyal guardians of our households."

C. 425 B.C. Athenian Concubines. A concubine is any woman living with a man on a permanent basis who has not gone through the formal betrothal and marriage rituals. An Athenian can have only one formal wife, and only her children can share in the inheritance at his death. Athenian concubines are often former slaves or foreigners, although some Athenian-born women are also concubines, perhaps because their guardians have died or they are too poor to attract an official husband. The concubines typically live in a separate home, although some share the wife's home.

C. 415 B.C. Sexual Relations in Athens. Athenian society countenances a double standard in matters of sexual relations. A man can legally have a wife, concubines, and have sexual relations with prostitutes (*hetaerae*). Women can have sexual relations only with a husband. This is particularly important in Athens, where legal matters of citizenship and inheritance will be thrown into doubt if the parentage of children is questioned. For this reason, penalties for adultery are very stiff. A man is legally allowed to kill any man discovered in his wife's bed. However, he may also accept the promise of payment of a stiff penalty, hold the offender prisoner until payment is assured, or physically torture him. Since the offender's family may seek revenge, financial penalties are a safer option.

Women adulterers, however, are legally required to be divorced and forbidden to take part in public religious rituals. Any man who catches her trying to participate in a public ritual is legally enjoined to tear off her clothes in public and beat her. The life of a woman so disgraced is almost unbearable.

C. 400 B.C. Lysimache Is Model for Aristophanes' Play. Lysimache is a priestess of Athena for 64 years in the late fifth and early fourth centuries B.C. She has been identified as the model for Aristophanes' play *Lysistrata*. (Both names—Lysimache and Lysistrata—mean "disbander of armies.")

C. 400 B.C. Childbirth in Ancient Greece. The Hippocratic writers of ancient Greece write very little about childbirth, indicating that doctors are not usually called on to attend a birth. Usually a midwife (maia) and female friends and neighbors come to help a woman in labor. When the child is born, these helpers set up a ritual cry of joy, bathe both the mother and the child, and wrap the baby in swaddling bands. If the baby is a boy, they hang an olive crown on the family's door. If it is a girl, a tuft of wool is hung, a reference to her future womanly duties in textile production. If for some reason it is decided that the baby should not be allowed to live, it seems the midwife is responsible for arranging its death by exposure. Usually, a child is exposed if it is illegitimate, sickly, or handicapped. Such a child is placed in a deserted spot, or perhaps near a crossroads where someone wanting a child may pick it up. Although there is no conclusive evidence, Greek baby girls may be more likely to be exposed at birth. A third-century comic poet writes the epigram: "Everybody raises a son even if he is poor, but exposes a daughter even if he is rich." The dowry required to find a husband for a daughter may be an incentive to limit the number of girls a family raises.

A fourth century B.C. law states that anyone present in the house at birth will be considered impure for three days. On the tenth day after birth, the baby is given a name at a ritual that includes carrying it around the household's *hestia* or hearth. Sometime thereafter, the mother visits the shrine of a birth-goddess, usually Artemis, to offer thanks and sometimes gifts of clothing.

C. 390 B.C. Mother of Important Chinese Philosopher Becomes Model for Chinese Female Behavior. Meng-tzu (known in the West as Mencius) (c.370–290 B.C.) is one of the most important Confucian philosophers in Chinese history. Nothing is known of his father, but his mother is credited with providing him with a splendid education. When he is a child, he imitates his surroundings, so she moves three times until she finds a suitable environment near a school. She is taken as a model for proper maternal behavior by later generations of Chinese, and stories about her are prominently featured in handbooks of female behavior.

C. 350 B.C. Aristotle and the Physiology of Women. Aristotle (384–322 B.C.) is a philosopher, not a doctor. Nevertheless, in creating his theories on animals, he speculates on female physiology. He believes that the main difference between the two sexes is the relative heat of their bodies. Men are hot and women are cold in physical nature. According to Aristotle, the hotter the body is, the more easily it can turn food into blood, flesh, and hair. Since men, being hotter, can create semen and women cannot, Aristotle says women are incomplete or deformed males. The woman's body can only turn blood into menstrual fluid. Unlike the Hippocratic doctors, Aristotle believes that menstruation can weaken the body. According to Aristotle, this lack of heat is also the explanation for women's smaller bodies and weaker intelligence. Aristotle also challenges the Hippocratics' belief in a "mobile" womb.

C. 350 B.C. First Nude Female Statue in Greece Sculpted. Around 350 B.C., the sculptor Praxitiles creates a monumental statue of Aphrodite in the nude. It is widely copied by later Hellenistic and Roman artists. Previously, Greek goddesses have always been portrayed fully clothed. (The only women represented nude are prostitutes; the youthful male body is considered to be artistically beautiful and is also represented nude.) In Hellenistic Greek culture, the naked female form becomes more acceptable as an object of art.

331 B.C. Alexander the Great Conquers Egypt. Alexander of Macedon conquers Egypt and establishes Alexandria as its capital. This marks the end of ancient, dynastic Egypt and the beginning of Hellenistic Egypt, also called "Ptolemaic Egypt" after the rulers of Egypt during this era, the Ptolemies.

C. 300 B.C. Herophilus and the Physiology of Women. Herophilus is a Greek physician who lives in Alexandria at the end of the fourth century and beginning of the third century B.C. He is the first (and last until the thirteenth century) to use dissection to study the human body. Although not much of his work is extant, commentators have quoted him so that something is known of his discoveries about female anatomy. Herophilus agrees with Aristotle that men are hot and women cold in nature. However, he notices a similarity between the testicles of men and the ovaries of women. However, like Aristotle, he believes that the woman's only contribution to conception is her menstrual fluid. Herophilus also writes an influential manual for midwives. This indicates that midwives are expected to be literate.

300 B.C. Dana, Chief Goddess of Ancient Ireland. Dana (or Danu) is the chief goddess of ancient Ireland, mother of the Tuantha De Danann—the People of Dana—a tribe of divine beings who are demoted to fairy folk in later times. Many other Great Mother goddesses the world over also carry the name Dana, or a variation of it (e.g., Danu, Danae, Dinah, Danu-Ana, or Anu).

300 B.C. Ise Shrine Dedicated to Japanese Sun Goddess. Ise Shrine, one of the most important Shinto shrines in Japan, enshrines Amaterasu o Mikami, the sun goddess and mythical ancestress of the Japanese imperial family. Imperial princesses become the high priestesses of Ise.

300 B.C. Ancient Ireland's Trinity of War and Death Goddesses. Ancient Ireland has a trinity of war and death goddesses whose distinction from each other has become blurred in present times with different sources giving different names for the three. Generally, Morrigan is considered to be the unified triple-goddess, with the three aspects named Badb (pronounced Beeve), Macha, and Ana. All the goddesses can take the shape of a crow (which they frequently do), and in human form they are giants. In the Ana-Badb-Macha trinity, Ana is the virgin maiden fertility goddess; Badb, the mother producing life from her boiling cauldron; and Macha, the aged crone who rules death. Before a battle, the Triple Goddess Morrigan washes the armor of those doomed to die, and during the battle she flies over the battlefield in her crow-form, searching for carrion (dead bodies) to eat. She uses the blood of slain warriors for her magic, and as Badb can bring the dead back to life by boiling them in her cauldron—the source of life, wisdom, inspiration, and spiritual enlightenment. So, as in most cultures, the goddess of death is also the goddess of life (and rebirth); and the goddess of life is also the goddess of death (and rebirth). It is all part of the cycle.

C. 212 B.C. Roman Law to Prevent Fancy Dress and Carriage Travel for Women. The *Lex Oppia* is passed during the emergency of Rome's war against Carthage (212–202 B.C.). It forbids women to wear finery and to travel in carriages. In 195 B.C. women strive to have the law repealed, provoking extensive debates in the Roman Senate that are rendered by the historian Livy.

C. 204 B.C. Claudia Moves Barge to Prove Chastity. Quinta Claudia, who is variously recorded to be a married woman or a Vestal Virgin, is suspected of unchastity. When the barge that carries the statue of the Great Mother up the Tiber River to Rome becomes grounded (a very bad omen), Claudia prays to the goddess to allow her to move the barge if she is chaste. She uses her hair as a tow rope and brings the barge safely to the temple.

204 B.C. Black Stone of the Goddess Cybele, Great Mother of the Gods. The religion of Cybele, Great Mother of the Gods, arrives in Rome from Phygia (in modern-day Turkey) in 204 B.C. when her meteoric black stone is carried into the city in a triumphal procession. It is believed that the Romans can defeat Hannibal if Cybele's stone is in Rome, and, in fact, 13 years later, they do just that. Cybele's temple stands on the Vatican until Christians take it over in the fourth century A.D.

C. 200 B.C. Galen Writes About Woman's Reproductive System. Galen, a medical author who lives in Rome in the late second century B.C., believes that men and women's bodies are the same, except for the reproductive organs. Women's reproductive organs, he says, are inverted because women, being colder, do not possess sufficient heat to project them out, as a man does. However, he does not see that as a flaw, but as nature's perfect plan for reproduction. Galen does not believe the Hippocratic theory that the womb can travel. However, he blames women's hysterical symptoms on a lack of sexual intercourse, which he says can affect a woman's reproductive system. Galen agrees with Aristotle that women are naturally inferior to men due to their physiology. For example, Galen says that a woman's lack of body hair, like a child's, is proof of her inferiority to men.

C. 200 B.C. Empress Lü in China's Han Dynasty. The Empress Lü is the consort of the founding emperor of the Han dynasty, Gaozu (reigns 202–195 B.C.). After his death, she is the power behind the throne, and she is an effective ruler. Later Chinese historians vilify her, in part because of her ruthlessness in

Cornelia

eliminating her rivals, and in part because her assumption of power seems to them to violate proper norms of female behavior.

200 B.C.   Roman Ideal of Womanhood. A famous tomb inscription celebrating the second century B.C. woman Claudia, succinctly states the Roman ideal:

"Friend, I have not much to say; stop and read it. This tomb, which is not fair, is for a fair woman. Her parents gave her the name Claudia. She loved her husband in her heart. She bore two sons, one of whom she left on earth, the other beneath it. She was pleasant to talk with, and she walked with grace. She kept the house and worked in wool. That is all. You may go."

C. 180 B.C.   Birth of Cornelia, Roman Woman. Cornelia (c.180 B.C.–c.105 B.C.) is the daughter of the Roman ruler Scipio Afri-

canus. She bears Tiberius Sempronius Gracchus 12 children, only three of whom survive. Her daughter marries a Roman national hero. When she is widowed, Cornelia refuses an offer of marriage from King Ptolemy of Egypt, devoting herself to the education of her two sons, Tiberius and Gaius Gracchus. She brings Greek philosophers from the city of Mitylene to educate them. When Tiberius and Gaius try to institute political reforms inspired by Greek democracy, it leads to violent political change at Rome. After her death, her sons' political opponents "discover" a letter attributed to Cornelia criticizing her younger son Gaius for his revolutionary activities. Scholars debate whether the letter is authentic, or a piece of propaganda.

At any rate, a marble statue of Cornelia seated is erected in a public place, apparently the first Roman statue so honoring a mortal woman. It becomes a model for later statues of Roman women.

Cornelia is the Roman ideal of a *univira*, a woman who has only one husband throughout her life.

C. 100 B.C.   Roman Property Law. Under Roman law, a husband can distinguish between the amount of the dowry the wife brings with her (which he has to give back in the event of divorce) and the amount of wealth that may have accrued to his estate as a result of owning her dowry. Laws are also passed that allow the husband to retain one-sixth of her dowry for the support of each child. Children, as always, are considered the property of the father. Marital faults can cost a woman another one-sixth or one-eighth of her dowry.

C. 100 B.C.   Marriage in Roman Society. Roman women, although not sequestered like some Greek women, are still defined by their membership in the household of first their fathers, then their husbands. In the usual form of marriage, the daughter passes from the manus (hand) of her father to the manus of her new husband. There, her legal status is almost the same as that of her own daughters. The paterfamilias (father of the family) has the power of life and death over everyone in the household. It is he who decides whether or not his wife's children will be exposed at birth. In principle, she has no say in the matter. In the case of divorce, the father has the right to retain the children.

A looser form of marriage ("without manus") exists in cases where for financial reasons the daughter's family does not wish to totally break its ties with the daughter. In this case, the wife is required to spend three nights in succession every year away from her husband.

C. 89 B.C. Illicit Love Celebrated in Rome. Set against the Roman ideal of the chaste and virtuous wife and mother is the demonic figure of the extravagantly wanton aristocratic woman. Poets of the late Republican era even begin to celebrate illicit love.

The noblewoman Clodia (born c.89 B.C.) seems to be the model for the character of "Lesbia," the object of passionate poetry by the author Valerius Catullus. Lesbia is a new type of Roman woman: one who chooses her own lovers and leaves them at her own whim. Clodia's position in society insulates her from public opinion, and she apparently lives a scandalous lifestyle. One of her lovers, M. Caelius Rufus, is prosecuted for violence in 54 B.C. The orator, Cicero, successfully defends Caelius by maintaining that Clodia has taught the young man evil ways, and is behind his prosecution because Caelius has left her.

Because of Rome's constant wars, and the custom of marrying young women to men at least ten years older, many Roman noblewomen become widows while they are still in the prime of life. Whether this, combined with the instability of the time, contributes to a rise in immorality among noblewomen is now hard to determine. However, the Emperor Augustus eventually exiles the poet

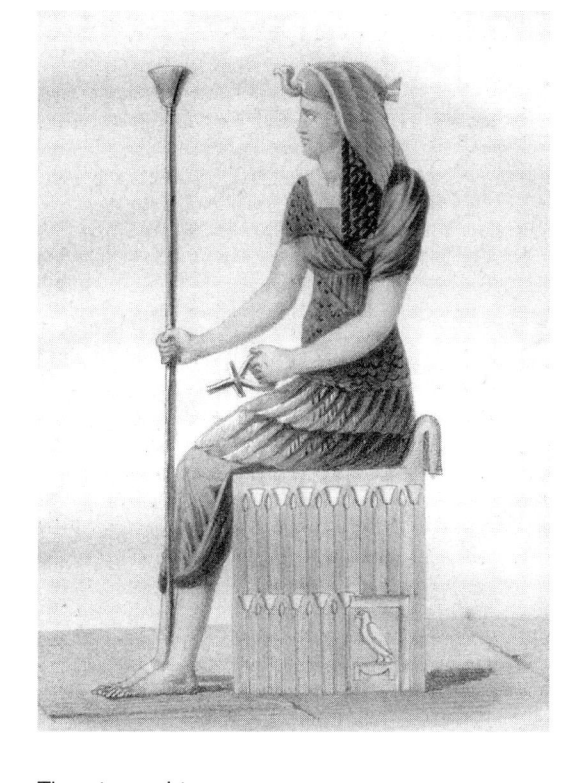

The priestess Isis.

Ovid because of his poetic manuals instructing men and women on the ways of illicit love.

80 B.C. Cult of the Ancient Egyptian Goddess Isis. The supreme deity of ancient Egypt, creator of all, known by many names, comes to be known primarily as Isis. She absorbs all the aspects of the other goddesses who are identified with her until she becomes the universal goddess. Her worship reaches Rome in about 80 B.C. where it flourishes until overtaken by Christianity four centuries later. As Isis has absorbed other goddesses, so is she absorbed by the Christian cult of the Virgin Mary. Some early Christians call themselves Pastophori, or "servants of Isis," which later develops into "pastors."

76 B.C. Rare Biography of Roman Woman, Tullia. The life of Tullia (76–45 B.C.), the daughter of the Roman orator Cicero, comes down through his letters. Hers is one of the few biographies of a private Roman woman in existence today. She is married in her teens to a man in his late thirties. He dies a natural death a few years later. Tullia and her mother contract a marriage to Cornelius Dolabella while her father (who is trying to find her a debt-free husband) is away, serving as governor of Cilicia. Tullia loses her first child, and she and Dolabella begin to live apart. When Tullia becomes pregnant by another, Cicero considers making Dolabella divorce her so that her own family can raise the child. However, he is unable to raise enough money to accomplish this (he has not yet succeeded in completely paying Tullia's dowry). Tullia dies in childbirth in 45 B.C., leaving her father heartbroken. She is only 31 years old.

C. 69–30 B.C. Cleopatra, Epic Queen of Egypt. Cleopatra (69–30 B.C.) lives an epic life at the crossroads of modern history. Mistress of two Roman rulers, the events of her reign decisively influence the shape of the Roman world, which becomes the foundation of modern, western civilization.

In 51 B.C., at the age of 18, she ascends to the throne as Cleopatra VII, having married her younger brother, Ptolemy XIII, according to ancient Egyptian custom. Because her brother is a minor, he rules with the assistance of a three-person regency council. This council perceives the strong-willed Cleopatra as a threat and deposes her. She flees to Syria, raises an army, and returns to Egypt's capital, Alexandria, ready to do battle against her brother and his council.

At this critical moment, in 48 B.C., Julius Caesar, dictator of Rome, arrives at Alexandria with a small force of soldiers. He declares that Cleopatra's father, Ptolemy XII (Ptolemy Auletes), has left a will putting the welfare of his royal children in the hands of the Roman Senate. Caesar will, therefore, set-tle the dispute between Cleopatra and her brother.

The council agrees to this, confident that they will be able to assassinate Cleopatra if she tries to enter Alexandria. Unable to enter the city safely, Cleopatra sends a large carpet to Caesar as a gift. When it is unrolled, Caesar, 52 at the time, is astonished and delighted to find the beautiful young queen wrapped inside it. It is said that they become lovers the same night. Contemporaneous Roman historians bear witness to Cleopatra's astonishing beauty and magical personal charm.

Despite his infatuation with Cleopatra, Caesar proposes the resumption of joint rule between Cleopatra and Ptolemy. This does not satisfy Ptolemy's advisors, who surround the city with troops. When Roman reinforcements arrive, Caesar decisively defeats the Egyptian force. Ptolemy drowns while trying to escape. Thus, Cleopatra becomes the sole ruler of Egypt. She also becomes the acknowledged mistress and protégée of Caesar, who spends more than a year enjoying her lavish hospitality.

According to the Roman historian Plutarch, Cleopatra bears Caesar a son, Caesarion, although some historians now dispute this claim. At the time, Cleopatra insists that Caesarion is indeed Caesar's child, his only son. She hopes that Caesarion will inherit Caesar's powerful position as dictator of Rome.

In 46 B.C., Cleopatra travels to Rome, apparently to participate in Caesar's enormous Triumph, a kind of parade and celebration for his victories in Egypt, North Africa, and Gaul (present-day France). Caesar dedicates a new temple to Venus and places Cleopatra's statue inside it. He also makes her a member of his family, which scandalizes the Romans, to whom Roman citizenship is a sacred honor, not lightly conferred on foreigners. Caesar also gives her a country-home outside of Rome, offending his virtuous wife, Calpurnia, and further scandalizing the Romans. Rumors fly that

Caesar plans to move the capital of the empire from Rome to Alexandria.

However, on March 15, 44 B.C., Caesar is assassinated by republicans who fear that he will establish a monarchy with himself as king. Caesar's will proclaims his nephew, the 18-year-old Octavian, not Cleopatra's son Caesarion, his heir. Cleopatra quickly flees with Caesarion by ship back to Alexandria.

Octavian and Marc Antony, Caesar's powerful friend and lieutenant, come to a power-sharing arrangement that includes another powerful Roman, Lepidus. This group is known as the "second triumvirate." Antony wins a glorious victory in 42 B.C. at Philippi that effectively puts him in control of the Roman Empire. Shortly thereafter, he requests that Cleopatra, now 28 years old, meet him in Tarsus to answer charges that she has helped the enemies of the second triumvirate. Cleopatra arrives in an enormous, gilded barge decorated to look like an enchanted forest. She quickly charms Antony as she had charmed Caesar. Antony spends years idling in luxury at Cleopatra's side while the security of Rome's eastern provinces deteriorates. Octavian eventually gains the upper hand, and Antony leaves Egypt hastily for Rome.

In 40 B.C., Octavian and Antony agree to a power-sharing arrangement that makes Antony ruler of the eastern part of the empire. Octavian takes Rome and the western provinces. To cement this agreement, Antony agrees to marry Octavian's half-sister, Octavia. In 37 B.C., Antony leaves Rome and brings Octavia with him only as far as Greece. He then summons Cleopatra to meet him at Antioch. There he consummates a marriage ritual with Cleopatra, one which is not recognized by Rome but is accepted by the eastern territories. Antony makes Cleopatra the ruler of all the territories formerly held by her ancestors, the Ptolemaic rulers of Egypt. She bears Antony three children, Alexander Helios, Ptolemy Philadelphus, and Cleopatra Selene.

Antony's infatuation with Cleopatra seems to impair his abilities both as a commander and as a ruler. He loses important battles and bestows countries he has not yet conquered on Cleopatra and her children. In 32 B.C., Antony formally divorces Octavia and orders her to leave his house in Rome, even though she has been faithfully caring for his Roman children. Octavian declares war on Cleopatra and calls Antony an agent of a foreign state.

In 31 B.C., Octavian and Antony face each other near the Greek city of Actium. Antony's force has superior numbers, but Octavian has the brilliant general Agrippa. Antony's fleet is soon blockaded in the Gulf of Actium. The Battle of Actium lasts only a few minutes. Antony's fleet is quickly destroyed. Seeing the day is lost, Cleopatra's ships raise their sails and run for Egypt. Antony, seeing this, shamefully abandons his fleet and land troops, chasing after Cleopatra's ship in a small, fast galley. Now a broken man, he and Cleopatra return to Alexandria. His abandoned troops and the various subjugated princes of the eastern empire pledge their allegiance to Octavian.

Both Antony and Cleopatra appeal to Octavian for mercy. He replies only to Cleopatra, saying that if she will expel Antony from Egypt, she can ask for anything. She refuses.

Finally, in 30 B.C., Antony faces Octavian outside Alexandria. On the day of the battle, both Egypt's navy and his own cavalry desert to Octavian. Antony rides back to Alexandria, convinced that Cleopatra has betrayed him. Cleopatra, fearing his anger, flees to her royal tomb. Antony is told that she has died. He tries to commit suicide by falling on his sword, a time-honored Roman custom, but he only fatally injures himself. The historian Plutarch relates that he is carried in agony to Cleopatra's tomb, where he dies in her arms.

Octavian's soldiers manage to penetrate Cleopatra's stronghold and take her prisoner. Although he promises not to harm her, Octavian plans to take her to Rome, no doubt to appear in chains at his Triumph. In one last act of desperation, she manages to obtain a poisonous snake, called an asp, hidden in a basket of figs. She writes a letter to Octavian begging for mercy for her children. By the time he receives the letter, she and her servants are all dead.

Plutarch, a historian who lives about 100 years after Cleopatra, describes her thus: "The charm of her presence was irresistible, and there was an attraction in her person and her talk, together with a peculiar force of character which pervaded her every word and action, and laid all who associated with her under its spell."

Cleopatra's tragic and remarkable life has been the subject of innumerable books, plays, films, and poems. She is the last of the Ptolemaic rulers of Egypt, which becomes only another exploited province of imperial Rome. Octavian becomes the celebrated Emperor Augustus. Egypt becomes Rome's bread basket. It will be centuries before Egyptians are ruled again by Egyptians.

58 B.C.   Berenice Rules in Egypt. Ptolemy XII (also called Ptolemy Auletes) rules Egypt at a time when Rome is beginning to consolidate its power over kingdoms that it has previously granted much autonomy. By borrowing heavily from a Roman money lender, he buys the Roman senate's agreement to allow Egypt to remain autonomous. However, when he decrees that the people of Egypt have to pay back the enormous debt he has incurred, a popular uprising occurs. Auletes flees, leaving his daughters, Cleopatra VI Tryphaena and Berenice, as coregents in his absence. Cleopatra VI is supposed to be the mother of Cleopatra VII, the most famous woman to bear the title Cleopatra, which means "the glory of her

race." Cleopatra VI dies shortly after being named coregent, leaving Berenice as sole ruler.

Auletes flees to Rome and attempts to obtain help from the Roman senate to regain his throne. Berenice tries to obstruct her father's machinations by sending her own representatives to the senate. However, Auletes arranges to have them assassinated when they arrive in Italy. He eventually obtains help from the Roman governor of Syria, recaptures his throne, and puts his daughter to death. Cleopatra VII is about 14 years old at this time.

C. 50 B.C. Occupations of Women. One of the principal jobs of a Roman woman is working wool, carding, spinning, and weaving. During the centuries of Roman wars and conquests, women are left alone to manage farms and businesses for long periods of time while their men are off fighting.

Slaves depend totally on the good will of their master and mistress. If a slave earns her freedom, she may have to yet earn enough money to buy her children from the master. Freedwomen can support themselves as craftswomen or entertainers; others may buy girl slaves or foundlings and raise them to the sex trade.

C. 50 B.C.   Terentia Will Not Finance Her Husband's Wars. All that is known of Terentia, wife of the famous Roman politician Cicero, is that Cicero writes letters to a friend complaining that Terentia will not loan him enough of her money to help him through his difficulties during the civil wars. Although they are not wealthy, Terentia's dowry has been enough to allow Cicero to live in Rome, where he can be active in affairs of the day. Due to this quarrel, the couple divorces in 46 B.C., and Cicero is obliged to return Terentia's dowry, which puts him in very difficult financial circumstances. In order to satisfy this debt, he marries the 17-year-old girl Publilia who is under his guardianship. Her dowry restores his fortune. He is 63 years old.

43 B.C. Hortensia. The widow of Servilius Caepio and the daughter of a Roman orator, Hortensia makes an impassioned plea before the triumvirs to end a tax on the women relations of men who have been proscribed by Rome for taking part in the civil wars. When the triumvirs drive the noblewomen from the court, public outrage forces them to grant the women's request. Before the civil wars, it is unheard of for a woman to plead her own case in a court. During the lawlessness and chaos of the wars, several women become notorious for speaking out in public.

C. 40 B.C. Livia Drusilla, Roman Role Model. Livia Drusilla is the daughter of two of Rome's most ancient noble families: the Claudians and Drusi. She is one of the most beautiful women in Rome. At a young age she is married to a man of equally noble parentage, Tiberius Claudius Nero, who is many years her senior. After the death of Julius Caesar, Livia's father, who had fought with the traitors Brutus and Cassius, is proscribed by the ruling authorities and commits suicide. In 40 B.C., Livia and her husband flee Italy in fear of the vengeance of Caesar's now powerful nephew, Octavian.

Two years later, Livia is only 19 when she is hastily divorced from her first husband, the aging Tiberius Claudius Nero, and marries Octavian, who will eventually become the first emperor of Rome, Augustus. Octavian also quickly divorces his first wife, Scribonia, who has borne him a daughter, Julia. It is 38 B.C., and Livia is pregnant with Nero's child. Nevertheless, her former husband plays the part of a father at her wedding and endows her with a dowry. When her second son, Drusus Claudius Nero, is born, he is quickly sent back to his father's house to be raised along with his brother, Livia's oldest son, Tiberius.

Although the alliance itself is not unusual, the haste with which it is accomplished is. Perhaps Octavian virtually abducts Livia, having fallen passionately in love with

her, or perhaps Octavian needs the alliance with a woman of the highest rank to help secure his position politically in those strife-ridden times. Octavian's two enemies, Marc Antony and Lepidus, have much more ancient and illustrious ancestors. Since her first husband seems to be a willing party to the match, it may also be supposed that the aristocracy by this marriage is throwing its support behind Octavian, the youngest of the three revolutionary leaders. The ailing, aged Nero dies a few years after the wedding.

After Nero's death, Livia accepts both her sons by him into her new household.

The Roman historian Suetonius relates that the home shared by Augustus and Livia on the Palatine Hill is small and austere by late-Roman standards. They own several unpretentious country villas. Livia personally supervises the affairs of the household, including the weaving of garments for the entire royal family. It is known that Augustus frequently consults with Livia about political decisions and takes her advice very seriously. In 18 B.C., during the debate in the senate on Augustus' Lex sumptuaria, meant to curb the extravagant lifestyles of the nobility, Augustus delivers a speech citing Livia as a model for the ladies of Rome, detailing her mode of life and even how she dresses. After Augustus' death, Livia's son Tiberius becomes emperor. Her grandsons, Caligula and Claudius, also become emperors.

In the realm of rumor and speculation, the string of tragedies which bedevil Augustus' family are laid at Livia's door by the acerbic Roman historian Tacitus. In particular, the deaths of Augustus' two grandsons and heirs to his throne, Caius and Lucius, less than two years apart, raise speculation that Livia is responsible for their deaths. Due to their loss, her son, Tiberius, becomes emperor after Augustus' death on August 23, 14 A.D. Augustus and Livia have been married for 52 years. In his will, Augustus leaves Livia one-third of his estate and directs the senate to bestow on her the title "Augusta." Livia dies 15 years later, in 29 A.D., at the age of 86. Her son, now Emperor Tiberius, refuses to honor the provisions of her will or to deify her, as the populace wishes. Her grandson, the Emperor Claudius, accomplishes this when he succeeds to the throne in 41 A.D.

In modern times, the poet Robert Graves' popular novels *I Claudius* and *Claudius the God* concoct an evil Livia based on the calumnies of Tacitus: an accomplished poisoner and manipulator who is behind virtually all the tragedies that befall Rome during her lifetime. Whether or not this is true is impossible to know. However, millions of people know this picture of Livia thanks to the popular television series, *I Claudius*, first broadcast in the 1970s.

39 B.C. Julia, Unconventional Roman Woman, Is Born. Julia, the daughter of Octavian (who will become the Emperor Augustus) and his first wife, Scribonia, is born in 39 B.C. Although her father shortly thereafter divorces her mother to marry Livia, as is the custom, he retains the right to make all decisions about his daughter's education and marriage. When she is 16, she is married to Augustus' nephew, Marcellus, the son of Augustus' own sister, Octavia.

Julia and Marcellus represent a new generation of Romans, ones for whom the terrible years of the Civil Wars are just dim memories. This generation is ready to enjoy the opulence of the newly-won countries of the eastern Mediterranean, especially Alexandrian Egypt. Augustus' severe laws on adultery and extravagance may be a reaction to this influx of luxury and, to Roman eyes, immorality.

Marcellus dies very young, in 23 B.C., and in conformance with Roman laws requiring remarriage, Augustus has to find another husband for his daughter. He chooses his old companion-in-arms, Marcus Agrippa, 24 years older than his daughter. Agrippa, who had been the architect of Marc Antony's defeat, is the second most powerful man in

Rome. Julia bears Agrippa two sons, Caius and Lucius (whom her father will adopt as potential heirs to the throne), and two daughters, Julia the Younger and Agrippina.

Julia, only 21, is now second only to Livia in prestige among the women of Rome. Julia seems to take pleasure in being everything Livia is not: where Livia is reputed to live modestly, Julia lives extravagantly and a coterie of followers grows up around her. Although Roman custom dictates that a matron should stay at home when her husband is sent abroad on the business of the country, Julia persuades Agrippa to take her with him on a tour of the eastern empire. She is greeted as a representation of the divine Venus (Greek: Aphrodite) at Paphos, the center of worship of the goddess. During Agrippa's absences on business, Julia begins to have affairs with the young men of her court, including Sempronius Gracchus, a descendant of the famous Gracchi.

Where Livia comes to represent the ideals of the party of the Claudii, the old conservative nobility, Julia embodies the party of the Julii, the youthful nobility. When Agrippa dies in 12 B.C., Augustus tries to reconcile these two factions by marrying Julia to her own half-brother, Livia's son Tiberius. To accomplish this, Tiberius is required to divorce his first wife, Agrippina, whom he dearly loves. Julia and Tiberius have a son who dies shortly after birth. The differences between them widen, and Julia resumes her affair with Sempronius Gracchus. Tiberius seems to know of this, but is powerless to expose her and bring disgrace on Augustus, who remains willfully blind to her behavior. The differences of the opposing factions solidify around the differences between Tiberius and Julia.

Tiberius, irked by honors Augustus and the senate have voted to one of Agrippa's and Julia's two sons (who have been adopted by Augustus), retires to private life on the island of Rhodes in 12 B.C. Tiberius, a fierce supporter of the laws against luxury, is actively disliked and little missed at Rome, where laws are soon passed to increase appropriations for public games. In 18 B.C., the party of Tiberius had helped pass a severe law against adultery, the *Lex Julia de adulteriis*, which allowed any citizen to denounce an unfaithful wife, even if her husband or father both refused to make the accusation. Julia's adulteries have escaped unpunished because of her unique position and the blindness of her father. Somehow, proof of Julia's adulteries is finally brought to Augustus' attention, and he is forced to apply his own law to his own daughter. He exiles Julia to the tiny island of Pandataria. Scribonia, the model of a Roman mother, chooses to join her daughter in exile. Julia is only 37 years old.

Nothing can persuade Augustus to forgive his daughter, even though the populace intercedes on her behalf many times. Despite her extravagance, she is a well-loved figure. Julia lives five years on the island, forbidden both wine and male companionship. Thereafter she is allowed to move to the mainland and lives under a kind of house arrest.

33 B.C. **Wang Zhaojun, Consort of Han Emperor, Refuses to Bribe a Court Painter.** A court painter portrays Wang Zhaojun, a beautiful consort of the emperor Yuandi, as ugly in his portrait of her. She does not bribe him to change the depiction. On the basis of the unflattering portrait, the emperor gives Zhaojun as a bride to a chief of the Xiongnu, a nomadic people to China's north. When Zhaojun is leaving the court, the emperor sees her beauty and his mistake, but it is too late. He cannot go back on his promise for fear of incurring the wrath of the powerful Xiongnu. The story of Wang Zhaojun has been the subject of countless poems and plays.

C. 31 B.C. **Marc Antony Abandons All for Cleopatra.** Antony and Cleopatra face Octavian, the future Emperor Augustus, and his brilliant general Agrippa in a naval battle near the Greek city of Actium. Despite his superior numbers, Antony loses the battle within minutes and shamefully deserts his troops to follow Cleopatra in fleeing back to the safety of Alexandria. The historian Plutarch later writes: "Here it was that Antony showed to all the world that he was no longer actuated by the thoughts and motives of a commander or a man, or indeed by his own judgment. What was once said as a jest—that the soul of a lover lives in someone else's body—he proved to be a serious truth. For, as if he had been born part of her, and must move with her wherever she went, as soon as he saw her ship sailing away, he abandoned all who were fighting and spending their lives for him.... He followed her that had so well begun his ruin and hereafter accomplished it."

C. 20 B.C. **Ovid and the Allegory of Princess Psyche.** The Roman poet Ovid (43 B.C.–17 A.D.) tells the allegorical story of the Princess Psyche. She is so famous for her beauty that crowds of people come from all around to gaze on her and pay her the kind of homage that is due to Venus (Greek: Aphrodite). Angered, Venus calls her son, Cupid (Greek: Eros), to wound her with one of his arrows and make her fall in love with some low being. However, Cupid, while performing this task, wounds himself with one of his arrows and falls in love with Psyche himself. Since she is now out of favor with Venus, Psyche finds that she has no suitors, despite the general adulation she receives. Her alarmed parents consult the Delphic Oracle and receive the following answer: "The virgin is destined for the bride of no mortal lover. Her future husband awaits her on the top of the mountain. He is a monster whom neither gods nor men can resist."

Psyche accepts her fate with dignity and is left alone on top of the mountain. A gentle wind bears her down to a beautiful palace with magnificent gardens. There, invisible voices tell her everything belongs to her; she is served by invisible hands and listens to music played by invisible performers. Her husband does not come until the dead of night and leaves before the dawn, so she never sees him, either. He charges her to make no attempt to see him.

Eventually Psyche grows so lonely, she begs her husband to let her bring her sisters for a visit. He reluctantly agrees. When the wind deposits them in her garden, the sisters are jealous of Psyche's good fortune. They pester her with questions about her husband and urge her to try to get a glimpse of the monster who they say may be preparing to eat her. Psyche, her anxiety aroused, brings a lamp and a knife to bed with her the next night. When her husband has fallen asleep, she lights the lamp and discovers not a monster, but the beautiful god Cupid. As she leans over him to look at him, a drop of oil falls on his shoulder and startles him awake. Without a word he spreads his wings and flies out the window. Psyche runs after him, but suddenly the palace and the gardens vanish.

Psyche wanders everywhere in search of her husband. The goddess Ceres (Greek: Demeter) takes pity on her and tells her to voluntarily surrender herself to the mercy of Venus. When Psyche attains Venus' presence the goddess is very angry with her. After reproaching her, Venus sets her three tasks.

The first is to separate into distinct piles a storehouse full of wheat, barley, millet, beans, and lentils all mixed together. Psyche begins to weep at the impossibility of the task. Suddenly, a horde of ants begins to attack the heap of grains. They sort every one into its own separate pile and then vanish.

The second task is to gather the golden wool from the back of a herd of wild rams. As Psyche is about to attempt this, the river god warns her of the danger and advises her to wait until the herd falls asleep in the noonday sun. Then she can easily go among them and gather bits of the fleece that have stuck to the bushes and to the trunks of trees.

The third task is to take a box to the goddess of the Underworld, Proserpina

(Greek: Persephone), and request her to fill it with beauty. Psyche is then to return and give the box to Venus. Since no mortals ever return from the Underworld, Psyche believes she is doomed. In desperation, she climbs a high tower and decides to throw herself off it. The tower itself speaks to her and instructs her in how to reach Proserpina safely and return. It also warns her not to look into the box that the queen of the dead will give her.

Psyche almost accomplishes the last task when she cannot resist the urge to open the box and take a little of the beauty for herself. Instead, she is enveloped by a deadly sleep. Cupid, now recovered from his wound, flies to her side, closes the box, and awakens her. He leads her back to Olympus, where he persuades Jupiter (Greek: Zeus) to intercede with Venus on Psyche's behalf. He agrees, and even has Mercury bring Psyche a cup full of divine ambrosia, which makes her immortal. She and Cupid are properly married and have a daughter named Pleasure.

18 B.C. Lex Julia Penalizes Childless Roman Couples. As the Roman nobility become fabulously wealthy, and as society absorbs the influence of eastern Hellenistic culture (symbolically consummated by the union of Marc Antony and Egypt's Cleopatra), the rigid standards of morality of the Roman Republic begin to decline. In addition, the political chaos caused by the Roman civil wars contributes to social chaos.

Against this background, the Emperor Augustus decrees the *Lex Julia* in 18 B.C. in order to penalize Roman citizens who remain childless. It affects women between the ages of 20 and 50, and men over the age of 25. Widows and widowers in these age groups are not allowed to remain unmarried. The law also penalizes citizens who commit adultery and citizens who marry outside of their social rank or status.

C. 14 B.C. Birth of Agrippina, Model Roman Matron. Agrippina the Elder, the daughter of

Julia and Marcus Agrippa, is born about 10 B.C. She marries Germanicus, a nephew of the Emperor Augustus by his widowed sister Antonia. Unlike her sister Julia the Younger, Agrippina leads the virtuous life of the traditional Roman matron. By the age of 26 she bears Germanicus nine children. In 4 A.D., Augustus orders Tiberius to adopt Germanicus, apparently hoping to unify the family and end strife about who will succeed the emperor.

After Augustus' death in 14 A.D., his wife's son, Tiberius, becomes emperor and Germanicus is sent to the Roman frontier in Gaul (present-day France and Germany), accompanied by Agrippina. In 16 A.D., against Tiberius' orders, Germanicus leads several campaigns into enemy territory and wins a number of costly victories against the barbarous tribes. He is given a triumph at Rome. These victories make him popular among the army and the populace.

Tiberius recalls the 33-year-old Germanicus from Gaul and sends him to the eastern side of the empire, to subdue troubles in Armenia. Along with Germanicus and Agrippina, Tiberius sends Cnaeus Piso, an older statesman, to advise Germanicus and probably to keep Tiberius informed of his adopted son's doings. This offends Germanicus. In addition, Agrippina and Cnaeus Piso's wife, Plancina, quarrel. This leads to the formation of two parties of supporters. Public opinion in Rome is drawn into the quarrel, with some accusing Tiberius and his mother, Livia, of obstructing and persecuting Germanicus.

In 19 A.D., Germanicus succumbs to a long illness at Antioch in Syria, destroying the hopes of the party that opposes Tiberius. Rumors circulate that Piso has poisoned Germanicus at the bidding of Tiberius and Livia. When Agrippina arrives in Rome with her husband's ashes, she leads a vehement campaign against Piso at Rome, stirring up public hatred against both Piso and Tiberius. It is even said that Piso has letters from Tiberius

Agrippina

instructing him to kill Germanicus. Although Piso professes his innocence, and assumes the emperor will protect him, he is condemned and his family is only narrowly saved by the efforts of Tiberius and Livia.

In 23 A.D., Tiberius' own son, Drusus, dies, leaving him without an heir. Agrippina's sons are the next in line. Agrippina's two oldest sons, Nero and Drusus, are presented by Tiberius to the senate. The Roman historian Tacitus records that, in 26 A.D., Tiberius refuses to allow Agrippina to remarry, presumably to prevent her from forming an alliance that may challenge his authority. As the head of her family, Tiberius has the power to decide Agrippina's fate.

After the death of Augustus' widow Livia in 29 A.D., Agrippina and her son Nero are accused of treason against Tiberius. Nero commits suicide and Agrippina is sent into exile. Later, her son Drusus is also imprisoned. In 33 B.C., Agrippina commits suicide by starving herself to death. Tacitus says of her, "Agrippina knew no feminine weaknesses. Intolerant of rivalry, thirsting for power, she had a man's preoccupations."

1 – 499 A.D.

15 A.D. Agrippina the Younger Is Born. Agrippina the Younger (15–59 A.D.) is one of nine children of Agrippina the Elder and Germanicus. By 33 A.D. her older brothers and her mother have all been driven into exile or suicide as a result of political maneuvering to designate a successor to the elderly Emperor Tiberius. Agrippina is married to Cnaeus Domitius Enobarbus, who is descended from one of the great aristocratic families of Rome.

When Tiberius dies in 37 A.D., Agrippina's youngest brother, 27-year-old Gaius (called Caligula), becomes emperor. That same year, she gives birth to her son Lucius Domitius Ahenobarbus (who will later be known as Domitius Nero). Caligula bestows vestal privileges on his three sisters: Agrippina, Drusilla, and Julia Livilla. This means, among other things, that at public games they will sit next to him at a place of honor. This is the first time that the women of the emperor's family are officially accorded a privileged position and a sacred character. At first, Caligula's reign is welcomed as a relief from the austerity imposed by the previous two emperors. But eventually, her brother's rule will become infamous for its wanton extravagance, cruelty, and madness.

Caligula exiles Agrippina in 39 A.D. and her husband dies in 40 A.D. Agrippina's son, Nero, is sent by Caligula to her sister-in-law to be raised. However, since Caligula has appropriated Agrippina's own fortune, Nero is raised in impoverished surroundings. After Caligula's assassination in January of 41 A.D., Agrippina's uncle, the new Emperor Claudius, recalls her. The impoverished Agrippina persuades her sister-in-law's husband, the wealthy Passienus Crispus, to divorce his wife and marry her. Shortly thereafter he dies, and Agrippina inherits his wealth.

The emperor's wife, Messalina, is bent on persecuting the remaining children of Germanicus, whom she sees as a threat to her power. Agrippina's sister, Julia Livilla, is accused of adultery with the philosopher Seneca and exiled. Somehow Agrippina survives the seven years of Messalina's ascendancy. After Messalina's execution for treason in 48 A.D., Claudius (perhaps with the aid of his freedmen) picks Agrippina to be the next empress. She is 33 years old.

Marriage between an uncle and a niece is regarded to be undesirable in Rome, so Claudius has to petition the senate to pass a law authorizing such marriages. Although the historian Tacitus claims that Agrippina is guilty of affairs with Claudius' freedmen, it does seem doubtful. Apparently her good reputation saves her from her sister's fate during the reign of Messalina.

During her six-year reign at Claudius' side, the laxity of the first seven years ends. The state finances and the imperial family's own fortune are reorganized, and the power of Claudius' freedmen to enrich themselves at his expense is curtailed. Agrippina has the title "Augusta" conferred upon her in her own lifetime. She is allowed to ride in a gilded coach within the precincts of the capitol, an honor reserved for priests and the images of the gods.

However, the question of succession continues to bedevil the imperial family. The aging Claudius' young children by Messalina, Britannicus and Octavia, stand in the way of Agrippina's son's line to the throne. In 50 A.D., she persuades Claudius to adopt her 11-year-old son. She also arranges Nero's marriage to Octavia in 53 A.D. Claudius dies in 54 A.D. at the age of 64, some say poisoned by the hand of Agrippina, who worried that he would make Britannicus his successor, instead of Nero. At this time Britannicus is 13 years old; Nero, 17 years old. Agrippina arranges for the pretorian guard to propose her son, not Britannicus, to the senate to succeed Claudius. The senate grudgingly confirms him. Because of his youth, Agrippina now holds supreme power as virtual regent.

Nero soon asserts his independence. A year later, he repudiates his wife, Octavia, and begins living with a freedwoman called Acte as if she is his legal wife. However, the laws of Rome forbid persons of his rank from marrying freedwomen. Agrippina tries to make Nero give up such a scandalous relationship, but to no effect. This is the first in a series of disagreements that will bring Nero to deeply hate his mother. In a way, their disaffection symbolizes the disaffection between the conservative, old aristocracy of Rome and the younger, luxury-loving nobles, many of whom are newcomers to the ranks of the aristocracy.

In 55 A.D., Claudius' son Britannicus dies suddenly. According to Tacitus, he is poisoned by Nero, who fears that Agrippina may groom Britannicus to take his place. Her power and influence is clearly on the wane. In 58 A.D., Nero leaves Acte for a beautiful, wealthy, and married noblewoman, Poppaea

Sabina. She is among the party of the new aristocracy and encourages Nero to break with his wife and mother. In 59 A.D., Poppaea convinces Nero to kill his mother, apparently because her opposition to their union will prevent Poppaea from ever becoming empress. With the collusion of one Anicetus, Nero invites his mother to visit him, sending her a large boat for transportation. The boat is designed to break apart and sink, making her death appear to be an accident. However, Agrippina discovers the danger in time, leaps overboard, and swims to shore. Her freedwoman is mistaken for her and is beaten to death. Somehow Agrippina makes her way to one of her villas. Anicetus is sent to finish what he has begun. He surrounds her villa with troops, finds her reclining on a couch speaking with a servant, and kills her. Tacitus says that she asks him to thrust her through the womb which has borne her son. The Roman historian Suetonius suggests that there may have been an incestuous relationship between Agrippina and her son.

19 A.D. **The *Lex Papia Poppea* Amends the *Lex Julia*.** The *Lex Papia Poppea* and the *Lex Julia* (18 B.C.) prevent offenders (those who are childless) from inheriting property and wealth, or cut their inheritances in half. They also reward women for having larger families. A woman who has three children is freed from her guardian. Augustus' law also allows citizens (except senators) to marry freedwomen and orders their children to be considered legitimate. If a freedwoman has four children, she is exempted from her obligations to her patron. Although free, the former slave usually enters freedom owing her previous master a certain amount of work. The new law relieves her of that obligation.

Augustus intends these measures to improve morality, purify society, and restore structure to the state. With this goal in mind, the law forbids marriage with those it calls immoral people: for example, actresses, prostitutes, or women convicted of adultery.

The *Lex Julia de adulteriis*, part of the larger *Lex Julia*, sets down death as a punishment for men caught in adultery. It also punishes men who rape a virgin or respectable widow by confiscating half their estate or administering corporal punishment. The law still, however, sanctions a man's right to kill a wife found in the act of adultery. The law is intended not to provide equality in the treatment of men and women, but to enforce a traditional standard of morality.

It is not clear if Augustus is really able to enforce the *Lex Julia*. The Roman historian Suetonius, writing 100 years later, says that Augustus is forced to mitigate some of its provisions due to popular outcry. For example, Suetonius says widows and widowers are allowed to remain unmarried for three years.

C. 21 A.D. Plotina Lauded as Model of Roman Womanhood. Plotina, the wife of the Emperor Trajan, is praised by several contemporaries as a model of Roman womanhood. Her attributes are that she devotes herself to her husband and is unswerving in her devotion to him. She is modest in attire and follows her husband's example of moving about on foot. Despite this self-effacing portrait, Roman historians say she does offer her husband advice on domestic matters and reproaches him for allowing his officials to extort money from provincial people. A letter from Plotina to her husband records her concern for the appointment of the proper person as head of the Epicurean school at Athens. She also accompanies her husband on campaigns, and is with him at his death.

C. 22 A.D. Valeria Messalina, Infamous for Treachery, Is Born. Roman women have come down to the present as basically two types: either completely virtuous, idealized matrons, or totally evil, adulterous villains. Valeria Messalina (22–48 A.D.), wife of the Emperor Claudius, is one of the latter type.

When she is only 16, she is married to the 50-year-old Claudius during the reign of Caligula. Claudius, a nephew of Augustus, has been kept in obscurity by the family. He is reputed to be slow-witted and clown-like, unable to assist at the simplest public duties. Claudius is drafted into being emperor by the Praetorian Guard after the assassination of his nephew Caligula. Claudius is in fact a historian and rules better than anyone expects. He is reputed, however, to be totally under the control of both Messalina and his freedmen.

Messalina persecutes the sisters of Caligula (Agrippina the Younger and Julia Livilla), whom Claudius has recalled to Rome from exile. Julia Livilla had been accused of adultery with the famous philosopher Seneca, and both had been sent into exile. For seven years, Messalina sells her influence to foreign allies and vassals, barters with contractors for public affairs, and indulges in ostentatious displays which violate Roman laws against luxury passed during the time of Augustus. The common people ascribe all the troubles of the time to Messalina, and by inference to Claudius' inability to rule his wife. There is so much dissent, Rome is on the brink of another civil war.

According to the Roman historians Suetonius and Tacitus, Messalina actually decides that she can dispose of Claudius and marry one of her lovers, Gaius Silius. In 48 A.D., when Claudius is out of the city for an official function, the pair celebrates a complete wedding ceremony. Suetonius reports that Claudius himself bestows a dowry on Messalina. Whether Claudius really intends to divorce Messalina and then give her to Silius is not clear. However, it seems that his freedmen convince Claudius of the danger and he orders her execution.

Messalina tries to commit suicide, but when she can't bring herself to do it, a soldier assists her. It is said that Claudius is informed of her death while at dinner and does not interrupt his banquet to inquire about the details of her death.

C. 37 A.D.   Drusilla Is Both Sister and Wife of Roman Emperor Caligula. Drusilla is one of the nine children of Agrippina the Elder and Germanicus. When her brother, Gaius (called Caligula), succeeds the Emperor Tiberius in 37 A.D., he arranges for her and her other sisters to receive special honors. When Gaius' first wife dies shortly afterwards, he decides to marry Drusilla, something that is scandalous to Romans, but a common practice in the Egyptian monarchical tradition of Alexandria. During an illness, he drafts a will in which he makes Drusilla heir of his goods and the empire itself, something that is unheard of. She dies suddenly in 39 A.D. of an unknown malady. Caligula declares her a goddess and has a temple built for her with a college of 20 priests, ten men and ten women. He declares her birthday a holiday and orders a statue of Venus carved in her likeness and placed in the Forum.

37 A.D.   Birth of Octavia, Who Will Die A Terrible Death. Octavia (37–62 A.D.) is the daughter of the Emperor Claudius and Messalina. Her mother becomes infamous for her infidelities and is executed for plotting to replace Claudius with one of her lovers. Her father remarries Agrippina the Younger, a woman whose goal is to place her own son, Nero, on the throne. In 48 A.D., Agrippina engineers the downfall of Octavia's fiancé, Lucius Silanus. He is accused of incest and banished. When 16-year-old Octavia is then betrothed to Nero, Silanus commits suicide. In 53 A.D. Octavia is married to Nero. Only two years later, Nero begins to defy his mother's influence and begins living with the freedwoman Acte. A few years later, he takes Poppaea Sabina, the wife of one of his close friends, as his mistress. Poppaea encourages Nero to free himself from the influence of both his mother and his wife. After arranging for his mother's death in 59 A.D., Nero divorces Octavia and banishes her in 62 A.D. The populace in Rome riots over this, replacing statues of Poppaea with those of Octavia. On June 6, 62 A.D., Nero orders Octavia to commit suicide. When Octavia resists, his soldiers bind her and open her veins, finishing the job by suffocating her. Her severed head is sent to Poppaea, who then marries Nero.

C. 40 A.D.   Chinese Historian Ban Zhao Is Born. Chinese historian Ban Zhao (c.40–115 A.D.), the earliest woman historian in China and perhaps in the world, is born. She is an author of *Precepts for Women* (*Nu jie*), a guide to proper female behavior. Together with her father and her brother, she writes the great *Han shu*, the definitive history of the Han dynasty.

50 A.D.   Maria the Jewess Establishes Alchemy. Maria the Jewess probably lives and works in Alexandria. She is referred to by a number of names, including Maria Prophetissa and Miriam the Prophetess, the name with which she signs her scientific writings. She writes extensively on her work, notably her invention of an apparatus for distillation. Her design, resembling a modern-day double boiler, is referred to as Maria's bath. The modern-day French-language term for double-boiler, *bain-marie,* is traced to Maria's design.

Maria believes that metals are living things, with either male or female gender. She invents an apparatus for processing metals, in a union she describes in sexual terms.

C. 60 A.D.   Icenian Warrior Queen Boudicca Leads Revolt Against the Romans. Boudicca is the wife of Prasutagus, king of the Icenians (a Celtic tribe in what is now England). During this time, the Romans are disarming tribes in Britain and colonizing the area with Roman settlers. When Prasutagus dies in 59 or 60 A.D., Boudicca takes command and leads a revolt against the Romans. Within a year, her rebel forces number over 120,000, and they attack and level several Roman villages, taking

Boudicca, queen of the Icenians.

no prisoners, but killing soldiers and citizens alike. By 61 A.D., the Romans have compensated for being taken off guard. The Roman cavalry defeats the poorly armed Icenian troops, but it is believed that Boudicca escapes capture and poisons herself.

C. 65 A.D. Building in Pompeii Built by Eumachia. A large structure is built in Pompeii by Eumachia, the priestess of Venus, according to the inscription on the building, which will be unearthed during excavations in later years. A statue, dedicated to her by the city's cloth cleaners, shows her in the costume of a respectable Roman matron. Scholars are not sure if the building is a warehouse, auction house, or meeting place.

Eumachia also wields political power. Her son, Marcus Numistrius Fronto, is mentioned in the inscription. He is running for

public office at the time the building is dedicated. At least 14 other women at Pompeii engage in business enterprises.

65 A.D. Death of Poppaea Sabina Is Result of Nero's Kick. Poppaea Sabina (d. 65 A.D.) is the wife of Rufius Crispinus, to whom she bears a son. Nevertheless, she becomes the mistress of one of the Emperor Nero's close confidantes, Marcus Salvius Otho. Poppaea divorces Crispinus and marries Otho, but soon becomes mistress to the emperor himself. Under her influence, Nero breaks away from the influence of his mother, Agrippina the Younger, and his wife, Octavia, the daughter of Emperor Claudius. Poppaea urges him on in the murder of his mother in 59 A.D. In order to marry Poppaea, Nero banishes and executes Octavia in 62 A.D. Three years later, Nero kicks Poppaea while she is pregnant, and she dies of her injuries.

98 A.D. First Account of Germanic Worship of Earth-Goddess Nerthus Written. The Germanic goddess Nerthus, or Mother Earth, is celebrated in a ritual procession described sometime around 98 A.D. by the Roman writer Tacitus (c.55–c.120 A.D.) in Germania, the first-known written account of Germanic religious rites. During this procession, all fighting ceases, weapons and iron tools are laid aside, and doors are opened in hospitality. Nerthus is one of the many aspects of Freya, the Great Goddess of northern Europe, who rules the heavens before Odin (or Woden) arrives from the East and, indeed, teaches Odin everything he knows about magic and divine power.

C. 100 A.D. Shamanesses in Shinto. Shinto, the indigenous religion of Japan, is based on the view of the world in which kami (divine spirits) interact with humans in both positive and negative ways. Since ancient times, some women fulfill the role of shamaness—a person having supernatural powers, able to communicate with and interpret the way of the kami.

Japan's early empresses, the legendary Himiko (reigns 180–248) and Jingu (reigns late 4th-early 5th centuries) practice shamanism. At times, shamanesses will go into a trance and, when in a state of possession, make predictions of future events or give advice to their followers.

C. 251 A.D. Birth of Wei Huacun, Chinese Daoist Leader. Wei Huacun (251–334 A.D.), an important Chinese Daoist leader, is born. She is highly educated, and although she is married, she lives apart from her husband. Daoist divinities reveal sacred texts to her, which she then transmits to the human world. This pattern of communication, where male divinities transmit texts to male humans through a female intermediary, remains common in Daoism.

267 A.D. Queen Zenobia Leads Independence Movement for Palmyra. The early years of Zenobia, a woman of Arab descent, are a mystery to modern historians. During this era, Roman control is weakening as the empire becomes too big and fragmented to maintain. As a result, the people of Palmyra (in the north of Syria) recognize that the Roman Empire can no longer provide adequate protection. Odainat rises to power as king of Palmyra during this period of autonomy, and with him rises his wife, Queen Zenobia. When Odainat is murdered in 267 A.D., Zenobia quickly takes his place and assumes control. During her reign, she commands military campaigns that result in the annexation of most of Syria and parts of Egypt. In 272 A.D., however, Zenobia is captured by the Romans and the independence movement for Palmyra is stopped.

300 A.D. Christians Take Over Temple of Cybele. The temple of the Great Mother goddess Cybele, which has stood on the Vatican in Rome since 204 B.C., is taken over by Christians (who later build St. Peter's basilica on the same site). At the same time, Chris-

tians declare the Christian sect of the Montanists, founded in the second century A.D. by a Cybeline priest named Montanus, to be heresy and kill many of its followers. Montanists believe that women are agents of the goddess and can preach and prophesy as well as men.

300 A.D. Kuan-Yin Transformed into Female Bodhisattva. Originally a male bodhisattva called Bodhisattva Avolokitesvara, Kuan-Yin is transformed into a female bodhisattva by the fourth century A.D. in China and comes to embody the feminine in Chinese and Japanese (as Kwannon) Buddhism. A bodhisattva is a "Buddha-to-be"; someone who, upon enlightenment, chooses to stay in human form, rather than become pure energy, so as to help all other humans attain enlightenment. Based on the Great Mother goddess of China, Kwai-Yin, who created the world and represents Boundless Compassion, so Kuan-Yin too becomes the most powerful and popular divine being in China, honored as the symbol of compassion in nearly every home.

C. 306 A.D. Constantine the Great Proclaimed Emperor of Rome While in Britain. It is a time of great confusion, political turmoil, and strife. The dying father of Constantine (Flavius Valerius Constantinus), declares his son his successor as emperor of the Roman Empire in 306 A.D. In 312 A.D., before the decisive Battle of the Milvian Bridge, Constantine has a vision in which he is told that if he paints a Christian symbol on the shields of his soldiers, he will be victorious. He does so and wins the battle.

Constantine's mother, Helena, is believed to have been a practicing Christian. Throughout his rule, Constantine grants more and more favors to followers of Christianity. It is Constantine who helps the early Christian fathers settle a divisive dispute on the nature of the Trinity, by presiding at the Council of Nicae in 325 A.D. However, Constantine does not accept baptism until 337 A.D., when he is on his deathbed.

Female pilgrim with staff and scrip.

C. 317 A.D. Zhong Lingyi Becomes First Chinese Buddhist Nun. Zhong Lingyi is ordained in 317 A.D. Many early nuns are noted for their learning and intellectual achievements. Early monastic institutions in China are places where women who want to pursue religion and learning independent of the constraints of family life can go.

C. 320 A.D. Religious Pilgrimages Include Women. Pilgrimages around Europe to religious shrines and to the Holy Land become fashionable in the fourth century. Pilgrim traffic develops between Britain and the Holy Land (present-day Israel), passing through Rome, Italy. Hospitals are founded along the way to provide refuge to the weary travelers. The Hospital of the Pellegrini at Rome can entertain 7,000 men and women pilgrims. To be admitted, pilgrims must have walked at least 60 miles and carry a certificate from a bishop or priest proving that they are true pilgrims. Women of all ranks participate in pilgrimages. Pilgrims carry a staff and a scrip, the pouch that is often decorated with an emblem of the pilgrimage.

324 A.D. Helena Contributes to Spread of Christianity in Western World. Helena (c.250–330), mother of Constantine the Great, is also considered by some to be the mother of Christianity. A devout Christian, she makes a pilgrimage to Jerusalem in 324 A.D. While there, she finds pieces of wood that she claims are remnants of the cross on which Jesus Christ had been crucified 300 years earlier. As a result of this experience, she founds the Church of the Holy Sepulchre in Jerusalem, and the Church of the Nativity in Nazareth, on the site where she believes Jesus was born. She founds many more churches, and is buried at first in Constantinople, but her body is moved around 850 A.D. to the Abbey of Hautvillers near Rheims, France. In the Eastern Orthodox church, her feast day is celebrated on May 21.

C. 370 A.D. Chinese Poet Su Hui Weaves Poems and Linguistic Puzzles into Brocade Fabrics. Su Hui (c.370 A.D.) is a skilled poet and weaver, the Chinese inventor of the palindrome. The palindrome she creates features Chinese characters woven in brocade in a square, 29 characters by 29 characters. The poems imbedded in it can be read from top to bottom, from right to left, or from left to right. Commentators find as many as 4,000 poems in the palindrome. Weaving is regarded by Chinese of Su Hui's time as quintessential women's work: Su Hui manages to express her literary skills while doing women's work.

382 A.D.   Vestal Virgins Forced to Leave Temple of Roman Goddess. The Roman goddess of hearth and home, Vesta, is served in her temple by a sisterhood of consecrated women called Vestal Virgins who keep the fire on Vesta's hearth burning, thus ensuring the safety of Rome. In 382 A.D., the now-Christian state of Rome withdraws all endowments and protections for pagan temples, including the 600-year-old hearth of Vesta. The Vestal Virgins are forced to leave the temple, and the fire that has burned for six centuries goes out.

C. 391–408 A.D.   St. Olympias Is Ordained Minister of Early Christian Church, Supports Radical Reformer St. John Chrysostom. St. Olympias (366–408 A.D.), a minister of the early Christian Church, risks arrest and other persecutions to support the outspoken reformer St. John Chrysostom (deposed archbishop of Constantinople), even after his banishment. At the age of 18, Olympias marries the prefect of the city of Constantinople. After his death two years later, she refuses to marry again despite tremendous pressures to do so because of her great wealth and personal charm. Instead, she begins giving her money to charities and in 391 becomes ordained as a minister of the Christian Church. Olympias is a strong supporter and friend of the archbishop of Constantinople, St. John Chrysostom—an outspoken reformer who earns many enemies by his attacks on corruption. In 403 Chrysostom is deposed from the archbishopric and a year later banished from Constantinople. In protest, Olympias organizes an attempt to burn down the cathedral. When arrested, she speaks out boldly to the authorities in support of Chrysostom, refusing to recognize his successor as archbishop, for which she is heavily fined. Although persecuted and driven from place to place until her death, Olympias never gives in to the authorities but continues in her tireless and courageous support of the radical reformer, St. John Chrysostom.

432 A.D.   Most Ephesians Believe "Our Lady" Is the Goddess Diana. One of the earliest Christian churches devoted to "Our Lady" is in Ephesus, but most of the people there believe "Our Lady" to be the goddess Diana, not Mary, the mother of Jesus. When the Council of Ephesus tries to end the worship of Diana in 432 A.D., the people riot against the bishops. Diana, goddess of the moon and wild animals and another aspect of the Queen of Heaven, is absorbed by the Greek goddess Artemis so that the two eventually become synonymous.

C. 451 A.D.   Patron Saint of Paris, St. Geneviève, Turns Back Atilla the Hun. The legendary patron saint of Paris, France, St. Geneviève (420–500 A.D.) is credited with turning back Atilla the Hun when he advances on Paris. When she is 15 years old, Geneviève takes vows and receives her veil as a dedicated virgin. When the Huns invade France and Atilla advances toward Paris, Geneviève tells the people not to abandon their homes. Fearfully, they finally agree and watch as Atilla turns away and attacks Orléans instead. They believe Geneviève's prayers have protected them, and her credibility as a prophet and holy woman is established. Later the people follow her as she leads a convoy up the River Seine to Troyes to bring back supplies when the Franks blockade Paris. She persuades the Frankish leader Childeric to accept her pleas on behalf of prisoners of war and, near the end of her life, convinces King Clovis of the Franks to release some prisoners and go easy on others. The people of Paris continue to look to Geneviève as their protector even after her death. In 1129, an epidemic of ergot-poisoning comes to an end when her relics are carried in a public procession, an event that is still celebrated each year in the churches of Paris. Her feast day is celebrated on January 3.

C. 480 A.D. **St. Brigid, Linked to Celtic Moon Goddess Bridgit, Founds First Convent in Ireland.** Little is known of the life of St. Brigid (c.450–c.523 A.D.). It is believed that she founds a convent at Kildare, the first Irish women's religious community. She is one of the patron saints of Ireland, venerated as highly as her co-patron, St. Patrick. Some feel that Brigid never existed as a person but was merely a Christianization of the Celtic triune moon goddess, Bridgit. Kildare, the site of the alleged convent, is a popular shrine to the goddess Bridgit before the Christianization of Ireland. St. Brigid's Feast Day—February 1—is the same day as the goddess Bridgit's feast. Fires are lit for both celebrations. St. Brigid's nuns allegedly tend a sacred fire that men are not allowed to approach, as do many priestesses in goddess temples. Miraculous stories of fertility magic grow up around the convent at Kildare, suggesting pagan roots. Even St. Patrick, a legendary figure himself whose

name means "father," may be a simple renaming of the goddess Bridgit's consort, the Dagda or "father." An old Irish verse refers to Brigid and Patrick as buried in one tomb. In Ireland, Sts. Brigid, Patrick, and Columba replace the pagan trinity of the triune moon goddess, Bridgit.

C. 496 A.D. **Clotild, Queen of the Franks, Converts the King to Christianity.** Clotild, alternately spelled Clotilda or Clotilde (c.475–545 A.D.), queen of the Franks, takes a notable part in the conversion of her husband, Clovis, to Christianity about 496. The conversion of the king has important consequences for the future of France in that it allies the Franks with the Roman Catholic Church. Clotild is born into the royal family of Burgundy about 475. She marries Clovis, who establishes the Kingdom of the Franks (present-day France), when she is about 18. She bears Clovis four sons. After her husband's death in 511, the queen devotes herself to religious pursuits, becoming famous for her piety and her generosity to the Church. Clotild, who dies on June 3, 545, is named a saint.

Part 2

SAINTHOOD & SORCERY
500 A.D. – 1499

Chapter 3

500 TO 999 A.D.

500–599

C. 500 A.D. Salic Law Prohibits Women from Inheriting Land. The Salians, the Germanic Franks living in Gaul (the area of today's France, Holland, and Belgium), issue a code of laws which prohibit women from inheriting land. Later in the sixth century, the so-called Salic Law is revised to allow a daughter to inherit land if her father has no male heirs. Nonetheless, the French for centuries cite the Salic Law as the authority for denying the crown of France to a woman.

C. 500 A.D. Confucianism Introduced to Japan. Confucianism, a Chinese social philosophy originated in the fifth century B.C., is not introduced to Japan until the sixth century A.D. This philosophy diminishes the status and authority of women. Confucius (551–479 B.C.), a Chinese scholar, devises an ethical system that aims at creating a harmonious society. He believes that by behaving in a manner consistent with one's rank in society, order will be established. Confucius believes that society ought to be organized hierarchically—older is superior to younger, and male is superior to female. In this hierarchy, then, young women have the lowest status. In Confucian philosophy, the autonomy of women is constrained by the "three obediences": a woman is to obey her parents when she is young, her husband after marriage, and her sons in her old age. While Confucianism theoretically means that women will be cared for by the men whom they are to obey, in practice, it is a philosophy that rationalizes the subjugation of women. The influence of Confucianism in the Japanese family system is particularly strong in the seventeenth through nineteenth centuries, when the government is attempting to centralize political authority.

500 A.D. Devi Is Supreme Deity of Hindu Religion. Devi, whose name simply means "Goddess," is the supreme deity of the Hindu religion. Without her, no other god or goddess has form or power. Therefore, all the gods and goddesses in the Hindu pantheon are really aspects of Devi, the source of all being. The earliest known text that speaks of the goddess as the supreme deity dates from perhaps 500 A.D.

500–600 A.D. Christians Seize Parthenon in Athens. Sometime during the fifth or sixth century A.D., Christians seize the Parthenon, the temple of the goddess Athena in Athens, Greece. They rededicate it as a temple of the Virgin Mary, mother of Jesus Christ.

C. 525 A.D. Theodora Marries Justinian, Future Byzantine Emperor. Theodora (497–548 A.D.) rises from obscure origins to become a powerful Byzantine empress through her marriage to Justinian. Two years after they marry, he becomes the Byzantine emperor Justinian I. Theodora is the daughter of a bear keeper at the circus in Constantinople (now Istanbul, Turkey). After a career as an actress or circus performer and possible courtesan, Theodora attracts the attention of Justinian, then a court official. For over 20 years until her death, the empress takes an active role in ruling the Byzantine Empire. A famous story relates that she urges Justinian to remain in Constantinople during the Nika (victory) rebellion in 532 rather than flee for his life. He accepts her advice and saves his throne. Theodora is remembered especially for recognizing the rights of women.

C. 526–535 A.D. Amalasuntha Not Effective in Governing Italy. Amalasuntha (498–535 A.D.), queen and regent of the Ostrogoths, fails in her attempt to govern Italy. She is the daughter of Theodoric the Great, Ostrogothic king of Italy, and her husband, by whom she has two children, dies in the early years of their marriage. At her father's death in 526, Amalasuntha assumes the regency for her son Athalaric. She follows a pro-Byzantine policy which angers the nobility of the Gothic court at Ravenna. When Athalaric dies in 534, Amalasuntha becomes co-ruler of Italy with her cousin, but she is deposed by the disaffected nobles in 535. In that same year, the queen is strangled in her bath while being held prisoner. She is deeply appreciative of ancient Roman culture and tries to elevate the tone of Gothic society by encouraging literacy and learning. However, she is unable to make changes in Gothic Italy during the nine years she holds power.

532 A.D. Theodora Encourages Justinian Not To Flee Constantinople During the Nika Rebellion. Large areas of Constantinople (now Istanbul, Turkey) are burned as mobs shout Nika! (Victory!). Theodora (497–548 A.D.) calms Justinian's panic, and challenges him to consider how he would feel if he fled for safety. Her argument convinces him to

remain in the city, and his forces prevail. Theodora dies of cancer in 438, and Justinian rules alone until his death in 565.

C. 552 A.D. Buddhism Spreads to Japan. The Buddhist religion, founded in India during the sixth century B.C., spreads to Japan and is established as the religion of Japanese rulers during the reign of Empress Suiko (reigns 592–628 A.D.). Buddhism offers advantages to women, particularly aristocrats. It provides women with an alternative to marriage as religious nuns and gives them opportunities for leadership as the abbesses of convents. Buddhism, which emphasizes the value of charitable work, gives women an opportunity to serve the sick and needy. Some Buddhist temples and convents serve as a refuge for women needing protection. Some Buddhist beliefs, however, restrict women and presume the inferiority of women. During menstruation and childbirth, women are considered unclean and so are excluded from some Buddhist rites. It is thought that women will have to be reborn as men before they can achieve salvation. This is because women are thought to be guilty of major sins, including jealousy, deceit, uncleanliness, and the ability to sexually arouse men.

C. 552 A.D. Radegund of Poitiers, Frankish Queen, Founds Christian Convent. Radegund of Poitiers (c.520–587 A.D.), a Frankish queen who becomes a nun, founds one of the earliest convents in Christendom in Poitiers, France. Born about 520 to the king of Thuringia in Germany, Radegund is captured when just a young child by Chlotar, a king in the northwestern area of the Kingdom of the Franks (present-day France). Chlotar has her educated in a Frankish convent and, when she comes of age, marries her. The deeply religious Radegund flees from her cruel husband and ultimately gains his permission to become a nun. The queen's convent, which opens in 552, becomes a center of Christian learning and a repository for famous relics. Known for her ascetic lifestyle and generosity toward the poor, Radegund dies on August 13, 587, in the convent she founded. Radegund is named a saint.

C. 567 A.D. Fredegund Causes Assassination that Leads to War in Frankish Kingdom. The ruthless Queen Fredegund (?–597 A.D.) brings war to the Frankish Kingdom (present-day France) through her involvement in the assassination of the king's previous wife. Fredegund is originally a servant in the household of Chilperic I, who is king in the northwestern area of the Kingdom of the Franks. She becomes his mistress, and then marries him after engineering the murder of his previous wife, Galeswintha, about 567. The murder begins her disastrous feud with Galeswintha's sister, Queen Brunhild of the eastern Franks. The feud leads to a half-century of warfare in the Frankish Kingdom. Fredegund dies around the year 597 and is remembered as reckless, ruthless, and cruel.

C. 567 A.D. Brunhild Marries Frankish King and Becomes Influential in Politics. Queen Brunhild (534–613 A.D.), who marries a king in the eastern area of the Kingdom of Franks (present-day France) in 567, exercises political influence in the Frankish Kingdom for nearly half a century. Brunhild, the daughter of a Visigothic king in Spain, marries King Sigebert. Within a year or two, Brunhild begins a feud with Fredegund, queen in the northwestern area of the Frankish Kingdom, who has engineered the murder of Brunhild's sister, Galeswintha. Seeking revenge for the murder, Brunhild, who exercises political influence as queen consort or queen mother for nearly 50 years, plunges the kingdom into bloody and vicious warfare. She is still engaged in political intrigue at the time of her death in 613, when she is probably 80 years old.

C. 580 A.D. Chinese Lady Chiaoguo Negotiates Surrender of Kingdoms. The Lady Chiaoguo, a woman from an aboriginal family in south China, is a political leader who is instru-

mental in negotiating the surrender of southern kingdoms during the Sui unification of China in the late sixth century. Her skilled diplomacy is credited with saving many lives.

592 A.D. Suiko Becomes First Woman Sovereign of Japan. Empress Suiko (554–626 A.D.) ascends to the throne through the assistance of her mother's family, the powerful Soga, becoming the first woman sovereign of Japan. Her duties are mainly those of a shamaness or priestess, including preparation of meals to offer the ancestral Shinto deities. She reigns at a time of conflict between conservatives, who continue to champion the Shinto religion, and other ruling families, like the Soga, who promote Buddhism. Suiko reconciles these conflicting interests by continuing to serve the Shinto deities and also serving as a patron to Buddhism. Her reign is a golden period for the establishment of Buddhist temples and the creation of Buddhist-inspired art.

While the more secular aspects of imperial rule are entrusted to Prince Shotoku, her nephew, Suiko nevertheless musters troops and dispatches emissaries to foreign countries. Two significant institutional achievements contribute to the centralization of the state during Suiko's reign. The first is the establishment of a recruiting and promotion system for government officials similar to the Chinese and Korean models. Called the cap-ranking system, it enables talented people, not just the nobility, to work for the government. The other is a set of moral injunctions, the Seventeen Article Constitution, promulgated in 604, to be observed by government officials. This document establishes an organized, government bureaucracy, with the emperor or empress at the top.

594 A.D. Muhammad, Founder of Islam, Marries Khadija. Twenty-five-year-old Muhammad (sometimes spelled Mohammed or Mahomet; c.570–632) marries the 40-year-old Khadija (c.564–619). Muhammad works for Khadija, a widow, probably as a camel driver. She encourages him to act on his religious visions, which eventually become the Koran, the basis for both the Islamic religion and Islamic law.

594 A.D.   Birth of Japanese Empress Saimei. Empress Saimei (594–661 A.D.) of Japan is born. During her first reign, 642–645, she is known as Empress Kogyoku. She relinquishes the throne to her brother, Emperor Kotoku; when he dies in 654, however, she resumes the throne, reigning under the name Empress Saimei. Her second reign is associated with military campaigns. She frequently sends military expeditions to the northern part of the main Japanese island to subdue the aboriginal population, the Ezo. She dies while seeing off her forces to Korea to aid the Paekche kingdom against invasion by the combined troops of the Chinese (Tang dynasty) and the Korean kingdom of Silla.

600 – 699

C. 600 A.D.   Abbesses Rule Double Monasteries. Abbesses rule double monasteries—Roman Catholic institutions for both men and women—during the seventh and eighth centuries A.D. The abbess has the authority of a bishop, although she cannot preside at Communion or administer other sacraments. Double monasteries have adjoining facilities for both monks and nuns, and flourish in these centuries. A notable administrator of a double monastery is Hilda of Whitby (614–680 A.D.). She establishes her monastery at Whitby in 657. From the ninth century on, the church discourages these establishments as seedbeds for immorality. In the twelfth century, double monasteries are revived for a brief period.

C. 600 A.D.   Japanese Society Begins to Shift from Matriarchal to Patriarchal Society. After Buddhist and Confucian ideas about the inferiority of women are introduced to Japan from China in the sixth century A.D., Japanese society begins to shift from a matriarchal to a patriarchal society. In ancient times, a woman-centered marriage pattern contributed to considerable religious and political influence by women. But with the growing acceptance of these new ideas, patriarchal law and practice begin to take hold. The Taika Reform of the mid-seventh century, based on Confucian-style laws, makes a significant contribution to this shift. Women are barred from becoming *kanri* (government officials), and a woman's share of the government-distributed land is set at two-thirds of that for a man.

610 A.D.   Frankish Nun Baudonivia Writes One of the Earliest Biographies by a Woman. Baudonivia, a Frankish nun at the convent established by Queen Radegund at Poitiers, completes *The Life of St. Radegund*. Writing some 20 years after the former queen's death, Baudonivia relies on information she obtains largely from people who knew her subject. Her biography is one of the earliest books about a woman *by* a woman.

C. 614 A.D.   Hilda, Abbess of Whitby, Is Born. Hilda (614–680 A.D.), abbess of Whitby, who plays an active role in establishing Christianity in England, is born. As a great-niece of the king of Northumbria, Hilda belongs to Anglo-Saxon royalty. She is baptised at the age of 13 but does not become a nun until she is 33. Thereafter Hilda serves as abbess of several English religious houses, the most famous being the double monastery at Whitby, where she governs both monks and nuns. She is an able and devout administrator, as witnessed by the fact that five monks of Whitby become bishops. She is also influential at the Synod of Whitby in 664, where Irish and Roman Catholic clergy settle their differences over rituals and ensure the unity of Christianity on the British Isles. When she dies in 680, she admonishes the nuns at her bedside to follow the teachings of the gospel.

622 A.D. Muhammad Replaces Female-Centered Religion with Islam. The three goddesses Al-Uzza, Al-Lat, and Menat (or Manat) make up the supreme religious trinity of pre-Islamic Arabia. They are worshipped as the supreme religious trinity of Arabia for centuries before Muhammad supplants them with the male-centered religion of Islam. They are three aspects of the same goddess: Al-Uzza is the young warrior; Al-Lat the fertile mother; and Menat the aged bestower of fate and death. Muhammad himself worships the triune goddess before overthrowing this female-centered religion and replacing it with the male-centered religion of Islam in 622 A.D.

C. 630 A.D. Birth of Nukata no Okimi, Japanese Poet. Nukata (or, Nukada) no Okimi (c.630 to c.690 A.D.), the most outstanding Japanese woman poet of her generation, is born. Her mother's family has a rich tradition of storytelling. Influenced by this background, she distinguishes herself at the imperial court for her literary skill. She is a Shinto priestess and an imperial consort. Her most famous poem is one in which she argues that autumn is aesthetically and emotionally more satisfying than spring. Twelve of her poems are compiled in the *Manyoshu* (c.759), the earliest extant collection of Japanese poetry.

632 A.D. Roman Church Moves Date of Easter, Named for Goddess of Springtime, Eostre. The Christian festival of Easter is named for the Anglo-Saxon goddess of springtime—Eostre. Many of Eostre's traditions are also absorbed by the Christian celebration, including the date (figured as the first Sunday after Eostre's original festival—the first full moon after the spring, or vernal, equinox), painted eggs, and the Easter Bunny (originally the moon-hare sacred to the goddess). Irish Christians continue to celebrate Easter on the date of the original festival of Eostre until the Roman Church imposes its calendar on them in 632 A.D. The Columbian foundation and its colonies in Britain persist in celebrating on the old date, however, for another 50 years. In Bohemia, Christ is celebrated on Easter Sunday and the goddess on Easter Monday, or Moon-day as opposed to the Sun-day.

C. 645 A.D. Empress Jito of Japan Is Born. Empress Jito (c.645–703 A.D.), who will complete the centralization of the Japanese state under imperial rule, is born. She initially assists her husband, Emperor Temmu, ascend to the throne by developing successful military strategies and commanding the troops stationed at Ise (the Ise Shrine, dedicated to the sun goddess, symbolizes imperial rule). Jito educates herself on matters of law and drafts regulations during Temmu's reign, which lasts from 673 to 686. To forestall power struggles following Temmu's death, Jito assumes the throne. She orders a national census in order to more effectively collect taxes. Also, she forms the army and drafts their training regulations and service codes. In 694, Jito establishes a new capital in Fujiwara.

While these achievements are relatively short-lived, she makes several long-term contributions. First, the goals of the Taika Reform are achieved (creating a government bureaucracy); during Jito's reign, the tribal (kingship) system is ended and the Japanese state is placed under a single sovereign, rather than many chieftains. Second, as a patron of Buddhism, Jito supervises efforts to proselytize throughout Japan. Finally, she is a patron of the arts. A poet herself, and contributor to the eighth-century compilation the *Manyoshu*, Jito also recognizes local artists and performers, particularly those skilled in the martial arts.

Jito abdicates in 697, installing her grandson, Emperor Mommu, who reigns from 697 to 707, on the throne. This is only the second abdication of a ruler in Japan, and the first time a minor accedes to the throne. She becomes the first to use the title "dojo-tenno" (ex-emperor), which enables her to continue wielding political power until her death.

C. 657 A.D.   St. Balthild Rises from Slave to Queen Regent of the Western Franks. When her husband, Clovis, dies, Balthild (sometimes spelled Bathild or Baldhild) becomes queen regent of the Western Franks for her son Clothar. Balthild is an English girl who is captured by the Franks and forced to be a slave for Erchinoald, mayor of the palace of King Clovis II. Eventually, she catches the notice of the king, and he marries her sometime around the year 648 A.D. They have three sons together—Clothar III, Theuderic III, and Childeric II—and when Clovis dies in 657, Balthild becomes queen regent for her son Clothar. As queen regent, she opposes the slave trade and encourages religious vocations, giving many gifts to monasteries and founding convents at Chelles and Corbie. When her regency comes to an end in 664, ambitious nobles force her to leave the court and retire instead to the convent at Chelles, where she lives as a nun until her death in 680. Her feast day is celebrated on January 30.

673 A.D.   St. Etheldreda Founds Double Monastery on Ely. Etheldreda (630–679 A.D.) founds, and then presides over until her death, a double monastery on the Isle of Ely, which becomes an important pilgrimage shrine in the Anglo-Saxon world. Her name is spelled various ways in Old English, such as Ithelthryth; she is also known in modern times as Audrey. She is the daughter of King Anna of East Anglia. She is married twice, but it is said she never consummates either union. In 672, her second husband releases her from her marriage vows and she instead takes her religious vows, becoming a nun at Coldingham. She gives land to St. Wilfrid for the founding of a monastery; then in 673 she returns to East Anglia to found her own double monastery on the Isle of Ely. Etheldreda presides over the monastery on Ely, caring for the poor and practicing medicine, until her death, probably of plague,

in 679. Her sister, St. Sexburga (or Seaxburh), succeeds her as abbess. Many miracles are attributed to Etheldreda and she becomes one of the most revered of the Anglo-Saxon saints. Her burial site is famous for its miraculous healing powers, and the monastery on Ely becomes an important pilgrimage center. The present Ely cathedral stands on its site. Her feast day is celebrated on June 23.

680 A.D.   Empress Gensho, Who Fosters Completion of Second Japanese National History, Is Born. Empress Gensho (680–748 A.D.) of Japan is born. She succeeds her mother, Empress Gemmei (661-721 A.D.), ascending to the throne in 715. During her reign, centralized rule is extended further into Japan with the promulgation of the Yoro Code in 718. In 720, Japan's second official national history, the *Nihongi* (or *Nihonshoki*, *Chronicle of Japan*) is completed, in accordance with the Empress Gensho's orders.

681 A.D.   Empress Gemmei Orders the Writing of the *Kojiki*, Japan's First National History. Empress Gemmei (661–721 A.D.) orders that the first national history of Japan be written from the transcription of orally transmitted tales. She ascends to the throne of Japan in 707. During her reign, the new capital in Nara is completed, and it becomes a cultural, as well as a political, center. The first attempt to replace the barter system with copper coins is made during her reign. However, Gemmei's most significant contribution is to Japan's cultural history with her command that the *Kojiki* (*Chronicle of Ancient Things*) be written. This three-volume work records the rise of the imperial clan and aristocratic families in Japan from the beginning of the universe to the reign of Empress Suiko (reigns 592–628) and is completed in 712.

690 A.D.   Wu Ze-tian Becomes Only Female Emperor of Imperial China. After receiving three successive petitions requesting her to ascend the imperial throne, Empress Wu proclaims herself emperor. Wu Ze-tian (624–705 A.D.) is initially in the harem of Emperor Tai Zong of the Tang dynasty in 637, but the emperor dies in 649. His son, Gao Zong, adopts Wu Ze-tian into his harem and has a daughter with her. Through manipulation, Wu Ze-tian becomes the empress of Gao Zong by strangling her own daughter and blaming it on the ruling empress, Wang. When Gao Zong later becomes physically frail, Wu Ze-tian takes over state affairs and begins formulating new policies that appeal to a wide variety of social groups. In 690, Wu Ze-tian proclaims herself emperor and renames herself Wu Zhou to signify the end of the Tang dynasty. Age and corruption lead to her depose in February 705. Wu Ze-tian dies later that year.

---

7 0 0 – 7 9 9

700 A.D. Japanese Law Permits One Wife, Numerous Concubines. The Japanese legal code of the eighth century A.D. specifies that a man may have only one wife, but it places no restrictions on the number of his concubines. In law, ceremony, and practice, Japanese men can be polygamous, but women cannot. Principal wives, generally from a man's first marriage, are distinguished by the honorific titles they are permitted, their husbands' residence with them, and the higher official positions occupied by their sons. Secondary wives, or concubines, lead a precarious life; while their husbands may continue to pay their household expenses, there are no assurances of marital relations. These assumptions characterize the marriage practices of men in the elite well into the twentieth century.

C. 700 A.D. Japanese Ideals of Feminine Beauty Develop. At the imperial court, Japanese ideals of feminine beauty develop. Women's clothing ceases to emulate Chinese styles and becomes more characteristically Japa-nese. Women at court wear 12-layer, loosely fitting robes, each of a slightly greater length, in a slightly different shade. Women of the lower classes wear simpler clothes, including short, sleeveless robes. Women's hair is ideally long (floor-length), glossy, and worn loosely. Cosmetics are an important part of the feminine ideal. Women shave their eyebrows and replace them with a thin, painted line. They wear white face powder and rouge. When girls reach puberty, they begin to blacken their teeth.

C. 700 A.D. Birth of Japanese Poet Sano no Chigami. Sano no Chigami is born in Japan about 700 A.D. Sano is a palace attendant of low rank who serves the High Priestess of the Shrine of Ise. In violation of a strict taboo against the presence of men in the palace of the priestess, she has a clandestine affair. The lovers are discovered, and she is sent into exile. She writes a series of 63 poems about her forbidden love which are included in the *Manyoshu,* the first great anthology of Japa-nese poetry published in 759.

C. 710 A.D. Birth of English Nun Lioba, Who Helps Christianize Germany. Lioba (c.710–782 A.D.), is born in Wessex, England, of a noble family. She becomes a nun upon completion of her education in an Anglo-Saxon convent. She is related to St. Boniface, the English monk who undertakes the Christianization of the Germans. In 748, she follows Boniface to Germany, where she aids his missionary effort and becomes abbess of the Benedictine convent at Bischofsheim. She is noted for her wisdom, piety, and charity in this position for 28 years. Upon her death about 782, she is buried near Boniface at his request.

729 A.D. Empress Komyo Becomes First Woman Not of Noble Blood to Serve as Imperial Consort in Japan. Through the influence of her family, the powerful Fujiwara, Empress Komyo (701–760 A.D.) becomes the first woman not of noble blood to serve as an

Benedictine abbess and nun.

imperial consort in Japan. A devout Buddhist, it is at her suggestion that Emperor Shomu, who reigns from 715 to 749, establishes government-sponsored Buddhist temples and convents throughout Japan. Komyo sponsors charitable foundations that minister to the poor and sick.

749 A.D. Empress Koken-Shotoku Begins First Reign. Empress Koken-Shotoku (718–770 A.D.) of Japan ascends to the throne for the first of her two reigns in 749 and becomes an ardent patron of Buddhism. During her first reign, the Great Buddha of Nara is cast and its hall constructed (still the largest wooden structure in the world). After her retirement from the throne in 758, she seeks the counsel of a Buddhist priest, Dokyo, and expresses frustration that tradition prevents her from marriage. She creates friction among court factions when she declares that, as the former empress, she will continue to make decisions (presumably with the assistance of Dokyo), regarding war, awards for meritorious

service, and the punishment of criminals. Opponents mount armies to depose Koken-Shotoku, but her forces triumph and she returns to the throne for a second time.

During her second reign, she seeks to consolidate the power of the throne by prohibiting unauthorized persons from reclaiming land for private purposes and officials from bearing arms. She continues to honor both the ancestral Shinto deities, as well as Buddhism. Well into the twentieth century, however, her assumed indiscretion with Dokyo is remembered as the reason for the long-standing practice to prohibit women from ruling as the sovereign of Japan.

C. 756 A.D. Yang Guifei, Notorious Chinese Imperial Concubine, Ignominiously Dies. Yang Guifei, concubine of the Tang dynasty emperor Xuanzong in China, is executed. She is a paradigm of the "state-toppling beauty," a beautiful woman who poses a threat to the political order. The story goes that Emperor Xuanzong becomes so besotted with her that he appoints her corrupt male relatives to important positions and, what is worse, neglects affairs of state. The result is the catastrophic rebellion of An Lushan in 755. The imperial troops are so certain that the root of the problem lies with Yang Guifei that they refuse to fight to defend the throne unless the emperor has her executed. The emperor makes his choice, and Yang Guifei meets her death. The tragic story has been the subject of countless poems, plays, and stories.

C. 759 A.D. Earliest Collection of Japanese Poetry, *Manyoshu*, Is Compiled. The *Manyoshu*, the earliest extant collection of Japanese poetry, includes over 4,000 poems written mostly by court nobility, both women and men. Twelve poems of Nukata no Okimi (c.630 to c.690 A.D.), the most outstanding Japanese woman poet of her generation, are among those included.

Empress Irene the Athenian

C. 768 A.D.   Chinese Courtesan Xue Tao, Famed for Literary Skills, Is Born. Xue Tao (c.768–831 A.D.), a famous calligrapher and poet in China as well as a courtesan, is born. In the China of Xue Tao's day, literary skills are part and parcel of the erotic charm which courtesans hold for their patrons. Thus there is considerable ambivalence on the part of men of the elite about educating their daughters in these skills. Many of the most accomplished women in China's history are courtesans.

780 A.D.   Byzantine Empress Irene Becomes Regent for her Son, Constantine VI. Empress Irene the Athenian (c.752–803 A.D.) rules as regent for her son, Constantine IV, until he comes of age in 790. When she does not yield complete power to him, Constantine IV has her exiled until 792, when he reconsiders and allows her to become his co-ruler for the next

five years. Irene, dissatisfied with this arrangement, rebels.

786 A.D.   Birth of Ardent Buddhist Empress Danrin. Danrin (786–850 A.D.), a Japanese imperial consort, is born. An ardent Buddhist, she is said to have invited the first lectures on Zen Buddhism in Japan.

794 A.D.   Fujiwara Family Reduces Emperor's Power in Japan through Marriages. Keibatsu, a system in which access to political or economic power is controlled through marriage alliances between influential families, is used by the Fujiwara family in Japan to reduce the emperor's power. The system works in this manner: the Fujiwara marry their daughters to the young men of the imperial family eligible to become emperor. A son born to such a couple is appointed crown prince. At approximately age 30, the emperor resigns and the crown prince ascends to the throne. He is then married to a Fujiwara daughter and the cycle repeats. In this system, the Japanese emperor is raised by the Fujiwara, and his major advisors are Fujiwara. By forcing the early abdication of the emperor, the influence of the Fujiwara advisors is increased. Daughters are valued more than sons by the Fujiwara because they serve as the link with the imperial family. It is, nevertheless, a system in which a woman's husband is chosen for her, without her consent. Keibatsu continues to be used throughout Japanese history as a means of achieving a relationship between warrior families in medieval Japan and relationships between business and political families in the twentieth century.

794 A.D.   Birth of Sugawara no Takasue, Japanese Writer. Japanese writer Sugawara no Takasue, author of *Sarashina Nikki* (*Sarashina Diary*), her confessional memoirs, is born. Writing in prose and poetry at the end of her life, Sugawara recalls her early passion for historical romances, and later, her focus on the prophetic interpretation of her dreams. Only after the death of her husband is Sugawara able to confront the realities of the world. Making religious pilgrimages, she becomes aware that the only true happiness in this world is to be achieved through religion.

797 A.D. Irene the Athenian Becomes First Woman in Recorded European History to Rule Alone. Irene the Athenian (c.752–803 A.D.) rules the Byzantine Empire in her own name for five years, the first woman sovereign recorded in European history. She dies in exile, having been deposed as sole ruler of the Byzantine Empire and ousted from Constantinople (today Istanbul, Turkey). Born in Athens about 752, Irene receives an education and marries the Byzantine emperor Leo IV. Upon his death in 780, she becomes regent for their young son Constantine VI. She later conspires against her son in order to retain control of the government, having him blinded and possibly murdered in 797. For the next five years, she controls the empire alone, the first woman in recorded European history to rule in her own name. Irene is instrumental in restoring the use of icons in the Byzantine Empire, a practice prohibited in the early eighth century. For this service to the Greek Orthodox Church, she is named a saint. Nonetheless, her enemies succeed in overthrowing her in 802, a year before her death.

8 0 0 – 8 9 9

800 A.D. Charlemagne Establishes the Holy Roman Empire. Charlemagne (Charles the Great, 742–814 A.D.), king of the Franks, acquires and conquers territory for the Frankish empire until it includes all of France, all of Germany and Austria except East Prussia, eastern Hungary and Croatia, the northwest corner of Spain, and all of Italy except Naples. To recognize this achievement, Pope Leo III crowns Charlemagne and revives the western Roman empire. The newly created Holy Roman Empire closely aligns with the Roman Catholic Church. Charlemagne attempts to bring together the Holy Roman Empire with the Byzantine Empire through marriage to Byzantine ruler, Irene, but she is overthrown in 802 and banished to the island of Lesbos, where she dies in 803.

800 A.D. Hindu Philosopher Shankara Composes Hymn Praising Shakti, Female Cosmic Energy. In Hinduism, shakti means "Cosmic Energy" and is believed to be the female form that is the active power of any deity—even a male god must have his shakti in order to act. This is described by the philosopher Shankara in the opening words of his hymn to the goddess called Saundaryalahari, or "Wave of Beauty," which he composes sometime between 800 and 1400 A.D. Mythologically, this force is represented by the goddess Shakti, an aspect of Devi (as are all goddesses, and gods, in one sense), and by the goddess-consorts and queens of each of the male gods.

C. FEBRUARY 819 A.D. Queen Judith Marries Louis I of Carolingian Empire. Judith, from the powerful Welf (or Guelph) family, becomes the second wife of Charlemagne's son, Emperor Louis "the Pious," who rules from 814 to 840 A.D. Her influence on her husband's government arouses some resentment, and her insistence on a portion of the realm for her son to rule endangers the kingdom. She succeeds, at an imperial meeting at Worms in 829, in gaining parts of Swabia, Alsace, and Burgundy for her son, Charles "the Bald" (823–877 A.D.). When Louis' sons from his first wife refuse to accept this new division with their half-brother, they unleash a civil war which gravely weakens the Carolingian Empire. Judith dies on April 11, 843, a few months before the empire is permanently divided into three parts. The eastern and western parts, which are separated by a middle realm of "Lotharingia," will become France and Germany.

C. 830 A.D. Birth of Japanese Poet Ono no Komachi. Ono no Komachi (c.830–?), one of Japan's best-known poets, is born. She ranks as one of the Six Poetic Sages. Most frequently, she writes about unhappy love—separation, unrequited love, and infidelity of men.

C. 841 A.D. Carolingian Noblewoman Dhuoda Writes Handbook for Her Son. Dhuoda, a member of the higher nobility in the Carolingian Empire (the Frankish Kingdom enlarged by Charlemagne), writes a handbook for her son's use at court, which emphasizes service to God and the ideals of noble existence. This small work gives remarkable insight into the life of a well-educated woman in the early medieval period, a time of great political unrest. Dhuoda is married to Bernard, a duke involved in the intrigues of the Carolingian courts. Her husband settles her in a little town in southern France and rarely visits her, although she gives birth to two sons—one in 824 and another in 841. Bernard takes the elder son, William, from Dhuoda when he is 14 to live at the court of Charles the Bald, the monarch of the western third of the empire (present-day France). Because Dhuoda mentions in the handbook that she is seriously ill, it may be that she dies shortly after the handbook is finished in 843.

C. 857 A.D. Queen Theutberga Resists Divorce Efforts of Her Husband, King Lothar II. Theutberga is the wife of King Lothar II of "Lotharingia," an area which covers the modern countries of Belgium, the Netherlands, Luxembourg, Switzerland, and parts of France and Germany; he reigns from 855 to 869. Their marriage remains childless and without heirs. Meanwhile, Lothar wants to marry his mistress Waldrada, by whom he has a son who can inherit his kingdom. In 857 Lothar accuses his wife of adultery so he can gain a divorce. Theutberga protests her husband's false accusations, and even undergoes the ordeal of hot water to prove the justness of her cause. Although the clergy in Lothar's kingdom agree to their king's divorce, Pope Nicholas I (858–867 A.D.) prohibits the same. This intervention signals an increasing control by the papacy of the laws of marriage. Therefore the dynasty ends with Lothar's death, while both Waldrada and Theutberga retire to monasteries. The Lotharingian middle realm is then destroyed by various competitors, and its remnants are fought over by France and Germany for the next thousand years.

877 A.D. Birth of Lady Ise, Japanese Poet. The Japanese court lady known as Lady Ise (877–940 A.D.) is born. She is considered one of the most accomplished poets of her time, and more than 500 of her poems are compiled in various anthologies. Her poetry is characterized by wit, and her love poems reflect great passion.

900 – 999

C. 900 A.D. Feminine Divinity Mazu Protects Chinese Seafarers and Fishermen. Mazu is one of the most important deities along coastal China and Taiwan. Legend has it that she is a young woman of the Lin family who lives during the Song dynasty. She saves her brothers (or her father: versions of her story differ) from a storm, and hence becomes a divinity who protects seafarers and fishermen. Like many female Chinese divinities and religious figures, the girl Lin never marries. Mazu is granted official honorific titles by the state, thus incorporating her into the official religion.

C. 900 A.D. Legend of Miaoshan Transforms Buddhist Nun into the Deity Guanyin. The legend of Miaoshan dates from the Song dynasty. Miaoshan is the earthly manifestation of the Buddhist deity Guanyin. Her story is characterized by the bitter struggle between the young woman who wants to live a religious life and her parents who want her to marry. The story has a happy ending: she succeeds in her religious vocation and converts her parents. Guanyin is one of the most important of all Chinese deities. Prayers to her about children are believed to be particularly efficacious.

JUNE 12, 918 A.D. Death of Aethelflaed, Who Repels Viking Forces and Helps Unify England. The daughter of Alfred the Great, king of the West-Saxons in what is now England, Aethelflaed (sometimes spelled Ethelfleda), dies on June 12, 918 A.D., just prior to the collapse of Viking opposition in the Midlands. Aethelflaed is given in marriage to Aethelred, earl of the West Mercians, sometime around 880. The marriage is part of Alfred's plan to create a unified England. Alfred the Great dies in 899. Aethelflaed's brother, Edward, is crowned King of Wessex about 900 and continues his father's policies.

Aethelflaed and her husband, who apparently act with equal authority, defend Mercia against invading Danes, Northmen, and Welshmen. Mercia and Wessex cooperate in erecting fortresses to defend against Viking incursions. The poor health of Aethelflaed's husband forces her to act as regent. After Aethelred's death in 911, "The Lady of the Mercians," as Aethelflaed is now called, rules Mercia alone for seven years. She leads troops into combat, increases the extent of the territory under her control, and builds a number of fortresses throughout Mercia.

The Battle of Tettennal in 909 results in a Viking defeat, and it is probable that Aethelflaed commands the Mercian contingent. In 911, the year her husband dies, she undertakes the reconquest of The Five Boroughs herself. Derby falls in 917. In 918, she faces a Viking invasion from the north. Aethelflaed forges an alliance with the Picts, Scots, and the men of Strathclyde. In the second Battle of Corbridge, the northern Vikings are defeated. The second of the Five Boroughs, Leceister, surrenders in 918. She is on the verge of negotiating the surrender of York when she dies on June 12, 918. Aethelflaed misses witnessing the collapse of Viking opposition in the Midlands by six months.

At her death, all Aethelflaed's subjects accept her brother, King Edward of Wessex, as their sovereign. Her efforts lead to the defeat of the Vikings and the political unification of England.

C. 922 A.D. Ritual Sacrifice of Slave Girl in Russia Reported. Ibn Fadhlan, an Arabian traveler and writer, witnesses the burial of a man, presumably a prominent Norse trader, along the Volga River in what is now Russia. He writes a detailed account of the ritual, in which a slave girl is drugged, killed, and cremated along with the deceased to serve as his companion in death. Such sacrifices of women at the burials of their husbands or masters occur in eastern Europe during the early medieval period. There are several reports of the voluntary self-cremation of widows at the funeral pyres of their husbands, known as *sati*, among the Slavic populations in the area from the sixth through the tenth centuries A.D. *Sati* suggests the complete subjugation of women to men in eastern Europe at the time. This practice ends with the coming of Christianity, but it survives until modern times in parts of India.

C. 935 A.D. Hrosvitha, Considered First German Woman Poet, Is Born. Hrosvitha (also Hrotsvit or Roswitha) (c.935–1000 A.D.) is born into the royal Saxon family. She enters the rich, independent nunnery of Gandersheim as a child. Hrosvitha gains a fine education, perhaps at the royal court, and becomes a canoness. She writes saints' lives, histories of the royal family and of her monastery, and, most importantly, dramas. These plays, some of the first since antiquity, draw on classical writers (especially Terence). She adapts their themes, transforming them into stories of Christian saints and martyrs. She also writes narrative poems based on Christian legends and is considered the first German woman poet.

C. 945 A.D. Princess Olga Becomes First Recorded Female Ruler in Russian History. When her husband Prince Igor I is assassinated in 945 A.D., Princess Olga serves as regent for her son until 964—the first female ruler in recorded Russian history. She is born in the Principality of Kiev, a region that eventually becomes part of western Russia (the Republic of Ukraine today). During her reign, she expands the borders of her land and converts to Christianity. She is probably baptized into the Orthodox Church in Constantinople (now Istanbul, Turkey) in 957. Her efforts to bring Christianity to Russia are brought to fruition by her grandson, Prince Vladimir, three decades later. For her service to the faith, Olga is named the first Russian saint of the Orthodox Church.

C. 950 A.D. Diary of Unhappy Court Lady in Japan. *Kagero Nikki* (*The Gossamer Years*) is a classic of Japanese confessional literature which depicts a court lady's unhappiness in her marriage. The name of the author is unknown; she is known only as the wife of Fujiwara Kaneie (928–990 A.D.) or the mother of Fujiwara Michitsuna (955–1020 A.D.). She is a secondary wife in a system of polygamy. Her position is, thus, uncertain, and she records in her diary her feelings of betrayal and rejection. While her son brings her satisfaction, her marriage brings her only frustration and bitterness. The major themes of her excruciatingly honest diary include the despair of sharing her husband with other women, her jealousy toward her rivals, her fights with her husband, and her resentment of a society in which a woman is obliged to be dependent on her father or her husband. The diary is influential in the work of later court ladies because of its representation of real life.

957 A.D. Birth of Japanese Poet Akazome Emon. The Japanese court lady Akazome Emon (957–1041 A.D.), is one of the foremost poets of her era and author of at least a portion of the important historical tale *Eiga Monogatari*, the story of the powerful Fujiwara family.

C. 960 A.D. Japanese Poet Izumi Shikibu, Known for Expression of Erotic and Buddhist Themes, Is Born. Izumi Shikibu (c.960–c. 1030 A.D.), the most accomplished Japanese poet of her era, is born. Her body of work includes more than 1,500 waka (31-syllable poems). She is involved in multiple marriages and love affairs with men at the court, and her poetry reflects her erotic experiences with overtones of Buddhist themes.

C. 975 A.D. Spanish Painter Ende Illustrates Manuscript Copy of the Beatus Apocalypse. Sometime around the year 975, the woman painter Ende illustrates a famous copy of *The Commentary on the Apocalypse of St. John* by Beatus of Liebana, now in Gerona. Her work is considered among the best in early medieval Spain. Ende apparently is attached to a Spanish convent as a manuscript illuminator. She may be a nun or a canoness (who lives in the convent but under partial vows).

C. 980 A.D. Russian Princess Ragnilda Refuses the Hand of Prince Vladimir, with Dire Consequences. Around this year, the proud princess Ragnilda (Rogneda), daughter of Ragvald, prince of Polatsk (a town in the area of western Russia, now in Belarus), refuses the hand of Vladimir, who rules the Principality of Kiev (a region in western Russia, now in the Ukraine). Ragnilda is contemptuous of Prince Vladimir because, although his father is of royal birth, his mother is a servant woman. A standard ritual in Russian marriage ceremonies requires the bride to remove the boots of the groom to demonstrate his absolute dominance over her. It is said that Ragnilda does not wish to pull off the boots of a low-born man. With this refusal, Vladimir takes decisive action. He attacks Polatsk, kills Ragvald and takes Ragnilda by force.

983 A.D.   Empress Adelaide Rules as Regent for Her Grandson. Adelaide or Adelheid (931–999 A.D.), daughter of the king of Burgundy, becomes coregent for her young grandson in 983 A.D. and sole regent in 991 until he is old enough to rule alone. She marries King Lothar II of Italy (reigns 946–950) in 947. When her husband dies, she is pursued by Berengar, who seeks to claim the Italian crown. The German king Otto "the Great" (reigns 936–973) invades Italy to rescue her, defeats Berengar, and becomes king of the Lombards and king of the Italians. He soon makes Adelaide his wife, and they further unite Italy and Germany in the new Roman Empire, when they are crowned emperor and empress in 962 in Rome. When their son and Otto's successor, Otto II (reigns 973–983), dies young, the empire threatens to fall apart in civil war over the rights of the young heir Otto III (reigns 983–1002), Adelaide's grandson. Adelaide helps create stability when she acts as coregent with her daughter-in-law Theophanu, until the latter forces her out of power. After Theophanu's death in 991, Adelaide returns as sole regent. When Otto reaches his majority in 996, his grandmother goes into retirement, dying on December 16, 999.

988 A.D.   Prince Vladimir of Russia Converts to Christianity and Outlaws Pagan Beliefs. Prince Vladimir of Russia erects a pantheon (temple to a group of gods) to the Old Russian pagan gods on top of a hill in Kiev. Only eight years later, in 988 A.D., Prince Vladimir is baptized as a Christian and declares Christianity the official religion. The hilltop idols are torn down and pagan beliefs, rituals, and traditions—along with their celebration of the feminine—are outlawed in favor of the patriarchal beliefs of Christianity.

NOVEMBER 1, 990 A.D.   Birth of Gisela, German Queen. Gisela (990–1043 A.D.), daughter of the duke of Swabia and a sister of the last king of Burgundy, is born. She inherits the duchy upon her father's death. After her first husband, Count Bruno of Brunswick, is murdered, she marries her second husband, Ernst von Babenberg, in 1012. Yet three years later Ernst dies in a hunting accident. In 1016 Gisela then marries Conrad, the heir to the German kingdom. This marriage is opposed by the emperor, Henry II (reigns 1002–24), and by some clerics, because the couple is too closely related. Nonetheless, after Conrad II becomes the German king (reigns 1024–39), she plays an influential role in government. At one point she even abandons her son from her second marriage when he rebels against the royal government. Her husband Conrad also adds Burgundy to the German Empire, partly on the rights of her claims of inheritance. She dies four years after their son becomes King and Emperor Henry III (reigns 1139–56).

$$\mathcal{C}hapter \, 4$$

1000-1299

1000–1100

c. 1000 In Italy, Trotula Writes Influential Treatise on Childbirth. A treatise on childbirth and the diseases of women, written at the medical center in Salerno, Italy, sometime in the eleventh century, is widely respected in medieval Europe. The treatise is signed by Trotula, whose identity is hotly debated. Some argue that Trotula is a learned female physician who teaches at the center; others believe that the treatise is really written by a man. Because of the general respect given to Trotula, known popularly as "Dame Trot," other texts on obstetrics and gynecology circulate under her name until the sixteenth century.

1000 Germanic Goddesses Known as Valkyries Rule Over War. During the eleventh century A.D., the Germanic goddesses known as Valkyries are called walcyries or waelceasig in Old Saxon, which means "corpse-eaters." The Valkyries rule over war and take the souls of slain warriors back with them to Valhalla (the Germanic heaven or paradise).

1000 Coatlicue, Mother of All Aztec Gods and Goddesses. Aztecs believe Coatlicue, "Lady of the Serpent Skirt," is the mother of all the other Aztec gods and goddesses, including the savior-god Quetzalcoatl, and the goddess of all women (the Mexican Aphrodite)—Xochiquetzal. Coatlicue is the creator, existing before all else. She is Mother Earth and goddess of the moon (though sometimes her daughter Coyolxauhqui is named as the moon-goddess). Bringer of all life, Coatlicue is also the mother of death, taking the dead back into her body again. She is commonly shown wearing a skirt of serpents, garlanded with skulls, hearts, and hands, and a vest of stripped human skin.

1000 Improved Lifestyles Lead to Surplus of European Women. Although a shortage of women seems to exist in ancient and early medieval times, women seem to begin outnumbering men in Europe during the High Middle Ages. In the absence of reliable census data, this conclusion can only be tentative. However, concerns on how unmarried women can support themselves arise in these centuries. One reason for a female surplus may be the increasing life expectancies of women, which begin to surpass those of men. Women may benefit in general by an improved diet, which includes larger quantities of the iron so necessary for their reproductive functions. They are also less taxed by hard physical labor in fields, as society becomes increasingly urbanized.

c. 1002 Sei Shonagon Writes Classic Literary Piece in Japan. Sei Shonagon, considered to be one of the most brilliant writers at a time when the literature of court ladies flourishes in Japan, writes the classic *Makura no Soshi* (*The Pillow Book*). Her book is the first of a genre known as *zuihitsu* (to follow the brush) that reflects the stream-of-consciousness approach. It includes short, eye-witness narratives, casual essays, impressions, lists, and imagined scenes. Purportedly, it is the list of jottings she keeps under her pillow. The charm of the book is the endearing idiosyncrasies of the author and the realistic glimpses into life at court. At one moment, the author is thrilled to bask in the presence of an empress whom she reveres; the next, she is ridiculing a courtier whom she finds too gauche. While romantic liaisons are frequently the major topic of women's literature of this period in Japan, Sei Shonagon shows herself to be a comic artist on this subject, revealing the realistic side of courtly love.

c. 1008 Murasaki Shikibu Writes *Genji Monogatari* (*The Tale of Genji*). Murasaki Shikibu, deemed the greatest master of narrative prose in the history of Japanese literature, writes *Genji Monogatari* (*The Tale of Genji*), considered the height of classic prose literature in Japan. Little is known of Murasaki's life, apart from the episodes she relates in her diary, *Murasaki Shikibu nikki*. She is a lady-in-waiting to the Empress Akiko and is known at court for her writing, her knowledge of the Chinese and Japanese classics, and her proficiency with musical instruments. *The Tale of Genji* is a long, narrative epic, featuring the romantic exploits of Prince Genji, a paragon of classical Japanese tastes and values. The book, therefore, becomes a kind of repository of Japanese aesthetics and ideals. Genji is an immensely charming, magnanimous, and sensitive individual, and it is from the depiction of his character that the book draws its strength.

1046 St. Margaret, Queen of Scotland, Is Born. St. Margaret (1046–1093), grand-daughter of English king Edmund Ironside, is born in Hungary in 1046 and educated on the continent. She finds refuge in Scotland after the Norman Conquest. There she marries King Malcolm III in 1070 and bears him six sons and two daughters. Margaret, a strong-willed and deeply religious woman, exercises considerable influence over Malcolm and the children. She is able to introduce reforms in the Scottish church, bringing its calendar and practices into conformity with Roman Catholicism. Her son David becomes one of the best Scottish kings and is also revered as a saint in Scotland. She and Malcolm found the Dunfermline abbey in 1072. Her piety and acts of charity, such as feeding orphans with her own spoon and washing the feet of beggars, are legion. Margaret's reign as queen is chiefly directed towards bringing Anglo-Norman manners and institutions, particularly those of the Western Church, into a fairly isolated Scotland.

MARCH 6, 1052 Death of Emma, Influential Wife and Mother of English Kings. Emma, the wife of two English kings and the mother of two more, dies on this date. The daughter of a Norman duke, Emma marries the Anglo-Saxon king Ethelred the Unready in 1002 and bears him two sons, one of whom is Edward the Confessor. A year after Ethelred's death in 1016, she marries Canute II, the Danish king who has conquered England. By him, she has a son named Harthacnut. Upon Canute's death in 1035, Emma works to procure the English crown for Harthacnut and holds a position of influence during his short and bloody reign (1040–42). When Edward the Confessor becomes king in 1043, Emma is forced into retirement in Winchester until her death. The queen probably commissions the *Encomium Emmae*, a book written in praise of her life. The work suggests that she has some learning and that she wields considerable authority.

c. 1079 **Birth of Japanese Writer Fujiwara no Nagako.** Fujiwara no Nagako is born, the Japanese author of *Sanuki no suke no nikki* (*The Diary of Lady Sanuki*). Lady Sanuki is lady-in-waiting to Emperor Horikawa and later to his son and successor, Emperor Toba. Distraught over Horikawa's death, and believing it her destiny to preserve his memory, Lady Sanuki writes about the emperor's last days.

1080 **Matilda, Beloved Queen of England, Is Born.** Matilda (1080–1118), daughter of Malcolm III and Margaret, king and queen of the Scots, is born in 1080 and educated in a convent under the supervision of her aunt, the abbess Cristina. In 1100, the Norman usurper Henry I marries her to legitimize his seizure of the English throne. As a descendant of Anglo-Saxon kings, she can help sway public opinion in his favor. After giving birth to a son and a daughter (the future Empress Matilda), Matilda retires from the royal court in 1103 and lives in Westminster outside London until her death in 1118. She is widely praised for her many charitable works in the vicinity of London, including the founding of a leper hospital and an Austin priory. A learned woman, she corresponds with important men of her time and patronizes writers and musicians.

1084 **Li Qingzhao, Chinese Poet, Excels in Ci.** Li Qingzhao (1084–c.1151) is a poet who excels in a form called *ci*. Ci are lyrical songs and are regarded in Chinese literary theory as a particularly feminine form. Li Qingzhao is its most renowned practitioner. She seems to have a happy marriage, and many of her poems are romantic, even erotic, poems addressed to her husband.

1 1 0 0 – 1 1 4 9

c. 1100 **Twenty Women Troubadours Write Popular Love Songs in France.** In southern France, the twelfth century is the age of the troubadours, aristocratic poet-composers who write songs mainly dealing with love. Not only are the names of 400 male troubadours known, but also those of 20 female troubadours (*trobairitz*). About two dozen of their songs survive, the last ones being composed in the early thirteenth century.

c. 1100 **Countess of Dia Becomes Famous Female Troubadour.** The Countess of Dia, often called Beatrix, becomes famous as a female troubadour in southern France during the twelfth century. Although she mentions some details of her life in the *vida* (short biography) accompanying her songs, the information is too fragmentary to identify her positively. Four or five of her songs are extant. She tells of her love for Count Raimbaut of Orange (whose identity is also a mystery), with forthrightness and sensitivity.

c. 1100 **Cathar or Albigensian Heresy Attracts Women in Southern France.** The Cathar or Albigensian heresy is popular among many Christians in the south of France, particularly women. Cathars teach a dualist doctrine that states that the universe is divided between two antagonistic forces: good found in spiritual things and evil found in material things. In order for persons to find salvation, they must lead simple and moral lives, avoiding the pleasures of the flesh as much as possible. Leadership is provided for the Cathars by the *perfecti* (the perfect ones), who practice extreme fasting and other means of self-deprivation. At first, women can belong to the *perfecti*, although they are gradually excluded from this inner circle. Nonetheless, women are attracted to the Cathar sect because it gives them a higher status than the Roman Catholic Church does. By the middle of the thirteenth century, the Cathars are wiped out by a crusade mounted against them under papal sanction.

c. 1100 **Marie de France, Earliest French Woman Poet, Writes Charming Verse Nar-**

ratives. Very little information is available about the life of Marie de France, the earliest known French woman poet. It is supposed that she is born in France, but lives in England, as do many French people after the Norman Conquest of 1066. Flourishing in the late twelfth century, Marie may be attached to the court of the Norman king of England, Henry II. She is famous for twelve *lais* (short narrative tales in verse) dealing with all aspects of love. Marie de France receives praise from literary critics throughout the centuries for her charming style and direct expression. Modern feminist scholars are attracted to her stories because the author takes the viewpoint that men and women are equal.

c. 1100   Courtly Love Places Women on Pedestals. Courtly love places women on pedestals in literature, if not in real life. The tradition of courtly love, a code of chivalric behavior for medieval knights in matters of love, arises in the south of France with the troubadours. The tradition moves into northern Europe largely through the influence of Eleanor of Aquitaine and Marie of Champagne. According to the rules of courtly love, a nobleman should perform great deeds to honor a noblewoman whom he loves, but cannot marry. Theoretically, he must worship his beloved from a distance, never becoming intimate with her. Although it is questionable whether the rules of courtly love are ever followed in real life, there is a vast body of medieval literature based on the courtly love ideal. In many stories, such as those about King Arthur, Queen Guinevere, and Lancelot, the lovers do commit adultery. Although women are placed on pedestals in these narratives, modern feminists question whether women are really honored.

1100   Guinevere Translated into Wife of King Arthur in Arthurian Legends. Guinevere, originally a Welsh goddess, is translated into the wife of King Arthur in the Arthurian leg-

ends of Britain. As the Triple Goddess, "first lady of these islands," Guinevere has to "marry" any man who will be king in order for him to rule; therefore, in many of the Arthurian stories, she is kidnapped by men who want to become king, including Arthur himself.

1100   Matilda, Descended from English Royalty, Marries Norman King Henry I. Henry I, son of the tyrant William II, marries Matilda (1080–1118) to legitimize his seizure of the English throne.

1100   Cult of the Virgin Honors Mary, Mother of Jesus. The popularity of Mary, the mother of Jesus, among medieval Christians in Europe leads to the Cult of the Virgin. Although a special position is given to Mary in the fifth century as the Mother of God, her veneration in the Roman Catholic Church reaches immense proportions by the twelfth century. Many cathedrals are dedicated to her; the *Ave Maria* ("Hail Mary") comes to be one of the most important prayers for Catholics; many altar paintings are completed of her. Because the Cult of the Virgin is attacked by the Protestants, it begins to disappear in the sixteenth century. Nonetheless, Mary still holds an important place in the Roman Catholic and Greek Orthodox Churches today.

1102   Birth of Empress Matilda, Who Briefly Seizes English Throne. Matilda (1102–1167), daughter of King Henry I of England and his first wife Matilda, is born. Betrothed to the Holy Roman Emperor Henry V, she is sent to the German court at the age of eight to be educated. When she marries Henry in 1114, Matilda is crowned empress. After her husband's death, the English barons agree to name Matilda the heir of Henry I as his only surviving child. In 1128, she marries Geoffrey Plantagenet, soon to become count of Anjou, by whom she has three sons. When her father dies in 1135, the barons renege on their earlier agreement and refuse to accept Matilda as their monarch because of her gender, choosing instead her cousin Stephen of Blois. During the civil war that breaks out, Empress Matilda is able to seize the throne briefly in 1141, but she is ultimately defeated. She alienates the English people with her ruthless measures to assert her power. After her eldest son becomes king of England as Henry II, she serves as his able counsellor. Matilda dies in 1167.

1118   Anna Comnena Leads a Conspiracy to Remove Her Brother, John, From Power in the Byzantine Empire. Anna Comnena (1083–1148) tries to undermine her brother, John, as ruler of the Byzantine Empire. Her efforts fail, and John retaliates by taking away her inherited property. Anna Comnena withdraws from the court completely, and devotes the remainder of her life to writing a history of her father's rule entitled *Alexiad.*

c. 1119   Sun Bu'er, Daoist Leader, Is Born. Chinese religious leader Sun Bu'er (1119–1183), a matriarch of the Quanjen school of Daoism, is born. It is said that she is able to wander freely (something that is not appropriate for a woman of the upper classes of her time) by adopting the pose of a mad woman. Among her contributions to Daoism are a series of texts dealing specifically with meditational practices for women. She is also a skilled poet.

1122   Eleanor of Aquitaine, Most Influential Woman of the Twelfth Century, Is Born. Eleanor, the lively and headstrong daughter of William X, the duke of Aquitaine, is the most influential woman of the twelfth century. In 1137 she inherits her father's vast lands in present-day southern France, making her the most powerful woman in Europe at the time. Her 15-year marriage to King Louis VII of France, which produces only two daughters, ends in 1152. Immediately after an annulment is approved by the pope, she marries the Henry Plantagenet, duke of Nor-

mandy, soon to become King Henry II of England. With him she has three daughters and five sons, two of whom (Richard the Lion-Hearted and John) become kings of England.

Maintaining residences both in England and France, Eleanor sponsors "courts of love" in Poitiers to debate points on the proper conduct of knights toward their ladies. What comes to be known as courtly love is much discussed in medieval Europe and spawns a large body of chivalric romance.

Eleanor becomes estranged from Henry and encourages her sons to rebel against him over political matters. This involvement causes her house arrest from 1174 until Henry's death in 1189. Thereafter she supports her sons, Richard I (the Lion-Hearted) and John as kings of England. She serves as regent while Richard is on the Third Crusade and manages to raise the enormous ransom demanded by the Germans for his release from captivity in 1192. At the end of her long life, she retires to the abbey of Fontevrault in France.

Eleanor's amazing and unconventional life is the subject of many books and a modern play that becomes the 1968 movie, *The Lion in Winter,* for which Katharine Hepburn wins the Academy Award for best actress for her performance as Eleanor.

1135   Matilda, Only Surviving Child of Norman King Henry I, Is Named His Successor. Matilda, wife of Geoffrey Plantagenet, is declared successor to her father, Henry I, upon his death in Normandy. However, her cousin, Stephen, son of Adela, daughter of William I, the Conquerer, raises an army in Normandy, comes to England, and declares himself king. After several years of civil war, Matilda agrees to allow Stephen to rule, on the condition that her son, Henry, be named successor. When Stephen dies in 1154, Henry II ascends to the throne.

1137 Eleanor, Daughter of William X, Duke of Aquitaine, Inherits Her Father's Land. At age 15, Eleanor of Aquitaine (1122–1204) gains control of Aquitaine, a vast land area adjacent to France. Later this year, she marries French king Louis VII, and Aquitaine is thus controlled by France. The couple divorces in 1152 after their marriage produces two daughters, but no male heir.

c. 1138 Anna Comnena, Early Woman Historian, Writes the *Alexiad*. At age 55, Anna Comnena (1083–1148), daughter of Byzantine emperor Alexius Comnenus, begins writing the *Alexiad*, a history of her father's reign. The book not only reflects life at the Byzantine court and discusses the policies of Alexius Comnenus, but it is considered one of the best histories of the First Crusade (1096–99). Anna is born in Constantinople (now Istanbul, Turkey) in 1083. When she is 14, she is married to a court official with whom she has four children. At the time of her father's death in 1118, Anna is involved in a conspiracy aimed at killing her brother and elevating herself to the throne in his place. The plot is uncovered, and Anna is sent to a convent where she spends the rest of her life studying and writing. Anna dies sometime around 1148 with the distinction of being an early female historian.

EASTER DAY 1146 Eleanor of Aquitaine Pledges Soldiers To Join the Crusade. Eleanor Aquitaine (1122–1204), moved by the religious orator, Abbé Bernard of Clairvaux at Vézelay, pledges soldiers for what would later be known as the Second Crusade.

1150 – 1199

1150 Hildegard of Bingen Founds Abbey and Writes Mystic Literature. Hildegard (1098–1179) founds an abbey at Rupertsberg, near Bingen on the Rhine River in Germany, and becomes renowned as one of the first important mystic writers. She is the last of ten children of a noble family, and at age five has her first vision. Her visions are perhaps connected to an illness (possibly migraines) that plagues her throughout her life. At the age of eight she becomes a religious by being enclosed with an anchoress who resides in a cell near the monastery of Disibodenberg. That cell develops into a small convent of nuns dependent on the larger abbey. The nuns elect Hildegard abbess in 1136. When around 1147 she is inspired to found a new convent, the monks of Disibodenberg resist, fearing the loss of prestige and assets. Nonetheless, in 1150 Hildegard and about 20 nuns establish themselves in a new abbey. At this time she also begins to gain fame through her writings concerning her mystical visions. Her first book, *Scivias,* deals with prophesies, mysteries, and directions about the religious life. She writes many other books, covering such diverse subjects as theology, religious music, vices and virtues, medicines, and cures for diseases. Her wide correspondence includes letters to many of the leading figures in Europe, as well as advice for and criticisms of popes and emperors. In her lifetime she is famous throughout Christendom, even making tours in order to preach and perform exorcisms. She dies on September 17, 1179. Whether she is officially canonized is unclear, but she is locally venerated as a saint.

c. 1152 Elizabeth of Schönau Writes of Religious Visions and Stories. At 12 years of age, Elizabeth enters the double monastery of Schönau, near St. Goarshausen on the Rhine, which is founded by her relatives six years before. In 1152 she begins to experience ecstatic visions, which are written down by her brother, who later becomes an abbot. Her writings resemble those of Hildegard of Bingen, with whom she is in communication. Her most famous work, *The Revelations of the Sacred Band of Virgins of Cologne,* elaborates the popular legend of 11,000 women who are martyred during the Roman Empire. She dies on June 18, 1165.

1152   Eleanor of Aquitaine Marries Her Second Husband, Henry Plantagenet. Eleanor of Aquitaine (1122–1204), an influential figure in the struggle for power between England and France, marries Henry Plantagenet, who became Henry II, king of England in 1154.

c. 1155   Death of Christine of Markyate, English Nun. Christine of Markyate (?–c.1155), who resides in a convent at Markyate in England built for her by the abbot of St. Albans, dies about 1155. She enters into religious life despite the strong opposition of her well-to-do parents and then wins great fame for prophecy and miracles.

1157   Birth of Hojo Masako, Influential Japanese Woman. Hojo Masako (1157–1225), the most powerful woman of medieval Japan, is born. She significantly strengthens the rule of the Kamakura Shogunate, the warrior government of medieval Japan, in which a military general, the shogun, governs on behalf of the emperor. She marries Minamoto no Yoritomo in 1177, during which time Yoritomo is bringing warrior groups of Japan under his control. In 1185, he decisively defeats his enemies and becomes Japan's first shogun. After his death in 1199, Masako takes Buddhist vows, but nevertheless, she becomes involved in the politics of choosing a successor to her husband. She becomes the regent for both their elder son Yoriie and younger son, Sanetomo, but later, with the assistance of her natal family, the powerful Hojo, she deposes both for their incompetence. Later, she exiles her father when he attempts to conspire against her. When the emperor declares war against Masako, she rallies warriors to defeat him and thus maintains the shogunate form of military government. Until her death, she rules the shogunate through the Hojo family regents. She is known as "the nun shogun."

c. 1160   Herrad of Landsberg Compiles an Encyclopedia. Herrad of Landsberg (or Hohenburg) (1120–1195), with 60 nuns and canonesses under her direction, compiles the *Hortus deliciarum* (*The Garden of Delights*), a richly illustrated encyclopedia covering much of the theological, historical, and scientific knowledge of her times. The oldest manuscript survives only in a modern copy, since the best medieval version is destroyed during the Franco-Prussian War. Herrad is the abbess of Hohenburg in Alsace. She dies on July 25, 1195.

1165   Birth of Mongolian Börte, Influential Wife of Genghis Khan. Börte is the wife of Genghis Khan (c.1165–1227), the great Mongol leader who rules most of Eurasia, including northern China. She is said to have a major influence on him. Women in Mongol society have greater authority (they can be camp leaders) and greater rights to property than do Chinese women.

c. 1170   Marie of Champagne Encourages Development of Courtly Love. Marie of Champagne (1145–1198), the daughter of King Louis VII of France and Eleanor of Aquitaine, cosponsors "courts of love" to debate points on the proper conduct of knights toward their ladies. When the marriage of her parents is annulled, Marie is raised by her father. In 1164, she marries Count Henry I of Champagne. The countess and her mother, with whom she has a close relationship, preside over famous "courts of love" at Poitiers in the 1170s. An important literary patron, Marie of Champagne encourages Chrétien de Troyes to write *Lancelot* and Andreas Capellanus, *The Art of Courtly Love.* She dies in 1198.

1174   Queen Eleanor of Aquitaine, Most Influential Woman of the Twelfth Century, Held in Captivity. Eleanor of Aquitaine (1122–1204) is under house arrest from 1174 until her husband, Henry II, king of England, dies in 1189. Eleanor, the lively and head-strong daughter of William X, the duke of Aquitaine, is the most influential woman of the twelfth century.

1178   Queen Tamara Crowned Co-Ruler of the Caucasian Kingdom of Georgia. King Giorgi, in an attempt to assure that his daughter will be acknowledged as ruler by his nobles and generals, has her crowned Queen Tamara (also spelled Thamar) (c.1156–1212). She sits on a throne to her father's right for six years until his death in 1184.

c. 1180   Japanese Warrior Tomoe Gozen Displays Prowess During Taira-Minamoto War. Tomoe Gozen, Japan's legendary woman warrior, is said to display military prowess equal to that of any man during the Taira-Minamoto War (1180–85). According to the thirteenth-century military romance, *Heike Monogatari*, Tomoe accompanies her husband, Minamoto Yoshinaka, commander of the Minamoto forces, when he flees from his previous allies, who accuse him of treachery and abuse of power. Tomoe, one of his last surviving companions, refuses to flee for her own life until she has taken the head of an enemy warrior to prove her military prowess. It is believed that she escapes. Her story is also recounted in a play, "Tomoe," attributed to the great playwright, Zeami.

1184   Queen Tamara Becomes Sole Ruler of Georgia. Queen Tamara (c.1156–1212) becomes ruler of Georgia when her father, King Giorgi, dies. Because there is no word in the Georgian language for queen, she is proclaimed King (*Mepe* in Georgian). Her monogram is used on the copper coins of Georgia during her reign.

c. 1190   Japanese Dancer Shizuka Gozen Demonstrates Loyalty to Her Lover. Medieval Japanese drama frequently depicts the tragic story of the shirabyoshi dancer, Shizuka Gozen. Shizuka becomes the lover of Mina-

The monogram of Queen Tamara of Georgia appears on copper coins during her reign.

moto no Yoshitsune, the brilliant general of the Taira-Minamoto War (1180–85). Minamoto no Yoritomo turns against his brother, Yoshitsune, whom he kills. Shizuka is apprehended and brought to Yoritomo, who forces her to dance for him. She finally does so, incorporating songs which attest both to her love for Yoshitsune and his military skill. She dances so beautifully that Yoritomo spares her life.

1192   Eleanor of Aquitaine Raises Ransom For Release of Her Son, Richard I, the Lion-Hearted. Eleanor of Aquitaine (1122–1204) serves as regent while her son, Richard I, the Lion-Hearted, king of England, is on the Third Crusade. While returning from Palestine (present-day Israel) in disguise, he is captured and held prisoner by Leopold, duke of Austria. Eleanor manages to raise the enormous ransom demanded for his release.

c. 1193   Clare of Assisi, Founder of Order of Franciscan Nuns, Is Born. Clare of Assisi (c.1193–1253) is born into a prosperous Italian family. Refusing to marry, she becomes a follower of Francis of Assisi, who founds the Franciscan Order dedicated to poverty and charitable works. In 1212, he permits her to establish a Franciscan convent in Assisi. Although Clare wants her nuns to beg in the streets as do the Franciscan monks, the Roman Catholic Church insists that they remain within convent walls. The "Poor

Clares," as members of her order are known, spread throughout Europe. In 1253, the year of her death, the Vatican approves Clare's rule for her order—the first religious rule written by a woman. Clare is later named a saint.

1199 John, Son of Eleanor of Aquitaine, Becomes King of England. John becomes king of England upon the death of his older brother, Richard I, the Lion-Hearted. Both are sons of Eleanor of Aquitaine (1122–1204), one of the most influential women of the twelfth century, who was also wife to two kings.

1 2 0 0 – 1 2 4 9

c. 1200 Medieval Women Find Employment as Midwives. Midwifery is an honored profession for women in medieval times, as it is in antiquity. Typically women learn midwifery through apprenticeships and earn handsome salaries in its practice. Midwives only intervene in the birth process when absolutely necessary, letting nature take its course. More than anything else, they give psychological support to their clients. Male midwives and doctors begin to squeeze women out of the profession in the seventeenth century.

c. 1200 Shelter for Repentant Prostitutes Opens in Paris. William of Auvergne, the bishop of Paris, France, opens the Filles-Dieu, a home for repentant prostitutes. Although the sex trade is condoned by government authorities, medieval prostitutes are scorned, as they are through the ages. Nonetheless, Christian doctrine offers all sinners, including prostitutes, the possibility of redemption. The Roman Catholic Church also recognizes that women are usually driven to prostitution because of destitution. This enlightened view leads to the Filles-Dieu. The institution shelters its residents and gives them work to establish themselves as respect-able citizens. It declines at the end of the thirteenth century. Other such institutions are established in European cities, where prostitutes flourish. They are often known as Magdalene Houses, based on the notion that Mary Magdalene is a repentant prostitute.

c. 1200 Ordinary European Women May Enjoy Economic "Golden Age." Non-elite women in Europe may enjoy a "Golden Age" regarding economic opportunities during the thirteenth and fourteenth centuries. The household is the center of production, both in town and country; and marriage is primarily an economic partnership, in which husband and wife work together. Thus women enjoy a rough equality with men in a time of trade expansion and urban growth. For example, women can run businesses. The "Golden Age" thesis is given influential support by Alice Clark in her study *Working Life of Women in the Seventeenth Century* (1919), which surveys conditions in England. She claims that as economic activities move out of the home with the onset of industrial capitalism, women's opportunities shrink. Women are increasingly restricted to the private sphere. In the 1990s, scholars note, however, that medieval women are always subordinate to men in their homes and that their business ventures are limited to small enterprises.

c. 1200 Women Shirabyoshi Contribute to Development of Noh Drama in Medieval Japan. Women shirabyoshi performances are a part of Japanese court and Buddhist temple festivities. In their songs and dances, characterized by a strongly marked rhythm, these women performers dress all in white, male attire which includes fans, court caps, and swords. Drums and small cymbals are the accompanying musical instruments. This form of traditional dance plays an important role in the development of classical Japanese noh drama.

c. 1200 Buddhist Sect Jodo Shinshu Established, Teaching that Women Cannot Enter Paradise. Jodo Shinshu, the True Pure Land sect of Buddhism, is established by Shinran (1173–1263), a Japanese Buddhist monk. He teaches that women, as women, cannot enter paradise. Shinran states that "women by nature are covetous and sinful." Shinran is the first Buddhist priest to be publicly married and have a family; thereafter, it becomes a more common practice in the Buddhist priesthood.

c. 1200 Nyonin Kinzei (No Women Allowed) Practices in Japan. *Nyonin kinzei* (no women allowed) practices in Japan exclude women from Buddhist sacred places and ceremonies because they are assumed to be impure. These Buddhist practices reinforce indigenous taboos associated with menstruation and childbirth.

APRIL 3, 1200 Queen Cunegunde Becomes a Saint through her Supposed Celibacy. Cunegunde (or Kunigunde) (c.980–1040), a Benedictine nun and widow of Henry II, is canonized on April 3, 1200, 50 years after her husband. For unclear reasons, she is the patron saint of Lithuania. Cunegunde is the daughter of the count of Luxemburg. She is crowned German queen in Paderborn on August 10, 1002, several months after her husband, Henry II (reigns 1002–24), is crowned king; but they are crowned together as Roman emperor and empress in Rome on February 14, 1014. Her Luxemburg relatives try to take advantage of her position to expand their power but are held in check by the political efforts of Cunegunde's husband. After her husband's death, she becomes a Benedictine nun at the Abbey of Kaufungen, where she dies on March 3, 1040. A marvelous marble monument by the sixteenth-century sculptor Tilman Riemanschneider marks her and her husband's tomb in the Bamberg Cathedral, which the imperial couple founds together. A popular tradition grows up around their child-

less marriage, that the couple leads a celibate life together. As a role model for this behavior, Cunegunde is canonized.

APRIL 1, 1204 Eleanor of Aquitaine Dies At 83. Eleanor of Aquitaine, wife of both King Louis VII of France and later of King Henry II of England, is a great influence on English and French kings. She is the mother of two English kings, Richard the Lion-Hearted and John. She inherited Aquitaine, an indepedent state adjacent to France, in 1137.

c. 1207 Marie of Oignies, Mother of Catholic Lay Order of Beguines. Marie of Oignies (1176–1238) inspires the development of the Catholic lay order of Beguines. She is born into a prosperous family of the Brabant, a region in the Low Countries (between what is now the Netherlands and Belgium). Although she is married when she is 14, Marie adopts a religious life in 1207 with the agreement of her husband. Taking no formal vows, she gives up all her earthly possessions, becomes celibate, and engages in charitable work among the oppressed poor. After her death in 1238, many women in northern Europe follow her example. These lay sisters of the Roman Catholic Church come to be called Beguines, and Marie of Oignies, the "mother" of the Beguines.

c. 1210 Birth of St. Mechtilde of Magdeburg, Popular Mystic Writer. St. Mechtilde of Magdeburg (1210–1290?) is born in Saxony to an aristocratic family, where she begins to have visions as a young girl. At the age of 23, she applies to a traditional convent. Customarily, a woman is presented by her parents along with a "dowry," but Mechtilde chooses instead to apply on her own without money and is rejected. Pursuing her desire to give up the wealth and comfort she is born to, Mechtilde becomes a Beguine. Beguines are religious women who do not take formal vows and who live by the principles of poverty, chastity, and service to others. Mechtilde believes that the Catholic Church has become indulgent and corrupt, and she chastises the Church in her spiritual writings. She chooses to write of her mystical experiences in her native tongue, Low German, rather than Latin, the language considered proper for serious religious works, so that more people will be able to read her words. This makes her works more accessible to a wider audience and leads to a great popular following, as well as harassment by critics in the Church. She enters the convent at Helfta (or Helfda) in Saxony, where she becomes known as one of the three great mystics there, influencing sister mystics Mechtilde of Hackeborn (c.1241–1298) and Gertrude the Great (1256–1302). She continues writing into old age, completing her final book by dictation when she is blind and ill. Her major work, *The Flowing Light of the Godhead*, collects many of her religious revelations, as well as other writings in prose and verse on the spiritual life. The exact date of Mechtilde's death is unknown; estimates range from 1282 to 1297.

1212 **Clare of Assisi Founds the Order of Poor Clares.** Clare of Assisi (c.1193–1235) establishes a Franciscan convent in Assisi. Although Clare wants her nuns to beg in the streets as do the Franciscan monks, the Roman Catholic Church insists that they remain within convent walls. The "Poor Clares," as members of her order are known, spread throughout Europe. In 1235, the year of her death, the Vatican approves Clare's rule for her order—the first religious rule written by a woman. Clare is named a saint in 1255.

JANUARY 18, 1212 **Queen Tamara of Georgia Dies.** Queen Tamara, who had ruled Georgia for 24 years, dies, and is succeeded by her 18-year-old son, Giorgi.

JUNE 15, 1215 **The Magna Carta Signed at Runnymede, England.** The Magna Carta is significant because it marks the beginning of a move away from monarchy toward parliamentary rule. The king is forced by the land barons to agree to grant them rights over their own territories. The Magna Carta clarifies some issues about a married woman's rights to inherit property upon the death of her husband.

NOVEMBER 1, 1215 **Fourth Lateran Council Decrees Marriage a Sacrament.** The delegates of the Fourth Lateran Council of the Roman Catholic Church, which is held in the Basilica of St. John Lateran in Rome, declare that marriage is one of the seven sacraments, or rituals, bestowing God's grace on Christians. Whereas marriage is previously considered a private arrangement, this decision by the council establishes the doctrine that a valid marriage can only exist if it is performed by a priest. The church also upholds the idea that the sanctity of marriage makes divorce impossible. A union can be broken only by annulment, a declaration that a marriage has never really existed. In enforcing monogamy and marital indissolubility, the Church gives greater stability to family life in the Middle Ages.

1226 **Ermesinde Becomes Ruler of Luxemburg.** Countess Ermesinde (1186–1247) becomes ruler of Luxemburg, governing until her son comes of age in 1237. Her father, Henry IV "the Blind," count of Namur and Luxemburg (reigns 1136–96), is quite old when his heir, Ermesinde, is born. When Henry dies, the already twice-married Count Thibault of Bar (reigns 1191–1214) weds the ten-year-old heiress, Ermesinde. Thibault successfully fights off other claimants to Ermesinde's lands and secures her inheritance. Within three months of Count Thibault's death in 1214, she marries Waleran, margrave of Arlon and duke of Limburg (reigns 1214–26), who also aggressively fights to defend and add to their lands. Upon her second husband's death in 1226, Ermesinde governs Luxemburg until their son, Henry V "the Blond" (reigns 1226–81), comes of age in 1237. She preserves peace with her neighbors, strengthens the administration, and increases the French influence in the realm. She dies on February 19, 1247.

1226   Blanche of Castile, Queen and Regent of France, Proves Her Ability to Rule. Blanche of Castile (1188–1252) rules France for the first time as regent for her minor son. The daughter of the king of Castile, Blanche marries King Louis VIII of France in 1200 and becomes the mother of eight living children. After her husband dies, Blanche serves as regent for her minor son Louis IX from 1226 to 1234. She rules France again when Louis is on crusade from 1248 to 1252, the year of her death. Known for her ability to manage state affairs, she works to bring stability and unity to France.

1235   Elizabeth of Hungary/Thuringia Named a Saint. Elizabeth of Hungary/Thuringia (1207–1231) becomes a saint through her ascetic life and ministry to the poor. She is considered the patron saint of bakers, based on a miracle tale of her converting bread into roses. At an early age, Elizabeth, the second daughter of King Andreas II of Hungary (reigns 1205–35), is betrothed to the heir of the Landgravate of Thuringia. Although her first betrothed dies, at 14 she marries his younger brother, Landgrave Ludwig IV of Thuringia (reigns 1217–27). She lives happily with her husband and bears him three children, including a male heir. But she refuses to take part in the lively court, and begins to lead an more ascetic and pious life, performing works of charity. Her behavior is influenced both by the example of Francis of Assisi and by the papal inquisitor Conrad of Marburg, who becomes her spiritual advisor. When her husband dies in Italy while preparing for a crusade, her brother-in-law, Henry "Raspe," seizes power as regent for her son, the five-year-old heir. Eventually Elizabeth retreats to Marburg, where she becomes a Franciscan Tertiary, a lay member of that mendicant religious order. Elizabeth dedicates the rest of her short life to fasting, prayer, and care

of the sick in a hospital she founds. She dies young, being buried on November 19, 1231. Only four years later, the church canonizes her.

c. 1238   Many Northern European Women Join the Beguines, a Catholic Lay Order. A lay sisterhood of Roman Catholic women attracts many members, known as Beguines, in northern Europe. Beginning in the Low Countries (present-day Netherlands and Belgium) through the influence of Marie of Oignies (1176–1238), this sisterhood spreads on the grassroots level throughout the Low Countries and into northern France and Germany. Although variations exist in their organization in separate locales, all Beguines take temporary vows to live in poverty, adopt chastity, and engage in charitable activities in urban settings. Most typically, they live in group homes known as beguinages. The Beguines have only informal ties with the official Roman Catholic Church through their confessors. Although begun by well-to-do women, the sisterhood attracts many poor women, who desire shelter and economic support without sincere religious motivations. As a result, the Church becomes increasingly suspicious of the Beguines. By the fourteenth century, the sisterhood is largely suppressed, although some beguinages still exist today.

1241   Birth of St. Mechtilde of Hackeborn, Teacher and Mystic. St. Mechtilde of Hackeborn (1241–1298), who serves as spiritual guide and mentor to the sisters of Helfta, is born. Mechtilde enters the convent at the age of seven and takes her final vows at the age of 17. With her beautiful singing voice, she becomes the choir director, as well as a teacher. Mechtilde is the mentor of St. Gertrude the Great and friend of St. Mechtilde of Magdeburg. Together, they are known as the three great mystics of Helfta. In one of Mechtilde's revelations, she hears Christ describe himself in such inclusive terms as father, mother, brother, and sister. She dies in 1298, after a three-year illness. Gertrude and another nun write a book about Mechtilde's teaching and spiritual experiences called *The Book of Special Grace*, which is published after Mechtilde's death. Gertrude writes of her, "There has never before been anyone like her in our monastery, and I fear there never will be again." Her feast day is observed on November 19.

1 2 5 0 – 1 2 9 9

c. 1250 Wife Beating Acceptable in European Society. Wife beating is condoned in European society in the High Middle Ages as a part of the natural order. The great theologian Thomas Aquinas writes in his *Summa Contra Gentiles* (1258–64) that a husband must instruct and govern his wife just as he does his children. There are limits to wife beating, however. In the English common law, a husband can use a stick no bigger in diameter than his thumb. The "rule of thumb" applies for centuries.

1256 Mystic St. Gertrude the Great Is Born. St. Gertrude of Helfta (1256–1302), often called "the Great," is born. She is brought to the convent of Helfta at age five and never leaves until her death in 1302. St. Mechtilde of Hackeborn is her mentor there, and together with their contemporary, Mechtilde of Magdeburg, they are known as the three great mystics of Helfta. With another nun, Gertrude writes a book about Mechtilde of Hackeborn's teaching and spiritual experiences, called *The Book of Special Grace*. Gertrude's own spiritual experiences, emphasizing the healing power of prayer, are described in *The Revelations of Gertrude and Mechtilde,* an important contribution to the field of medieval mysticism. Her feast day is observed on November 16.

c. 1270 Book on Craft Guilds Reveals Women Guild Members. Etienne de Boileau compiles his *Book of Crafts*, detailing the regulations of about 100 craft guilds in Paris, France, and it reveals that some guilds are open to women. Craft guilds, associations to regulate the quantity and quality of goods produced in various European cities, flourish in the High and Late Middle Ages. Membership is generally restricted to male craftsmen, but in some locales (Paris, Cologne, Rouen, and a few other French towns), women are permitted to join. Boileau explains that several guilds in Paris are open only to women who work in exclusively female trades, such as dressmaking. However, most regulations permit female members only if they are widows of master craftsmen.

1270 Death of Princess Margaret of Hungary, Dominican Nun. Margaret of Hungary (1242–1270), the daughter of King Bela IV of Hungary who devotes her life to pious deeds as a Dominican nun, dies. As a young girl, Margaret is raised in the care of Dominican nuns. Refusing a royal marriage, she takes religious vows at the age of 12 in the convent built for her near the present city of Budapest. Because she does not want to be treated like a princess, she not only does all the tasks of a nun, but insists on performing the lowliest and most unpleasant ones. After her death in 1270, many miracles are attributed to her. Margaret is canonized in 1943.

c. 1275 Japanese Poet Abutsu Ni Writes Travel Diary. Abutsu Ni (?–1283), a Japanese court lady, writes a poetic travel diary, *Izayoi Nikki (Diary of the Waning Moon)* on the occasion of her travel to Kyoto to seek inheritance rights for herself and her children. An accomplished waka (verse of 31 syllables in five lines) poet herself, she is a secondary wife of the most prestigious court poet of the day, Fujiwara no Tameie and bears him two sons. Following his death, there is an inheritance dispute with his first wife and her children. Abutsu Ni seeks to claim not only his property for herself and her children, but also his poetry manuscripts and his authority as a teacher of poetry.

C. 1285 Japanese Buddhist Convent Established to Provide Sanctuary for Women. Tokeiji, a Japanese Buddhist convent, is established by Kakusan Shido (1252–1306), a widow of the ruling Hojo family. It is the best known of the *kakekomidera* (refuge temples) or *enkiridera* (divorce temples), which provide refuge for women fleeing from their husbands during the thirteenth to the nineteenth centuries. After serving in the temple for two years, a woman can be granted a divorce by the *jisha bugyo* (commissioner of shrines and temples), despite her husband's objections. The convent establishes a bureaucratic procedure for granting divorces, which includes a written statement of the wife's grievances, and just cause has to be proven to gain a divorce. Furthermore, the temple does not deal with the women themselves, but their parents. During the Tokugawa period (1600–1868), Tokeiji is

one of two imperially sanctioned temples, and it is thought that they harbor several thousand women. During this later period, only the wives of commoners, not samurai warriors, can be granted asylum.

C. JUNE 25, 1291 Death of Eleanor of Provence, Queen of England. Eleanor of Provence, queen of England, dies in the convent of Amesbury where she has been a nun during her last years. A daughter of the count of Provence, a powerful ruler in the south of France, Eleanor marries King Henry III of England in 1236. The foreign queen is immensely unpopular because of her expensive lifestyle and her success in convincing her husband to give vast sums of money to her French relatives. Between 1259 and 1265, she secures financial aid and soldiers to help Henry subdue the English barons rebelling against his rule. After Henry's death in 1271, she continues to exert political influence by advising her eldest son, Edward I.

Chapter 5

1300 TO 1499

1 3 0 0 – 1 3 0 9

c. 1300 Italian Scholar Novella D'Andrea Gives Lectures at the University of Bologna. Sometime in the fourteenth century, Novella d'Andrea, the daughter of a professor at the University of Bologna, Italy, lectures in his absence. Because she is a woman at a male institution, however, she does not appear before her audience, but speaks from behind a curtain. It is feared that her beauty will distract the students.

1300 Women's Sports During the European Renaissance. During the Renaissance in Europe, between 1300 and 1600, women in the peasant class play various forms of soccer and stoolball, and run in foot races. These activities usually are associated with harvest celebrations and spring rites. Women of noble rank ride horses and hunt. They are the only women permitted by law to play court tennis in 1388.

1307 *Towazugatari (An Uninvited Confession)*, **Famous Japanese Autobiography.** *Towazugatari (An Uninvited Confession)*, the autobiography of Lady Nijo, is written. A narrative of the years 1271–1307, her story begins with a description of how she becomes the concubine of the retired emperor at the age of 14; it ends, a number of love affairs later, with an account of her

life as a wandering Buddhist nun. Nijo lives at a time when court life is in eclipse and the warrior class is becoming increasingly prominent. The remarkable aspect of her life and her account is that it encompasses both worlds.

1 3 1 0 – 1 3 1 9

JUNE 1, 1310 Marguerite Porete, Author of *The Mirror of Simple Souls*, **Executed for Heresy.** Marguerite Porete, probably a Beguine (a member of a lay sisterhood popular in the Middle Ages), is burned at the stake for heresy. Although little is known of her life, Marguerite is from Hainaut, a region at the border of France and Belgium. Between 1285 and 1295, she writes *The Mirror of Simple Souls*, which describes her mystical union with God and suggests that an individual can attain salvation through faith without the assistance of priests and sacraments. In the spring of 1310, theologians at the Sorbonne in Paris judge her writings to be heretical. Shortly thereafter, she suffers the death penalty at the hands of secular authorities. Despite the church ban against it, *The Mirror* continues to be read as an anonymous work.

c. 1318 Birth of Countess Margaret "Maultasch" of Tyrol. Margaret (1318–1369), the daughter of Henry, count of Tyrol, duke of

Carinthia (reigns 1295–1335), and once briefly king of Bohemia, is born. When Henry seeks a husband for his only legitimate child and heiress, he settles on John von Luxemburg, younger son of the current king of Bohemia. The 12-year-old Margaret marries the eight-year-old John in Innsbruck on September 16, 1330. When her father dies five years later, Emperor Ludwig "the Bavarian" (reigns 1314–47) and the Austrian Habsburg family try to seize Margaret's lands. Margaret loses Carinthia to the Habsburgs but successfully defends Tyrol. Soon, however, she tires of her Luxemburger husband and his relatives. On November 2, 1341, Margaret locks her husband, John, out of Castle Tyrol and tells him to leave her lands forever. Margaret then marries Ludwig von Wittelsbach, margrave of Brandenburg (reigns 1324–51), the son of Emperor Ludwig. Excommunicated by the pope, plagued by the Black Death, and attacked by the Luxemburgers, the young couple nonetheless manages to hold onto their lands. Margaret shares rule with her husband, and after his death in 1361 passes it on to their son, who dies 16 months later. Without an heir, Margaret signs Tyrol over to the Austrian Habsburg dynasty. Margaret then retires, perhaps under force, to Vienna, where she dies on October 3, 1369. The origin of her contemporary sobriquet, "Maultasch," literally "Pocket-mouth," remains uncertain. Historians doubt it relates to some facial deformity; more likely it defames her as a woman of loose morals or bad character.

c. 1318   Alessandra Giliani Studies Anatomy in Italy. Alessandra Giliani is described as a skillful dissector in reports about activities at the Anatomy School in Bologna, Italy. Giliani devises the technique of injecting dye into blood vessels by drawing blood from veins and arteries and refilling them with colored liquids that later solidify, enabling scientists to study blood flow.

---

1 3 2 0 – 1 3 2 9

c. 1322   Jacqueline Felicie Forced to Cease Medical Practice in Paris. Jacqueline (or Jacabina, or Jacoba) Felicie, a physician in Paris, France, is forced to cease the practice of medicine. A trial is held in Paris, France, to consider her case, appealing an earlier condemnation of her practice of medicine in the city. Although there are eight witnesses testifying to the superiority of her work, the judgement goes against Felicie. The Paris faculty of medicine argues that she practices without a license, for she has not been trained at a university. This indicates that universities, from which women are excluded, are beginning to control the medical profession. Women cannot become licensed physicians until the nineteenth century.

1323   Countess Loretta Becomes Regent of Sponheim. Countess Loretta becomes regent of Sponheim, a small collection of territories on the central Mosel River, upon her husband's death in 1323. She governs until her son comes of age in 1331. She aggressively defends the rights of her territories, especially against her rival, the archbishop of Trier, Baldwin von Luxemburg (reigns 1307–54). Her most famous exploit occurs in May or June 1328, when she captures the archbishop as he sails down the Mosel River near her territories. She holds him prisoner for weeks, until he pays a large ransom and guarantees her rights to properties in the area. Although she is briefly excommunicated for kidnapping a cleric and has to personally go to Avignon to be absolved by the pope, she has successfully defended her lands. She dies in 1346.

c. 1328   Salic Law of Succession Prohibits Passing of the French Crown Through a Woman. The French cite the Salic Law, which was promulgated in the early medieval period and prohibits women from inheriting land, as the authority for denying the crown of

France to anyone—man or woman—whose claim to the throne is through a woman. That is, the Salic Law of Succession rules out a person whose descent from a French king can be traced only through the female line. The French use this means to discredit the attempt of King Edward III of England, the son of a daughter of French king Philip IV, to become their monarch when the Capetian dynasty dies out with the death of Charles IV, the Fair, in 1328. Instead, Philip VI of Valois, the son of a brother of Philip IV, becomes the French king.

1330 – 1339

1332   Chinese Empress Ma Is Born. Empress Ma (1332–1382), the wife of Zhu Yuanzhang, the founding emperor of the Chinese Ming (1368–1644) dynasty, is born. Like her husband, she comes from a poor peasant background. By the fourteenth century, most Chinese women of the elite have bound feet. The empress, not being a member of the elite, has large natural feet, which is a subject of much sensitivity. She is said to be very influential with her husband, exercising political power in the only way deemed appropriate for women in the late imperial period: from behind the scenes.

1340 – 1349

1346   English Queen Philippa of Hainaut Supports Husband Edward III during the Hundred Years' War. Philippa of Hainaut (1314–1369), queen of England, supports her husband, Edward III, while he fights the French during the Hundred Years' War (1337–1453), allegedly leading English troops against Scottish invaders in 1346. Philippa is born of noble parents in the Low Countries (present-day Netherlands and Belgium). At the age of 14, she marries Edward III, king of England. With him she has seven

sons and five daughters. A popular queen, Philippa is especially noted for participation in elegant court functions, for her generosity toward the poor, and for fostering the wool industry. A generally accepted story relates that she leads English troops against Scottish invaders in 1346 during her husband's absence on the continent. A more famous tale is recorded by her friend Froissart. According to this noted historian, she joins Edward at the siege of Calais in 1347. After the town surrenders to the English, the pregnant Philippa saves six of its leading citizens from the death penalty by kneeling before the king and pleading on their behalf. The queen dies in 1369.

1346   Birgitta of Sweden, Famous Medieval Mystic, Founds Catholic Order. Birgitta of Sweden (1303–1373) founds the Roman Catholic Order of St. Saviour, whose members are called the Brigittines. Birgitta is born into an aristocratic Swedish family, and at age 14, marries the Swedish nobleman Ulf Gudmarrson, by whom she has eight children. After her husband's death in 1344, she devotes herself to a life of piety and austerity. Birgitta also writes *Revelations*, an account of her supernatural visions, which begin when she is ten years old. In 1349, she leaves Sweden and moves to Rome where she lives until her death on July 23, 1373. Because of her social position, Birgitta's advice is sought by popes, kings, and queens, who respect her mystical powers. She attains unusual authority in public affairs during her lifetime. S is named a saint in 1391.

c. MARCH 25, 1347   St. Catherine of Siena, Italian Mystic and Author, Is Born. Catherine of Siena (1347–1380), a mystic and author who influences public issues of her day, is born to an artisan in the Italian town of Siena. At age 18 she joins the Dominican Order as a tertiary (a lay member) and dedicates herself to works of charity. Experiencing divine visions, she believes herself destined to take part in public affairs and corresponds with leading men of the day; almost 400 of her letters survive. Her influence is most readily apparent in the pope's return to Rome in 1377, a move which restores the independence and credibility of the Roman Catholic Church. The papal court is located in Avignon under the control of French kings for much of the fourteenth century. Catherine writes a classic dialogue about her religious doctrines entitled *A Treatise on Divine Providence* and 26 prayers. Dying in 1380, she is named a saint in 1461.

1 3 6 0 - 1 3 6 9

c. 1364 Birth of Christine de Pisan, First Professional Woman Author. Christine de Pisan (c.1364–c.1430), the first woman to support herself as an author, is born near Venice. At the age of five, she moves with her family to Paris, where her father becomes astrologer to King Charles V. When she is 15, she marries Etienne du Castel, a secretary at the French court. Etienne dies in 1389, leaving his widow with three young children. Faced with the need to support herself and her family, Christine decides to educate herself and become an author. She is the first known professional woman writer, receiving commissions for her manuscripts from aristocratic patrons. In all, Christine writes 15 volumes, including lyric poems, a biography of Charles V, and treatises on various subjects. After her death about 1430, only her poetry is consistently published; the rest of her writings are neglected.

Modern feminists rehabilitate her works, recognizing Christine as a pioneer in the championship of women. In 1399, Christine writes the long poem "Letter to the God of Love," in which she objects strenuously to the negative image of women projected in much literature. Subsequently, she publishes *The Book of the City of Ladies* (1404), a collection of stories about virtuous women throughout history, and *The Treasure of the City of Ladies* (1405), a handbook on proper conduct

of women of all classes. Her last work is a poem celebrating Joan of Arc's victory over the English at Orleans and expressing her satisfaction that a woman has saved France.

1 3 7 0 - 1 3 7 9

c. 1373 Margery Kempe, Author of First Autobiography in English, Is Born. Margery Kempe (c.1373–c.1438), an unusual religious mystic who writes the first autobiography in English, is born. The daughter of John Brunham, a well-to-do merchant in the English town of Lynn, she marries John Kempe, another Lynn businessman, when she is about 20. The couple has 14 children. After the birth of the first, Kempe suffers from acute depression, but recovers after having a direct vision of God. Her divine revelations, which apparently continue until her death, usually come upon her during periods of uncontrolled weeping. In 1413, she convinces her husband to live separately and thereupon embarks on the life of a holy woman. She goes on numerous pilgrimages on the European Continent and even travels as far as Jerusalem. Although Kempe is illiterate, at the end of her life she dictates her autobiography, *The Book of Margery Kempe*, which has the distinction of being the first autobiography in English. There is no record of her after 1438. As in her own time, the debate still rages on whether Margery Kempe is a genuine visionary or simply a psychotic housewife.

1 3 8 0 - 1 3 8 9

1381 Birth of St. Colette, Reformer of Poor Clare Order. Nicolette Boylet, known as Colette (1381–1447), is born in Corbie, France, the daughter of a carpenter. She becomes a Franciscan tertiary (a person who lives in the world but is closely associated with an order of monks) and begins to live alone as a hermit at the age of 21. In a vision, St. Francis calls her to help the Poor Clare nuns return to their original strict rule of life. Colette speaks with the papal claimant, Peter de Luna, in Nice, France, in 1506 about her calling. He is so impressed he admits her to the Poor Clare order and authorizes her to make her reforms and to found new convents. She has no training for this work and is strongly resisted by many of the existing Poor Clare nuns. But with faith and determination, Colette perseveres, and she founds 17 new convents and reforms several others; they are now known as the Poor Clares of the Colettine reform and are located throughout the world. Her feast day is celebrated on March 6.

1384 Jadwiga, Child Queen of Poland. Jadwiga (Hedwiga) (c.1374–1399), at the age of ten, is crowned ruling queen of Poland upon the death of her father Louis I, the king of Poland and Hungary, in the absence of male heirs. In 1386, the pious young queen elects to marry Jogaila (Jagiello), the grandduke of Lithuania, as a means of converting the largely pagan Lithuanians to Christianity. The marriage establishes the Jagellonian dynasty, which rules the Polish-Lithuanian union for nearly two centuries. Jadwiga is a patron of scholarship, financing the Jagellonian University at Cracow, which becomes the center of Polish culture. She dies in 1399.

c. 1388 Margrethe of Denmark Rules a Unified Scandinavia. Margrethe of Denmark (1353–1412) rules a unified Scandinavia between 1388 and 1412. The politically astute daughter of the king of Denmark marries the king of Norway, with whom she seems to share governing responsibilities, in 1363. Upon her father's death in 1375, Margrethe rules Denmark as regent for her young son Olaf. After her husband's death in 1380, she takes over sole control of Norway in the same manner. Olaf dies in 1387, and Margrethe continues her regencies in Denmark and Norway. The queen becomes the head of a unified Scandinavian state when the Swedes name her "Sovereign Lady and Ruler" in 1388. She continues in this position until her death in 1412. One of Scandinavia's most eminent monarchs, Margrethe is noted for strengthening the royal power over the nobles.

1 3 9 0 – 1 3 9 9

c. 1390 Dorotea Bocchi Teaches Medicine in Italy. Dorotea Bocchi (or, possibly Bucca) is appointed professor of medicine at the University of Bologna, Italy, to succeed her father. She hold this post 40 years.

c. 1393 Julian of Norwich, English Mystic, Writes on Idea of Christ as Mother. Julian of Norwich (1343–c.1416), the most famous of all the medieval recluses in England, writes *Revelations of Divine Love,* expounding on the idea of Christ as mother. Although details of her youth are scant, some scholars believe that she is attached to a convent before she becomes a recluse. Her wide learning, particularly in the scriptures, suggests that she has an excellent education. When she is 30, Julian experiences divine visions. Nearly 20 years later, she writes about them in the classic text entitled *Revelations of Divine Love.* The work attracts considerable attention on the part of feminists in the 1990s, because Julian writes so profoundly on the idea of Christ as mother. Just when she becomes a recluse is not known, although this may occur after the book is finished in 1393. At any rate, Julian lives in an isolated cell attached to the church wall of St. Julian in Conisford at Norwich for years. Because of her reputation for wisdom and divine inspiration, Julian is often consulted for advice. This English mystic lives until at least 1416, possibly until 1419.

c. 1393 Merchant in Paris Writes Handbook on Household Management for Bride. An anonymous merchant in Paris writes a handbook on household management under the name *Le Menagier de Paris* (the goodman or husband of Paris). Probably in his 50s, the author wishes to instruct his young bride, who is only 15, in her domestic duties. His treatise gives insight not only into housekeeping in the Middle Ages, but also into medieval moral standards. Although he stresses the necessity of mutual affection in a marriage, the husband makes clear that his wife must obey him without question.

1399   **Christine de Pisan Inaugurates the** *querelle des femmes* **(debate on women).** Christine de Pisan (1364–c.1430), a French author, writes the long poem "Letter to the God of Love," which can be taken as the beginning of the *querelle des femmes* (debate on women). In this work, she objects strenuously to the negative image of women in medieval literature, particularly in the popular *Romance of the Rose* by Jean de Meun. Christine's attack on misogyny (hatred of women) triggers a lively exchange of letters among the foremost French scholars of the day. Some agree with Christine's position; others criticize it. The *querelle des femmes* is continued by various literary scholars throughout Europe for centuries.

The story of Joan of Arc is presented in many literary works. The version illustrated by Edwin J. Prittie was published in 1930.

1 4 0 0 – 1 4 1 9

1400   **Aztec Civilization Thrives in Mexico.** During the 1400s and early 1500s, Aztec civilization thrives in Mexico. The Aztec empire has its capital at Tenochtitlan, on the site of present-day Mexico City. Aztec women are responsible for cooking the food for the family, and for weaving the cloth for their clothing. Aztec women marry at about age 16, and men at about age 20. Boys are educated by their fathers and at formal schools, where they receive general, religious, and military education. Some girls are also educated, particularly at religious schools, but most learn weaving, cooking, and other domestic skills at home. Aztec women wear loose blouses without sleeves and wrap skirts. The wealthier Aztec families have cotton clothing; others wear fabrics made from the coarser fibers of the native maguey plant.

1412   **Joan of Arc, the Maid of Orleans, Is Born.** French patriot Joan of Arc (1412–1431) is born in Domrémy in northeastern France. Joan is raised in a normal peasant household. Sometime around the age of 13, she begins having visions of St. Michael, St. Catherine, and St. Margaret, whose voices she also hears. For several years, Joan does not tell anyone about her divine revelations. However, the voices instruct her to prepare herself for battle, because they claim that she is destined to save France from the English in the last stages of the Hundred Years' War. Therefore, Joan learns to ride horseback, wear armor, and use a sword. In 1429, she sets out on her mission.

1418   Italian Scholar Isotta Nogarola Is Born. Humanist scholar Isotta Nogarola (1418–1466) is born into a noble family of Verona, Italy. As a young woman, Nogarola is trained in the new humanistic learning of the Renaissance, including mastery of Greek and Latin. Although some scholars praise her intellectual accomplishments, many others severely criticize her interest in secular knowledge as unseemly for a woman. Therefore, when she is 23, Nogarola retreats into a "book-lined cell" in her Veronese home, where she devotes her remaining 25 years to sacred studies—more acceptable for females according to conventional wisdom of the time. She writes many letters, orations, and treatises. Her career makes it clear that upper-class women of the Renaissance are encouraged to undertake humanistic studies, but not to become serious-minded scholars.

1 4 2 0 – 1 4 6 9

1420   French Queen Isabeau of Bavaria Signs Treaty of Troyes. Isabeau of Bavaria (1371–1435), queen of France, mishandles French affairs during the Hundred Years' War and in 1420 signs the disastrous Treaty of Troyes. The daughter of the duke of Bavaria, Isabeau marries King Charles VI of France in 1385. The queen leads a scandalous life at the dissolute French court. Because of the king's periodic attacks of insanity, she is frequently named regent. Her capricious policies are disastrous for France, which is engaged in the Hundred Years' War (1337–1453) against England. In 1420 she signs the Treaty of Troyes, by which the English king Henry V is named heir of Charles VI instead of her son (later Charles VII). Charles VII's right to the throne is restored by Joan of Arc in 1429. Isabeau dies in 1435 despised by both the French and English.

1420   Tang Saier Leads Rebellion in China. Tang Saier, a Chinese widow, leads a rebellion with religious overtones in north China. She claims that she can cut paper horses and soldiers which will later come to life. Although the rebellion is put down, Tang Saier is never captured. Women frequently play an important role in sectarian religious groups, which often advocate equality of the sexes as a way of attacking the hierarchical structure of Chinese society.

APRIL 29, 1429   Joan of Arc Leads Liberation Forces. Joan of Arc (1412–1431) presents herself before Charles VII, the rightful king of France who has been denied his throne by his enemies. The English at this point are controlling most of France. Charles gives Joan permission to liberate the city of Orléans from a siege. Wearing all-white armor, she leads an advance force into Orléans, and by June, the English retreat. Her military victory gives her the title of "the Maid of Orleans" and opens the way for the French to ultimately free their country from foreign domination. With a force of 12,000 troops, Joan leads Charles VII through English-held territory to the cathedral at Reims for his coronation. Charles declines to support further military exploits, however, and Joan continues her military efforts independently. In 1430, she is captured and sold to the British.

MAY 30, 1431   Joan of Arc, Savior of France, Is Burned at the Stake. Joan of Arc (1412–1431), the young girl who becomes the national heroine of France, is burned at the stake as a heretic by the English. In 1430, Joan is captured and imprisoned in Rouen, a city held by the English. There she is condemned by an English-dominated church court for heresy. After her martyrdom in 1431, Joan is acquitted as a heretic by another church court in 1456 and proclaimed a saint in 1920.

1451   Isabella of Castile, Future Queen of Spain, Is Born. Isabella, daughter of King John

II of Castile and Leon, becomes the queen of Spain when she succeeds her brother in 1474. Her husband, Ferdinand of Aragon, reigns with her jointly from 1479.

c. 1460   Juliana Barnes Writes About Natural History. Juliana Barnes (or, possibly Berners) is the prioress of Sopewell Nunnery at St. Albans in England. According to many historical narratives, Dame Juliana is the author of rhymes and essays on hunting, hawking, and fishing. The *Treatyse perteynynge to Hawkynege, Huntynge, Fyshynge, and Coote Armiris*, which later forms part of the *Book of St. Albans*, has been attributed to her.

---

1 4 7 0 – 1 4 7 9

1472   Fresco Painter Honorata Rodiana Dies. Honorata Rodiana, the first female fresco painter, dies. She works for the ruler of Cremona in Italy until one of his courtiers attempts to rape her. She flees, disguised as a man.

c. 1479   Anna von Nassau Acts as Regent for the Duchy of Brunswick-Lüneburg. Anna von Nassau (1440–?) acts as regent for her son, Henry, the duke of Brunswick-Lüneburg. Anna is the daughter of Duke John IV of Nassau-Dillenburg. In 1467 she marries the new Duke Otto of Brunswick-Lüneburg (reigns 1464–71). After his death, others at first take over the regency for their young son. In 1473 Anna marries the 71-year-old Count Philip of Katzenelnbogen (reigns 1444–79), who has banished his first wife for witchcraft. Anna survives a few years of intrigue and rivalry over power within his court, including an attempted poisoning. After Philip's death in 1479, Anna returns to Brunswick-Lüneburg to act as regent for her son, Henry (reigns 1471–1520). Until he comes of age in 1486, she is a frugal ruler who promotes religious reform.

JANUARY 20, 1479   Queen Isabella Begins to Create a United Spain with Her Husband

Queen Isabella

Ferdinand of Aragon. Isabella (1451–1504), queen of Castile, and her husband Ferdinand, king of Aragon, rule their countries jointly from 1479 to 1504 and thus lay the groundwork for a united Spain. Isabella marries Ferdinand of Aragon in 1469, with whom she has five children. In 1474, she is named queen of Castile. After her husband becomes king of Aragon on January 20, 1479, the couple rules their countries together. The queen leads military campaigns to end Moorish rule on the Iberian Peninsula (present-day Spain and Portugal), completing the task in 1492 with the conquest of Granada. In that same year, she approves the voyage of Christopher Columbus to the New World, which results in the beginning of the Spanish overseas empire. A devout Catholic, Isabella expels both the Jews and Moors from her land to ensure that all its citizens are Christian. She is criticized for using the Spanish Inquisition as an instrument of political control; nonetheless, her rule is noted for the peace and stability it brings Spain. Isabella dies in 1504.

1480–1489

NOVEMBER 30, 1485 Renaissance Poet Veronica Gambara, Who Presides over Flourishing Court, Is Born. Veronica Gambara (1485–1550), the daughter of an aristocratic Italian family, is born. She marries the count of Corregio, a tiny city-state in Italy. Widowed in 1518, the countess thereafter devotes herself to the upbringing of her two sons and the governance of Corregio. Her court, over which she presides for nearly a half a century until her death in 1550, becomes an important center of the Italian Renaissance. Most notably, Veronica is a patron of the famous artist known as Corregio. She also achieves distinction as an author; 50 poems, many of them sonnets in the style of Petrarch, and over 130 letters are still in existence.

c. 1486 Publication of *Malleus Maleficarum* Begins Centuries of Persecutions for Witchcraft. The papal bull "Summis desiderantes," issued on December 5, 1484, appoints two German Dominicans, Henry Krämer (who Latinizes his name to Institoris) and Jacob Sprenger, as inquisitors to root out heresy and disbelief. The two pursue a special mission, however, as shown in their book, *Malleus Maleficarum (The Hammer of Witches)*, published in 1486. This book contributes to the hysteria that sweeps over Europe and makes its way to Salem, Massachusetts, in 1692.

The Hammer of Witches is an encyclopedia of contemporary knowledge about witches as well as a handbook of methods for investigating the crime of witchcraft. While acknowledging that both men and women can be tempted by the devil to use magical powers for evil, these authors maintain that women

are more at risk. In their views, backed by biblical, theological, historical, and anecdotal evidence, women are vulnerable since they are more superstitious, more sexually insatiable, more vain, and less clever than men. The pacts with the devil are usually sealed by sexual intercourse. Then witches have the power to harm in many ways: cause storms, slay farm animals, kill infants in the womb, make women barren, and deprive men of their "virile members." The last part of the book details how witches can be accused, questioned (using torture), sentenced, and executed. Helping Krämer and Sprenger in their efforts, secular and religious governments throughout Europe increasingly pass laws and begin criminal actions against witches. This book encourages several hundred years of witch-hunts, leading to the persecution, arrest, torture, and execution of tens of thousands of people, most of whom are women.

The almost universal European persecution of witches reaches its height between 1580 and 1660. Germany has the worst record, where authorities execute more than 3,000 women. In the British American colonies, approximately 40 people (mostly women) are executed for witchcraft before 1710.

c. 1488 Catherine Sforza Gains Fame as a "Warrior Woman" in Italy. Catherine Sforza (1462–1509) gains fame as a *virago* (warrior woman) in Renaissance Italy. The illegitimate daughter of the Duke of Milan, Catherine marries the Count of Forli-Imola, two small city-states in northern Italy, and gives birth to six children. After her husband's assassination in 1488, she governs his territory as regent for their son. Known for her vindictive and bloody rule, the countess leads troops in warfare against her enemies. For several months, she bravely withstands the siege of Forli undertaken by a papal army, but capitulates to these superior forces in 1500. She is taken captive to Rome, but allowed to spend the rest of her life in retirement.

1 4 9 0 – 1 4 9 9

c. 1490　Beatrice d'Este Presides over a Brilliant Court in Milan. Beatrice d'Este (1475–1497) presides over a brilliant court in the powerful city-state of Milan during the Italian Renaissance. She is born as a member of the celebrated Este family of Ferrara, Italy, and marries Lodovico "il Moro" Sforza, the duke of Milan, in 1490. For six years, the duchess rules with her husband over one of the most magnificent courts of the Italian Renaissance. She dies during the birth of their third child in 1497.

1490　Properzia de Rossi, Renaissance Sculptor, Is Born. Properzia de Rossi (1490–1530), a successful sculptor in Renaissance Bologna, is born in Bologna, Italy. She begins her artistic career by carving intricate scenes on peach and cherry stones and eventually turns to working with marble, creating portrait busts and low-relief panels for churches in Bologna. Probably because a woman sculptor is highly unusual in her time, Properzia is the subject of much unfounded gossip. It is said that her panel *Joseph and Potiphar's Wife* (c.1520) is a study depicting her own rejection by a lover.

JANUARY 29, 1499　Catherine von Bora, Future Wife of Martin Luther, Is Born. Catherine (Katherine) von Bora is born. She becomes a German Catholic nun, but leaves the convent during the Protestant Reformation led by German clergyman, Martin Luther. In 1525, she marries Luther.

Part 3

QUEENS, EMPRESSES
& REGENTS 1500 – 1799

Chapter 6

1500 TO 1599

1 5 0 0 – 1 5 0 9

c. 1500 Female Cottage Industry Workers Earn Less than Male Colleagues. A system of home-based manufacturing, often called cottage or domestic industry, begins to develop in the Late Middle Ages, and from around 1500 to 1750, female workers in the industry earn less than their male counterparts. The industry reaches enormous proportions in some western European countries, principally Great Britain, in the Early Modern period. The system involves the production of goods in the homes or cottages of rural workers under the direction of merchant-capitalists, centering on the making of textiles. The merchant-capitalists supply the workers with raw materials such as wool or flax, pay them wages for producing finished cloth, and then sell the finished product for profit. Scholars have debated on the impact of cottage industry on women. Some argue that men and women are equal in their work, which depends on cooperation in the family unit, even though production decisions are no longer made by family members. Others point out that women always do the lowest-paying tasks and receive wages from one-third to one-half of those of men. For example, men do the highly paid job of weaving, while women earn less in carding and spinning.

c. 1500 Chinese Peasant Women Earn Money by Creating Textiles. A sixteenth-century peasant woman in south China can often earn as much money in textile work as a man can in the fields, so she is more likely to work indoors at textiles than outdoors in the fields. A peasant woman may have bound feet, though she is less likely to than a woman of the elite. She is also less restricted in her movements than a woman of the upper classes.

c. 1500 Blind Women Musicians Contribute to Japanese Folk Music. Goze—blind, itinerant, women musicians—make a significant contribution to the spread and development of folk music in Japan. They travel throughout Japan, singing popular ballads, accompanying themselves on *shamisen* (stringed instruments), and reciting Buddhist and Shinto teachings. Some are thought to have supernatural powers for casting spells, healing the sick, and enhancing fertility.

1507 Margaret of Austria Named Governor of the Netherlands. Margaret of Austria (1480–1530) is married several times for Habsburg family politics, until she is installed as governor of the Netherlands. Known as Margaret "of Austria" or Margaret "of Savoy," she is the daughter of Maximilian I (who as Holy Roman Emperor reigns from 1493 to 1519). In 1483 she is promised in marriage to the Dauphin of France, who soon becomes King

Charles VIII (reigns 1483–98). Charles breaks the engagement and makes a more politically advantageous marriage with Duchess Anne of Brittany (reigns 1488–1514), who is supposed to have married Margaret's father, Maximilian. Maximilian then promises Margaret to Prince Juan of Castile-Aragon, but her husband dies a few months after the wedding. Next Margaret marries Duke Philibert of Savoy, with whom she enjoys an idyllic relationship until his sudden death in 1504, reportedly from a cold drink taken after an overheated hunt. Finally, Maximilian installs Margaret as governor of the Netherlands in 1507, with her own court at Mecheln. Until her death there in 1530, she is a patron of the arts and diligently works for peace between France and the empire.

1509   Henry VIII Marries First Wife Catherine of Aragon. Shortly before he becomes king of England in 1509, Henry VIII marries Catherine of Aragon (1485–1536), daughter of Ferdinand of Aragon and Isabella of Castile, as his first wife. The couple has six children, of whom only a daughter (the future Mary I) survives infancy. In 1527, Henry will request an annulment of their marriage because he wishes a male heir to the throne and Catherine then is past childbearing age.

---

1 5 1 0 – 1 5 1 9

1510   Nun Lea Ráski Becomes First Woman Writer in Hungarian. Lea Ráski, the daughter of a noble Hungarian family, lives in the sixteenth century and becomes the first woman writer in Hungarian. In 1510, she writes a life of Princess Margaret entitled *Legend of Blessed Margaret.* This is the first work written by a woman in Hungarian. Probably early in her life, she becomes a Dominican nun, entering the convent that is established near present-day Budapest for Princess Margaret of Hungary in the thirteenth century. Lea seems to be engaged as a scribe in the convent.

Teresa of Ávila

MARCH 28, 1515   Birth of Teresa of Ávila, Spanish Nun and Mystic. Teresa of Ávila (1515–1582), the daughter of a noble family in Ávila, Spain, is born. When she is 21, she enters the Carmelite convent in her home town. In her middle age, she undergoes a religious awakening and begins to have mystical visions. She decides to lead a reform of the Carmelite Order, eventually establishing 16 convents of the Discalced, or Barefoot, Carmelites, who live under a rule of extreme austerity. She writes a number of classic works on her experiences, the most notable being *The Interior Castle,* about the techniques necessary to enter into communion with God. Dying in 1582, Teresa of Ávila is named a saint in 1622.

OCTOBER 31, 1517   Protestant Reformation Begins, But Does Not Immediately Change

Attitudes Toward Women. The theologian Martin Luther (1483–1546) posts his "Ninety-five Theses" on the door of a church in Wittenberg, Germany, triggering the Protestant Reformation. There is much debate on the impact of the Protestant Reformation on women. Protestants teach that each individual is responsible for his or her own soul without the need of clerical intervention. They support the concept of "the priesthood of all believers." Because all Christians should be able to read the Bible, it is essential that both boys and girls be literate. This doctrine encourages education for women, at least on the elementary level. Furthermore, Protestants do not consider the celibate life as especially virtuous, so married women can have a better self-image of themselves. On the other hand, Protestants close avenues for unique female experience by abolishing convents and the veneration of the Virgin Mary. They are also strongly patriarchal in teaching that the husband must have mastery over his wife. Most Protestant sects deny women the right to preach. In the short run, the Protestant Reformation does not change attitudes toward women. Nonetheless, some Protestant doctrines will eventually encourage their emancipation.

1519   Isabella d'Este Promotes Culture in Mantua During Italian Renaissance. Isabella d'Este (1474–1539), advisor to her son who rules the city-state of Mantua, encourages the growth and development of arts and letters. She is a member of the celebrated Este family of Ferrara, Italy. In 1490, she marries Francesco Gonzaga, the marquis of Mantua, by whom she has six children. Possessing great diplomatic skill, the marchioness takes an active role in Mantua's government. When her husband dies in 1519, she becomes a trusted advisor for her eldest son, who takes over control of the city-state. Isabella is chiefly remembered for the cultural flowering she brings about in Mantua during the Italian

Renaissance, particularly for her patronage of artists and learned men.

---

1 5 2 0 – 1 5 2 9

1521   Maria von Habsburg Becomes Queen of Hungary and Bohemia. Maria von Habsburg (1505–1558), the daughter of Philip "the Handsome" and Johanna "the Mad," whose union creates the kingdom of Spain, becomes queen of Hungary and Bohemia. She is not yet a year old when her grandfather, Emperor Maximilian I (reigns 1493–1519), betroths her to the as-yet-unborn king of Hungary, Ludwig II (reigns 1516–26). They wed in Vienna in 1514, reside in Innsbruck until 1521, and then leave for Hungary, where Maria is crowned with her husband. Just five years later, however, Ludwig II dies at the catastrophic Battle of Mohács, where the Ottoman Turks crush the Hungarian armies and occupy most of the country.

DECEMBER 23, 1523   Katherine Schütz Marries Priest, Becomes Lutheran Reformer. In the free imperial city of Strasbourg, Katherine Schütz marries the Catholic priest Matthew Zell, who is 20 years her senior. They thereby defy the Catholic Bishop of Basel and create a Lutheran community with other married priests. After the death of their two children as infants, she devotes her efforts to preaching, arguing theology, writing (including publishing tracts and a book of hymns), and aiding the poor and the persecuted in Strasbourg. She remains active after the death of her husband in 1548, until her own passing in 1562.

1524   Courtesan Gaspara Stampa, Italian Renaissance Poet, Is Born. Gaspara Stampa (1524–1554), one of the finest poets of the Italian Renaissance, is born in Padua, Italy, as a member of a middle-class family. Most of her short life is spent in Venice, where she becomes a courtesan, a high-ranking

Catherine von Bora

prostitute dedicated to giving wealthy men sexual pleasure and intellectual companionship. She is remembered for her lyric poems on love and its frustrations, written in the style of Petrarch.

1525   Former Nun Catherine von Bora Marries Martin Luther, Founder of Protestantism. Catherine (Katherine) von Bora (1499–1550), a former nun, becomes the wife of former monk Martin Luther, leader of the Protestant Reformation. Von Bora takes vows as a nun when she is 16 years old. In 1523, after the Reformation ideas of Martin Luther reach her nunnery, she and eight others escape. Uncertain how to live, she soon offers to marry Martin Luther himself, who is 16 years older than she. Surprised at first, the great reformer soon feels led to accept. Their betrothal on June 13, 1525, is followed four weeks later by their wedding. Catherine

becomes the model wife and mother for the new Protestant religions; Luther praises her as compliant and accommodating. She supervises his health and behavior, takes over his household in his former monastery (looking after the numerous guests of her famous husband), raises several of his nephews, and bears three sons and three daughters. After Luther's death in 1546, warfare sweeps over her household, and she dies on December 20, 1550, while fleeing her persecutors.

c. 1525   Argula von Grumbach Argues in Favor of Lutheranism. As the Reformation ideas spread over Bavaria in the 1520s, Argula von Grumbach soon begins to write in favor of Lutheran reforms. Argula von Stauffer, from a Bavarian noble family, marries Frederick von Grumbach in 1516, and soon bears him two daughters and two sons. Her activities promoting the cause of Protestantism bring condemnation by Catholics and anger from her family. Yet she also gains the support of Protestants, even meeting Martin Luther himself in 1530. Her husband dies in that same year. Argula remarries two years later, but her second husband dies after a year and a half. The rest of her life is spent in relative quiet on her estates. Her last mark on history is when the duke of Bavaria briefly imprisons her in 1563 for a second time, on the charge of persisting in circulating books and ideas contrary to the Catholic religion.

1527   Marguerite of Navarre Encourages Renaissance Culture in France. The court of Marguerite of Navarre (1492–1547) is a center of the French Renaissance, as well as a refuge for persecuted writers and supporters of reform in the Roman Catholic Church. Born on April 11, 1492, into the French royal family, Marguerite's close relationship to her brother, King Francis I, makes her one of the most influential women in France during the sixteenth century. In 1527 she marries Henry II, king of Navarre, and her court encourages Renaissance culture in France. Not only a literary patron, Marguerite writes many works herself, including plays, poems, stories, and spiritual meditations. Her most famous work is the *Heptaméron*, a collection of 72 short stories.

---

1 5 3 0 – 1 5 3 9

1531 Maria von Habsburg Becomes Governor of the Netherlands. Emperor Charles V (reigns 1519–56),the brother of Maria von Habsburg, queen of Hungary and Bohemia, installs her as governor of the Netherlands. Maria leaves Hungary after her husband, King Ludwig II, is killed in battle and the Ottoman Turks occupy much of the country. She supports her brother in strengthening the Dutch economy, raising armies, and building fortresses, as well as trying to suppress any Protestant tendencies. When Charles V resigns his throne in 1556, she also surrenders her position and follows him to Spain. She dies there on October 18, 1558.

1533 Henry VIII Annuls His Marriage to Catherine of Aragon Despite Her Protests. Henry VIII, king of England, breaks with the Roman Catholic Church and succeeds in getting his marriage to Catherine of Aragon (1485–1536) annulled through the newly-established Anglican Church. In 1527, Henry requests an annulment from the Catholic Church because he wishes a male heir to the throne and Catherine then is past childbearing age. Catherine offers vigorous protests to an annulment, and the pope refuses to grant one. In 1536 Catherine dies in exile in the English countryside, where she has been forced to live after her marriage is annulled.

c. 1535 Birth of Sofonisba Anguissola, Italian Painter. Sofonisba Anguissola (c.1535–1625), the first distinguished woman painter of modern times, is born in Cremona, Italy. Her father decides to educate his six daughters on the same level as his only son, in contrast to the prevailing views of the day that women ought to prepare only for domestic duties. Consequently, Anguissola is able to develop her considerable talent for painting under capable instructors. Michelangelo, the great master, encourages her in her artistic career. Establishing a reputation as a fine portraitist, Anguissola goes to Spain in 1559 at the invitation of King Philip II to serve as painter for the Spanish court. She remains in Spain until 1580, when she marries and moves to Sicily. After her husband's death, she marries again, dying in her 80s in 1625. At least 50 of her works, most of them portraits, still exist.

c. 1535 Angela Merici Founds the Company of St. Ursula, Catholic Teaching Order. Angela Merici (1474–1540) founds the Company of St. Ursula, a religious congregation of noncloistered women, in Brescia, Italy, dedicated to teaching girls. At first, the Ursulines live at home and engage in prayer and charitable activities. In 1626, however, they are forced by the Roman Catholic Church to become nuns, living in cloisters and achieving fame in the education of girls. Angela Merici is named a saint in 1807.

MAY 19, 1536 Henry VIII Has His Wife Anne Boleyn Beheaded. The second wife of king Henry VIII of England, Anne Boleyn (1507–1536) is beheaded after being convicted for infidelity and treason. Boleyn is born into the English nobility. When she attends the court of the king, Henry VIII, she catches his eye. In 1533, Henry procures an annulment of his marriage to his first wife, Catherine of Aragon (1485–1536), and marries Boleyn, hoping the marriage will produce the desired male heir. Later that year, Boleyn gives birth to a daughter, the future Elizabeth I. When Boleyn gives birth to a stillborn son in 1536, Henry, desperate for a male heir, turns against her and charges her with infidelity and treason. Boleyn is convicted by a court probably prejudiced against her and beheaded on May 19, 1536.

OCTOBER 12, 1537 Jane Seymour Bears Male Heir for King Henry VIII. Jane Seymour (1509–1537) gives birth to a male heir, Edward, for King Henry VIII of England, but she dies of childbirth complications 12 days later. Seymour becomes Henry VIII's third wife 11 days after the execution of his second (Anne Boleyn) in 1536. For years, the king is most anxious for a legitimate male heir to succeed him on the throne. Upon the death of Henry VIII in 1547, the son becomes King Edward VI, but he does not live beyond his sixteenth year.

1538 Duchess Elizabeth of Brunswick-Calenberg Becomes Regent. Duchess Elizabeth is regent of Brunswick-Calenberg from her husband's death in 1538 until their son and heir, Erich II, comes of age in 1540. As ruler, she converts her country to Lutheranism. Elizabeth is the daughter of Joachim I, the Elector of Brandenburg (reigns 1499–1535), and his wife Elizabeth (1485–1545), the sister of the king of Denmark, who soon abandons her husband for the sake of the Protestant religion. At 15, the younger Elizabeth marries Duke Erich of Brunswick-Calenberg (reigns 1495–1538), who is 40 years older, and who keeps a concubine before and after she bears four children to him. Her husband's death in 1538 leaves Elizabeth as regent for five years for their 12-year-old heir, Erich II (reigns 1540–84). When her son assumes power, she marries Duke Poppo of Henneburg and soon becomes caught both in dynastic wars with Wolfenbüttel over Brunswick and the wars of the Reformation. She dies in 1558.

1538 Vittoria Colonna, Italian Poet, Publishes First Collection. Vittoria Colonna (1492–1547), an influential woman in Renaissance Italy, achieves distinction as a poet when her first book of poetry, which is well-received by the critics, is published. She is born in Rome as a member of one of Italy's greatest families. In 1509 she marries the marquis of Pescara, thus becoming a marchesa and moving to Naples. She rarely spends time with her husband, a military man active in the field. Widowed without children in 1525, the marchesa lives in various convents for the balance of her life but never takes the veil. She has many influential acquaintances, including high officials in the Roman Catholic Church. Her most celebrated friend is the artist Michelangelo, with whom she exchanges letters and poems. Colonna presses vigorously for reform in the Catholic Church, although she never accepts Protestantism. A collection of her poetry, published in 1982, includes 390 pieces. They reveal the poet's deep spirituality and considerable learning.

1 5 4 0 – 1 5 4 9

1542 Tarquinia Molza, Virtuoso Italian Singer, Is Born. Tarquinia Molza (1542–1617), a famous virtuoso singer in Renaissance Italy, is born. In addition to her singing, she composes musical pieces for voice, lute, viol, and harp. From 1583 to 1589, she is a member of a group of four "lady singers" organized by the Duke of Ferrara at his court. Tarquinia is dismissed from this celebrated group, one of the first professional groups for female musicians, because of her scandalous lifestyle.

DECEMBER 11, 1542 Mary, Future Queen of Scots, Is Born. The daughter of James V, King of Scotland, Mary Stuart's two older brothers both died in infancy. Her father dies when Mary is a few days old, making her sole heir to the crown of Scotland. Mary is crowned queen while still an infant, She holds the title from 1542 until 1567. Her mother, Mary of Guise, serves as regent for her daughter, who is sent at the age of five to France to be raised at the court of Henry II. The young Queen of Scots marries Francis, the heir to the French throne, in 1558 and serves as queen consort of France briefly before her young husband's death in 1560. She returns to Scotland in 1561.

1548   Birth of Odani no Kata, Twice a Victim of Marital Politics in Medieval Japan. Odani no Kata (1548–1583), famed as the greatest beauty of her time, is born. She is the younger sister of Oda Nobunaga, the great warrior who seeks to unify Japan under his rule. One of his strategies for strengthening relations with his allies is to practice *keibatsu*, marital politics. When Odani is 15 years old, Nobunaga arranges her marriage with his ally, Asai Nagamasa. In 1570, however, her husband turns against Nobunaga. Three years later, Nobunaga's forces kill Asai in battle. Nobunaga spares the lives of his sister and her three young daughters, but orders that her two infant sons be put to death. Odani lives in seclusion for a decade, until her nephew, Oda Nobutaka, orders her to marry his ally, Shibata Katsuie. Within a year of their marriage, their castle is under siege. While her daughters escape, Odani chooses to die with her husband in the flames of the castle.

1 5 5 0 – 1 5 5 9

C. 1552   Lavinia Fontana, Italian Painter, Is Born. Lavinia Fontana (c.1552–1614), who excels in painting portraits and religious scenes, is born in Bologna, Italy. Her father, the painter Prospero Fontana, teaches her his craft. She marries Gian Paolo Zappi, a fellow student in her father's studio, who gives up his own career to care for their numerous children and allow Lavinia time for painting. She gains renown throughout Italy for her portraits and religious scenes, moving to Rome in 1603 with her family and becoming one of the official painters of the papal court. There are 135 known works by Lavinia Fontana.

1553   Queen Mary I Tries to Reestablish Roman Catholicism in England. Mary Tudor (1516–1558), the daughter of King Henry VIII of England and his first wife Catherine of Aragon, attempts to destroy the Anglican Church and restore Roman Catholicism to England once she becomes queen. When Henry arranges the annulment of his marriage to Catherine and establishes the Anglican Church (Church of England), Mary remains loyal to her Catholic mother. After her half-brother Edward VI dies in 1553, she succeeds to the throne as Mary I. During her five-year reign, the queen persecutes Protestants in a futile attempt to destroy the Anglican Church and reestablish Roman Catholicism in England. Because about 300 Protestants are killed, the queen becomes known as "Bloody Mary." Although married to Philip II, king of Spain, in 1554, she dies childless in 1558.

JULY 1, 1553   Lady Jane Grey Serves as Queen of England for Nine Days. Upon the death of Edward VI, Lady Jane Grey (1537–1554) becomes queen of England, a reign that lasts nine days. A great-granddaughter of King Henry VII of England, Lady Jane Grey is raised as a Protestant and is well-educated. She becomes the tool of politicians anxious to retain the Protestant Anglican Church upon the death of Edward VI in 1553. There is danger that Catholicism will once again be made the official religion of England. Lady Jane is named queen of England in July of that year, but holds the title for only nine days before the Catholic Mary Tudor takes the throne as Mary I. In 1554, Lady Jane and her husband, Lord Guildford Dudley, are executed for high treason at the order of the queen.

C. 1555   Louise Labé, French Renaissance Poet, Writes Notable Love Sonnets. Louise Labé (1425–1565), the well-educated daughter of a wealthy ropemaker, publishes a volume of her works, including a number of highly-praised and passionate love sonnets. She is a strong advocate of better education for women. Her unconventional behavior leads to unverifiable legends about her, such as that

Queen Elizabeth

she fights on horseback in a battle. Born in Lyon, France, and married to another rope-maker of Lyon, Labé forms a literary circle in her home, which becomes a center for French Renaissance poets.

c. 1557   Birth of Tanyangzi, Who Teaches a Religion Harmonizing Daoism, Buddhism, and Confucianism. Tanyangzi (c.1557–1580), a religious teacher from an elite family who live in Suzhou, is born. Her teachings combine Daoism, Buddhism, and Confucianism in a way that is typical of the syncretic thought of her time. She is said to ascend heavenward and attain immortality in broad daylight. She attracts as her disciples a number of men from prominent families, who write copiously about her.

1558   Queen Elizabeth I Supports Protestantism and Brings Peace and Prosperity to England during the "Elizabethan Age." Elizabeth Tudor (1533–1603), the daughter of King Henry VIII of England and his second wife Anne Boleyn, rules England between 1558 and her death in 1603, a period often called the "Elizabethan Age." During her long reign, she successfully overcomes many external and internal obstacles. The "Virgin Queen," as the never-married Elizabeth is called, dedicates herself to bringing peace and prosperity to her country. Before Parliament in 1558, she explains her resolve to remain single in view of her royal duties: "I have long since made choice of a husband, the kingdom of England..." The queen supports the Protestants by restoring the Anglican Church, undoing the Roman Catholic policies of her half-sister Mary I. In 1587, Elizabeth condones the execution of Mary Stuart, queen of Scots, because of plots to depose her and elevate the Catholic Mary to the English throne. Spain, which desires the return of Roman Catholicism to England, supports the undermining of Elizabeth's rule. In the following year, her position is secured when the English defeat the Spanish Armada, which is sent to invade England. Under her guidance, England emerges as a European power.

1559   Margaret, Duchess of Parma, Is Named Governor of the Netherlands. Margaret von Habsburg (1522–1586), duchess of Parma, becomes governor of the Netherlands. Margaret is the illegitimate daughter of the Holy Roman Emperor Charles V (reigns 1519–56) and a mistress, Jean van den Gheynst. Her father first marries her to Alexander de Medici in 1536; a year later she briefly takes over the government in Florence after his murder. In 1538 she is next married to Ottavio Farnese, who becomes duke of Parma (reigns 1547–86); but her husband quarrels with her father and allies with the king of France. The successor of Charles V, Margaret's half-brother King Philip II of Spain (reigns 1556–98), names her as governor of the Netherlands in

1559. Although she quickly becomes caught between quarrelling factions of nobles and bureaucrats, as well as Catholics and Protestants, she soon asserts her authority. In 1567 when Philip sends the duke of Alba, his army, and brutal oppression to the region, she resigns. From 1580 to 1583 Philip brings her back, although she has to share power as governor with her son, Alexander Farnese, who dies in 1592. Again dissatisfied with the limits on her authority, she withdraws from the government, dying soon after, in 1586.

1 5 6 0 – 1 5 6 9

c. 1561   Birth of Noted English Literary Patron Mary Sidney. Mary Sidney (c.1561–1621) is born into an aristocratic family in England, marrying Henry Herbert, the earl of Pembroke, at the age of 16. Always close to her brother, the noted poet Sir Philip Sidney, she has a life-long passion for literature. As the Countess of Pembroke, Mary Sidney is a great patron of learning. She edits and publishes her brother's poems after his death in 1586. Her most notable accomplishment is the completion of his translation of the Psalms into English. She dies in 1621.

1561   Mary, Queen of Scots, Returns to Scotland. When Mary Stuart's husband, King Francis of France, dies after less than one year on the throne, his mother, Catherine de Medici, is restored to power as Queen Regent. Reluctantly, Mary decides to return to Scotland. Queen Elizabeth I of England, perceiving Mary as a threat, refuses Mary permission to enter Scotland via England, and even attempts to intercept Mary's ship at sea. Mary escapes and enters safely at Leth, proceeds to Edinburgh and takes up residence at Holyrood Palace.

c. 1563   Counter-Reformation Does Not Change Attitudes Toward Women Within the Roman Catholic Church. The Council of Trent (1545–63), a series of meetings held in northern Italy by high officials of the Roman Catholic Church, decides on the policies of the Counter-Reformation. This reform movement, often called the Catholic Reformation, is designed to meet the threat posed to Catholicism by the Protestant Reformation. Although the Church stops abuses, it does not change any of its doctrines to counter Protestant criticism. Those traditions which give women special solace are reaffirmed. Convents continue to provide an alternate lifestyle for women, and the veneration of the Virgin Mary continues to express the feminine principle in the liturgy. Although the Church is hesitant to condone nuns working outside the cloister, new orders do bring some of them into the world, particularly the Daughters of Charity.

1564   Maharanee Durgawati of India Dies at Battle of Narhi. An opponent of Mughal expansionism, Maharanee Durgawati of Gondwana, India, dies at the battle of Narhi resisting an invasion by Akbar the Great. In 1562, Akbar the Great ascends the Mughal throne. He faces a potent foe in Maharanee Durgawati of Gondwana, who has ruled Gondwana since the death of her husband in 1548. The role of elite women in India is in transition during the sixteenth century; they exert increasing independence in the spheres of politics and warfare. Like her male predecessors, Durgawati enlarges her domain through military conquest. In 1564, a Mughal army invades Gondwana, and a game of cat and mouse begins. Durgawati's force marches to the mountain village of Narhi, and Mughal troops seize the mountain passes. Leading a counterattack, Durgawati and her troops rout the enemy. Durgawati plans a nocturnal surprise attack, but the plan is rejected by the majority of her chiefs. As a result, the next day the Mughals easily recapture the cliffs. Durgawati leads her outnumbered army into battle, and her troops repulse three Mughal attacks. On the second day of the battle, Durgawati's army is overwhelmed. Wounded and fearing capture, Durgawati takes her own life. She is a benevolent ruler, renowned for her great beauty and greater military skill. Gondwana is absorbed into the Mughal Empire.

OCTOBER 6, 1565   Marie de Gournay, the French "Minerva," Is Born. Marie le Jars de Gournay (1565–1646) is born as the eldest in a family with six children in Paris, France. Her father, an influential court official, purchases a feudal estate in Picardy, from which Marie gets the name by which she is known: de Gournay. In 1580, her widowed mother moves her children to the castle at Gournay, where Marie educates herself. When she is 18, she is enamored by the *Essays* of Michel de Montaigne. Moving back to Paris in 1588, she wins the friendship of this famous writer, who considers her an adopted daughter. Marie decides to remain single and to support herself and her family by her literary efforts. Known as the French "Minerva" (a woman of great wisdom or learning), she is a financial success as a writer of treatises on various subjects. Her *Equality of Men and Women* (1622) and *Complaint of Ladies* (1626) demand better education for women. She is best known for editing the works of Montaigne after his death. Marie de Gournay is hostess for a salon in Paris. The salonières (women of the salons) are subjected to some ridicule for aspiring to rise above their place in the domestic sphere. In England, such women are called bluestockings, a term carrying a negative connotation. Although Marie de Gournay is scorned as a bluestocking, her salon is attended by important figures of Parisian society.

1567   Birth of Yodogimi, Tragic Japanese Heroine. Yodogimi (c.1567–1615), a tragic heroine of medieval Japan, is born. She is the daughter of Odani no Kata, who is herself a victim of marriage politics. At the age of 20, Yodogimi becomes the "bedtime attendant," or concubine, of 51-year-old Toyotomi Hideyoshi. Hideyoshi is the military leader who seeks to unify Japan under his authority. While Hideyoshi is alleged to be solicitous toward Yodogimi, he is, nevertheless, the man who is responsible for the deaths of her mother, stepfather, and brothers. Two years later, Yodogimi gains power as the mother of Hideyoshi's only child, a male heir. The child dies at the age of two, but Yodogimi later gives birth to another boy, Hideyori. Hideyoshi dies in 1598, when the boy is still young. Yodogimi then seeks to rally the allies of the Toyotomi family in support of her son, Hideyori. Ultimately, she is unable to do so. During a siege of their castle by the forces of Tokugawa Ieyasu in 1615, Yodogimi and Hideyori commit suicide.

---

1 5 7 0 – 1 5 7 9

1572   Queen Catherine de Médici Takes Part in the French Religious Wars between Catholics and Protestants. Queen Catherine de Médici (1519–1589) is intimately involved in the religious wars between the dominant Catholics and the Protestant Huguenots in France. Although she tries to balance the warring factions and maintain peace, she approves the infamous massacre of Protestants on St. Bartholomew's Day. Despite this black mark, she is credited with holding France together during a period of intense internal discord. The daughter of the Duke of Urbino in Italy, she marries Henry of Valois in 1533. Henry serves as king of France from 1547 until his death in 1559. The couple has four sons and five daughters. The queen serves as regent for her young sons Francis II and Charles IX between 1559 and 1574. Her strong political influence is still felt during the reign of her son Henry III between 1574 and 1589.

1573   Qin Liangyu, Who Helps Emperor Ming Defeat the Invading Manchus, Is Born. Qin Liangyu (1573–1648), a military heroine at the time of the transition between the Ming and Qing dynasties in China, is born. She is educated by her father the same as her brothers. She marries an aboriginal chieftain named Ma Qiancheng, who is granted a title by the Ming state. When he dies, she inherits his title. In 1630 when the invading Manchus are threatening the capital, the Emperor Ming summons her to help defend it.

DECEMBER 8, 1573   Sophia Brahe Assists in Calculation of Lunar Eclipse. Sophia Brahe (1556–1643), Danish student of astronomy, assists her brother, astronomer Tycho Brahe (1546–1601) in observations leading to their calculation of the lunar eclipse. Sophia also becomes an excellent horticulturist, and assists her brother frequently in his astronomy research.

1 5 8 0 – 1 5 8 9

1581   Catherine de Médici Introduces Italian Dance to the French Court. Catherine de Médici (1519–1589) of Florence, Italy, who becomes queen of France in 1547, commissions a group of Italian dancers to come to Paris for a royal wedding. They create the *Ballet Comique de la Reine,* one of the first ballets ever produced.

FEBRUARY 8, 1587   Mary Stuart, Forced to Flee Scotland for England, Is Executed. Mary Stuart (1542–1587), known as Mary, Queen of Scots, is executed, an act that is condoned by her cousin, Elizabeth I, queen of England, in order to preserve her own position. Elizabeth keeps Mary under house arrest for 18 years because she is aware that there are Catholic plots to give the English crown to the Queen of Scots. Elizabeth has supported Protestantism in England throughout her reign. In 1587, she condones the execution of the Catholic Mary Stuart in order to protect her own position. Mary meets her fate with great dignity at the age of 44.

Mary, Queen of Scots

C. 1588   Birth of Madame de Rambouillet, Inaugurator of Salon Society in Paris. Catherine de Vivonne (c.1588–1665), who as Madame de Rambouillet inaugurates salon society in Paris and stimulates the intellectual life of France, is born into the French nobility. At the age of 12, she marries Charles d'Angennes, afterwards marquis de Rambouillet. Disgusted with the coarseness of the French court in the early seventeenth century, she establishes a salon in her Parisian townhouse to elevate the tone of high society. There members of the aristocracy—both male and female—and men of learning meet to engage in serious conversation, particularly on literary matters. Through her role as hostess, Madame de Rambouillet has a great influence on the development of French literature. After her death in 1665, salon society flourishes in France and other European countries.

1 5 9 0 – 1 5 9 9

c. 1590 Du Liniang Is Popular Heroine of Chinese Play. Du Liniang is the fictional heroine of the romantic drama *Peony Pavilion,* one of the most popular of Chinese plays, written by Tang Xianzu about 1590. In the play, she pines away and dies from lovesickness but is revived by the passion of her lover, Liu Mengmei. She is a particularly popular figure among women in late imperial China.

SEPTEMBER 12, 1590 Maria de Zayas, Popular Spanish Novelist, Is Born. Maria de Zayas (1590–1661), a popular novelist in Spain in the seventeenth century, is born into a noble family in Madrid. Little is known of her life, although it is thought that she lives in Zaragoza because her novels are published there. She is considered the most important of the minor Spanish novelists of the seventeenth century. Her works are widely read in her time; in them, she criticizes the subjugation of women in Spanish society.

c. 1591 Veronica Franco, Italian Renaissance Poet, Opens Women's Shelter. Veronica Franco (1546–1591), an Italian Renaissance poet, opens a refuge, or shelter, for women of the streets in Venice, Italy. Her poetry is neglected for centuries, but she is now known as an able writer with a concern for social issues of particular interest to women.

c. 1593 Renowned Italian Painter Artemisia Gentileschi Is Born. Artemisia Gentileschi (c.1593–c.1652), a renowned painter in Italy and England, is born in Rome. Her father, the well-known artist Orazio Gentileschi, teaches her to paint in his studio. A notorious trial, in which one of her instructors is found guilty of raping Gentileschi, serves to blacken the young woman's reputation. In 1612, the same year as the trial, Gentileschi marries and moves to Florence with her husband. Although the couple eventually separates, they have a daughter. By the time she is 23, Gentileschi has established herself as an artist to the extent that she is made a member of the Florentine Academy, an unusual honor for a woman. Her dramatic canvases, often dealing with narrative and Biblical subjects, attract wealthy clients. In addition to Rome and Florence, the artist also works in Genoa, Naples, and London. She is considered the greatest of all Italian women artists. She dies sometime around 1652.

1594 Dutch Painter Clara Peeters Is Born. Clara Peeters (1594–c.1657), the first Dutch woman to paint still lifes, is born. She specializes in scenes of food and tableware and is particularly skilled in depicting reflected light.

c. 1599 Beatrice Cenci Is Beheaded, Later Inspires Percy Bysshe Shelley. Beatrice Cenci (1577–1599), an Italian beauty, is beheaded by order of Pope Clement VIII and inspires the central figure of a play by Percy Bysshe Shelley. The dramatic poetic play, *Cenci,* published in 1819, recounts the tragedy of the Cenci family. Beatrice, with her stepmother and brother, plot the murder of Count Francesco Cenci, Beatrice's father. All three are arrested, tortured, and beheaded.

OCTOBER 28, 1599 Birth of Sister de L'Incarnation, Religious Educator in Quebec. Marie Guyart (Sister de L'Incarnation) (1599–1676), who plays a vital role in the educational and religious life of Quebec, is born in Tours, France. Throughout her early life she demonstrates unusual spirituality. Despite urges to remarry following the death of her husband in 1619, she withdraws into secluded meditation and prayer. On March 15, 1620, she experiences a mystical and emotional conversion, resulting in her decision to withdraw from the world. However, her sister and brother-in-law call her to assist them with

Beatrice Cenci

their failing business. Under Guyart's leadership, the business prospers, yet she remains haunted by religious visions. In 1632, though heartbroken at leaving her son, she enters the Ursuline cloister at Tours. She takes her vows in 1633, becoming Sister de L'Incarnation, and teaches religious doctrine for six years. From her reading of the Jesuit Relations and continuing visions, she concludes that her vocation is in Canada. Sister de L'Incarnation's business experience proves invaluable as she is called upon to arrange financial agreements and oversee the construction of the first Ursuline convent in Quebec. While she governs the Quebec Ursulines, she also runs a boarding school for Native Indian and French girls, writes several religious works in Native languages and in French, and writes over 12,000 letters. Finally, she provides an opposing framework to the Bishop of Quebec. In fact, he cannot impose his authority over the Ursulines until after her death in 1676.

1 6 0 0 – 1 6 0 9

c. 1600 Salon Society Offers Educational Opportunities to Aristocratic European Women. Salon society, in which hostesses hold receptions in their salons or drawing rooms for the purpose of intellectual conversation, is originated by Madame de Rambouillet in Paris in the early seventeenth century. Spreading from France throughout Europe, salon society flourishes in the seventeenth and eighteenth centuries. Both men and women of aristocratic and bourgeois backgrounds participate. By stimulating women through intellectual exchange, salon society offers them unique opportunities for extending their education. The salonières (women of the salons) are subjected to some ridicule for aspiring to rise above their place in the domestic sphere. In England, such women are called bluestockings, a term carrying a negative connotation.

1600 Geisha and Prostitutes Are Licensed by the Japanese Government. Geisha (female artists/entertainers) and prostitutes are licensed by the Japanese government to work in entertainment districts of major cities in Japan. In order to maintain standards of public morality, the government sets aside parts of the cities of Kyoto (Shimabara) and Edo (Yoshiwara), where women entertainers and prostitutes are fenced into walled areas in which they are licensed to work. In the restau-

The salon of Madame de Rambouillet in Paris.

rants and tea houses of these licensed quarters, men have parties where they eat, drink, and are entertained by women. Geisha are trained in traditional arts of dance and music. While they are skilled in the arts of charm and conversation, they are not supposed to engage in

THE LIVES OF COLONIAL INDENTURED SERVANTS AND SLAVES IN SEVENTEENTH-CENTURY AMERICA

1600 Seventeenth-century colonists in British North America needed labor to work their plantations and they favored white indentured servants over African or Native American slaves. English females and males agreed to work in the fields as indentured servants. They tended to be young, and they signed a written contract to serve between four and seven years in return for their passage to the New World. Indentured servants were entitled to "freedom dues" when their time of service expired. Freedom dues often included two suits of clothes, a few tools, food, and in the first half of the seventeenth century, a small plot of land. A few women married into wealthy families when freed. Helenor Stephenson came to Maryland to work for Sir Edmund Plouden and later married William Brainth-

waite, a wealthy relative of the colony's proprietor Lord Baltimore. However, many women found servitude oppressive and unending. Unwed mothers (women could not marry without their master's permission), after being secured to a post and whipped, were forced to serve extra time for the inconvenience they created for their masters. Few African slaves were imported before 1680 to the American mainland. Because of their small numbers, they often experienced similar working and living conditions to that of indentured servants. Faced with the prospects of a short life in the southern colonies due to malaria, yellow fever, and various other deadly diseases, newcomers died in large numbers regardless of their race or gender.

sexual activities (a geisha may, however, enjoy a relationship with her patron). Yujo (women of pleasure) are more clearly prostitutes. While the licensing of pleasure quarters ends with the fall of the government in 1868, the practices continue to modern times. Feminists work to make prostitution illegal and are successful in 1957.

JULY 29, 1600 **Anna Pappenheimer and Her Family Executed for Witchcraft.** Anna Pappenheimer and her family are executed for witchcraft in Bavaria, a region of present-day Germany. Around this time beggars, itinerants, and vagabonds are often targets of government campaigns to clean up society. When the duke of Bavaria declares a witch-hunt, 60-year-old Anna Pappenheimer (the daughter of a grave-digger), her husband, Paul (a cleaner of latrines), their three sons, and two others are rounded up. Under torture, they finally confess to such crimes as flying on sticks,

making magic potions, causing storms, having intercourse and making pacts with the Devil, practicing ritual dismemberment and cannibalism, as well as committing robberies, arsons, and hundreds of murders. Their punishment is carried out before thousands of onlookers (and their 11-year-old youngest son, who will be executed weeks later). First, officials rip their skin with red-hot pincers. Then, in a rare part of the penalty, the officials tear off the mother's breasts and rub them around her and then her sons' mouths. The officials next take them by cart in a procession for over half a mile to the place of execution. There the men's limbs are broken with the wheel, her husband is impaled, and finally all are tied to stakes and burned alive.

C. 1603 **Izumo no Okuni Originates Kabuki Theater of Japan.** According to popular accounts, Izumo no Okuni (1572–?) is believed to originate kabuki, the combination of dance, drama, and music which dominates Japanese theater throughout the Tokugawa period (1600–1868). Okuni is an attendant at Izumo Shrine, a major Shinto center, and later achieves acclaim as the leader of a successful women's theater troupe. Performing in Kyoto in 1603, her troupe combines current songs and dances with popular fashion and dramas in which the women impersonate men. These performers, known as "Okuni kabuki," are soon copied by other groups of itinerant female entertainers. Viewed as offensive to public morals, the government suppresses these performances and thereafter, women are prohibited from appearing on stage.

1603   James I, Son of Mary Queen of Scots, Succeeds Elizabeth I on the Throne of England. James, son of Mary Queen of Scots, becomes James I of England and James VI of Scotland, beginning a union of the two countries. During his reign, colonies in America, including his namesake, Jamestown, are established.

c. 1607   Italian Musician Francesca Caccini Serves Tuscan Court. Francesca Caccini (1587–1640), who enjoys a long professional career as a singer and composer, serves the Tuscan court as a highly-paid musician from 1607 to 1627. A member of an Italian family of distinguished musicians, she is born and lives in Florence, although she makes her first singing appearance at the French court in 1600. In addition to singing, Francesca plays the lute, guitar, and harpsichord. She also composes music, her most famous work being the opera *La liberazione di Ruggiero*. After her first husband dies in 1626, Francesca may have married again. She dies in 1640.

1607   Birth of Madelaine de Scudéry, Author of Novels about Parisian High Society. Madelaine de Scudéry (1607–1701), who writes popular novels about high society in Paris, France, is born. Her lengthy novels are

extremely popular because the characters are based on important society figures, easily recognized by her readers. She moves to Paris at a young age to join her brother, the successful dramatist Georges de Scudéry. There she holds a literary salon in her home, establishing herself as a successful hostess, and gains renown as an author. Treasuring her own independence by remaining single, she advocates the education of women in her novels. She dies on June 21, 1701. Although her works are no longer read, Madame de Scudéry has an impact on the development of the novel, particularly because of her masterful character analysis.

MAY 6, 1607   First English Settlers Sail Into the Chesapeake Bay in North America. Three ships—*Susan Constant, Godspeed,* and *Discovery*—stop at Cape Henry at the entrance to the Chesapeake Bay. The ships sail about 60 miles (97 kilometres) up the river to establish the colony of Jamestown on May 24. The colonists give the river the name James River. Both the colony and the river are named for King James I of England. Under the leadership of Captain John Smith, the colonists struggle to survive swampy conditions, impure drinking water, and disease. After several years, they successfully grow their own food, and recruit women to join the all-male settlers. These two factors greatly improve living conditions and prospects for survival.

DECEMBER 30, 1607   Native American Pocahontas Saves Life of Colonist John Smith. Twelve-year-old Pocahontas (c.1595–1617), the daughter of chief Powhatan of the Algonquians, rescues Captain John Smith—captured by the Powhatans in 1607 and held for execution—and saves the Jamestown colony from attack by Powhatan Indians, according to Smith's *Generall Historie of Virginia, New England, and the Summer Isles,* published in 1624. Historians now believe that this may have been staged and that the Powhatans

Pocahontas

never intended to kill Smith. Yet, Pocahontas does play an important role in maintaining peaceful relations between the fragile Jamestown colony and the Powhatans. She brings much needed food as well as information about her father's plans. After Smith returns to England, relations between Jamestown and the Powhatans deteriorate. Captain Samuel Argall has Pocahontas abducted and held captive in 1613. During her captivity, she converts to Christianity and marries widower John Rolfe in 1614. The Virginia Company realizes that Pocahontas (now called Rebecca) can be useful in promoting immigration and investment in the colony. In 1616, the company sends Pocahontas, John Rolfe, and their one-year-old son to England as an example of the peaceful relations between the Native Americans and the colonists. In England, she visits the queen and

other important dignitaries. Unfortunately, she contracts a fatal illness and dies in 1617. Relations between the Powhatans and the colonists deteriorate further after the deaths of both Pocahontas and her father.

c. 1609   Mary Ward Founds Successful but Short-lived Catholic Teaching Order. Mary Ward (1585–1645) founds a short-lived Roman Catholic order for lay female teachers—The Institute of the Blessed Virgin Mary—patterned on the Jesuits. According to the rules of the institute, the sisters are to live outside convent walls and to dedicate themselves to instructing girls. Between 1616 and 1628, Ward's sisterhood opens schools in various cities on the European continent, including Cologne, Rome, and Vienna. Although the congregation is quite successful, it is dissolved in 1631 because the Church judges that it allows women excessive freedom. Ward is born in England, but because the Roman Catholic Church is outlawed in her native land, she moves to northern France at the age of 21 to enter the convent of St. Omer, run by English Jesuits. Spending her last years in England, Ward dies in 1645.

JULY 28, 1609   Dutch Artist Judith Leyster Is Born. Judith Leyster (1609–1660), an artist who paints scenes of everyday Dutch life, is born into a middle-class Dutch family. She receives instruction in painting from established artists, including the Dutch master Franz Hals, and becomes well-known for her *genre* scenes (scenes of everyday life). In 1636 she marries Jan Miense Molenaer, a fellow painter. The couple, who has at least one son, enjoy professional success in Amsterdam. After her death in 1660, the name of Judith Leyster is largely forgotten, although many of her works are misattributed to male painters such as Franz Hals. In the twentieth century, feminist art historians work to restore her reputation.

1 6 1 0 – 1 6 1 9

1610   St. Jeanne-Françoise de Chantal and St. Francis de Sales Found the Order of the Visitation of the Virgin Mary. St. Jeanne-Françoise (Jane Frances) de Chantal (1572–1641) founds, along with St. Francis de Sales (1567–1622), the Order of the Visitation of the Virgin Mary for single or widowed women who cannot be admitted into other religious orders because of their age, health, or financial situation (in those days, a "dowry" is required for admittance to most orders). In 1600, after eight years of marriage, Jeanne-Françoise Frémyot de Chantal herself is left a widow with four children. To survive, she moves in with her father-in-law, who treats her badly. In 1604, at the age of 32, she meets St. Francis de Sales, who becomes her spiritual director and friend. Together they develop a plan to begin their new religious order. The first convent in their Order of the Visitation of the Virgin Mary is founded in 1610 with Jeanne-Françoise in charge. The order receives criticism from the religious establishment for being too "easy" (since it is designed for those who cannot handle the severe life of the stricter orders), and many of the women admitted to the order are difficult to deal with, being ill or elderly or from the poor, uneducated classes. But Jeanne-Françoise copes decisively with all this and goes on to found over 80 other convents before her death in 1641. Her feast day is December 12.

1613   Russians Elect Anastasia Romanov's Great-Nephew Michael Czar. The marriage of Czar Ivan IV to Anastasia Romanov in 1547 establishes the foundation for the Romanov dynasty. Michael Romanov, the son of Anastasia Romanov's nephew, wins election as czar in 1613, beginning an era of imperial rule that lasts until 1917.

1614   Birth of Englishwoman Margaret Fell, "Mother of Quakerism." Margaret Askew Fell (1614–1702), who helps establish the Society of Friends, or Quakers, and becomes known as the "mother of Quakerism," is born in Lancashire, England. She becomes the wife of Thomas Fell, a prominent judge in Lancashire and an official in the Puritan government of Oliver Cromwell during the mid-seventeenth century. The couple has nine children. For a number of years beginning in 1651, they allow George Fox to use their home, Swarthmoor (Swarthmore), as the center for the Society of Friends, also known as the Quakers. This radical Protestant sect, organized by Fox, is based on the idea that humans are guided by their own "inner light" and do not need clerical guidance in the search for salvation. Quakers give women unusual freedom in religious life. Margaret Fell helps the development of the Quaker movement by preaching, fund-raising, and letter-writing. She continues such activities after her husband's death in 1658, suffering imprisonment for four years, from 1664 to 1668. An impassioned advocate of the right of women to preach, she publishes the tract *Women's Speaking Justified, Proved and Allowed of by the Scriptures*, in 1666. In 1669 she marries Fox, although he spends little time at Swarthmoor and travels widely on behalf of the Quaker cause until his death in 1691.

1616   Native American Pocahontas Sent to England. The Virginia Company realizes that Pocahontas (now called Rebecca after her conversion to Christianity) can be useful in promoting immigration and investment in the colony of Virginia. They encourage her to travel with her husband John Rolfe, and their one-year-old son to England as an example of the peaceful relations between the Native Americans and the colonists. In England, she visits the queen and other important dignitaries. Unfortunately, she contracts a fatal illness (reportedly smallpox) and dies in 1617. Relations between the Powhatans and the colonists deteriorate further after the deaths of both Pocahontas and her father.

c. 1618   Birth of Liu Rushi, Chinese Courtesan, Poet, and Editor. Liu Rushi (c.1618–1664), a poet and editor, is born in China. One of the most accomplished courtesans of her day, she understands that the best way for a woman in her position to achieve security and prominence is through liaisons with successful men. She courts the famous scholar Qian Qianyi and proposes to him that she become his concubine. The two of them live and work together until his death. At his death in 1664, she commits suicide.

1619   The London Company Begins to Recruit Women to Join the Jamestown Settlement. The London Company, a group of merchants who financed the settlement in Jamestown in search of treasure and agricultural lands, begins recruiting women to become wives of bachelor colonists. Their goal is to make the Jamestown colony a permanent and stable settlement.

Margaret Lucas Cavendish, Duchess of Newcastle.

1 6 2 0 – 1 6 2 9

DECEMBER 1621   European Women Settlers Arrive in Virginia. During August and September of 1621, 57 women settlers leave the Isle of Wight bound for the settlement at Jamestown, Virginia, and arrive by Christmas. The daughters of artisans, gentry, and tradesmen, these "young, handsome, and honestlie educated Maides" are sent to the colony by the Virginia Company in an effort to appease its unhappy settlers and to "tye and roote the Planters myndes to Virginia by the bonds of wives and children." In December, all 57 (remarkably) arrive safely aboard three ships, *The Marmaduke, Warwick,* and *Tiger.* A good number of them "were well married before the comming away of the Ships" the next spring. Life in the Virginia colony is hard and often short; those women who survive the Indian

attack of March 1622 most likely succumb in the starving winter of 1622–23.

c. 1623   English Author Margaret Cavendish Is Born. Writer Margaret Lucas Cavendish (c.1623–1673) is born into an aristocratic English family. She marries William Cavendish, the duke of Newcastle, at the age of 22. At the time of the Puritan rule between 1648 and 1660, the couple has to flee their home and live in exile on the European continent because of their royalist sympathies. With the restoration of the monarchy in 1660, they return to England. Margaret Cavendish pursues her literary career with great diligence, but her works are ignored. Indeed, her contemporaries call her "Mad Madge" on account of her eccentric behavior and dress. In all, the Duchess of Newcastle writes 14 volumes, including scientific treatises, poems, and plays.

In recent years, feminists have studied her neglected writings for the light they shed on the situation of seventeenth-century women in England. Of particular interest is her autobiography, *The True Relation of My Birth, Breeding and Life* (1656). Margaret Cavendish dies in 1674.

1 6 3 0 – 1 6 3 9

1631   Birth of Katherine Phillips, Founder of Influential London Literary Salon. Katherine Phillips (1631–1664), who writes poetry under the pseudonym "Orinda," is born. She is the founder of a London literary salon called the Society of Friendship, which includes such luminaries as Jeremy Taylor and Henry Vaughn.

1632–1653   Taj Mahal Built as Memorial to Mogol Emperor's Wife. The Taj Mahal is built by Shah Jahan, Mogol Emperor (1628–1657), in memory of his favorite wife Mumataz Mahal, who dies while giving birth to their fourteenth child. Constructed in Agra, India, the mausoleum is well-known for its characteristic crowning architecture, consisting of a large dome and four smaller octagonal kiosks. The pointed and slightly bulbous dome measures 58 feet in diameter and stands at a height of approximately 210 feet.

1632   Chinese Poet Ye Ziaolan Dies Very Young. Ye Ziaolan (1616–1632), whose poetry becomes famous in the south of China, dies at the age of 16. The daughter of an elite family, Ye Ziaolan's literary aspirations are encouraged by both of her parents. When she dies, she becomes a cult figure among south Chinese literary leaders who are as entranced by the pathos of her life as they are by the beauty of her poetry.

1633   French Woman Louise de Marillac Cofounds the Daughters of Charity. Louise

Mumataz Mahal is honored by her husband with this memorial, the Taj Mahal.

de Marillac (1591–1660) cofounds with Vincent de Paul the Daughters of Charity, a Catholic nursing order in France. This lay order, made up of women who dedicate themselves to visiting, feeding, and nursing the needy, pioneers in bringing women into religious service outside convent walls. Highly successful in attracting members not only in France but throughout the world, the Daughters of Charity is today the Catholic Church's largest congregation of women. Louise de Marillac is born into a powerful French family and marries Antoine Le Gras in 1613, by whom she has a son. After she is widowed in 1625, Louise turns to charitable works under the direction of the Roman Catholic priest Vincent de Paul. Dying in 1660, Louise de Marillac is named a saint in 1934.

C. MAY 1634   Frances Lady Berkeley, Wife to Two Colonial Governors of Virginia, Is Born. Frances Lady Berkeley (c.1634–1696) is born and baptized at Hollingbourne Church, Kent, England. She comes to Virginia with her parents about 1650. An influential figure in society and politics, Berkeley marries two men who serve as colonial governors. After her first husband, Samuel Stephens, dies, she marries Sir William Berkeley, Virginia's governor from 1641 to 1652 and 1660 to 1677. The Berkeley home at Green Spring, Virginia (four miles north of Jamestown), is a center of political influence and intrigue, and Lady Berkeley is a central figure in the powerful Green Spring faction. When Bacon's Rebellion flares in 1676, Frances Lady Berkeley goes to England to act as representative for her husband. A woman of action, she returns to the colony with 1,000 redcoats and orders to crush the rebels.

C. 1637   Puritan Leaders Persecute Anne Marbury Hutchinson for Preaching Antinomianism. The leaders of the Massachusetts Bay Colony expel Anne Marbury Hutchinson (1591–1643) for preaching heretical Antinomian (radical Puritan) views. Antinomians believe that God chooses them for salvation and no one can perform "good works" to gain salvation. Antinomians differ from Puritans in that God speaks directly to them, thus freeing them from having to obey church or civil laws. The colony's leaders see Anne as a threat to their community on three levels: political, theological, and social. First, the colony is a fragile settlement that continues to have problems with Native Americans. Naturally, the community leaders worry about internal divisions while they face external enemies. Second, Anne's Antinomian beliefs pose a serious threat to Puritanism. She condemns many Puritan ministers and she has the audacity to speak directly to God. Third, by holding meetings in her house, where she teaches men and women, she violates social norms. As a woman, Anne should not presume to teach men. Banished from the colony, Anne; her husband, William; and their 11 children settle on an island in Narragansett Bay. William dies in 1642, and Anne along with six children moves to a Dutch colony in an area that will later be called New York City. There, Native Americans kill Anne and all but one child during a raid in 1643.

1638   Sibylle Schwarz Writes Poetry. Sibylle Schwarz or Schwarzin writes poetry, inspiring some literary critics to hail her as the "Pomeranian Sappho." She is born into an aristocratic family in Pomerania (an area in present-day Germany and Poland) and receives a good education. After her premature death of dysentery at the age of 17 on July 31, 1638, her poems are published. Her writings deal with the feelings of turmoil caused by the Thirty Years War, which has driven her family from their estates.

1 6 4 0 – 1 6 4 9

1644–1912   The Manchus Rule China as the Ch'ing Dynasty. When leaders of the Ming dynasty, in control of China since 1368, ask Manchus from Manchuria for support in quelling internal rebellion, the Manchus invade China and take control of the country.

C. 1645   Deborah Moody, First Woman to Own Land in Colonial America. Deborah Moody (c.1580–c.1659) becomes the first woman to receive a land grant in colonial America when she is given title to land in Kings County (now Brooklyn), New York. She is also the first colonial woman to vote.

C. 1646   Birth of Glückel of Hameln, Jewish Merchant Who Writes Her Memoirs. Glückel of Hameln, who records her life as a Jewish merchant in Germany in her memoirs, is born in the year 5407 of the Jewish calendar in Hamburg into a Jewish merchant family.

Betrothed at 12 and married at 14 to Chayim Hameln, she remains happily married until her husband's death in 1689. She is forced to take over the family business, pay off her husband's debts, and raise the eight of their 12 children who are not yet married. Since she already is an advisor for her husband's business in gold and gems, she adapts quickly and through hard work manages to do well. Her memoirs, published as *The Memoirs of Glückel of Hameln*, vividly describe the events of her life, family, and community up to 1719. Glückel dies on September 19, 1724.

c. 1648   First Plea for Women's Suffrage in America by Margaret Brent. Margaret Brent (c.1601–1658), a lawyer and landowner in the colony of Maryland, requests the vote for herself. A capable businesswoman who serves as Lord Baltimore's attorney in the colony of Maryland, Brent manages her own sizable estate as well as her sister Mary's, and for a time, manages her brother, Giles's, affairs. Governor Leonard Calvert names Brent his executrix, responsible for settling his complicated estate after his death. Because of her frequent appearance in the Maryland Assembly (legislating body) and her powerful position in the community, clerks often mention her as, "Margaret Brent, Gentleman." As the proprietor's attorney, executrix to the late governor, and one of the largest landowners, Brent believes, in January of 1648, she deserves, "a vote in the howse for herselfe and voyce allso." The assembly denies her request. In 1658, Brent dies at her plantation in Virginia, owning thousands of acres in both Virginia and Maryland.

1649   *Keian no ofuregaki* (Instructions of the Keian Era) Promulgated in Japan. The Tokugawa shogunate (1603–1867) issues the *Keian no Ofuregaki* (Instructions of the Keian Era), a set of detailed instructions on how people of the peasant class should conduct their daily lives. Rural women help farm, prepare clothing and food, spin thread, weave cloth, and sew clothes. They also engage in

silkworm raising. The ordinance directs peasants on issues of morality. For women, this means the Confucian admonition to obedience and chastity.

1650 – 1659

c. 1650   Early American Poet Anne Dudley Bradstreet Publishes First Collection. Anne Dudley Bradstreet (c.1612–1672), the best known early American poet, publishes her first collection of poems, *The Tenth Muse Lately Sprung Up in America.* Anne marries Simon Bradstreet in 1628, and together they immigrate with John Winthrop's Puritans to the Massachusetts Bay Colony in 1630. While raising eight children, she writes poetry. John Woodbridge, Anne's brother-in-law, writes the preface to assure the reader that a woman wrote the poems and she did not neglect her family while she busied herself with her writing. He writes, "it is the work of a woman, honored, and esteemed where she lives, for her gracious demeanor, her eminent parts, her pious conversation, her courteous disposition, her exact diligence in her place, and discreet managing of her family occasions, and more than so, these poems are the fruit but of some few hours." Another edition of her poetry, *Several Poems Compiled with Great Variety of Wit and Learning*, issued posthumously in 1678 and reprinted in 1758, includes some of her finest work.

1654   Queen Christina of Sweden Abdicates Her Throne. Christina (1626–1689), who is crowned queen of Sweden in 1644 during an era when tensions between Protestant Sweden and the pro-Catholic Holy Roman Empire of Europe are very high, abdicates her throne. In 1630, Sweden enters the Thirty Years' War against the forces of the Holy Roman Empire. Economic malaise, widespread hunger, high taxes, and revolutions across Europe make the task of ruling as the Swedish monarch very difficult. Furthermore, Christina is not inter-

Queen Christina

ested in confronting these problems. In 1651, Christina announces her intention to abdicate, but public response delays her actual abdication until 1654. After 1654, she goes into self-imposed exile and converts to Catholicism. The true motivation for her religious conversion is the subject of much debate. In Rome, Christina socializes with scholars, cardinals, and nobles. Some historians believe Christina wants to use her Roman contacts as a way of positioning herself to become a candidate for another monarchy, possibly as queen of Naples.

c. 1655   Verlinda Stone Apprises Lord Baltimore of Puritan Threat. Verlinda (Virlinda) Graves Stone (c.1615–1675) informs Lord Baltimore about the Puritan threat to peaceful coexistence and religious toleration in Maryland. In 1648 Verlinda and her husband,

Captain William Stone, and their seven children emigrate to Maryland from Virginia when Lord Baltimore appoints William governor. The Puritans, who are invited into the colony by Governor Stone, form their own council (thus creating a rival government in the colony) in 1652. Governor Stone mounts an attack in 1655 to dissolve the council, but he miscalculates the Puritans' forces. Stone is wounded and taken prisoner. Verlinda writes to Lord Baltimore to apprise him of the desperate situation. Peace and religious toleration are restored in 1657. William Stone dies in 1660, and Verlinda continues to manage the large estate she inherits from him. When she dies in July of 1675, Verlinda has a will leaving slaves, silver items, land, and pigs to her children, an unusual act for a woman at that time.

c. 1656   Birth of Luisa Roldán, Court Sculptor for Spanish Kings. Luisa Roldán (c.1656–1704), who is named court sculptor for the Spanish kings Charles II and Philip V, is born in Seville, Spain. Her father is the sculptor Pedro Roldán, who maintains a family workshop in which Luisa, a sister, and two brothers are trained in sculpture. Later her husband and son also join the group, but it is Luisa who obtains royal commissions. She creates magnificent pieces in polychromed wood and terra cotta.

c. 1656   Kateri Tekakwitha, First Native American Beatified by the Roman Catholic Church, Is Born. Mohawk Indian Kateri Tekakwitha (c.1656–1680), called the "Lily of the Mohawks," is born. She is the daughter of a prominent Mohawk chieftain. Her mother, a Christian, is a captive Algonquin slave who is officially "adopted" into the Mohawk tribe upon her marriage to the chief. In 1660, when Tekakwitha is four years old, a smallpox epidemic kills both her parents and leaves her half-blind and scarred. She is taken in by her father's brother, the new chief, and his childless wife. As a young adult, she refuses marriage (a very unusual stance in Mohawk society) and is baptized as a Christian on Easter Sunday, 1676. She takes the Christian name Kateri, or Katherine, upon her baptism. Because of her refusal to marry and her conversion to Christianity, she is harassed by the other members of the tribe and eventually forced to flee to Sault Mission in Canada. There she becomes a severe mystic, engaging in extreme penances which eventually lead to her early death at the age of 24. She appeals to the Church to let her establish a Native American convent near Sault Mission, but the white male hierarchy simply laughs at the idea. Known as "the Saint" at Sault Mission while still alive, she is named the "Protectoress of Canada" among Christians in that country soon after her death. So many posthumous miraculous healings are attributed to her that she comes to be called the "Thaumaturge" or "Healer of the New World." She is declared venerable by the Roman Catholic church in 1942, then blessed in June of 1980. The movement for canonization continues.

JUNE 19, 1656 New England Authorities Execute Anne Hibbins as a Witch. Governor John Endicott sentences Anne Hibbins (?–1656) "to hang till she was dead" for witchcraft, and the sentence is carried out on this date. New England executes approximately ten individuals as witches before her, but Anne's wealth makes this case peculiar. The previous cases involve social outcasts (much like Anne), but they are poor. Anne's husband leaves her a sizable estate when he dies in 1654. Anne Hibbins and her husband, William, immigrate to the Massachusetts Bay Colony in the early 1630s. William becomes a fine upstanding citizen and serves as magistrate, member of the Court of Assistants, saintly church member, and merchant. While William conforms to social norms, Anne refuses to do so. She fights openly with men, thus angering many people in the community. The Boston Puritan church excommunicates Anne Hibbins in 1640.

Because of her husband's standing in the colony, people tolerate Anne. When William dies in 1654, he leaves Anne unprotected against the enemies she has made.

C. 1658 Marguerite Bourgeoys Advances Religious and Educational Innovations in New France. Beginning in 1658 in the colony of New France (now Quebec), Marguerite Bourgeoys chaperones girls sent from France as brides for colonists, recruits French and Canadian girls as teachers, and organizes a boarding school in Montreal as well as a school for Native girls. Bourgeoys is born in Troyes, France. In 1640, she joins a non-cloistered congregation of teachers attached to a Troyes convent directed by Mother Louise de Chomedy de Sainte Marie, the sister of Governor Maisonneuve of Ville-Marie (Montreal, Quebec, Canada). Maisonneuve refuses to introduce a religious community to Montreal, but agrees to bring Bourgeoys in 1653, if she will devote herself to educating children. Many of her first years in New France are dedicated to resolving health issues in the colony. With her subsequent advancement of educational and religious innovations, she becomes one of the most important figures in colonial life in New France. She spends the last two years of her life in meditation and prayer. Despite the fact that she is revered as a saint when she dies in 1700, she is not canonized until 1982.

1660 Royal Society in England Is Founded. Scientists who meet weekly from November to June form the Royal Society in London. The goal of the organization is to provide a forum of discussion of scientific subjects. Over 250 years later, in 1945, Kathleen Yardley Lonsdale (1903–1971), a British scientist, becomes the first female Fellow of the Royal Society.

1 6 6 0 – 1 6 6 9

C. JUNE 1, 1660 Mary Barrett Dyer Executed for Her Quaker Beliefs. Mary Barrett Dyer (c.1610–1660) is executed in Boston for her Quaker beliefs. She marries William Dyer (or Dyre), a Puritan, in London in 1633. The following year, the couple immigrates to the Massachusetts Bay Colony. Mary Barrett Dyer follows the teachings of Anne Hutchinson, who is banished from the colony in 1637; the colony expels Mary Dyer soon after. Mary and William move to Newport, Rhode Island, where they have five sons: Samuel, William, Mahershallalhashbaz, Henry, and Charles. Mary returns to England, where she is persuaded by the teachings of George Fox, the founder of the Society of Friends (Quakers). When she returns to New England in 1657, authorities arrest her under a new law forbidding Quakerism, but release her when her husband (still a Puritan) promises to take her out of the colony. Mary, along with two other Quakers—William Robinson and Marmaduke Stephenson—returns to Boston to challenge the outlawing of Quaker teachings. The court eventually sentences all three to death by hanging.

1662 Catharina Regina von Greiffenberg Becomes a Religious Writer. Austrian-born German Catharina Regina von Greiffenberg (1633–1694) becomes a religious writer, publishing *Geistlichen Sonette, Lieder und Gedichte (Spiritual Sonnets, Songs and Poems)*, which establishes her fame. Catharina is born into the family of the barons of Seyssenegg in Lower Austria. In 1663 both the fear of Turkish invasions and persecution because of the Protestant beliefs of her family force her to flee Austria for Nuremberg, Germany. While there, her uncle proposes marriage to her. After some hesitation because of her asceticism, and some difficulty in gaining church permission, she consents in 1664. They return to Austria to live until her husband's death in 1679, whereafter she settles in Nuremberg until her own death on April 8, 1694.

1664 Margaret Fell Imprisoned for Preaching Quakerism. Margaret Fell (1614–1702), at age 50, is sentenced to four years in prison for preaching Quakerism. Fell helps the development of the Quaker movement by preaching, fund-raising, and letter-writing. Margaret Fell is often called "the mother of Quakerism."

C. 1665 Marie-Catherine Desjardins Recognized as Important French Literary Figure. With the performance of her play *The Favorite Minister*, Marie-Catherine Desjardins (1640–1683) is recognized as an important French novelist and playwright. Desjardins is born into a poor family in the lower ranks of the French nobility. Paris is her home from 1655, where she supports herself as an author, gaining recognition as a novelist, poet, and playwright. Writing 20 popular novels, Desjardins excels in presenting her characters with psychological depth. The best known of her three plays is *The Favorite Minister* (1665), performed at the command of Louis XIV before his court at Versailles. Desjardins sometimes writes under the pseudonym Madame de Villedieu. After a tragic love affair, in 1677 she marries Claude-Nicolas de Chaste, with whom she has a son.

1666 Quaker Preacher Margaret Fell Publishes Tract Advocating Women's Right to Speak in Public. An impassioned advocate of the right of women to preach, Margaret Fell (1614–1702), the "mother of Quakerism," publishes the tract *Women's Speaking Justified, Proved and Allowed of by the Scriptures*. At this time, she is imprisoned for her Quaker beliefs for four years (from 1664 to 1668).

1 6 7 0 – 1 6 7 9

C. 1670 Aphra Behn Becomes First Professional Woman Writer in England. After her husband dies, Aphra Behn (1640–1689) becomes the first professional woman writer in England. During her youth, she spends several years in Surinam (Guiana). In 1664, she marries a Mr. Behn, a Dutch merchant in London, but is widowed apparently in the following year. For a short time, Behn serves as a paid spy for the English government. As this occupation is insufficient for her support, she turns to writing as a profession. Her plays, numbering at least 14, are successful in the 1670s, but are also notorious, because they are largely licentious bedroom farces, so popular during the Restoration period. In 1682 Behn is forced to quit her career as playwright. She also writes witty poems and prose fiction. Her best-known novel is *Oroonoka* (1688), based on her experiences in Surinam. She dies in poverty in 1689 but gains enough respect to be buried in Westminster Abbey.

c. 1670 Native Women Enable Expansion of Fur Trade in Canada. From the earliest beginnings of the European fur trade in Canada, Native women are crucial to its functioning. European male fur traders find that they cannot survive in the Canadian bush without female companions who provide the food, make the clothing, and dress the furs for trade. Through marriage to aboriginal women, European fur traders also gain alliances with important trading families, thus enabling the exploitation of existing trade networks among the First Nations. Though the practice of intermarriage between First and Second Nations inhabitants wanes significantly in the nineteenth century, non-Native fur traders in Northern British Columbia continue the practice into the 1920s. In areas of the country where the fur trade and its associated families found colonies (such as at Red River and Victoria, B.C.), these Native women are central to the colonial elite. Christian missionaries and non-Native middle-class women challenge the social positions of these First Nations women. Lady Amelia Conolly Douglas, the Cree-Irish wife of Victoria's Governor James Douglas, is one such woman. Married to Douglas when he is a fur trader, she works with him at out-

posts such as Fort St. James in British Columbia's central interior. As he rises through the ranks of the company and eventually becomes governor of the colony of British Columbia, she rises in rank with him. Despite her position within the colony, the pressure of Anglican missionaries forces the Douglases to remarry in the Christian tradition and, to a certain extent, forces Amelia to fade from public life.

1670 Actress Marie Champmeslé Debuts Famous Role. Marie Desmares Champmeslé (1642–1698) plays the title role of Bérénice in Racine's famous play written for her. One of the most well-known French actresses of the seventeenth century, Champmeslé is the first actress to perform the role.

1671 St. Rose of Lima Is Named First Catholic Saint in the Americas. Isabel de Flores y del Oliva (1586–1617), known as Rose, is the first person in the Americas to be canonized (declared a saint) by the Roman Catholic Church. Rose is born to poor Spanish parents in Lima, Peru, in 1586. She works hard to help support her family, growing flowers and doing needlework. She refuses to marry and at age 20 becomes a Dominican tertiary (a person who lives in the world but is closely associated with an order of monks). Living in a summerhouse in her parents' garden, she spends long hours praying and inflicting severe penances on herself. The self-inflicted cruelty of her life raises questions of the true health and holiness of her spiritual mission, but she does achieve great successes in the realm of social services. Besides praying and suffering penances, Rose also gives a great deal of her energy to caring for the sick, poor, Indians, and slaves, and she is considered to be the founder of social service in Peru. Her feast day is celebrated on August 23.

c. 1673 French Thinker Francois Poulain de la Barre Publishes Book on Intellectual Equality. Francois Poulain de la Barre pub-

FEMALE LAWYERS, DOCTORS, LANDOWNERS, AND BUSINESSWOMEN WORKED IN EACH OF THE AMERICAN COLONIES

C. 1680 Colonial court records reveal many women buying or selling land, and suing or being sued for debts, during the seventeenth and eighteenth centuries. English law gave a married woman's husband the right to control her property; therefore, more single or widowed women are found acting on their own behalf. Elizabeth Haddon led a group of people who settled in New Jersey in 1680. Physician Mary Venderdonck of Maryland had to sue former Governor Fendall in 1661, after he hired her to attend three servants and then refused to pay. And Margaret Brent, whose name appears in the Maryland court records 124 times between 1642 and 1650, was the consummate colonial female lawyer and landholder. Yet, some married women represented their absent husbands, managed the family business alongside their husbands, and operated their own businesses. Sarah Bland's husband, John, was a prosperous London merchant who owned a good deal of property in Virginia. With her husband's permission, Sarah sailed for Virginia in 1678 to manage the estate. In Delaware, Anna Joung—acting as her husband's attorney in 1680—successfully sued John Taylor for slander (Taylor told others that Jacob Joung had hired Indians to kill Christians). Hannah Penn—proprietor William Penn's wife—acted as her husband's attorney and handled all of his finances as well as the governance of the province after his stroke in 1712 until 1718. Colonial women—married, single, or widowed—were tavern and ferry operators, merchants, doctors, nurses, midwives, farmers, landowners, and lawyers.

lishes *The Equality of the Sexes*, in which the French philosopher declares that "the mind has no sex." He is among the first thinkers to support the idea that women have intellectual powers equal to those of men. His work stimulates the betterment of women's education in succeeding centuries.

1676 **Puritan Mary Rowlandson Writes Popular Indian Captive Narrative.** After being captured by Wampanoag Indians and then freed, Puritan settler Mary White Rowlandson (1636–1678) writes what becomes a famous account of her captivity. A settler in Massachusetts Bay Colony, Rowlandson is captured during "King Philip's War" when King Philip (Metacomet) attacks the colonists. Rowlandson is held captive for 11 weeks and released after her husband pays a ransom.

MAY 29, 1677 **Treaty of Middle Plantation Is Endorsed.** Cockacoeske (?–1686), queen of the Pamunkey Indians, endorses the Treaty of Middle Plantation, ushering in peaceful relations between the colonists and the Indians of Virginia's coastal plain. A leader of considerable influence and acumen, she works within the context of Virginia's colonial government to recapture the Pamunkey's former political power during her 30-year reign. In the Treaty of Middle Plantation, all subscribing tribes pledge their allegiance to Cockacoeske as well as to the English king, Charles II (who presents her with a silver badge and a scarlet robe, possibly as a reward for her loyalty during Bacon's Rebellion). When the Pamunkey queen dies in 1686, she is succeeded by her niece, Ann.

1678 **French Author Madame de Lafayette Writes Classic Novel *La Princesse de Clèves*.** Marie-Madelaine Pioche de la Vergne de Lafayette (1634–1693) publishes her masterpiece, *La Princesse de Clèves*. This work is noted for its psychological insight in presenting a heroine struggling between her own desires and her duty. Although the background of the novel is an earlier era, it reflects the manners and morals of the French court in the author's own day. A member of the French aristocracy, she is baptized on March 18, 1634. In 1655, she marries the Count de Lafayette, by whom she has two sons. While her husband remains on his country estate, Madame de Lafayette lives independently in Paris from 1659 on. There she opens a famous literary salon and writes several novels. After the death of her longtime friend, the Duc de la Rochefoucauld, Madame de Lafayette spends the last decade of her life withdrawn from society.

1678   **Italian Elena Cornaro, First Woman to Earn Doctorate in Philosophy.** Elena Cornaro (1646–1684), the daughter of a powerful Venetian family, is awarded a doctorate in philosophy by the University of Padua when she is 32 years old—the first woman to achieve this distinction. Cornaro carries out her studies in private and never attends the university. Refusing a wealthy marriage, she lives in association with a Benedictine convent as an adult. The degree does not allow her to teach at the university.

---

1 6 8 0 – 1 6 8 9

1682   **Birth of Madame de Tencin, Mother of French Mathematician and Philosopher Jean d'Alembert.** Madame de Tencin (1682–1749) is born Claudine Alexandrine Guérin in Grenoble. She marries the Marquis de Tencin and moves to Paris. She gives birth to the future philosopher and mathematician, Jean d'Alembert, whose father is reputed to be the poet Destouches. Madame de Tencin hosts one of the first prominent salons that helps to spread the ideas of the Enlightenment. She dies in Paris in 1749, having helped found the salon movement.

Lady Mary Wortley Montagu poses for a portrait wearing a Turkish costume.

C. MAY 26, 1689   **Mary Wortley Montagu, Literary Correspondent, Is Born.** Mary Pierrepont Wortley Montagu (1689–1762), who establishes a literary reputation in England through her letters, is born. The daughter of an English aristocrat, she is 23 years of age when she elopes with Edward Wortley Montagu against her father's wishes. From 1716 to 1718, the couple lives in Constantinople (now Istanbul, Turkey), where Edward serves as English ambassador. While there, Mary learns about smallpox inoculation. Upon returning to England, she popularizes the technique despite heated opposition from the medical profession. For the next two decades, Mary is active in English literary circles. In 1739 she moves to Italy, living apart from her husband, but returns to England the year before her death in 1762. Her literary reputation rests on her entertaining and finely crafted letters, which are addressed chiefly to her sister, husband and daughter throughout her adult life. In them, she records much about contemporary events and customs, particularly about the daily lives of women. Her vast correspondence, totalling 900 letters, is published after her death.

1 6 9 0 – 1 6 9 9

1692   Identity of Mother Goose is a mystery. *Who is the real Mother Goose?* Some theorize that she was Elizabeth Foster (1665– ?), married to Isaac Vergoose in Boston. The Vergooses had 16 children, and Mrs. Vergoose told stories to them. According to the legend, *Mother Goose's Melodies* were published in 1719 by a son-in-law who was a printer. However, no copies remain in existence.

A French legend asserts that the mother of Charlemagne, "Goose-footed Bertha," was Mother Goose. The first printed use of the name was probably in 1697, by publisher Charles Perrault. He produced "Contes de Ma Mère L'Oye"—"Tales of My Mother Goose."

The rhymes known today as Mother Goose were first published by John Newbery in the late 1700s in London, England.

1692   Luisa Roldán, First Female Spanish Sculptor to Work at Madrid Court. Luisa Roldán (1656–1704), the daughter and wife of sculptors, is the first female Spanish sculptor to work at the court in Madrid, Spain, when she is appointed to serve under King Charles II. She continues her work under King Philip V. Though never adequately compensated, she is known for her professionalism and is remembered particularly for her sensitive sculpture of St. Catherine.

FEBRUARY 1692   Witch Hunt in New England Begins With Accusations. The witch hysteria in New England begins when teenag-

ers accuse Tituba, Sarah Good, and Sarah Osborne of witchcraft. The Paris family, headed by a prominent minister, owns Tituba, a Carib Indian slave. The court does not sentence Tituba to death because she confesses to many crimes of witchcraft and implicates others. Sarah Solart Poole Good is born into a prominent family but suffers severe financial setbacks, and by 1692, she and her second husband are nearly destitute. From the start, Good staunchly denies the witchcraft allegations and tries to place the guilt on Osborne. Her husband suspects she may be a witch and vocalizes his concerns. Authorities arrest Sarah Good's four-year-old daughter, Dorcas, but release her after approximately eight months. Sarah Good is not so lucky. The court sentences her to death; she is 38 years old. Sixty-year-old Sarah Osborne denies being a witch also. She enjoys a much higher social standing than does Good or Tituba, but it does not help her situation. She dies in prison awaiting trial.

c. 1694   Mary Astell Calls for Improved Education for Women in Her Treatise. Between 1694 and 1697, Mary Astell (1666–1731) publishes the treatise *A Serious Proposal to the Ladies* in two volumes. In it, Astell calls for the establishment of private institutions where single women live together for a time and receive quality education. Born into a middle-class English family, Astell never marries and is associated with female intellectual circles in London, England. Believing that women are denied opportunities to develop their minds, she wishes to combat the stereotype that they are vain and frivolous creatures. Although her proposal attracts much interest among her contemporaries, it is not realized before her death in 1731. It does, however, anticipate the coming of women's colleges in the late nineteenth century to a certain extent.

1696   Death of Madame de Sévigné, Famous for Correspondence. Marie de Rabutin-Chantal de Sévigné (1626–1696), who writes 1,700

Eudoxia Feodorowna prepares to wed Peter the Great.

famous letters to her married daughter between 1669 and 1676, dies. In the letters, she reports in a witty and conversational tone the events and gossip surrounding the court of Louis XIV in France. This correspondence, published after her death, is said to raise the genre of letter writing to the level of a fine art. The daughter of a French baron, she is orphaned at the age of six and raised by her uncle, who provides her with a superior education. In 1644 she marries Marquis Henri de Sévigné. Widowed in 1651, Madame de Sévigné thereafter devotes herself to her two children and literary interests in Paris.

1697   Marie du Deffand, Hostess of Influential Salon in Paris, Is Born. Marie du Deffand (1697–1780) is born to noble parents in the Château de Chamrond in Burgundy. She is a religious skeptic who enjoys a life of pleasure

and sexual fulfillment. A good friend of Voltaire, du Deffand also exercises her considerable intelligence in intellectual pursuits. She establishes a salon in Paris where women and men are treated equally, unlike most salons where men do all the talking. She takes Julie de Lespinasse as her protégé, but the two quarrel and du Deffand ends her days alone in Paris in 1780.

c. 1698   Mademoiselle Maupin, French Opera Singer, Captivates Audiences. Mademoiselle Maupin (first name unknown) (1670–1707), a French soprano, captivates Paris opera goers with her performances. The daughter of a secretary to the Count of Armagnac in France, she rises to fame as an opera singer in Paris, reaching her peak as a soprano between 1698 and 1705. Although she never has musical training, she compensates for this lack with her physical beauty and natural talent. She is known for her tempestuous behavior, including fighting duels with men, and her many lovers, both male and female. She leaves her husband, whom she marries young, but returns to him before her death in 1707. Théophile Gautier bases his novel *Mademoiselle Maupin, double amour*, on her colorful life.

1698   Peter the Great Abolishes Custom of Isolating Aristocratic Russian Women at Home. Russian Tsar Peter the Great insists that female members of the royal family attend a diplomatic reception, a break with the customary isolation of aristocratic Russian women in the home. For centuries, such women live in the women's section of the house, known as the *terem*, and socialize only with relatives. Although his marriage in 1689 to Eudoxia Feodorowna was unhappy, Peter's modern views on women had a powerful influence on Russian society. Under his rule, the *terem* was gradually eliminated and Russian women enjoyed greater social freedom.

1699   Birth of Marie-Thérèse Rodet, Who Reigns Over Important Salon. Marie-Thérèse Rodet (1699–1777) is born in Paris, France. Orphaned as a child, her godmother marries her to a rich old businessman, Pierre Francois Geoffrin, who does not love her. Now Madame de Geoffrin, she begins to frequent the salon of Madame de Tencin, and when de Tencin dies in 1749, Madame de Geoffrin moves the whole salon to her own house. Her husband objects to the expense, but she overrules him, and he grudgingly pays for the lavish dinners. Once a guest asks her, "Who was that old man at the end of the table who never said anything?" She replies, "That was my husband. He's dead." After her husband really dies, her salon becomes the most important intellectual meeting place in Paris. She begins financing the works of many great thinkers, and her money saves the *Encyclopedia* from ruin after it is banned by royal authorities. She also collects paintings, thus subsidizing the work of many artists. She dies in Paris in 1777.

Chapter 8
1700 TO 1799

1700 - 1709

c. 1700 Limited Opportunities for European Women in Public Sporting Events. Between 1700 and 1800 in Europe, women participate in races, golf, archery, and cricket. By the end of the eighteenth century, local clubs are established so women can challenge each other.

In terms of public entertainment, there are very few women who fence, wrestle, box, or ride in races. These events are geared more to the pleasure of the spectator rather than to acceptance of women athletes.

c. 1700 Confucian Manual for Women's Behavior Published. *Onna Daigaku* (*The Great Learning for Women*), a Confucian manual for ethics and the proper behavior of women, is published. Although its authorship is uncertain, the manual is usually attributed to Kaibara Ekiken (1630–1714). It is also speculated that the manual is adapted from a work by his wife, Kaibara Token (1652–1713), who is herself a scholar. The text is a popular manual for the education of young women, particularly as they are prepared for marriage. A specific code of behavior is prescribed for women. A woman is expected to be obedient and respectful at all times: to her parents as a daughter, to her husband and his family after marriage, and to her sons as a widow. Her place is at home; she is supposed to be diligent in her household labors. A woman can be summarily divorced for disobedience, jealousy, ill health, failure to produce a child, or even personal habits that are found offensive. The text defines the position of women and their role within the narrow confines of the Japanese family system and marriage practices.

1700 Ballet Technique Becomes Less Restrictive, and Costumes Become Freer. Before 1700, female ballet dancers wore long, heavy skirts and tight corsets. Ballet slippers had heels. Because of these restrictive costumes, women were limited in their ability to leap, twirl, or perform other rapid or lively steps— these were reserved for the freer male dancers. In the 1700s, this gradually changes. Ballerinas shorten their skirts and begin to wear ballet slippers without heels. With the rise of Romanticism in the 1800s, many ballet stories include delicate, lightweight characters. Ballerinas begin to dance on their toes in these roles, and the fluffy tutu is introduced.

1700 Merchants in Southern China Educate Their Daughters. In the rich regions of South China in the eighteenth century, merchants often educate their daughters to make them more desirable as brides. Education includes needlework, often embroidery rather than the more utilitarian spinning and weaving that is the work of a less affluent woman. But a family who is ambitious in its plans for the marriage of their daughter also teaches her

CONDITIONS FOR WOMEN IN AMERICA'S COLONIAL SOUTH—PRIVILEGED PLANTATION MISTRESSES AND AFRICAN AMERICAN SLAVES.

c. 1700 In the colonial South, the lifestyle of women depended mainly on their class and race. Classes ranged from plantation mistress, the middling class (small farmers, servants, and laborers), and free African Americans to indentured servants and slaves.

On plantations, the mistress oversaw the household work (in a large house she could be responsible for 20 servants). Mistresses also cared for sick slaves and attended to house guests. Middling class women were responsible for their households and tended gardens and dairies. In the South, one-fourth of indentured servants were women. They worked six days a week, 14-hour days. If they got pregnant, their owner could legally add from nine months to two years extra time onto their contracts.

African-American slave women performed key economic and social roles, often under circumstances even more difficult than indentured servants. Besides laboring in the fields, caring for their families, and being culturally significant in the slave community, slave women also specialized in essential jobs, such as tanning hides, weaving, and sewing. This was key to the economic success of many plantations.

some reading and writing. When a young man's family selects a bride, they are interested in a young woman who will make a good mother. Because early childhood education is the responsibility of the mother, some literacy is desirable in a bride from the upper classes.

c. 1701 Elizabeth Haddon Estaugh Founds New Jersey Plantation. Elizabeth Haddon (later Estaugh) (1680–1762) founds Haddonfield, New Jersey, a 500-acre plantation. At 21 years old, Haddon is one of the youngest female landowners in the New World. In 1702, she marries the Quaker minister John Estaugh. Together they develop their land, and after his death in 1724, she continues to manage the estate on her own.

MARCH 8, 1702 Anne Becomes Queen of England. Queen Anne (1665–1714) rules England from 1702 to 1714 after the deaths of her older sister Mary II and her brother-in-law William III. The daughter of King James II of England, Anne is a staunch Protestant despite her father's pro-Catholic leanings. She marries George, prince of Denmark, in 1683.

Of their many children, only one son survives infancy, but dies at the age of ten. Queen Anne is totally dependent upon her ministers because of her chronic illnesses and her limited capabilities.

1703 Birth of Kaga no Chiyo, Haiku Poet. Kaga no Chiyo (1703–1775), a famed haiku poet in Japan, is born. *Chiyo Ni kushu* and *Matsu no koe* are collections of her poems.

c. 1704 New England Woman Details Trip in Journal. Sarah Kemble Knight (1666–1727), a Puritan author, records her arduous journey from Boston to New York to settle the estate of her cousin. The journal, published long after her death, reveals an independent, resourceful, brave, and shrewd woman.

1704 Aurora von Königsmarck Named Provost of Quedlinburg Abbey. Maria Aurora von Königsmarck (1662–1728) of the Swedish nobility, who rises through the ranks of courtiers in the German courts through her gift for languages, musical talent, cultivated manners, and cultured beauty, becomes provost of the abbey at Quedlinburg, a post she holds from

1704 to 1718. Her success seems assured when she becomes the mistress of Frederick August "the Strong," Electoral Prince of Saxony (reigns 1694–1733) and the king of Poland from 1697. August is renowned both for his physical strength and his reputed 350 illegitimate children from many extramarital affairs. Befriending August's wife, von Königsmarck briefly forms the center of cultural life in Dresden. Von Königsmarck's son by August, Marshal Maurice of Saxony (1696–1750), later becomes famous as a commander in the French army. Rather than be married off to some petty noble, the usual fate of current and former mistresses, she seeks instead to become Abbess of Quedlinburg, which she enters in 1698. August's need of cash, however, leads him to sell the abbey to neighboring Brandenburg-Prussia. When the new owners and the resident nuns cannot agree on her election as abbess, von Königsmarck has to settle for the title of provost, which she holds from 1704 to 1718. Despite her new obligations in Quedlinburg, she travels and leads a rather secular life until her last few years, when she retires to the abbey. She dies there on February 16, 1728, leaving too little to pay the costs of her funeral.

1706　Birth of Gabrielle-Emilie du Châtelet, Lover and Financial Supporter of Voltaire. Gabrielle-Emilie Le Tonnelier de Breteuil, later Gabrielle-Emilie du Châtelet (1706–1749), is born to noble parents in Paris. She marries in 1725 at age 19, but is far more interested in study and philosophy than in marriage. A feminist before the word is invented, she writes, "If I were king, I would give to women all the rights of humanity, especially those of the intellect." She is a great admirer of Voltaire, and after the two meet in 1733 they become lovers. Madame du Châtelet provides Voltaire with financial support and a place to stay at her chateau at Cirey, and the two become inseparable friends for 15 years, traveling together and debating philosophy.

During this time Madame du Châtelet translates Newton's *Principia* from Latin, the first and still the best translation into French. However much Voltaire respects her intellect, though, he grows tired of the love affair and in 1748 tells her that he "no longer regarded her as a woman." She sickens and dies the following year at age 43.

c. JULY 10, 1706　Virginia Witchcraft Trial Takes Place in Lynnhaven River. In Princess Anne County, Virginia, accused witch Grace Sherwood is tried for witchcraft by being bound and thrown into the western branch of the Lynnhaven River to see whether she will sink or float. Sherwood floats, indicating her guilt. She also receives an unfavorable report from a panel of matrons charged with detecting physical evidence of her suspected relations with the devil. Despite these marks against her claim of innocence, Sherwood survives the ordeal without further punishment. She dies of natural causes in 1740. In present-day Virginia Beach, the spot where her trial took place is still called Witch Duck Point.

1707　Birth of Marie Sallé, French Choreographer. Marie Sallé (1707–1756), the first female choreographer in France, is born. Also a costume designer, she performs in both her native France and in England, where she is criticized for appearing in simple Greek drapery as a boy in Handel's *Alcina* and for having a female lover.

1708　Rachel Ruysch, First Female Court Painter in Düsseldorf. Dutch artist Rachel Ruysch (1664–1750) is invited to serve as court painter in Düsseldorf, Germany, becoming the first woman to hold this appointment. She remains in Düsseldorf in this capacity until 1716. Ruysch is remembered for her detailed flower paintings. She enjoys such a wide reputation in her own time that she is able to give paintings as dowries for her daughters.

1710 - 1719

C. 1713 Anne Finch Writes Poetry on Condition of Aristocratic Women in England. Anne Kingsmill Finch (1661–1720) writes many poems on themes often dealing with the beauty of rural life and also the injustice suffered by women of her class. Only one volume of her work is published during her lifetime, in 1713. Born into an aristocratic family in England, she marries Heneage Finch at the age of 23. After William of Orange is named king of England during the Glorious Revolution of 1688, the couple remains loyal to the exiled James II and suffers economic hardships as a result. Eventually, Heneage inherits the title of earl of Winchilsea and an estate at Eastwell. Anne, now the Countess of Winchilsea, becomes the center of a literary circle at Eastwell. She dies in 1720.

1714 Birth of Chinese Peasant Poet He Shuangqing. He Shuangqing (1714–?), an eighteenth century peasant poet in China, is born. She is greatly admired by a circle of male literary leaders, who collect and publish her poetry. Her admirers value the directness and the simplicity of her work. She is reported to learn her literary skills by listening to a maternal uncle, who is a village teacher.

MAY 17, 1718 Birth of Maria Agnesi, Italian Mathematician. Maria Agnesi (1718–1799), the first important woman mathematician in Europe, is born. She moves with her family to Bologna, Italy, where her father accepts a position as professor of mathematics at the university there. A precocious child, she already delivers theses on philosophical questions before the learned men of Bologna when she is 14. From age 20 on, she lives in seclusion in her father's house, devoting herself to the study of mathematics, principally conic sections and the versed sine curve, and writing her best-known work, *Analytical Institutions for the Use of Italian Youth* (1748). In 1749, she is appointed honorary lecturer at the University of Bologna, although she never actually lectures. Upon her father's death in 1752, she devotes herself to religious activities, eventually becoming a nun.

1720 - 1729

C. 1720 Italian Painter Rosalba Carriera Introduces Use of Pastels in Portraits. Rosalba Carriera (1675–1757), an Italian painter, introduces the use of pastels, a medium that allows for speed in execution and subtlety in colors, in portraits. The daughter of a middle-class family, Carriera is born in Venice. Beginning her artistic career by creating designs for lace and decorating snuffboxes, Rosalba turns to portrait painting while in her 20s. Her work becomes so popular that she receives many commissions from royal patrons throughout Europe, including Louis XV of France and Augustus III of Poland. In 1720, she is elected to the French Academy of Painting and Sculpture, a rare honor for a woman. Never married, Rosalba's life-long companion is her sister Giovanna, who serves as her assistant in the studio. Rosalba is bereaved by the loss of her sister in 1737 and suffers blindness in the last decade of her life.

1720 Elizabeth Chudleigh Is Born. Elizabeth Chudleigh (1720–1788), countess of Bristol (England) is born. Beautiful and uneducated, Chudleigh conceals a previous marriage when she marries the second Duke of Kingston. Following his death, she is accused of bigamy by her husband's nephew. Chudleigh provides the inspiration for William Thackeray's works *Esmond* and *The Virginians*.

NOVEMBER 1720 Masculine Pirate Anne Bonney Captured and Sentenced to Death. One of the most sensational events in the annals of crime occurs with the capture of pirate Anne Bonney. The illegitimate daughter of an Irish attorney, Bonney frequents the waterfront in Charleston, South Carolina, wearing men's clothing. In 1719 she elopes with James Bonney to the Bahamas, where she meets and falls in love with the pirate Calico Jack Rackham. Rackham offers to buy a divorce from her husband, and when James Bonney refuses, Anne and Rackham seize a ship. Allegedly, the crew members are ignorant of Anne Bonney's gender, which seems unlikely. Aboard the ship, another woman, Mary Read, is disguised as a sailor. Bonney discovers Read's identity, and the two become a team. In November of 1720, Rackham's ship is captured, but Bonney and Read wound several Royal Navy sailors during the battle. Both women are sentenced to hang. Asked whether the condemned have anything to say, Bonney and Read shout, "Milord, we plead our bellies!" As both are pregnant, the court cannot condemn the unborn children. Bonney delivers her baby and escapes, never to be seen again.

NOVEMBER 1720 **Pirate Mary Read Arrested for Piracy.** Along with her fellow crew members, pirate Mary Read is captured and sentenced to death. Born in England, Read joins the Royal Navy when she is 14. During the War of the Spanish Succession, she serves with distinction in the army. With the Peace of Utrecht, Read signs on a Dutch ship known as a merchantman. When the vessel is captured by the pirate Calico Jack Rackham, Read joins his crew. Anne Bonney, another female pirate and the partner of Rackham, soon discovers Read's identity, and the two become friends. Read falls in love with a crew member and reveals her gender. When her lover quarrels with a shipmate, the two opponents are set ashore to settle their differences. Being an experienced swordswoman, Read insists on taking his place. After a fierce struggle, Read kills her opponent. In 1720, when Rackham's ship is captured by the Royal Navy, the entire crew is sentenced to death. Both pregnant, Read and Bonney reveal their identities to the court. British law forbids the

sentencing to death of pregnant women. Read's sentence is commuted. She dies in childbirth on April 28, 1721.

c. 1721 **Mary Digges Takes Vows to Become First American Nun.** Mary Digges (1696–?) leaves her home in the colony of Maryland to train to become the first American educated in Europe as a Catholic nun. The documents of Holy Sepulchre in Liege describe Mary as a "canoness regular" in 1721. Her father, William Digges (c.1650–1697), a Protestant, holds several important political offices in Maryland after he immigrates to Maryland from Virginia in 1679. Mary's grandfather is Governor Edward Digges of Virginia. Mary's mother, Elizabeth Sewall Wharton (a widow), marries William Digges before 1679.

1721 **Madame du Pompadour, Unofficial Ruler of France and King's Mistress, Is Born.** Madame du Pompadour (1721–1764) is born Jeanne Antoinette Poisson in Paris to middle class parents. Despite her common birth, her family calls her "queenie" and teaches her all the social graces that a young noblewoman should learn. She marries Le Normant d'Etoiles in 1741, but she retains an ambition, openly stated, to be the king's mistress. By 1745, the beautiful and talented Poisson catches the eye of King Louis XV, who calls her "the most delicious woman in France." After the death of his previous mistress, the two become lovers. The king names her the Marquise de Pompadour, thus making her a noblewoman; gives her a private apartment at his palace of Versailles; and names her his official mistress. Madame du Pompadour, as she becomes known, enlivens court life with balls and banquets, and she directs and stars in professional-quality theater productions. She also acts as a patron and protector of many great writers and artists, including Voltaire, who calls her, "sincere and tender Pompadour." The immense power she wields over the king allows her to control military and government policies, earning her the enmity of many nobles, who despise her for her common birth. In fact, she becomes the virtual ruler of France for almost 20 years until her death at Versailles in 1764.

1729   Commemorative Medal Honors French Composer Jacquet de la Guerre. Elisabeth-Claude Jacquet de la Guerre (1666–1729), a French composer and harpsichordist, is the first female musician in France to have a commemorative medal struck in her honor. Much of her work does not survive, but she is so famous during her lifetime that the medal in her memory is issued shortly after her death.

MAY 2, 1729   Empress Catherine the Great Is Born. Catherine the Great (1729–1796), who helps develop Russia into a major European power during her reign as empress from 1762 to 1796, is born in Germany as Sophia Friederica Augusta, princess of Anhalt-Zerbst. In 1745 she is taken to Russia at the invitation of the empress Elizabeth Petrovna to marry the grand duke Peter, the heir to the throne. The young German princess takes the name of Catherine for her royal role. Her marriage to the incompetent Peter is a failure, but the couple has a son, later the emperor Paul I. In 1762 Peter takes the throne, but within six months Catherine replaces him as sole Russian monarch through a palace revolution. Whether she is involved in the subsequent murder of Peter is a moot question.

Among her more important acts are the reform of local government and the extension of Russian territory to the Black Sea and into Poland. A well-educated woman, the empress corresponds with some of the most distinguished intellects of her day, including the French thinkers Voltaire and Diderot. In 1764 she opens the Smolny Institute, a secondary school for girls of noble birth, in St. Petersburg, thus showing her concern for better female education in Russia.

1 7 3 0 – 1 7 3 9

1731   Giuseppa Eleanora Barbapiccola Translates Work of Descartes Into Italian. Giuseppa Eleanora Barbapiccola (fl. 1731) translates René Descartes's *Principles of Philosophy* into Italian. Nothing is known of her formal education, although she is reported to be proficient in science and languages.

1732   Julie de Lespinasse, Hostess of Famous Enlightenment Salon, Is Born. Julie de Lespinasse (1732–1776) is born, the illegitimate daughter of two nobles in Lyon. Unacknowledged by her parents, de Lespinasse grows up in poverty but moves to Paris, where she meets the famous Madame du Deffand, who runs a salon where the greatest minds of the Enlightenment meet to discuss philosophical issues. De Lespinasse is young, beautiful, and intelligent, and her work as du Deffand's assistant makes her extremely popular—so popular, in fact, that the jealous Madame du Deffand fires her. Friends give de Lespinasse money to start her own salon, which features only simple tea and cake in contrast to the elegant and highly formal settings at most other salons. However, her salon hosts gatherings of Europe's most distinguished thinkers, and de Lespinasse presides over its discussions as hostess. She dies in Paris in 1776.

1732   Birth of Arakida Reijo, Japanese Historical Novelist. The Japanese poet and novelist Arakida Reijo (1732–1806) is born. As a young writer, she becomes proficient in a variety of kinds of poetry, but the historical novels she later writes are the works for which she is particularly known. These novels depict the life of Japanese aristocracy in the eleventh and fourteenth centuries.

c. 1736   Birth of Molly Brant, Influential Mohawk During the American Revolution. Molly Brant, who plays an important role in negotiations during the American Revolution and exercises an influential role in Mohawk tribal life, is born. Her Mohawk Indian name is Konwatsi' tsiaienni, meaning "someone lends her a flower." The sister of the Mohawk chief, Joseph Brant, and later wife of the British Indian agent, Sir William Johnston, Molly Brant is the leading matron of the extensive and important Six Nations Tribe. She renders invaluable assistance to the Crown by encouraging the Six Nations to keep its alliance with England when the Revolutionary War forces the Mohawk to relinquish its ancestral territories in New York State for a new home in Upper Canada. She continues to work for the best conditions of the Mohawk tribe's settlement throughout her life and remains a staunch loyalist to the Crown.

1736   Birth of Ann Lee, Founder of Shaker Community in the United States. Ann Lee (1736–1784) is born in Manchester, England, the daughter of a blacksmith. At about age 23, Lee is forced to marry Abraham Stanley, also a blacksmith, against her will. When all four of their children die in early childhood, Lee joins the "Shaking Quakers," or "Shakers," certain that marriage and sex are evil. She persuades her husband to become a Shaker also, and she develops a reputation for street preaching, for which she is imprisoned in 1770. To escape persecution, Lee and a band of followers emigrate to the United States in 1774, and establish a Shaker community at Niskayuna, New York (near Albany) in 1776.

c. 1738   Eliza Lucas Pinckney Develops Cultivation of Indigo. Eliza Lucas Pinckney (1722–1793), a successful Colonial agriculturalist, develops the cultivation and marketing of indigo in South Carolina. Lucas (later Pinckney) moves to South Carolina when her father inherits a plantation near present-day Charleston. From the age of 16, she helps her father with management of his plantation property. She experiments with indigo, a crop that previously proved impossible to raise in South Carolina. Her efforts are so successful that by 1747, South Carolina planters are able to export 100,000 pounds of indigo dye to England. For approximately 30 years, indigo bolsters the economy of South Carolina. The industry declines during the Revolutionary War. After the death of her husband in 1758, Pinckney successfully manages their seven plantations in South Carolina.

1740 – 1749

1740   Maria Theresa Becomes Only Female Ruler of Habsburg Empire. Maria Theresa, Archduchess of Austria (1717–1780), becomes the only female—but possible the greatest—ruler of the Habsburg Empire. Since her father, Emperor Charles VI (reigns 1711–40), has no male heirs, he convinces the European powers to agree to the Pragmatic Sanction, a treaty that guarantees to his daughter the inheritance of the vast collection of Habsburg territories in Central Europe. When he dies, Maria Theresa is only 23, pregnant with her second child, and completely unprepared for rule. Breaking the Pragmatic Sanction, King Frederick II of Prussia seizes the province of Silesia, and so begins the War of the Austrian Succession (1740–48). Maria Theresa rises to the emergency. She rallies the support of her people, defeats the attacking armies, and gains the emperorship for her husband and then her son. Silesia, however, remains with Prussia, despite her efforts in the Seven Years' War (1756–63) to retake it. Meanwhile, she reforms her lands, somewhat in the manner of an enlightened despot: she revises the tax system, improves the bureaucracy, establishes a more humane legal code, and begins the foundation of universal elementary education for all her subjects, boys and girls. She maintains an active schedule, even while bearing 16 children (the most famous—or infamous—of whom becomes Queen Marie Antoinette of France). In her later years, she shares rule with her son and heir, Joseph II (1741–1790), until her death on November 28, 1780.

Catherine the Great assumes her role as empress.

SEPTEMBER 10, 1740 Birth of Mary Willing Byrd, Manager of Westover Plantation. Mary Willing (1740–1814) is born in Philadelphia. In January 1761 she weds William Byrd III of Virginia and during her 16 years of marriage, bears ten children. After her insolvent husband commits suicide on New Year's Day 1777, Mary Willing Byrd faces the task of settling his estate, satisfying numerous creditors, and preserving an inheritance for her children. Despite the fact that British troops land three times at Westover, her Charles City County plantation, and that she is suspected of having Loyalist sympathies and engaging in illegal commerce, Byrd survives the American Revolution without being brought to trial. At her death in March 1814, she is able to provide financially for her children and grandchildren.

1741 Elizabeth Petrovna Ascends to Russian Throne. Elizabeth Petrovna (1709–1762) becomes empress of Russia. The daughter of Peter the Great and Catherine I, emperor and empress of Russia, Elizabeth is born near Moscow. In 1741, at the age of 32, she ascends the Russian throne as a result of a conspiracy. Empress Elizabeth Petrovna is known for licentiousness and tyrannical government; nonetheless, she encourages the development of education and the arts, founding both the University of Moscow (1755) and the Academy of Fine Arts in St. Petersburg (1758). Elizabeth supports the Austrians during the European wars of the mid-eighteenth century and enhances her country's position in international affairs. When she dies in 1762, she is succeeded by her incompetent nephew, the grand duke

Peter. Within six months, however, the throne is seized by the bride whom Elizabeth has selected for Peter: Catherine the Great.

1742   Wilhemina Writes Memoirs of Life at Prussian Court. Wilhemina Fredericke Sophie von Hohenzollern records life at the courts of Potsdam and Bayreuth in her memoirs. Covering her life up to 1742, her recollections paint an insightful, if at times fanciful, portrait of the Prussian court and her beloved brother Frederick. She is born into the court of the first Hohenzollern king in Prussia; her father soon becomes the frugal and martial King Frederick William I (reigns 1713–40), and her brother later takes throne as Frederick II "the Great" (reigns 1740–86). She dies on October 14, 1758.

1743   Madame du Barry, Mistress of King Louis XV, Is Born. Madame du Barry, born Marie Jeanne Bécu (1743–1794) in the village of Vaucouleurs, France, is the illegitimate daughter of a peasant woman and a Catholic monk. She moves to Paris as a child and spends eight years in a convent, then works several years as a salesgirl in an exclusive shop. Her incredible beauty is legendary among the Parisian noblemen, who call her "the Angel." One of them, Count Jean du Barry, makes her his mistress and trains her to be a courtesan to the rich and powerful. She formally marries his brother, Count Guillaume du Barry. By 1768, she catches the attention of Louis XV and becomes his official mistress.

1743   Birth of Etta Palm d'Aelders, Prominent Spokesperson for Women's Rights in France. Etta Palm d'Aelders (1743-1830) is born in Holland. She moves to Paris before the French Revolution, and after 1789 becomes a prominent spokesperson for women's rights. She particularly advocates equality before the law in cases of adultery and divorce, and she advocates a public role for women through supervision of public welfare and child care. She survives the revolution and dies in 1830.

Hannah More

FEBRUARY 2, 1745   Birth of Hannah More, British Religious Writer. British author Hannah More (1745–1833) is born. She begins her writing career at the age of seventeen, when she publishes the dramatic work, "The Search After Happiness." She is remembered for her poetry and drama but particularly for her religious writing. As a figure of moral authority, her influential monthly publication, *The Cheap Repository,* is designed to counteract political writings of the time. It has an estimated circulation of one million per issue in London between 1795 and 1798. She also writes tracts for moral and religious education, including *Village Politics* (1792) and *Coefebs in Search of A Wife* (1809). More dies on September 7, 1833.

1748   Madame de Geoffrin Hosts Influential Salon During the Enlightenment. Madame

SALON SOCIETY

c. 1750 Salons were social and intellectual gatherings hosted by women of means in their homes during the mid-to late-eighteenth century in France. Each woman, or *salonière*, invited a select group of intellectuals (called *"philosophes"*), nobles, and businesspeople to meet for refreshments and conversation in her drawing room. There, she presided over the gathering, encouraging and directing conversation and debate on philosophy, science, social issues, literature, and politics. In effect, the salons were the forum by which the philosophy of the Enlightenment spread to the nobility and middle classes. They were also places where the *philosophes* like Voltaire, Diderot, and Montesquieu could debate each other and so develop the Enlightenment itself. The elegant settings and fine foods attracted France's powerful elites to the salons, where they were exposed to the new currents of critical thought and material progress through learning.

de Geoffrin (1699–1777) conducts one of the most important salons during the French Enlightenment. Born Marie Thérèse Rodet in Paris, France, at 14 she marries a wealthy older man, Pierre Francois Geoffrin, who is a lieutenant in the National Guard and a founder of glass manufacture. Her husband provides her with money to make her home a luxurious salon for artists and intellectuals. Very quiet, Monsieur Geoffrin is known as "the old gentleman who sat in a corner saying nothing." Although Madame de Geoffrin is not well-educated (she cannot even spell), she reigns over one of the most important salons in Paris during the Enlightenment, from 1748 until her death. She refers to her salon in the Rue Saint-Honore as an "institution" and the attendees, who include disciples

of Rousseau and Voltaire and the future king of Poland, call her "Mamma." Unlike the philosophers who come to her home, Madame de Geoffrin is very religious. Because she dislikes arguments, she forbids the discussion of politics and religion at her salon. Most debates concern literature and philosophy, and intellectual women and royalty also flock to her home. Her role as a salon leader is proof that upper-class women do participate in the Enlightenment.

1748 Birth of Olympe de Gouges, French Revolutionary Feminist. Olympe de Gouges (1748–1793) is born Olympe Gouze in Montauban, France, to a poor family. She later moves to Paris, where she becomes an actress and takes on the more noble-sound-ing name Olympe de Gouges. She becomes an active feminist in France and plays a significant role in the French Revolution, demanding equal rights for women in the new French Republic. She is guillotined for treason on November 3, 1793.

1 7 5 0 – 1 7 5 9

1750 **Women's Important Contributions to Early Colonial Economies Do Not Guarantee Equal Rights and Status.** In the colonial era, homes are mini-factories which produce soap, candles, cloth, and food. If a woman is not a good planner, the whole family suffers. Women also tend to the family's health care needs. They deliver babies because male doctors consider it beneath their dignity. Although women are crucial contributors to colonial society, they face double standards. For example, while adulterous men generally receive fines, women are often put on trial and have their names published in the newspaper. Two terms, "Feme Sole" and "Feme Couvert," indicate the formal position of women. As Feme Sole, single women can own a business, conduct their own legal affairs, own property, or keep their wages. However, after marriage, a woman's legal identity is completely merged with her husband's. As Feme Couvert, women cannot own property. Colonial women are defined completely by their relationships to males: they are either daughters, sisters, wives, or someone's mother.

Women's labor is considered inferior to men's work. Midwives are often not paid. If a woman performs the role of a doctor, she is called a nurse. Male doctors have more respect and prestige. Girls are hired out as servants, whereas boys become apprentices and receive superior educations. Wages also differ in the 1700s; for example, women innkeepers are paid one-half as much as men.

JANUARY 1, 1752 **Birth of Elizabeth "Betsy" Griscom Ross in Philadelphia, Pennsylvania.**

Elizabeth Griscom, known as Betsy, is the daughter of Samuel Griscom, a builder who constructed a large part of Independence Hall in Philadelphia. She marries John Ross in December 1773, and establishes a flag-making business after his death in 1776. A story, of doubtful accuracy, recounts her stitching of the first flag for the newly created United States of America in 1776.

1755 **Birth of Marie Antoinette, Unpopular Queen of France.** Marie Antoinette (1755–1793) is born in Vienna, daughter of the Holy Roman Emperor Frances I and Empress Maria Theresa. In 1770, when she is 14, she marries the heir to the French throne, and in 1774 becomes queen upon his succession to the throne as Louis XVI.

Marie Antoinette is very unpopular with the French people, who view her as a foreigner. They believe her to be arrogant, promiscuous, and a bad influence on the king. Her life as queen is surrounded by scandal and rumors, and when the French Revolution breaks out in 1789, she is the target of much hatred. During the period of constitutional monarchy (1789–91), she urges the king to resist the revolutionaries.

1755 **French Portrait Painter Marie Anne Elisabeth Vigée-Lebrun Is Born.** Elisabeth Vigée-Lebrun (1755–1842), who becomes one of the most celebrated French portrait painters of the eighteenth and nineteenth centuries, is born Marie Anne Elisabeth in Paris. Her excellent sense of color and her ability to paint flattering yet believable portraits make her a favorite artist of the French royal court and nobility. She paints memorable portraits of Queen Marie Antoinette as well as of Madame du Barry. Despite her favor with the royal court, she survives the French Revolution and continues her work, leaving excellent portraits of many of the era's most prominent women, including Germaine de Staël. Her portraits are not limited to women, however.

Hannah Adams

In the early 1800s, she paints the Prince of Wales and Lord Byron.

1758 Hannah Adams, First American Woman Author, Is Born. Hannah Adams (1755–1831), the first woman author to support herself with her writing, is born in Medfield, Massachusetts. Her first book, *View of Religions* (later *Dictionary of Religions*), was published in 1784.

1758 Marie Lavoisier, Great French Chemist, Is Born. Marie Lavoisier (1758-1836) is born Marie Anne Paulze. Her father arranges her marriage to 28-year-old Antoine Lavoisier when she is 14. Antoine is already a chemist, and he recognizes his wife's great intelligence, teaching her Latin and English. She uses these language skills to translate important scientific works from England. Marie and Antoine collaborate on all their experiments,

discovering oxygen and discrediting the then-current notion that combustion is the result of the release of a substance called "phlogiston." The two also formulate the "Law of the Conservation of Matter" and apply inorganic chemistry to physiological phenomena.

Marie Lavoisier opens a scientific salon in Paris. She also uses her artistic skill to illustrate their books. During the French Revolution, Antoine is arrested and executed for being a royal employee of Louis XVI, and she is imprisoned. After her release she edits and writes *Memoirs of Chemistry* (1805), publishing it in Antoine's name since female authors have a difficult time publishing. She remarries in 1805 but separates in 1809. As a woman alone, she has a difficult time working as a scientist, and she dies poor and unhappy in 1836. Nevertheless, her work in chemistry provides a crucial building block for nineteenth-century advances in the field.

1758 Anna Amalia Becomes Regent for Saxe-Weimar. Anna Amalia of Brunswick (1739–1807) becomes regent for Saxe-Weimar after the death of her husband. She governs until 1775, when their son, Carl August, comes of age. As regent, Anna Amalia's encouragement of the arts provides the foundation for Weimar as a center of German culture, culminating in her son's invitation to Johann Wolfgang von Goethe to live and work in Weimar. The dowager duchess remains active in the principality's intellectual and social life until her death on April 10, 1807.

1758 Pauline Léon, Radical French Activist, Is Born. Pauline Léon (1758-?), a radical activist during the French Revolution, is born in Paris. She credits her father, a chocolate manufacturer, with raising her with strong principles. After her father's death on the eve of the French Revolution, she helps her mother with the business and with raising her four siblings. She then becomes actively involved in the Revolution, protesting the aristocracy and tyranny. On March 6, 1792, Léon leads a delegation of "citoyennes de la ville de Paris" and presents to the Legislative Assembly a petition with 300 signatures concerning women's right to bear arms and engage in military maneuvers. Léon believes that women are as essential as men in the armed defense of the Revolution. She participates in the storming of the Bastille, and in 1793 she founds and is president of the Society of Revolutionary Republican Women. The society initially cooperates with, but eventually conflicts with, the radical Jacobin establishment. In October 1793, the National Convention shuts down Léon's society on the grounds that its members threaten public order. Women are then banned from any political action and denied the right to assemble in public. The following month she marries Theophile Leclern, a spokesman for the radical Parisian Sans-culottes. Both are arrested in April 1794 and serve prison terms until August of that year. No new heroines arise to speak out for women's issues during the Revolution. However, the Society of Revolutionary Republican Women serves as a prototype of the political clubs for women that flourish during the Revolution of 1848. Léon is remembered for her attacks on the bourgeoisie and her championship of the interests of working women.

JANUARY 6, 1759 **Wedding of Martha and George Washington.** Martha Dandridge Custis (1732–1801), the wealthy young widow of Colonel Daniel Parke Custis, is married to George Washington. During the Revolutionary War, Martha Washington often accompanies her husband, commander in chief of the American army, to army encampments. In 1789, George Washington becomes the first president of the United States.

1 7 6 0 – 1 7 6 9

1760 **Birth of Deborah Sampson Gannett.** Deborah Sampson Gannett (1760–1827) is born in Plympton, Massachusetts, the oldest of three daughters and sons. In 1782, dis-

A portrait of Deborah Sampson Gannett.

guised as a man, Gannett becomes the first woman to enlist in the U.S. Army.

SEPTEMBER 27, 1760 **School for African American Children Opens in Colonial Virginia.** The Bray's Associates School "for the Education of Negroes in the Christian Faith" is founded in Williamsburg, Virginia, with Anne Wager (?–1774), an elderly widow, as the only teacher. During its first year, the Bray's School opens its doors to 24 scholars, both slave and free, ranging in age from three to ten. Beginning at seven o'clock on winter mornings, six o'clock in the summer, Wager teaches her pupils reading, writing, and religion, keeping them "diligently to their Business during the Hours of Schooling." With her death in 1774, the school is closed.

1761   English Silversmith Hester Needham Bateman Registers Own Hallmark. Hester Needham Bateman (1709–1794) of England is the first female silversmith to register her own hallmark, "H.B." She works with her husband, John, until his death in 1760, then carries on his business as her own. She is now regarded as one of the greatest eighteenth-century silversmiths.

1763   French Empress Josephine Is Born. Born in Martinique, Marie Josephine Rose Tascher later becomes the wife of Napoleon. She first marries at age 16 Viscount Alexander de Beauharnais, a French gentleman of rank, in 1779. Josephine returns with him to France, where she becomes a favorite of Marie Antoinette. The Viscount is executed at the guillotine in 1794. On March 9, 1795, Josephine marries Napoleon.

1763   British Historian Catherine Sawbridge Macaulay Publishes Most Famous Work. Catherine Sawbridge Macaulay (1731–1796?), a distinguished British historian, publishes between 1763 and 1783 her most famous work in eight volumes: *History of England from the Accession of James I to that of the Brunswick Line.* Although this study is controversial in light of its radical republican sympathies, it is immensely popular. Her early exposure to ancient Greek and Roman history inspires the enthusiasm for republican ideals found in her historical books. In 1760, she marries the Scottish physician George Macaulay and is widowed six years later. In 1778, Catherine Macaulay marries William Graham. Among her last books is *Letters on Education* (1787), an appeal for better education for women.

1764   Smolny Institute Founded in Russia. Empress Catherine the Great (1729–1796) opens the Smolny Institute, a secondary school for girls of noble birth, in St. Petersburg, thus showing her concern for better female education in Russia. She helps develop

After her husband, Viscount Alexander de Beauharnais, is executed, Josephine marries Napoleon.

Russia into a major European power during her reign as empress from 1762 to 1796.

1765   Swiss Artist Angelica Kauffmann Moves to London. Angelica Kauffmann (1741–1807) moves to London, where from 1765 to 1780, she works, becomes a founding member of the Royal Academy of Art, and is romantically pursued by the academy's president, the painter Joshua Reynolds. The daughter of a travelling Austrian artist, Kauffmann is born in Chur, in modern-day Switzerland. She decides to go to Italy and become an artist, and is helped by her father, who runs her business affairs. Proving her talent early, she is admitted into the Florentine Academy by 1762. She refuses to allow herself to be limited to portraits, and excels at historical paintings in the Neoclassic style. As one of the most successful and famous artists in her adopted city of Rome, she dies on November 5, 1807.

1766　Birth of Germaine de Staël, Leading Figure of French Romantic Movement. Germaine de Staël (1766–1817) is born Germaine Necker in Paris, the daughter of a powerful royal official and an important salon hostess. Unlike most women of the time, she receives an excellent education and becomes an impassioned believer in Enlightenment ideas. Brilliant and talented in music, art, and writing, she marries the Swedish ambassador and becomes Madame de Staël. When the French Revolution (1789–99) begins, de Staël manages to keep her salon open when many others are forced to close, but she eventually flees to Switzerland during the Reign of Terror (1793–94). She returns to Paris in 1795, where she remains until 1800. The Emperor Napoleon, who hates intelligent women, then harasses her until she goes once again into Swiss exile in 1803. From 1805 to 1814, Napoleon's police force her to move from country to country to escape persecution. It is during this period that de Staël writes two major works: a novel, *Corinne*, and a nonfiction work, *On Germany*. Napoleon sees *Corinne* as a direct challenge to his anti-feminist Napoleonic Code, and bans *On Germany*. Nevertheless, the works of de Staël are immensely popular. They help found the movement of French Romanticism, in which artistic minds challenge the political and social order of the day, not through the world of politics but through a world of creative imagination. After Napoleon's downfall, de Staël returns to Paris, where she dies in 1817.

1767　British Activist Children's Author Maria Edgeworth Is Born. Maria Edgeworth (1767–1849), daughter of British inventor and writer Richard Lovell Edgeworth (1744–1817), is born in Oxfordshire, England. In 1782, Maria accompanies her father to Ireland, and completes his memoirs after his death. Maria assists the Irish people during the famine of 1846, and publishes more than twenty books during her lifetime, including *The Absentee* (1812), and *Ormond* (1817). She chronicles Irish life in *Castle Rackrent Belinda* (1801), *Leonora* (1806), *Tales from Fashionable Life* (1809, 1812), and her last novel, *Helen* (1834).

c. 1768　Anne Catherine Hoof Green Publishes Maryland's Sole Newspaper. Anne Catherine Hoof (c.1720–1775) becomes "printer and postmaster" of the Province of Maryland a year after the death of her husband, Jonas Green, who previously holds the position. The Greens' newspaper, the *Maryland Gazette*, is Maryland's only newspaper until 1773.

1768　Madame du Barry Becomes Mistress of King Louis XV. Madame du Barry (1743–1794) becomes the official mistress of King Louis XV following the death of Madame du Pompadour. She remains the official favorite until the king's death in 1774, when she is dismissed from court.

c. 1769　William Blackstone Publishes Work on English Common Law, Viewing Women as Minors. William Blackstone (1723–1780) summarizes English common law in his monumental work *Commentaries on the Laws of England*, published in four volumes. Common law is the unwritten law of a country based on centuries of custom, usage, and legal decisions. In England, as in other European countries, women are typically viewed as perpetual minors in common law. A married woman is considered a *feme couvert* (protected woman), who has to turn over control of her property to her husband. A woman's rights to her property can be guaranteed by equity law, but this involves expensive legal action at the time of marriage and is not a viable option for most wives. A single woman over 21 years of age is considered a *feme sole*, who can make contracts and control her own property. Some wives are given this independent status by court decree.

1769 **Elizabeth Montagu, "Queen of the Bluestockings," Publishes Work on Shakespeare.** Elizabeth Robinson Montagu (1720–1800), a noted literary critic in London, England, publishes one of her more important works, *Essay on the Writings and Genius of Shakespeare.* She is born in York, England, on October 2, 1720. At age 22 she marries Charles Montagu, a wealthy aristocrat. Called the "queen of the bluestockings" (intellectual women), Elizabeth Montagu makes their townhouse the center of intellectual society in London during the mid-eighteenth century and gains a reputation as a literary critic. Upon her husband's death in 1775, she interests herself in architectural projects.

1 7 7 0 – 1 7 7 9

C. 1770 **Elizabeth Chudleigh Establishes Brandy Distillery in Russia.** Englishwoman Elizabeth Chudleigh (1720–1788) establishes a brandy distillery in St. Petersburg, Russia. Having created a scandal at the English court because of her licentious behavior, Chudleigh lives most of her life in Europe, and during the late 1770s becomes a favorite in the court of Catherine II in Russia.

C. OCTOBER 3, 1771 **Christiana Campbell's Williamsburg Tavern Serves Famous Patrons.** Campbell's Tavern in Williamsburg is advertised in the *Virginia Gazette.* Williamsburg entrepreneur Christiana Burdett Campbell (1722–1792) runs a popular establishment behind the capitol, offering lodging, gambling, and food to her patrons. Campbell is the daughter of John Burdett, a Williamsburg tavernkeeper, and the widow of one of the town's apothecaries. During the 1760s and 1770s, George Washington is a frequent visitor to Campbell's establishment, where "gen-

teel Accommodations" and the "very best Entertainment" are available. Business declines when the state capital moves to Richmond in 1780. Campbell (remembered by a Yorktown merchant as "a little old Woman about four feet high; & equally thick") closes her business by 1783.

OCTOBER 25, 1771 **Death of Catherine Kaidyee Blaikley, Williamsburg Midwife.** Catherine Kaidyee Blaikley (1695–1771), a Williamsburg midwife, dies. During her career, she delivers "upwards of three Thousand Children."

1774 **Julie Postel Founds Religious School for Girls in Normandy.** Julie Postel (1756–1846), at the age of 19, opens a school for girls in Barfleur, Normandy, the center for underground religious activity in opposition to the clergy imposed by the official state-controlled religious establishment of that time in France. Like other women during times of political upheaval throughout history, Postel is allowed to administer the Eucharist, a sacramental privilege usually reserved for men. When the political and religious situation settles down, Postel continues her teaching and, at the age of 51, takes vows and becomes Sister Mary-Magdalene. She then founds the Sisters of the Christian Schools of Mercy, a religious education order, and serves as its director until her death in 1846 at age 90.

1774 **Marie Antoinette Becomes Queen of France.** Marie Antoinette (1755–1793) becomes queen of France upon the succession of her husband to the throne as Louis XVI. Her life as queen is surrounded by scandal and rumors questioning her loyalty to France. When the French Revolution breaks out in 1789, she is the target of much hatred and accusations of favoritism to her native Austria.

1774 **Clementina Rind Publishes the *Virginia Gazette*.** The House of Burgesses in Virginia appoints Clementina Rind (1740–1774) pub-

Marie Antoinette

lic printer in her own right, and she publishes the *Virginia Gazette*. Arguably the most famous woman of affairs in eighteenth-century Virginia, Rind is the wife of the public printer in Williamsburg. With her husband's death, she assumes publication of his newspaper, the *Virginia Gazette,* and control of his printing business. Rind's paper includes foreign, domestic, and shipping news, essays, poems, and advertisements, in accordance with the *Gazette*'s motto: "Open to ALL PARTIES, but Influenced by NONE."

1774   Birth of Elizabeth Ann Seton. Elizabeth Ann Bayley Seton (1774–1821) is born into a wealthy New York City family. In 1797, Seton founds the Society for the Relief of Poor Widows with Small Children, and herself is widowed with five children six years later. She converts to Catholicism, and is credited with launching the Catholic school system in the United States. Seton also establishes the Sisters of Charity, the first religious order in the United States. In 1975, Seton is made a saint, the first native-born U.S. citizen to be so canonized.

1775   Birth of Mary Martha Sherwood, Children's Author. Mary Martha Butt Sherwood (1775–1851), British author, is born. She publishes religious stories, beginning with *The Traditions* (1794). In 1803, she marries Captain Henry Sherwood and accompanies him to India. She later writes the three-part work, *The History of the Fairchild Family* (1919, 1842, and 1847). Sherwood is a very prolific writer, publishing over 300 stories, tracts, and articles before her death in 1851.

JULY 8, 1775   Mary Draper Ingles Abducted by Shawnees. Mary Draper Ingles (1732–1815) is taken from her farm near present-day Blacksburg, Virginia, by a Shawnee raiding party. Caught in the upheaval of the French and Indian War, Ingles, her two young sons, and her sister-in-law begin the long march west with their captors to the Ohio Valley. When her sons are sent off to be adopted by Indian families, Ingles begins plotting her escape. After 42 days on the run and nearly 500 miles of travel, Ingles finally reaches a German farm on the New River. Reunited with her husband, Ingles bears four more children and lives to be 83.

JULY 27, 1775   Second Continental Congress Authorizes Army Medical Department with Female Nurses and Matrons. The Second Continental Congress authorizes a Medical Department for the new army of 20,000 men and establishes three hospitals to support the northern, middle, and southern theaters of operation. Each hospital is composed of a medical staff that follows the army and provides medical support as needed, including a director, chief physician, four surgeons, an

Steventon Parsonage, the birthplace of Jane Austen.

apothecary, 20 surgeon's mates, a clerk, two storekeepers, a nurse for each ten patients, and a nurse matron (to supervise the nurses and oversee the wards) for every 100 patients.

General George Washington specifically requests female nurses and matrons so that men can be freed for battle. A nurse is authorized one-fifteenth of a dollar per day, or two dollars per month, plus a daily ration, while a matron receives one-half of a dollar per day, or 15 dollars per month, and a daily ration. By contrast, senior surgeons are paid four dollars per day, or 120 dollars per month, plus six daily rations, and surgeon's mates receive 50 dollars per month. By the end of the war, a nurse's pay increases to eight dollars per month.

DECEMBER 16, 1775 Birth of Jane Austen, English Novelist. Jane Austen (1775–1817), English novelist, is born at Steventon, Hampshire, England, the seventh child and second daughter of Reverend George and Cassandra

Leigh Austen. Jane and her older sister Cassandra are educated at home, and Jane begins writing stories at an early age. At age 21, she begins *Pride and Prejudice* (completed in 1797), followed by *Sense and Sensibility* (1798), and *Northanger Abbey* (1798). All three works are rejected for publication, and Jane stops writing. In 1811, when Austen is age 35, *Sense and Sensibility* is finally published, and she begins writing again. *Pride and Prejudice* is published next, followed by *Mansfield Park. Emma* appears in 1815. Her health begins to fail, and she completes *Persuasion* during the final year of her life. She dies on July 18, 1817, and is buried at Winchester Cathedral.

1776 Laura Bassi Named Physics Professor at University of Bologna. Laura Bassi (1711–1778), the daughter of a well-to-do lawyer in Bologna, Italy, is appointed professor of experimental physics at the University of Bologna. Bassi is a pioneer female physicist; as a woman teacher of male students at the university level, she is unique for her time. Receiving an excellent education as a child, she is awarded a philosophy degree from the University of Bologna in 1732. In that same year, she is also named a lecturer in universal philosophy at the university, as well as a member of the prestigious Academy of Sciences in Bologna. In 1738 Bassi marries one of her colleagues, Guiseppe Veratti. The couple has twelve children. Throughout her long career, Bassi is an active teacher and researcher in the field of physics. Her studies on electricity are particularly noteworthy.

1776 Some Female Property Owners Gain Suffrage. Holders of property worth over 50 pounds, including some women, are granted the right to vote in New Jersey.

1776 Shaker Leader Mother Ann Lee Establishes Community in New York. Mother Ann Lee (1736–1784), with a small band of followers who emigrated with her from England in 1774, establishes a Shaker community at Niskayuna, New York (near Albany).

MAY 1776 Beginning of Traditional Story About the Making of the First American Flag. Elizabeth "Betsy" Ross (1752–?), widow of John Ross, is a successful upholsterer and flag-maker in Philadelphia, Pennsylvania. According to folk history, George Washington, accompanied by Colonel George Ross and Robert Morris, engages Ross to make the first American flag, the "Stars and Stripes."

NOVEMBER 16, 1776 Margaret "Molly" Corbin Takes Wounded Husband's Place in Battle. Accompanying her husband to Fort Washington, New York, Margaret "Molly" Corbin (1751–1800) stood alongside him as he lay mortally wounded. She immediately took his place and without hesitation reloaded his cannon and took responsibility for his battle station. In July 1779, Molly Corbin was awarded a full military pension by the

Supreme Council of Pennsylvania. The Continental Congress additionally decided that she was entitled to half of a soldier's disability pay for life.

C. 1777 Colonial Woman Manages Land in Virginia. When her husband dies, Mary Marshall Bolling (1738–1814) assumes management of their estate in Petersburg, Virginia. Because she does not remarry, Bolling is able to take advantage of a legal system that authorizes single women and widows to exercise control over property. In the 37 years of her widowhood, Bolling controls plantations, slaves, tobacco warehouses, a gristmill, and much of the land on which the town of Petersburg is built.

JANUARY 18, 1777 Mary Katherine Goddard, Printer, Is Commissioned to Print Declaration of Independence. In Baltimore, Maryland, Mary Katherine Goddard, a printer and newspaper publisher, is commissioned to print the first official copies of the Declaration of Independence. The Continental Congress had moved to Baltimore from Philadelphia. Goddard is also Baltimore's postmaster.

NOVEMBER 14, 1777 Ann Neill Advertises Opening of Her General Store in Virginia. Ann Neill announces the opening of her general store in the *Virginia Gazette*. Neill's general store stocks small household wares, musical instruments, ladies' hats, pocket pistols, liquor, groceries, and other diverse items. By 1779, Neill is also selling her own brand of dentifrice (toothpaste).

C. 1778 Hannah Lee Corbin Proposes Suffrage for Widowed Women Landowners. Hannah Lee Corbin (1728–1782) complains to her brother, Richard Henry Lee, a leader of Virginia's delegation to the Continental Congress, that she is a victim of taxation without representation and, as a propertied widow, should have the vote. Corbin is born in Westmoreland County, Virginia. An unconventional woman, she applies the principles of the American Revolution to the condition of women. In the 1760s, she becomes a Baptist, despite the fact that the Anglican religion is compulsory and Baptists are regarded as members of a dissenting religious sect. Widowed at the age of 32, Lee preserves her children's inheritance by apparently living with (and not marrying) Dr. Richard Lingan Hall, with whom she has two children.

1778   Birth of Suzanne Theodore Vaillande Douvillier, First Female Choreographer in the United States. Suzanne Theodore Vaillande Douvillier (1778–1846), the first female choreographer in the United States, is born in France. Educated in Paris, she is the first ballerina to gain celebrity in America through performances in New York, Philadelphia, Charleston, and New Orleans. In 1808, she appears on the stage in male attire, probably the first woman to dance in cross dress in the United States. She is well-known on the east coast of America and has few rivals during her long career.

1778   Birth of Elizabeth Macquarie, Supporter of Women and Aborigines in Australia. Elizabeth Henrietta Campbell Macquarie (1778–1835), who works for women and Aborigines in early New South Wales, Australia, is born. Her husband, Lachlan Macquarie, is appointed Governor of New South Wales, Australia, in 1809, and the couple moves there. She takes a strong interest in Aboriginal affairs as patroness of the Native Institution and supporter of the Methodist Mission to the Aborigines. In 1816 she is appointed to the chair of the Female Orphan School, which had deteriorated markedly since the departure of Anna Josepha King in 1807. She sets to work to restore the institution to its former vigor, involving herself with every aspect of its management. In doing so, she clashes with the powerful Reverend Samuel Marsden and becomes the victim of a series of public sexist

insults from this cleric. Elizabeth Macquarie is also involved in agriculture and, with her friend Elizabeth Macarthur, is said to pioneer hay-making in the colony. Although she dies on March 11, 1835, her architectural knowledge and taste can be detected in many of the buildings that are the Macquaries' legacy to the colony, and several features of Sydney's landscape are named for her.

1779   Elisabeth Vigée-Lebrun Paints Portrait of Marie Antoinette. Elisabeth Vigée-Lebrun (1755-1842) paints a memorable portrait of the French queen Marie Antoinette, who is so pleased with it that she accepts the artist as a personal friend. At the outbreak of the French Revolution (1789–99), Vigée-Lebrun flees France for Italy.

JULY 1779   "Captain Molly" Receives Military Pension. Margaret "Molly" Corbin (1751–1800), an American Revolutionary War heroine, is the first woman to receive a military pension. She is called "the first woman to take a soldier's part in the Revolution" for her courageous acts of heroism. Suffering permanent disability due to the loss of one arm, Corbin began a series of appeals to the government for financial assistance. In July of 1779, the Supreme Council awarded her a thirty dollar grant; Congress also approved a military pension, including all military benefits given to a Revolutionary War veteran. Corbin also registered with the Invalid Regiment, created in 1777 for those wounded in service. She remained with the Invalid Regiment until it was disbanded in 1783.

1 7 8 0 – 1 7 8 9

c. 1780   Madame Roland Establishes Herself as Revolutionary *Salonière* and Thinker. Madame Roland (1754–1793), formerly Marie "Manon" Philppon, hosts an important salon where revolutionary politicians and thinkers debate during the French Revolution (1789–

99). She marries Jean-Marie Roland, who becomes a prominent moderate in the French Revolution and is Minister of the Interior in 1792–93. As an outspoken feminist, Madame Roland presses for women's political and social rights. When the radical Jacobins—led by Maximilien Robespierre, Georges Jacques Danton, and Jean Paul Marat—crack down on their political opposition, they include many prominent feminists in their list of prisoners, including Madame Roland. She is executed in November 1793, ostensibly for treason but actually because the Jacobins want to suppress feminist elements in the revolution.

1780   Women Found Revolutionary War's First Relief Organization. Esther Reed (1746–1780) and Sarah Franklin Bache, daughter of Benjamin Franklin, found the first relief organization of the American Revolution. They form a committee of 35 women in Philadelphia, Pennsylvania, whose purpose is to raise money to purchase clothing and supplies for soldiers serving in the Continental Army.

1782   Princess Ekaterina Dashkova Encourages Development of Russian Language and Literature. Ekaterina Romanovna Vorontsova Dashkova (1744–1810) is appointed director of the St. Petersburg Academy of Arts and Sciences by Empress Catherine the Great. Dashkova holds this position from 1783, when she formally takes over the post, until 1796. In this role, Dashkova encourages the development of Russian language and literature. A member of an influential Russian family in St. Petersburg, she is married in 1759 to Prince Mikhail Dashkov but is widowed three years later. Princess Dashkova then travels for over a decade throughout Europe. Upon her return to Russia, she assumes her appointed position at the St. Petersburg Academy of Arts and Sciences. Princess Dashkova is instrumental in the establishment of the Russian Academy, whose purpose is to promote the study and use of the Russian language. As the first president of this institution, she directs the publication of a Russian dictionary. A writer and editor herself, Ekaterina is a prominent patron of literature until Catherine's death in 1796. Forced to leave St. Petersburg by Emperor Paul I, she loses her position of influence.

MAY 20, 1782   Deborah Sampson Gannett Enlists in the U.S. Army. Deborah Sampson (later Gannett) (1760–1827) disguises herself as a man and uses the name Robert Shurtleff (Shirtliff) when she enlists in the Continental Army, becoming the first woman to enlist in the U.S. Army. She is remarkably adept at hiding her identity, but is discovered to be a woman when she is hospitalized with a fever. She is discharged by General Henry Knox at West Point, New York, on October 25, 1783. Returning to her home in Massachusetts, she marries Benjamin Gannett and together they raise three children. In 1797, Herman Mann publishes her story in the book *The Female Review*.

JUNE 17, 1782   Last Regular Execution for Witchcraft in Western Europe. In Glaris, a Protestant district of Switzerland, Anne Goeldi is executed for witchcraft. A local doctor accuses her of witchcraft, claiming she has cast evil spells on his son. In what turns out to be the last regular trial for witchcraft in Western Europe, she is found guilty, then hanged.

C. 1784   Sacajawea (Bird Woman), Guide for Lewis and Clark, Is Born. Sacajawea (1784?–1812?) is born in Idaho into the Lemhi (Shoshone) tribe, but is kidnapped at age ten by the Hidatsa tribe. In 1804, she is purchased or won by fur trader Toussaint Charbonneau, who is hired that same year by Meriwether Lewis and William Clark to serve as interpreter for their expedition. Sacajawea and their two-month-old son accompany him; Sacajawea proves invaluable as an interpreter and guide. She speaks Shoshoni and Siouan, and guides the group safely through the wilderness.

Statue of Sacajawea that stands on the grounds of the state capital in Bismarck, North Dakota.

1784   Hannah Adams, First American Woman Author, Publishes Her First Work. Hannah Adams (1755–1831), the first woman author to support herself with her writing, publishes her first book, *View of Religions.* By the time it reached its fourth edition, the title was changed to *Dictionary of Religions.*

1787   Mary Wollstonecraft Publishes *Thoughts on the Education of Daughters.* Mary Wollstonecraft (1759–1979), English author and intellectual, publishes *Thoughts on the Education of Daughters.* Wollstonecraft, who marries William Godwin in 1797, is ostracized for her radical ideas. She dies after giving birth to a daughter, Mary Wollstonecraft Godwin (later Shelley).

FEBRUARY 23, 1787   Educator Emma Hart Willard Is Born. Educator Emma Hart Willard (1787–1870) is born at Berlin, Connecticut, into a family of seventeen children. She receives her early education at the Berlin village academy, and begins her life's work as an educator at age 17. In about 1809, she marries Dr. John Willard, and in 1814, opens a boarding school for female students in Middlebury, Vermont. In 1821, Willard founds the Troy (New York) Female seminary.

1789   Louise Keralio-Robert Becomes Leading French Female Journalist and Revolutionary. At the start of the French Revolution, Louise Keralio-Robert (1758-1821) opens a revolutionary newspaper. As a revolutionary feminist, she pushes for a larger public role for women and joins the Fraternal Society of Patriots of Both Sexes. As a young adult, Keralio-Robert edits anthologies of women writers and advocates Enlightenment ideas. She argues incessantly for women's education in France, a nation that educates only wealthy women. She survives the anti-feminist purge of the French Revolution in 1793 and dies quietly in 1821.

1789   Olympe de Gouges Writes *The Declaration of the Rights of Woman and Citizen.* At the start of the French Revolution, Olympe de Gouges (1748–1793) is outraged that the *Declaration of the Rights of Man and of the Citizen* drafted by the French revolutionary government, which guarantees basic civil liberties to all men, totally neglects women's rights. In response, she writes *The Declaration of the Rights of Woman and Citizen,* systematically applying the *Rights of Man* to all people. Her 17-point document demands that the Revolution recognize women as political, civil, and legal equals of men. The declaration also provides a sample marriage contract that emphasizes free will and equality in marriage.

APRIL 30, 1789   Martha Washington Becomes First Lady. Martha Dandridge Cus-

Martha Washington

Ann Hasseltine Judson

tis Washington (1732–1801) becomes the first "First Lady" in the United States when her husband, George Washington, is inaugurated as the first president.

OCTOBER 5, 1789 Women's March on Versailles Changes Course of French Revolution. During the so-called October Days of October 5-7, 1789, the French Revolution gains new momentum due to the actions of a crowd of poor Parisian street women. Starting with a demonstration by female street vendors, the March on Versailles quickly gathers momentum as poor women in need of food gather and march on the royal palace at Versailles, 20 miles away. The crowd of armed women murder the royal guards and seize the royal family, dragging them back to Paris. This means that the king is subject to the threats and coercion of the revolutionary crowds instead of safe in his country palace. The Women's March on

Versailles marks a crucial turning point in the French Revolution, and it is the result of spontaneous mob action by women without male leadership or control.

DECEMBER 22, 1789 American Missionary Ann Hasseltine Judson Is Born. Anne Hasseltine is born in Bradford, Massachusetts, and educated at Bradford Academy. She marries dedicated missionary Adoniram Judson on February 12, 1812, and on February 14th the couple leaves for Calcutta, India.

1 7 9 0 – 1 7 9 9

c. 1790 Carmelite Monastery Founded in Maryland. Sister Bernardina (formerly Anne) Matthews and her two nieces, Sisters Mary Eleanora (Susanna) and Mary Aloysia (Ann Teresa) Matthews, along with Clare Joseph Dickinson, found the Carmelite

Monastery in Port Tobacco, Maryland. The monastery currently makes its home in Baltimore, Maryland.

C. 1790   Publication of *The Dream of the Red Chamber*, Famous Chinese Novel. *The Dream of the Red Chamber,* a Chinese novel whose main characters are two young women, is published. The action in this best-loved of all Chinese novels, written by Cao Xueqin, centers around a group of young upper-class female cousins of the elite. The plot revolves around the question of which of two cousins— Lin Daiyu or Xue Baochai—the young male hero, Jia Baoyu, will marry. The world of these well-educated and refined women is contrasted to the dull and corrupt world of the adult male. Baoyu's refusal to take his proper place in that dull and corrupt world leads his family into precipitous decline.

1791   Marie Lee Fights Off Bandits. Bandits attempting to steal armaments intended for a Revenue Cutter Service (precursor to the U.S. Coast Guard) ship are thwarted by Marie Lee, a shipping company employee.

1791   Birth of Japanese Artist Otagaki Rengetsu. Otagaki Rengetsu (1791–1875), a Japanese poet, calligrapher, potter, and painter, is born. Her poetry is known for the use of imagery drawn from everyday life.

DECEMBER 4, 1791   Birth of Jane Franklin, Founder of Scientific Institutions in Australia. Lady Jane Griffin Franklin (1791–1875), who establishes scientific institutions in Australia, is born. She marries John Franklin in 1828, and in 1836 he is appointed Lieutenant-Governor of Van Diemen's Land (Tasmania), Australia. Soon after their arrival, Jane fosters scientific knowledge by establishing (in her husband's name) the first Royal Society for the Advancement of Science outside Britain. In 1839 she finances the creation of the Hobart Botanical Gardens and Museum of Natural History. In the same year

she establishes the agricultural settlement of Willingham. Her other notable achievement is the founding of a public college, Christ's, in 1840. Franklin is far too forceful to be popular and attacks from the colonial press force her to abandon her scheme to set up a Tasmanian Society for the Reformation of Female Prisoners. The press also strongly disapproves of her involvement in the political squabbles of the colony and the growing tendency of prominent colonials to use her as a conduit to the Lieutenant-Governor. She invests her surplus energy in travel. She is the first woman to achieve a variety of physical feats, including climbing Mount Wellington, and travelling overland from Melbourne to Sydney and from Hobart to Macquarie Harbour. After her husband's recall in 1843, she travels internationally until her death, in England, in 1875.

1792   Théroigne de Méricourt, Radical Political Activist during the French Revolution. Théroigne Anne Josephe de Méricourt (1762–1817) is a radical political activist nicknamed the "Amazon of Liberty" during the French Revolution. A singer by profession, she is a member of the Fraternal Society of Patriots of Both Sexes during the early stages of the Revolution. She participates in the Women's March in October 1789, and in 1790 she is part of a short-lived society called *Amis de la loi*, which is dedicated to teaching the people their rights. In 1790 she goes to Belgium, where she is arrested for inciting revolution and put in an Austrian prison. After her release in 1791, she returns to Paris and is greeted with honor and acclaim. She tries unsuccessfully to found a women's society and later becomes an ardent advocate of an armed female battalion. In a speech before the *Societé fraternelle,* she asks for a women's battalion, "a company of Amazons," but she fails to attract middle-class women to this cause. On August 10, 1792, she takes part in the attack on the Tuileries. Once honored for her heroism, by 1792 she is denounced by the

Mary Wollstonecraft

Jacobins, who call her a "She-devil in ruffles." In 1793, she sides with the Girondins in their split with the Jacobins, and is then flogged nearly to death. She goes insane and dies in a French asylum in 1817. The Jacobins' treatment of de Méricourt is typical of the backlash against women by the end of the Revolution. By 1792 women are barred from organizing clubs and protesting in public.

1792   Mary Wollstonecraft Publishes *Vindication of the Rights of Woman*. Mary Wollstonecraft (1759–1797), English author and intellectual, publishes *Vindication of the Rights of Woman*, considered the most important of the feminist works of the late eighteenth century.

Born in 1759, Wollstonecraft witnesses the abuse of her mother by an alcoholic father, who squanders what little money the family

had. At first she earns a living at sewing and teaching, two of the occupations open to young women. She makes her way as a writer and translator, and marries William Godwin in 1797. Wollstonecraft is ostracized for her radical ideas, and dies after giving birth to their daughter, Mary Wollstonecraft Godwin (later Shelley). Mary Shelley becomes famous as the author of *Frankenstein.*

1793   Death of South Carolina Agriculturist Elizabeth Lucas Pinckney. Prominent South Carolina plantation manager Eliza Lucas Pinckney (1722–1793) was also the mother of two sons who both signed the Declaration of Independence, and a prominent citizen of South Carolina. President George Washington served as a pallbearer at her funeral.

JANUARY 3, 1793   Birth of Suffragist Lucretia Coffin Mott. Prominent Quaker minister and women's rights leader Lucretia Coffin (1793–1880) is born in Nantucket, Massachusetts. Around 1811 she marries James Mott, Philadelphia abolitionist, and devotes her life to anti-slavery and women's rights causes. With Elizabeth Cady Stanton (1815–1902) she calls the first women's rights convention in Seneca Falls, New York, in 1848. Mott gives the opening and closing addresses at the convention. She dies November 11, 1880.

FEBRUARY 1, 1793   Society of Revolutionary Republican Women Founded in Paris. A group of patriotic working class women led by Claire Lacombe and Pauline Léon form the Society of Revolutionary Republican Women in Paris. The group meets at the library of the radical Jacobin Club and has as its stated objective, "deliberation on the means of frustrating the projects of the Republic's enemies." In reality, the society focuses on pushing for a more radical, egalitarian revolutionary government. Its specific demands are for the arrest and execution of all enemies of the Republic, price controls on foodstuffs, and government regulation of the supply of consumer goods. In short, the

Lucretia Coffin Mott

women of the society reject the idea of a free-market economy and of political leniency. The group helps the Jacobins overthrow their political enemies in June 1793, and in September the women pressure the government into complying with their demands. The government passes a law requiring all women to wear the revolutionary tricolor cocade to show their loyalty. However, once the Jacobins feel secure in power, they turn on the more radical elements in the revolution that champion the rights of common people. As part of this purge, the government bans all women's political clubs on October 30, 1793. Over the next week, many prominent female revolutionaries are arrested and executed, including the leadership of the Society of Revolutionary Republican Women.

APRIL 30, 1793   French Government Authorizes Women in Army Only as Cantinières. The French government bans women from traveling with or serving in the French army, except for women termed "absolutely necessary." These "necessary" women are cantinières. They are married to soldiers in the unit and often wear a uniform, but they receive no pay. They earn their living by selling food and drink (usually alcohol) to the soldiers. They carry their wares on a wagon or pack animal and wear a characteristic brandy barrel on a shoulder strap. They go into battle with their units, and many are killed, wounded, or captured, and several are cited for bravery. In 1906, the army forbids women to serve as cantinières, claiming they are a bad moral influence.

JULY 1, 1793   Charlotte Corday Assassinates Jacobin Leader Jean Paul Marat. Charlotte Corday (1768–1793), a sympathizer of the Girondist movement in France, fatally stabs the opposing Jacobin leader, Jean Paul Marat. After King Louis XVI and Marie Antoinette are guillotined, the revolution in France becomes more radical. On one side are the extreme leaders Maximilien Robespierre, Georges Jacques Danton, and Jean Paul Marat, known collectively as the Mountain because they are seated on high benches at the rear of the National Convention. As the Mountain, these three wield the power in the Jacobin Club. In opposition to the Jacobins are the Girondists, who take their name from the government department of their leaders. In June 1793, the National Convention in France expels and arrests many Girondists. In response, the Girondists stage further rebellions. Although the Girondists are eventually defeated in the Convention, a sympathizer, Charlotte Corday, fatally stabs Jean Paul Marat while he bathes. This assassination inspires many works of art—paintings, poetry, and songs. It is said that Charlotte Corday, born Marie Anne Charlotte Corday D'Armont, plans to assassinate either Robespierre or Marat, but her opportunity comes when she is granted a meeting with Marat while he is in the bath. Corday is immediately apprehended. She is executed four days later.

OCTOBER 16, 1793   Queen Marie Antoinette Guillotined in France. Marie Antoinette (1755–1793), queen of France since 1774, is executed. In the midst of the French Revolution (1789–99), it becomes clear that the French monarch will fall. On the night of June 20, 1791, King Louis XVI and Marie Antoinette attempt to flee the country, but are recognized and captured. The king is executed at the guillotine on January 21, 1793. Marie Antoinette remains a prisoner until October 16, 1793, when she goes to the guillotine as well. She dies with a grace and simple dignity that wins over many of her former enemies, but she remains a notorious and unpopular figure in French history.

NOVEMBER 3, 1793   French Feminist Olympe de Gouges Executed for Treason. Olympe de Gouges (1748–1793) is guillotined in France for treason. In 1789 she publishes *The Declaration of the Rights of Woman and Citizen* in response to the French Revolution's *Declaration of the Rights of Man and of the Citizen*. She is arrested during the general crackdown on feminists in 1793.

1794   French King's Mistress, Madame du Barry, Is Guillotined. Madame du Barry (1743–1794) is executed by guillotine during the Reign of Terror. In 1768, she becomes the official mistress of King Louis XV following the death of Madame du Pompadour. The tribunal of the French Revolution finds her guilty of wasting the treasures of the state and orders her execution.

1797   Birth of Eugénie Niboyet, Early Supporter of Female Suffrage. Eugénie Niboyet (1797–1893), a leading advocate of women's right to vote, is born in Paris. She marries and becomes active in the Society of Christian Morals. In 1830 she converts to Saint-Simonism, also converting her husband and her

son, Paulin. Niboyet rises in the Saint-Simonian hierarchy, but when Prosper Enfantin begins preaching sexual liberation, she leaves the movement in protest. She soon becomes associated with the followers of Charles Fourier, successfully arguing for a policy of sexual restraint. She becomes a friend of Flora Tristan and associates with the feminist republican newspaper *The Women's Gazette* in 1836-38. In 1847 she publishes *Women's Voice*, a newspaper calling for women's suffrage. In June the government closes down the paper and Niboyet flees to Switzerland. She follows the feminist debate in writing, but takes no active part in it until 1878, when she attends the International Congress of Women's Rights in Paris. She dies in 1893.

1797   Elizabeth Ann Seton Founds the Society for the Relief of Poor Widows with Small Children. Elizabeth Ann Bayley Seton (1774–1821) founds the Society for the Relief of Poor Widows with Small Children. She later converts to Catholicism and becomes, in 1975, the first native-born U.S. citizen to be made a saint.

1798   Kementyna Tonska Hoffmanowa, Advocate of Polish Language and Literature, Is Born. Kementyna Tonska Hoffmanowa (1798–1845), who struggles to preserve Polish language and literature, is born in Warsaw, Poland, then within the Russian Empire. She begins activities to preserve the Polish language and literature in the face of efforts by the Russian rulers to wipe them out. Writing numerous children's works in Polish, she takes great interest in the development of Polish schools. In 1829, she marries the noted historian and patriot Karol Hoffman. Subsequently, Kementyna Tonska Hoffmanowa and her husband have to flee from Russian persecution in their native land and settle in Paris. A collection of her works in 15 volumes goes through many Polish editions.

Part 4

WINNING THE RIGHT TO EDUCATION & THE VOTE 1800 – 1929

1 8 0 0 – 1 8 0 4

1800 **Caroline Milhaud, Prominent French Feminist and Scientist.** Caroline Milhaud is a pioneer feminist and scientist of nineteenth-century France. She believes that modern social sciences can correct social ills and eliminate class conflict. Milhaud supports the theory of positivism, which promotes the study of society in order to discover "positive" social laws. A member of the middle class, she conducts interviews with working women to understand their lives and seek scientific solutions to their dilemmas. Like other positivist reformers, she tries to repair the separation that has developed among women of different classes.

1800 **Anna Josepha King Founds Australia's First Female Orphanage.** Anna Josepha Coombe King (1765–1844) establishes and operates Australia's first female orphanage. A woman of fairly humble birth, she sets sail from England for Norfolk Island (Australia) a few days after her marriage to the penal colony's superintendent, Philip Gidley King, in 1791. The family goes to England in 1796 but returns three years later when Philip King is appointed Governor of New South Wales. In her time as Governor's Lady, Anna Josepha King plays a very strong role in the governance of the colony, acquiring the hostile nickname "Queen Josepha." She also works independently for Sydney charities, in particular the Female Orphan School, which is founded, at her instigation, in 1800. She controls both the internal daily operation of what becomes known locally as "Mrs. King's Orphan School" and its broader management. Its account books and even its daily shopping lists are in her handwriting.

1800 **Chinese Scholar Wang Zhaoyuan Annotates Famous Ancient Text.** Wang Zhaoyuan (1763–1851) produces annotated editions of the Han dynasty scholar Liu Xiang's *Biographies of Virtuous Women*. Wang Zhaoyuan is a scholar who participates in the school of evidential scholarship (*Kaozheng*), which flourishes in China in the eighteenth century. One of the primary goals of this school is the study of ancient texts.

1800 **Sweet Betsy from Pike Represents American Pioneer Women.** One of the most popular songs to come out of the California Gold Rush, "Sweet Betsy from Pike," tells of a character named Sweet Betsy from Pike County, Missouri, who travels by covered wagon across the prairies and mountains to California. Surviving cholera epidemics, raids by Native American tribes, snowstorms, and the alkali water of the deserts, Sweet Betsy exemplifies all the pioneering women of the early nineteenth century who venture into the frontier and thrive there.

1800 Egyptologists Regard Ancient Egypt's God Neter as Male. Egyptologists persistently refer to the supreme being of ancient Egypt, known as Neter (or Nu), as a male god, despite much evidence that she was in fact worshipped as a goddess. Nineteenth-century French Egyptologist Auguste Mariette, who achieves the Egyptian ranks of Bey and Pasha (courtesy titles of authority and respect), ignores the clear indications that Neter is female and writes instead of the one male "God." The tradition of regarding Neter as male continues for nearly a century after Mariette, coming into question only in the latter half of the twentieth century.

1800 Hindu Saint Ramakrishna Revives Worship of Kali. Kali, known to most Westerners only in her Destroyer aspect, is one of the principal deities of the Hindu pantheon. An aspect of Devi (as are all Hindu goddesses and gods, in one sense), Kali is the Mother Goddess who both gives and takes away life. Kali is considered the source from which all life flows, and also the one who takes all life back into herself to then be reborn. In the Hindu religion, existence is seen as a spiraling cycle including life, death, and rebirth, and as the goddess of all three, Kali best represents this belief. Kali is also believed to have created Sanskrit, the first written language. In the nineteenth century, the Hindu saint Ramakrishna has a mystical experience wherein Kali reveals herself to him, and after this experience he revives the worship of Kali with his teachings.

SEPTEMBER 6, 1800 Birth of Catharine Beecher, Promoter of the Teaching Profession in America. Catharine Beecher (1800–1878), who devotes herself to the improvement of women's lives and the promotion of the teaching profession, is born in New York. She is insistent that education is "a true profession for women," as important as their responsibilities in the home as mothers. She encourages and trains young American women to go as teachers into the newly settled parts of the country. She also writes influential books, including *Treatise on Domestic Economy* (1843) and *Letters to the People on Health and Happiness* (1855). She does not support women's suffrage, which she does not believe will solve women's problems. Rather, she urges women to work toward economic independence and to work together to demand that women's unpaid work in the home be given the same respect as men's paid labor.

1801 Convict Margaret Catchpole Transported to Australia. After a daring escape from an English jail in 1800, Margaret Catchpole (1762–1819) is recaptured and sentenced to Australia for life, arriving in the colony of New South Wales at the end of 1801. Convicted of stealing a horse for her lover, a notorious smuggler, Catchpole is assigned as a servant to a series of prominent families in and around Sydney. Although she is pardoned for her crime in England in January 1814, she chooses not to return to England. As a free woman she accumulates some modest property comprising a parcel of land, some livestock, and a retail store. She declines to marry the man who "kept me company"; an unusual decision for the time and place, but one that safeguards her hard-won independence. (Under eighteenth-century British law, a woman's property reverts to her husband upon marriage.)

1801 Statue of Demeter Moved to Museum in England, Causing Riot. Two Englishmen, Clark and Cripps, cause a riot in Eleusis, Greece, when they take the image of the goddess Demeter away and put the statue into a museum in Cambridge, England. Demeter is the goddess of the cornfield and fertility in both plants and humans.

FEBRUARY 11, 1802 Lydia Maria Child, American Author and Abolitionist, Is Born. Lydia Maria Francis Child (1802–1880), American abolitionist and writer for children,

Lydia Maria Francis Child

is born in Medford, Massachusetts. Her first novel, *Hobomok,* is published in 1824. From 1826, she serves as editor of *Juvenile Miscellany,* one of the first magazines for children in America and the forerunner of *Harper's Young People.* In 1828, she marries David Lee Child. Her abolitionist work includes *An Appeal in Faovr of That Class of Americas Called Africans* (1833); she also edits, with her husband, *National Anti-Slavery Standard* from 1841 to 1849. Her anti-slavery position causes both her career and her social position to suffer; she is ostracized, and her books are returned to the publisher.

1803   Flora Tristan, French Socialist Thinker and Author, Is Born. Flora Tristan (1803–1844) is born to a wealthy Peruvian father and a French mother. The French government seizes her father's wealth as alien property upon his death and refuses to recognize his

marriage to his wife, declaring Tristan to be illegitimate. At age 18 she begins working in a print shop and soon marries the owner, André Chazal, largely to escape poverty. They have three children, but in 1825 Tristan leaves Chazal to escape his abuse. She travels to England as a "ladies' companion," and to Peru to restore her connections to her father's family. She writes a book about her travels, *Peregrinations of a Pariah* (1838), and also uses this background as a basis for her novel, *Méphis* (1838).

Tristan returns to Paris in 1835 to try to regain custody of her children. After Chazal sexually abuses their eldest daughter, Tristan wins a court custody case in 1837. In 1838, however, Chazal shoots Tristan in the back while she walks on a Paris street. Although the crime is clearly premeditated, an all-male jury acquits him because Tristan has publicly embarrassed him with her writings. Tristan recovers, though doctors are unable to remove the bullet, and it causes her constant pain and health problems. She becomes involved with organized feminist and socialist groups, petitioning the government to legalize divorce and to abolish capital punishment.

In 1844 while on a public speaking tour of France, Tristan falls ill and dies, still plagued by her husband's bullet.

1804   Napoleonic Code Enshrines Female Inequality in French Law. The Napoleonic Code is finished at the bidding of Napoleon I, enshrining female inequality in French law for more than a century. It removes the few gains women make during the French Revolution and makes women legally subordinate to men. It allows divorce under limited circumstances, but clearly favors husbands over wives. Under the code, a woman owes obedience to her husband, and is legally required to live with him unless he brings his mistress to live in their household. A woman who leaves her husband can be forcibly returned by the police. Women cannot vote, sit on juries, serve as legal witnesses, or sit on chambers of commerce or boards of trade. The code reflects both Napoleon's own misogyny and the prevailing male attitudes toward women. After Napoleon's final downfall in 1815, the restored French king Louis XVIII outlaws divorce entirely, and keeps the anti-woman aspects of the code in place.

JULY 10, 1804 Birth of Emma Smith, Active in Mormon Church. Emma Hale Smith (1804–1879), an early convert to the Church of Jesus Christ of Latter Day Saints (Mormonism) as defined by her husband, Joseph Smith, is born. With her husband, she survives persecution and helps the church to grow for 17 years. One of her tasks is to edit the first hymnal for the group. With other Mormon women, she creates the social welfare arm of the church—the Relief Society—which is still active today. After Joseph Smith's death, she rejects claims of the church to his property and his revelation on plural marriage. She remains in Nauvoo, Indiana, with her five children, and remarries (to Lewis Bidamon). In 1860, she helps to found the Reorganized Church of Jesus Christ of Latter Day Saints.

JULY 18, 1804 Elizabeth Gould, English Artist of Australian Fauna, Is Born. Artist and naturalist Elizabeth Coxen Gould (1804-1841) is born. Educated in England, she is a knowledgeable zoologist and ornithologist, competent linguist, talented musician, and gifted pictorial artist. After working briefly as a governess in London, she marries the poorly educated taxidermist John Gould in 1828. Three years later John Gould publishes *A Century of Birds from the Himalayan Mountains,* whose most notable feature is 80 color plates painted by Elizabeth Gould. Between 1832 and 1837 he publishes the five-volume *The Birds of Europe,* again illustrated by his wife. The couple travels to New South Wales, Australia, in 1838, leaving the three youngest of their four children in England. When they arrive in Hobart (Tasmania), a fifth child is

born. To further John's ornithological career, they begin to travel around rural New South Wales. Each time they stop, Elizabeth is left in camp while John goes out and shoots native birds and mammals. He then takes the carcasses to Elizabeth, who paints and describes them. Her surviving letters reveal the anguish of her separation from her children and her exhaustion from producing some 600 illustrations under extremely primitive conditions. In 1840 they return to England, where she dies the following year at the age of 37 while giving birth to her sixth child. Her two Australian books, *The Birds of Australia* and *The Mammals of Australia,* both originally published in London, are highly valued as magnificent examples of illustrative art. Their authorship is still attributed solely to John Gould.

SEPTEMBER 1, 1804 French Author George Sand Is Born. George Sand (1804–1876), the pen name for Amandine Aurore Lucie Dupin Dudevant, is born in Paris. She grows up in the small French village of Nohant. Her father serves under Napoleon, but her mother is a low-born, poorly educated working woman. This combination of backgrounds produces a rebellious heiress and writer. Well-educated and intelligent, she marries the Baron Dudevant. In 1831, she leaves her tyrannical and brutish husband to live an independent life with her two children in Paris.

Her first novel, *Indiana,* appears in 1832. It deals with the plight of a woman trapped in a loveless marriage. In her novels, Sand creates heroines who seek love, assert their rights to sexual happiness, and often fail to find this happiness with men.

She also writes novels that deal with common people. For example, *Francois the Waif* (1847) tells the story of a poor rural teen who raises an abandoned child and then marries him. She also addresses social problems such as poverty and class conflict in *Consuelo* (1842).

In her personal life Sand is known as a rebel who defies social convention. She prefers to dress in men's clothes, smokes cigars, and has several love affairs. While she flouts societal restrictions on women herself, she accepts those restrictions for most women. She argues for equal education for women, but denounces female suffrage. In 1848 when the feminist newspaper *Women's Voice* calls for her to run for office as the best-known woman in France, Sand turns the offer down with contempt, publicly insulting the paper and its editor.

Throughout the reign of Napoleon III, Sand gives financial aid to political exiles and stands in opposition to the regime. Even so, she is a favorite of the Empress Eugenie, who gives her protection and patronage. She stands for peace in 1870 and opposes the Paris Commune, favoring a moderate republican government. She dies in 1876 as one of France's greatest literary figures.

1 8 0 5 – 1 8 0 9

1805 **Birth of Jeanne Déroin, Advocate for Women's Suffrage in France.** Jeanne Déroin (1805-1894), a seamstress who later campaigns and writes for the emancipation of French women, is born in Paris. Although married and a mother, she uses her given name rather than that of her husband, Desroches. She explains to a court that she does not wish to implicate her husband, a civil servant, in her efforts to eliminate servitude for women. She is a socialist and briefly belongs to the utopian movement, the Saint-Simonians, during the 1830s. With Suzanne Voilquin and Desiree Gay, Déroin founds a women's newspaper, *La Femme Nouvelle* (*The New Woman*). They reject the Saint-Simonian idea of "free love" and insist instead on the greater importance of women's economic independence from men.

During the revolution of 1848 in Paris, Déroin writes for another women's newspa-per, *La Voix des Femmes* (*The Women's Voice*) and calls for women's formal participation in public affairs. In her 1849 periodical, *L'Opinion des Femmes* (*Women's Opinion*), she presents her vision of this participation: male privilege will end, women will vote, and women's moral superiority will triumph over male violence. This same year, she petitions the Democratic-Socialist party to become a candidate for the Legislative Assembly, an action that is declared unconstitutional. Also in 1849, she helps found a national federation of workers' associations that includes both male and female workers. The police suppress the associations in 1850, and Déroin is sentenced to six months in jail for "conspiracy to overthrow the government by violence." The French government declares women's memberships in political clubs illegal and regards publicly active women as "disorderly."

In 1852, Déroin flees to England along with other men and women who oppose the consolidation of Louis-Napoleon's grip on political power. She spends the rest of her life in London and remains committed to her dream of freedom, equality, and representation for women and the working class.

1805 **Birth of Pauline Roland, Leading French Feminist.** French feminist Pauline Roland (1805–1852) is born in Normandy. She learns of the teaching of the Saint-Simonians by reading their newspaper, and in 1833 she leaves her home in Falaise to join them in Paris. She is a regular contributor to the *Women's Tribune* in 1834. Although at first rejecting the Saint-Simonian theories of sexual liberation, she eventually decides to have children. Roland bears four children by two different lovers but takes full responsibility for their upbringing, giving them her last name. In 1847 she leaves her lover of 12 years, but he refuses to give her any of the community property.

During the Revolution of 1848, she writes a column for the journal *The Representative of the People*. By then she also repudiates her earlier beliefs on sexuality, writing instead that "marriage must be founded on fidelity." In 1850 she is attempting to form a group to work for female suffrage when she is arrested and charged with trying to overthrow the government. Her arrest order reads: "For many years she has been promulgating communist-socialist opinions. An unmarried mother, she is the enemy of marriage, maintaining that subjecting the woman to the control of the husband sanctifies inequality." She spends six months in jail, and during Louis-Napoleon's general arrests of subversives in December 1851 she is again arrested and deported to Algeria, where she dies of disease in 1852.

1805   **French Chemist Marie Lavoisier Publishes Memoirs of Chemistry.** French chemist Marie Lavoisier (1758-1836) writes and edits *Memoirs of Chemistry*, publishing it in her husband's name since female authors have a difficult time publishing. Marie and her husband, Antoine, both chemists, work together in this field throughout their marriage, collaborating on experiments. During the French Revolution, Antoine is arrested and executed for being a royal employee of Louis XVI, and Marie is imprisoned. It is after her release that she publishes *Memoirs of Chemistry*. Her work in chemistry provides a crucial building block for nineteenth-century advances in the field.

DECEMBER 30, 1805   **Birth of Marie d'Agoult, Great French Author Known As Daniel Stern.** Marie d'Agoult (1805–1876), one of France's greatest authors under the male pen name Daniel Stern, is born in Frankfort-am-Main as Marie de Flavigny. She is the daughter of wealthy exiled French nobility and receives a classical education as well as fencing lessons. In 1827 she marries the Count d'Agoult in an arranged marriage, and spends three years at the court of Charles X, where her husband has a position. When the 1830 Revolution topples the king, she and her husband retire to their country home. Marie d'Agoult separates from her husband in 1832, and in

Elizabeth Barrett Browning

1834 she begins a ten-year affair with composer Franz Liszt. In 1835 she becomes pregnant, and she and Liszt leave Paris together for Switzerland. They have three children together. During this period, Marie begins writing articles under the pen name Daniel Stern. In 1844 she leaves Liszt due to his numerous affairs with other women, turning to writing. As Daniel Stern, she publishes *Moral Sketches* in 1849, and *History of the Revolution of 1848* in three volumes from 1850 to 1853. In 1857, she publishes *Joan of Arc* and, in 1860, she co-writes an opera with Rossini, who praises her as a great pianist in her own right. During the 1860s, d'Agoult concentrates on writing poetry and publishing in Europe's leading literary journals. In addition to writing, she runs a prominent Parisian salon. She dies in 1876 in Paris.

1806 **Elizabeth Barrett Browning, Victorian Poet, Is Born.** Elizabeth Barrett Browning (1806–1861), one of the most well-known British poets of the Victorian era, is born in Durham, England. She is educated at home, and her strict father is proud of his daughter's accomplishments in classical Greek, Latin, and several modern languages. In 1819, he arranges for the printing of a long poem written by 13-year-old Elizabeth Barrett. In 1821 she injures her spine in a fall and by 1838 is a permanent invalid. She spends most of her time in a darkened room, where she writes poetry and love letters. The poet Robert Browning admires her *Poems* (1844) and begins a correspondence with Barrett. The two writers finally meet in 1845 and become engaged later that year. Although aged 40, Barrett fears her father's opposition to the marriage, and she and Browning wed in secret in 1846. The newlyweds then run off to Italy where Barrett Browning's health improves, but she never sees nor speaks to her father again.

　For the remainder of her life, Barrett Browning lives in the villa of Casa Guidi, overlooking Florence. She bears a son in 1849 and continues her writing. The Brownings also entertain many famous English and American artists and writers at their home. In 1850 Barrett Browning publishes *Sonnets from the Portuguese,* a sequence of 44 sonnets recording the growth of her love for Browning. He calls her "my little Portuguese" because of her dark complexion. The 43rd sonnet begins with the now-famous line, "How do I love thee? Let me count the ways." Barrett Browning also writes poems protesting unjust social conditions, such as "The Cry of the Children," about child labor in England, and she appeals for political freedom for Italy, which remains under Austrian rule until 1861.

1806 **French Writer Josephine de Gaulle Is Born.** Josephine de Gaulle (1806–1886), a successful French writer, is born. In her works,

Germaine de Staël

she holds up the domestic sphere as an ideal for women while also criticizing the marketplace and men.

1807 **Germaine de Staël Publishes First Major Work, *Corinne.*** Germaine de Staël (1766–1817), a leading figure in the French Romantic movement, publishes the first of her two major works, a novel, *Corinne.* Her second work, the nonfiction *On Germany,* is published in 1810. *Corinne* challenges societal values that force women to live in subservience to men. The Emperor Napoleon I (1769–1821) sees *Corinne* as a direct challenge to his anti-feminist Napoleonic Code, and he bans *On Germany.* However, de Staël's books are immensely popular, and they help found the movement of Romanticism in France. De Staël dies in Paris in 1817.

1807 **Suffrage in New Jersey Limited to "White Male Citizens."** The New Jersey legislature passes an act to limit suffrage to "white male citizens." Women in New Jersey are able to vote up until this legislation is enacted.

c. FEBRUARY 6, 1808 Revolutionary War Veteran Anna Maria Lane Granted Pension. Anna Maria Lane (?–1810) is granted a pension by the Virginia General Assembly. The only known female veteran of the Revolutionary War living in Virginia, Lane is granted $100 a year for life: two and one-half times the amount awarded to her husband, John. Lane performs "extraordinary military services" and receives a wound at the battle of Germantown (fought on October 4, 1777, six miles northwest of Philadelphia) that leaves her lame for life.

1810–1814

c. 1810 Désirée Veret, Advocate of Female Workers' Rights, Is Born. Désirée Veret (c.1810–1890), an early advocate of female workers' rights and suffrage, is born to poor parents in Paris, France. She becomes a Saint-Simonian and writes for the *Women's Tribune*, but she rebels against Prosper Enfantin's paternalism and leaves the Saint-Simonian movement in 1832. Instead, she turns increasingly to the ideas of Charles Fourier, who argues first and foremost for female emancipation. She fights for female suffrage in 1848–49, backing Jeanne Déroin's candidacy for office. She also becomes increasingly class conscious, claiming the rights of women workers. She organizes a union of seamstresses in 1848, but the government crushes the group and she flees to Belgium to avoid persecution. She dies in 1890.

AUGUST 8, 1810 Birth of Mary Gove Nichols, American Reformer for Women's Health. Mary Gove Nichols (1810–?),a reformer interested in women's health in all areas, including marriage, is born in New Hampshire. Nichols lectures and lives all over the United States and England, where she dies. As a young woman, Nichols has two interests: writing and health care. She teaches herself as much as she can from her brother's schoolbooks and later works and learns from the health reformer Sylvester Graham, whose ideas on diet greatly influence her own. She is one of the first women in America to give other women lectures on their bodies and their health. At the same time, she writes articles for medical journals and short stories for magazines and newspapers. Nichols is immediately attracted to hydropathy's ("water cure") promise of better health for women. She studies and practices hydropathy in New York, where she meets her second husband, the reformer Thomas Low Nichols, and Edgar Allen Poe, who admires her fiction. The Nicholses believe in "free love," defining it around two main ideas: women have a right to say "no" to sexual activity, even in marriage; and a woman has a right to choose when and with whom she has a child.

1811 Birth of Delia Bacon, Who Alleges Shakespeare Is a Fraud. Delia Bacon (1811–1859), who calls William Shakespeare "Will the Jester," is born. She devotes herself to proving that Shakespeare did not write the plays that are credited to him, basing this idea on the notion that the works of Shakespeare would have to have been written by someone knowledgeable about ancient history, law, and science. Bacon finds support from Ralph Waldo Emerson, who helps her get an article published in *Putnam's Monthly,* and Nathaniel Hawthorne. Her accusation lives on and continues to inspire scholars who either refute or support her notion.

JUNE 4, 1811 Harriet Beecher Stowe, Author of *Uncle Tom's Cabin,* Is Born. Harriet Beecher Stowe (1811–1896), best known for her first novel, the antislavery work *Uncle Tom's Cabin,* is born. After the success of *Uncle Tom's Cabin* in 1852, Stowe continues to write, focusing on the New England of her girlhood. Stowe is also involved in women's

Harriet Beecher Stowe

rights and in school reform. On the issue of slavery, she supports the colonization movement, not immediate emancipation; while she supports women's rights, she does not see suffrage as the most important battle for women to fight. None of her books after *Uncle Tom's Cabin* is as popular as that novel, but she continues to write novels exploring the society in which she lives. Among her works are *The Minister's Wooing* (1859); *The Pearl of Orr's Island* (1862); and *Oldtown Folks* (1869). Her later books include *Lady Byron Vindicated* (1870), in which she recounts Lady Byron's separation from her husband, poet Lord Byron.

c. 1812   Trugernanner, Tasmanian Aborigine, Is Born. Trugernanner, often called Truganini (c.1812-1876), considered the last full-blood Tasmanian Aborigine to survive European invasion, is born in southeast Van Die-

men's Land (Tasmania). In 1829, after her mother is killed by sailors, her uncle shot by a soldier, her sister abducted by sealers, and her prospective husband murdered by timber-getters, she and her father move to Bruny Island mission. There she acts as guide to the Protector of Aborigines, G.A. Robinson, and teaches him Aboriginal languages and customs. Robinson's records of this instruction provide the best surviving ethnographical record of traditional Tasmanian society. In 1835 Trugernanner is moved to Flinders Island where, with 100 other Aborigines, she is to be "christianised and Europeanised." The program is unsuccessful, and the mission's mortality rate is high. In 1839, she and 15 other Aborigines visit Port Phillip (Victoria) with Robinson. From there, with two men and two women companions, she joins a party of whalers near Portland Bay. Two years later the Aborigines are collectively charged with the murder of two of the Europeans. The two men are hanged and the three women sent back to Flinders Island. In 1847 Trugernanner manages to return to her own land and resume her traditional lifestyle. When she eventually moves to Hobart in 1874 she is the last surviving full-blood Tasmanian Aborigine. She dies in Hobart two years later and is buried at the old female penitentiary at midnight in an attempt to protect her remains from scientific collectors. Nevertheless, her body is exhumed in 1878 and is publicly displayed in the Tasmanian Museum from 1904 to 1951.

1813   Camilla Collett, Norwegian Author, Is Born. Camilla Collett (1813–1895), author of the first Norwegian realistic novel, is born in Kristiansand, Norway, the daughter of a clergyman. She is also a pioneer in Norway for women's rights. Her brother, Henrik Wergeland (1808–1845), is considered Norway's greatest poet.

JUNE 22, 1813   Laura Secord Provides Vital Information to British Army. Canadian Laura Secord (1775–?) overhears two American officers discussing military plans while they are dining at her house during the War of 1812. She immediately begins a 30-kilometer trek on foot from Queenston to Beaver Dams to warn the British officer, James Fitzgibbon, that the Americans are planning to attack his outpost. Two days later, the Americans are ambushed by Indians at Beaver Dams and 400 men surrender to Fitzgibbon. Although Secord is perceived by many as a heroine, she receives little recognition. In 1828, her husband is rewarded for her actions by a series of local offices. She is widowed and penniless in 1841 and teaches school in order to earn a living. Finally, at the age of 85, she receives a small reward from the Prince of Wales.

1814 **Emma Hart Willard Publishes "Plan for Improving Female Education."** American Educator Emma Hart Willard (1787–1870) publishes an *Address to the Public,* where she sets forth her "Plan for Improving Female Education." The governor of New York recommends the plan to the state legislature, and urges Willard to move her Wateford, Vermont, school for girls to New York State. She moves to Waterford, New York, where the legislature has created an institute dedicated to the improvement of female education. Willard founds the Troy Female Seminary in nearby Troy, New York, in 1821.

Elizabeth Cady Stanton

1 8 1 5 – 1 8 1 9

NOVEMBER 12, 1815 **Birth of Elizabeth Cady Stanton, American Reformer and Suffragist.** A reformer and suffragist, Elizabeth Cady Stanton (1815–1902) is born in Johnston, New York. When she marries Henry B. Stanton, an antislavery reformer, the word "obey" is eliminated from the ceremony. In 1840, Stanton begins working with Lucretia Coffin Mott (1793–1880) on the issue of suffrage for women. In 1848, Stanton is a key force in the passage of a New York state law guaranteeing property rights to married women. Also in

1848, Stanton and Mott, with Mary McClintock, Jane Hunt, and Martha Wright (1806–1875), organize the now-famous Women's Rights Convention at Seneca Falls, New York. Stanton's skills as a writer result in the *Declaration of Sentiments,* which comes out of the Women's Rights Convention. Stanton patterns the *Declaration of Sentiments* after the Declaration of Independence, stating that men *and women* are created equal, and demanding that women be permitted to vote. In 1851, Stanton begins a collaboration with Susan B. Anthony (1820–1906); the two publish a weekly newspaper, *The Revolution,* from 1858 to 1860, and, in 1869, create the National Women Suffrage Association, with Stanton as president. In 1888, Stanton and Anthony extend their efforts on behalf of suffrage for women, forming the International Council of Women. With Ida Harper, Matilda Gage, and Anthony, Stanton writes the first four volumes of the six-volume *A History of Woman Suffrage* (1881–1922).

1816 Sr. Mary-Magdalene Postel Establishes Sisters of the Christian Schools of Mercy. Sr. Mary-Magdalene Postel (1756–1846) founds the Sisters of the Christian Schools of Mercy, a religious education order, and serves as its director until her death in 1846 at age 90. At the age of 19, known then as Julie Postel, she opens a school for girls in Barfleur, Normandy, the center for underground religious activity in France. When the political and religious situation settles down, Julie continues her teaching and, at the age of 51, takes vows and becomes Sister Mary-Magdalene.

1816 Mary Reiby, Australia's First Highly Successful Businesswoman. Mary Haydock Reiby (1777–1855) is Australia's first highly successful businesswoman; she is worth about £20,000 and owns 1,000 acres of land. At age 13 and dressed as a boy, she is arrested in England for stealing a horse. Her female identity is revealed during the trial and she is sentenced to New South Wales, Australia, for seven years. She arrives in 1792 and works as an assigned servant for two years before marrying Thomas Reiby. The couple establish themselves as business developers despite exclusion from the trade cartel that controls colonial business. When Thomas dies in 1811, it becomes clear that Mary has been the driving force behind their success. While raising their seven children alone, she builds up her holdings until, by 1816, she is said to be worth about £20,000 and owns 1,000 acres of land. During the 1820s she is responsible for building a considerable number of elegant and substantial domestic and commercial properties in the heart of Sydney.

JANUARY 8, 1816 French Mathematician Sophie Germain Wins Prestigious Award. Although her parents disapprove, Sophie Germain (1776–1831) teaches herself science and mathematics—so well, in fact, that she wins the gold medal of the French Academy of Sciences. In 1794, the Ecole Centrale des Travaux Publique opens in Paris. Barred as a woman from attending lectures, Germain obtains lecture notes from another student. In 1804, she begins a correspondence with the eminent mathematician Carl Friedrich Gauss. By the beginning of the nineteenth century, mathematicians are turning to research on the vibration of elastic surfaces, and Napoleon orders the Academy of Sciences to hold an essay competition on the subject. Sophie Germain submits her entry on September 21, 1811, and it is rejected. In 1813, Germain's second essay receives an honorable mention. In 1816, her third essay exposes the laws of vibrating elastic surfaces by describing a fourth-order partial differential equation. Germain is awarded a gold medal, worth 3,000 francs, on January 8, 1816, but because she is a woman, she is denied membership in the French Academy of Sciences. Sophie Germain dies in 1831.

APRIL 21, 1816 Charlotte Brontë, British Author, Is Born. Charlotte Brontë (1816–1855), oldest of the noted Brontë sisters, is born in England. Charlotte is the third child born to the Reverend Patrick Brontë and his wife Maria Branwell. After Charlotte, the Brontës add a son and two more daughters, Emily Jane (1818–1848) and Anne (1819–1849) to their family. Their life is difficult, and two of the eldest children die while away at school. The three younger girls enjoy writing, and publish poetry under the pseudonyms of Currer, Ellis, and Acton Bell respectively. In October 1847, Charlotte, as Currer Bell, publishes her masterpiece, *Jane Eyre*. In December 1847, Emily publishes *Wuthering Heights* in a single volume with Anne's work, *Agnes Gray*. In 1848, Anne publishes *The Tenant of Wildfell Hall*. On December 19, 1848, Emily Brontë dies; Anne dies less than six months later on May 28, 1849. In her loneli-

Charlotte Brontë

ness, Charlotte completes *Shirley,* and publishes it in 1849. Her third work, *Villette,* is published in 1853, and she marries her father's curate, Mr. Arthur Bell Nicholls, in June 1854. Their married life is brief, however; Charlotte dies March 31, 1855.

1817   New South Wales Established as Wool-Producing Area by Elizabeth Macarthur. Elizabeth Macarthur (1767–1850) establishes New South Wales, Australia, as a wool-producing area. Macarthur leaves England for Botany Bay, Australia, with her husband, John Macarthur, in 1789. When her husband flees the country during a period of political unrest in 1809, she takes over the management of their property for eight years and becomes the first person to establish New South Wales as a wool-producing area. She develops an English market for Australian wool, and after her hus-

band's death in 1834, she passes on to her sons the wool empire she has started.

1818   Mary Shelley Writes Classic Novel *Frankenstein.* English author Mary Wollstonecraft Shelley (1797–1851) produces the novel *Frankenstein,* which is an immediate success and has since become a classic. Shelley claims the idea for the novel was derived from a dream following a discussion with the poet Percy Bysshe Shelley about ghost tales. This novel is Mary Shelley's vision of a world without women, a male-centered world of violence. Dr. Frankenstein symbolizes the egoist of the new industrialist age. He circumvents the natural role of the mother to create life—a monster. Shelley is the daughter of the feminist Mary Wollstonecraft and the philosopher William Godwin. At age 16 she runs off with the poet Percy Bysshe Shelley, who is already married. Pursued by scandal and debt, the lovers move frequently. The couple settles in Lerici, Italy, and although they claim they do not believe in marriage, they wed after Shelley's first wife dies in 1816. Like her mother, Mary Wollstonecraft, who wrote *Vindication of the Rights of Woman,* Mary Shelley criticizes male-dominated society. After Percy Shelley's death, Mary Shelley continues to write to support herself and her children and in 1835 writes her autobiographical novel, *Lodore.* Eventually, she returns to England where she dies in 1851.

1818   Birth of Biddy Mason, Former Slave Who Becomes Prominent Californian. African American slave Biddy Mason (1818–1891) is born. When Robert Smith and his family emigrate to California in 1851, his slaves Biddy Mason, her three daughters, Hannah (who may be Mason's sister), and Hannah's children go with them. In California the slaves encounter free blacks for the first time, including Robert Owens, a respected businessman in Los Angeles. When Smith attempts to move his slaves to Texas, a slave state, Mason turns to Owens for assistance.

Owens manages to convince the law to intervene, and on January 19, 1856, Mason's suit for freedom is heard before Judge Benjamin Hayes. Although blacks were prohibited from testifying against whites in California courts, Judge Hayes hears Mason's plea in his chambers and ultimately pronounces that she and all of her family are "entitled to their freedom and are free forever."

Mason becomes a midwife in Los Angeles, saves her money, and begins to purchase lots in the city. As her wealth grows, she becomes known as a friend to the poor. She is a founder of the First African Methodist Episcopal Church of Los Angeles. When she dies in 1891, the *Los Angeles Times* obituary praises her for her good works and notes that an "old settler of Los Angeles" has passed away. In 1991 a memorial to Biddy Mason is dedicated on the site of her original home in downtown Los Angeles.

1818   **Eliza O'Flaherty, Australian Author and Actress, Is Born.** Australian Eliza Winstanley O'Flaherty (1818–1882), the first Australian woman performer to succeed overseas, is born in England. She migrates to New South Wales, Australia, in 1833 and makes her first stage appearance there the following year. After some early experimentation, she specializes in tragic and dramatic roles, notably Juliet, Desdemona, Portia, and Lady Macbeth. She marries theater musician Henry Charles O'Flaherty in 1841, prior to a successful season in Hobart and Launceston. Returning to Sydney, Australia, the following year, she causes a scandal by appearing in the title role of *Richard III*. After her husband's death in 1854 she begins a new career as writer and editor under the name Mrs. Eliza Winstanley, though several of her novels—none notable—are serialized under the pen name Ariele. She finally abandons her acting career in 1864 to work as editor of the weekly *Fiction for Family Reading*. Her fame rests on her theatrical career as the first of

many woman performers who begin their careers in Australia and go on to succeed in Europe and America.

1818   **Birth of Maria Mitchell, American Astronomer.** Maria Mitchell (1818–1889), one of the first female astronomers in the United States, is born. In 1847, she becomes the first woman to have a comet named after her. While assisting her father, William Mitchell, in his observatory, Maria Mitchell helps make thousands of observations of meridian altitudes of stars for the determination of time and latitude, and of moon culminations and occultations for longitude. On the night of October 1, 1847, Maria Mitchell discovers an unknown comet; as a consequence, she gains worldwide fame and is awarded a gold medal by the King of Denmark. In 1848 Mitchell becomes the first, and until 1943, the only, woman elected to the Academy of Arts and Sciences in Boston, Massachusetts. Her later accomplishments include being appointed in 1849 as one of the original contributors computing data for the *American Ephemeris and Nautical Almanac,* a work that provides tables of data stating the exact locations of celestial bodies at specific points in time. In 1850, she is elected to the American Association for the Advancement of Science. When Matthew Vassar founds a women's college to rival the best men's college in the United States, Mitchell is offered a teaching position. She accepts, and Vassar builds her an observatory with a 12-inch telescope, the third largest in the country. She eventually becomes one of the best-known professors at Vassar College, refusing the conventional grading system and refusing to report students' absences. In 1873, she is the founder of the Association of the Advancement of Women, as well as vice-president of the American Social Science Association.

AUGUST 13, 1818   **Women's Rights Advocate Lucy Stone Is Born.** Lucy Stone (1818–1893), the first woman to receive a college degree in

Massachusetts, is born. She marries Harry Blackwell, brother of Elizabeth Blackwell, and keeps her own name as a protest of restrictive property laws for married women.

1819 **German Musician Clara Schumann Is Born.** Clara Schumann (1819–1896), a German composer and pianist, is born. She is the first person to edit the letters of her husband, Robert Schumann, the renowned composer. Her collection of correspondence between 1827 and 1840 appears in 1885. Clara Schumann is also the first woman, with the help of Johannes Brahms, to prepare a complete edition of Robert Schumann's works (1881-93). She puts aside her own promising career in music for the sake of her husband's career, and after his death in 1856, turns increasingly to teaching. She is appointed principal piano teacher, the first woman to hold this post, at the Hoch Conservatory in Frankfurt in 1878.

1820 – 1824

C. 1820 Birth of American Activist and Leader Harriet Tubman. Harriet Tubman (c.1820–1913) is born into slavery in Corchester, Maryland. She escapes to Philadelphia, Pennsylvania, in 1849, and devotes herself to helping more than 300 slaves gain their freedom.

1820 Birth of Anna Sewell, Author of *Black Beauty*. Anna Sewell (1820–1878), English writer, is born. Sewell publishes only one work, *Black Beauty: Autobiography of a Horse* (1877), which is later made into a feature film.

FEBRUARY 15, 1820 Birth of Susan B. Anthony, American Social Reformer and Suffragist. Social reformer Susan Brownell Anthony (1820–1906) is born in Adams, Massachusetts. She is educated at Bartenville, New York, and at Friends' Boarding School in West Philadelphia, Pennsylvania. Early in her career, between the ages of 15 to 30, she works as a teacher. The young Anthony is a liberal Quaker, becoming active in the antislavery and temperance movements. Strongly opposed to the use of alcohol, Anthony founds the first temperance organization in the United States—Women's Temperance Society—in 1852. From 1856 to 1861, she rallies support for the antislavery movement through the Anti-Slavery Society. With Elizabeth Cady

Susan Brownell Anthony

Stanton, Anthony publishes a weekly newspaper, *The Revolution*, with the motto: "The true republic—men, their rights and nothing more; women, their rights and nothing less." During the Civil War (1861–65), Anthony serves as both the organizer and secretary of the Women's National Loyal League, an organization dedicated to freeing slaves.

Convinced that social reforms will not happen until women can vote, Anthony and Elizabeth Cady Stanton turn their efforts to the cause of women's suffrage, founding the National Woman Suffrage Association (NWSA) in 1869 to push for an amendment to the U.S. Constitution. In 1872, Anthony attempts to cast a vote in New York State in the presidential election. She is arrested and fined $100, which she refuses to pay. In 1878, when Senator A. A. Sargent introduces an amendment to the U.S. Constitution that will extend suffrage to women, it becomes known as the "Susan B. Anthony Amendment." It will not be ratified until August 26, 1920.

In 1888, Anthony organizes the International Council of Women, with representatives from 48 countries; in 1904, she establishes the International Woman Suffrage Alliance in Berlin, Germany. She is known as a lecturer, as well as for writing a large part of four of the six volumes comprising the work entitled *History of Woman Suffrage*. She is elected to the American Hall of Fame in 1950. On July 29, 1979, the U.S. government issues a one-dollar Susan B. Anthony coin, making her the first U.S. woman to have her likeness on a coin in general circulation.

MAY 1821   American Educator Emma Hart Willard Founds Troy Female Seminary. Emma Hart Willard (1787–1870) founds Troy Female Seminary in Troy, New York. It is the first endowed school for girls in the United States.

1823   Birth of Mother Joseph. Esther Pariseau (1823–1902), who will become Mother Joseph, is born in Montréal, Québec. In 1856, she travels with four other nuns to the territory of Washington, where she spends nearly 50 years designing and building hospitals and schools. From Oregon to Alaska, Mother Joseph establishes more than 20 institutions open to people of all faiths. The American Institute of Architects labels her the "first architect of the Pacific Northwest." In 1977,

Mother Joseph, Statuary Hall, U.S. Capitol.

Mother Joseph is the first American nun to have her statue placed in the National Statuary Hall in the U.S. Capitol building in Washington, D.C.

C. 1824   Women Participate in Labor Strike Along with Men. In Pawtucket, Rhode Island, women workers participate in a strike (along with men) for the first time in recorded U.S. history. A total of 202 female workers strike in support of brother weavers protesting the simultaneous reduction of wages and the extension of the work day.

1824   Mississippi Supreme Court Allows Husbands to Beat Wives. The Supreme Court of Mississippi becomes the first state court to recognize a husband's right to beat his wife. Mississippi wants husbands to enforce "domestic discipline." Although in the late nineteenth century some states adopt anti-wife beating laws, no real enforcement policies exist. These laws are on the books, but criminal sanctions are rarely assessed.

In the colonial era, the legal system allows a husband to punish his wife as long as he beats her with a stick no thicker than his thumb. In the early 1800s, on the rare occasion when a man is finally brought to court for severely beating his wife, judges routinely dismiss the case. Until the Civil War, neither the government nor the courts try to stop domestic violence.

1 8 2 5 – 1 8 2 9

C. 1825   Women Go on Strike Alone, Without Men. Women workers participate in a strike alone (without men) for the first time in the United States when the United Tailoresses of New York City walk off their jobs. They form a union and demand an increase in wages.

1825   Utopian Socialist Saint-Simonians Argue for Women's Liberation. The utopian socialist group known as the Saint-Simonians, which follows the teachings of Claude Henri, the Count of Saint-Simon, considers women's liberation a central part of its program. However, by 1830 the group reorganizes as a religion, with a mystical young banker named Prosper Enfantin at its head. Enfantin argues for sexual liberation of women as a step toward total female liberation. He believes that the group will one day find "The Woman" who will save humanity and usher in a new era of peace and prosperity. Enfantin's radical views on sexuality alienate the public and many followers, while his refusal to accept women as political equals angers many female group members. His trial and imprisonment in 1832 essentially ends the Saint-Simonian religion. However, the group's initial writings draw a whole generation of French women into feminism, including Pauline Roland, Claire

Démar, Jeanne Déroin, and Suzanne Voilquin.

1825   Frances Wright Establishes Commune, Nashoba, for Emancipation of Slaves. Frances Wright (1795–1852) establishes the Tennessee commune, Nashoba, to promote the gradual emancipation of slaves. Wright is the daughter of an upper-class Scottish family who devotes her life to the cause of emancipation of slaves and the improvement of women's status. At age 30, she uses part of her inheritance to buy 320 acres of marshy swamp in western Tennessee, inspired by the Scottish industrialist and philanthropist Robert Owen, who establishes a commune, New Harmony, in Indiana. At Nashoba, Wright plans for a long-range emancipation that will allow slaves to work for five years, earn back their purchase price, and learn a trade to support themselves. The slaves will then be freed and colonized in some foreign place, such as California, Texas, or Haiti. Seven years earlier, in 1818, Wright had voyaged to the United States and published her favorable impressions of the country in her *Views and Manners in America* (1821).

Wright invites other free thinkers to visit Nashoba, and she becomes outspoken in her attacks on capitalism, organized religion, private property, and marriage. She also helps edit the weekly liberal newspaper, *Free Inquirer*, from 1828 to 1830 and lectures throughout the United States. She is one of the first women to speak in public to a large secular audience of both sexes and to argue that women must be granted an equal role in public life.

Critics condemn Wright as the "Red Harlot of Infidelity," but thousands gather wherever she speaks. In 1830, she closes Nashoba due to miserable climate conditions, disease-breeding mosquitoes, the discontent of the slaves, and financial problems. Nonetheless, Wright succeeds in freeing over 30 slaves. After closing Nashoba, she moves to Paris, marries, and has a daughter. Craving

Rebecca Webb Lukens

independence, Wright returns alone to the United States in 1835 and lives in relative obscurity until her death in 1852. Her daughter inherits Nashoba's land but rejects her mother's feminist and liberal beliefs.

1825   Rebecca Webb Lukens Becomes First Female Manager in American Iron Industry. Rebecca Webb Lukens (1794–1854), the daughter of the founder of the Brandywine Rolling Mill, becomes the first female manager in the American iron industry when she takes over this mill on the death of her husband. In 1890 the mill is renamed Lukens Mills, and she becomes the first woman to have a steel mill named after her.

SEPTEMBER 24, 1825   Birth of Frances E. W. Harper, African American Literary Figure, Abolitionist, and Feminist. Frances E. W. Harper (1825–1910), a prominent African American abolitionist, feminist, and author,

is born in Baltimore, Maryland. She publishes her short story, "The Two Offers," in *The Anglo-African Magazine,* making her perhaps the first African American to publish a short story anywhere. She also publishes books of poetry.

She marries Fenton Harper in 1860 and moves to Columbus, Ohio. For four years she is absent from the abolitionist movement because of her family obligations. After the death of her husband in 1864, she resumes her activities, becoming involved in the woman's suffrage movement and joining the American Woman Suffrage Association (AWSA).

In 1869, Frances Harper publishes her third and most renowned book, *Moses: A Story of the Nile.* As a result of her extensive traveling in the South as a lecturer for abolition and women's rights, Harper publishes her fifth book, *Sketches of Southern Life,* in 1872. In addition, Harper publishes three serialized novels, and in 1892, she becomes the first African American woman to publish a widely acclaimed novel, *Iola Leroy* or *Shadows Uplifted.* Harper dies in 1910 at the age of 85.

OCTOBER 31, 1825   Catherine Spence, "The Grand Old Woman of Australia," Is Born. Australian Catherine Helen Spence (1825–1910), an author, publicist, social worker, electoral reformer, and suffragist, is born in Scotland. She migrates with her family to Adelaide, South Australia, in 1839. By 1854, she publishes (anonymously) *Clara Morison,* the first novel about Australia written by a woman. She writes eight works of fiction before discarding the genre in 1889. All of her novels are strongly feminist and one of them, *Handfasted,* is considered as "calculated to loosen the marriage tie...too socialistic" for publication until the late twentieth century. From the early 1870s Spence channels her massive energies into aid for destitute and delinquent children and the education of girls. She is the author of the first social studies text used in Australian schools. She is also a strong proponent of electoral reform, advocating a modified version of Thomas Hare's system of proportional representation (the "Hare-Spence system") to provide minority groups with parliamentary representation. Spence is a Unitarian preacher, a speaker of note, and a prodigious source of newspaper and journal articles. In 1893-94 Spence lectures extensively in the United States and Europe. From the early 1890s she espouses the cause of womanhood suffrage. She is vice-president of the Women's Suffrage League of South Australia when women obtain the vote there in 1894. She then turns her attention to suffrage in other colonies and, in 1897, becomes Australia's first woman political candidate when, at the age of 72, she unsuccessfully contests a position on the Federal Convention. When Catherine Spence dies in 1910, she is mourned as "The Grand Old Woman of Australia."

MAY 5, 1826 Birth of Eugenie de Montijo, Empress of France. Eugenie Marie de Montijo (1826–1920), who becomes empress of France, is born in Granada, Spain. She is descended from Spanish and Scottish nobility and is educated in France, Spain, and England. Her mother, the Countess of Montijo, leads a life of scandalous promiscuity until she is forced to leave Spain in 1849, but Eugenie is very chaste and fervently religious. Eugenie and her mother spend much time at their Parisian townhouse, where they meet the Emperor Napoleon III. Eugenie marries Napoleon III in 1853, soon after the Second Empire of France is proclaimed.

As empress, Eugenie gains international attention and praise and represents the height of womanhood at mid-century. Dressed in hoops, crinolines, and silks, she sets fashion around the world and helps the French silk industry. She also is respected by many feminists for her motherly behavior and fortitude in the face of her husband's many marital infidelities. She serves as a symbol of motherhood in her constant attention to her only child. She always has her son at her side in her portraits, and the whole family sometimes poses together. A devout Catholic, she is pious and charitable, visiting orphanages and sponsoring hundreds of philanthropic societies around the country.

Eugenie believes in the right to education for women and sponsors advanced courses taught by university professors. She presides at Ministerial Councils in her husband's absence, and in 1866 she advances a decree that states, "Women are authorized to take the examinations of the facultes." This guarantees that women cannot be turned down by reason of their sex at any university in France. She then sends her own nieces to attend university courses.

The empress is criticized for her extravagance and for her attempts to delay a more liberal government in France. She urges a warlike policy on the eve of the Franco-Prussian War. After Napoleon III's fall in 1870, the two go into exile. Following the emperor's death in 1873, Eugenie lives in England for a time, then returns to Madrid, where she dies in 1920.

MAY 23, 1826 Frances Fuller Victor, Who Helps to Define the American West, Is Born. Victor (1826–?), an American writer and historian, is born. Like her younger sister, Meta Fuller, Frances Fuller Victor supports herself as a writer from her early teens, and she helps to define historical accounts of the American West. She writes dime novels and contributes to magazines, but her most important contribution may be as the only woman on the staff of *Bancroft's History of the Pacific States* series.

1828 Birth of Maria Deraismes, Leading Figure of French Republican Feminism. Maria Deraismes (1828-1894), a leading French feminist in the nineteenth century, is born in Pontoise, France. Her liberal republican father gives her a boy's education in philosophy, law, political economy, and languages as well as the fine arts. By 1861 her parents die, leaving her an independent and wealthy heiress. She contributes to Léon Richer's newspaper *Women's Rights* and gives public speeches on women's rights during the 1860s. She is a founding member of the Association for the Rights of Women, and after its forced dissolution becomes involved in electoral politics, publishing her own political newspaper and backing candidates for office with her money and writing. In 1882 she becomes the first woman freemason, eventually founding her own lodge. She also leads a campaign for female suffrage and speaks out against scientific testing on animals. She dies in 1894.

1828 **First All-Woman Strike by U.S. Textile Mill Workers.** Dover, New Hampshire, is the site of the first recorded strike by textile mill women in the United States. Several hundred women denounce company fines for tardiness and for talking on the job, among other rules, including required church attendance and the threat of blacklisting for the failure to give two weeks notice before quitting. The strike makes newspapers from the North to the South. Some poke fun at the women for objecting to the ban on talking. The employers advertise for better-behaved women to apply for work. In the end, the strike is lost and the strikers gain nothing.

JULY 27, 1828 **Ranavalona I of Madagascar Launches Coup d'Etat, Unleashing Mass Genocide.** Upon the death of her pro-European husband, King Radama, Ranavalona of Madagascar launches a coup d'etat in which all of the king's relatives are murdered. To secure her hold on the throne, Ranavalona declares herself to be a man. Ranavalona's policies contrast markedly with those of her husband. In November 1828, she repudiates the Anglo-Malagasy Friendship Treaty. In addition, slavery is reintroduced as a social and economic feature of Malagasy life. Ranavalona seeks to conquer the Sakalava tribe. This forces the Sakalava to look for assistance. In August 1829, a French military expedition defeats

Ranavalona's forces, an experience that leaves the queen bitter. On September 23, 1829, she gives birth to a son, Rakoto, who becomes heir apparent; his father is one of Ranavalona's generals. On June 18, 1835, Ranavalona I expels all foreign missionaries, and the persecution of Malagasy Christians begins. Many are enslaved, boiled alive, dismembered, or poisoned as mass genocide spreads across the island. Other victims include the queen's political opponents. In 1845 all Europeans are enslaved, and in 1857, they are expelled. Ranavalona I dies in 1861, and Rakoto ascends the throne. He ends the genocide, which has claimed one million of the island's two million inhabitants as victims.

C. 1829 **Salome Lincoln Leads Textile Workers in Strike.** Sixty young New England textile workers walk out of their mill in Taunton, Massachusetts, to protest a wage cut. Salome Lincoln, a young country preacher, is chosen as their leader. Lincoln, a weaver at 15 and a preacher at 20, finances her preaching activities by her mill work. The strikers meet in a hall near the village green and Lincoln urges them to vow to not return to work until the pay cut is rescinded. However, the strike is lost, as one by one, the strikers return to work. Everyone returns except Lincoln.

1 8 3 0 – 1 8 3 4

1830 **Harriet Taylor and John Stuart Mill Work Together for Women's Emancipation.** Harriet Hardy Taylor (1807–1858) begins her association with the English reformer and philosopher John Stuart Mill (1806–1873) to work toward the emancipation of women. Harriet Hardy is the daughter of a domineering surgeon. At age 18, Harriet marries John Taylor, a manufacturer and Unitarian Radical 11 years her senior. The couple has three children, including one daughter, Helen, who later becomes an outspoken feminist. In 1830, Harriet Taylor meets John Stuart Mill. The

Godey's Lady's Book, the first women's magazine in the United States, features fashion plates, essays, and fiction.

intense emotional and intellectual bond that develops between them quickly becomes central to both their lives. Honoring her duty to her husband and children, as well as her attachment to Mill, Harriet works out a suitable agreement; she functions as John Taylor's wife to outward appearances but meets with Mill for private dinners in her home and joins him for occasional trips to the seaside. (Their relationship is platonic.)

After 20 years of this unconventional triangle, John Taylor dies. Two years later, in April 1851, Harriet marries Mill. On the eve of their marriage, Mill writes an essay entitled "A Renunciation of the Rights of Husbands." In this piece, he vows to reject the patriarchal rights that the law gives a husband over the person and property of his wife. When Harriet dies in Avignon, France, in 1858, Mill buys a

cottage close to her burial site and makes daily pilgrimages to her grave. He credits Harriet with inspiring his commitment to feminism and suffrage. He dedicates his most important work, *On Liberty,* to her. In 1869, he writes *The Subjection of Women* at the request of Harriet's daughter, Helen. Many of the book's ideas appear in Harriet's shorter 1851 article, "Enfranchisement of Women," written anonymously as a response to the birth of the American suffrage movement. Mill's own text on the need for sex equality is praised by feminists as their definitive manifesto. Mill is the first member of Parliament to propose a bill granting women the right to vote, in 1867. He loses his bid for reelection the following year due to his outspoken feminism.

1830 *Godey's Lady's Book* **Begins Publication.** Sarah Josepha Hale (1788–1879) is editor of

Godey's Lady's Book, the first women's magazine in the United States. Founded by Louis Antoine Godey (1804–1878), the magazine features fashion plates and essays and stories by many of the noted writers of the time, including Ralph Waldo Emerson, Henry Longfellow, Edgar Allen Poe, and Nathaniel Hawthorne. Hale, a writer herself, is the author of the children's poem, "Mary Had a Little Lamb."

APRIL 21, 1830 **Birth of Clémence Royer, French Philosopher and Scientific Writer.** Clémence Royer (1830–1902), France's leading female philosopher and scientific writer, is born in Nantes, France, the illegitimate daughter of a royalist officer. Her parents marry in 1837, giving her legitimacy. Royer spends much of her early childhood in exile with her family after the French Revolution of 1830, but she returns to France and a religious education in 1835. Her father's death in 1849 leaves her without money, and relatives press her to marry. Instead, she teaches piano and French lessons to earn money to support her own studies. She reads extensively, loses her religious faith, and develops a keen interest in science. In 1857, she moves to Switzerland and begins a career as a writer and public speaker, arguing that "nothing prevents a woman from being a chemist, pharmacist, electrician, mechanic, engineer, or agronomist. Woman is free to be what she wants to be." Royer is best known for her translation into French of Charles Darwin's *On the Origin of Species,* but she also writes scores of articles, encyclopedia entries, and several books on political science, economics, anthropology, philosophy, and biology. She publicly argues for tax reform and women's education, and the police keep her under careful watch as a subversive. Her books include *Theory of Taxes* (1868), *Origin of Man and of Society* (1869), and *History of the Heavens* (1901). Toward the end of her life, the example Royer sets helps make women's education and professional

Mary Mapes Dodge

careers a reality, and she receives official government recognition, including an official banquet in 1897 and the Legion of Honor in 1900. Royer dies in 1902.

DECEMBER 10, 1830 **Birth of American Poet Emily Dickinson.** Emily Elizabeth Dickinson (1830–1886), American poet, is born in Amherst, Massachusetts. At age 23, she withdraws from all social life to live in seclusion. During her lifetime, she writes over 1,000 poems but only one or two are published while she is alive. Her sister, Lavinia, publishes three volumes of Emily's poetry (1891–96). In 1914, another volume, *The Single Hound,* is published, followed in 1945 by *Bolts of Melody.*

1831 **Birth of Mary Mapes Dodge, American Author.** Mary Mapes Dodge (1838–1905), American author and editor, is born in New York City. She is widowed at a young age, and supports herself and her two young sons with her writing. Her first book, *Irvington Stories,* is a collection of short stories for children. Her most famous work, *Hans Brinker and the Silver Skates* (1865), is begun as a short serial but develops into a full novel. The French version is awarded the Montyon Prize by the French Academy. In 1870, Mapes becomes editor of *Hearth and Home,* a weekly publication with which Harriet Beecher Stowe is also associated. In 1873, the children's magazine *St. Nicholas* is founded, with Mapes as managing editor.

1832 Founding of Feminist Newspaper *The Women's Tribune.* *La Tribune des Femmes* (*The Women's Tribune*) is founded in 1832 by two young seamstresses in their early 20s, Désirée Veret and Reine Guindorf. They allow only women to write for the paper, and all work is unpaid. This places a serious strain on authors and staff, and both Veret and Guindorf have to leave to find paying work, leaving the paper in the hands of Suzanne Voilquin. The paper calls for "equality among us, of rights and duties," arguing that "with the emancipation of women will come the emancipation of the worker." The paper stops publishing in 1834 when Voilquin leaves France, but it marks the first feminist newspaper written by women alone.

1832 Suzanne Voilquin Helps Found Women's Newspaper, *The New Woman.* Suzanne Voilquin belongs to a group of Saint-Simonian women who found a women's newspaper, *La Femme Nouvelle* (*The New Woman*). Voilquin, Desiree Gay, Reine Guindorf, and Jeanne Déroin are all young working women who sign their articles using only their first names, meant as a symbolic protest against masculine control.

Voilquin has a poor, unhappy childhood and is raised by her strict, pious mother. She learns to read from a brother who has started training for the priesthood and continues her education in a convent until overwork makes her ill. She then falls in love with a medical stu-

dent, but her father refuses to sanction the marriage. The student seduces and abandons Suzanne, who then contemplates suicide.

After her father's business fails, she and her sister go to work in an embroidery factory. Her marriage to a man named Voilquin does not lead to happiness. Suzanne Voilquin discovers she has a disease (possibly venereal disease contracted from her husband) that prevents her from having a healthy child, and her husband sails for America with another woman. Abandoned, Voilquin decides to dedicate her life to fighting for the rights of mothers. She becomes involved with the utopian socialist group known as the Saint-Simonians, but she dislikes the leader Enfantin's theory of free love.

The Saint-Simonian women's movement in 1830s France is the most sophisticated of its day. It addresses the total situation of women, not just working class rights. These feminists believe in maternity as the common link for female solidarity and advocate economic independence for women. In 1833, Voilquin travels East with other Saint-Simonians in search of the Mother, or female Messiah. Arriving in the midst of a plague, the Saint-Simonians are decimated, but Voilquin survives and travels to Egypt, where she works as a tutor, learns Arabic, studies medicine in the hospitals of Cairo, and helps women in the harems. In 1836, she returns to France and organizes a society for unmarried mothers whose babies she delivers for free. During the Revolution of 1848 she participates in *Le Club des Femmes* (The Women's Club) and writes for its daily newspaper, *La Voix des Femmes* (*The Women's Voice*). After a lifetime of participation in the development of the "Woman Movement," Voilquin dies in relative obscurity in Paris.

1832 George Sand Publishes First Novel. George Sand (1804–1876), the pen name for French author Amandine Aurore Lucie Dupin Dudevant, publishes her first novel,

Indiana. It deals with the plight of a woman trapped in a loveless marriage.

1832 Italian Ballerina Marie Taglione Goes Up on Point in Performance.

Marie Taglione (1804–1884), an Italian ballerina born in Stockholm, Sweden, is the first woman to go up on point on stage. She impresses audiences in Paris when she goes up on her toes in the Romantic ballet *La Sylphide*. Trained by her father, a dancer and choreographer, Taglione tours throughout Europe and is known for her graceful and apparently effortless movements.

NOVEMBER 26, 1832 American Surgeon Mary Edwards Walker Is Born.

Mary Edwards Walker, M.D. (1832–1919), an Army surgeon during the Civil War and a women's dress reformer, is born in Oswego, New York. In 1853 she enters the Syracuse Medical College; by her graduation in 1855, she is committed to wearing reform dress and begins to lecture on hygiene, dress reform, and women's rights.

At the outbreak of the Civil War, Walker travels to Washington, D.C., to offer her services as a physician to the Union army, clothed in a unique costume—men's pants covered by a loose-hanging dress that falls to the knees. Walker's strange outfit and her womanhood lose her both an army commission and a civilian contract. In 1862, she leaves an unpaid post as a volunteer physician in the Patent Office Hospital to attend the Hygieo-Therapeutic College in New York City, from which she receives her second medical degree.

In 1863, back in Washington, Walker helps to establish the Women's Relief Association, providing lodging and support for women who come to the Union capital in search of enlisted relatives. The same year, she is finally appointed a civilian contract surgeon (the first such woman), assigned to the 52nd Ohio Regiment. Walker adopts her fellow officers' uniform of pants, tunic, and greatcoat so that she can perform her duties more effectively. She frequently crosses Con-

federate lines to attend to wounded civilians and is captured and imprisoned as a spy in April 1864 and is held for four months. In May 1865, she is relieved of her duties as contract surgeon for the Union army. Her persistence in seeking a post-war commission, however, results in her being accorded the recognition of the Congressional Medal of Honor for Meritorious Service.

With the end of the war, Walker resumes the lecture circuit. She lectures in England during 1866 and 1867. By the late 1870s, Walker adopts a form of attire styled closely after men's clothing. She is arrested on a number of occasions for appearing in public in men's clothes, despite her insistence that women be freed to wear trousers for reasons of comfort and hygiene.

Walker is not welcomed by the mainstream women's rights movements because of her radical dress reform views. She also alienates suffragists by insisting that the fight for a Constitutional amendment granting women the right to vote is unnecessary as that right is already secured by the Constitution itself.

In 1917, Walker and 910 other recipients of the Congressional Medal of Honor lose their citations in a bureaucratic review. However, in 1976, Senate Resolution 569 reinstates Walker's medal, declaring her "a woman one hundred years ahead of her time [who] pursued many occupations including teaching, lecturing, and writing on women's rights, and campaigning for women's suffrage and other progressive reforms;...the only woman in the history of the United States to have ever received the Nation's highest award for valor...."

Walker's published works include a pamphlet on suffrage called "Crowning Constitutional Argument" (1907); *Hit* (1871), about dress and health reform; and *Unmasked, or the Science of Immorality* (1878).

NOVEMBER 29, 1832 American Author Louisa May Alcott Is Born.

Louisa May Alcott

romances such as *The Dove in the Eagle's Nest* (1866).

1833   Anne Drysdale and Her Partner Caroline Newcombe, Pioneer Australian Graziers. Anne Drysdale (1792–1853) secures the license of the Boronggoop run, a 10,000-acre cattle property, and she and Caroline Elizabeth Newcombe (1812–1874) build a new homestead equipped with two unusual luxuries: a piano and glazed windows. Drysdale is born in Scotland, where she gains some experience as a farmer. She emigrates to Australia for health reasons in 1840. While in Melbourne, she meets Caroline Elizabeth Newcombe, a governess, who arrives from England in 1833. Their ranch is so successful that, in 1843, they extend their interests by acquiring the Coryule run on the Bellarine Peninsula. When this property is freeholded in 1848, they build themselves a stone mansion overlooking Port Philip Bay. They sell the Boronggoop run one year before Drysdale's death at Coryule in 1853. Newcombe continues to work the station and takes a lively interest in local religious and philanthropic affairs. She marries the Reverend Davy Dodgson in 1861 but chooses to be buried beside Drysdale at Coryule after her death in 1874. Their remains are later moved to the Geelong cemetery.

FEBRUARY 22, 1833   American Author Rebecca Sophia Clarke (Sophie May) Is Born. Rebecca Sophia Clarke (Sophie May) (1833–1906), American author of popular series of girls' stories, is born in Norridgewock, Maine, of a well-to-do family that dates to Revolutionary War times. She wants to be a teacher, but deafness forces her to return to her home to live with her sister Sarah. She decides to write for a newspaper friend but under another name; it is her whimsy that leads to her pseudonym. Since she may or may not write, she becomes Sophie May. Sophie May is unusual in that her fictional characters appear to be more like real children who are both good and naughty, a refreshing change for this time

Louisa May Alcott

(1832–1888), daughter of American teacher, writer, and transcendentalist Amos Bronson Alcott, is born in Germantown, Pennsylvania. Alcott serves as a nurse during the American Civil War, and later publishes *Hospital Sketches,* a collection of her letters from this era. Alcott edits *Merry Museum,* a magazine for children, in 1867. In 1868, her novel, *Little Women,* brings her great success. Other works include *An Old-Fashioned Girl* (1870), *Little Men* (1871), *Aunt Jo's Scrap-Bag* (six volumes, 1872–82), and *Jo's Boys* (1886).

1833   Birth of Charlotte Yonge, Children's Author. Charlotte Mary Yonge (1833–1901), author, editor, and novelist, is born in England. From 1851 to 1900, Yonge edits the monthly children's periodical *Monthly Packet.* In 1853, she publishes her most famous work, *The Heir of Redclyffe.* Her themes feature high moral values. Other works include *Heartsease* (1854), *The Daisy Chain* (1856), and historical period. Six volumes comprise her Little Prudy books, including *Little Prudy* (1864) and *Little Prudy's Cousin Grace* (1864), detailing the everyday life of three-year-old Prudy and her friends and relatives. Between 1868 and 1870, May writes a new series entitled Dolly Dimple, including *Dolly Dimple At School* (1869) and *Dolly Dimple At Play* (1869). Many contemporary critics praise her work while others find fault, perhaps because she writes stories rather rapidly and with relatively slight plots. Her stories are gentle and appealing to readers, with a moral tone presented in a light and amusing style.

AUGUST 6, 1833 Saint-Simonian Claire Démar Commits Suicide. Claire Démar (1800–1833), a Saint-Simonian whose radical ideas on sexuality isolate her from society, commits suicide in Paris. Virtually nothing is known of Démar's parents, her early life, or even her real name. She calls herself a "woman of the people," and certainly comes from a background of poverty. She joins the Saint-Simonians around 1830 and becomes an advocate of total sexual freedom for men and women, arguing that only by long association can two people decide if they are fit to be married. She denounces the Saint-Simonian leader Prosper Enfantin for being too interested in control of women rather than their liberation, and her radical stance alienates most of her associates. Her controversial ideas on sexuality result in her isolation from society, and even radicals and socialists shun her. Unable to bear the societal pressure, she commits suicide.

c. 1834 Madame Tussaud Establishes Wax Museum. Marie Tussaud (1761–1850), known as Madame Tussaud, founds her famous London waxworks in Baker Street. She is the first woman to make her name as a wax-modeller and operator of wax museums. She and her brother learn wax-modelling in Bern, Switzerland, where they grow up. They move to Paris in 1770, where her brother opens two

museums. When he dies in 1794, Tussaud inherits his museums. By that time she has established her reputation as a modeller, even making death masks from guillotined people of prominence. Emigrating to England in 1802, she travels throughout Britain, making models and exhibiting her work for 33 years.

1835 – 1839

1835 Sister Euphrasia Pelletier Founds Institute of the Good Shepherd. Sister Euphrasia Pelletier (1796–1868) founds the Institute of the Good Shepherd, a religious order directed toward rescue work for women in danger. When Rose Virginia Pelletier is 18 years old, she joins the Institute of Our Lady of Charity and Refuge at Tours, France, and takes the name of a fifth-century saint, Euphrasia. Eleven years later, in 1825, she is made Mother Superior of the house and soon after is sent to Angers to start up a new convent there. She does this, returns to Tours, then decides that radical changes need to be made in the organization. Despite strong opposition and accusations of innovation, ambition, and insubordination (all considered sins against the rule of obedience), Euphrasia perseveres. In 1835, official approval is given to her new organization, the Institute of the Good Shepherd, at Angers. Like the Institute of Our Lady of Charity and Refuge, the Institute of the Good Shepherd is directed toward rescue work for women and those in "moral danger." During the 33 years Euphrasia directs the Institute of the Good Shepherd, 110 convents are opened on four continents. The institute continues to thrive after Euphrasia's death; 100 years later, over 10,000 nuns are members of the order. Her feast day is celebrated on April 24.

1835 Writer Harriet Jane Hanson Robinson Begins Work in Mill at Early Age. Harriet Jane Hanson Robinson (1825–1911) becomes a bobbin tender in a textile mill in Lowell, Massachusetts, when she is ten years old. Robinson is a frequent contributor to *The Lowell Offering,* the literary magazine of the textile mill operatives. She is a prolific contributor and her writings take a positive tone regarding mill work and conditions. In addition to writing for *The Offering,* Robinson writes five other published works. Her memoirs, *Loom and Spindle,* are considered the best book of reminiscences about the early days of the mill.

1835   Birth of Empress Dowager Cixi Blamed for Collapse of Qing Dynasty. Cixi (1835–1908), who begins her rise to political power in China as the imperial consort, is born. Through her masterful manipulation of court politics, she is, for the final decades of the Qing dynasty, the real power behind the throne. Unfortunately, the Empress Dowager's political acumen does not extend to governing the country, and she is often blamed for a series of political and diplomatic catastrophes which culminate in the collapse of the Qing dynasty in 1911.

JANUARY 5, 1835   Birth of Olympia Brown, First Woman Minister. Olympia Brown (1835–1926) is born in Michigan. She marries John Willis, but keeps her own name. In 1863, Brown becomes the first woman to be ordained by full authority of her denomination (Unitarian).

C. 1836   Grimké Sisters Lecture on Abolitionists and Women's Rights Themes. Angelina Emily Grimké (1805–1879) and her sister, Sarah Moore Grimké (1792–1873) are children of a slave-owning father in South Carolina. Both convert to Quakerism and become involved in the abolitionist movement. In 1868, Angelina publishes "An Appeal to the Christian Women of the South," a pamphlet advocating the abolition of slavery; many Southern postmasters destroyed copies rather than deliver them.

Empress Dowager

Sarah also publishes extensively. Her works include "Epistle to the Clergy of the Southern States," (1827); "Letters on the Condition of Woman and the Equality of the Sexes" (1838); and a translation of French poet Alphonse Lamartine's "Joan of Arc" (1867). Sarah is silenced during a Quaker meeting for voicing her anti-slavery views. The experience strengthens her resolve to fight for the abolitionist cause and for a woman's right to voice her opinions.

Grimké sisters. Angelina Emily Grimké (left) and her sister, Sarah Moore Grimké (right).

c. 1836   Sarah Bagley, First Known Female Union Organizer in the United States. Probably born in New Hampshire, Sarah Bagley first emerges in history in 1836 in Lowell, Massachusetts, where she begins working in a textile mill. She quickly becomes an activist, organizer, and strike supporter and develops a reputation as a fiery public speaker. She conducts free classes for other mill workers, works for the 10-hour day movement, organizes around other political issues, pressures the state legislature to hold public hearings on the working conditions in the textile mills, and is a prolific writer. Bagley regularly writes for both *The Lowell Offering* and *The Voice of Industry*. *The Lowell Offering* is the publication containing the literary efforts of the textile mill operatives. However, Bagley's submissions are soon rejected because they are critical of the factories and their owners. She is a leader of the Lowell Female Labor Reform Association,

one of the earliest unions for working women to organize on more than a local basis. Under Bagley's leadership, the association purchases *The Voice of Industry* and lets it serve as a vehicle that gives a more honest and less romanticized look at factory life. Bagley disappears from known records in the mid-1840s. She most probably is blacklisted because of her union and strike activities. She reemerges in late 1846 as the first telegraph operator.

1836   Jane Franklin Founds Scientific Institution in Australia. Australian Jane Franklin (1791–1875) establishes the first Royal Society for the Advancement of Science outside Britain, in Van Dieman's Land (Tasmania), Australia.

OCTOBER 3, 1836   Cornerstone of First Building of Mount Holyoke Seminary Is Laid. American educator Mary Lyon (1797–

Mount Holyoke Seminary

1849), raises the funds to found Mount Holyoke seminary in South Hadley, Massachusetts. The cornerstone for the first building is laid, and classes convene in the fall of 1837. The seminary eventually becomes Mount Holyoke College, the first four-year college for women in the United States. Mary Lyon serves as principal of the seminary from 1837 to 1849, publishing a number of works on women's education, including "Tendencies of the Principles Embraced and the System Adopted in the Mount Holyoke Seminary" (1840).

1837   Reine Guindorf, Who Helps Found French Women's Newspaper, Commits Suicide. Reine Guindorf (?–1837), a working class woman and Saint-Simonian, commits suicide. In 1832, along with Suzanne Voilquin, Desiree Gay, and Claire Demar, she organizes a women's newspaper, *La Femme Nouvelle* (*The New Woman*), the first consciously feminist venture in France. The writers sign only their first names as a protest against masculine power, and Guindorf writes under the pseudonym of Marie-Reine. The paper's short-lived success is due in part to the popularity of the utopian socialist Saint-Simonians, but these women do not agree with the Saint-Simonians on all issues. Guindorf and the other women especially dislike the Saint-Simonian belief in free love, and instead focus on working class women and the need to emancipate all women from male oppression. These women argue for women's associations on the basis of gender. They see in their sexual nature and reproductive lives a power and basis for unity. They challenge male criticism of "feminine shriekings"— women who speak publicly about social issues. Guindorf eventually gives up her duties on the newspaper to teach at a night school for poor women. In 1837 she commits suicide by throwing herself into the Seine, leaving behind a husband and 15-month-old child; she has fallen in love with another utopian socialist and refuses to live in hypocrisy with her husband.

1837   **Queen Victoria Commences Rule of Great Britain, Ushering in Victorian Era.** Alexandria Victoria (1819–1901) becomes Queen Victoria of England at the age of 18 when her uncle, King William IV, dies. Her reign lasts for 63 years, the longest reign of any British monarch. During her reign, Britain reaches the height of its power with industrial expansion at home and imperial expansion abroad. This period comes to be known as the Victorian Era.

Since Britain is a constitutional monarchy, Victoria's role is only to warn, advise, or encourage the prime minister, but Victoria sets the moral tone of the country. Adulterous kings and queens have preceded her, but she restores the public's faith and respect for the monarchy. In February 1840 she marries her cousin, Prince Albert of Saxe-Coburg-Gotha. Their happy marriage produces four sons and five daughters. The queen and the prince consort are models of marital stability and sobriety. In public, Victoria gives the impression of maternal devotion by always appearing with her children at ceremonial functions. She deliberately sets an example of virtue and good behavior for her subjects. In 1861 Albert dies. Victoria withdraws from social activities and dresses in mourning for several years. In 1897, her Diamond Jubilee is celebrated as a great "festival of empire." Victoria dies in 1901, and her eldest son becomes King Edward VII.

1837   **Oberlin College Admits Women.** Oberlin College in Ohio, founded in 1833 and always open to all students, admits its first women students; Antioch College in Yellow Springs, Ohio, will also admit women beginning in 1852.

AUGUST 17, 1837   **Birth of Charlotte L. Forten-Grimké, Author and Educator Committed to Racial Justice.** Charlotte L. Forten-Grimké (1837–1914), the granddaughter of the famous abolitionists Charlotte and James Forten, is born. Her father, Robert Forten, is committed to racial uplift and refuses to allow his daughter to attend a segregated school. Therefore, she is privately tutored until the age of 16. While living with abolitionist Charles Lenox Remond, Charlotte Forten attends the integrated schools of Higginson Grammar in 1855 and Salem Normal School in 1856. After completing her education, Forten becomes a teacher at the all-white Episcopalian Grammar School and teaches there in 1856 and from 1860 to 1861. It is at this time that she develops her writing ability. Many of the poems she writes deal with her feelings about racism and her lifelong commitment to seeking justice for African Americans. Recommended by her friend John Greenleaf Whittier, Forten receives a teaching position at St. Helena Island, where she teaches from 1862 to 1864.

After the Civil War, Forten works for the New England Freedman's Union Commission for six years (1864–71). In 1873, she is chosen from over 500 applicants to work as a clerk in the Treasury Department. Five years later, in December 1878 and at the age of 41, Forten marries the 28-year-old nephew of Sarah and Angelina Grimké. She continues her commitment to racial justice and becomes an active member in the Anti-Slavery Society and one of the founding members of the National Association of Colored Women. Charlotte Forten-Grimké dies after a recurring illness at the age of 72, on July 23, 1914.

1838   **Birth of Victoria Claflin Woodhull.** Victoria Claflin, later Woodhull (1838–1927), activist, businesswoman, and publisher, is born in Homer, Ohio. In 1870, Woodhull is the first woman candidate for U.S. president.

1838   Liliuokalani, Last Queen of Hawaii, Is Born. Hawaii's Queen Liliuokalani (1838–1917) is born. In 1893, after only two years as queen, Liliuokalani abdicates the throne under pressure from European and mainland U.S. interests. When her efforts to maintain her crown are opposed by the U.S. Marines and others, she steps down.

1838   Caroline Chisholm Helps Women Migrants in Australia. Caroline Jones Chisholm (1808–1877) devotes her adult life to helping women migrants in Australia. Born in England, she marries East India company employee Archibald Chisholm and converts to his religion, but her marriage contract stipulates that she be allowed to work. They are posted to Madras, India, where Caroline Chisholm founds a Female School of Industry for the Daughters of European Soldiers. In 1838 she and her three children remain in Australia after her husband returns to India. Chisholm devotes herself to the welfare of women immigrants, meeting every migrant ship, sheltering the women in her home, and finding them employment. In 1841, she opens her Female Immigrants Home and sets up Sydney's first free employment registry. Riding her white horse, Captain, Chisholm escorts women to jobs on pastoral stations. After her death, her headstone is inscribed with the words: "The emigrant's friend."

1839   Infant Custody Act Passed by British Parliament. The British Infant Custody Act of 1839 gives women custody of their children under the age of seven. Prior to this time, in the event of separation, the children are automatically placed in the custody of the father, no matter how unfit he may be.

1839   Georgiana Molloy Classifies Native Western Australian Plants. Georgiana Kennedy Molloy (1805–1843) is a botanist who classifies and catalogues native Western Australian plants. She arrives in Western Australia a few months after her marriage to John Molloy in 1829. They settle first in a leaky canvas tent on a remote property at Augusta, and by 1839 they move to another property on the Vasse River some 60 miles to the north. For Georgiana Molloy, life in the colonies is a nightmare. She has no domestic help, no female company, and none of the facilities to which she is accustomed. She worries constantly that domestic drudgery leaves her no time to educate and care for her three children. She eventually suffers a nervous breakdown after her youngest is killed when he falls into a well near the house. Molloy eventually manages to resume her life by becoming involved in a hobby that had fascinated her in her youth: botany. She collects, describes, and labels native Western Australian plants and sends seeds back to England where they are propagated, cultivated, and scientifically named in a number of botanical gardens. Her work is greatly admired and a number of her original collections are still held at the Kew Herbarium in London. A plant, the scented boronia *Boronia molloyae,* is named for her.

1839   Birth of Mary Louisa Molesworth, British Children's Author. Mary Louisa Molesworth (1839–1921), called the "Jane Austen of the Nursery," is born. She publishes extensively for children, including *The Cuckoo Clock* (1877), *The Tapestry Room* (1879), and *The Ruby Ring* (1904).

1839   Jane Franklin Finances Establishment of Botanical Gardens and Museum in Australia. Australian Jane Franklin (1791–1875) finances the creation of the Hobart Botanical Gardens and Museum of Natural History in Australia. In the same year, she establishes the agricultural settlement of Willingham. Her other notable achievement is the founding of the public Christ's College, in 1840.

JUNE 26, 1839   Birth of Emma Miller, Australian Suffragist. Emma Holmes Miller (1839–1917), a prominent suffragist in Queensland, Australia, is born in Derbyshire, England. She migrates to Queensland with her second husband in 1879. Throughout her life, Miller fights fearlessly for equality, freedom of speech, secularism, and pacifism. Above all, she believes in industrial unionism. A seamstress by trade, she helps organize a female workers' union in Brisbane in 1890 and the following year appears before a royal commission of inquiry into factory conditions. Miller joins the Australian Workers Union and is its first woman organizer in western Queensland. She also becomes involved in parliamentary politics as the first woman member of the Brisbane Workers Political Organisation. Miller is foundation president of the Women's Equal Franchise Association from 1894 and of the Women Workers Political Organisation from 1903. During the Queensland General Strike of 1912 she leads a large group of women demonstrators against mounted police, allegedly dismounting and injuring the police commissioner by puncturing his horse with a hat pin. During World War I she campaigns against conscription from her position as president of the Queensland branch of the Women's Peace Army. "Mother Miller" dies on January 22, 1917, and her marble bust is unveiled at the Brisbane Trades Hall in 1922.

SEPTEMBER 6, 1839   French Socialist Louise-Léonie Rouzade Is Born. Louise-Léonie

Rouzade (1839–?), a leading female socialist of the late nineteenth century, is born in Paris as Louise-Léonie Camusat. Her father is a Republican watchmaker, and her grandfather had been a revolutionary in 1789. She works as an embroiderer and marries Auguste Rouzade in 1850. Her husband encourages her to write, and she publishes two obscure metaphysical pamphlets before publishing a series of utopian novels in 1872. In *The World Turned Upside Down* (1872), her heroine Celestine is kidnapped and taken to a Middle Eastern harem. She leads a women's revolt and sets up a new code of laws whose first article is "men must honor women." In *The Voyage of Theodose to the Island of Utopia*, the hero is shipwrecked on an island where men and women are equals. In 1878 Rouzade becomes actively involved in feminism, being introduced to socialism in 1879. She begins speaking at socialist banquets, and her public speaking is extremely skillful. In 1880 she founds The Union of Women, a political group that calls for the joint emancipation of women and labor. However, male socialists are unwilling to make demands for female emancipation part of their programs, and socialism suffers from a split between male and female workers that Rouzade is unable to heal.

Chapter 11

1840 TO 1849

1840 – 1844

c. 1840   Augusta Maywood, First American Dancer to Win International Fame. Augusta Maywood (1825–1876), a ballerina trained in both Philadelphia and Paris, is the first American dancer to win international fame. She performs at the Paris Opera beginning in 1838, and by 1840 she is dancing throughout Europe and widely acclaimed. She is the first American woman to form her own traveling ballet company. She tours the continent with her own managers, partners, decors, and costumes, and she is particularly popular in Italy, where she performs to wide acclaim in the 1840s and 1850s. A colorful personality, she makes a fortune before retiring to a villa near Lake Como in Italy.

1840   Baptism of Pocahontas Placed in Capitol Rotunda. A painting depicting the baptism of Pocahontas (1595?–1617), the daughter of Native American chief Powhatan, is installed in the U.S. capital rotunda. In the scene, which takes place around 1613, one sees John Rolfe standing immediately behind the kneeling Pocahontas. Rolfe and Pocahontas, who took the name Rebecca after her baptism, are married in 1614. Also visible are members of Pocahontas's family, including her sister and infant seated on the floor and her brother, standing immediately behind Rolfe and looking away from the ritual being performed.

Painting entitled *Baptism of Pocahontas.*

1840   Debut of Textile Workers' Publication *The Lowell Offering.* Young female textile mill operatives (workers), most of them under 30 years old, are encouraged to form cultural groups or clubs, commonly referred to as improvement circles. Out of one such circle comes *The Lowell Offering*. It carries original articles, stories, and poems of various kinds written by women workers in the cotton mill factories. It especially encourages items that reflect positively on factory life and the factory system. *The Lowell Offering* is accepted as the voice of the mill workers. Printed by William Schouler, an agent of the mill owners, it does not criticize factory conditions, nor does it encourage factory operatives to unite to change these conditions. It is edited by Harriet Farley and Harriet Curtis, both former operatives. Their choice of articles for the paper reflects Farley's and Curtis' belief that women cannot impact their wages, hours, or working conditions. They contend, as do the paper's articles, that by continuing to meet in improvement circles, women who study can protect their dignity and prove they are equal in culture to women who stay at home. Besides, they contend, as long as the mind and soul are free, it doesn't matter what happens to the body. The paper attracts national as well as international attention. Public debate and alternative publications soon make it known that this newspaper is not the voice of all cotton mill workers and that many have criticisms of the factory system as well as a willingness to organize.

1840   Ernestine Rose Petitions for Married Women's Property Rights. Ernestine Rose (1810–1892) writes the first petition for a law granting married women the right to own property. The petition is reviewed by the New York State Legislature in Albany, New York, and leads in 1848 to a law safeguarding the property of married women.

1840   Nakayama Miki Establishes New Japanese Religion. Nakayama Miki (1798–1887) founds the Japanese religion known as Tenrikyo. Religious from her youth, Miki devotes herself to the worship of Shinto deities and acts of compassion. At the age of 40, she claims to receive a revelation from a deity and accepts the divine wishes to come under its

possession. Thereafter, Miki sees as part of her religious mission to give away her family's possessions to needy people. Approximately 20 years after her initial revelation, Miki begins to practice faith healing. She is the author of *Mikagura uta* (*Songs for the Sacred Dance*) and the *Ofudesaki* (*Tip of the Divine Writing Brush*), which are considered the scriptures of Tenrikyo. Miki also teaches her disciples dances to perform before God. The leaders and disciples of Tenrikyo are persecuted until after World War II (1939–45), when the constitution defends religious freedom. Tenrikyo is an active religion today, and as its founder, Miki is referred to as Oyasama (Beloved Parent) and is believed to eternally reside in the world, extending to it her protection. Some scholars identify the Japanese "new religions," of which Tenrikyo is the first, as a means of feminist expression. In this interpretation, the fact that Miki gives away her family's possessions is viewed as an attack on patriarchy.

1841   British Author Juliana Horatia Ewing Is Born. Juliana Horatia Gatty Ewing (1841–1885), author of stories for children, is born in England. She is the daughter of Alfred Gatty (1813–1903), a vicar and author, and Margaret Gatty (1807–1873), creator in 1866 of *Aunt Judy's Magazine* for children, where Juliana publishes her first stories. In 1867, Juliana marries composer Alexander Ewing. Her published stories include *Melchior's Dream* (1862), *The Brownies* (1870), *Lob-lie-by-the-Fire* (1873), *Jackanapes* (1884), *Jan of the Windmill* (1884), and *The Story of a Short Life* (1885).

1841   Ann Lohman Arrested for Aborting a Quickened Fetus. Ann Lohman, known professionally as "Madame Restell, female physician and professor of midwifery," is arrested in New York City for aborting a quickened fetus—one that is showing signs of life. Lohman operates a clinic in lower Manhattan, and after a sensational trial, she is found guilty of violating the law. She uses the exposure to expand her clinic in New York and to open clinics in Boston and Philadelphia. She is arrested again in 1845 when one of her patients dies. She is convicted and sent to prison. In 1878, years after her release, when facing trial again for selling contraceptives, she commits suicide.

APRIL 21, 1841   Jennie Kidd Trout, First Licensed Woman Doctor in Canada, Is Born. Jennie Kidd Trout, a pioneering Canadian doctor, is born at Kelso, Scotland. Her family moves to Canada and she grows up near Stratford, Ontario. Shortly after her marriage to publisher Edward Trout in 1865, she decides to become a doctor. At the time, no Canadian medical school admits women, so she enrolls at the Women's Medical College of Pennsylvania. She graduates in 1875 and subsequently passes the Ontario registration exams. Trout becomes the first Canadian woman licensed to practice medicine. She fights great opposition in regards to the admission of women to medical schools and becomes a fervent promoter of women in medicine. Jennie Kidd Trout later helps to endow the Women's Medical College of Kingston in 1883. She is one of the most significant contributors to breaking down the barriers to the entry of women into medicine in Canada.

1842   Death of Marie Anne Elisabeth Vigée-Lebrun, French Portrait Painter. Elisabeth Vigée-Lebrun (1755–1842), one of the most celebrated portrait painters of the eighteenth and nineteenth centuries, dies in Paris after living out the French Revolution in Italy and touring Europe.

1842   Birth of Ellen Swallow Richards, Pioneer in Environmental Science. Ellen Swallow Richards (1842–1911), regarded as the founder of ecology, is born. She earns a bachelor's degree in science from Vassar College in 1870 and another in chemistry in 1873 from Massachusetts Institute of Technology (MIT), where she then teaches chemistry for five years with-

out title or salary. MIT refuses to confer the Ph.D. in chemistry which she earns during this period. She then becomes an instructor in chemistry and mineralogy at the newly founded MIT Woman's Laboratory, followed by instructor of sanitary chemistry at MIT from 1884 to 1911. Richards analyzes water and gas for the state of Massachusetts and also specializes in the analysis of metals and minerals.

1843   French Socialist Flora Tristan Writes *The Workers' Union.* French socialist Flora Tristan (1803–1844) writes her most acclaimed work, *The Workers' Union*, in which she argues that only by organizing can workers protect themselves from capitalism. In 1844, while on a public speaking tour of France, she falls ill and dies, still suffering from the effects of being shot by her husband in the back in 1838.

1843   Sojourner Truth, Former Slave and Powerful Orator, Begins Her Mission. Born a slave called Isabella, Sojourner Truth (c.1797–1893) renames herself, representing with her name her mission to travel and preach. The only thing known about her early life is her statement that she converses with God from early childhood. The slave Isabella escapes from her master and is sheltered by the Van Wagener family of New York State. In 1827, after the New York State Emancipation Act makes her a free woman, one of her first acts is to sue, successfully, for the return of her son, who has been sold illegally to an Alabama slaveholder.

She lives for a while in a religious commune and utopian community in Northampton, Massachusetts, where she meets the anti-slavery activist Frederick Douglass. For ten years, until 1843, she lives quietly, until her voices instruct her to change her name to Sojourner Truth and begin travelling and preaching.

Although she is illiterate, Sojourner Truth is famous as an extremely skillful speaker. In 1850, she collaborates with Olive

Gilbert on the autobiography of her life as a slave, *The Narrative of Sojourner Truth,* which is sold at her lectures. She understands the connections between racial and sexual discrimination, and often speaks at women's rights conventions. A particularly powerful speech she gives in 1851 is recounted many years later by the writer and reformer Frances Dana Gage, who includes the now famous words, "Ar'n't I a Woman?," though contemporary newspaper accounts of the speech do not include this phrase.

During the Civil War, Sojourner Truth helps solicit supplies for Negro volunteer regiments. President Lincoln receives her at the White House in 1864. After the Civil War, she continues to campaign for women's rights, eventually retiring to Battle Creek, Michigan, where she dies in 1883.

1844   Birth of Sarah Bernhardt, Great French Entertainer. Sarah Bernhardt (1844–1923) is born Rosine Bernard in Paris, France. She is the daughter of a wealthy courtesan and madame of Dutch Jewish origin. Bernhardt studies acting at the Paris Conservatory from 1860 to 1862. She stars in her first play at the Comédie Française, Racine's *Iphigenie,* in 1862. She does poorly, attracting public notice not for her acting but for her temper. She leaves the Comédie Française after breaking her parasol over the stagemaster's head and punching another actress. For years she continues a disappointing career and briefly leaves Paris to bear an illegitimate son, Maurice.

In 1868, Bernhardt finally achieves success, charming the Imperial family. Her new success brings her money, fame, a new house, and a crowd of influential friends and lovers, including George Sand, Leon Gambetta, Prince Napoleon, and Théophile Gautier. She has triumph after triumph in such plays as *La Tosca, Hernani,* and *Phedre,* and conquers London in 1879. Outside of France, she is best known for her performance in *Camille,* and in 1912 she appears in the motion picture

Sarah Bernhardt

Queen Elizabeth. She makes her first New York City appearance in 1880 and her last in 1918. During a 1907 visit to America, she has to perform in a tent to combat the monopoly of the theatrical syndicate.

Bernhardt fills her house with exotic animals and art. She becomes a cult figure in the 1870s, inspiring outrageous acts of devotion from her fans. She continues to act and to lead a life of extravagance and sexual freedom among Paris's avant-garde community. She eventually becomes an independent actress and manager. A leg injury in 1914 results in an amputation, but she continues to act and dance in patriotic performances throughout World War I. When she dies in 1923, while rehearsing yet another play, 250,000 Parisians come to pay homage to the "Divine Sarah." Her writings include her autobiographical

Memories of My Life (1907) and *Art of the Theater,* published in 1924 after her death.

1 8 4 5 – 1 8 4 9

1845   Female Labor Reform Association Founded. The Female Labor Reform Association is first formed by 12 cotton mill workers in Lowell, Massachusetts. Within six months membership is over 500, and it is the first union for working women to organize on more than a local basis. Sarah Bagley, the first recorded trade union organizer in the United States, is one of the founders and its first president. She and other representatives regularly travel to other New England cities and form new chapters of the association while they sell subscriptions to their publication *The Voice of Industry.* Since mill operatives regularly work 12-, 14-, or 16-hour days, six days a week, the association supports the 10-hour day movement. Their activities include gathering thousands of signatures on petitions, testifying before public hearings, and supporting the strike activities of other workers and chapters.

1845   Birth of Edmonia Lewis, African American sculptor in America. Edmonia Lewis (1845–c.1909), the daughter of an African American father and a Native American (Chippewa) mother, is born. Educated at Oberlin College in Ohio, she is the first black female sculptor in America. Lewis also studies in Rome and exhibits with Harriet Hosmer's group of women sculptors. She settles in Rome in the 1880s, and little is known of her later life.

NOVEMBER 7, 1845   The *Voice of Industry* Becomes Vehicle for Mill Workers to Express Dissatisfaction. *The Voice of Industry* carries a notice inviting female cotton mill operatives of Lowell, Massachusetts, to use the publication as "a medium of communication" and a way of voicing their complaints about the factory system. *The Voice of Industry* differs from its con-

temporary, *The Lowell Offering,* in that it is critical of the mill owners, the unhealthy working conditions in the factories, the low wages, and other poor conditions.

c. 1846   First Female Telegraph Operator. Union organizer Sarah Bagley becomes the first female telegraph operator. She is also believed to be the first female union organizer, an activity she engages in beginning in 1826.

1846   English Painter and Illustrator Kate Greenaway Is Born. Illustrator of books for children, Catherine Greenaway (1846–1901), known as Kate, is born. Her best-known works include U*nder the Window: Pictures and Rhymes for Children* (1879), *Kate Greenaway's Birthday Book* (1880), *Mother Goose* (1991), and *The Language of Flowers* (1884). In 1955, the "Kate Greenaway Medal" is established, awarded annually to the most distinguished illustrator of children's books.

1846   French Legal Reformer Jeanne Archer Schmahl Is Born. Jeanne-Elisabeth Archer (later Schmahl) (1846–1915), who lobbies for legal reform for women in France, is born. She is one of the young women who goes to Edinburgh to study medicine in the wake of Sophia Jex-Blake (1840–1912). In 1869, Jex-Blake and four other female students pressure the University of Edinburgh in Scotland to admit them to medical training. The University at Edinburgh refuses to allow the women to finish their medical studies, and Archer therefore moves to Paris to study. She never completes her medical degree and instead becomes involved in the Parisian women's movement during the late 1870s, under her married name of Madame Henri Schmahl. She opposes the anticlerical republican women's rights group led by Maria Deraismes and believes that the mixing of religion and politics with the "Woman Question" is responsible for the movement's lack of success in France. She forms her own group, The Forerunner, and during the 1890s campaigns to amend the laws concerning women. The French Civil Code denies married women control over their property and wages, and a wife needs her husband's written permission to work outside the home. Schmahl and The Forerunner help secure the passage of the first French Married Women's Property Act as well as legal recognition of women's capacity to testify in official public acts and to sit on juries. Schmahl then devotes her energy to the pursuit of woman suffrage and in 1909 founds the French Union for Woman Suffrage.

1847 Eugénie Niboyet Publishes French Newspaper *Women's Voice.* In France, Eugénie Niboyet (1797–1893) begins publishing *Women's Voice,* a newspaper calling for women's suffrage. In June, the French government closes down the paper and Niboyet flees to Switzerland. She follows the feminist debate in writing, but takes no active part in it until 1878, when she attends the International Congress of Women's Rights in Paris.

1847 The Statue "The Greek Slave" Becomes Symbol to U.S. Antislavery Movement. "The Greek Slave," a nude statue of a woman in chains, becomes a symbol to the antislavery movement in the United States. It is also the first nude, female statue to be reluctantly accepted by Americans as art. Hiram Powers, a respected American sculptor, works on "The Greek Slave" between 1841 and 1847. When finished, the original statue and at least six marble copies are exhibited across the United States and in England. Because it is explained to the public as a representation of the Greek nation in a war for independence, the statue of a naked young woman with chained hands and feet is hailed as high art, and women and children are encouraged to view it. Those opposed to slavery in the United States also find the statue a powerful symbol. Elizabeth Barrett Browning writes a much-reprinted poem about the statue; many other writers, including Nathaniel Hawthorne, also praise it. The discussion and exhibit of the statue helps

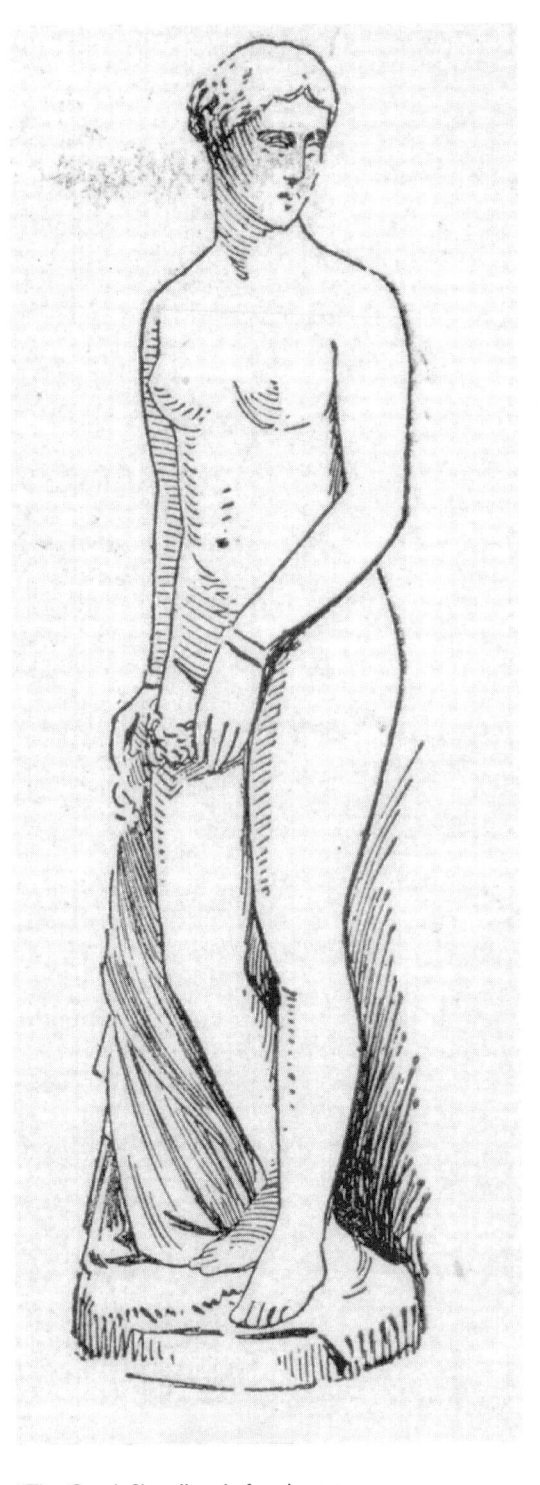

"The Greek Slave," nude female statue.

to make nudity in art more acceptable to a previously resistant middle-class taste.

1847   First Female Lithographer in the United States. Frances Flora Bond Palmer (1812–1876) becomes the first female lithographer in the United States. Born and trained in England, she settles in New York City in the 1840s and opens a lithographic printing and publishing business with her husband. In 1849, she joins the staff of the firm of Nathaniel Currier. A creative lithographer, she draws directly on stone.

AUGUST 25, 1847   Birth of Elizabeth Flynn Rodgers, First Woman Member of Knights of Labor. Elizabeth Flynn Rodgers (1847–1939), a housewife and mother of 12 when she first joins the Holy Order of the Knights of Labor, is born. She becomes the first female member of that labor organization. (The Knights recognize housewives as workers and therefore consider them eligible for membership.) She and her husband, George, a union iron molder, live in Chicago, where she heads the Knights' women's Local Assembly No. 1789. Rodgers is also one of the few women to be elected to the highest post a woman can hold—master workman. In that capacity, she represents 40,000 members, both men and women. Before the Knights admit women, Rodgers organizes a union of working women and serves as their president for two years. As a member of the Knights, Rodgers serves as a judge in their district court and represents her own Knights' assembly at district meetings. At the 1886 national convention, Rodgers is nominated for the position of general treasurer, but declines the nomination.

OCTOBER 1, 1847   English Radical and Theosophist Annie Besant Is Born. Annie Wood Besant (1847–1933), who earns a reputation as a radical, free thinker, supporter of family limitation, socialist, and Theosophist, is born in England. Throughout her life, she is affected by the strong and conflicting religious

Annie Besant

experiences of her childhood. Her father, who dies when she is five, is an agnostic; her mother is a deeply religious Anglican; and the spinster who "adopts" Annie Wood after her father's death is of "low-Church" Calvinist leanings. At 14, she visits Paris, where she falls under the spell of the Catholic church, but after a disastrous marriage to an Anglican minister, she loses her religious faith for a while. In 1867, she marries Rev. Frank Besant, who strikes her when she suggests they practice "family limitation" (contraception). They separate in 1873, and Annie Besant supports herself and her daughter, Mabel, by writing for *National Reformer*, a journal for "free thinkers," and by public speaking. Her radical speeches provoke violent reactions from some but adulation from others. Her beauty, passion, and brilliance attract Charles Bradlaugh, a leading secularist (the

Victorian term for radical atheist). Unable to divorce her husband, Besant forms a romantic as well as intellectual relationship with Bradlaugh. They both support Irish home rule, attack Christianity, and advocate family limitation as a cure for poverty. In 1877 they stand trial for publishing a pamphlet on contraception but are acquitted of "obscene libel." In 1884 Besant meets the author and socialist George Bernard Shaw, who rejects her proposal of a "free marriage." As a socialist, she writes articles on poverty, slums, sweatshops, and prostitution, and she supports the Matchmakers' Strike of 1888.

By the time she writes her autobiography (1893), Besant has embarked on the last great crusade of her life—Theosophy. Deeply interested in Eastern mysticism, she joins the circle led by Madame Blavatsky, edits the organization's magazine, and becomes its leader after Blavatsky's death. She also founds a Hindu college in India, supports the Indian nationalist movement against the British government, and founds the Indian Boy Scouts.

Maria Mitchell

OCTOBER 1, 1847   Comet Named After Woman for First Time. American astronomer Maria Mitchell (1818–1889) becomes the first woman to have a comet named after her. While assisting her father, William Mitchell, in his observatory, Maria makes a discovery of her own—an unknown comet. As a consequence, she gains worldwide fame as an astronomer.

1848   Desiree Gay Helps Found The Women's Club in France. During the Revolution of 1848, Desiree Gay and her colleagues form *Le Club des Femmes* (The Women's Club) to work for female autonomy from men, women's suffrage, and women's political freedom. In 1832, Gay and a group of Saint-Simonian women found a women's newspaper, *La Femme Nouvelle* (*The New Woman*). Although they are Saint-Simonians, they downplay the aspect of free love preached by

this group of utopian socialists and insist instead on the greater importance of women's economic independence from men. Gay argues for women's right to work and to be self-supporting, but she also defends the traditional sectors of women's employment, such as ribbon selling, from male infiltration.

Gay especially believes that women are united through maternity, a quality unique to their sex. According to Gay, "Women's banner is universal, for...are they not all united by the same bond, Maternity?" In addition to organizing The Women's Club, Gay also serves on the national workshop council and proposes a series of services for working class women. However, the conservative political victory in April 1848 leads to a backlash against feminists and the working class. The government soon closes down the national workshops, and workers like Gay take to the streets to protest during the "June Days" insurrection.

The new French government declares an end to women's membership in political clubs and begins harassing women's newspapers. Women like Gay who play a public role symbolize the disorderliness of a revolution that the men in power want to put behind them. Gay flees to Belgium, and the French feminist movement of 1848-49 collapses.

1848 Birth of Hubertine Auclert, French Suffragist. Hubertine Auclert (1848–1914), who becomes a leading French suffragist, is born. Although her parents die when she is still a child, they leave her enough money to support herself. This allows her to work for women's civil rights, a cause for which she is recruited by Maria Deraismes in the early 1870s. Auclert becomes convinced that women can never gain civil equality unless they first gain the right to vote. Deraismes and Léon Richer forbid her to bring the issue up publicly, so, in 1878, she breaks with them. She has already formed her own group, the Society for Women's Rights, in 1876, but changes its name to The Society for Women's Suffrage in 1883 to better reflect its goal. From 1881 to 1891 she publishes *The Citizen*, a newspaper dedicated to female suffrage. She also writes for a variety of other journals and writes several books. She is most famous, though, for her publicity-grabbing tactics, which she calls the politics of "the assault." She goes on a tax strike, registers to vote and to run for office, and calls on women to boycott the government census until women become full citizens. She also pushes for labor legislation that will help working women, and by 1900 she convinces most middle-class feminists of the importance of suffrage. She dies in 1914, without seeing women gain the vote.

1848 New York State Passes Law Guaranteeing Property Rights to Women. The state of New York passes a law that permits married women to hold and to dispose of property;

Elizabeth Cady Stanton (1815–1902) is a key force in the law's passage. Similar laws are soon adopted by other states, beginning a trend that will ultimately extend full civil rights to women.

FEBRUARY 1848 Society for Women's Equality, the Vesuvians, Is Formed in France. During the chaos of the February Revolution in France in 1848, many men and women form political clubs or societies. The Vesuvians are a radical group of poorly-paid young working women who form in Paris. They demand total equality in marriage, politics, and even dress: they wear loose pants similar to the American feminists' "bloomers." They also demand female military service. Their constitution states that "the Republic recognizes neither masters nor slaves: it sees only children who are equally free." The Vesuvians also argue that husbands should share equally in household chores or face legal punishment, stating "husbands and wives are like associates, friends united by interests and affection. Neither should be a master." More moderate feminists shy away from them, and male cartoonists satirize their controversial dress and ideas in an attempt to ridicule all demands for women's rights. The group is suppressed in June 1848.

FEBRUARY 17, 1848 Birth of Louisa Lawson, Founder of Australia's First Feminist Paper. Feminist and suffragist Louisa Albury Lawson (1848–1920) is born into a poor rural family in New South Wales, Australia. She marries Neils (Peter) Larsen, a gold digger, in 1866. The couple selects 40 acres at Eurunderee, anglicizes the Larsen name to Lawson, and produces five children. Louisa Lawson supports them by working the farm while her husband is away prospecting. In 1883, she takes the children to Sydney where she does sewing and washing and takes in boarders. In 1887 she saves enough to buy the near-defunct *Republican* newspaper, which she runs for a year with the help of her gifted son, Henry. Lawson then starts *The Dawn*, Australia's first feminist journal. The paper is a commercial success and, by 1889, has ten employees. However, her insistence on employing only women leads to conflict with the printers' union, which does not permit women members. She is accused of anti-unionism and her reporters are thrown out of a New South Wales Tailoresses' strike meeting in 1896. *The Dawn* hosts The Dawn Club to offer women the opportunity to practice public speaking. Its offices and printery also accommodate the Womanhood Suffrage League, of which Lawson is a council member. In 1900 she suffers an accident from which she never recovers. Her problems are exacerbated by the stress of protracted legal battles with the New South Wales Post Office over ownership of a patent mailbag fastener. *The Dawn* folds in 1905 and Lawson supports herself by selling her poetry. She dies in the Gladesville Hospital for the Insane in 1920.

FEBRUARY 22, 1848   Revolution of 1848 Breaks Out in Paris. When street riots overthrow King Louis-Philippe I in February 1848, France becomes a republic. During the period from February to April, many French women form clubs, engage in journalism, call for women's rights, and even run for political office. The temporary Provisional Government refuses to allow women any new rights, claiming that only an elected legislature can do so. In April, elections based on universal male suffrage return a conservative legislature and government that proceeds to crack down on radicals and feminists. This culminates in the bloody June Days, when government troops brutally suppress an uprising of poor Parisian women and men, killing over 2,000. Although the revolution gives women a brief window of opportunity to agitate for their rights, they make no concrete gains from it. The male Republican leadership refuses to grant women equal rights, and the Republic falls to a military coup after only three years.

JULY 19, 1848   Women's Rights Convention In Seneca Falls. Three hundred women and men gather on July 19–20 in the Wesleyan Chapel in Seneca Falls, New York, for "A Convention to discuss the social, civil, and religious condition and rights of Woman." Elizabeth Cady Stanton (1815–1902) is a key force in the reform community in western New York State. Along with Lucretia Mott, Stanton organizes the now-famous Women's Rights Convention at Seneca Falls, New York. Stanton's skills as a writer result in the *Declaration of Sentiments* which comes out of the Women's Rights Convention. Stanton patterns the *Declaration of Sentiments* after the Declaration of Independence, stating that men *and women* are created equal, and demanding that women be permitted to vote. One hundred men and women, including abolitionist Frederick Douglass, sign the document on July 20, the final day of the convention.

JULY 30, 1848   Birth of Ellis Rowan, Painter of Australian Flora and Fauna. Marian Ellis (Ellis) Ryan Rowan (1848–1922), who discovers and paints Australian flora and fauna, is born. Although she receives no formal art training, she starts painting flowers in her youth and continues to do so through a four-year New Zealand posting that follows her marriage to Frederic Rowan in 1873. By this time Ellis Rowan is exhibiting her work. Between 1879 and 1893 she holds exhibitions in Australia, India, England, Europe, and the United States and is awarded ten gold medals, 15 silver, and four bronze. After her husband's death in 1892, Rowan travels widely, gaining particular acclaim in London. Between 1916 and 1918 she visits Papua New Guinea, finding and illustrating unclassified flowers and searching for endangered birds of paradise. She succeeds in painting 47 of the 52 known species. Her many successes, however, exact their toll. In order to discover rare or unknown plants and animals, she works in unexplored territory, often under very primitive conditions. She routinely travels alone or with local native guides. By 1920 her health is broken by fatigue and repeated bouts of malaria. Further, her success is often resented by other artists who claim that flower painting is not "real" art. Nevertheless, several colonial governments acquire her paintings, and a collection now hangs in the National Library in Canberra, Australia.

1849   Swedish Writer Ellen Key, Advocate of Radical Reforms for Marriage and Motherhood, Is Born. Ellen Sofia Karolina Key (1849-1926), a writer who publishes controversial works on marriage and motherhood, is born in Sundsholm, Sweden. She is the eldest child of a Swedish landowner, a political radical of Scottish ancestry, and his wife, a Swedish noblewoman. Educated at home, Key travels widely throughout Europe with her father during her early adulthood. She becomes a school teacher in Stockholm to support herself and lectures at the Workers' Institute in Stockholm for several years. Although she never marries, she has keen insight into the problems of wives and mothers. Key criticizes the Catholic and Lutheran churches' views of sex for procreation within marriage only, and she calls for the open acknowledgment of the sexual aspect of love. Key campaigns for radical reforms in the marriage laws to grant women's work within the home adequate social and economic recognition. She suggests that the economic support of women during their childbearing years should be the responsibility of the government, not husbands, since dependence on individual men leads to women's subordination within marriage. Key proposes formal training for motherhood and insists that motherhood be recognized by the government as the female equivalent of male military service. Her ideas find wide support among leaders of the women's movement throughout Northern Europe. Curiously, Key does not support women's suffrage. In her 1896 speech

"The Abuse of Women's Strength," she attacks women's desire to vote. According to Key, women can achieve their maximum development as individuals through their contributions to society as mothers. In her middle age, she begins to publish the controversial works that bring her international fame, including *The Century of the Child* (1900) and *Love and Marriage* (1904).

1849   Jeanne Déroin Becomes Leading Advocate for Women's Suffrage in France. The Parisian Jeanne Déroin (1805–1894), in her periodical, *L'Opinion des Femmes* (*Women's Opinion*), presents her vision of women's participation in public affairs: male privilege will end, women will vote, and women's moral superiority will triumph over male violence. Also this year, she petitions the Democratic-Socialist party to become a candidate for the Legislative Assembly, an action that is declared unconstitutional. She also helps found a national federation of workers' associations which includes both male and female workers. The police suppress the associations in 1850, and Déroin is sentenced to six months in jail for "conspiracy to overthrow the government by violence."

1849   Elizabeth Blackwell, World's First Trained, Registered Woman Doctor. At age 28, Elizabeth Blackwell (1821–1910) graduates at the top of her class at Geneva Medical College of New York State and becomes the world's first trained, registered woman doctor. The daughter of an abolitionist, she is raised to be bold and outspoken. She believes that women doctors will help other women whose "modesty" and "delicacy" keep them ignorant of their bodies and adequate healthcare. All of the colleges she writes to for admission disagree, however, until the Geneva Medical College accepts her in 1847. After graduation, she works in a hospital in Paris, France, where she contracts an eye infection. The partial loss of her eyesight destroys her plans for a career

Elizabeth Blackwell

in surgery, but she manages to complete her medical training in a London hospital.

Upon her return to America, Blackwell is not allowed by other doctors to practice her profession. She begins giving lectures on female health that attract a small following of interested patients. In 1853 she opens a dispensary in New York City where she treats female illnesses, sexual diseases, and pregnancy complications. The dispensary at 64 Bleecker Street soon becomes the New York Infirmary for Indigent Women and Children. During the Civil War she trains and dispatches nurses to war fronts, and in 1868 she opens the Infirmary Medical School for women. Blackwell does not consider herself a feminist or part of a general movement. Rather, she sees herself as special and believes that most women should become mothers, not doctors. She also argues that female doctors should pursue only the areas of

family practice, obstetrics, and gynecology. She returns to England while in her 40s and is active in such causes as spiritualism, psychology, and anti-vivisectionism.

1849   Amelia Jenks Bloomer Founds Reform Publication *The Lily.* Amelia Jenks Bloomer (1818–1894) begins to publish *The Lily*, a periodical that provides a forum for reformers prominent in the temperance movement. Bloomer introduces woman's rights activists Elizabeth Cady Stanton and Susan B. Anthony to each other in 1850, and the two also contribute their views to *The Lily*.

In the pages of *The Lily's* first issues, Bloomer articulates her support for the actress Fanny Kemble, whose decision, for reasons of health and comfort, to wear "pantalettes" under a modified long dress creates a public furor. In 1851, *The Lily* continues its advocacy of the healthful and liberating potential of reform costume by promoting an ensemble that is brought to Bloomer's attention by Elizabeth Smith Miller, a cousin of her friend Elizabeth Cady Stanton. Both Stanton and Bloomer adopt Miller's "short dress" and "Turkish trousers," and the costume becomes known popularly as the "Bloomer Costume" through its promotion in Bloomer's publication. Newspapers throughout the country make capital of the eccentricity of the costume and of those who wear it, eliciting either intense interest or unmitigated scorn from their readership. While Bloomer, Stanton, Susan B. Anthony, and Lucy Stone number among the costume's most vocal proponents for several years, all eventually give up wearing and championing it. They fear that widespread caricatures of reform dress as the hobbyhorse of an "un-sexed" group of women extremists seeking to insinuate themselves into men's sphere of society by emulating male attire may damage the cause of woman's rights.

Though she sells *The Lily* in 1853, Bloomer continues to promote the causes of temperance and women's rights and suffrage through lecture tours, published articles, and legislative lobbying. In 1856, she works for suffrage legislation in Nebraska and Iowa. In 1871, she is elected president of the Iowa Woman Suffrage Society and helps to lay the groundwork for the Iowa legal code of 1873, which grants married women property rights previously denied to them. She dies in Council Bluffs, Iowa, on December 30, 1894.

1849 **Property Rights Extended to Women in California.** The first state constitution in California extends property rights to women in their own name. California becomes the 31st state the next year, in 1850.

APRIL 1849 **Margaret Fuller Reports on Siege of Rome.** When American reformer Margaret Fuller (1810–1850) travels to Europe in 1846, publisher Horace Greeley asks her to send dispatches to the *New York Tribune*. Three years later, Fuller finds herself in Rome as the city is besieged by the French Army and sends reports of the bombardment to the *Tribune*.

JULY 1849 **Lydia Sayer Hasbrouck, American Physician and Journalist, Adopts Pantaloons for Clothing.** Lydia Sayer Hasbrouck (1827–1910), concerned for physical freedom, sets aside the tightly-fitted bodices and floor-length, voluminous skirts that are the period's fashion and adopts in their place the knee-length dress and pantaloons that become known as the "Bloomer costume." Lydia Sayer obtains her medical degree during the early 1850s from the American Hydropathic Institute in New York City. She subsequently divides her time between a medical practice in Washington, D.C., and journalism, contributing regularly to newspapers in Washington, Baltimore, and Philadelphia. Returning to her home territory on a lecture tour in 1856, Sayer remains in Middletown, New York, to take up the editorship of a new, feminist periodical called *The Sibyl: A Review of the Tastes, Errors, and Fashions of Society*, published by John Hasbrouck. The two are married on July 27, 1856,

Sarah Orne Jewett

three weeks after they produce the first issue of *The Sibyl*. Lydia Sayer Hasbrouck is elected to the Middletown Board of Education in 1880, one of the first women in the country to hold elected office. She dies in Middletown on August 24, 1910.

SEPTEMBER 3, 1849 **Birth of Maine Author Sarah Orne Jewett.** Sarah Orne Jewett (1849–1909), an author whose works depict life in her native state, is born in South Berwick, Maine. She writes several novels and collections of stories, beginning with *A Country Doctor* in 1884, which detail the flora and fauna and the customs of the local people, especially the women, in late nineteenth-century New England. She is remembered particularly for her autobiographical collection of interrelated stories, *The Country of the Pointed Firs*, first published in 1896. She dies in South Berwick in 1909.

Frances Eliza Hodgson Burnett

OCTOBER 1849 Astronomer Maria Mitchell Appointed as Contributor to *American Ephemeris and Nautical Almanac.* American Astronomer Maria Mitchell (1818–1889) becomes one of the original contributors computing data for the *American Ephemeris and Nautical Almanac,* a work that provides tables of data stating the exact locations of celestial bodies at specific points in time.

NOVEMBER 24, 1849 Birth of Children's Author Frances Hodgson Burnett. Frances Eliza Hodgson Burnett (1849–1924), best known as a children's author, is born in Manchester, England. She later immigrates to the United States and becomes an American citizen in 1905. Her writing career begins at the age of ten, but her first published works are two stories, "Hearts and Diamonds," and

"Miss Carruthers Engagement," which appear in *Godeys Ladys Book* in 1868; she is 18 and receives 35 dollars for these manuscripts. She marries Swan Burnett, a doctor; bears two sons, Lionel and Vivian; and finally, after many years of separation, files for divorce. Frances Burnett is out of sync with her Victorian times. Married, divorced, self-supporting, she is driven by the need to publish to make money. She leads a flamboyant life and is publicly criticized for her behavior. She dresses extravagantly, smokes, and appears to have numerous relationships with men, from her editors to playwrights to actors. Burnett marries Stephen Townsend, her business manager and an actor/playwright, in 1900, but the marriage does not survive. Most of her prolific writing career is in the publishing of adult novels and in writing plays in both England and the United States. At the request of her son, she writes what becomes one of her most famous books, *Little Lord Fauntleroy* (1886), which is first published in *St. Nicholas Magazine* and sets a fashion for boys' clothes. The book is later made into plays, films, and other collectable items for children. In fact, Burnett sues the British playwright Seebohm for violating the Copyright Act of 1842 by writing a play version with text taken directly from her book. The courts decide in her favor and establish the precedent for authors to control the use of their work. The Society of British Authors honors her with a certificate and a diamond ring and bracelet to mark this occasion. *The Little Princess* (1905) and *The Secret Garden* (1911), the two books for which she is most famous, are made into plays, films, video, and CD-ROM productions. She begins her life in poverty and, through her writing, earns the money necessary for the things she values in life. She consistently gives money to family and friends and to charities for young boys.

Chapter 12

1850 TO 1859

1 8 5 0 – 1 8 5 4

1850 Elizabeth Barrett Browning Publishes *Sonnets from the Portuguese.* British Victorian poet Elizabeth Barrett Browning (1806–1861) publishes *Sonnets from the Portuguese,* a sequence of 44 sonnets recording the growth of her love for her husband, the poet Robert Browning, who calls her "my little Portuguese" because of her dark complexion. The 43rd sonnet begins with the now-famous line, "How do I love thee? Let me count the ways." Barrett Browning also writes poems protesting unjust social conditions, such as "The Cry of the Children," about child labor in England, and she appeals for political freedom for Italy, which remains under Austrian rule until 1861.

1850 Elizabeth Smith Miller Introduces Reform Dress to Amelia Bloomer, Who Promotes the Look. Elizabeth Smith (1822–1911) abandons her fashionable skirts and corseted waists for a "short dress" and "Turkish trousers" gathered at the ankles. Her self-reform arises, as she describes it, from "years of annoyance" with the "long heavy skirt" and "dissatisfaction" with herself for "submitting to such bondage." Her father's cousin, Elizabeth Cady Stanton, and Amelia Bloomer both adopt the ensemble. Bloomer lauds it in her reform paper *The Lily* in 1851, giving rise to its identification as the "Bloomer costume."

1850 African American Author Frances E. W. Harper Begins Teaching Career in Ohio. Frances E. W. Harper (1825–1910) starts her teaching career as the first female teacher at the Union Seminary in Ohio, founded by the African Methodist Episcopal Church. Harper also uses her literary talents to further the abolitionist and women's suffrage causes. By 1846, Harper publishes her first book of poetry, *Forest Leaves.* She moves to Philadelphia, Pennsylvania, in 1854 and becomes heavily involved in the abolitionist movement. Also that year, she publishes her second book, *Poems on Miscellaneous Subjects,* which has several reprintings and sells over 12,000 copies. The abolitionist theme is central in her work. She later joins the Maine Anti-Slavery Society, becoming its first female orator. After three years traveling in the North speaking out against slavery, Harper returns to Philadelphia in 1857 and serves as lecturer for the Pennsylvania Anti-Slavery Society.

1850 Su Sanniang Participates in Taiping Rebellion. Su Sanniang is a rebel who participates in the Taiping rebellion in China (1850–60). She is a female knight-errant who roams the countryside around Guilin in southwestern China. After avenging her husband's death, she throws her lot in with the rebels. Her military prowess, and the remarkable fact that she defeats generals of the Qing dynasty, is celebrated in poetry.

Female Medical College of Pennsylvania

OCTOBER 12, 1850 Opening Lectures at Female Medical College of Pennsylvania. The Female Medical College of Pennsylvania (FMCP), the first women's medical school in the world, offers its first courses.

OCTOBER 23–24, 1850 First National Women's Rights Convention Held at Worcester, Massachusetts. Over 1,000 men and women attend the first National Woman's Rights Convention, planned by Lucy Stone (1818–1893) and Lucretia Mott (1793–1880). National attention is directed at the women's rights movement in the United States as a result, and annual meetings are held for the next ten years.

1851 Emilia Pardo Bazan, Spanish Naturalist Author, Is Born. Emilia Pardo Bazan (1851–1921), a leading naturalist, or realist, writer in

Spain, is born. Like the French naturalist Emile Zola, Bazan rejects romantic versions of people's lives. Instead, her novels describe the power of nature to destroy whole families. *The Manor of Ulloa* (1886) realistically portrays village life and the decay of aristocratic families. Bazan boldly addresses themes of illegitimacy, ignorance, and sloth. In her sequel, *Mother Nature* (1887), she tackles the taboo subject of incest. Bazan is also a feminist who rejects the intellectual limits placed on upper-class Spanish women. She edits journals, engages in notorious literary debates, and champions improved education for girls. Because of her aristocratic social status, Bazan shocks society when she accepts a university post. By the end of the century she becomes interested in psychology, which she applies to character development in her novels.

1851 Reformers and Suffragists Elizabeth Cady Stanton and Susan B. Anthony Begin Productive Collaboration. Elizabeth Cady Stanton (1815–1902) begins a collaboration with Susan B. Anthony (1820–1906); the two publish a weekly newspaper, *The Revolution*, from 1858 to 1860, and, in 1869, create the National Women Suffrage Association, with Stanton as president. In 1888, Stanton and Anthony extend their efforts on behalf of suffrage for women, forming the International Council of Women. With Ida Harper, Matilda Gage, and Anthony, Stanton writes the first four volumes of the six-volume *A History of Woman Suffrage* (1881–1922).

JANUARY 11, 1851 Taiping Rebellion in China. The advent of the Taiping Rebellion contributes to a redefinition of women's rights in China. Hung Hsiu-ch'üan, a failed scholar and teacher who declares himself to be the brother of Jesus Christ, inaugurates the Taiping Tienkuo (Heavenly Kingdom of Great Peace). The Taiping Revolution spreads quickly throughout China, absorbing 18 provinces. From the Taiping capital of Nanking, Hung issues a series of edicts. Women are declared to be the equal of men and enjoy access to all civil and military posts in the kingdom. One hundred thousand women join the Taiping army as soldiers and officers. Prostitution and polygamy are outlawed, and women gain equal access to land. The practice of foot-binding, the most visible example of female oppression, is prohibited. Internal dissension and government pressure lead to the collapse of the Taiping Revolution in 1864. Despite this defeat, however, the Taiping Revolution profoundly affects the Chinese perception of women's rights.

MAY 29, 1851 African American Orator Sojourner Truth Gives Powerful Speech on Discrimination. Born a slave called Isabella, Sojourner Truth (c.1797–1893) gives a particularly powerful speech on racial and sexual discrimination at a women's rights convention in Akron, Ohio. Her words are recounted many years later by the writer and reformer Frances Dana Gage, who includes the now-famous words "Ar'n't (Ain't) I a Woman?," though contemporary newspaper accounts of the speech do not include this phrase.

C. 1852 Dr. Harriet N. Austin Introduces the "American Costume." Harriet N. Austin (1825–1891), M.D., originates a loose-fitting style of reform dress for women known as the "American Costume." In 1851 Austin, a health reformer, dress reformer, and women's rights advocate, receives her medical degree from the American Hydropathic Institute in New York City, a member of its first graduating class.

In 1852, Austin joins the practice of James C. Jackson, M.D., at the Glen Haven Water Cure near Syracuse, New York. She writes in 1858 that "Health cannot be had without habitual exercise out of doors...and the dress of women positively forbids this.... Women can ... never take their proper rank till they adopt and wear a dress at least so unlike their present as the Reform Dress...." Both

Austin and Jackson campaign zealously for women's release from the "bondage" of constrictive fashionable clothing as a prerequisite for intellectual freedom and full citizenship. Soon after she takes up her post at Glen Haven, Austin herself gives up wearing the corseted bodices and long skirts in fashion, and continues to wear some form of reform dress until her death in 1891. She originates a set of garments that becomes known as the "American Costume." "The Dress," she writes, "may be of any material....[Bodices] ... may be worn [plain or with trimmings].... But all ... should be so loose as to leave the lungs ... unobstructed in their action.... The skirt does not reach below the knee, and is a little less full than a long dress skirt.... The appearance of the skirt is improved ... by adding an outer skirt a little more than half as long as the first.... The best style of pantaloons ... is much the same as gentlemen's.... I am satisfied that the only rational manner of supporting the pants is by elastic suspenders. They must have support from the shoulders, and there must be the capability of yielding in stooping...."

In 1858, Jackson and his wife move with their son, Giles, and with Austin, whom they legally adopt in 1855, to Dansville, New York. There, they take possession of an abandoned sanatorium, which they rename "Our Home on the Hillside." Austin appears to treat both women and men patients, an unusual circumstance during the nineteenth century when women physicians are grudgingly allowed only the circumscribed territory of "women's and children's diseases" in deference to concerns of propriety.

During her years at Glen Haven and Dansville, Harriet Austin publishes tracts on various health and dress reform issues. She edits newsletters published by her own institutions and contributes to such national publications as *The Sibyl* and *The Water-Cure Journal*. She is one of the founding members of the National Dress Reform Association, serving terms as its president and its secretary.

Rosa Marie Rosalie Bonheur

1852   Woman Granted Official Permission to Dress as Man. In Paris, France, Rosa Marie Rosalie Bonheur (1822–1899), the French artist known for her vivid depiction of animals in her paintings, is the first woman to be granted official police permission to wear male attire. Bonheur initially dresses as a man in order to be allowed to observe anatomy at Paris slaughter houses, but her male attire later becomes a trademark.

1852   Susan B. Anthony Founds First Temperance Organization in the United States. Susan B. Anthony (1820–1906), a liberal Quaker strongly opposed to the use of alcohol, founds the first temperance organization in the United States—the Women's Temperance Society.

1852   Publication of *Roughing It in the Bush*, Account of Pioneer Life in Canada. Susanna Strickland Moodie (1803–1885) writes an influential and popular account of pioneer life in Canada, entitled *Roughing It in the Bush*. Born on December 6, 1803, at Stowe House, near Bungay in Suffolk, England, she is the youngest in a literary family. Along with her sister, Catherine Parr Traill, Moodie becomes one of Canada's most famous gentlewoman emigrants from the British Isles. Emigrating to Canada in 1832, Moodie and her husband settle near Peterborough, Canada West. In *Roughing It in the Bush*, Moodie warns emigrants that Canada is not the paradise that it is promoted to be in England and that the settler's life is a harsh one. Her struggles as a pioneer, liberal ideas, attachment to the finest of contemporary British values, and mistrust of "Yankee influences" from America make her a legendary figure in Canada. Moodie also contributes to the *Literary Garland* and *The Victorian Magazine*.

APRIL 1852   Publication of Antislavery Novel *Uncle Tom's Cabin*. American author Harriet Beecher Stowe (1811–1896) publishes *Uncle Tom's Cabin*. Neither she nor the public is really prepared for the immense popularity of the work. The novel's focus on what slavery does to families, and Stowe's emphasis on what women's reactions to slavery are and can be, help to energize antislavery activity by women in the United States, England, and around the world. The novel is an immediate best-seller and has remained in print continuously since 1852, with translations into more than 100 languages.

1853   Eugenie de Montijo Becomes Empress Eugenie of France. Eugenie Marie de Montijo (1826–1920) of Spain marries Napoleon III, soon after the Second Empire of France is proclaimed. As empress, she gains international attention and praise and represents the height of womanhood at mid-century.

1853   Elizabeth Blackwell Opens a Dispensary for Women. Dr. Elizabeth Blackwell (1821–

House where Harriet Beecher Stowe wrote *Uncle Tom's Cabin.*

1910) opens a dispensary in New York City where she treats female illnesses, sexual diseases, and pregnancy complications. The dispensary at 64 Bleecker Street soon becomes the New York Infirmary for Indigent Women and Children. Blackwell, at age 28, graduates at the top of her class at Geneva Medical College of New York State. She becomes the world's first trained, registered woman doctor, although she is prevented from practicing medicine by other doctors.

FEBRUARY 1853 **The First Women's Rights Newspaper, *Una*, Premiers.** Published in Providence, Rhode Island, and edited by Paulina Kellogg Wright Davis (1813–1876), the *Una* is the first newspaper of the women's rights movement. Its masthead carries the slogan, "A Paper Devoted to the Elevation of Woman." Davis publishes the *Una* at her own expense until 1855.

1854 **Marie L. Shedlock, Master British Storyteller, Is Born.** Marie L. Shedlock (1854–1935), British author, is born. Shedlock is regarded as a master storyteller and is noted

for her work, *Art of the Storyteller,* which she publishes in 1915.

1854 **Scottish Writer Margaret Oliphant Publishes Pamphlet Exposing Unfair Laws.** Margaret Oliphant (1827–1897), one of the most popular and prolific writers in Victorian England, publishes *A Brief Summary in Plain Language of the Most Important Laws Concerning Women.* This pamphlet explains the unfair laws concerning women and exposes the need for reform. Oliphant is a member of the original audiences attending lectures for women at Bedford College, London, in 1849. She later makes large financial donations to Bedford and to Girton College, Cambridge, which she helps to found. As a popular writer, Oliphant publishes over 120 novels and historical works and 300 articles in magazines and journals. Throughout the 1860s she addresses the need to reform the laws concerning women's property. After her husband's death in 1859 and the death of her daughter, Oliphant cares for her widowed brother's children and her own two sons, all of whom rely on her writing for financial support. She later writes in her autobiography that her vast literary output is motivated by financial need. Despite her struggles, Oliphant does not identify herself as a feminist. In an article written for the *Edinburgh Review,* Oliphant argues that in marriage, the couple, not the individual, matters.

1854 **Florence Nightingale and Her Nurses Care for British Troops during Crimean War.** Florence Nightingale (1820–1910) commands a party of nurses during the Crimean War (1854–56), in which British soldiers are dying from poor medical care, disease, and malnourishment. Sidney Herbert of the British military helps Nightingale obtain a commission to raise and equip a team of 38 nurses to care for British troops. After the war, Nightingale returns to England a national heroine. She then devotes her energies to transforming the British army into a modern, sanitary, and effi-

Florence Nightingale

cient institution. She also establishes schools of nursing and nursing corps and publishes the best-selling *Notes on Nursing* in 1859.

Nightingale challenges old superstitions and advocates such novel ideas as fresh air and sunshine, substantial nourishment, and friendly visitors to aid a patient's recuperation. She does not support the women's rights movement, nor does she applaud such women as Elizabeth Blackwell who become doctors. She prefers to carve out a separate space for women as nurses.

1854   Catherine Spence Publishes Novel about Australia. Australian Catherine Helen Spence (1825–1910) publishes (anonymously) *Clara Morison*, the first novel about Australia written by a woman. She writes eight works of fiction before discarding the genre in 1889. All her novels are strongly feminist.

1 8 5 5 – 1 8 5 9

1855   Boöena Nemcová Writes Famous Czech Novel *Granny*. Barbora Panklova Nemcová (1820–1862) writes the famous Czech novel *Granny*, the story of an old grandmother who keeps alive the Czech national heritage for future generations. Nemcová is born in Bohemia, the Czech province of the Habsburg Empire, but she anticipates the creation of the independent nation of Czechoslovakia in 1918. Although she grows up in a German environment in Bohemia, she develops an intense Czech consciousness. Married to Josef Nemec in 1837, she begins writing in Czech under the pen name of Boöena Nemcová.

1855   Young Women's Christian Association (YWCA) Is Started. Two groups in Great Britain are founded—a Prayer Union and the General Female Training Institute (a home for nurses returning from the Crimean War, forming the foundation of the Young Women's Christian Association (YWCA). The two organizations expand their activities and merge in 1877 as the Young Women's Christian Association. YWCAs also send missionaries to other parts of the world—including India, China, Japan, Korea, parts of Latin America, and (less often) Africa.

DECEMBER 2, 1855   Eliza Clark Garrett's Will Establishes Garrett Biblical Institute. Eliza Clark Garrett (1805–1855), following her death, leaves proceeds in her will to establish the Garrett Biblical Institute, a theological institution for the Methodist Episcopal Church in Chicago, Illinois. Garrett dedicates her life to religious education.

1856   Kate Douglas Wiggin, American Author and Educator, Is Born. Kate Douglas Wiggin (1856–1923), author and kindergarten teacher, is born. In 1903, Wiggin publishes *Rebecca of Sunnybrook Farm*, which later is adapted into a play and a feature film, starring

Eliza Clark Garrett

child actress Shirley Temple. In 1911, Wiggin publishes *Mother Carey's Chickens*.

JANUARY 19, 1856   African American Slave Biddy Mason Wins Freedom in Lawsuit. Former slave Biddy Mason (1818–1891) wins her suit for freedom before Judge Benjamin Hayes in a Los Angeles, California, court. Although blacks are prohibited from testifying against whites in California courts, Judge Hayes hears Mason's plea in his chambers and ultimately pronounces that she and all of her family are "entitled to their freedom and are free forever." Mason encounters free blacks for the first time in California when her owner emigrates there, and when he wants to move everyone to the slave state of Texas, Mason brings her lawsuit for freedom.

FEBRUARY 21, 1856   National Dress Reform Association Established. The first organiza-

tional meeting of what becomes the National Dress Reform Association (NDRA) is held over two days in Homer, New York. Those in attendance at this first meeting—men and women from ten states—resolve that: "… in advocating Reform in Dress for Woman, our object is not to advocate for her positions of singularity, eccentricity, immodesty, or to get her out of her 'appropriate sphere'; but to enable her to act with that freedom needful to find out what her 'appropriate sphere' is…and, seeing a clear connection between her dress and her present condition, we are determined to discard a dress that is only adapted to 'womanly helplessness.'" Their priorities include ridding women of long skirts and tight corsets and bodices.

The NDRA survives until 1865, holding annual dress reform conventions every year except for 1862. Membership, which is estimated at its height to include 6,000 to 8,000 women alone, is open to all men and women over the age of 12.

FEBRUARY 28, 1856   Birth of Elizabeth Glendower Evans, American Labor Organizer and Reformer. Elizabeth Glendower Evans (1856–1937), an active reformer, suffragist and labor organizer, is born. She marries in 1882 but is widowed in 1886. That same year she is appointed to the Massachusetts reformatory system's board of trustees. In 1911, she works with Florence Kelley and heads up the campaign in Massachusetts that results in the first minimum wage law for women passed in the United States. Evans is an active member of the Women's Trade Union League and participates in many strikes. These include the 1910 weavers' strike in Roxbury, Massachusetts, and the 1912 textile workers' strike in Lawrence, Massachusetts. For over 25 years she is a contributing editor to *La Follette's Weekly Magazine*, a reformist labor publication put out by Senator Robert and Belle La Follette. She also lobbies on behalf of the American Women's

Suffrage Association and is a national director of the American Civil Liberties Union.

JULY 1856 Periodical *The Sibyl,* Promoting Dress Reform and Women's Rights, Is Founded. Lydia Sayer, M.D., a physician and journalist who champions women's rights, and John Hasbrouck, a Middletown, New York, publisher and newspaper editor, join forces to produce the first issue of *The Sibyl: A Review of the Tastes, Errors, and Fashions of Society.* This periodical provides a sympathetic forum for a variety of reform agendas, as well as editorial commentary on those beliefs and prejudices that mid-nineteenth-century reform movements seek to revise.

C. 1857 Luna Elizabeth Sanford Kellie, American Agrarian Reformer, Is Born. Luna Elizabeth Sanford (c.1857–1940), a western pioneer who fights for agrarian reform, is born in Pipestone, Minnesota, the eldest of five children. In 1874 her family settles in St. Louis, where she marries James Kellie. In 1876 she moves to Nebraska to homestead near her father. Kellie lives in a sod house, contends with grasshopper plagues, almost starves, watches family members die, does demanding physical work, and raises 11 children. She also works with various reform organizations.

When devastating winds destroy her family's wheat crop, Luna Kellie's "egg and milk" money pays the household expenses. Unfortunately, despite her hard work, the family loses their farm. Kellie blames the railroads for her family's failure and turns to politics.

In 1894, she is elected the state secretary of Nebraska's Farmers' Alliance and gains national attention. She is a staunch Populist and opposes political fusion with either the Democrats or the Republicans. She lectures for the alliance and publishes the newspaper *Wealth Makers*, later called the *Prairie Home*, in 1895. It rallies support for the non-fusionist cause.

Emmeline Pankhurst

Kellie continues to be involved in agrarian reform until 1900. Thereafter, disillusioned by lack of progress, she sells her newspaper and returns to farming. In 1918 her husband dies, and during the Great Depression she loses her farm and moves to Arizona, where she once again tries to homestead. Unfortunately, ill health thwarts her efforts, and she dies in Phoenix.

1857 English Suffragist Emmeline Goulden Pankhurst Is Born. Emmeline Goulden Pankhurst (1857–1928), leader of the movement for women's suffrage, is born in Manchester, England. In 1879, she marries Richard Marsden Pankhurst, a barrister who authors the first women's suffrage bill in England, and of the Married Women's Property Acts of 1870 and 1882. In 1889, Emmeline Pankhurst founds the Women's Franchise

League, and in 1903, with her daughter Christabel (1880–1958) founds the Women's Social and Political Union. Emmeline is frequently imprisoned for her militant tactics on behalf of the cause of women's suffrage, and is force fed during hunger strikes she undertakes while in prison. She publishes an autobiography, *My Own Story*, in 1914.

1857   Birth of American Journalist Ida Minerva Tarbell. Ida Minerva Tarbell (1857–1944), American journalist, is born in Erie County, Pennsylvania. She studies at Allegheny College and the Sorbonne in Paris, and joins the staff of *McClure's Magazine* in 1894. She publishes biographies of Napoleon, Madame Roland, and Abraham Lincoln. Her investigation of the tactics used by John D. Rockefeller in building the Standard Oil Company is published in book form as *History of the Standard Oil Company* in 1904. She denounces his empire-building business tactics, and contributes significantly to the efforts to pass antitrust legislation in the United States. Her works on women's rights include *The Business of Being a Woman* (1912) and *The Ways of Women* (1915). She publishes her autobiography, *All in the Day's Work*, in 1939.

1857   Married Women's Property Bill Passes in the U.S. Congress. The Married Women's Property Bill passes in the U.S. Congress, beginning to redress the grievances of married women whose property and children have been under the complete control of husbands, no matter how abusive or negligent. Clause 21 allows a deserted wife to keep her earnings; Clause 25 empowers a wife to inherit and bequeath property; Clause 26 allows a separated wife to sue, be sued, and make contracts.

1857   Delia Bacon Alleges William Shakespeare Is a Fraud. With the support of writer and diplomat Nathaniel Hawthorne, Delia Bacon (1811–1859) publishes her 700-page volume entitled *The Philosophy of the Plays of Shakespeare Unfolded*. Her premise is that Wil-

Selma Attiliana Lovisa Lagerlöf

liam Shakespeare did not write the plays that are credited to him.

C. JUNE 4, 1857   Laskshmi Bai of India Renounces Alliance to British Crown. Laskshmi Bai (c.1820–1858) renounces her alliance to Great Britain, the colonial power in India, and emerges as the Indian Mutiny's most competent military leader. Bai dies leading her troops on June 17, 1858, during the Battle of Gwalior. Her body is easily recognized—a striking woman attired in male clothing, fully armed. She is often compared to France's Joan of Arc.

1858   Selma Lagerlöf, Swedish Writer, Is Born. Selma Attiliana Lovisa Lagerlöf (1858–1940) is born. She publishes her best-known work, *The Miracles of Antichrist*, in 1899. In 1909, she becomes the first woman to win the

George Eliot

Nobel Prize for literature, and in 1914 is named the first woman member of the Swedish Academy.

1858 **Susan B. Anthony and Elizabeth Cady Stanton Found Newspaper** *The Revolution.* Susan Brownell Anthony (1820–1906) and Elizabeth Cady Stanton (1815–1902) publish a weekly newspaper, *The Revolution,* with the motto: "The true republic—men, their rights and nothing more; women, their rights and nothing less." When they cease publication in 1860, *The Revolution* has over $10,000 in debts, which Anthony pays off through her public speaking engagements.

1858 **English Writer George Eliot Publishes First Novel.** One of the greatest writers of the nineteenth century, George Eliot, the pseudonym of Mary Ann Evans (1819–1880), pub-

lishes her first novel, *Scenes of Clerical Life.* It is followed by *Adam Bede* in 1859; by the time she publishes *The Mill on the Floss* in 1860, her true identity is revealed. However, she continues to use her male pseudonym for her subsequent novels, *Silas Marner* (1861) and *Middlemarch* (1872).

Eliot's novels portray aspects of ordinary life and examine ordinary people—parsons, country girls, undistinguished scholars, and aristocrats. Her masterpiece, *Middlemarch,* criticizes women's aspirations to be like men in their quest for money and place. Although she never publicly supports the women's rights movement in England, she is admired by most feminists. The death of George Henry Lewes, the man with whom she lives for years, in 1878 leaves Eliot griefstricken and lonely. She weds John Cross in 1880 shortly before her death.

1858 **Young Women's Christian Association Begins in the United States.** In the United States, the Young Women's Christian Association (YWCA) begins when evangelical Protestant women form a prayer circle in New York City. Eventually calling themselves the Ladies' Christian Union, they work for the welfare of self-supporting young women. In 1871, younger women break off to focus on housing and employment opportunities and became the Young Women's Christian Association of the City of New York. Similar organizations spring up throughout the urban United States. While never abandoning their religious commitments, these groups concentrate their efforts on young women moving to the city from rural areas. Community YWCAs provide a variety of services including employment programs, housing, recreation, education, religious activities, travelers' aid, health programs, cafeterias, and free libraries.

JUNE 1858 **Margaret Gaffney Haughery Establishes Steam Bakery.** Margaret Gaffney Haughery (1813–1882) becomes the first woman to establish a steam bakery in the

American South when she opens the D'Aquin Bakery in New Orleans. One of her innovations is packaged crackers, and her bakery soon becomes the city's largest export business. She is remembered not only as a successful entrepreneur but as a generous philanthropist in this city.

AUGUST 10, 1858 Birth of Anna J. Cooper, African American Educator and Feminist. Anna J. Cooper (1858–1964) is born into slavery in Raleigh, North Carolina, of mixed parentage. At the age of ten, Cooper is awarded a scholarship to attend the St. Augustine Normal School and Collegiate Institute. But because she is a female, Cooper has to fight in order to take Latin and Greek classes. Graduating from St. Augustine in 1877, she later marries the Rev. A. C. Cooper. After the death of her husband in 1881, Cooper attends Oberlin College in Ohio. Along with Mary Eliza Church and Ida A. Gibbs (Hunt), Cooper is one of the first three African American women to earn a B.A. from an American college. She is the only African American female graduate in the class of 1884 at Oberlin College. Three years later, in 1887, Cooper receives her M.A. in mathematics from Oberlin, and soon afterwards applies for a teaching position at Wilberforce University. However, she is turned down because it is unheard of for a woman to teach classical subjects. Cooper finally is awarded a position at Wilberforce when a new administration takes over the school and works there only one year, teaching Latin and Greek.

Cooper returns to North Carolina and becomes very active in a teacher's organization and community outreach program at St. Augustine. Having jeopardized her teaching career because of her community work, she leaves North Carolina and accepts a teaching position at Washington, D.C.'s Colored High School, which later becomes known as the M Street School. She is principal there from 1902 to 1906, and her credo is "Education for Ser-

vice." With the help of white philanthropists and the local African American clergy, Cooper founds Frelinghuysen University, an interdenominational Bible college, in April 1906.

In 1910, Cooper returns to the M Street School and writes *A Voice From the South*, which establishes her as a feminist. She returns to her hometown, Raleigh, North Carolina, and becomes a leader of the National Association of Colored Women. A prominent speaker, she frequently speaks at feminist and educational conferences. She becomes the only female member of the American Negro Academy, the black think tank of its day. In 1914, Cooper begins work on a Ph.D. at Columbia University, then transfers to the University of Paris. In 1925, she successfully defends her thesis on French policies during slavery. When she is 72, she becomes the president of Frelinghuysen, the university she founded. She dies on February 27, 1964, at the age of 105, in Washington, D.C.

AUGUST 19, 1858 English Writer Edith Nesbit Is Born. English author Edith Nesbit (1858–1924) is born in London, England. She writes *The Treasure Seekers* in 1899, and becomes best known for her children's novels of the "Bastable Children," among them *The Five Children and It* (1902) and *The Railway Children* (1906). Other works include *The Enchanted Castle* (1907), *The Wonderful Garden* (1911), and *The Magic World* (1912). She is a cofounder (with her husband, Hubert Bland, and a circle of literary friends that includes H. G. Wells and George Bernard Shaw) of the Fabian Society, a socialist organization, in London in 1884.

1859 Birth of Julia Brainerd Hall, Collaborator on Development of Electrolytic Process. American researcher Julia Brainerd Hall (1859–1925), who shares the invention, development, and marketing of the electrolytic aluminum process, is born. Graduating from Oberlin College in 1885, Hall is granted a diploma from the literary program, but she also earns more than enough credits for a degree in science and chemistry. In accordance with expectations for women in the late nineteenth century, immediately after graduation she becomes responsible for her siblings upon her mother's death. Hall's younger brother, Charles Martin Hall, earns a degree in chemistry from Oberlin in 1889. Julia and Charles are lifelong companions and colleagues, sharing both home and laboratory. They work together as a team on a series of patents which results in a feasible and inexpensive process for the production and marketing of electrolytic aluminum. This discovery leads to the establishment of the Pittsburgh Reduction Company, the predecessor of ALCOA, the Aluminum Company of America. Although Julia Hall's work in the capacity of research engineer is well-documented, her brother Charles remains the sole recognized inventor and developer of the electrolytic process.

1859   Birth of Carrie Chapman Catt, U.S. Reformer and Pacifist. American reformer and pacifist Carrie Chapman Catt (1859–1947) is born in Ripon, Wisconsin. She is educated at Iowa State College. Widely recognized for her organizational skill, Catt is credited for helping to pass suffrage referenda in many states, including Colorado (1893), Utah and Idaho (1896), Washington (1910), California (1911), Kansas, Oregon, and Arizona (1912), Nevada and Montana (1914), and New York (1917). In 1920, after the amendment to the U.S. Constitution is finally passed and women are guaranteed the right to vote, Catt reorganizes the National American Woman Suffrage Association into the National League of Women Voters. From 1925 to 1932, 11 international women's organizations come together under Catt's leadership as president to work for world peace as the National Committee on the Cause and Cure of War.

1 8 6 0 – 1 8 6 4

**1860   French Feminist Author Jenny d'Héri-
court Publishes** *Woman Affranchised*. French
author Jenny d'Héricourt (1830–1890)
responds to the masculinist writings of Pierre
Proudhon and Jules Michelet with her book
Woman Affranchised. She argues that "woman
has the same rights as man" and demands
women be allowed to sit on juries, boards of
trade, and chambers of commerce. She also
wants women to be legal witnesses and to
have equal access to education and the professions. During the 1870s, she engages in
public speaking on women's issues, but her
abrasive personality, her inflammatory language, and her refusal to agree that women's
primary role is that of wife and mother alienates her from many liberals and feminists.
She dies in 1890.

**1860   Emma Smith Helps Establish Reorga-
nized Mormon Church.** Emma Smith
(1804–1879), widowed first wife of Mormon
leader Joseph Smith, helps to found the
Reorganized Church of Jesus Christ of Latter Day Saints.

**1860   Birth of Charlotte Gilman, American
Feminist and Writer.** American writer Charlotte Gilman (1860–1935) is born in Hartford, Connecticut, and raised by her mother.
She is educated at the Rhode Island School of

Emma Smith

Design. In 1898 Gilman writes *Women and
Economics*, now recognized as a feminist landmark. She founds, edits, and writes for the
journal *Forerunner* (1909–16) and publishes
The Man Made World (1911) and *His Religion
and Hers* (1923). She commits suicide upon

receiving the news that she is suffering from an incurable cancer.

1860   Phoebe Anne Mosey, Known As Annie Oakley, Is Born. Phoebe Anne Mosey (1860–1926), who becomes Annie Oakley, is born. She is a skilled markswoman from childhood, and achieves renown in the late 1880s when she tours with Buffalo Bill's Wild West show as a sharpshooter.

1861   Civil War in the United States Disrupts Suffragists' Cause. American women turn their attentions to efforts in support of the U.S. Civil War (1861–65), temporarily suspending efforts to win the vote.

1861   Publication of Harriet Jacobs' *Incidents in the Life of a Slave Girl.* Harriet Jacobs (1813–1897), writing under the pseudonym Linda Brent, publishes *Incidents in the Life of a Slave Girl,* the most comprehensive autobiography written by a former slave. Jacobs describes what it is like to be a female slave and fugitive in the South and the North. Her autobiography brings to the forefront the continued sexual harassment many female slaves experience. Once Jacobs gains her freedom, she becomes very active in the abolitionist movement. When the Civil War starts, she is involved in raising money and gathering supplies for the contraband black refugees who travel to union territory. She moves to Alexandria, Virginia, in 1863 with her daughter to set up emergency relief and primary medical care for black refugees. She also founds the Jacobs Free School to educate them. Two years later, Jacobs moves to Savannah, Georgia, and continues her work with refugees. In 1868, she travels to England and raises enough money to establish a home for black orphans and the aged in Savannah. However, because of an increase in acts of violence against African Americans in the South, Jacobs and her daughter move to Massachusetts, and then Washington, D.C., where she continues her work with freed slaves. She works in the newly

established schools for former slaves and at Howard University. In the spring of 1897, Harriet Jacobs dies at her Washington, D.C., home and is buried in Mount Auburn Cemetery in Cambridge, Massachusetts.

1861   Dorothea Dix Named Head of Army Nursing Corps. Dorothea Lynde Dix (1802–1887) is appointed by U.S. Secretary of War Edwin Stanton to head the Army Nursing Corps. She organizes this group according to rigid standards: nurses have to be religious, of a high moral character, 30 years old or older, and plain. Dix serves as head of the Corps until 1866.

1861   Susan B. Anthony Founds Women's National Loyal League. During the Civil War (1861–65), Susan B. Anthony (1820–1906) serves as both the organizer and secretary of the Women's National Loyal League, an organization dedicated to freeing slaves.

1861   Ann Preston Founds Women's Hospital in Philadelphia, Pennsylvania. Ann Preston, M.D. (1813–1872) and her patients are barred from many of Philadelphia's hospitals, so Preston founds Women's Hospital in the Fairmount section of the city.

1861   Certain Swedish Women Gain Suffrage. Single taxpaying women win the right to vote in municipal elections in Sweden.

APRIL 12, 1861   Emma Edmonds Enlists in Union Army, Becomes Successful Spy. Born in Canada, Emma Edmonds enlists in the Union army on the first day of the U.S. Civil War (1861–65). Serving as a nurse, she is soon recruited as a spy. Edmonds disguises herself as a male African American. She is ordered to report on troop numbers, fortifications, and enemy plans at Yorktown. In her pocket she carries a loaded revolver. Conscripted into a labor gang, Edmonds makes detailed sketches of Yorktown's defensive works. She also hears General Lee comment that the fortifications

Nellie Melba

will not withstand a siege. Returning to Union lines, she reports to General McClelland. Edmonds next crosses Confederate lines as an Irish peddler. Near the Chickahominy River she discovers a Confederate camp, where she peddles her wares and assesses the size, disposition, and intentions of the enemy. Stealing a Confederate horse, she returns to Union lines. Emma Edmonds undertakes a total of at least 11 missions, each one successfully. She is promoted to "Detective" and given the job of uncovering southern spies. After participating in the battles of Bull Run, Williamsburg, Fair Oaks, Richmond, and Antietam, Edmonds' health falters. She is invalidated out of the army.

MAY 19, 1861   Birth of Australian Soprano Nellie Melba. Dame Nellie Melba (1861–1931), one of the world's greatest operatic

sopranos, is born Helen Porter Mitchell in Melbourne (hence "Melba"), Australia. In 1880 her father buys a sugar mill in north Queensland, where Melba marries Charles Armstrong in December 1882. Fourteen months later, she takes her infant son to Melbourne where she studies with Pietro Cecchi. Melba makes her debut there four months later. She moves to London in 1886 but has little success until taken up by Mathilde Marchesi in Paris. Melba's operatic career begins in Brussels in 1887, and from that time her success is assured. She is feted throughout Europe and the United States, though her name is most frequently associated with Covent Garden. An unfortunate liaison with Philippe, Duke of Orleans, and persistent rumors about her drinking habits have no effect on the enormous popularity of her splendid soprano voice. Melba returns to Australia for a season in 1902 and is received with adulation. Her next visit involves a 10,000-mile Australian tour in 1909. She buys a property in Victoria and spends increasing amounts of time in Australia, where she teaches singing, gives "Concerts for the People," and publishes the "Melba Method." In the intervals, she maintains her international career, cuts over 100 gramophone records, and, in 1920, becomes the first artist of international standing to make live radio broadcasts. In 1924, at Geelong, she gives the first of a series of worldwide final performances. These continue until late 1928, and the term "doing a Melba" becomes part of the Australian language. She dies in Sydney in 1931.

1862   First French Woman to Earn Bachelor's Degree. Julie Victoire Daubié (1830–1874) becomes the first French woman to earn a bachelor's degree. Daubié is born in an iron works in the Vosges mountains. Her father, an employee of the works, dies when Daubié is nine months old. She lives a life of poverty but studies hard and gains her teaching certificate in primary education in 1844. She works as a

During the U.S. Civil War, women play many roles. These Union women staff the hospital tents set up near a battle-field. Julia Ward Howe's "The Battle Hymn of the Republic" becomes their rallying hymn.

schoolteacher but also researches and writes on social questions. In 1859 Daubié wins first prize in an essay contest of the Imperial Academy of Lyon with her study, "Poor Women, by a Poor Woman." The 800-franc prize allows her to study for her degree, and in 1861 she becomes the first woman to pass the baccalaureate examinations. Despite resistance due to her sex, she receives her bachelor's degree in 1862. The same year, she publishes *On Progress in Primary Education.* In 1868 she publishes her masterful sociological study, *Poor Women in France,* which has a major influence on public debate. When the Third French Republic is founded in 1870, Daubié demands the right to vote, but the government refuses. She returns to her native village to

work on her doctoral thesis, but she falls ill and dies at Fontenoy-le-Château in 1874, before she can complete her final degree.

1862 Society for the Professional Training of Women Founded in France. French feminist Elisa Lemonnier (1805–1865) founds the Society for the Professional Training of Women in response to the lack of economic opportunities for women in France. She experiences firsthand the prejudice against working wives when she is forced to shut down her lingerie shop in Bordeaux. She joins her husband in supporting the Saint-Simonian movement. The couple donates their small inheritance of 50,000 francs to the utopian group in Bordeaux, but Elisa Lemonnier dislikes the group's belief in free love. She even separates from her husband, Charles, because of his support of the "new morality" promoted by the Saint-Simonian leader, Enfantin. She instead focuses on the ideals of economic equality for women. During the Revolution of 1848 Lemonnier joins Suzanne Voilquin, Desiree Gay, and Jeanne Déroin to form *Le Club des Femmes* (The Women's Club) and writes for the club's socialist daily newspaper, *La Voix des Femmes*. She and Gay also organize a club of linen seamstresses to provide the workers with retirement income and disability insurance. By the summer of 1848, the conservative political victory puts an end to the feminist and socialist activities and goals of such women as Lemonnier. In 1862 she founds the Society for the Professional Training of Women, raising the money for her project from Parisian ladies who each contribute 25 centimes. By "professional," Lemonnier does not mean the liberal professions. The first school is a workshop for dressmaking; then follow institutes for bookbinding, commerce, and industrial design. The Lemonnier plan always includes some general studies along with technical training for working-class women. Her society grows and other schools open in the provinces.

1862   Dressmaker Elizabeth Keckley Begins Work at White House. Former slave Elizabeth Keckley is hired to make inaugural gowns for Mary Todd Lincoln, wife of U.S. President Abraham Lincoln, and the daughters of Andrew Johnson. She soon becomes the First Lady's confidante and servant. After the Civil War (1861–65), Keckley decides to collaborate with James Redpath on a book about her experiences. The resulting work, *Thirty Years a Slave and Four Years in the White House*, loses her Mary Todd Lincoln's friendship.

1862   Julia Ward Howe Publishes "The Battle Hymn of the Republic." Julia Ward Howe (1819–1910) writes the "The Battle Hymn of the Republic" and publishes it in the *Atlantic Monthly* magazine. It becomes the theme song

Kady Brownell, member of Union Army regiment.

for the Union forces during the Civil War (1861–65).

JULY 1862   Kady Brownell Marches With Union Army. When the First Rhode Island Regiment encamps in Maryland, Kady Brownell, wife of orderly sergeant Robert S. Brownell, resolves to be more than a water-carrier. When the company goes to rifle practice, Kady accompanies them, practicing daily with her husband and others in the camp. A battle breaks out, and Kady stands firm at the line of fire, holding the colors and giving the men a rallying point. She courageously helps wounded soldiers, reenlists with her husband in the Fifth Rhode Island Regiment, and, at the close of the Civil War (1861–65), her discharge is signed by A.E. Burnside.

c. 1863   Birth of Kishida Toshiko, Japanese Political Activist for Women's Rights. Kishida Toshiko (1863?–1901), a writer, political activist for women's rights, and Japan's first woman orator, is born. Because she excels in her study of the Chinese and Japanese classics, Toshiko is the first commoner to serve as a lady-in-waiting to an empress, Shoken (1850-1914). Toshiko leaves court, however, in 1882 to embark on a national lecture tour, sponsored by the Jiyuto (Liberal Party). In her lectures, she speaks of women as participants in the establishment of a new Japanese society. She criticizes the marriage system, in which women have no right to divorce; the concubine system; and inadequate educational opportunities for girls. She attacks the Confucian values expressed in the three obediences, in which women are to be under the control of their fathers, husbands, or sons, throughout their lives. Toshiko encourages women to organize discussion groups and lecture societies as a means of promoting equal rights for women. The Peace Preservation Law of 1887, which prohibits women from engaging in political activities (it is thought that Toshiko, in particular, is meant to be the target of this legislation), effectively ends her speaking career on women's rights. She continues to contribute poems and essays to the periodical, *Jogaku Zasshi*, and is said to make a fortune in real estate dealings.

1863   Birth of American Author Gene Stratton Porter. Gene Stratton Porter (1863–1924), American author, is born in Wabash County, Indiana. She achieves great popularity with her 1909 novel, *A Girl of the Limberlost*.

1863   Mary Edwards Walker, M.D., U. S. Army's First Woman Contract Surgeon. Mary Edwards Walker, M.D. (1832–1919) becomes the first woman to be appointed a civilian contract surgeon in the U.S. Army, assigned to the 52nd Ohio Regiment during the Civil War (1861–65). Walker adapts her fellow officers' uniform of pants, tunic, and greatcoat so that she can perform her duties more effectively. In May 1865, she is relieved of her duties as contract surgeon for the Union army. Her persistence in seeking a post-war commission, however, results in her being accorded the recognition of the Congressional Medal of Honor for Meritorious Service.

In 1917, Walker and 910 other recipients of the Congressional Medal of Honor lose their citations in a bureaucratic review. However, in 1976, Senate Resolution 569 reinstates Walker's medal, declaring her "a woman one hundred years ahead of her time [who] pursued many occupations including teaching, lecturing, and writing on women's rights, and campaigning for women's suffrage and other progressive reforms;...the only woman in the history of the United States to have ever received the Nation's highest award for valor...."

1863   Jessie Wilcox Smith, American Illustrator, Is Born. Jessie Wilcox Smith (1863–1935) is born. An illustrator of children's books, she illustrates Robert Louis Stevenson's *A Child's Garden of Verses* (1914), and Louisa May Alcott's *Little Women* (1915).

1863   Olympia Brown Is First Woman Ordained Minister. Olympia Brown (1835–1926) becomes the first woman ordained as a minister by full authority of a denomination, the Unitarian Church. Brown serves congregations in Wisconsin, Massachusetts, and Connecticut for 21 years as a full-time pastor. Married to John Willis and mother of two, Brown uses her own name.

1863   Naturalist Amalie Dietrich Collects Specimens in Australia. Amalie Nellem Dietrich(1821–1891) is an avid, skilled, and fearless collector of plant and animal specimens in eastern Queensland, Australia. Her interest in natural history stems from her marriage, around 1846, to chemist Wilhelm August Salomo Dietrich, who collects and sells plant and animal specimens. The couple undertakes long collecting trips in northern Europe before separating in 1853. Amalie Dietrich then moves her daughter and her prepared collections to Hamburg, Germany, where the merchant J. C. Godeffroy agrees to sponsor a field trip to Australia to collect for his private museum. She lands in Brisbane, Australia, in 1863, four years after the colony is separated from New South Wales, and collects throughout eastern Queensland. Her adventures in the new colony are hair-raising; her list of dissections includes a 22-foot crocodile. Dietrich collects plants, insects, corals, shells, mammals, fish, birds, and Aboriginal bones. Around 1870 she visits the southern colonies, returning to Hamburg three years later. Though regarded as eccentric, probably due to her lack of concern about her appearance, her work in Australia attracts international recognition. She is elected Fellow of the Entomological Society of Stettin and wins a gold medal for her Australian wood specimens. Several Australian plant and animal species are named for her, notably *Acacia dietrichiana, Bonamia dietrichianus, Nortonia amaliae,* and *Odynerus dietrichianus.* Some of her plant specimens are held at the National Herbarium in Melbourne.

1863   **Birth of American Psychologist Mary Calkins.** Mary Whiton Calkins (1863–1930), American psychologist and philosopher, is born. After earning a B.A. from Smith College with a concentration in the classics, Calkins begins teaching Greek at Wellesley College in 1887. In 1888, she is offered the new position of instructor in psychology there, contingent upon a year's training in the discipline. Consistent with university policy toward women in 1890, Calkins is granted special permission to attend classes in psychol-

Mary Whiton Calkins

ogy and philosophy at Harvard University and in laboratory psychology at Clark University in Worcester, but is denied admission to their graduate studies programs. She is also denied permission to attend regular Harvard seminars until faculty members William James and Josiah Royce (1855-1916), as well as Calkins's father, intervene on her behalf.

Returning to Wellesley in the fall of 1891, Calkins establishes the first psychology laboratory at a women's college in the United States. In 1895, Calkins requests and takes an examination equivalent to the official Ph.D. exam. Her performance is praised by James as "the most brilliant examination for the Ph.D. that we have had at Harvard." Nevertheless, Calkins is still denied admission to candidacy for the degree. With the creation of Radcliffe

College in April 1902, Calkins is one of the first four women to be offered the Ph.D., but she refuses it in protest. In 1905, Calkins becomes the first woman president of the American Psychological Association. In 1918, she becomes the first woman president of the American Philosophical Association. Calkins teaches at Wellesley College until her retirement in 1929, and publishes four books and more than 100 papers in psychology and philosophy. In 1909, Columbia University awards Calkins a honorary Doctor of Letters (Litt.D.) and in 1910, Smith College grants her the Doctor of Laws (LL.D.). Calkins dies in 1930.

1864   Octavia Hill Rents Low-Cost Housing to the Poor in England. Octavia Hill (1838-1912) receives a loan from the artist John Ruskin and begins her venture of buying apartment houses to rehabilitate and manage in order to provide low-cost housing for thousands of poor people in Victorian England. Hill not only rents apartments to the poor, but also intervenes in their lives. According to her, the poor need to build their characters by learning frugality and thrift. She also trains teams of rent collectors to teach middle-class household management skills to the poor. Hill is born in London and begins teaching at her mother's school by age 13; at 14, she manages a workshop for poor girls. She studies art with John Ruskin, who supports her efforts on behalf of the poor. Because of her success, the Church of England asks Hill to manage its properties. Eventually, she manages property for over 3,000 persons. Hill serves on the Central Council of the Charity Organization Society and on the Royal Commission on the Poor Laws. She distrusts organized charity and emphasizes personal relationships, business-like practices, and self-help. A believer in beauty and recreation, Hill helps to establish and preserve London's "green-belt" of parks and playgrounds.

1864   Birth of English Entertainer Vesta Tilley, Male Impersonator. Vesta Tilley (1864-1952), an English music hall star, is born. She is the first woman to make her career on the English stage by wearing male attire, consisting of a top hat and tails. This outfit, later popularized in the twentieth century by such famous film stars as Marlene Dietrich and Judy Garland, comes to signify complex gender relations from the point of view of both the performer and the spectator. Tilley first dresses as a man at the age of five and goes on to make her name as a male impersonator.

1864   French Sculptor Camille Claudel Is Born. Camille Claudel (1864–1943), a French sculptor who is thought to greatly influence the work of her lover, the internationally famous Auguste Rodin, is born. Although her own work remains obscure, Claudel's life becomes the subject of a feature film. The movie *Camille Claudel* is produced in 1989 and directed by Bruno Nuytten.

1 8 6 5 – 1 8 6 9

1865   Birth of Jeanne Bouvier, French Activist for Working Class. Jeanne Marie Bouvier (1865–1964), a prominent activist for working class and women's interests in France, is born. She grows up south of the city of Lyons. After her father's wine barrel-making business fails and her father turns to drinking, Bouvier becomes the family wage earner at age 11. She first works in a silk factory, winding thread on bobbins from five in the morning until eight at night, with two hours for meals. She is proud of her ability to survive on her own, and in her autobiography, she writes, "I didn't complain. Misery had knocked on my door and my thirteen hours in the factory would pay me 50 centimes." She also crochets shawls and scarves to earn extra money for her family. By 1879 her mother finds jobs as domestics for both of them in Paris. Bouvier eventually becomes a seamstress, working a 12-hour day for a couturier and in the evenings for private clients. She pays for her financial security with poor health and spends several months in hospitals at different times. Her experiences make Bouvier aware of the negative impact of industrialization on the laboring classes. During World War I she runs workshops that employ only women to make shirts, slacks, and ground cloths for the soldiers. Bouvier is remembered as a prominent French feminist and union organizer.

1866   **French Writer Olympe Audouard Petitions for Women's Rights.** French author Olympe Audouard (1830–1890) tries to publish a political review, but the government forbids it on the grounds that a woman is not a full citizen. In response she writes *War on Men* and petitions the legislature for full civil rights. In 1860 she separates from her husband, but she doesn't obtain a divorce until 1885, after France legalizes divorce in 1884. After her separation, she travels around the world, supporting herself by writing travel books. She publishes the literary review *The Butterfly* starting in 1862. She becomes a leading proponent of legal divorce, leading the Minister of the Interior to remark in 1873, "the theories of Madame Olympe Audouard are subversive, dangerous, and immoral."

1866   **English Physician Elizabeth Garrett Anderson Certified to Practice Profession.** Elizabeth Garrett (1836–1917) receives her certificate to practice medicine from the Society of Apothecaries, placing ahead of her seven male classmates on the certification exam. She completes her M.D. at the University of Paris in 1870. In March 1859, Garrett hears a speech given by Elizabeth Blackwell, the world's first woman doctor. Garrett then decides to become the first practicing woman doctor in England. Her father supports her plan to study medicine, while her mother sobs over "the disgrace." Unfortunately, Elizabeth Garrett finds all the schools and hospitals

closed to her. In 1860 she begins training as a nurse at Middlesex Hospital and gains admission to medical lectures and even the dissection room. When Garrett places first in an exam for medical students, the male students protest her presence and have her expelled by convincing the all-male faculty that they are subject to ridicule from other schools for sharing their benches with a woman. Garrett then applies for matriculation at London University but is rejected. Instead, she qualifies for licensing as a doctor through the Society of Apothecaries—a back door into medical practice. Garrett returns to London, and in 1871 she marries the steamship merchant James Anderson, but she insists on the right to continue her career. Mrs. Garrett Anderson, as she prefers to be called, works through three pregnancies, operating and lecturing. Among her patients is the moral reformer Josephine Butler, who expresses the enormous satisfaction she derives from getting medical attention from a member of her own sex. In 1872, Garrett Anderson founds the New Hospital for Women, run by and for women. After her death, it is renamed the Elizabeth Garrett Anderson Hospital.

1866   **Women Allowed to Attend French Universities.** While presiding over French Ministerial Councils in her husband's absence, Empress Eugenie of France succeeds in getting a decree passed that states, "Women are authorized to take the examinations of the faculties." This guarantees that women cannot be turned down by reason of their sex at any university in France. She then sends her own nieces to attend university courses. Born in Spain as Eugenie de Montijo, the empress is the wife of Napoleon III.

1866   **Mary Helen McKillop Establishes Sisterhood in Australia.** Mother Mary Helen McKillop (1842–1909), in conjunction with Father Tenison-Woods, establishes the Sisterhood of St. Joseph of the Sacred Heart at Penola, South Australia. Members are committed to poverty and the education of the children of the poor. McKillop becomes its first member and superior as Mother Mary of the Cross. The movement spreads rapidly within South Australia but is soon caught up in conflict between Tenison-Woods, by then director of Catholic education, and a group of priests. McKillop, on a visit to Rome, obtains approval from the Pope, the highest authority in the Catholic Church, to establish her own religious order. She returns to Australia in 1875 and spends the next 25 years establishing schools, convents, and charitable institutions throughout Australia and Asia. The cause for her beatification and canonization is formally introduced on February 1, 1973. She is beatified in January 1995 and is expected to become Australia's first saint.

1866   First Dean of Women's Medical College. Ann Preston, M.D. (1813–1872), one of the first women doctors in the United States, is promoted from professor of physiology and hygiene to the new position of dean at the Female Medical College of Pennsylvania (FMCP) in Philadelphia. As such, she is the first dean of the first women's medical college in the United States.

MAY 1, 1866   The American Equal Rights Association Forms. At the close of the Eleventh National Woman's Rights Convention, the American Equal Rights Association is founded by Elizabeth Cady Stanton and Susan B. Anthony, with Lucretia Mott as president. The association is dedicated to winning suffrage for both African Americans (then known as Negroes) and women.

JULY 28, 1866   Birth of Beatrix Potter, English Writer and Illustrator for Children. Helen Beatrix Potter (1866–1943), a leading writer and illustrator of classic children's stories, is born to a wealthy family of leisure, the first child and only daughter of Helen and Rupert Potter. She spends most of her first 30 years of life in the third floor nursery of her

Beatrix Potter

parents' London home, seldom allowed downstairs to join her parents for meals and not permitted to leave home without her governess. During vacations in Scotland, she and her younger brother Bertram walk about the farmlands and woods. Young Beatrix Potter sketches the plants and animals, and captures wild animals for pets. She becomes devoted to art as a discipline rather than a diversion during her teen years, and her parents allow her special tutors for art lessons. As Potter grows up, she tries to assert her independence, but her parents expect her to take over the handling of household affairs and tend to their health. During her late teens she suffers a mysterious illness—possibly a nervous reaction to her confined life—and becomes nearly paralyzed.

In 1900 a family friend suggests that Potter write a children's book. Her first book, *The Tale of Peter Rabbit*, is published in 1901. From 1903 to 1913, she publishes one to two books a year. Potter illustrates all of her stories, which include *The Tailor of Gloucester* (1903), *The Tale of Benjamin Bunny* (1904), *The Tale of Jemima Puddle-Duck* (1908), and many others.

Potter's parents disapprove of her engagement to her publisher, Norman Warne, in 1905, but Warne dies suddenly from leukemia before they can marry. Potter finds solace in the purchase of a farm in Near Sawrey. There she has independence from her parents and is free to study the nearby farmers and shepherds. In 1913, again against her parents' wishes, she marries the attorney William Heelis and devotes herself to marriage and farming. She gives up publishing but still sketches and writes for her own pleasure. Potter also campaigns for the preservation of the English countryside.

1867　Marie Sklodowska (Marie Curie), Renowned French Scientist, Is Born. Physical chemist Marie Sklodowska (later Marie Curie) (1867–1934) is born in Warsaw, Poland, to a family of intellectuals. She works to put her sister through medical school, then in 1892 travels to Paris, France, to study physics at the prestigious university the Sorbonne. In 1895 she finishes her thesis on the study of X-rays and marries her classmate Pierre Curie the same year. Pierre Curie obtains a chair in general physics at the Sorbonne, and the two collaborate on experiments. Marie Curie gains fame for discovering the radioactive properties of thorium and for isolating the metal radium. She wins a Nobel Prize in physics in 1903 and in chemistry in 1911. When her husband is killed by a truck in 1906, Marie Curie takes over his chair at the Sorbonne, the first time a woman receives such a prestigious university post in France. During World War I, she

organizes the French Army medical service's radiological services. Marie Curie dies in 1934.

1867　Emily Howard Stowe, First Woman Doctor in Canada. Emily Howard Stowe (1831–1903) becomes Canada's first practicing female physician. Denied entry into any Canadian medical school, she receives her degree from the New York Medical College for Women.

Stowe is born into a Quaker family in northern Canada, and after working for several years as a schoolteacher, she resolves to become a physician. The medical community disdains women's involvement in medicine, and no medical school in Canada admits women. The leading medical journal in the country, *Canada Lancet*, states this view: "As wives, mothers, sisters, and dainty little housekeepers we have the utmost love and respect for them; but we do not think the profession of medicine, as a rule, a fit place for them." Denied entry into the Toronto School of Medicine, Stowe enrolls in a homeopathic school, the New York Medical College for Women, in 1865 and receives her degree in 1867. Stowe returns to Toronto to practice but is denied a license under the medical licensing act, which refuses approval to homeopaths. Additional courses at a Canadian medical school are required for Stowe to get her license. Since Canadian medical schools are still not admitting women, Stowe has little choice but to practice medicine without a license for several years. In 1870, Stowe is finally admitted to the Toronto Medical School to complete her qualifying courses. There, she and another female medical student are harassed by both faculty and students who heap garbage and refuse on their seats, cover the walls with misogynist (anti-woman) graffiti, and verbally and intellectually abuse them. Having completed her courses, Stowe returns to her practice but it is not until 1880 that the College of Physicians and Surgeons grants her license. Stowe goes on to found the

Dominion Women's Enfranchisement Association, an organization established to fight for women's suffrage at the federal level.

1867 Metta Victoria Fuller Writes First Detective Novel by a Woman. Metta Victoria Fuller (1831–?) writes *The Dead Letter,* the first detective novel by a woman. Fuller is 13 when her first published writing appears. In her teens she is known as the "Singing Sybil" for her poetry. She earns her living by writing in a variety of genres, including temperance tales: *The Senator's Son* (1851) and *Fashionable Dissipation* (1853) are very popular. In 1860, Fuller publishes *Maum Guinea,* an anti-slavery novel that is popular in England and among Union soldiers. After her marriage to Orville Victor in 1856, she writes many "dime novels" (many under pseudonyms).

FEBRUARY 7, 1867   Birth of Laura Ingalls Wilder, Author Famous for Little House Series of Life on American Frontier. Laura Elizabeth Ingalls Wilder (1867–1957), who makes a major contribution to children's literature with her autobiographical Little House series, is born in Pepin, Wisconsin, the second child of the Ingalls family. Her early years there become the setting for *The Little House in the Big Woods* (1932), the first of her series on frontier life in America and a Newbery Honor book. These autobiographical stories of her childhood are a fascinating contribution to American women's literature. Her father yearned for the open prairie lands, and the family's move to Kansas in a covered wagon becomes part of *Little House on the Prairie* (1935). Ingalls marries Almanzo Wilder on August 25, 1885, in De Smet, South Dakota, and writes of his ninth year on the family farm in *Farmer Boy* (1933). Her teaching and their courtship is portrayed in *These Happy Golden Years* (1943). *On the Banks of Plum Creek* (1937) is published when she is 70, and it becomes a Newbery Honor book. *By the Shores of Silver Lake* (1939) also wins a Newbery Honor. *The Long Winter* (1940) records the

blizzard of 1880-81 in De Smet. *Little Town on the Prairie* (1941) tells of Ingalls' teenage years on the homestead and it, too, becomes a Newbery Honor book, her fifth. The Little House series, encompassing ten books, and the heroine Laura Ingalls Wilder stand as the epitome of the American frontier story. Throughout her writing career, Ingalls Wilder depends heavily on the criticism and assistance of her daughter, Rose Wilder Lane. The Laura Ingalls Wilder Award is established in 1954 by the Childrens Services Division of the American Library Association to be given every five years to an author who, over a period of years, makes a substantial and lasting contribution to literature for children. Over 20 million copies of her books have been sold; they have been translated into more than 20 languages, and a major television series was based on the stories she created. People travel from all over the world to visit the sites of the Little House books. Laura Ingalls Wilder dies in 1957 and is posthumously inducted into the South Dakota Cowboy and Western Hall of Fame in 1978.

1868   French Entertainer Sarah Bernhardt Achieves Success. After years of a disappointing career, actress Sarah Bernhardt (1844–1923) finally achieves success, charming the Imperial family in France. Her success brings her money, fame, a new house, and a crowd of influential friends and lovers, including George Sand, Leon Gambetta, Prince Napoleon, and Théophile Gautier. She has triumph after triumph in such plays as *La Tosca, Hernani,* and *Phedre,* and she conquers London in 1879. Outside of France, she is best known for her performance in *Camille,* and in 1912 she appears in the motion picture *Queen Elizabeth.* She makes her first New York City appearance in 1880 and her last in 1918. When she dies in 1923, while rehearsing yet another play, 250,000 Parisians come to pay homage to the "Divine Sarah." Her writings include her autobiographical *Memories of My Life*

(1907) and *Art of the Theater*, published in 1924 after her death.

1868 **Elizabeth Blackwell Establishes Infirmary Medical School for Women.** Elizabeth Blackwell (1821–1910), the world's first trained, registered woman doctor, opens the Infirmary Medical School for women.

1868 **Frances Hodgson Burnett Publishes First Works.** An Englishwoman who becomes an American citizen, Frances Eliza Hodgson Burnett (1849–1924), best known as a children's author, publishes her first works. These are two stories, "Hearts and Diamonds" and "Miss Carruthers Engagement," in *Godeys Ladys Book*. Burnett is eighteen and receives 35 dollars for these manuscripts. She later writes *Little Lord Fauntleroy* (1886), which is first published in *St. Nicholas Magazine* and sets a fashion for boys' clothes; *A Little Princess* (1905); and *The Secret Garden* (1911).

1868 **Augusta Lewis Troup Founds Working Women's Association and Women's Typographical Union Number 1.** With suffrage activists Elizabeth Cady Stanton and Susan B. Anthony, Augusta Lewis Troup (1848–1920) establishes the Working Women's Association in New York City. The same year, she also founds the Women's Typographical Union Number 1, and in 1870, she is elected corresponding secretary of the National Typographical Union, a job that involves organizing, developing contacts with women printers, and analyzing problems in the printing industry. As part of her job, Troup surveys conditions in the industry and presents her findings in a well-documented report to the next convention. She honestly describes to her union brothers the situation for women as they are ostracized by their male coworkers and paid 40 percent of what their male coworkers are paid, yet support their union brothers and refuse to be used as scabs and strike breakers. The Women's Typographical Union lasts for only nine years, but Augusta Lewis Troup contin-

ues to be active in labor, suffrage, and social reform issues.

1868 **Julia Ward Howe Founds Two New England Women's Groups.** American writer and reformer Julia Ward Howe (1819–1910) founds both the New England Woman Suffrage Association and the New England Women's Club. In 1908, Howe becomes the first woman to be elected to the American Academy of Arts and Letters. Born in New York City, Howe is the author of "The Battle Hymn of the Republic," which is first published in the *Atlantic Monthly* magazine in 1862. It becomes the theme song for the Union forces during the Civil War (1861–65).

1868 **Lucy Osburn Introduces Nightingale System of Nursing to Australia.** After completing her studies at the Nightingale Training School, Lucy Osburn (1835–1891) introduces the Nightingale System of nursing to Australia as superintendent of the Sydney Infirmary and Dispensary. Osburn spends her childhood in England, where she learns several languages and becomes an accomplished horsewoman. In the late 1850s she works for three months at the Kaiserwerth Hospital at Dusseldorf before visiting hospitals in Austria and Holland. She then attends the Nightingale Training School at St. Thomas's Hospital, London, in 1866 and studies midwifery at King's College Hospital. The following year she responds to an appeal from the Premier of New South Wales, Australia, for trained nurses to work in Sydney. Osburn is appointed Lady Superintendent of the Sydney Infirmary and Dispensary and arrives in the colony with five trained nurses in March 1868. Conditions at the infirmary are appalling, and Osburn's attempts to improve them are frequently frustrated by the doctors and the hospital board. In 1870, she is attacked in the New South Wales Legislative Assembly on religious grounds. The hospital is investigated by the Windeyer Royal Commission on public charities in 1873, and her work is completely vindicated. From that time on conditions gradually improve, and when Osburn resigns in 1884, she has successfully introduced the Nightingale System of nursing and nurse training into Australia. She returns to continue her distinguished career in England, where she dies in 1891.

1868   **First Women to Sell Stocks.** Victoria Claflin Woodhull (1838–1927) and her sister Tennessee open an office on Wall Street in New York City from which they are the first women to sell stocks and bonds. They convince wealthy financier Cornelius Vanderbilt to back them, thus becoming the first female stockbrokers in the United States.

JANUARY 1868   *The Revolution* **Begins Publication in New York City.** Susan B. Anthony, Elizabeth Cady Stanton, and Parker Pillsbury begin publication of *The Revolution*, a radical periodical devoted to the cause of women's rights. The three will collaborate for three years to publish this weekly newspaper, under the motto, "Men, their rights and nothing more; women, their rights and nothing less."

FEBRUARY 1868   **Caroline Seymour Severance Establishes New England Woman's Club, Sparking Woman's Club Movement.** With her friend Dr. Harriot Hunt, Caroline Seymour Severance (1820–1914) founds the New England Woman's Club. In time the Woman's Club Movement will have thousands of members, and Severance will come to be called the "Mother of Clubs."

After moving to California in 1875, Severance rekindles her interest in the suffrage cause, becoming a leader in the campaign for a suffrage amendment in 1895. That campaign fails, but the California suffragists regroup and wage a successful campaign in 1911, leading to the passage of the California Suffrage Amendment in October of that year. Severance registers to vote within a month of the amendment's passage and votes first in a Los Angeles mayoralty election in 1911.

MARCH 14, 1868   **Birth of Emily Murphy, Canadian Advocate of Women's Legal and Property Rights.** Emily Murphy (1868–1933), who plays an important role in the achievement of women's rights, is born at Cookstown, Ontario, into a prominent legal family. She becomes a productive contributor of book reviews and articles to a variety of Canadian magazines and newspapers. She later adopts the pen name "Janey Canuck" and publishes four popular books of personal accounts. Throughout her life Murphy is able to combine her family life, her passion for writing, and a multitude of reform activities. She becomes actively involved in the establishment and proliferation of many professional and volunteer women's organizations. A self-taught legal expert, Murphy soon becomes the first woman police magistrate for Edmonton, then Alberta, and finally for the British Empire. She is a great opponent of narcotics, prostitution, and organized crime. Challenged by a lawyer that she is not a person in the eyes of the British Empire, "Judge Murphy" embarks on a decade-long quest to have women declared legal persons and thereby eligible for appointed positions. This successful campaign is spearheaded by Murphy; however, she never receives the Senate appointment she hopes for, and she dies of diabetes in 1933.

MARCH 19, 1868   **American Athlete Senda Berenson Is Born.** Senda Berenson (1868–1954), a nineteenth-century athlete who promotes gymnastic activities for women, is born. She begins teaching physical training at Smith College in Massachusetts in 1892. She helps organize gymnastic activities and introduces fencing in 1895. Shortly after James Naismith introduces the game of basketball, Berenson introduces her version of the game, modified for women, in the fall of 1892, and women's basketball spreads like wildfire across the United States.

DECEMBER 1868 Women's Suffrage Amendment Introduced in U.S. Congress. Senator S. C. Pomeroy of Kansas introduces an amendment to the U.S. Constitution to grant women suffrage. It will be over fifty years before the amendment is ratified and American women win the vote.

1869 Arabella Aurelia Babb Mansfield, First American Woman Lawyer. Arabella Aurelia Babb Mansfield (1846–1911) is the first female lawyer to be admitted to the bar. She and her brother, who is three years her junior, attend Iowa Wesleyan University, and receive their degrees in three years in a graduation class of three. Arabella, known as "Belle," is valedictorian and her brother salutatorian. Belle and her husband, John Mansfield, take the Iowa bar exam together in 1866. Belle Mansfield is not immediately admitted to the bar, although her husband is, and must wait until later in the day. The Iowa Code states only that "any white male person" can be admitted, and Belle Mansfield argues her own case before Judge Francis Springer, who makes an interpretation of the statute's language to mean that "the affirmative declaration [for males] is not a denial of the right of females." It will be another three years before the statute is officially amended to specifically allow women to be admitted to the bar.

1869 Passage of Indian Act in Canada. The Canadian Parliament passes a new Indian Act that is designed to more closely govern Native people. Among other clauses, the new act seeks to define who is an Indian and develops two categories: "status" and "non-status." Status Indians are permitted to live on reserves, collect annuities laid out in treaties, and hold band membership, while non-status Indians lose all these privileges, however much they may identify themselves as Native. In its definitions, the Indian Act determines that any status-Indian woman who marries a non-status man will lose her status, and her children will be denied it as well. In practical terms, this means that such women are denied access to reserve housing and sometimes even prohibited from visiting their families on reserves. They lose all access to treaty payments and other benefits derived from holding status. Beginning in the 1970s, Native women join together to protest this aspect of the act, staging a "Women's Walk" to Ottawa and appealing to the United Nations Human Rights Committee, which declares the Canadian government in violation of the International Covenant on Civil and Political Rights. In 1985 in Canada, Bill C-31 repeals the clauses denying "Indian" status to any woman (and her children) who marries a non-status Indian man from the Indian Act, and Native women begin the long process of reintegrating themselves and their families into reserve communities.

1869 Women Granted Suffrage in Wyoming Territory. American suffragists experience their first victory in the territory of Wyoming. Women are granted full and equal suffrage and are permitted to hold office within the territory. Legislators believe that by extending suffrage to women, more women will be attracted to settle in Wyoming. When Wyoming is admitted to the Union in 1890, it becomes the first state to grant women full voting rights in its state constitution.

FEBRUARY 27, 1869 Birth of Alice Hamilton, Authority on Industrial Diseases. Alice Hamilton (1869–1970), a physician and the founder of the discipline of industrial medicine, is born in New York City. She receives her degree from the University of Michigan Medical School in 1893 and focuses on identifying the source of toxic substances in factories and mines. Hamilton is the first woman to win the Lasker Award, a United States Public Health Service award, and she is recognized in the mid-1930s for her work in industrial medicine. She dies on September 22, 1970, in Hadlyne, Connecticut.

Idawalley Zoradia Lewis

MARCH 1869 Idawalley Zoradia Lewis, **Lighthouse Keeper.** Idawalley Zoradia Lewis (1842–1911) takes over as lighthouse keeper in Narragansett Bay, Rhode Island, when her father dies. She saves 18 lives during her years on the job. In 1879, the U.S. Congress gives her a special award, and she is the recipient of a number of rewards and honors from organizations around the world. In 1879, she is finally awarded the official title of keeper of the light—even though she has been doing the job for ten years.

MAY 1869 **Establishment of National Woman Suffrage Association.** The movement for women's suffrage divides into two factions. The more radical National Woman Suffrage Association—led by Elizabeth Cady Stanton and Susan B. Anthony and based in New York—seeks to gain women's suffrage through an amendment to the U.S. Constitution. Five months later, the more conservative American Woman Suffrage Association is formed with headquarters in Boston, Massachusetts.

JULY 1869 First National Union of U.S. Women Workers Established. Women shoe binders form the Daughters of St. Crispin, the first national union of women workers in the United States. The union is the female counterpart to the all-male Knights of St. Crispin. Thirty delegates attend their first national convention in July 1869, representing 11 lodges. By December 1869, the union has 24 lodges and applications from 14 more.

NOVEMBER 1869 **Establishment of American Woman Suffrage Association in Boston.** The American Woman Suffrage Association—led by Lucy Stone, her husband Henry Blackwell, Julia Ward Howe and others—seeks suffrage (the vote) first for black males, and then for women through amendments to state constitutions. Five months earlier, the National Woman Suffrage Association—led by Elizabeth Cady Stanton and Susan B. Anthony—was formed.

Chapter 14

1870 TO 1879

1870-1874

1870 Association of the Rights of Women Formed in Paris. Founded in Paris, the Association of the Rights of Women is the first middle-class, republican feminist organization in France. Its founding members are Léon Richer, Maria Deraismes, and the socialist Louise Michel, but the group loses its working-class and socialist members during the repression following the Paris Commune. Thereafter it is solidly middle class, devoted to working within the system to achieve legal, peaceful change. However, the government forces it to dissolve in 1875, despite its moderate nature.

1870 Berthe Morisot Becomes Leading French Impressionist Painter. French artist Berthe Morisot (1841–1895) exhibits her paintings for the first time in the Impressionist exhibition. Morisot is the third daughter of Edme Tiburce Morisot and Marie-Josephine-Cornelie Thomas. Raised in a bourgeois household, she and her sisters are encouraged by their mother to study art. Since women are not admitted to state fine art institutions in France until the end of the nineteenth century, the sisters receive private lessons. In 1868 Morisot meets the artist Edouard Manet and poses for his painting "Le Balcon." Madame Morisot and her daughters begin to attend Madame Auguste Manet's Thursday soirees, where they meet such famous figures as Zola, Degas, Baudelaire, and others. Berthe Morisot joins the Impressionists Manet, Monet, and Renoir in their commitment to the aesthetic of apparent spontaneity. The Impressionists use everyday subjects, less realistic brushwork, and have a fascination with light. Morisot exhibits her paintings in seven of the eight Impressionist exhibitions during the 1870s and 1880s. In 1874 she marries Eugene Manet, brother of Edouard Manet and also a painter, and the couple has one child, Juliet. Morisot is just one of many women working as professional artists during this period. As a woman, she is not allowed into the Parisian cafes where the free exchange of ideas takes place, but she is close friends with the leading male artists of her day. She does not consider herself a feminist confronting institutionalized sexism and even avoids the separate women's art world that emerges, known as the Union des Femmes Artistes. Like other Impressionists, she is attacked by the mainstream press and public but praised by the radical papers. In 1894 the French State purchases one of her paintings for the Musee de Luxembourg, and a retrospective exhibition of her work is held a year after her death.

1870 Margaret Knight Invents Grocery Store Bag. Margaret Knight (1838?–1914) is working in a paper bag factory in Springfield, Massachusetts, when she gets her first patent. It is

Maria Montessori

for an attachment for bag-folding machines to create a square-bottom bag—the grocery store bag. Knight is awarded a total of 27 patents for such inventions as a window frame, a clasp for holding robes, and improvements to a shoe-cutting machine.

1870   Victoria Woodhull and Tennessee Claflin Launch Newspaper. Victoria Claflin Woodhull (1838–1927) and her sister Tennessee begin a weekly newspaper, *Woodhull and Claflin's Weekly,* that is "run by female brains and hands." Always controversial, *Woodhull and Claflin's Weekly* publishes the first English translation of Karl Marx's *Communist Manifesto.* Two years later, Victoria Woodhull runs for president of the United States.

1870   Women Granted Suffrage in Territory of Utah. Women are granted full and equal suffrage in the territory of Utah. They enjoy this right until 1887, when the Edmunds-Tucker Act revokes women's right to vote. (It also revokes the voting rights of polygamous men.) When Utah becomes a state in 1896, women's suffrage is included in the state constitution.

1870   Italian Physician and Educator Maria Montessori Is Born. Maria Montessori

(1870–1952), pioneering educator and physician, is born in Ancona, Italy. In 1896, she becomes the first woman in Italy to receive a medical degree, after which she begins her work with children. In 1906, she opens her first Casa dei Bambinin ("children's house") in a run-down area of Rome. In 1909, she publishes her ideas about education in *Il metodo della pedagogia scientifica* (translated as *The Montessori Method* in 1912). Her emphasis is on the child's own natural motivation and creative potential. Her success leads her to open schools in Italy, Spain, Asia, and the Netherlands.

1870   Ada Cambridge, Australia's First Significant Woman Poet. Ada Cambridge (1844–1926) moves to Australia, becoming the country's first significant woman poet. Born in England, where she publishes two religious books, Cambridge marries George Cross, an Anglican parson, and migrates to Australia in 1870. In her early years in Australia she writes poetry, but her international reputation rests on the novels she begins to publish, such as *Up the Murray*, which first appears as a serial in the *Australasian* in 1875. Cambridge eventually publishes five volumes of poetry and 30 novels. Her books repeatedly attack the institution of marriage, which she uses as a symbol for the old social order. Cambridge becomes a prominent figure in the emerging Australian literary scene which she describes in her autobiographical *Thirty Years in Australia* (1903). In 1913 she returns to England, where her husband dies four years later. Cambridge then returns to Victoria, Australia, where she lives until her death in 1926.

JANUARY 8, 1870   *The Woman's Journal* Premiers. Edited by Lucy Stone, Henry Blackwell, and Mary Livermore, *The Woman's Journal* begins publication. Thirty years later, in 1900, it is adopted at the official publication of the National American Woman Suffrage Association.

APRIL 3, 1870   Birth of Sara Conboy, American Union Leader. Sara Agnes Conboy (1870–1928), who enjoys a short but distinguished career as a union woman, is born. Her activism is highlighted in 1915 when she is elected Secretary-Treasurer of the United Textile Workers of America. In addition to her union activities, Conboy is involved in a number of civic and social groups, particularly those which allow her to tap her union resources and activities. In 1920, she is the American Federation of Labor's representative to the British Trade Union Congress in Portsmouth, England. President Warren G. Harding appoints Conboy to the 1921 Conference on Unemployment. In 1923, she is elected to the New York State Housing Commission. Conboy also serves on the executive board of the National Commission on Prisons and Prison Reform and is chair of the advisory board on vocational training in the New York public schools.

DECEMBER 25, 1870   Birth of Helena Rubinstein, Creator of Modern Cosmetics Industry. Cosmetics entrepreneur Helena Rubinstein (1870–1965) is born in Krakow, Poland, the daughter of wealthy merchants. After dabbling in medical studies in Switzerland, she flees to rural Victoria, Australia, in 1894 to avoid an unwanted marriage. According to legend, she takes along 12 pots of homemade face cream. Her skin stays so beautiful in the harsh Australian climate that soon people are asking for the cream. Rubinstein opens a beauty salon in Melbourne in 1902 to market her cosmetic, Creme Valaze. Within two years she moves to a fashionable Melbourne address where she operates as a beauty consultant, developing a range of products. After a brief visit to Europe in 1905, she returns to open the Valaze Institutes and an agency in New Zealand. Rubinstein continues to develop new cosmetic products, including waterproof mascara, and new techniques for selling them. She introduces the idea of a trained cosmetics saleswoman who can demonstrate products in department stores and help create demand. When Rubinstein leaves for Europe in 1908 she has £100,000 to invest in salons in London and Paris. She sets up her New York salon in 1916, then moves into San Francisco, Boston, Philadelphia, Chicago, and Toronto. At this stage she also begins to sell her products through selected department stores. After the war, Rubinstein travels widely to expand her business and indulge her voracious appetite for collecting art, jewelry, and antiques, while glorying in bitter and ingenious feuds with other beauticians. While undeniably eccentric and reputedly mean, her gifts are lavish; Rubinstein gives all her Australian assets to her sisters. She perpetuates her name outside the cosmetic industry by setting up, in 1953, a Pavilion for Contemporary Art in Tel Aviv, and in 1957 she endows a travelling art scholarship in Australia. Married twice, with two sons, she never retires. Her biographer records that, in her last years, she operates her business from a spectacular lucite bed with built-in fluorescent lights. When Helena Rubinstein dies in New York in 1965, the value of her business is estimated at over $60 million.

1871   Anne Carroll Moore, American Author and Critic, Is Born. Anne Carroll Moore (1871–1961), author and book critic, is born. Moore influences growth in children's book publishing and encourages new writing and art. Among her works is *Nicholas and the Golden Goose,* published in 1932.

1871   Anti-Suffrage Party Formed in the United States. Wives of many prominent U.S. politicians, military officers, and businessmen found the Anti-Suffrage Party to fight against women's suffrage.

1871   Elizabeth Dmitrieff Organizes *Union des Femmes* and Participates in Paris Commune. Elizabeth Dmitrieff (1851–?) founds the *Union des Femmes* and participates in the Paris

Commune, the revolutionary municipal government. She is born Elizabeth Kouchelev in the Russian province of Pskov, where her father, a former Hussar officer, harshly treats his serfs. This inspires in his daughter a spirit of militant rebellion. During the 1860s, she is attracted to revolutionary ideas about the emancipation of serfs and women. Dmitrieff is well-educated and speaks several languages, but she has to attend university in Switzerland, since Russian universities are closed to women. She then enters into a "marriage of convenience" with Colonel Tomanovsky, an older, sickly man who gives Elizabeth a social position and freedom to pursue her interest in women's emancipation.

In Geneva, Dmitrieff befriends young Russian revolutionaries and then goes to London in 1870 to meet Karl Marx. Marx sends Dmitrieff to Paris (without her husband) in 1871 to investigate the revolutionary activities of the working class. There she forms the *Union des Femmes* and recruits militant women from proletarian backgrounds to support the cause of the revolution and the Commune. She serves at ambulance stations and canteens, and defends the barricades from the Versailles troops. During the "bloody week" of May 1871, she and 120 other women hold off the army for four hours at the Place Blanche.

After the defeat of the Commune, Dmitrieff flees Paris while the police search in vain for her. Other female activists (the *Petroleuses,* or "incendiaries") are arrested and tried for their militancy against the government. Dmitrieff eventually returns to Russia, remarries after the death of her husband, and dies in Siberia.

1871   *Petroleuses* Accused of Setting Fire to Paris. The *Petroleuses* are accused of setting fire to Paris during the final days of the Paris Commune of 1871. *Petroleuses,* the French term for incendiaries, are the women who participate in the Paris Commune, the revolutionary municipal government. Women, mainly working-class and socialist, participate in demonstrations, defend the barricades from the Versailles army, and care for the wounded. Because they store kerosene in case of emergency, they are immediately suspected of starting the fires. Also, after the Commune is defeated and order is reestablished, women and feminists become a target of political oppression. Enemies of the Commune suspect any woman seen carrying a basket, box, or milk bottle to be an arsonist.

1871   Louise Michel Takes Part in Paris Uprising. Louise Michel (1830–1905) participates in the uprising of the Paris Commune, the revolutionary municipal government, wearing a National Guard uniform and using her considerable skills at oration to inspire the workers. Born in Vroncourt, France, Michel is the illegitimate daughter of a domestic servant and her employer's son. The nobles her mother serves raise Michel like their own daughter, but following their death she begins a career as a schoolmistress, moving to Paris in 1856. She becomes involved with the socialist movement and grows into a dedicated revolutionary. In the 1871 uprising, she is a member of the rebel 61st battalion and helps set fire to government buildings during the final battles. Michel's strong will and revolutionary fervor earn her the nickname "The Red Virgin." After the Commune, the government tries her and sentences her to life imprisonment in New Caledonia. She lives in a prison colony there from 1873 to 1880, participating in the native Kanakan uprising in 1878. In the general amnesty of 1880, she receives a pardon and returns to France to be greeted by enthusiastic crowds.

She becomes a popular speaker, and champions anarchism instead of socialism, having been converted in prison. She serves two jail terms in the years 1882–86 and leaves France in 1890 for voluntary exile in England. She returns occasionally for speaking tours. She dies in France during a speaking tour in

1905. Louise Michel remains a heroine of socialists and anarchists alike, though she rejects Marxism. Instead, she wants "a spontaneous rising of the people against injustice and exploitation."

1871   Mother Mary Harris Jones Begins Involvement in Labor Movement. Mary Harris Jones (1830–1930) becomes involved with the Chicago, Illinois, chapter of the Knights of Labor. As an organizer, "Mother Jones," as she begins to be called, is interested in all working people but takes a special interest in miners; she is also known as "the Miner's Angel." During the course of her life, Jones is involved in every major labor strike in the United States. She is a founding member of the Industrial Workers of the World.

MARCH 18, 1871   Paris Commune, Revolutionary Government of Paris, Is Formed. The workers and National Guards of Paris revolt against the French government and form the Paris Commune. The revolt of the Paris Commune (March 18-May 28,1871) once again gives women a chance to be politically active. Largely socialist in nature, the Commune proposes free child care, social welfare, and the right to work. However, survival is its top priority in the civil war with the French government, so questions of formal rights for women are left aside until after victory. Women do form large cooperative workshops, schools, and vigilance committees. They also participate in policy debates and fight in the defense of the city. Government troops crush the revolt in May, killing 20,000 rebels and deporting 50,000 more. The French Third Republic uses the Commune as an excuse to forbid socialist and feminist activities during the 1870s.

1872   Elizabeth Garrett Anderson Establishes New Hospital for Women. Elizabeth Garrett Anderson (1836–1917) founds the New Hospital for Women in England, run by and for women. After her death, it is renamed the

Elizabeth Garrett Anderson Hospital. Garrett Anderson receives her certificate to practice medicine from the Society of Apothecaries, placing ahead of her seven male classmates on the certification exam. She completes her M.D. at the University of Paris in 1870. In 1871 she marries the steamship merchant James Anderson, but she insists on the right to continue her career.

1872   Married Women Gain Rights in Oregon. Abigail Duniway (1838?–1915) speaks before a joint session of the Oregon legislature and convinces lawmakers to pass laws granting married women certain rights: the right to start and operate a business on their own, without their husbands' involvement; and the right to protect their property if their husbands leave. Later, she wins women the right to sue and to control the money they earn. In 1883, she convinces the legislature to amend the state constitution to give women the vote, but the amendment is defeated in the general election.

1872   American "Free Love" Advocate Victoria Woodhull Runs for President. One of the most admired and despised women of the nineteenth century, Victoria Claflin Woodhull (1838–1927) is the first woman to run for president of the United States. Her advocacy of "free love," which she believes to be her "inalienable, constitutional and natural right...to love as long or as short a period as I can..." is not well-received in the suffrage community. She is abused in the press, where she is labeled "The Terrible Siren" and persecuted by the public moralist Anthony Comstock. Eventually, she turns to religion and away from free love, moves to England, and marries for the second time. She lives long enough to become interested in aviation before her death in 1927.

1872   Birth of Mary Anderson, American Labor Activist. Mary Anderson (1872–1964), one of the best-known members of the

Victoria Claflin Woodhull

Women's Trade Union League (WTUL), is born. She comes to the United States in 1889 at the age of 16. Her early employment experiences include a job as a shoe worker, and she becomes president of the Stitchers Local 94. She also carries membership on the International Boot and Shoe Workers Executive Board. After Anderson joins the WTUL, her activities expand and she participates in and supports numerous strikes nationwide. These include the Hart, Schaffner, and Marx strike of 1910 in Chicago; the copper miners' strike of 1913 in Calumet, Michigan; and the spar miners' strike in 1916 in Rosiclare, Illinois. In 1920 the Women's Bureau of the Department of Labor is established, and Anderson is named its first director, serving in this capacity until 1944. With Anderson at the helm of the Women's Bureau, the WTUL and the bureau work closely together, each supporting the other's fund-raising efforts. Mary Anderson dies on January 30, 1964.

1872 Mary Putnam Jacobi Establishes Association for the Advancement of Medical Education of Women. Mary Putnam Jacobi (1842–1906), a physician with a particular interest in women's education and health, founds the Association for the Advancement of Medical Education of Women. Born in London, England, Jacobi is the first woman to be admitted to the New York College of Pharmacy (from which she graduates in 1863) and to the Ecole de Médécine in Paris (graduating in 1868).She is also the first woman to be elected to the New York Academy of Medicine (1880). In addition, she organizes the first consumers' organization in America, the National Consumers' League, which works to abolish sweatshops.

1872 Birth of Higuchi Ichiyo, Japanese Author. Higuchi Ichiyo (1872–1896), the first important woman writer in modern Japan, is born. In her approximately 20 stories and more than 3,800 poems, she writes about her own unfulfilled love and the unhappy, circumscribed lives of the women in her age.

FEBRUARY 18, 1872 Mary Williams Dewson, American Economist, Is Born. American economist Mary Williams Dewson (1872–1962), best known for writing legal briefs used in Supreme Court proceedings in support of minimum wage legislation, is born. She does economic research for the Women's Educational and Industrial Union until 1910 and serves as superintendent of the Girls' Parole Department of Massachusetts until 1912. She is best known for her work with Felix Frankfurter in preparing evidence in support of minimum wage legislation when it is challenged before the U.S. Supreme Court. Dewson is also very involved with the National Consumer's League. From 1919 to 1924 she is the league's research secretary, and from 1925 to 1931 she is president of the New York Con-

Alessandra Kollontai

sumer's League. Politics also interest her, and in 1928 she works with Eleanor Roosevelt and develops state women's political caucuses. In 1933, Dewson becomes director of the Women's Division of the Democratic National Party. The same year, she is named a member of the President's Committee on Economic Security. At this time she also serves on the Consumer's Advisory Board as well as the Social Security Board.

APRIL 1, 1872 Birth of Alessandra Kollontai, Prominent Woman in Early Soviet Union. Alessandra Mikhailovna Domontovich Kollontai (1872–1952), the most prominent woman in the early years of the Soviet Union (most of present day Eastern Europe, including Russia), is born in St. Petersburg, the daughter of a Russian general. In 1893 she marries V. L. Kollontai, a fellow member of the nobility, but leaves both her husband and young son in 1896 to study at the University of Zurich in Switzerland. Her concern for the oppressed masses leads her to accept socialist doctrines. A prolific writer at the turn of the century, Alessandra Kollontai advocates free love and full equality for women. Around 1914, she joins the radical Bolshevik party under the leadership of Vladimir Lenin. After the Bolsheviks take over Russia in 1917, Kollontai is the most influential woman in the new Soviet Union, becoming Commissar of Social Welfare and then head of *Zhenotdel,* the women's section of the ruling communist party. She is the first woman to be fully accredited as an ambassador in modern times, serving as a diplomat in Norway, Mexico, and Sweden. Kollontai retires from government service in 1945.

NOVEMBER 1872   Susan B. Anthony Tries to Vote in Presidential Election. Susan B. Anthony (1820–1906) and 15 other women attempt to cast their votes in Rochester, New York in the presidential election. (Anthony attempts to vote for Ulysses S. Grant.) Anthony is arrested and fined $100, which she refuses to pay. African American orator Sojourner Truth also demands a ballot in Grand Rapids, Michigan, but her demand is refused.

1873   Colette, Modernist French Author of Post-World War I Era, Is Born. Colette (1873–1954), a French writer whose most famous works are four autobiographical novels (1900–1904) about a girl named Claudine, is born Sidonie-Gabrielle Colette in St. Sauveue-en-Puisaye, near Auxerre, France. Her mother encourages her tenderness for every plant and animal, and Colette's novels often express a closeness to nature. Colette is forced to write each day by her husband Willy, who publishes her work as his own. Colette tires of this and of catering to Willy's many mistresses. She breaks away and becomes a music hall and cafe dancer but continues to write. Colette participates in

Colette

many society circles including the celebrated one of Natalie Barney, the American expatriate and lesbian intellectual.

Many of Colette's stories, which deal with themes of sex, incest, adultery, and lesbianism, are considered shocking and depraved. Besides her autobiographical works, her writings include *The Vagabond* (1910); *Cheri* (1920), which details the affair between an older woman and her 25-year-old male lover; *The Ripening* (1923); *Sido* (1929); and *The Cat* (1933).

During the Nazi occupation of Paris, Colette has to hide her Jewish husband. Meanwhile she produces *Gigi* (1944), which tells the story of a young courtesan-to-be. In 1944 she also publishes *From My Window,* a simple tale of daily happenings in her Parisian neighborhood. The book offers recipes for rations and other wartime survival techniques.

The majority of Colette's writings are sensitive and sensual, portray women in love, and have vivid descriptions of sexual desire.

1873   Birth of Sara Josephine Baker, Pioneer in Children's Health Care. Sara Josephine Baker(1873–1945) physician, child health pioneer, and founder of the Bureau of Child Hygiene in New York City (1908), is born. In 1894, Baker passes the state regents examination and enters the Women's Medical College of the New York Infirmary for Women and Children, after a year of private study. She receives her M.D. degree four years later, second in a class of eighteen. She is appointed assistant to the health commissioner in 1907; she is also one of those who apprehends the notorious disease carrier "Typhoid Mary" Mallon. Throughout her life, Baker works on behalf of public health issues, helping to decrease the infant mortality rate on New York's east side. When she refuses a lectureship at New York University because the institution does not admit women to its graduate program, the university changes its policy. Recognized as an authority on child hygiene, Baker goes on to earn a Doctorate of Public Health in 1917, the first woman to do so.

1873   Young Women's Christian Association Begins Missionary Work. Influenced by the Young Men's Christian Association (YMCA), Young Women's Christian Association (YWCA) groups with student members focus their energies on bible study and supporting missionaries overseas. Tensions grow between the community YWCAs and student YWCAs. The former tend to be based in northeastern cities and stress meeting the needs of women; they also prize their independence from the YMCA. Student YWCAs, based in the midwest, are more likely to work closely with YMCAs and also remain strongly evangelical. The two factions merge in 1906 to become the Young Women's Christian Association of the United States of America, with the stated purpose as follows: "to advance the physical, social, intellectual, moral and spiritual interests of young women; [and] to participate in the work of the World's Young Women's Christian Association."

JANUARY 1873   Women's Periodical, *The Delineator*, Begins Publication. The Butterick Publishing Company begins publication of *The Delineator*, a women's periodical. *The Delineator*, featuring fashions for women and girls and practical articles on domestic topics, is published monthly until April 1937.

APRIL 22, 1873   Prolific Virginia Writer Ellen Glasgow Is Born. Ellen Anderson Gholson Glasgow (1873–1945), who writes 20 novels and numerous essays, poems, and short stories, is born in Richmond, Virginia. Although women are not allowed to attend the University of Virginia, Glasgow takes and passes the political economy exam given to male students. While seeking her first publisher, she is told to stop writing, go home, and have babies. Her first novel, *The Descendant* (1897), shocks the literary world and her family with its proposal for a new kind of woman. Her third novel, *The Voice of the People* (1900), blends history and realism and becomes a bestseller. Her fifth novel, *The Deliverance*, is published in 1904. *Barren Ground* (1925), her fourteenth novel, presents the woman as victor instead of victim. *The Sheltered Life* (1932) becomes her most popular work with both the public and critics. In 1942 she wins a Pulitzer Prize for her nineteenth novel, *In This Our Life*. Glasgow never marries, although she has relationships with several different men. Her long-hidden autobiography, *The Woman Within*, is finally published in 1954.

JUNE 4, 1873   Birth of Constance Applebee, Founder of First Periodical about Women's Sports. Sportswoman and coach Constance M. K. Applebee (1873–1981), affectionately known as "The Apple," is born in Chigivall, England. In 1901, she comes to America to study at the Sargent School in Boston, where

Constance M. K. Applebee, age 90.

she meets Harriet Ballentine, who invites her to teach field hockey at Vassar College. Between 1902 and 1903, Applebee coaches field hockey at Smith, Mt. Holyoke, Wellesey, Vassar, and Bryn Mawr colleges. In 1904 she is hired as the director of outdoor sports at Bryn Mawr College. During the 1920s, she founds, publishes, and edits the *Sportswoman*, the first periodical to focus on women's sports, which continues publishing for ten years.

In 1922, Applebee presides at the inaugural meeting of the United States Field Hockey Association (USFHA). She is instrumental in creating international competition by sending teams to England as well as hosting teams from England. Applebee is still coaching at the age of 95; she dies on January 26, 1981, at the age of 107.

OCTOBER 1873 Association of the Advancement of Women Established. Astronomer Maria Mitchell (1818–1889), the first woman to have a comet named after her, founds the Association of the Advancement of Women. Mitchell is on the faculty of Vassar College.

1874 Russian Woman Sofia Kovalevskaya Earns Doctorate in Mathematics. Sofia Krukovskaya (1850–1891) earns a doctorate in mathematics at the University of Göttingen, Germany. The daughter of a Russian general, she is born in Moscow and marries Vladimir Kovalevsky in 1868 in an arrangement whereby the groom gives the bride her freedom immediately after the ceremony. Such "fictitious marriages" are a common means for emancipated Russian women to circumvent the severe restrictions placed on their movement at the time. Kovalevsky agrees to allow Sofia Kovalevskaya to study abroad, an ambition that her traditional family does not condone. Although German universities do not admit female students, Kovalevskaya studies mathematics under German professors. In 1874, she is granted a doctorate in mathematics from the University of Göttingen, the first such degree awarded to a woman in modern times. Recognized for her pioneering work in differential equations, she is named to the faculty of the University of Stockholm in 1884.

1874 French Physician Madeleine Pelletier, Advocate of Birth Control, Is Born. Madeleine Pelletier (1874–1939), one of the first women doctors practicing in Paris in the early twentieth century, is born. She obtains her medical education in spite of objections and harassment, and as a doctor provides women with information on birth control. In 1939 she is arrested for performing abortions. Throughout her career, she advocates abortion and contraception as essential rights for women. As more and more public officials in France promote increasing family size to boost the French population, Pelletier becomes outspoken in her denunciations of such "barbar-

Astronomer Maria Mitchell and students in front of Vassar College Observatory, c. 1878.

ism." She believes that individual well-being is more important than intensive reproductivity. Pelletier is active in left-wing politics and serves on the executive committee of the French Socialist Party (SFIO). She insists on the importance for socialist women of putting the "Woman Question," especially female suffrage, before all other concerns. She establishes her own journal, *La Suffragist,* and exhorts French women to adopt the militant tactics of the Women's Social and Political Union (WSPU) in England.

1874   Sophia Jex-Blake Establishes Medical School in London. Sophia Jex-Blake (1840–1912) opens her own medical school, the London School of Medicine for Women. The school has on its teaching staff both Elizabeth Garrett Anderson and Elizabeth Blackwell, the first women doctors in Britain and the United States, respectively. Jex-Blake is driven to open the school after the experience she has at age 29, when she and four other female students pressure the University of Edinburgh in Scotland to admit them to medical training in 1869. The women spend two years there as special students but are forbidden to do the necessary clinical work at the university-affiliated infirmary. Opposition to Jex-Blake and her group at the University of Edinburgh focuses on the women's admission to anatomy classes. The dissection of corpses is considered unsuitable for women to experience, especially in mixed company. Jex-Blake eventually receives a medical degree at Berne, Switzerland, and is admitted to medical practice. By 1880 it is possible for women to obtain a medical education and license in Britain, and by

London School of Medicine for Women

1891, there are 101 women doctors in practice. In April 1895, Jex-Blake is an honored guest at the ceremonious final opening to women at the University of Edinburgh Medical School.

MARCH 29, 1874 First Lady Lou Henry Hoover Is Born. Lou Henry Hoover (1874–1944), future wife of U.S. President Herbert Hoover, is born in Iowa. She earns a degree in geology from Stanford University, the first woman to do so, and coauthors a translation of a text on metallurgy with her husband.

NOVEMBER 30, 1874 Birth of Canadian Novelist Lucy Maud Montgomery, Creator of *Anne of Green Gables* **stories.** Lucy Maud Montgomery (1874–1942), a Canadian novelist whose *Anne of Green Gables* stories are perennial classics, is born. Montgomery is an extraordinary woman who fights for her objectives throughout her life. She maintains her determination to write and publish despite total discouragement by her family. She is one of the first women to hold a professional position on a newspaper in Halifax, Nova Scotia. Most of her childhood and adolescence are spent in her grandparents' home in Cavendish, Prince Edward Island. She writes poetry and short stories that are published but rarely earn her money. Finally Montgomery writes her best-known novel, *Anne of Green Gables* (1908), that establishes Anne Shirley, the protagonist, as a central character of childhood. This is followed by several more Anne stories, including *Anne of Avonlea* (1909), *Anne of the Island* (1915), and *Anne of Ingleside* (1939). These classic stories are read throughout the world by young women and made into films, plays, musicals, television miniseries, and even a ballet. Montgomery's contract with L. C. Page of Boston is very unfair, and eventually she sues the publisher and wins. She marries Ewan Macdonald in 1911 and raises two boys. Her husband is a minister, and the duties of a minister's wife are a heavy burden to Montgomery's free spirit. She creates another series character in *Emily of the New Moon* (1923). In 1923 she is invited to become a member of the prestigious Royal Society of Arts in England, the first Canadian woman so named, and in 1935 she is named an officer of the British Empire. *Jane of Lantern Hill* (1937) is one of Montgomery's last books, and in it she is more optimistic in her style.

1875 – 1879

1875   **Anne Whitney Wins Commission to Sculpt Public Memorial.** Anne Whitney (1821-1915), an American artist educated in New York, Philadelphia, and Rome, is the first person to win a commission to sculpt a memorial to Charles Sumner, in Boston. When it is discovered that she is a woman, however, the commission is revoked. Whitney goes on to complete the piece anyway, and it now stands outside the Harvard Law School in Cambridge, Massachusetts. Remembered for her often politically charged work, Whitney is a friend of the major women's rights leaders of her day and supports both abolition and women's suffrage.

1875   **Lydia Estes Pinkham Makes a Name by Selling Patent Medicines.** Lydia Estes Pinkham (1819–1883) is the first American

woman to establish her reputation by selling medicine, in Boston, Massachusetts. She decides to combat her family's poverty by selling an herbal mixture she calls "Lydia E. Pinkham's Vegetable Compound." Although the mixture has no evident curative powers, it becomes very popular and earns its maker fame and prosperity.

APRIL 29, 1875   **Birth of Australian Artist Margaret Preston.** Margaret Rose McPherson Preston (1875–1963), an Australian painter who helps persuade Australians to accept non-realist art, is born at Port Adelaide. She studies painting in Sydney, under Frederick McCubbin in Melbourne, and under HP Gill in Adelaide. She exhibits and teaches from 1894 on but, between 1904 and 1907, visits Munich and Paris to broaden her understanding of nontraditional and non-European painting. Back in Adelaide, Preston shares a studio with her intimate friend Gladys Reynell and the couple moves to London in 1912. There and in Paris, Preston gradually breaks with academic realism and develops a style based on color theory. In 1918 they work with shell-shocked soldiers in Britain, and the following year Preston is invited to exhibit at the Carnegie Institute. She meets her ex-soldier future husband on the voyage home and the couple settles permanently in Sydney, though she continues to travel widely to exhibit and to absorb and experiment with new styles and techniques. In the late 1920s and 1930s she publishes a series of 27 articles to explain her ideas. Preston holds three major one-woman shows in 1929, 1936, and 1953 and, through her painting and writing, plays a significant part in broadening Australian ideas about and attitudes toward non-realist art. For the most part, her work is international and experimental, but from 1940 she advocates the development of a "national" Australian style based on Aboriginal art. She pursues this idea through her own painting for the rest of her life. Margaret Preston dies at Mosman, Sydney, in 1963.

Illustration from *The Delineator*.

SEPTEMBER 26, 1875 Mary Dreier, Supporter of New York Women's Trade Union League, Is Born. Mary Dreier (1875–1963), an activist in many women's issues, is born in Brooklyn, New York. Her family is independently wealthy and she grows up to become a member of society. In 1909, she makes it possible for Leonora O'Reilly to devote full time to National Women's Trade Union League (NWTUL) work by providing her with a lifetime annuity. Dreier serves the New York branch of the NWTUL as president for nine years, from 1906 to 1915. For four years, from 1911 to 1915, she is a member of the New York State Factory Investigating Committee. In 1915 she is appointed to the board of education, but she resigns this position to work for the suffrage movement. Dreier combines her interest in many issues with activism. She is chair of the Industrial Section of the New York State Woman's Suffrage Party, chair of the Outlawry of War Committee of the NWTUL in 1921, chair of the New York State Conference for the Ratification of the Federal Child Labor Amendment in 1937, and chair of the War Labor Standards Committee in 1942.

1876 American Feminist and Historian Mary Ritter Beard Is Born. Mary Ritter (1876–1958) is born in Indianapolis, Indiana. In 1900, she marries Charles Austin Beard, and the two collaborate on several publications dealing with the economic and historical development of the United States. The two publish *History of the United States* (1921) and

The Rise of American Civilization (1927). Mary Beard, an ardent activist for women's rights, becomes involved in the fight for women's suffrage. After the birth of their son in 1907, Mary joins the National Women's Trade Union League, and organizes strikes and protests. From 1913 to 1917, with Alice Paul, she works for the Congressional Union, which later becomes the National Women's Party. Her publications include *Woman's Work in Municipalities* (1915), *On Understanding Women* (1931), and her landmark, *Women As a Force in History* (1946).

1876 German Painter Paula Modersohn-Becker Is Born. Paula Modersohn-Becker (1876–1907), a significant German artist of the twentieth century, is born. She is the first German painter to be introduced to an English-reading public through poetry, in a poem published in Adrienne Rich's collection *The Dream of a Common Language* in 1979. Modersohn-Becker, who dies following the trauma of childbirth, is now regarded as one of the most powerful figure painters of the twentieth century, although during her lifetime her work is regarded as crude and shocking.

1876 Hubertine Auclert Becomes Leading French Suffragist. Hubertine Auclert (1848–1914) becomes a leading French suffragist, forming her own group, The Society for Women's Rights, which she renames The Society for Women's Suffrage in 1883 to better reflect its goal. From 1881 to 1891 she publishes *The Citizen*, a newspaper dedicated to female suffrage. She dies in 1914, without seeing women gain the vote.

JUNE 22, 1876 Birth of French Fashion Designer Madeleine Vionnet, Originator of Bias Cut. Madeleine Vionnet (1876–1975), pioneering fashion designer and dressmaker, is born at Chilleurs-aux-Boix, just outside of Paris. Vionnet is apprenticed to a neighborhood seamstress at the age of 11 and, at the age of 17, goes to work at a small coûture

house in Paris. Within three years, she marries, suffers the birth and death of a daughter, and leaves her husband, a boldly independent step for a young woman in late nineteenth-century society. She begins a new life in London where she joins the atelier of Kate Reily, an English dressmaker who copies the latest designs from Paris for her English clients. Vionnet remains with Reily from 1895 to 1900, when she returns to Paris and takes a position at the atelier of the Callot sisters, whose designs she had copied while in Reily's employ. During the next seven years, Vionnet works as the "première" dressmaker at the House of the Callot Soeurs. The eldest Callot sister's self-proclaimed mission, "to put the form of the woman at the center of her art," guides Vionnet throughout her career.

In 1907 Vionnet moves to another prestigious atelier, the House of Doucet. She boldly introduces a line of dresses that are to be worn without corsets. Though critics repudiate her unconventional designs (Doucet's sales staff refuses to sell her clothes), she persists in her campaign to rid women of their "deforming armor." She begins to cut fabrics for her dresses "on the bias" (or diagonally across the weave) because it gives her clothing greater elasticity. Clothes cut on the bias drape the body with fabric, rather than armoring it, and articulate the body's natural curves, rather than obscuring them.

In 1912 Vionnet opens her own fashion house and, with the exception of the period of World War I (1914–19), during which she closes her doors, she continues to work under her own name for another 20 years. Her concern for the liberation of the female body seems to be paired with a feminist concern for the welfare of working women. In her own atelier she provides her employees with healthful working conditions and generous salaries and benefits.

1877 First Women's Rowing Club Established. Wellesley College starts a women's rowing club. Women begin participating in rowing competitions in the late 1800s, but it does not become an Olympic sport until 1976.

MARCH 4, 1877   Birth of Mabel Edna Gillespie, American Labor Activist. Mabel Edna Gillespie, an active member of the Women's Trade Union League, is born. After attending Radcliffe and working as a social worker, Gillespie joins the Women's Trade Union League (WTUL) in 1903. She then participates in several strikes, including the Fall Rivers strike for the eight-hour day and the 1912 Lawrence strike by textile workers. In 1909 Gillespie becomes secretary of the Boston WTUL. She also twice serves on the executive board of the WTUL (1911–17 and 1919–22). From 1904 to 1909 Gillespie is executive secretary of the Buffalo branch of the New York Consumer's League. As a member of the Child Labor Commission, she conducts investigations of New York canneries and Boston child labor violations. Gillespie organizes newsstand, garment, hat, and jewelry workers as well as stenographers. From 1912 to 1919 she is the employees' representative on the Minimum Wage Commission. In 1918, she becomes the first woman elected to the executive committee of the Massachusetts American Federation of Labor and is elected vice president of the group that same year. With her own educational background, she understands the importance of education and helps establish the Boston Trade Union College in 1919. In 1921, she becomes a member of the joint administrative committee of the Bryn Mawr Summer School for Women Workers.

1878   Passage of England's Matrimonial Causes Act. The Matrimonial Causes Act of 1878 enables abused wives to obtain separation orders to keep their husbands away from them. Until this law, English common law gives a husband the right "to give his wife moderate correction...by domestic chastisement," and the right to restrain his wife physically to prevent her from "disobeying his rightful authority."

1878   Birth of Nelly Roussel, Critic of France's Patriarchal Society. Nelly Roussel (1878–1922), who writes radical critiques of the French government and patriarchal society, is born. When she is in her early 20s and the mother of three children, she begins writing on the women's movement in France. She is married to the sculptor Henri Godet, and she considers herself a free thinker. Roussel writes for the all-woman staffed daily newspaper, *La Fronde,* contributing columns on women's issues. In 1903 she emerges as a powerful public speaker for the *Ligue pour la Regeneration Humaine,* which advocates contraceptive advice and devices for working-class women. She believes in women's right to control their own fertility, but this controversial stance conflicts with the French government's campaign to increase the population. She tours the country, giving lectures in which she criticizes the French Civil Code and its patriarchal laws. She appeals to women of all classes to "declare war on today's society" and even invokes the threat of a national birth strike. She bases her claims for women's emancipation on the value of motherhood, which she regards as a "social," or state, function. She also calls for sex education for girls before they marry. Roussel criticizes *masculinisme,* a term she uses to describe male supremacy. She opposes French socialists who put class issues above gender. Roussel insists that all women share a common oppression as the "eternal victims" of society.

1878   Lillian Moller Gilbreth, American Pioneer of Industrial Engineering, Is Born. Lillian Moller Gilbreth (1878–1972), among the most important woman engineers, is born. She joins forces with Frank Bunker Gilbreth in 1904 through marriage and business partnership. Together they pioneer scientific management and industrial engineering—particularly time-and-motion studies—through writing and research, and in their consulting firm.

During that period, they also produce and raise 12 children. Their life story is recorded in the film *Cheaper by the Dozen*. Moller Gilbreth obtains her Ph.D. in psychology from Brown University in 1915 and publishes *The Psychology of Management*, a classic in the history of engineering thought and a foundation of modern scientific management theory. When her husband dies in 1924, Moller Gilbreth continues for almost 50 years as head of Gilbreth, Inc. Her specialty is the integration of psychology and human factors with time-and-motion work. In 1935, she becomes a full professor of management in the School of Mechanical Engineering at Purdue University in Indiana. In 1941, she is named head of the Department of Personnel Relations at Newark School of Engineering, and she becomes visiting professor of management at the University of Wisconsin at Madison in 1955.

1878 "Susan B. Anthony Amendment" Proposed in U.S. Congress. The "Susan B. Anthony Amendment," which will extend suffrage to women in the United States, is first proposed in Congress by Senator A. A. Sargent.

c. 1879 First Woman Elected to American Institute of Mining and Metallurgical Engineers. Ellen Swallow Richards (1842–1911) becomes the first woman to be elected to the American Institute of Mining and Metallurgical Engineers. As a holistic thinker and systems analyst, she gains an international reputation as an environmental scientist and engineer. Her home becomes a consumers' testing laboratory as she redesigns and remodels to embody her innovations in the area of pure air and water. As an extension of these solutions to sanitary engineering problems, Richards also becomes an authority in safety and in the analysis of food and human diet, leading to the new fields of domestic science, home economics, and safety engineering— milestones in an era when modern sanitation

methods and safety standards have not yet become the norm.

1879 "The Grand Lady of France," Juliette Lamber, Publishes *The New Review*. Juliette Lamber (1836-1936) publishes *The New Review* from 1879 to 1889 in France. Her patriotic writings and speeches gain her the title "The Grand Lady of France." Lamber is born to a middle-class family of doctors. She marries Alexis de Messine in 1853 and they move to Paris, but the marriage is unhappy. Lamber soon obtains a separation and becomes involved with literary women in Paris, notably George Sand, Daniel Stern, and Jenny d'Héricourt. She argues publicly against female vanity and luxury, and for women's education.

In 1858, Pierre Proudhon publishes his strongly anti-feminist *On Justice*, and Lamber is so outraged that she writes a counter, *Anti-Proudhonian Ideas on Love, Woman, and Marriage* (1858). In it she disproves Proudhon's ideas so well that she becomes an instant celebrity. She argues for equal rights for women, and especially for equal access to education, but she accepts the notion that men and women should have different gender-based duties.

In 1868 she manages to remarry, to her lover, the banker and Republican Edmond Adam. Thereafter she is known as "Madame Adam." Following the Franco-Prussian War, Lamber becomes increasingly patriotic, arguing for a war of revenge to take back France's lost provinces. She runs a Republican salon starting in 1877, and during World War I, she argues against pacifist feminists and supports the war effort. She dies in 1936, just short of her 100th birthday.

1879 Aletta Jacobs, First Woman Doctor in Holland and Birth Control Pioneer. Aletta Jacobs (1854–1929), the first woman admitted to a university in Holland, graduates and becomes the first woman doctor in her country. After her 1879 graduation, she begins her medical practice in Amsterdam and comes into close contact with the poor women of the working classes. She gives free lectures on hygiene and the nursing of infants and provides free medical advice and treatment to poor women and their children. Jacobs concludes that too many pregnancies endanger the lives of these women and of their babies. She begins a long correspondence with a German doctor who educates her about contraception. Jacobs then opens a clinic in 1882 to give contraceptive advice to patients (such advice is free for poor patients). Many of her male colleagues oppose such a clinic and the contraceptive, "Dutch cap," that she provides to patients.

Jacobs also becomes active in the international campaign against state-regulated prostitution, and she leads the international women's peace movement. She is the first woman in the Netherlands to claim the right to vote (1883) and is a cofounder of the Dutch Women's Suffrage Society (1883) and of the International Woman Suffrage Alliance (1902). Jacobs does not start out as a feminist or as a birth control pioneer. Rather, it is her experiences as a physician and her contacts with feminists in other countries that lead her to activism and to open the first birth control clinic in Europe.

Frances Willard, Statuary Hall, U.S. Capitol.

1879   Birth of Hsiang-ning Ho, Chinese Feminist. Hsiang-ning Ho (1879–1972), a Chinese feminist brought up in Hong Kong, is born. She is one of the first women in China to bob her hair as a sign of independence, just one of many feminist acts Ho engages in while living in Kuomintang in the early 1920s. From 1949 through 1959, she is head of the Overseas Chinese Affairs Commission in Peking, and in 1960 she is made Honorary Chairwoman of the China Women's Federation.

1879   Dorothy Canfield Fisher, American Novelist and Essayist, Is Born. Dorothy Canfield Fisher (1879–1958), American writer, is born in Lawrence, Kansas. She marries John Redwood Fisher in 1907, and five years later

publishes her first work, *The Squirrel-Cage.* As a children's author, Fisher is best remembered for *Understood Betsy,* published in 1917. First lady Eleanor Roosevelt names Canfield one of the ten most influential women in the United States, and the state of Vermont establishes the Dorothy Canfield Fisher Children's Book Award in her honor in 1957.

1879   Frances Willard, President of Woman's Christian Temperance Union (WCTU). American educator and reformer Frances Willard (1839–1898) becomes president of the Woman's Christian Temperance Union (WCTU), established in 1874 to fight the use of alcohol. Willard believes that curing society's ills will be best accomplished through women's suffrage. WCTU becomes the largest women's organization in the United States by 1880.

Willard plays an important role in education for women in Illinois. She serves as president of the Evanston (Illinois) College for Ladies until it merges with Northwestern University, when she becomes dean of the Women's College. A statue of Frances Willard represents the state of Illinois in Statuary Hall in the U.S. Capitol in Washington, D.C.

1879 Birth of Japanese Social Reformer Yamada Waka. Social reformer Yamada Waka (1879–1956), an advocate for the protection of mothers, is born. Seeking employment abroad to restore her family's financial situation, Waka is forced into prostitution in the United States, from 1897 to 1903. She is rescued by and married to Yamada Kakichi (1865–1934), who returns with her to Japan and educates her. With his encouragement, Waka begins publishing translations and essays in *Seito* (*Bluestocking*) and, later, *Shufu no Tomo* (*Housewife's Friend*). She is a participant in the "debate on the protection of motherhood," in which she takes the traditionalist position of elevating the status of motherhood and advocating for the government to provide financial support to poor mothers. She is most famous, however, for her popular column in the mass-circulation daily *Tokyo Asahi Shimbun*, in which she responds to letters from troubled women. Waka serves as president of the *Bosei Hogo Remmei* (Motherhood Protection League) from 1934 until 1937, when it is finally successful in persuading the national legislature to provide financial aid to poverty-stricken mothers of small children. She also establishes a refuge for mothers and children in Tokyo. After World War II, Waka manages a retraining center for former prostitutes.

MAY 19, 1879 Nancy Astor, First Woman Member of Parliament in Great Britain, Is Born. British politician Nancy Witcher Lang-

horne Astor (1879–1964) is born in Danville, Virginia. Her father is an officer in the Confederacy during the U.S. Civil War (1861–65). After a brief marriage in Boston around the turn of the century, she travels to England and marries the wealthy Waldorf Astor in 1906. He becomes a British peer and is elected to Parliament in 1910. Nancy Astor supports his work, and when he dies in 1919, she is elected to take his place as Member of Parliament (MP). Another woman, Constance Markiewicz (1868–1927), is elected MP in 1918 (the year British women win the vote and the right to serve in Parliament). But with other members of her party from Ireland, she refuses to meet in England. So when Nancy Astor is introduced into Parliament in 1919, she becomes the first woman to actually serve, and she remains the only woman until 1921. Although elected as a Tory, she refuses throughout her career to vote along party lines. She follows her own instincts and moral sense, supporting issues affecting women and the family and urging strict controls on drinking. She is strongly anti-Communist but speaks out against McCarthyism. She serves in Parliament until 1945 and then withdraws completely and somewhat bitterly from political life. She dies on May 2, 1964.

OCTOBER 14, 1879 Birth of Australian Author Stella Miles Franklin. Stella Maria Miles Franklin (1879–1954), who fosters Australia's literary heritage, is born at Talbingo, New South Wales, Australia. Franklin publishes her first, and best-known, novel *My Brilliant Career* (1901), a semi-autobiographical book that depicts a teenage girl's rebellion against the constraints of womanhood and marriage. It provokes an ambivalent response and its sequel, *My Career Goes Bung*, is not published until 1946. Franklin moves to Sydney, but her journalistic career is thwarted by her rejection of sexual advances from a very influential journalist and poet. In 1906 she sails for America, where an introduction from

Vida Goldstein gains her admission to feminist circles in Chicago. She works for the National Women's Trade Union League and helps edit *Life and Labor*. Her novels, *On Dearborn Street* and *The Net of Circumstance*, are written at this time. In 1915 she sails for England and works in Macedonia as a volunteer during World War I. She returns to Australia in 1928 and settles in Melbourne, where she fosters the work of young Australian writers and works tirelessly for greater recognition for the Australian literary heritage. Franklin publishes much of her work under male pseudonyms; six novels as "Brent of Bin Bin." She is awarded the Prior Memorial Prize in 1936 and 1939. In 1948 she establishes Australia's most prestigious literary prize: the Miles Franklin Award for Australian Fiction. She dies in Drummoyne in 1954 and some of her work is published posthumously.

Chapter 15

1880 TO 1889

1 8 8 0 – 1 8 8 4

c. 1880 **Birth of Rebecca Beck August, Activist in Needle Trades Industry.** Rebecca Beck August, a rank and file organizer, is born. She emigrates from her native Latvia first to London and then to Chicago. She begins her work career in a London tailor shop in 1893, the start of a 53-year career in the needle trades industry. In 1904, upon arrival in Chicago, she goes to work at Hart, Schaffner, and Marx. While working there, she protests a pay cut and is immediately fired. It is possible that she is one of the young women who ignite the big clothing worker's strike in Chicago over this very same pay cut. Her union organizing activity carries over into other aspects of her life. She helps found the Hebrew Trades Council and a woman's branch of The Workman's Circle, which becomes known as Ladies Branch Number 3. While in Chicago, she is influenced by her acquaintance with Jane Addams and is a frequent visitor to Hull House. In 1910 she moves to Seattle and becomes very active with the International Workers of the World and their fight for the 8-hour day. Additionally, she is an active member of the Amalgamated Clothing Workers of America. Upon retirement in 1948, she helps establish a Retired Members Club.

1880 **Birth of Aunt Molly Jackson, American Folk Historian.** Mary Stames (1880–1960), or

"Aunt Molly Jackson" as she is called, is born. She is a country balladeer and folk historian active in rural Kentucky, the wife and daughter of miners. Her work takes her on a nationwide tour seeking to raise funds for miners' relief. It is said that once, when she comes upon a group of hungry children in a rural hollow in Bell County, Kentucky, she takes her rifle and heads to the local company store. There, at gunpoint, she demands and receives some meager supplies for the family. She is "discovered" by Theodore Dreiser and John Dos Passos when they investigate the oppression of striking miners in Harlan County, Kentucky, in 1931.

1880 **Ruth Sawyer, American Children's Author, Is Born.** Ruth Sawyer (1880–1970), American author influenced by Irish folklore, is born. In 1936, her *Roller Skates* wins the Newbery Medal. Sawyer receives the Caldecott Medal in 1945 for *The Christmas Anna Angel,* and again in 1954 for *Journeycake, Ho!*

1880 **First Woman Elected to New York Academy of Medicine.** Mary Putnam Jacobi (1842–1906), the first woman to be admitted to the New York College of Pharmacy (from which she graduates in 1863) and to the Ecole de Médécine in Paris (in 1868), becomes the first woman to be elected to the New York Academy of Medicine.

1880   Actress Maggie Moore Founds the J. C. Williamson Theatrical Empire. Margaret Virginia (Maggie) Sullivan Moore's (1851–1926) gift for acting founds the J. C. Williamson theatrical empire in Australia. Born in the United States of Irish/Australian parents, Moore is an established actor when she meets and marries comedian J. C. Williamson in 1873. The next year the couple sails for Australia, where they open in Melbourne with a hugely successful season of *Struck Oil*. By October 1875, when they leave for England, Europe, and the United States, the couple is rich and famous. In 1879, they begin another Australian tour and, by 1880, lease a major Melbourne theater for their lavish productions. There, J. C. Williamson Ltd. becomes the most successful entrepreneurial company in the history of Australian theater. Much of its success is based on Moore's enormous popularity as an actress, and she is reputed to earn the bulk of the fortune they invest in the company. By 1897, Williamson is living with the dancer Mary Weir. Moore sues for her share of their combined fortune but wins little other than the right to perform in *Struck Oil*. She divorces him in June 1899, leaves Australia, and marries Harry Roberts in New York in 1902. She returns under contract to J. C. Williamson Ltd. in 1908 and spends most of the next 12 years working for the company in Australia. In August 1924, the 50th anniversary of her first Australian performance is celebrated with a lavish jubilee in Melbourne. The next year she retires to live with a sister in California, where she dies after an accident in 1926.

JUNE 1, 1880   Birth of Jeannette Rankin, First Woman Elected to U.S. House of Representatives. Jeannette Pickering Rankin (1880–1973), the first U.S. Congresswoman, is born near Missoula, in the Montana Territory. She is educated at Montana University and the New York School of Philanthropy, and she becomes an ardent suffragist and pacifist—two threads that wind through the rest of her life. Campaigning around the country for women's voting rights hones her political skills. In 1914, she is appointed legislative secretary of the National American Woman's Suffrage Association; her efforts help bring the vote to Montana women in 1914. In 1916, Rankin is elected as a Republican to Congress (taking office in 1917), becoming the first female member of the U.S. House of Representatives. When the issue of the United States' entering World War I is brought to a vote, the pacifist Rankin joins 56 other members in voting no. This vote, and legislation she sponsors for women's rights—including a bill to grant married women independent citizenship—and children's rights, make her unpopular at home. She leaves Congress after one term. In 1919, she is a delegate to the Second International Congress of Women, and she spends the next two decades working for organizations promoting peace and freedom. Rankin is reelected to the House of Representatives in 1940 and casts the only vote against the United States' entering World War II. Again, her pacifism costs her reelection. For the rest of her life she studies pacifism and feminism. In 1967 she forms the Jeannette Rankin Brigade to oppose the Vietnam War; 5,000 women join her in the Jeannette Rankin March on Capitol Hill in Washington, D.C., in 1968 to protest U.S. involvement in Vietnam. Jeannette Rankin continues her activism until her death by heart attack on May 18, 1973.

1881   First Russian Woman Executed for Political Crime. Sofia Perovskaya (1854–1881) is the first Russian woman to be executed for a political crime. Her father is governor of St. Petersburg at the time. A rebel against her father's conservatism as a young woman, Perovskaya develops radical political ideas through lecture courses and discussion groups in St. Petersburg. She becomes an ardent advocate of women's rights and social reform in tsarist Russia. Engaged in spreading anti-government propaganda among the peasants in the countryside, she is forced into an underground existence in the mid-1870s. Finally, Perovskaya joins the People's Will, a terrorist group planning to kill Tsar Alexander II. She takes a leading part in three assassination attempts, the third being successful in 1881. In that year, at the age of 27, Sofia Perovskaya is hanged.

JUNE 26, 1881   American Rural Educator Jessie Field Shambaugh Is Born. Jessie Field Shambaugh (1881–1971), considered the "Mother of 4-H," is born. Raised on a farm near Shenandoah, Iowa, Shambaugh at an early age is accompanying her father to the meetings of the local Farmers Institute. Trained as a teacher, she decides that she can influence rural education more by becoming a county superintendent of schools and in 1906 is elected the superintendent of schools of Page County, Iowa.

Shambaugh has 130 schools under her control, and in each school she sets up Girls' Home Clubs and Boys' Corn Clubs. She works with local teachers to develop a more enlightened course of study. In her courses she replaces abstract textbook questions with practical, everyday farming problems. She writes several books, including *Farm Arithmetic,* which she gives away free of charge.

In 1910 Shambaugh begins organizing summer camps where boys can learn how to judge livestock, test new farm machinery, and take classes in scientific farming. In 1911 she establishes similar camps for girls, called the "Camps of the Golden Maidens."

In 1912 Shambaugh resigns as superintendent to become the national secretary of the YMCA's Small Town and Country Work division. In this capacity, she sets up rural YMCAs throughout the nation.

After her marriage to Ira W. Shambaugh in 1917, she resigns. Later she hosts the radio program "Mother's Hour," giving advice on child care, and continues to work with 4-H

clubs. At the time of her death, people consider her the "Mother of 4-H."

SEPTEMBER 28, 1881   Birth of Eleanora Sears, American Sportswoman. Eleanora Sears (1881–1968), an active sportswoman who loves to participate in a variety of sports, leading to her being considered the first American all-around "sportswoman," is born. She ignores the social expectations and constraints placed on women of these times and does things like play in polo matches dressed in men's trousers rather than a skirt, much to the chagrin of the men (and women). Sears is credited, along with May Sutton Bundy, with changing the tennis dress style to a more comfortable level.

Sears wins championships both in tennis and squash. In 1928 she wins the first U.S. women's squash racquets singles championship. She also rides, sails, golfs, swims, and competes in long distance walking. Sears dies on March 26, 1968.

OCTOBER 18, 1881   Canadian Doctor Elizabeth Bagshaw, Birth Control Advocate, Is Born. One of Canada's first woman doctors, Elizabeth Bagshaw is born near Cannington, Ontario. She practices for 60 years, but she is best known for her 30 years as the medical director of the Hamilton Birth Control Clinic. While "rising relief costs" cause her great concern, her main motivation is her genuine concern for the plight of working-class women facing repeated unwanted pregnancies. Founded and financed by a wealthy widow, the clinic often distributes contraceptives free of charge. Despite opposition from medical colleagues and local clergy, Bagshaw continues to work with dedicated volunteers to promote inexpensive and reliable contraception. She receives many honors throughout her life, including an honorary doctorate from McMaster University in Hamilton.

1882   First Birth Control Clinic in Europe Established. Aletta Jacobs (1854–1929), the first woman doctor in Holland, opens the first birth control clinic in Europe. After providing free medical care and advice to poor working class women and their children in Amsterdam, Jacobs concludes that too many pregnancies endanger these women's lives. She begins a long correspondence with a German doctor who educates her about contraception and opens her clinic in 1882 to give contraceptive advice to patients. Many of her male colleagues oppose such a clinic and the contraceptive, "Dutch cap," that she provides.

1882   Birth of Sister Bertilla Boscardin, Protector of Children During World War I. Anna Francesca Boscardin (1882–1922), an uneducated Italian peasant girl who becomes a nun and cares for hospitalized children during World War I, is born. At the age of 16, she is accepted into the Sisters of St. Dorothy at Vicenza, Italy. She takes the name Bertilla and is put to work in the kitchen. After three years, she is promoted to nurses' aide in a children's ward at a hospital in Treviso. During World War I (1914–18) air-raids in 1917, Bertilla's dedicated, protective care of the hospitalized children earns her the attention and praise of hospital authorities. But the mother superior of the Treviso convent does not appreciate Bertilla and sends her to work in the laundry. A higher superior, however, rescues Bertilla from the washtubs and puts her in charge of the children's isolation ward at the hospital. Through hard work, devotion, and tender care of others, Bertilla rises from a life of menial labor and neglect to one of responsibility, authority, and great respect. Her feast day is celebrated on October 20.

1882   First Woman Freemason. French feminist Maria Deraismes (1828–1894), founding member of the Association for the Rights of Women, becomes the first woman freemason, eventually founding her own lodge. She also leads a campaign for female suffrage and speaks out against scientific testing on animals.

1882   Bertha Mahony, American Children's Author, Is Born. Bertha Mahony (1882–1969), cofounder of the first magazine devoted exclusively to reviews and criticisms of children's literature, is born. Mahony founds *Horn Book Magazine* with Elinor Whitenye in 1924, and later forms Horn Book Inc., an award-winning publishing company specializing in children's books.

1882   Harriet Jane Hanson Robinson Founds National Women's Suffrage Association of Massachusetts. Textile mill worker and writer Harriet Jane Hanson Robinson (1825–1911) and her daughter organize the National Women's Suffrage Association of Massachusetts.

1882   Birth of Japanese Social Activist Kubushiro Ochimi. Feminist and social activist Kubushiro Ochimi (1882-1972) is born. In 1916, she joins the *Kyofukai* (Japan's Women's Christian Temperance Union) and becomes active in its campaign against prostitution. She also works for women's suffrage and is a major organizer of the 1930 Zen *Nihon Fusen Taikai* (All-Japan Women's Suffrage Conference). After World War II, she continues to work for the Kyofukai's campaigns against prostitution and for world peace.

1882   Fukuda Hideko Becomes One of First Women's Rights Activists in Japan. Inspired to work for women's rights after hearing a speech by orator Kishida Toshiko, Fukuda Hideko (1865–1927) becomes one of the first such activists in Japan, as well as a socialist, pacifist, educator, and writer. She is active in the Freedom and Peoples' Rights Movement (seeking a Western-style democracy in Japan) and a women's lecture society. Between 1885 and 1889, Hideko becomes involved in a movement that opposes Japan's foreign policy in Korea, an activity for which she is imprisoned. Thereafter, in order to earn money for herself and her family, Hideko opens a women's technological school to enable young women to become self-supporting. Between the years 1901 and 1907, she turns increasingly to the politics of socialism, which she comes to believe will be the best vehicle for the liberation of women. In 1904 she publishes her autobiography, *Warawa no han shogai* (*Half of My Life*). In 1907 Hideko begins her most ambitious project, the publication of *Sekai Fujin* (*Women of the World*), a journal that publishes Japan's most prominent socialists and whose purpose is to improve the status of women in Japanese society. Hideko publishes articles on the Japanese marriage system, the Peace Police Law, *eta* (outcasts in Japanese society), women's movements in foreign countries, socialist theory, strategies to promote economic independence for women, women's suffrage, and women's education.

APRIL 10, 1882   Frances Perkins, American Public Official, Is Born. Fannie Coralie Perkins (1882–1965), the first female cabinet member in the United States, is born. She changes her name legally to Frances Perkins and keeps her name even after her 1913 marriage. Well-educated and hard-working, she becomes secretary of the New York Consumer's League in 1910 and works to improve the conditions of undernourished children and sweatshop laborers. Her work with the Consumer's League and the Committee on Safety of the City of New York leads to several new laws protecting workers. Perkins is a strong suffragist, marching in demonstrations and giving speeches on street corners, but throughout her life she opposes the Equal Rights Amendment. In 1918 she is appointed to the New York State Industrial Commission, and at $8,000 a year, she is the highest-paid state employee in the nation. Perkins works for several state agencies over the next decade, always pushing for rights for workers and women. When Franklin Roosevelt (1882-1945) becomes President of the United States in 1933, he appoints her Secretary of Labor,

Cosima Wagner

making her the first female cabinet member in the nation. During her tenure, she drafts the Social Security Act and the National Labor Relations Act. After resigning in 1945, Perkins concentrates on writing and public speaking. In 1956 she becomes a professor at the Cornell School of Industrial Relations. She remains on the faculty until her death on May 14, 1965.

1883   Cosima Wagner Becomes Director of Bayreuth Festival. Cosima Wagner (1837-1930), the daughter of Franz Liszt and the wife of Richard Wagner, is the first woman to serve as director of the Bayreuth Festival, in Bayreuth, Germany, which is dedicated to Richard Wagner's work. She assumes this position after the death of her husband, to whom she has devoted her life. Rigidly adhering to what she feels are Wagner's intentions, she controls all aspects of the opera productions until she hands over direction to their son Siegfried in 1906.

1883   Olive Schreiner Writes Famous "New Woman" Novel, *The Story of an African Farm.* Olive Emilie Albertina Schreiner (1855-1920) publishes her first novel, *The Story of An African Farm* (1883) under the pseudonym "Ralph Iron," but readers soon learn the author's true identity. This best-selling novel contains the most celebrated fictional representative of the so-called "new woman." The heroine, Lyndall, breaks convention by bearing an illegitimate child and refusing to marry. In London, Schreiner is acclaimed as a genius and is eagerly met by writers Oscar Wilde and George Moore and by socialist radicals Eleanor Marx and Karl Pearson. She joins the avant-garde society called The Fellowship of the New Life to help promote socialist politics and sexual equality, and devotes herself to feminism. She writes essays on prostitution and contraception and speaks publicly on women's issues. Schreiner is born in Cape Colony (now part of South Africa), the ninth child of a strict, impoverished Wesleyan missionary. Her harsh childhood inspires her commitment to "helping weak things against the strong." In 1881 she moves to England to study medicine but instead embarks on a literary career. At 34, she returns to South Africa, and in 1894 marries Samuel Cronwright, who takes her last name. Schreiner's anti-imperialist beliefs result in her imprisonment during the Boer War, the looting of her home, and the burning of her writings. She publicly criticizes the powerful South African politician Cecil Rhodes (who once courts her) and the atrocities committed by whites in Africa. Her book *Woman and Labour* (1911) is hailed as the "Bible of the Women's Movement." Despite her early fame, Schreiner dies alone in a boardinghouse in Africa in 1920.

1883   Dutch Physician Aletta Jacobs Claims Right to Vote. Aletta Jacobs (1854–1929), the first woman admitted to a university in the Netherlands and the first woman doctor in her country, is the first woman in the Netherlands to claim the right to vote. She is a cofounder of the Dutch Women's Suffrage Society and of the International Woman Suffrage Alliance (1902).

1883   Birth of Edith Clarke, Renowned American Electric Power Expert. Edith Clarke (1883–1959), an electric power theorist and mathematician, is born. She is the first woman to earn a master's degree in electrical engineering, from Massachusetts Institute of Technology (MIT) in 1919. Her undergraduate work at Vassar is in math and physics, and upon graduation in 1908, Clarke teaches these subjects for three years before enrolling in civil engineering at the University of Wisconsin. She leaves after a year to work for American Telephone and Telegraph (AT&T), supervising the group of women who perform calculations for the research engineers in electrical technology. After obtaining her master's degree, she finds no one willing to hire a woman electrical engineer until General Electric offers her a job identical to the position she holds at AT&T overseeing calculations. Frustrated after two years by the lack of recognition of her engineering qualifications, Clarke accepts an opening as an instructor at Constantinople Women's College in Turkey. Upon her return, General Electric finally hires her as an electrical engineer to analyze power transmission problems. Her major contributions in this field include the development of symmetrical components, often called Clarke components, and the publication of the major textbook in the specialty of power transmission. After retiring from General Electric in 1945, Edith Clarke becomes a professor of electrical engineering at the University of Texas and is the first woman to be elected a fellow of the American Institute of Electrical Engineers (now IEEE, the Institute of Electrical and Electronic Engineers).

1883   Suffrage Gained by Women in Washington. Suffrage is granted to women in the territory of Washington; the territorial suffrage acts are declared unconstitutional in 1887 by the territorial supreme court.

AUGUST 19, 1883   Birth of Gabrielle (Coco) Chanel, French Fashion Designer. Gabrielle (Coco) Chanel (1883–1971), a fashion designer who makes comfort and "casual elegance" in women's clothes fashionable from the 1910s through the 1960s, is born in Saumur, France. She begins her career in 1909, in Paris, remaking and selling women's hats purchased in Paris department stores. At her second shop, which she opens four years later in the resort town of Deauville, she adds to her popular line of hats and accessories an array of sports clothing and beachwear, including pullover sweaters and jackets adapted from menswear. Her fashions, executed in generous swathes of fabric, seek to free women from the constraints of corseting and form-fitting construction. "I make fashions women can live in, breathe in, [and] feel comfortable in," she once comments.

During World War I, the limited availability of textiles and the practical demands for comfort and mobility made by women—now a substantial part of the labor force—leads Chanel to introduce the line of clothing that leaves her most lasting mark on the fashion world. Using jersey, she produces garments without fitted waists or bodices. She designs jersey skirts that flout convention with raised hemlines and increase their wearers' mobility by eliminating cinched-in waistlines. The historian Valerie Steele suggests that Chanel's use of jersey (utilized previously in men's sweaters and underwear), like her adaptations of men's fashions for women, grows out of an aesthetic that privileges the simple over the elaborate; and powerful, "masculine" functionality over frivolous, "feminine" ornamentation.

After the war, Chanel continues to produce garments that simply and comfortably clothe her clients and shape contemporary tastes. In the mid-1920s, she designs the first "little black dress," austere and unembellished, which comes to embody the "new modern woman," as *Vogue* magazine declares in 1926. Chanel's use of jersey becomes so prolific that she begins to produce it herself in 1935 in her own textile factory. Simple woolen suits with cardigan jackets and plain or pleated skirts become her trademark and maintain their popularity throughout her career. By the mid-1930s, her business becomes so successful that she has more than 3,000 employees in England and France.

With the commencement of World War II in September of 1939, Chanel goes into retirement. Her affair with a high-ranking German officer brings her widespread disdain in France. Her comeback, 15 years later, receives an initially lukewarm reception. However, by 1956 she refashions her trademark Chanel suit into a tailored suit of trimmed wool which catapults her back into favor. Chanel effectively popularizes the principles of functional and comfortable fashion that nineteenth-century dress reform advocates so stridently called for.

The Chanel house, under the direction of a series of strong male designers, remains a strong force in the fashion industry of today with a commitment to the vision of its founder.

SEPTEMBER 14, 1883   Margaret Higgins Sanger, Founder of Planned Parenthood, Is Born. American birth control advocate Margaret Sanger (1883–1966) is born in Corning, New York. In 1953 she is the founder and first president of the International Planned Parenthood Federation.

C. 1884   Kate Gleason, Student of Mechanical Engineering. Kate Gleason (1865–1933) is the first woman on record to register and study mechanical engineering in the United States, at Cornell University in 1884–85 and 1888–89. Although she never obtains a degree, she practices engineering for many years at her father's firm, Gleason Machine Tools Company, winning renown for her original design of worm gears and helping the company to become the leading manufacturer of specialized gears.

1884   One of First African American Women to Earn Bachelor's Degree. Anna J. Cooper (1858–1964) is one of the first three African American women to earn a B.A. from an American college. She is the only African American female graduate in the class of 1884 at Oberlin College in Ohio.

1884   Edith Nesbit Cofounds the Fabian Society. Edith Nesbit (1858–1924), author of popular children's novels in the early 1900s, cofounds (with her husband, Hubert Bland, and a circle of literary friends that includes H. G. Wells and George Bernard Shaw) the Fabian Society, a socialist organization, in London, England.

1884   Birth of Cornelia Meigs, American Children's Author. Cornelia Lynde Meigs (1884–1973) is born in Rock Island, Illinois. Among her many works are *Kingdom of the Winding Road* (1915), *Rain on the Roof* (1925), *Trade Wind* (1927), *Incredible Louisa*, which is published in 1933 and wins the Newbery Medal in 1934, and *Railroad West* (1937). Her dramatic works include the Drama League Prize-winner, *The Steadfast Princess* (1916) and *Helga and the White Peacock* (1922).

FEBRUARY 28, 1884   Birth of Emma Callaghan, Australian Aboriginal Nurse and Civil Rights Activist. Emma Jane Foot Callaghan (1884–1979), an Australian Aboriginal (native people of Australia) nurse and civil rights activist, is born at La Perouse Aboriginal Reserve, Sydney, of the Dharawal tribe. Callaghan is educated only to third grade. However, inspired by Retta Dixon, later founder of the Aborigines' Inland Mission, Callaghan decides to become a nurse. She

studies midwifery at Bellbrook Reserve, an Aboriginal facility, under the clan's women elders. She stays on to nurse there because the nearest hospital does not accept Aboriginal patients. At Bellbrook she learns the local language, translates biblical stories, and registers births and deaths. She works for the Aborigines Protection Board and campaigns for civil rights for Aborigines. Callaghan dies in Sydney, and her last home is preserved by the New South Wales State Government as a memorial to her work.

OCTOBER 11, 1884   Eleanor Roosevelt, Who Revolutionizes Role of the Political Wife, Is Born. American First Lady Anna Eleanor Roosevelt (1884–1962), who takes full advantage of her position to champion the rights of women and minorities, is born. Known as Eleanor, she is the niece of the 26th U.S. president, Theodore Roosevelt (1858–1919), and the wife of the 32nd president, Franklin Delano Roosevelt (1882–1945). Eleanor Roosevelt is well-known and respected for her work for international cooperation, civil rights for minorities, and equal status for women. Although she does not participate in the suffrage movement as a young woman, in the 1920s she works with the League of Women Voters and the Women's Trade Union League.

In 1929, Franklin D. Roosevelt (FDR) wins the governorship of the State of New York. Because he loses the use of his legs during a bout with infantile paralysis (polio) in 1921, FDR sends his wife on countless official inspection trips to act as his "ambassadress." Her personal reports from the field during the height of the Great Depression help shape the state's social policies. In 1932 FDR wins his first term as president. He is elected three more times, dying of a brain hemorrhage on April 12, 1945. For 12 eventful years, encompassing the country's struggle with the Great Depression (1929–39) and entry into World War II in 1941, Roosevelt transforms the role of president's wife from that of an official hostess to that of a vibrant political activist.

In 1936, at the urging of her close friend, the journalist Lorena Hickock, Roosevelt begins writing a daily syndicated newspaper column, "My Day," in which she comments on current issues and champions the cause of civil rights. The column often deals with the everyday minutiae of life in the White House and is syndicated to scores of daily newspapers throughout the United States. Roosevelt takes full advantage of her access to FDR and his appointees to make sure women are represented and considered in policy decisions. After the United States' entry into World War II in 1941, FDR sends Roosevelt on numerous personal missions to meet American troops in the field.

After FDR dies, Roosevelt is appointed a delegate to the newly formed United Nations (UN). In 1948, she is widely acclaimed for her part in writing and passing the UN's Universal Declaration of Human Rights. During the 1950s, she speaks out against McCarthyism. Just before her death on November 7, 1962, she serves on the National Commission on the Status of Women. In addition to books for children, she publishes three volumes of autobiography: *This Is My Story* (1937), *This I Remember* (1949), and *Autobiography* (1961).

1 8 8 5 – 1 8 9 2

1885 **Birth of Lucy Diggs Slowe, Prominent African American Educator.** Lucy Diggs Slowe (1885–1937), an American educator particularly dedicated to the advancement of black women, is born. She is the first principal of Shaw Junior High School in Washington, D.C., in 1919. At Howard University, which she enters in 1904, she is one of the founders and the first vice-president of Alpha Kappa Alpha, the first sorority among black college women. She receives an MA in English from Columbia University in 1915 and goes on to

become dean of women at Howard University in 1922. She serves as the first secretary of the National Council of Negro Women (1935) and as the first president of the National Association of College Women (1923–29).

1885 **Ogino Ginko, First Japanese Woman Doctor of Western Medicine.** Ogino Ginko (1851–1913) becomes the first Japanese woman licensed to practice Western medicine. Her medical career follows a divorce from her first husband, on the grounds of childlessness. Her inability to bear children, however, is caused by a venereal disease that she contracts from him. In 1882 Ginko graduates from Kojuin, a private medical school for men. Ultimately overcoming objections, she is allowed to take the medical qualifying examination and establishes a practice in 1885. Ginko serves as the physician for Meiji Girls' School and contributes to the women's magazine *Jogaku zasshi*.

JANUARY 5, 1885 **Birth of Isabella McCorkindale, Australian Temperance Campaigner and Feminist.** Temperance advocate Isabella McCorkindale (1885–1971)is born. She migrates from Scotland to Queensland, Australia, as an infant and is state educated. McCorkindale joins the Women's Christian Temperance Union (WCTU) in 1911 and makes temperance her life's work. By 1917 she is the movement's organizing secretary and from 1920 to 1924, director of the Queensland Temperance Alliance. McCorkindale spends the next three years lecturing in Britain, Canada, and the United States. On her return she becomes national director of education and research for the WCTU, a position she holds almost continuously until 1969. As director, McCorkindale edits the movement's journal, *The White Ribbon Signal*, from 1948 and publishes huge numbers of pamphlets and several books. She continues to travel widely, becoming world vice-president of the WCTU in 1947-59 and president 1959-62. McCorkindale's passionate involvement with temperance stems from her belief that male alcoholism leads to family poverty and violence against women. Accordingly, she is active in feminist circles. She works for the League of Women Voters and helps organize the 1946 Australian Women's Charter Conference. In 1950 she is a delegate to the United Nations Status of Women Conference in New York. After a life of intense work and great international success, McCorkindale states her motivation in simple, if ambitious, terms. She writes that she has wanted to "make the world a better place."

DECEMBER 31, 1885 Muriel Heagney, Australian Advocate of Equal Pay for Women, Is Born. Muriel Agnes Heagney (1885–1974), who devotes her life to winning equal pay for women, is born in Brisbane, Australia. She is raised in Victoria, where she joins the Richmond Political Labor Council in 1906. After spending World War I campaigning against conscription, Heagney visits Russia and works briefly for the International Labour Organisation in Geneva. In 1923 she organizes a national conference on maternity allowances and is elected to the Central Executive of the Victorian Labor Party. During the Great Depression (1929–39), Heagney forms the Unemployed Girls' Relief Movement, which provides work at sewing centers and a jam factory. In 1937, she founds the Council of Action for Equal Pay. During World War II (1939–45), the Australian government sets up a Women's Employment Board to index women's wages in war-related industries to the percentage of male output they achieve. Not surprisingly, women achieve equal, or near-equal, pay in these industries (never more, despite the board's findings) and Heagney hopes her battle is over. Clearly, however, the board's role is to ensure that low-paid women are not preferred in "male" industries after the war. From the late 1940s, women return to their traditional jobs at 54 percent of the male rate. So the fight contin-

ues and, in this period, Heagney largely works through women's organizations within the Labor Party. She writes three books: *Are Women Taking Men's Jobs?* (1935), *Equal Pay for the Sexes* (1948) and *Australia at the Cross Roads* (1954). Heagney's life work is consummated in May 1974 when Australian women win an adult minimum wage. She dies in poverty in Melbourne one week later.

1886 Catherine Webb Founds Battersea Branch of Women's Co-operative Guild in England. Catherine Webb (1859–1947), a leader in the English co-operative movement, is the founder of the Battersea branch of the Women's Co-operative Guild in London. Webb is also remembered for her histories of the co-operative movement throughout England.

1886 Publication of Frances Hodgson Burnett's *Little Lord Fauntleroy*. Frances Eliza Hodgson Burnett (1849–1924), best known as a children's author, publishes *Little Lord Fauntleroy* in *St. Nicholas Magazine*. The work, which she writes at the request of her son, sets a fashion for boys' clothes. It later inspires plays, films, and collectable items for children. Born in Manchester, England, Burnett later immigrates to the United States and becomes an American citizen in 1905.

1886 Head Tax on Chinese Immigrants Established in Canada. Chinese community development in Canada is curtailed through legislation especially designed to keep Chinese women from immigrating. A "head tax" is established, taxing every immigrant to Canada from China. Demands for the exclusion of Asian immigrants reach a fever pitch in Canada, especially in British Columbia, the western province that is the Canadian destination for many immigrants from Asia. In 1904 the head tax on immigrants from China is raised to $500, a fee that prohibits many Chinese from entering Canada. Chinese women are the hardest hit, since the tax is high enough to prevent most men from bringing their wives with them and absolutely prohibits single women from coming to Canada. Women who are brought into Canada tend to be wives of merchants or concubines whose incomes from the sex trade, domestic service, or waiting tables goes to the support of the families of their sponsors back in China. The Chinatown district and the "red light district" of prostitution occupy the same city area in Vancouver, British Columbia. This contributes to widespread racist beliefs about the "immorality" of the Chinese and prompts Canadian authorities to come down especially hard on Chinese women. The limited numbers of Chinese women who immigrate to Canada during these years impedes the development of families in the Chinese community in British Columbia. The Chinese community remains almost a male-only preserve.

1886   **Sara Jeanette Duncan Contributes to Canadian Journalistic and Literary History.** Sara Jeanette Duncan (1861–1922) is best known for her contributions to the journalistic and literary history of Canada. During the 1880s, Duncan establishes her career by becoming the first woman employed full-time by the *Toronto Globe* (1886–87) and then by the *Montreal Star* (1887–88). In the fall of 1888, she departs on a round-the-world trip resulting in her first novel, entitled *A Social Departure* (1890). Her novels *The Imperialist* and *Cousin Cinderella* present brilliant studies of attitudes and mores in contemporary Canadian society. She dies at Ashford, England.

1886   **German Opera Singer Lilli Lehmann Stars in Wagner Première.** Lilli Lehmann (1848–1929), a German soprano known internationally for her performances in Wagnerian roles, stars in the première of Wagner's *Tristan and Isolde* at the Metropolitan Opera House in New York City.

1886   **Birth of Hiratsuka Raicho, Founder of Japanese Feminist Organizations.** Hiratsuka

Raicho (1886-1971), a feminist, pacifist, and consumer advocate, is born. In 1911 she is a founder of *Seitosha* (Bluestocking Society) and the first editor of its publication, *Seito*. In it, she writes eloquently on the history and status of women. She is particularly interested in the role of literature in women's self-fulfillment. In 1919, Raicho is one of the founders of the *Shin Fujin Kyokai* (New Women's Association), which campaigns for an extension of women's legal rights, higher education, and welfare. In particular, it seeks repeal of the clause of the Peace Preservation Law, which prohibits women from public, political activity. Raicho retires, for a time, from public activity but reemerges in the 1930s, when she becomes active in the organization of consumer unions.

1886   **Yajima Kajiko Establishes First Women's Organization in Japan.** Yajima Kajiko (1833–1925) founds the first women's organization in Japan, the Japan's Women's Christian Temperance Union (WCTU). She leaves her violent and alcoholic husband after ten years of marriage to become a teacher and administrator in Christian girls' academies. Influenced by American women missionaries and Mary Leavitt, a speaker for the Women's Christian Temperance Union of the United States, Kajiko establishes a similar organization in Japan and serves as its director for 35 years. Under the organization's banner of "purity, peace, and temperance," she leads more than 10,000 members in crusades of social consciousness. In 1890, during the first session of the Japanese Diet (national legislature), Kajiko appeals for a law to make plural marriage a crime (the "one-man, one-woman law"). Later, she petitions against the articles of the Peace Preservation Law that are discriminatory against women. Her conviction that social problems, particularly abuses of prostitution, require reform legislation leads the WCTU to become a staunch advocate of women's suffrage. While serving as the director of the WCTU, Kajiko works for the reform of prostitution, legislative protection of women and children, assistance to war widows and their children, and earthquake relief. Because of the universality of the WCTU's concerns and its ties with sister organizations in other countries, Kajiko and the WCTU also work for international peace. At the age of 90, Yajima Kajiko attends the Washington Conference on the Limitation of Armaments and presents a petition for peace signed by more than 10,000 Japanese women.

1886 Japanese Author Wakamatsu Shizuko's Translation Earns Her Recognition. Japanese translator and author Wakamatsu Shizuko (1864–1896) is best known for her translation of F. H. Burnett's novel *Little Lord Fauntleroy.* Shizuko is a writer for *Jogaku Zasshi* (*Women's Journal*), specializing in the topic of women's education. She is a member of the Women's Christian Temperance Union and helps raise money for the campaign to abolish licensed prostitution. Through her articles in the English-language journal *Japanese Evangelist,* she introduces English-speaking audiences to Japanese culture.

1886 Birth of Japanese Actress Matsui Sumako. Matsui Sumako (1886–1919), Japan's first Western-style actress, is born. In 1909 she joins the drama group Bungei Kyo-kai, which introduces Western theater into Japan. Her first major role is Ophelia in *Hamlet.* She is best remembered for her 1911 portrayal of Nora in Ibsen's *A Doll's House,* which contributes to the controversy over the emerging feminist movement in Japan. She also performs the roles of Anna Karenina, Salome, and Carmen.

1886 Leonora O'Reilly Organizes Women Workers. At the age of 16, Leonora O'Reilly (1870–1927) joins the Knights of Labor and organizes the New York Working Women's Society. Her efforts and the society are responsible for the enactment of the country's first factory inspection law.

SEPTEMBER 10, 1886 American Writer Hilda Doolittle, Known as H.D., Is Born. Hilda Doolittle (1886–1961), American poet and novelist who is known as H.D., is born in Bethlehem, Pennsylvania. She publishes many volumes of poetry, including *Sea Garden* (1916), *The Walls Do Not Fall* (1944), *Flowering of the Rod* (1946), and *Helen in Egypt* (1961). Among her novels are *Palimpsest* (1926), *Hedylus* (1928), *Bid Me to Live* (1960), and *Tribute to Freud* (1965).

1887 Women's Suffrage Revoked in Utah. Women's suffrage is revoked under the Edmunds-Tucker Act in Utah from 1887 to 1896.

1887 Alexandra Gripenberg Dedicates Her Life to Feminist Movement in Finland. The well-educated daughter of a Finnish senator and baron, Alexandra Gripenberg (1857–1911) decides to devote all her energy to the feminist movement in Finland, serving as president of the Finnish Women's Association for 20 years. When women's suffrage is introduced in Finland in 1906, she is elected to the national assembly. Gripenberg writes a history of the feminist movement in both the Finnish and Swedish languages.

1887 Lillian H. Smith, Noted Canadian Children's Librarian, Is Born. Lillian H. Smith (1887–1983), noted children's librarian, is born in Canada. She writes *The Unreluctant Years: A Critical Approach to Children's Literature,* which wins the Clarence Day Award in 1953.

1887 Frances Marion, "Dean of Hollywood Screenwriters," Is Born. Frances Marion (1887–1973), whose screenwriting talent and activity during the 1920s and 1930s earn her the moniker "Dean of Hollywood Screenwriters," is born. She is the first woman war correspondent commissioned by General John Pershing to cover battles and women's war activities during World War I (1914–19). Although Marion is determined to be a screenwriter, studio executives first hire her as an actress because of her beauty. Marion also works as a stunt horse rider and writes most of Mary Pickford's successful films, including *Rebecca of Sunny Brook Farm* (1917) and *Polly-anna* (1920). She writes two of Lillian Gish's films, *The Scarlet Letter* (1926) and *The Wind* (1927). She also writes *The Son of the Sheik* (1926), which stars Rudolph Valentino.

In 1925 Marion forms Frances Marion Pictures and writes screenplays for the great stars, including Greta Garbo, Norma Talmadge, and Douglas Fairbanks. Her most popular hits are *Camille* (1936), *Anna Christie* (1930), *Dinner at Eight* (1933), and *Stella Dallas* (1937). Most of her films tend to be action dramas, fast-paced, with gangsters and gun battles. She rarely writes romantic "woman's pictures." Marion wins Academy Awards for screenwriting for *The Big House* (1930) and *The Champ* (1931). During the 1930s she makes the difficult transition from silent to sound pictures and is signed on as a contract writer for Metro-Goldwyn-Mayer (MGM). Marion also directs, paints, and writes several novels and her autobiography, *Off With Their Heads* (1973).

1887 **Peace Preservation Law Prohibits Japanese Women from Participating in Political Organizations.** Article five of the Peace Preservation Law of 1887 in Japan prohibits women and minors from joining political organizations and attending meetings where political speeches are given. Even women's participation in the academic study of political subjects is prohibited by this legislation. The law ends the early feminist movement in Japan. Opposition to this law is initiated by the *Shin Fujin Kyokai* (New Women's Association) in 1920, and the organization finally wins the repeal of the law in 1922.

1888 **Leonora Barry Elected Knights of Labor Master Workman.** Leonora Barry (1849–1930) is elected Master Workman—the highest position a woman can hold—at the national Knights of Labor convention. Barry heads a district assembly of nearly 1,000 women Knights of Labor in upstate New York. At the same convention, the Knights becomes the first labor organization to establish a Department of Women's Work and appoints Barry as its first General Investigator. In that capacity she organizes new assemblies, travels extensively (unheard of for a woman alone during that time period), and answers hundreds of letters, telegrams, and other requests for help from women workers. Her reports to the annual conventions of 1887, 1888, and 1889 are models of detail about the lives of working women. She pays particular attention to the garment industry. She also compiles the first nationwide statistics on women workers. Barry faces much opposition to her work. As expected, some of it comes from male Knights, but it also comes from Catholic priests who denounce her as a "lady tramp" because she travels, speaks publicly, and encourages women to organize and join unions.

1888 **German Soprano Lotte Lehmann Is Born.** Lotte Lehmann (1888–1976), a German opera singer who settles in America toward the end of her career, is born. She is the first woman to appear successfully in all three soprano roles (Sophie, the Marschallin, and Octavian) in Richard Strauss' *Der Rosenkavalier*. She is also the first woman to sing the starring roles in the premières of Strauss' *Die Frau ohne Shatten* (in Vienna in 1919) and *Intermezzo* (in Dresden in 1924).

1888 **Susan B. Anthony Organizes International Council of Women.** American reformer Susan B. Anthony (1820–1906) organizes the International Council of Women with representatives from 48 countries, and in 1904 she establishes the International Woman Suffrage

Alliance in Berlin, Germany. Anthony is well-known as a lecturer, as well as for writing with Elizabeth Cady Stanton (1815–1902) the first four volumes of the six-volume work entitled *A History of Woman Suffrage*. She is elected to the American Hall of Fame in 1950. On July 29, 1979, the U.S. government issues a one-dollar Susan B. Anthony coin, making her the first U.S. woman to have her likeness on a coin in general circulation.

1888　Birth of Kamichika Ichiko, Japanese Feminist and Socialist. Kamichika Ichiko (1888–1981), a Japanese feminist, socialist, and opponent of prostitution, is born. Initially active in *Seitosha* (Bluestockings), a women's literary organization, Ichiko is interested in literature and the public discussion of women's issues. She becomes infamous for her role in the Hikage Teahouse Incident, a scandal in which she stabs her lover, the anarchist Osugi Sakake, who is having an affair with Ito Noe, another feminist and leader of Seitosha. After a two-year prison sentence, Ichiko returns to writing and socialist political activities. In 1950, she launches a weekly publication, *Fujin Times*, in which she advocates improvement in the status of women. In 1951 she becomes the chair of the Council for Women and Youth in the Department of Labor. Ichiko serves in the House of Representatives in the Diet (Japan's national legislature) from 1953 to 1969. During this time, she leads a campaign to make prostitution illegal and is the author of the Anti-Prostitution Act, which passes in 1956.

1888　Miyake Kaho's Literature Probes Modern Japanese Society. Miyake Kaho (1868–1943) is a writer who describes the effects of modernization on Japanese women. Her novel *Yabu no uguiso* (*The Warbler in the Grove*), published in 1888, examines the influences of modernization on women of different social classes. She also writes poems and short stories on similar themes. Kaho edits and contributes articles on women's issues to *Josei nihonjin*

(*Japanese Women*), a magazine published by her husband, Miyake Setsurei.

1888　National Council of Women in the United States Established. The National Council of Women in the United States is formed to promote the advancement of women in society. The group is also set up as a clearing-house for various women's organizations.

1888　Publication of Australia's First Feminist Paper, *The Dawn*. Feminist Louisa Albury Lawson (1848–1920) establishes *The Dawn*, Australia's first feminist journal. The paper is a commercial success and, by 1889, has ten employees. However, Lawson's insistence on employing only women leads to conflict with the printers' union, which does not permit women members. She is accused of anti-unionism and her reporters are thrown out of a New South Wales Tailoresses' strike meeting in 1896. *The Dawn* hosts The Dawn Club to offer women the opportunity to practice public speaking. Its offices and printery also accommodate the Womanhood Suffrage League of which Lawson is a council member. *The Dawn* folds in 1905, and Lawson supports herself by selling her poetry. She dies in the Gladesville Hospital for the Insane in 1920.

APRIL 5, 1888　Birth of Fannia Mary Cohn, Union Organizer, Leader, and Educator. Fannia Mary Cohn (1888–1962), an educator for the International Ladies Garment Workers Union (ILGWU), is born. She emigrates to the United States from Minsk, Russia in 1904 at the age of 16. Her first job is in New York City in a garment factory. In 1909, she joins the ILGWU and until 1914 is an executive board member of the Kimona, Wrappers, and House Dress Workers Local 41. From 1911 to 1914 she is chair of the executive board. In addition to being a union leader, Cohn is also an active organizer. In 1915 she becomes a general organizer for the ILGWU in Chicago. This same year she organizes strikers at the Herzog Garment Company into local #59 and is then elected president of the local. In 1916, she becomes the first woman to serve as a vice president of a major union when she is elected vice president of the ILGWU, an office she holds until 1925. In addition to these activities, Cohn is an educator who promotes worker education classes. In 1921 she founds the Workers Education Bureau of America. This same year she helps establish the Brookwood Labor College.

1889 Enid Bagnold, British Children's Author, Is Born. Enid Bagnold (1889–1981), author of books for children and young adults, is born. Her works include *Alice and Thomas and Jane* (1930) and *National Velvet* (1935), which is made into a feature film starring Elizabeth Taylor in 1944. Bagnold receives the Award of Merit Medal from the American Academy of Arts and Letters in 1956.

1889 Bertha von Suttner Publishes Popular Pacifist Novel. Austrian writer Bertha von Suttner (1843–1914) publishes the novel *Lay Down Your Arms*. It becomes a European bestseller, promoting the cause of pacifism. In the novel, the heroine loses two husbands to the battlefield and faces the emotional devastation of war. Von Suttner anonymously publishes *The Machine Age* in 1898. This social critique attacks the barbarism of a culture where women are treated solely as sex objects and where death and killing are honored above life and love. Bertha von Suttner wins the Nobel Peace Prize in 1905 for her career devoted to the cause of peace and women's rights. She heads the Austrian Peace Society and lobbies internationally against the arms race. Early in her career, she works in Paris as a secretary to Alfred Nobel, the Swedish dynamite magnate and philanthropist.

1889 Birth of Kawasaki Natsu, Women's Movement Activist in Japan. Kawasaki Natsu (1889–1966), an activist in Japanese women's organizations, is born. She begins her career as a faculty member of Japan's most prestigious

women's colleges, teaching writing. In 1921 she is a cofounder of Bunka Gakuin (Culture Academy), a coeducational school for the creative arts. From 1921 to 1934, she writes a popular advice column for the *Yomiuri shimbun*, a high-circulation newspaper in Tokyo. Natsu is also a participant in women's rights organizations, including *Shin Fujin Kyokai* (New Women's Association) and *Fusen Kakutoku Domei* (Women's Suffrage League). During World War II, the Japanese government appoints her to committees concerned with welfare and women's issues. In 1947 Natsu is elected to the House of Councillors (the upper house of the Diet, Japan's national legislature). She helps organize peace organizations and social reform groups, cofounding the *Nihon Fujin Dantai Rengokai* (Japan Federation of Women's Groups) in 1953 and the annual *Hahaoya Taikai* (Mothers' Conference) in 1955.

MARCH 14, 1889 Marguerite de Angeli, Award-Winning American Author/Illustrator of Children's Books, Is Born. Marguerite Lofft de Angeli (1889–1987), an author/illustrator of children's books who is honored with the Regina Medal for the body of her work in 1968, is born in Lapeer, Michigan. She spends her early years in Lapeer and later bases *Copper-Toed Boots* (1938) on her own family life. Her family moves to Pennsylvania in 1902; she marries John Dailey de Angeli in 1910 and subsequently raises five children. Her major contributions to children's literature are her warm, universal stories of children from various cultures and her carefully crafted illustrations. She publishes illustrations in *St. Nicholas Magazine*, *The American Girl*, *The Country Gentleman*, and *The Ladies Home Journal*. Her book *Henners Lydia* (1936) focuses on the Pennsylvania Dutch culture and *Yonie Wondernose* (1944), a Caldecott Honor book, on Amish traditions. The Mennonites, particularly the teaching methods of schoolmaster Christopher Dock, are the subject of *Shippack*

School (1939), which incorporates German Fractur Schriften in the illustrations. *Thee, Hannah!* (1940) tells a story of Quaker life and strong abolitionist traditions. De Angeli's *Bright April* (1946) is considered the first modern children's book about a black child and racial prejudice. She wins the Newbery Medal for *The Door in the Wall* (1949), set in thirteenth-century England where young Robin, a handicapped protagonist, learns to value his own inner strengths in spite of his crooked leg. Another historical novel, *Black Fox of Lorne* (1956), is a Newbery Honor book. Her *Book of Nursery and Mother Goose Rhymes* (1954), containing lavish illustrations, is a Caldecott Honor book. The Lapeer City Branch Library Board renames its library in her honor on August 22, 1981. She is named Distinguished Daughter of Pennsylvania in 1958.

APRIL 18, 1889 Birth of Jessie Street, Australian Feminist and Internationalist. Australian feminist Lady Jessie Mary Grey Lillingston Street (1889–1970) is born in India. She is educated in England and at the University of Sydney, Australia, from which she graduates with a bachelor's degree in 1910. After graduation, she works for the suffrage movement in England before moving to America where, in 1915, she establishes a home for wayward girls. She returns to Australia in 1916 to marry Kenneth Street and involve herself in Australian feminism. Jessie Street's achievements include the introduction of contraceptive information into university medical courses, the establishment of the Family Planning Association, the United Australian Associations of Women, and the Australian Women's Charter Conference of 1943. Street is a member of the Australian League of Nations Union and visits Russia on many occasions. During World War II (1939–45), Street devotes herself to the Sheepskins for Russia campaign and the Australia-Russia Friendship Society, and she is a member of the Aliens Control Committee, which reviews internment decisions. After the war, she is the only woman member of the Australian delegation to the San Francisco Conference, which draws up the United Nations Charter in 1945. In 1947 Street represents her country on the UN Status of Women Commission, which elects her vice president and delegate to the first meeting of the Human Rights Commission (Geneva, 1947). A politically hostile post-war Australian government prevents her trip to Geneva and removes her from the commission in 1949. Street devotes the remainder of her life to the causes of peace and Aboriginal rights. She dies in Sydney in 1970.

Chapter 16
1890 TO 1899

1890 German Women Teacher's Union Established. Helene Lange (1848–1930) founds the German Women Teacher's Union to challenge the male monopoly in teaching careers.

1890 Beatrice Webb Cofounds Fabian Society. Beatrice Potter Webb (1858–1943) is a founding member—with her husband Sidney Webb; H. G. Wells; and George Bernard Shaw—of the Fabian Society, a group of socialist reformers who believe in gradual reform through state intervention as opposed to violent revolution. They also believe that once the problems of the working class are resolved, the problem of women's rights will solve itself. Beatrice Potter is the independent-minded daughter of a wealthy Englishman, although she suffers from chronic psychosomatic illness which reappears frequently during her adulthood. Emotionally neglected by her mother, she finds comfort among the servants and grows up with a sense of social guilt. Potter begins working as a social investigator by helping her brother-in-law, Charles Booth, with his studies of life in poverty-ridden East London. She disguises herself and works in a sweatshop, and writes of her experiences in Booth's book. In 1890 she marries Sidney Webb. Her marriage to a man from the lower middle class shocks and alienates many of her friends and even some family members. The couple, however, remains committed to a life-time of reform, participation in politics, and writing.

1890 Czech Poet Eliska Krásnohorská Establishes Minerva Society. Eliska Krásnohorská (1847–1926), a Czech poet, founds the feminist group the Minerva Society in Prague, the capital of Bohemia within the Habsburg Empire. The Minerva Society seeks higher education for Czech women. Krásnohorská is also editor of the *Women's Gazette* in Prague.

1890 Birth of Theda Bara, "Vamp" of Silent Film Era. Theda Bara (1890–1955), an actress known for playing the part of seductress in her films, is born Theodosia Goodman in Cincinnati, Ohio. She enjoys a brief stage career before she moves to Hollywood to try her luck in the new medium of silent film. Her first substantive part is as a vampire in *A Fool There Is* (1915). She tells her man, "Kiss me, my fool," and he does. Bara represents a new female film character: the "Vamp." With her waist-length dark hair and darkly kohled eyes, she becomes the American screen's first sizzling sex goddess and is billed as "the daughter of Egypt." Her image of exotic sexuality contrasts the Victorian wholesomeness of such stars as Mary Pickford and Lillian Gish. Fox studios immediately signs her as a star in such spectaculars as *Romeo and Juliet* (1916), *Madame Du Barry* (1917), *Cleopatra* (1917), and *The She Devil* (1918). In these expensive costume dramas, Bara plays the seductress who uses sex for selfish or evil purposes and who drives men to drink, ruin, and slavery. Her personification of "daring sex" becomes one of the greatest box-office attractions from 1916 to 1920. Unfortunately, Bara becomes a prisoner of her own legend, and in the postwar era, the vamp becomes outdated. However, Bara inspires imitators, and the damaging myth that women are "femmes fatales" and sexual predators still remains central to popular culture.

1890   Gossip Columnist Hedda Hopper Is Born. Hedda Hopper (1890–1966), the rival of gossip columnist Louella Parsons and equally feared, is born Elda Furry to Quaker parents in Pennsylvania. At 28, she marries DeWolf Hopper and moves to Hollywood. Her husband stars in films and becomes a ladies' man. In 1922, the couple divorces, and Hopper begins a new career as a supporting actress and social butterfly. In 1936, she hosts the *Chit Chat Radio Hour,* and she has her own gossip column two years later. For the next 28 years, Hopper's gossip columns contain information about the stars that is often inaccurate and unnecessarily cruel. Actress Joan Bennett once sends Hopper a skunk in the mail, but Hopper points to her mansion in Benedict Canyon, Hollywood, and declares, "That's the house that fear built." She hosts Sunday morning rituals whereby the leading ladies of Hollywood call on her for breakfast to win her favor. By the time of her death in 1966, the era of powerful gossip columnists has come to a close, for sensational news items have become commonplace and the sensibilities of the American public are not so easily outraged.

1890   First Woman in Buffalo Bill Wild West Show. Calamity Jane (1852–1903), the stage name of Martha Jane Cannary Burke, is the first woman to perform in the Buffalo Bill Wild West Show. She joins the group in the far western United States in the 1890s and

travels with them throughout America. She also appears with Buffalo Bill when he takes his Wild West Show to England in 1893.

1890   Merger Forms National American Woman Suffrage Association. The American Woman Suffrage Association and the National Woman Suffrage Association merge to become the National American Woman Suffrage Association (NAWSA). Elizabeth Cady Stanton is president of the newly formed organization; she is succeeded in 1892 by Susan B. Anthony. The strategy of NAWSA shifts from amending the U.S. Constitution to seeking the vote for women at the state level, through state referenda. In 1920, after the passage of the 19th Amendment to the U.S. Constitution, guaranteeing women the right to vote, the two million members of NAWSA are reorganized as the National League of Women Voters.

1890   Wyoming Is First State to Provide Women's Suffrage. Wyoming becomes a state, and its state constitution provides women's suffrage. Wyoming thus is the first state to extend equal political rights to women.

1890   Birth of Japanese Feminist and Socialist Yamakawa Kikue. Yamakawa Kikue (1890-1980), Japanese socialist and feminist ideologue, is born. She writes articles in women's, socialist, and intellectual magazines about the rights of women workers. In her book *Musansha undo to fujin no mondai* (1928; *The Proletarian Movement and Problems of Women*), she tries to integrate women's demands for equal pay for equal work and maternity rights with the socialist agenda. In the "debate on the protection of motherhood," Kikue argues that political and cultural strategies for the liberation of women are naive. Only through the overthrow of capitalism, she argues, will women achieve equality. After World War II, Kikue joins the new Japan Socialist Party and serves as the first director of the new Women's and Minor's Bureau in the Ministry of Labor.

1890 Women Textile Workers Play Prominent Role in Japan's Industrial Revolution. During Japan's industrial revolution, industry gains the greatest momentum in the cotton and silk spinning industries, which depend primarily on female labor. Labor relations in the textile mills are exploitative and working conditions are deleterious to the laborers' health.

1890 Uemura Tamaki, Japan's First Woman Christian Minister, Is Born. Educator, Christian activist, and Japan's first woman Christian minister, Uemura Tamaki (1890–) is born. She begins teaching at *Joshi Eigaku juku* (now Tsuda Women's University). With Hani Motoko (1873–1957), she establishes a school, *Jiyu Gakuen* (Freedom Academy), in 1921. Tamaki studies theology at the University of Edinburgh and returns to Japan to serve as a minister of the *Nihon Kuristo Kyokai* (Japan Christian Church), the influential union of Protestant sects. She is also active in Japan's Young Women's Christian Association (YWCA) and in peace movements after World War II.

1890 Kozai Shikin Works for Women's Rights in Japan. Kozai Shikin (1868–1933), a novelist, essayist, and participant in Japan's early women's movement, attends *Meiji Jogakko* (Meiji Girls' School), a Christian women's post-secondary school. The school's president, Iwamoto Yoshiharu, is the editor of *Jogakku zasshi,* for which Shikin writes stories and essays on contemporary women's issues. With Fukuda Hideko, Shikin is a participant in the liberal wing of the Japanese women's movement.

1890 Emma Miller Organizes Union in Australia. Australian activist and suffragist Emma Holmes Miller (1839–1917), a seamstress by trade, helps organize a female workers' union in Brisbane. The following year, she appears before a royal commission of inquiry into factory conditions. Miller joins the Australian Workers Union and is its first woman organizer in western Queensland. She also becomes involved in parliamentary politics as the first woman member of the Brisbane Workers Political Organization. Miller is foundation president of the Women's Equal Franchise Association from 1894 and of the Women Workers Political Organization from 1903. During the Queensland General Strike of 1912, she leads a large group of women demonstrators against mounted police, allegedly dismounting and injuring the police commissioner by puncturing his horse with a hat pin. During World War I (1914–19), she campaigns against conscription from her position as president of the Queensland branch of the Women's Peace Army. "Mother Miller" dies in 1917, and her marble bust is unveiled at the Brisbane Trades Hall in 1922.

FEBRUARY 23, 1890 Birth of Lotte Lyell, Australia's First Woman Film Star. Lotte Edith Cox Lyell (1890-1925), an Australian film star, director, producer and script writer, is born in Sydney. Lyell becomes a professional actress with Edwin Geach's company in 1907. With her partner Raymond Longford, she joins Spencer's Pictures in 1911 and acts in five films in her first year in the industry. Between then and 1925, Lyell makes at least 32 films, most of which she scripts and codirects (with Longford); she acts in all but three. A number of these are among the most successful ever made in Australia: *The Mutiny on the Bounty* (1916), *The Sentimental Bloke* (1919), *Ginger Mick* (1920), *Rudd's New Selection* (1921) and *Fisher's Ghost* (1924). As Australia's first film star, she creates the image of the bush girl that is favored throughout the heyday of the Australian industry. On the other hand, she does not hesitate to undertake more daring roles and pioneers sympathetic treatment of unmarried mothers and other "wicked" women. Lyell is an accomplished swimmer and horsewoman and often uses these skills in her films. Spencer's is eventually taken over by Australasian Films, and to bypass that company's distribution policy, Lyell forms a business partnership with Longford as Longford-Lyell Productions. They make three films and the last of these, *Fisher's Ghost* (1924) and *The Bushwackers* (1925), are the only two, of all her films, that credit her as scriptwriter and assistant director. Lyell dies of tuberculosis in Sydney in 1925. Australasian Films cancels Longford's contract the following year.

C. JUNE 1890 Midwestern Agrarian Reformer Mary Elizabeth Clyens Lease Speaks Out Against Kansas Senator. Mary Elizabeth Clyens Lease (1850–1933), widely known for her oratory skills on behalf of debt-ridden Kansas farmers, delivers 160 speeches charging that Kansas Senator John Ingalls has not supported the Farmers' Alliance. Ingalls' reelection bid is unsuccessful.

Legend has it she tells Kansas farmers to "raise less corn and more hell." Lease also advocates woman suffrage, currency reform, nationalization of the railroads, and birth control. Before Lease dies of chronic nephritis, she becomes president of the National Society for Birth Control.

AUGUST 7, 1890 Birth of Elizabeth Gurley Flynn, Founding Member of Industrial Workers of the World. American laborer Elizabeth Gurley Flynn (1890–1964), the "Rebel Girl" celebrated in song by balladeer Joe Hill, is born. Flynn's union activity begins at a very early age. Her mother is a member of the Knights of Labor and her father is an active socialist. During her childhood she has regular contact with feminists, socialists, anarchists, and Irish revolutionists. At the age of 15, Flynn is a founding member of the Industrial Workers of the World (IWW), whose members are often referred to as "Wobblies." At the age of 16, she is arrested for the first time. The following year she participates in her first strike and barnstorms the country for the IWW. The next year she meets her hus-

band, Jack Archibald Jones, another Wobbly; their marriage lasts a little over two years. While married, each spends time in jail. Soon after they officially separate, she begins a 13-year relationship with Carlo Tresca, an editor and anarchist.

Flynn works hard within the Wobblies to change some of their attitudes toward women. However, she does accept their basic tenet that the problems of women cannot be separated from those of the working class. Flynn participates in several historic strikes, including the 1909 strike of New York City waistmakers; the 1912 strikes of Lowell and Lawrence textile mill workers; the 1913 strike of the Paterson, New Jersey, silk workers; the 1916 Mesabi Range miners' strike; and the 1926 Passaic, New Jersey, textile workers' strike. She is also involved in the defense of balladeer Joe Hill and is a pallbearer after his execution. Joe Hill writes his song "Rebel Girl" about Flynn. In 1952 Flynn is tried and convicted under the Smith Act in New York City and then spends 30 months in a West Virginia federal women's prison.

SEPTEMBER 10, 1890 Elsa Schiaparelli, French Fashion Designer, Is Born In Italy. Elsa Schiaparelli (1890–1973), who integrates elements of contemporary art, bold colors, inventive accessories, and simple lines to create fashions from the late 1920s through the mid-1950s, is born in Rome. Her gifts as a writer, sculptor, and painter emerge early, but she is inclined instead to "invent dresses or costumes." It is in large part, however, her knowledge of contemporary artists and their art that sets her apart from other fashion designers. She writes in her autobiography *Shocking Life*, published in 1954, "It is the time when abstract Dadaism and Futurism were the talk of the world, the time when chairs looked like tables, and tables like footstools...." In 1928, Schiaparelli produces her first "invention," a black, short-sleeved sweater knitted with the pattern of a butterfly bow around the neckline. The success of these sweaters emboldens her to experiment further with a quirky illusionism.

Schiaparelli promotes the "architectural" character of clothing. She designs garments that recover the natural placement of the waist, lowered during the Flapper era of the 1920s. During the early 1930s, she popularizes the squared, padded shoulder, accentuating the breadth of the upper torso.

Her designs for clothing and accessories are noted for their simplicity of line and for their boldness of color and conception. She expands her line of "inventions" in the 1940s to include perfumes, the first of which—"Shocking"—is characteristically exotic and conceived of color. The perfume is sold in a bottle accented in the color that she originates and which becomes her signature—shocking pink.

Schiaparelli collaborates with noted painters and photographers. Salvador Dali, in particular, is a frequent visitor to her home and workshop. Schiaparelli retires in 1954.

OCTOBER 9, 1890 Birth of American Evangelist Aimee Semple McPherson. Aimee Semple McPherson (1890–1944), one of the greatest evangelistic successes of the early twentieth century, is born at Ingersoll, Ontario, Canada. At the age of 17, she marries Robert Semple, a Pentecostal missionary, who dies in China in 1912. After his death, Aimee Semple returns to the United States. Shortly thereafter, she marries H. S. McPherson and begins to conduct a series of tent revivals along the East Coast of the United States. Catapulted by her evangelistic success, she moves to Los Angeles in 1918, where she later opens her 5,000-seat, 1.25 million-dollar Angelus Temple of the Four Square Gospel. "Sister Aimee's" theatrical pulpit techniques make her one of the most publicized revivalists in the world. She tours the United States, Canada, and Australia. After divorcing McPherson in 1926, Aimee Semple McPher-

son disappears and is presumed drowned. She reappears weeks later claiming to have been kidnapped, apparently trying to cover her affair with a radio manager. During the 1920s, she launches a continent-wide religious campaign, combining evangelism and drama. Her ability to attract followers is enhanced by her use of the media and its infatuation with her personal life, particularly her mysterious disappearances, moral and financial scandals, court cases, and marriages. In Western Canada, "Sister Aimee" runs several churches and a bible school. During the Great Depression (1929–39), she discovers the radio as an evangelistic vehicle and soon becomes a well-known radio preacher. Aimee Semple McPherson dies of an accidental drug overdose in 1944.

1891 Esther Forbes and Florence Cranell Means, Both American Children's Authors, Are Born. Esther Forbes (1891–1967), author of *Johnny Tremaine* (1943), is born in Westboro, Massachusetts. Forbes also writes *Miss Marvel* (1935), *Paradise* (1937), *The General's Daughter* (1939), and *Paul Revere and the World He Lived In,* for which she won the Pulitzer Prize in 1942.

Florence Cranell Means (1891–1980), author of books for young adults about members of minority groups, is born. Means's book, *The Moved-Outers,* wins a Newbery Honor Book Award in 1946. The work tells the story of Japanese Americans who are imprisoned by the U.S. government during World War II. Means also wins a Nancy Bloch Annual Award in 1957 for *Knock at the Door, Emmy,* a book that deals with intercultural relations.

1892 Olympia Brown Founds Federal Suffrage Association. Olympia Brown (1835–1926), first woman ordained minister in the United States, founds the Federal Suffrage Association to campaign for women's suffrage. She is president of the organization in 1920 when American women finally win the vote.

1892 Sophia Haydn Designs Women's Building for World's Columbian Exposition. Sophia Haydn (1869–1953), the first woman to graduate in architecture from the Massachusetts Institute of Technology in Cambridge, Massachusetts, wins the competition to design the Women's Building at the World's Columbian Exposition in Chicago. The Exposition, held in 1892–93, commemorates the 400th anniversary of Christopher Columbus's discovery of America. Haydn's design is for an Italian Renaissance exhibit hall with skylights. Devastated by the pressure of supervising such a large construction project and negative critical response to her work, Haydn never designs another building.

1892 Harriet Stratemeyer Adams, Author of Nancy Drew Books, Is Born. American author Harriet Stratemeyer Adams (1892–1982) is born. Under the pseudonym Carolyn Keene, Adams creates the *Nancy Drew* series of mysteries for young adults. Adams also writes *Barton Books for Girls.* In 1979, she wins the Edgar Award from the Mystery Writers of America.

1892 Helen Dove Boylston, American Children's Author and Nurse, Is Born. Helen Dove Boylston (1895–1984), a nurse and author of books for children, is born. Her works include a series of books about nurses, the first of which is *Sue Barton, Student Nurse* (1936). Boylston also develops the *Carol* series, beginning with *Carol Goes on the Stage.*

1892 Jeanne Chauvin, First Woman to Complete Legal Training in France. A pioneer in the legal profession in France, Jeanne Chauvin becomes the first woman to complete legal training in the country. She arrives early at her class every morning accompanied by her mother and writes her dissertation on the professions open to women. In 1892 she completes her legal training, but opposition to her is so strong that a riot halts the examination of her thesis. The French Bar remains closed to

women until 1901. Chauvin is told that to be admitted to the bar would be "contrary to the progress of civilization." After a 1900 decree opens the legal profession to women on the same terms as men, Chauvin is admitted to practice. By 1914 only 28 women have taken their oaths in court as lawyers, and only about 12 are practicing law. In 1925 Chauvin receives the Legion of Honor, one of France's highest awards.

1892 Florence Kelley Named First Female Factory Inspector for Illinois. Florence Kelley (1859–1932) is appointed the first female factory inspector for the state of Illinois and helps in the passage of the Illinois Factory and Workshop Inspection Act of 1893. In 1899 the National Consumers League (NCL) is established, and Kelley becomes its general secretary.

1892 Mary Kenney O'Sullivan, First Female AFL Organizer. Mary Kenney (later O'Sullivan) (1864–1943) becomes the first female organizer hired by the American Federation of Labor (AFL). In the five months she holds that position, she travels between many New York, Massachusetts, and Pennsylvania cities. She finds that organizing women is hard work and doesn't meet with the same results as organizing men. While Samuel Gompers, president of the AFL, is satisfied with her results, other members on the AFL executive council are not. Her commission as organizer is not renewed.

1892 American Anarchist Emma Goldman Admits Role in Assassination Plot. Emma Goldman (1869–1940), an American labor reformer, women's rights activist, and staunch pacifist, admits conspiring with Alexander Berkman to assassinate Henry Frick during the Homestead Strike. Berkman is sentenced to 25 years in prison but Goldman is never indicted. In 1893 Goldman, or "Red Emma" as she is often called, is convicted of inciting a riot at a Union Square demonstration in support of Eugene V. Debs and the railway strike. She is imprisoned until 1894. When President William McKinley is killed in 1901, his assassin, anarchist Leon Czolgosz, says he is influenced by Goldman's writings. She is arrested but later released when there is no evidence to link her to the assassination.

1892   Publication of First Widely Acclaimed Novel by African American Woman. Abolitionist and feminist Frances E. W. Harper (1825–1910) becomes the first African American woman to publish a widely acclaimed novel, *Iola Leroy* or *Shadows Uplifted.*

1892   Susan B. Anthony Contributes to *A History of Woman Suffrage*. Susan B. Anthony (1820–1906), along with Elizabeth Cady Stanton (1815–1902), works with Ida Harper and Matilda Gage on the first four volumes of a six-volume work entitled *A History of Woman Suffrage.*

1892   Deguchi Nao Establishes Japanese Religion Omoto. Deguchi Nao (1837–1918) founds the Omoto religion in Japan. In 1887 Nao's husband dies, leaving her and their eight children destitute. She begins to support her family by doing menial work. Her troubles increase when her elder son attempts suicide and then disappears, and two of her daughters begin to suffer psychological disturbances. In 1892 Nao herself begins to experience visions and utter oracles in trances, claiming that a god speaks to her. After exorcism fails, Nao decides to serve the god through acts of devotion and asceticism. Although she has no formal education, she begins writing down the divine messages she receives. These writings, called *ofudesaki*, become the core of Omoto teachings. They reveal the reappearance of a god who has suffered suppression from evil deities for many centuries. The deity expresses the view that the corrupt view will presently cease, to be replaced by pristine peace. Like other Japanese "new religions," Omoto is viewed as being subversive because of its criticism of the emperor system as the ideological foundation for state-supported Shinto.

APRIL 13, 1892   Gladys Moncrieff, Popular Australian Actress, Is Born. Australian stage performer Gladys Lillian Moncrieff (1892–1976) is born in north Queensland. Moncrieff plays lead roles for the Williamson Company in Sydney from 1914, but her immense popularity is confirmed by a two-year run begun in 1921 of *Maid of the Mountains,* in which she routinely takes 18 curtain calls. She marries actor Thomas Moore in 1924 and, during a honeymoon in England, makes her first ten gramophone recordings. She returns to Australia as one of the highest-paid performers in the history of Australian theater. As her manager, Moore persuades her to move to England in 1926–27 but, despite stage and recording successes, Moncrieff is homesick. She returns to Sydney, where she is referred to by audiences as "Our Glad," an artist of unprecedented popularity. She makes her farewell tour of Australia and New Zealand in 1958–59, and her last public performance is on television in Brisbane in 1962. She dies in Queensland in 1976.

APRIL 20, 1892   Birth of Grace Cossington Smith, Australian Post-Impressionist Artist. Australian painter Grace Cossington Smith (1892–1984) is born in Sydney. She studies drawing with Anthony Rubbo in Sydney, and after two years in Europe, she returns to Australia in 1914 and begins to paint. Her canvas "The Sock Knitter" (1915) is the first fully post-impressionist work hung in Australia. From then, Smith exhibits regularly in New South Wales and her first solo exhibition is hung at the Grosvenor Galleries in 1928. All her work is executed in a small hut in the garden of her family home until the death of her father in 1938, when she attaches a large, well-lit studio to the house. Apart from another European visit in 1949–50, Smith spends the rest of her life in Australia. Her subject matter is broad: she paints crowd scenes and public events, and there are a few biblical works. Her most valued canvases, though, are the late interiors of her own home at Turramurra. These gentle, private works lovingly depict "golden light entering doors and windows from the verandahs and the leafy garden, spreading into corners, corridors and cupboards," notes D. Thomas in the catalog of the 1973 Sydney exhibition of Smith's work. Smith herself says: "my aim had always been to express form in color—color within color, vibrant with light." Art museums throughout Australia begin collecting Grace Cossington Smith's work from the 1940s, but the quietness and simplicity of her life and personality delays wide public recognition until the 1960s. She is appointed to the Order of the British Empire in 1973, the year a retrospective of her work, organized by the Art Gallery of New South Wales, tours Australia. Grace Cossington Smith dies at Roseville in 1984.

SEPTEMBER 1892 American Athlete Senda Berenson Creates Rules of Women's Basketball. Senda Berenson (1868–1954) introduces her version of the game of basketball, modified for women, to Smith College in Massachusetts. Women's basketball spreads like wildfire across the United States.

1893 Birth of Mary Pickford, "America's Sweetheart" of Silent Film Era. American actress Mary Pickford (1893–1979) is born Gladys Mary Smith in Toronto, Ontario. Only five feet tall, she plays the role of little girl well into her 30s. She appears in such silent films as *Tess of the Storm Country* (1922) and *Little Annie Rooney* (1925). With her long blond locks, Pickford becomes known as "the girl with the curl." Her film image as the helpless and chaste young heroine also wins her the title of "America's Sweetheart," and she becomes the highest-paid actress of the 1920s. Audiences love her as the naive, tragic little orphan at the mercy of a hard, cruel world.

In real life, Pickford takes charge of her business and career. In 1919 she, Douglas

Fairbanks, and Charlie Chaplin form their own studio, United Artists. Pickford becomes star, studio owner, executive producer, and director. She keeps her credit as director/producer off the screen to protect her public image and popularity. American audiences prefer women as virginal victims, not independent businesswomen. When she falls in love with leading man Fairbanks, she worries that their double divorce and marriage will result in public scandal. The public, however, applauds this union of America's two favorite screen idols. By the early 1920s, Pickford's image of the naive girl loses popularity with the rise of the sexy flapper. When she tries other roles, however, the public rejects her. Her adult role in *Coquette* won her the Academy Award for Best Actress in 1929. In the prime of life, Pickford retreats from her film career. She is the first performer ever to become a millionaire from the craft of acting. Her autobiographical writings include *My Rendezvous with Life* (1935) and *Sunshine and Shadow* (1955).

1893 Screenwriter Anita Loos, Who Creates Blond Bombshell Stereotype, Is Born. Anita Loos (1893–1981), an American screenwriter who originates the blond bombshell stereotype in *Gentlemen Prefer Blonds*, is born. Even as a child, Loos is her family's breadwinner. Her father is a newspaperman, and she longs to follow his lead and be a writer. She begins her career as a child actress and eventually becomes one of Hollywood's leading screenwriters. At age 16, Loos sells her first script to director D. W. Griffith, which becomes *The New York Hat* starring Mary Pickford. She pens the titles for many silent films, and between 1912 and 1915 she writes the scripts for 101 films. The "flapper" garb of bobbed hair and sailor dresses are attributed to Loos. She continues to write scripts for "talkies," including *Red-Headed Woman* (1932), *San Francisco* (1936), and *The Women* (1939).

Loos is famous for the art of "wise-cracking," and other writers try to imitate her witty repartee. In 1925 she publishes her novel *Gentlemen Prefer Blonds*, which becomes a movie in 1928. The character of Loreli Lee is a stereotyped caricature of the "dumb blond." The book runs through 85 editions and is translated into 14 languages, including Chinese.

Loos loathes domesticity but refuses to call herself a feminist. Indeed, many of her scripts are misogynistic, and she contributes to Hollywood's negative representations of womanhood. In addition to movie scripts, Loos writes plays, novels, and her memoirs. Before her death at age 88, Loos jokes, "Gentlemen may prefer blonds, but they marry brunettes."

1893   Birth of Gossip Columnist Louella Parsons. Louella Parsons (1893–1972), a gossip columnist with the power to make and break the careers of Hollywood stars, is born in Freeport, Illinois. She marries John Parsons at 17 and moves to Iowa. Her husband decides that she is too immature for marriage and places her in a boarding home. She escapes with her baby daughter, taking a job as a story editor for the Essanay Movie Company and settling in Chicago.

Parsons writes her first columns for Chicago and New York newspapers before moving to Hollywood in 1926. She demands the unheard-of salary of $250 per week from publisher William Randolph Hearst. Soon, her column is syndicated to nearly 1,000 papers worldwide. Known as the "hatchet woman," Parsons quickly becomes the most important, powerful, feared—and respected—woman in Hollywood.

Parsons also appears in such films as *Hollywood Hotel* (1937), *Without Reservations* (1946), and *Starlift* (1951). In 1949 she is voted the best-loved woman commentator. She is the only columnist ever invited to place her hands and feet in the cement outside Grauman's Chinese Theater. During the

1950s, she hosts the *Jergens-Woodbury Journal* over the ABC radio network. She also writes for *Photoplay*, the leading fan magazine, and for *Modern Screen*. Parsons's 1944 autobiography, *The Gay Illiterate*, becomes a bestseller. Like her rival, columnist Hedda Hopper, Parsons loses most of her power in Hollywood during the relaxed moral climate of the 1960s.

1893   Bertha Lamme Feicht Earns Engineering Degree. Graduating from Ohio State University, Bertha Lamme Feicht (1869–1954) becomes the second woman in the United States to earn an engineering degree. Her major is mechanical engineering with a minor in electricity. She begins working at Westinghouse Electric and Manufacturing Company immediately after graduation, joining her brother, Benjamin, also a mechanical engineer, in the engineering department. For 12 years, Lamme designs motors and generators for Westinghouse in the East Pittsburgh plant. As a woman, she operates in spite of very limited access to the shop floor to test or implement her designs. Much of her work involves calculations for machine design. Lamme marries her supervisor, Russell S. Feicht, in 1905 and retires at that time in order to care for her home and family, as is expected of a woman during this period.

1893   National Council of Women of Canada Established. The National Council of Women of Canada (NCWC) is founded by Lady Aberdeen to unite Canadian women's organizations under a single umbrella. Although principally urban, anglophone, and middle-class, the NCWC becomes the champion of women and children while focusing on issues such as mother's allowance legislation, child welfare, equal divorce treatment, increasing the age of consent for marriage, and enhanced legal remedies for deserted wives. Nevertheless, this conservative organization puts off entering the bid for suffrage in 1910. During the 1920s, the reform-oriented organization declines in membership due to its

Actress Mae West

continued focus on motherhood and protection of home life as stabilizing factors in society. Despite this decline, the NCWC remains a dedicated lobbyist for women's issues throughout the years. It maintains an influential role in the creation of the Royal Commission on the Status of Women as well as demanding women's rights in Canada's constitution during the 1980s.

1893 **American Actress and Sex Symbol Mae West Is Born.** Mae West (1893–1980), who brings sex out of America's closet and onto the big screen, is born. West begins her acting career in American vaudeville, where she is first known as "The Baby Vamp." Her introduction of the "shimmy" to the stage helps propel her to infamy. By the mid-1920s West writes and performs in her own stage plays, concentrating on sexual innuendo. Her play

The Constant Sinner (1926) is attacked by prudish critics but plays 385 sold-out performances. Finally, the play is raided and West is jailed for ten days. She also writes a play called *The Drag* in which she pleads for "intelligent understanding" of homosexuality. This play sells out to New Jersey audiences, but West is forbidden to bring the play to Broadway.

In 1933 Paramount studio faces financial troubles and asks Mae West to adapt her successful Broadway play, *Diamond Lil*, to the big screen. The movie version, *She Done Him Wrong* (1933), launches West, as well as her unknown costar, Cary Grant, into stardom. West is a "sex goddess" who never once disrobes or uses profanity on the screen. Her writing relies on her wit, wisecracks and innuendos.

West writes and stars in three more films and in 1934 earns the largest salary in the United States, second only to publisher William Randolph Hearst. Hearst objects to West's films, and the powerful publisher urges strict censorship rules on Hollywood films. The development of the Production Code in 1934 hurts West's popularity at the box office. At age 78, she makes her comeback in *Myra Breckinridge* (1970). At 85, Mae West stars in her own film, *Sexette* (1978). As a sex symbol, she is not afraid to parody her own image. More than 60 years after her first film, her image remains instantly recognizable as an archetype of American feminine sensuality.

1893 **English Composer Ethel Mary Smyth's *Mass in D* Premieres.** *Mass in D* by Ethel Mary Smyth (1858–1944), England's first significant female composer, is performed at the Albert Hall in London, England. Smyth is also known for her active role in the women's suffrage movement, for which in 1911 she writes the *March of the Women*, and for her nine largely autobiographical books.

1893 **Women Win Vote in Colorado.** Suffrage is granted to women in Colorado, which becomes the 38th state in 1876. Suffragist

Carrie Chapman Catt (1859–1947) is instrumental in organizing the lobbying forces in Colorado to win the vote for women.

1893 **Hawaiian Queen Liliuokalani Overthrown by Bloodless Revolution.** Queen Liliuokalani, monarch of the territory of Hawaii, is overthrown by a bloodless revolution led by nine Americans, two Britons, and two Germans, with the help of U.S. Marines. Queen Liliuokalani is the last of the royal family of King Kamehameha to rule in Hawaii. Kamehameha unifies the local chiefs of Hawaii in 1795.

1893 **Birth of Ichikawa Fusae, Leader of Japanese Women's Suffrage Movement.** Japanese feminist, suffragist, and politician Ichikawa Fusae (1893–1981) is born. Fusae later claims in her autobiography that her motivation to participate in the women's movement is her father's cruelty to her mother. Early in her career, she works as a grade school teacher and a newspaper reporter. Concerned about the harsh conditions in which women factory workers labor in her hometown of Nagoya, Fusae is a cofounder of the *Shin Fujin Kyokai* (New Women's Association). In 1921, Fusae goes to the United States, not long after women there win the vote, to work with Alice Paul and the National Women's Party. She becomes convinced of the necessity of educating women about the political dimensions of their daily lives. Fusae returns to Japan in 1924 and organizes the *Fusen Kakutoku Domei* (Women's Suffrage League). As leader of this organization, she works for the next 16 years to persuade legislators to extend women's political rights. During World War II, in spite of government harassment, Fusae continues to work on women's war-related issues, particularly the scarcity of food. After the war, after being briefly purged by the U.S. military occupation, she becomes a participant in the discussions that result in the 1947 constitution granting women the vote and equal rights. Fusae is elected to serve five terms in the

House of Councillors (the upper house of the national legislature). She remains an independent, never affiliating with a political party. She fights for clean government, free of the influence of big business. In 1945, Fusae establishes the *Nihon Fujin Yukensha Domei* (Japan League of Women Voters).

1893 **New Zealand, First Country to Grant Suffrage to Women.** New Zealand becomes the first nation to grant women the vote.

1893 **National Council of Jewish Women Organized.** The National Council of Jewish Women (NCJW) is formed as a social service group to help persons of all races and religions.

1893 **Birth of Elizabeth Coatsworth, American Author.** Elizabeth Coatsworth (1893–), American children's author, is born. Her first work is *The Cat and the Captain* (1927), followed by *The Cat Who Went to Heaven* (1930), which won the Newbery Medal.

1893 **Wanda Gág, American Artist and Author, Is Born.** Wanda Gág (1893–1946), author and illustrator of *Millions of Cats* (1928), is born. Gág also translates and illustrates *Tales from Grimm* (1936) and *Snow White and the Seven Dwarfs* (1938).

1894 **Rachel Field, American Children's Author, Is Born.** Rachel Field (1894–1942), American children's author, is born. Her first work, *Hitty, Her First Hundred Years,* is published in 1929 and Field becomes the first woman to receive the prestigious Newbery Medal from the American Library Association. She later publishes *Calico Bush* (1931) and *Hepatica Hawks* (1932).

1894 **Elizabeth Morgan Moorage Is Delegate at AFL Convention.** Elizabeth Morgan Moorage is the only female delegate to the American Federation of Labor (AFL) convention. Morgan is the secretary and prime mover of the Ladies Federal Labor Union #2703. An

English immigrant, she is a child laborer in Birmingham, England. In 1881, Morgan becomes a charter member of the Chicago Knights of Labor. She forms the Illinois Women's Alliance, a women's coalition of suffrage, temperance, health, housing, and child labor reform groups. These groups were instrumental in passing the Compulsory Education Act of Illinois. When Congress begins its investigation into sweatshop conditions, Morgan is its first witness. She is married to the activist Tommy Moorage, who is one of the founders of the Chicago Trades and Labor Assembly.

1894 Luna Elizabeth Sanford Kellie, American Agrarian Reformer, Gains National Attention. Luna Elizabeth Sanford Kellie (c.1857–1940) is elected the state secretary of Nebraska's Farmers' Alliance and gains national attention. She is a staunch Populist and opposes political fusion with either the Democrats or the Republicans. She lectures for the alliance and publishes the newspaper *Wealth Makers*, later called the *Prairie Home*, in 1895. It rallies support for the non-fusionist cause.

1894 World's Young Women's Christian Association Forms. Representatives of national associations from Great Britain, Norway, Sweden, and the United States form the World's Young Women's Christian Association. Initially based in London, the World's (later just World) YWCA moves its headquarters to Geneva in 1930.

By the 1920s, the YWCA in the United States moves away from evangelical Protestantism, adopts the principles of the Social Gospel, and becomes active in public affairs. It pioneers studies of conditions for working women and stresses leadership training for women. The YWCA expands beyond the needs of native-born, white women by developing programs for African Americans, immigrants, and adolescent girls. Initially adopting a policy permitting segregation at

the local level in both the South *and* the North, YWCA members vote in 1946 to integrate all facilities. The struggle to desegregate the autonomous local associations is a challenge for decades after.

1894 Birth of Martha Graham, American Modern Dance Pioneer. Martha Graham (1894–1991), regarded as one of the most influential figures in modern dance, is born in Pittsburgh, Pennsylvania. She spends her childhood in California and studies with Ted Shawn at the Denishawn School (which Shawn cofounds with his wife, Ruth St. Denis) in Hollywood. Graham performs, choreographs, and teaches through the 1920s, founding the Martha Graham School of Contemporary Dance in 1927. In 1932 she becomes the first dancer to receive a Guggenheim Fellowship. Among Graham's best-known works are dances based on the lives of famous women, such as Joan of Arc; Mary, Queen of Scots; Emily Dickinson; and Charlotte and Emily Brontë. After 1938, she choreographs to music expressly composed for her work by Aaron Copeland (*Appalachian Spring*), Gian-Carlo Menotti, and Samuel Barber. Graham choreographs over 180 works before her retirement in 1969. She receives numerous awards, including the Presidential Medal of Freedom in 1976. Martha Graham receives the Samuel H. Scripps American Dance Festival Award in 1981 for her lifelong dedication to modern American dance.

JANUARY 7, 1894 Jean Crook Devanny, Australian Novelist and Political Activist, Is Born. Jane (Jean) Crook Devanny (1894–1962), an Australian novelist whose sexually frank works draw criticism, is born in New Zealand. She marries Hal Devanny in 1911 and bears a son and two daughters. Her first novel, *The Butcher Shop* (1926), explores the theme of sexual oppression in marriage. Jean Devanny and her family migrate to Sydney in 1929 in the hope of improving her son's health, but the child dies in 1934. She joins the Australian Communist Party (ACP) in 1930, becomes secretary of Workers' International Relief, and attends that organization's conference in Berlin in 1931. From that time, she juggles the demands of family, authorship, and party activism. Devanny is a superb platform speaker and an extremely efficient organizer, but the sexual frankness of her novels and her life draw criticism from inside and outside the party. Her frankness is not echoed by colleagues, and a cloud of innuendo surrounds her expulsion from the ACP in 1940. Devanny's decision to write her autobiography may have influenced her reinstatement four years later. She leaves the party in 1950, apparently over its condemnation of her novel *Cindie* (1949), which portrays the life of an Islander woman working on a north Queensland sugar plantation. Devanny publishes 20 books as well as many articles and short stories, and her work is published in Australia, England, the United States, Germany and Russia. She is also active in writers' organizations and corresponds regularly with other Australian feminist and social realist writers. She spends the last 20 years of her life in north Queensland, rejoining the party in 1957. Jean Devanny dies of leukemia in Townsville in 1962.

MAY 6, 1894 **Eleanor Grinnell Coit, Advocate of Workers Education, Is Born.** Eleanor Grinnell Coit (1894–?), a pioneer in the field of workers education and the establishment of residency schools for workers, is born. A college-educated woman, she joins the Industrial Department of the Young Women's Christian Association (YWCA). While with the YWCA, she uses her knowledge and skills in teaching classes in industrial history for unorganized women workers. She is also a field worker for the Children's Bureau of the U.S. Department of Labor. In 1929, Coit becomes educational secretary of the Affiliated Schools for Workers and in 1934 becomes the director. At the same time, the name of the group is changed to the American Labor Education Service.

1895 **Gynecological Procedures Performed to Treat Mental Illness in Canada.** At a time when mental illness in women is believed to be rooted in their reproductive systems, Dr. Richard Maurice Bucke (1837–1902) pioneers ovariotomies (removal of the ovaries) as a treatment for mental illness in Canada. Bucke is a trained psychiatrist who is superintendent at the London (Ontario, Canada) Asylum for the Insane in the late nineteenth century. Over a five-year period, he and his assistant, Dr. Alfred Thomas Hobbs, operate on 228 women correcting prolapsed uteri, repairing torn perineum, and performing dilatation, curettage, cervical amputation, and ovariotomies. With expectations that these measures will produce mental cures, Bucke and Hobbs declare the procedures successful. Subsequent studies show otherwise.

1895 **Mathilde Maria-Felixovna Kschessinskaya, First Russian Ballerina to Dance the 32 *Fouettés*.** Mathilde Maria-Felixovna Kschessinskaya (1872–1971) dances the 32 *fouettés*, a challenging balletic step, in St. Petersburg, becoming the first Russian ballerina to do so. In the same year she also becomes the first Russian to dance the role of Aurora, and she receives the title of "prima ballerina assoluta." She flees her homeland during the Russian Revolution (1905–6) and settles in Paris, France, where she opens her own ballet school in 1929.

1895 **Elizabeth Cady Stanton Publishes *The Woman's Bible*.** Elizabeth Cady Stanton (1815–1902), American social reformer and suffragist, publishes *The Woman's Bible*. The National American Woman's Suffrage Association's leaders regard the work as radical, and work to distance the organization from Stanton. Stanton, who had resigned as president of NAWSA in 1892, is no longer included among the dignitaries at the head table at NAWSA conventions and events.

1895   Birth of Ito Noe, Japanese Feminist and Anarchist. Japanese writer, feminist, and anarchist Ito Noe (1895–1923) is born. Noe becomes a member of the *Seitosha* (Bluestockings) in 1912. Her background differs from other members of the group—she is younger; less well-educated (only the compulsory high school education, as opposed to college); a member of the working class, rather than the professional, middle class; and she follows the wishes of her parents in a marriage they arrange for her. Membership in Seitosha enables her to break with her arranged marriage and, in 1915, work for the organization as the editor of its magazine, *Seito*. Under her editorship, the magazine changes from a basically literary publication to one that addresses contemporary women's issues. In 1916 its publication ends, because of both government suppression and a division of opinion in Seitosha (between the literature advocates and the women's rights advocates). Thereafter, Noe becomes involved in anarchist activities. In 1921, she helps to establish *Sekirankai* (Red Wave Society), a women's socialist group. It calls for the abolition of capitalism (which it sees as the source of women's oppression), equal wages, mothers' welfare, and the abolition of prostitution. Two years later, after the birth of her seventh child, Ito Noe and her anarchist lover, Osugi Sakae, are murdered by the military police.

1895   Carol Ryrie Brink, Children's Author, Is Born. Carol Ryrie Brink (1895–), American author, is born. Brink's first work for children is *Anything Can Happen on the River* (1934), but she is best known for her 1935 historical novel, *Caddie Woodlawn*. The story of the spunky daughter of a Wisconsin pioneer settler, *Caddie Woodlawn* wins the Newbery Medal.

JUNE 10, 1895   African American Actress Hattie McDaniel Is Born. Hattie McDaniel (1895–1952), the first African American to receive an Academy Award, is born to Henry and Susan Holbert McDaniel in Wichita, Kansas. She becomes one of Hollywood's screen legends as a domestic servant in the 1930s and 1940s. At 15, McDaniel wins a drama medal from the Women's Christian Temperance Union for her recitation of "Convict Joe." She then tours with a black orchestra and appears in the musical *Show Boat*. An accomplished blues singer, McDaniel is the first black woman to sing on the radio and becomes known as "Hi-Hat-Hattie." Her siblings, actors Etta and Sam McDaniel, lure their sister to Hollywood. Her physical features that resemble the ideal "mammy" stereotype typecast her as an endearing maidservant for film roles. She is never allowed to sing in films. In 1939, she wins the Academy Award for Best Supporting Actress for her role as "Mammy" in *Gone With the Wind*. Civil rights groups protest Margaret Mitchell's pro-southern novel and ask McDaniel to turn down the award. She refuses, saying "I'd rather play a maid than be one." In fact, McDaniel is barred from the film's premiere in Atlanta because of the objections of Southern audiences.

McDaniel's career, including appearances in some 300 pictures, begins to decline in the late 1940s. She appears on television in the *Amos 'n Andy Show* and the *Eddie Cantor Show*. She stars as "Beulah" on radio and television. Her deteriorating health, dissolving marriage, and inability to bear children contribute to the depression McDaniel suffers. Finally, losing her battle against breast cancer, Hattie McDaniel dies at the age of 57 on December 26, 1952.

1896   Idaho Women Gain the Vote. Idaho voters are persuaded, in part due to the efforts of Oregonian Abigail Duniway (1838?–1915), to grant women the vote.

1896 Fannie Farmer Publishes *The Boston Cooking-School Cook Book.* Fannie Farmer (1857–1915) publishes *The Boston Cooking-School Cook Book* and introduces the concept of precise measurement. The cookbook assumes no previous knowledge of cooking on the part of its reader. The publisher, Little, Brown & Co., has little faith in Farmer's approach and requires her to pay for the first printing. In 1902 Farmer opens her own cooking school, and to date millions of copies of her book, in several editions, have been sold.

1896 Birth of Lillian Gish, American Actress. Lillian Gish (1896–1993), a leading actress of the silent film era, is born in Ohio. She begins her stage career at age six and in 1912 she becomes a silent film actress, appearing in the first modern feature motion picture, *Birth of a Nation* (1915). She is famous for her long blonde hair and angelic face, and on screen, her delicacy and virtue win the adoration of thousands of fans. In her films, she usually plays a young maiden in peril, threatened by male seduction or abuse, but always virtuous in the end. Between 1919 and 1921, Gish appears in all but two of director D. W. Griffith's films, including *Broken Blossoms* (1919), *Way Down East* (1920), and *Orphans of the Storm* (1921). In *Orphans* she costars with her younger sister, Dorothy. Dorothy Gish also writes several films for her sister and Lillian Gish directs as well.

Though a major box office attraction for many years, Lillian Gish by 1930 becomes too old-fashioned for Hollywood. She returns to the stage but continues to appear in films in her middle and old age. In 1970 she receives a special Oscar for her cumulative work in film. In 1987 she stars in her 104th film, *The Whales of August,* with Bette Davis; Gish is 91 at the time. Though she weds countless times on screen, Gish never marries in real life. Her independence and devotion to her career gives rise to unfounded rumors of an incestual relationship with her sister, Dorothy. Gish confesses: "What kind of a wife would I have made? ... I was devoted to the studio. I loved many beautiful men but I never ruined their lives."

1896 French Producer-Director Alice Guy Screens First Film. Alice Guy (1873–1968), one of the world's first producer-directors of films, screens her movie, *La Fée aux Choux* (*The Cabbage Fairy*), for the first time at the International Exhibition in Paris, France, by the Gaumont film company. Guy goes on to make numerous one-reelers for Gaumont, even experimenting with sound as early as 1905. In 1910, she founds her own studio and production company, Solax, in Paris, and serves as its first president and director-in-chief. The French government awards her the Legion of Honor in 1953.

1896 National Association of Colored Women's Clubs Organized. The National Association of Colored Women's Clubs (NACWC) is founded. The NACWC is set up as a federation of various black women's clubs involved in civic and social service, education, and philanthropy. Among the founders meeting in Washington, D.C., are Mary Church Terrell, Ida B. Wells Barnett, Margaret Murray Washington, Fanny Jackson Coppin, Frances E. W. Harper, Charlotte Forten-Grimké, and Harriet Tubman.

1896 Ann Nolan Clark, American Children's Author and Nurse, Is Born. Ann Nolan Clark (1896–), American children's author, is born. In 1941, Clark publishes *In My Mother's House.* In 1952, her *Secret of the Andes* wins the Newbery Medal.

JANUARY 4, 1896 Suffrage Granted to Women in Utah. Utah achieves statehood, and suffrage is restored to women under the new state constitution. Women had the right to vote in the territory of Utah from 1870 to 1887, when the Edmunds-Tucker Act can-

celed the right to vote for women and polygamous men (men with more than one wife).

APRIL 4, 1896 **First Intercollegiate Women's Basketball Game Played.** The first intercollegiate women's basketball game is played between Stanford University and the University of California–Berkeley, two years after Senda Berenson introduces women's basketball at Smith College. Later the same year, the University of Washington plays Ellensburg State.

OCTOBER 31, 1896 **Birth of Ethel Waters, African American Singer and Actress.** Singer and actress Ethel Waters (1896–1977), who overcomes poverty and becomes one of the first African American women to star on Broadway, is fathered by a white man, John Waters, and born to Louise Anderson, an adolescent. Sally Anderson, Ethel Waters' grandmother, raises her in Chester, Pennsylvania, where Anderson is a domestic servant. Drawing upon her incredible singing skill and talent, Waters—billed as the "Sweet Mama String Bean"—first becomes a stage singer, creating a new style of singing popular music and attracting recording labels and the theater. Later becoming an actress, she appears in theatrical productions such as *Rhapsody in Black* of 1931, *As Thousands Cheer, At Home Abroad, Porgy and Bess,* and *Mamba's Daughters,* a 1939 production that allows her to become one of the first African American women to land a starring role on Broadway. When her roles in *Cabin in the Sky* and *The Member of the Wedding* are made into motion pictures, Waters is catapulted into everlasting fame. For her role in *Pinky* (1949), a film that focuses on the issue of African Americans passing as white, she receives an Oscar nomination for best supporting actress.

Waters is similarly successful in radio and television. When cast in the *Beulah* television series, Waters receives the praise of critics despite the criticism that the show receives. Unfortunately, Waters cannot escape the seg-regated practices characteristic of the pre-Civil Rights era. When she is injured in an automobile accident in Alabama, she is refused proper medical treatment because she is African American.

In 1951, Waters publishes a candid autobiography entitled *His Eye Is on the Sparrow,* based on a song that she makes popular. With an overwhelming spiritual belief, Waters continues to perform even as her health declines, until her death in 1977.

1897 **Publication of *Travels in West Africa*.** Mary Henrietta Kingsley (1862–1900) causes a popular sensation with her publication of *Travels in West Africa.* Accused by her critics of being pro-cannibalist, Kingsley insists that Africans must be respected as human beings. She especially opposes the efforts of missionaries to convert, or westernize, Africans. After her parents' deaths, 30-year-old Kingsley feels useless and decides to move to West Africa, where she begins to study African customs, religions, laws, fauna, and trade conditions.

Kingsley explores Africa by canoe in 1894 and 1895, returning with stories of her bravery in the face of dangerous animals. She sleeps in native huts rather than in the houses of Europeans and admires the freedoms of African women, which she says English women lack. She even climbs the 13,760 feet of Mount Cameroon.

Kingsley does not support the late nineteenth-century feminist movement. During the Boer War she volunteers as a nurse, taking her third and last trip to Africa. She dies of enteric fever caught while nursing prisoners. She is given a military and naval funeral and is buried at sea. During her brief career, she becomes such an expert on the continent of Africa that she lectures before scientific societies and gives testimony before government commissions. In England, medals for research are instituted in her memory at the Liverpool School of Tropical Medicine and the African Society.

1897 Establishment of Canadian Women's Institute for Farm Women. Adelaide Hunter Hoodless (1857–1910), a tireless campaigner for women's education in domestic science, founds the first Women's Institute for farm women, in Stoney Creek, Ontario, Canada. She establishes classes in home economics at the Young Men's Christian Association (YMCA) at Hamilton, Ontario, in the 1890s and at the Ontario Agricultural Institute at Guelph, Ontario, in 1904. The organization is now incorporated in the Associated Country Women of the World, which has over eight million members. Adelaide Hoodless dies on a lecture platform, seeking more funds for her work.

1897 First American Female Professional Photographer Opens Studio. Gertrude Stanton Käsebier (1852–1934), the first American female photographer to gain international recognition as a professional artist, establishes her first studio in New York City. She goes on to become a significant force in the circle around photographer Alfred Stieglitz. In international exhibitions she wins numerous medals and citations, and her photographs are widely reproduced from 1898 until 1910.

1897 Hani Motoko, Japan's First Woman Newspaper Reporter. Initially hired as copy editor of the newspaper *Hochi shimbun*, Hani Motoko (1873–1957) becomes Japan's first woman newspaper reporter when she is promoted in 1897. A leading Japanese journalist, publisher, and educator, Hani is in the first graduating class of Japan's pioneer public higher school for women, Tokyo Women's Normal School. As a newspaper reporter, she writes about women, education, and religion. In 1901 she marries her colleague at the newspaper, Hani Yoshikazu (1880–1955), who becomes her partner in journalistic and educational ventures. In 1903 Hani Motoko inaugurates *Katei no tomo* (*Friend of the Household*), becoming its sole editor and writer. In 1921 the Hanis found *Jiyu Gakuen* (Freedom Acad-

emy). Initially it is an all-girls boarding school striving to cultivate "good wives and wise mothers," who can run a household without depending on servants.

1897 Birth of Charlemae Hill Rollins, American Author, Illustrator, and Librarian. Charlemae Hill Rollins (1897–1979), influential American author and librarian, is born. During her career, Rollins compiles a list of books that combat stereotypes and sets criteria for minority literature. Some of her notable works are *We Build Together* and *The Magic World of Books*.

DECEMBER 14, 1897 Birth of Margaret Chase Smith, U.S. Congresswoman. Margaret Chase Smith (1897–1995), who serves effectively in the U.S. Congress for over 30 years, is born in Skowhegan, Maine. She works at office jobs until 1930, when she marries. In 1936 her husband is elected to the U.S. House of Representatives. Unwilling to play the part of the congressional wife, Smith becomes his paid full-time secretary. When he suffers a heart attack in 1940, she is elected in his place. She is a popular and effective representative, answering every letter, keeping every appointment, and visiting her home state at least once a month. Smith is elected to the Senate in 1948 and reelected in 1954, 1960, and 1966. A strong voice for military preparedness and an independent thinker, she becomes in 1950 the first Republican to speak out against the abuses of anti-Communist Senator Joseph McCarthy (1908–1957). In 1964 she campaigns for the presidency of the United States but does not win her party's nomination. Smith runs a low-budget campaign, stressing her moderate political stance and downplaying gender. After losing her Senate seat in 1970, she travels across the country as a university lecturer. In 1972 she publishes an autobiography, *Declaration of Conscience*. Her former constituents show their continuing respect for her by naming two bridges in her honor in March 1995. Smith dies on May 29, 1995, at

Margaret Bondfield

the age of 97. She is active until the very end of her life, sponsoring programs for the Margaret Chase Smith Library in her hometown of Skowhegan, Maine.

1898   British Labor Leader Margaret Bondfield is Delegate to Trades Union Congress. Margaret Grace Bondfield (1873–1953), as a member of the Independent Labour Party in England, is the only female delegate to the Trades Union Congress (TUC); she becomes its first woman chairperson in 1923. Bondfield is apprenticed to a draper in Somerset, England, at the age of 14. By age 19, she moves to London and is working the standard 74-hour week. Interested in women's and workers' rights, she joins the National Union of Shop Assistants and in 1909 publishes a pamphlet, *Socialism for Shop Assistants*. She cofounds the National Federation of Women

Workers, lectures around the country on radical issues, and speaks as a pacifist during World War I. Bondfield continues with the TUC, becoming chairperson in 1923. That same year she is elected Member of Parliament. She becomes Minister of Labour in 1929, the first woman cabinet minister in British history, and becomes more conservative on unemployment issues. Bondfield retires from Parliament in 1938 but continues to work with trade unions. Her union work takes her to Mexico and the United States to study labor conditions there, and she travels throughout the United States and Canada in the 1940s, lecturing. In 1948 she is made a Companion of Honour. Margaret Bondfield publishes an autobiography, *A Life's Work* (1949), and dies on June 16, 1953.

1898   Marriage of Russian Activists Nadia Krupskaya and Vladimir Lenin. Nadezhda (Nadia) Konstantinova Krupskaya (1869–1939) marries Vladimir Lenin while the two are in exile in Siberia for their revolutionary views. Born in St. Petersburg, Krupskaya meets Lenin in the early 1890s while engaging in socialist activism, for which both are arrested and exiled. Even though the couple marries, Nadezhda, known simply as Krupskaya, never takes her husband's name. For 16 years she lives with Lenin abroad, principally in Switzerland, as he organizes the radical Bolshevik party. She serves as her husband's secretary and works on Bolshevik publications. After the Bolsheviks take over Russia in 1917, Krupskaya actively participates in the educational affairs of the new Soviet Union. Upon Lenin's death in 1924, she briefly opposes the new dictator Stalin, but thereafter remains aloof from politics until her death in 1939.

1898   Publication of *Women and Economics*. American feminist Charlotte Gilman (1860–1935) writes *Women and Economics*, now recognized as a feminist landmark.

1898 American Photographer Berenice Abbott Is Born. Berenice Abbott (1898–1991), an important early photographer who is known for her images of New York City buildings scheduled for demolition, is born. Having studied sculpture in New York, Paris, and Berlin, Abbott works as an assistant to the photographer Man Ray in Paris between 1923 and 1925, returning to the United States in 1929 to take up a career in photography. Her photographs of New York architecture appear in her book, *Changing New York* (1937).

1898 Birth of Canadian Comedienne Beatrice Lillie. Beatrice Lillie (1898–1989), a popular Canadian-born actress and singer, is born. She is such a well-known comic stage artist in London and New York that in the 1920s she is often compared to Charlie Chaplin, then at the height of his international popularity. He himself calls her his "female counterpart." Lillie is remembered for her humorous songs, especially as rendered in the numerous revues in which she appears, beginning in 1914, and for her work on Broadway and in films. She continues to perform well into old age.

1898 Meiji Civil Law Code Promulgated In Japan. The Meiji Civil Law Code, the law of the Japanese nation state, is promulgated. This code makes the patriarchal family, rather than the individual, the legally recognized entity; only men are legally recognized persons. Married women are not able to bring legal action independently; they are classified in the same category as the deformed and mentally incompetent. Husbands are totally free to dispose of their wives' property as they like and free to operate under the sexual double standard by which only wives can be punished for adultery. Property can be inherited only by the oldest son. Thus, while women political activists had hoped that the new civil law code would bring them a measure of equality, it brings instead the legalization of inequality and a decline in the status of women.

JULY 2, 1898 Lizzie Arlington, First American Woman to Sign Baseball Contract. Lizzie Arlington becomes the first woman to sign a contract in the professional minor leagues, where she plays for several years. Women play baseball at the turn of the century in all-women's leagues.

JULY 24, 1898 Birth of American Aviator Amelia Earhart, First Woman to Fly Across Atlantic Ocean. Amelia Earhart (1898–1937), an aviator and adventurer, is born in Atchison, Kansas. On June 17, 1928, she becomes the first woman passenger on an airplane to fly across the Atlantic Ocean—from Newfoundland, Canada, to Burry Point, Wales. On July 6, 1930, she sets the woman's speed record in an airplane when she flies 181.18 miles per hour. Two years later, on May 22–23, 1932, Earhart is the first woman to fly an airplane across the Atlantic Ocean. Later that year, on August 24–25, she flies from Los Angeles, California, to Newark, New Jersey, setting the woman's nonstop transcontinental speed record. When Earhart attempts to fly over the Pacific Ocean in July 1937, her plane is lost in the South Pacific near Howland Island in the Mariannas. She is presumed dead, although days of searching the seas turn up no evidence of her; her navigator, Fred Noonan; or the wreckage of her plane. Earhart is awarded the Lindbergh Medal in 1928; the American National Geographic Society Award Medal, presented by President Herbert Hoover, in 1932; and over 40 other medals and awards.

c. 1899 Lin Heier Participates in Chinese Boxer Rebellion. Lin Heier is a member of the Red Lantern Society, a group of young female Chinese rebels who participate in the anti-western Boxer Rebellion (1899–1901). The rebels are called "Boxers" because they believe that traditional martial arts techniques will protect them from western bullets.

1899 Publication of Controversial Children's Book *Little Black Sambo*. Helen Brodie

Cowan Watson Bannerman (1862?–1946) publishes *Little Black Sambo*. Bannerman is author and illustrator of the work, written for her two young daughters the previous year; it is so loved by all that she submits it to a publisher. The book later becomes the subject of much controversy in both England and the United States. Libraries in both countries often remove it to historical collections because it is considered racist. The name Sambo is considered a derogatory term for an African American child, and although the book is set in India, the story is identified with children of color in the United States. Born in Edinburgh, Scotland, Bannerman is educated by her father, an army chaplain, and through correspondence courses. She marries William Bannerman, who is a doctor in the military and with whom she shares 30 years in India.

1899   **Publication of Kate Chopin's *The Awakening*.** Kate O'Flaherty Chopin (1850–1904) publishes her major work, *The Awakening*. The novel describes a woman's dreams and her illicit affair. Chopin is heavily criticized for writing such an explicit novel. *The Awakening* is reprinted in 1972.

1899   **Lady Augusta Gregory Cofounds Irish Literary Theatre.** Lady Augusta Gregory (1852–1932) cofounds, with William Butler Yeats and Edward Martyn, the Irish Literary Theatre in Dublin. This important center for the literary and artistic movement known as the "Irish Renaissance" later attains international fame as the Abbey Theatre. Lady Gregory dedicates her energies to the restoring of Irish culture and to political independence.

1899   **Ida Kaminska Founds Yiddish Theaters.** Ida Kaminska (1899–), an actor and benefactor in Yiddish theater, founds the Warsaw Jewish Art Theater and the Ida Kaminska Theater, both in Warsaw, Poland. Forced to leave Europe because of anti-Semitism, Kaminska moves to New York City, where she continues her work on behalf of Yiddish drama.

1899   **Birth of Japanese Feminist Yamataki Shigeri.** Japanese feminist and social reformer Yamataki Shigeri (1899-1977) is born. She begins as a writer for the women's magazine *Shufu no tomo* (*Housewife's Friend*). In 1924, Shigeri and Ichikawa Fusae establish the *Fusen Kakutoku Domei* (Women's Suffrage League), the main organization of Japanese women campaigning for suffrage. In addition to campaigning for women's political rights, the organization also becomes involved in consumer activism, leading a drive for lower gas prices in 1927. Faced with growing government suppression in the 1930s, Shigeri turns to the more moderate issues of assisting mothers and widows. With Yamada Waka and others, Shigeri forms the *Bosei Hogo Remmei* (Motherhood Protection League) in 1935. Shigeri continues to work on women's issues during World War II and is active after the war in promoting new rights for women. In 1952, she founds *Chifuren* (National Federation of Regional Women's Organizations) and serves as its president. The objectives of the organization include elevating the status of women and promoting social welfare. The organization is particularly active in consumer protection issues. With the backing of Chifuren, Shigeri is elected to the House of Councillors (the upper house of Japan's national legislature) in 1962 and 1965.

1899   **Japanese Literary Figure Miyamoto Yuriko Is Born.** Miyamoto Yuriko (1899–1951), a feminist novelist and leader of Japan's proletarian literary movement, is born. Women's issues are at the center of her literature. Beginning in the 1920s, she writes a series of autobiographical novels that address the institution of marriage, traditional ideas about the relations between men and women, and human fulfillment. In 1930 Yuriko joins the All-Japan Proletarian Artists' Association and becomes the coordinator of its women's committee and editor of *Hataraku fujin* (*Working Women*). In 1931 she joins the Japanese Communist Party. In the following years, leftist activities are severely repressed by the government, and her publications become the targets of censorship. She is repeatedly arrested and imprisoned through the 1930s. Yuriko writes little fiction during World War II but concentrates, instead, on essays of literary criticism, frequently on the works of women writers. Following the war, she returns to her political activities and again publishes novels and short stories. Yuriko helps to establish the *Shin Nihon Bungaku Kai* (New Japanese Literature Association), a group of writers committed to anti-imperialist, democratic movements. She is also the founder of the *Fujin Minshu Kurabu* (Women's Democratic Club).

1899 Japanese Activist Yamamuro Keiko Works with Salvation Army to Rehabilitate Prostitutes. Yamamuro Keiko (1874–1916), a Japanese activist in Christian social reform movements, marries Yamamuro Gumpei, the founder of the Japanese branch of the Salvation Army, and begins working in that organization with the rehabilitation of prostitutes. Keiko graduates from Meiji Jogakko (Meiji Girls' School), a Christian women's post-secondary school. Before her marriage, she campaigns with the Kyofukai, Japan's Women Christian Temperance Union.

1899 National Consumers League Organized. The National Consumers League (NCL) is formed in the United States to research and educate the public about product safety and standards. The NCL addresses consumer issues such as insurance, credit, health, wages, communications, and labor standards.

1899 Kate Seredy, Hungarian Children's Author and Illustrator, Is Born. Kate Seredy (1899–1975), Hungarian author and illustrator, is born. Her first work, *The Good Master*, is published in 1935. It is followed by *The White Stag*, published in 1937. It wins the Newbery Medal in 1938.

1 9 0 0 – 1 9 0 4

c. 1900   4-H Program Organized from Agricultural and Home Economics Clubs. What is now known as 4-H begins at the turn of the century in several places at the same time. Thus, no one individual is named as founder of 4-H nor is any one place identified as the site where 4-H first begins. The goal in the early years is to extend agricultural and home economics education to rural youth by organizing boys' and girls' clubs and through "learning by doing" activities. Corn clubs are among the first activities for boys, followed by pig clubs and cotton, poultry, and other agriculture-related projects. Canning clubs and home economics subjects such as clothing, home improvement, and foods are among the early projects for girls.

Some of the pioneers in girls' 4-H programs include Jessie Field Shambaugh, who with O. H. Benson, organizes corn clubs in Iowa and begins to use a 3-leaf clover emblem for awards; Marie Cromer of South Carolina, who founds the first canning clubs; Ella Agnew of Virginia, who becomes the USDA's State Agent of Girls' Tomato Clubs; and Mary Cresswell of Georgia and later Gertrude L. Warren, who are appointed by the USDA to provide leadership to girls' homemaking programs.

Through the years, the overall objective of 4-H remains the same—the development of youth as individuals and responsible and productive citizens. The four "H"s stand for Head, Heart, Hands, and Health. The 4-H Pledge: I pledge my head to clearer thinking, my heart to greater loyalty, my hands to larger service and my health to better living—for my clubs, my community, my country, and my world. Today's 4-H program is for all youth—urban as well as rural—of all racial, cultural, economic and social backgrounds. 4-H-type programs patterned after the U.S. program are conducted in 82 countries around the world.

1900   British Fiction Writer Elizabeth Goudge Is Born. Elizabeth Goudge (1900–), British author of work for children and adults, is born. She publishes her first work, *Island Magic*, in 1934. In 1944, Goudge receives the Metro-Goldwyn-Mayer Literary Award for *Green Dolphin Street.* In 1947, she receives the Carnegie Medal for outstanding children's book published in the United Kingdom for *Little White Horse.* Among her other works are *Pedlar's Pack, Towers in the Mist,* and *The Bird in the Tree.*

1900   French Author Colette Publishes First Autobiographical Novel. Colette (1873–1954), a leading modernist French author of the post-World War I era, publishes the first of her four autobiographical novels (1900–1904) about a girl named Claudine. Besides her autobiographical works, her writings

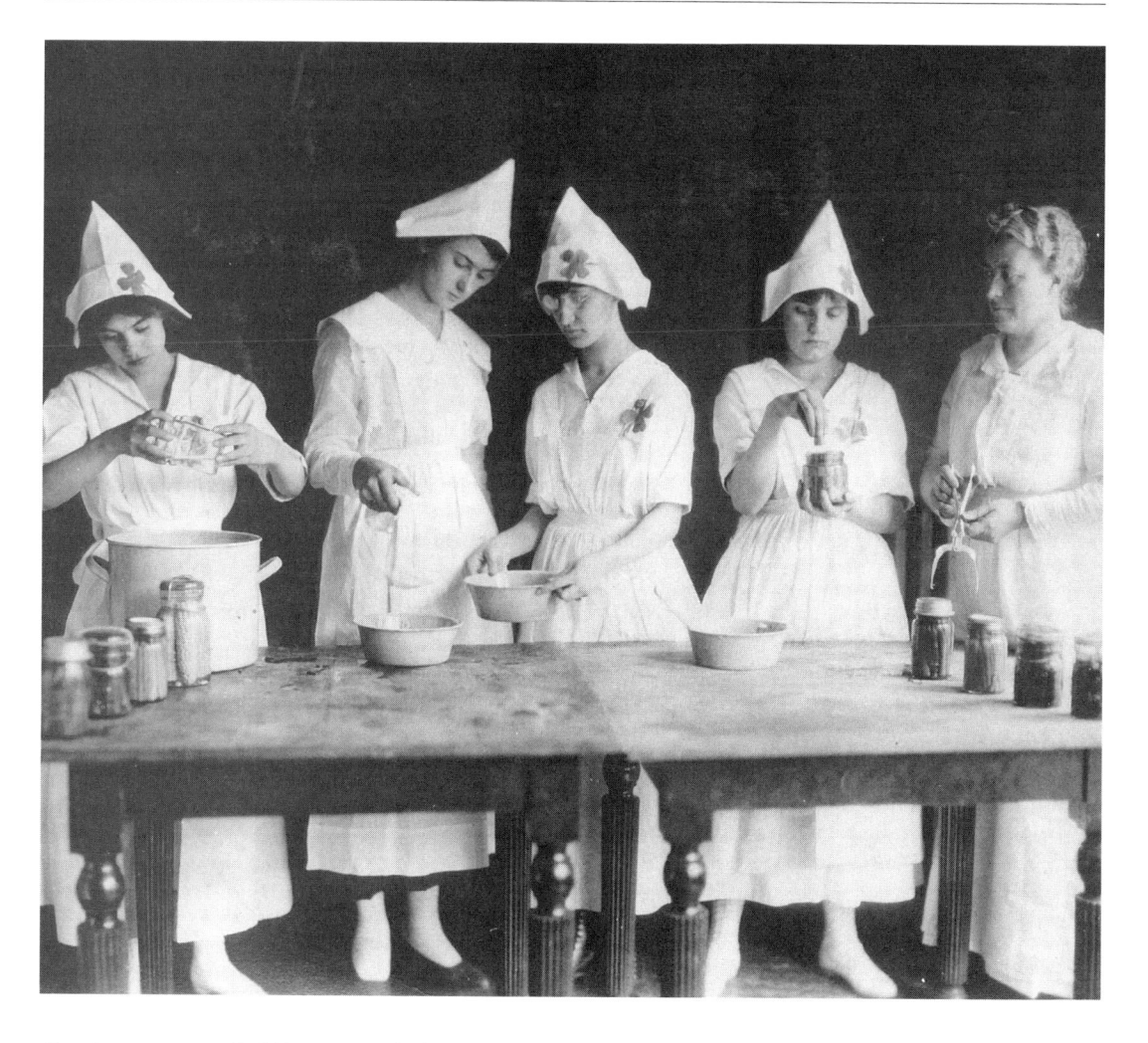

Canning team, an early 4-H activity, with their leader at Cedar Rapids, Iowa, in 1915.

include *The Vagabond* (1910); *Cheri* (1920), which details the affair between an older woman and her 25-year-old male lover; *The Ripening* (1923); *Sido* (1929); and *The Cat* (1933). She later produces *Gigi* (1944), which tells the story of a young courtesan-to-be, and *From My Window* (1944), a simple tale of daily happenings in her Parisian neighborhood. The majority of Colette's writings are sensitive and sensual, portray women in love, and have vivid descriptions of sexual desire.

1900 **British Children's Author Enid Blyton Is Born.** Enid Blyton (1900–) is born. Blyton publishes her first book, *Real Fairies,* in 1923; it is followed by more than 400 works. Among the best-known are *The Famous Five* and *The Secret Seven.*

1900 **Tango Introduced in United States and Europe.** American ballroom dancers Irene and Vernon Castle introduce the tango, the first of many Latin American dances to gain popularity in the United States and Europe.

1900 **Tsuda Umeko Founds University in Japan.** Tsuda Ume (or Umeko), (1865–1929), a leader of women's education in Japan, founds *Joshi Eigaku Juku* (now Tsuda Women's University). In 1871, Umeko is sent by the Japanese government with four other young girls to attend school in the United States. The intention is to raise the girls in the United States for ten years and then return them to Japan to serve as models for Japanese women, most likely as teachers. For the next 11 years, Umeko lives with an American couple in Washington, D.C., studies in private girls' schools, and is baptized a Christian. In 1882 she returns to Japan and begins teaching at the new school for daughters of the nobility, the *Kazoku Jogakko* (Peeress' School). Umeko again goes to the United States in 1889, where she studies biology and education at Bryn Mawr College in Pennsylvania until 1892. Returning to Japan to resume teaching in 1900, Umeko starts her own women's university. The school makes a significant contribution to women's higher education and the promotion of English-language instruction by preparing women as secondary-school English teachers. In 1905, Umeko is one of the principal organizers of the Japanese branch of the Young Women's Christian Association. A leader of nineteenth-century Japanese feminism, Umeko agrees with women's rights to a higher education, the need to make economic independence available to women, and the authority of the wife and mother in the home, but she stops short of advocating women's involvement in politics and suffrage.

1900 **"Go Down, Old Hannah" Begs Sun Not to Rise.** The African American work song, "Go Down, Old Hannah," begs the sun (called Old Hannah) not to rise any more, or, if she does rise, to "set the world on fire." Dating at least from the time of lease-labor plantations in 1900, or even earlier to the times of slave labor in the 1800s, the song continues to be sung well into the twentieth century by African American prisoners in Texas prison camps. Hannah is one of the names by which the Great Mother (or Grandmother) Goddess of life, fertility, and death, revered for millennia throughout the world, is known.

JUNE 18, 1900 **American Author Laura Zametkin Hobson Is Born.** Laura Zametkin Hobson (1900–), American novelist, is born in New York City. In 1947, she publishes her best-seller about anti-Semitism, *Gentlemen's Agreement*. Her other works include *The Trespassers* (1943), *The Celebrity* (1951), *First Papers* (1964), and *Consenting Adults* (1975).

1901 **Publication of Beatrix Potter's *The Tale of Peter Rabbit*.** British writer and illustrator Helen Beatrix Potter (1866–1943) publishes her first book, *The Tale of Peter Rabbit*. From 1903 to 1913, she publishes one to two books a year. Potter illustrates all of her stories, which include *The Tailor of Gloucester* (1903), *The Tale of Benjamin Bunny* (1904), *The Tale of Jemima Puddle-Duck* (1908), and many others. She gives up publishing after her marriage to attorney William Heelis in 1913, but still sketches and writes for her own pleasure. She also campaigns for the preservation of the English countryside.

1901 **Chinese Gynecologist Ch'iao-chih Lin Is Born.** Ch'iao-chih Lin (1901–), the first Chinese woman to receive a degree in gynecology from an English university, is born. She intends to become a pediatrician but is distressed at tending to dying infants and switches to gynecology.

1901 **Gardner Museum Founded.** Isabella Stewart Gardner (1840–1924), an American art collector, founds the Gardner Museum in Boston, Massachusetts. Gardner, who takes a personal interest in the varied collection of art displayed there, presides over the museum, living on the top floor, for the next 20 years.

1901   First Woman to Photograph Nude Male. Imogen Cunningham (1883–1976) becomes the first woman to photograph a male nude when she photographs her husband naked on Mt. Rainier. The pictures are censored for many years. Cunningham is mainly known for her photographs of plants and flowers.

1901   Birth of Helen Kalvak, Canadian Inuit Artist. Helen Kalvak (1901–1984), the first Inuit woman to chronicle the life of her people in her art, is born. She begins drawing in her late 60s. Traveling throughout Canada's Northwest Territories, Kalvak creates over 3,000 pictures that vividly convey the traditional culture and activities of the Copper Inuit, stressing their spiritual life, legends, and ceremonies. She is honored in 1975 with membership in the Royal Canadian Academy of Arts.

1901   Publication of Stella Miles Franklin's *My Brilliant Career.* Australian author Stella Maria Miles Franklin (1879–1954) publishes her first, and best-known, novel, *My Brilliant Career,* a semi-autobiographical book that depicts a teenage girl's rebellion against the constraints of womanhood and marriage. It provokes an ambivalent response, and its sequel, *My Career Goes Bung,* is not published until 1946.

DECEMBER 16, 1901   American Anthropologist Margaret Mead Is Born. Margaret Mead (1901–1978), American anthropologist and author, is born in Philadelphia, Pennsylvania. She works as a curator of ethnology at the American Museum of Natural History in New York City, undertaking expeditions to New Guinea and Samoa. She writes about her work there in *Coming of Age in Samoa* (1928) and *Growing Up in New Guinea* (1930). She later publishes *Male and Female* (1949) and *Growth and Culture* (1951), in which she argues that gender differences are shaped by culture rather than heredity.

Helena Rubinstein

1902   Birth of American Geneticist Barbara McClintock. Barbara McClintock (1902–1992), Nobel Prize-winning geneticist, is born. Although her parents discourage her from attending college, she eventually enrolls in Cornell University's College of Agriculture, where she begins her work with maize, or Indian corn. Her work earns her the Nobel Prize in 1982.

1902   Helena Rubinstein Opens Her First Beauty Salon. Starting with one product, a homemade face cream, Helena Rubinstein (1870?–1965) opens a small beauty shop in Melbourne, Australia. Two years later she is a rich woman, the founder of what will become the modern cosmetics industry.

1902   Elizabeth Christman Cofounds Local 1 of International Glove Workers Union.

American labor union activists Elizabeth Christman and Agnes Nestor found Local 1 of the International Glove Workers Union. Christman serves the local as shop steward and treasurer from 1905 to 1911 and as president from 1912 to 1917. She is also secretary-treasurer of the International Ladies Garment Workers Union from 1916 to 1931, and vice president from 1931 to 1933. President Herbert Hoover appoints her to the Organization on Unemployment Relief and representative to the Code Authority of the National Industrial Recovery Administration. In 1936 President Franklin D. Roosevelt appoints Christman to the Commission on Vocational Guidance. In 1940 she becomes a member of the Advisory Committee of the Women's Bureau of the U.S. Department of Labor.

1902   Publication of Edith Nesbit's *The Five Children and It*. English author Edith Nesbit (1858–1924) publishes what becomes one of her best-known children's novels, *The Five Children and It*. In 1906 she publishes another popular classic, *The Railway Children*.

1902   Florence Rena Sabin, First Woman Faculty Member at Johns Hopkins. Medical researcher Florence Rena Sabin (1871–1953) becomes the first female faculty member at Johns Hopkins University in Baltimore, Maryland. In 1917 she becomes Johns Hopkins' first female full professor. In 1924–26, Sabin serves as the first female president of the American Association of Anatomists. She is also the first woman elected to the New York Academy of Sciences and the first female member of the Rockefeller Institute.

1902   Women Gain Suffrage in Australia. Women of European descent are given the vote in Australia.

1902   Australian Vida Goldstein Runs for National Election. Vida Jane Mary Goldstein (1869–1949) is the first woman to run for office in a national election in the British

Statue of Florence Rena Sabin, M.D., in the U.S. Capitol building.

Empire. Born and educated in Victoria, Australia, Goldstein begins her public career by helping her mother collect signatures for the huge Woman Suffrage Petition of 1890. Throughout the ensuing decade she involves herself in public affairs, absorbs parliamentary procedures, and learns to be a first-class public speaker. In 1902 Goldstein travels to the United States, where she becomes secretary of the International Woman Suffrage Conference and attends a Conference of the International Council of Women. Australian women win the federal vote in 1902, and Goldstein returns to this country to become the first woman in the British Empire to stand for a national election. She fails to gain a seat in the Senate but polls a creditable 51,497 votes.

Louise Beavers during a visit to the home of President James Monroe.

Attributing her failure to women voters' lack of political education, she tackles this problem vigorously through her paper *Women's Sphere* and launches her second paper, the weekly *Woman Voter*, in 1909. During 1911, at the invitation of the Women's Social and Political Union, she visits England, where her speeches draw huge crowds. Goldstein runs unsuccessfully for federal parliament five times between 1903 and 1917. Her candidacy is hampered by her refusal to align herself with a political party and by persistent rumors that she believes in "free love." In 1917, she loses votes through her anti-war stance: she chairs the Peace Alliance and forms the Women's Peace Army in 1915. After the war, Goldstein concentrates mainly on internationalism to resist war and to promote equality. Vida Goldstein dies in Melbourne in 1949.

MARCH 8, 1902   **Louise Beavers, African American Actress, Is Born.** The first African American woman to receive a starring motion picture contract, actress Louise Beavers (1902–1962) is born in Cincinnati, Ohio. Both her great-grandfather and grandfather were slaves at Ash Lawn, home of U.S. president James Monroe. Beavers believes that her grandfather may have served as carriage driver there.

As an adolescent, Beavers performs on stage in minstrel shows but promotes herself as a concert singer. She transcends stage acting by becoming a screen actress when she lands roles in *Gold Diggers* (1923) and *Uncle Tom's Cabin* (1927). In 1934 Beavers becomes the first African American woman to receive a starring motion picture contract. Her role as "Delilah" in *Imitation of Life* (1934) escalates her to fame and allows her to become a popular screen domestic servant. This portrayal of African American subservience becomes the center of controversy when Sterling Brown, a professor at Howard University, publicly debates Fannie Hurst, the white author of the novel upon which the film is based. Beavers' portrayal in this film establishes her as a dramatic screen actress whose talent rivals that of white screen stars. Some critics even contend that she deserves an Academy Award for her performance.

During her career, Beavers appears in some 125 films: "Nearly all of [my] roles have been maids roles—just pleasant, likeable Negro maids—plump and happy and quick to laugh." She admits that she has to perfect the Southern accent usually characteristic of her part because she has never traveled South and that she must engage in forced-feed diets to remain large enough in size to assume these roles. A domestic servant on the screen, Beavers is actually unskilled in cooking, and studio officials reportedly hire cooks to prepare food for her performances.

Beavers is often referred to as an example of wasted talent, since Hollywood will not provide venues by which she can display her talent beyond the role of domestic servant. Beavers, like many black actresses, responds by turning such limited roles into unparalleled performances.

1903   Rose Schneiderman Begins Career as Union Activist by Organizing Shop. American union activist Rose Schneiderman (1882–1972) and a coworker organize their shop and establish Local 23 of the United Cloth Hat and Cap Makers of North America. Schneiderman is elected its first president and the following year is elected to the executive board of the Cap Makers' Union. In 1905, during a capmakers strike, she joins the New York chapter of the Women's Trade Union League (WTUL) and is elected vice president in 1907 and president in 1917. She is vice president of the National WTUL from 1919 to 1926 and president from 1926 to 1947.

1903   Gertrude Barnum, Founding Member of Women's Trade Union League. Gertrude Barnum (1866–1948) helps found the National Women's Trade Union League (WTUL). As a WTUL representative she participates in and supports numerous strikes, such as the textile workers' strike in Fall Rivers, Massachusetts, and the corset makers' strike in Troy, New York, in 1905. In 1911, Barnum is named a special representative with the International Ladies Garment Workers Union (ILGWU).

1903   English Women Stage Demonstrations in Hyde Park. One of the organizations leading the fight for women's suffrage in England is the National Women's Social and Political Union, whose slogan is "Votes for Women." Led by suffragists Emmeline Goulden Pankhurst (1858–1928) and her daughter Christabel Harriette (1880–1958), the Union stages parades, demonstrations, and engages in tactics such as window-breaking to gain attention for their cause. Women in England win the vote in 1928, the year Pankhurst dies.

1903   Margaret Dreier Robins Begins Involvement in Unionism. Margaret Dreier Robins (1869–1945) begins her union activism when she serves as chair of the legislative committee of the Woman's Municipal League in New York from 1903 to 1905; she becomes president of the New York Women's Trade Union League in 1905.

1903   Mary Kenney O'Sullivan, First Vice President of WTUL. While attending the American Federation of Labor (AFL) convention, Mary Kenney O'Sullivan (1864–1943)

A demonstration for women's suffrage in Hyde Park, London, staged by the Women's Social and Political Union.

becomes cofounder of the National Women's Trade Union League (WTUL) and serves as its first vice president.

1903   Marie Curie, First Woman to Win Nobel Prize. French scientist Marie Curie (1867–1934) becomes the first woman to receive a Nobel Prize when she wins the award in physics, an honor she shares with her husband, Pierre, and a colleague at the Sorbonne, A. H. Becquerel. The prize is awarded for their discovery of radioactivity. When her husband dies in 1906, Marie Curie is appointed to fill his chair at the Sorbonne, becoming the first woman in France to receive professorial rank. Marie Curie is also the first person to win two Nobel Prizes: she is awarded the prize for chemistry in 1911, an honor she earns for the isolation of pure radium.

1903   Hani Motoko Publishes Japanese Women's Magazine. Hani Motoko (1873–1957) inaugurates *Katei no tomo* (*Friend of the Household*) in Japan, becoming its sole editor and writer. With her husband, Hani Yoshikazu (1880–1955), she parts from the publisher in 1908 and continues the magazine as *Fujin no tomo* (*Women's Friend*). Appealing to lower- and middle-class housewives, the magazine articulates the belief that the home is the most important social unit, and its improvement will result in social reform and

Marie Curie in her laboratory, 1921.

progress. The magazine never advocates women's rights or revision of the social and political order. Under the motto "education in daily life," the magazine addresses issues of marriage, the education of children, health concerns, and household finance.

JANUARY 7, 1903   Birth of American Author Zora Neale Hurston. Zora Neale Hurston (1906–1960), African American author, is born in Eatonville, Florida, where she spends the first nine years of her life until the death of her mother. In *Dust Tracks on a Road* (1942), Hurston writes about her childhood years in Florida. Her other works include *Jonah's Gourd Vine* (1932), *Their Eyes Were Watching God* (1937), *Moses, Man of the Mountain* (1939), and *Seraph on the Suwanee* (1948).

APRIL 10, 1903   Birth of Clare Boothe Luce, American Writer and Public Official. Nationally known journalist, playwright, and politician Clare Boothe Luce (1903–1987) is born in New York. During the 1930s she works as an editor at *Vogue* and *Vanity Fair* magazines and as a writer, producing a novel, several well-received plays, and freelance columns. Raised modestly, she marries the millionaire Henry Luce, publisher of Time-Life publications. The Luces are passionate, talented, intelligent, and wealthy.

Boothe Luce is a foreign correspondent for *Life* magazine during World War II (1939–45). In 1943 she is elected to the U.S. House of Representatives as a Republican from Connecticut. There she fights for racial equality in the military and in the workplace,

Clare Boothe Luce

and becomes a strong anti-Communist. In the late 1940s, after the death of her daughter, she retires from elected office, converts to Roman Catholicism, and turns her attention again to writing. President Dwight Eisenhower appoints her Ambassador to Italy in 1953, and she oversees peaceful settlements of longstanding territorial disputes. No American woman has held a diplomatic post at this level before. She receives many honors at home and abroad, including the Hammarskjold Medal in 1966 and the Medal of Freedom in 1983. Clare Booth Luce dies on October 9, 1987.

SEPTEMBER 7, 1903 **Margaret Dorothea Landon, American Author, Is Born.** Margaret Dorothea Landon, author of *Anna and the King of Siam,* is born in Somers, Wisconsin. She researches the relationship between the Siamese King Mongkut and Mrs. Anna Leonowens. The king's letters, written in Siamese, are housed in the Library of Congress, where Landon discovers them. Her work is later adapted into a major musical play entitled *The King and I.*

NOVEMBER 1903 **National Women's Trade Union League Founded.** A small group of working women, social reformers, and settlement house workers form the National Women's Trade Union League (WTUL). The founders recognize the need for an independent organization to help women form unions since the male-dominated unions of the day are not responding to the needs of working women.

C. 1904 **Daisy Bindi, Australian Aboriginal Activist, Is Born.** Aboriginal activist Daisy Bindi (c.1904–1962) is born on a cattle station near Jigalong Aboriginal Reserve in Western Australia. Her Aboriginal name is Mumaring; she later adopts her partner's family name, Bindi. Daisy Bindi starts work as a child on Ethel Creek Station and subsequently lives on a number of cattle properties worked by the Nyangumarda. Angered by her employment conditions, she responds in 1945 to Clancy McKenna's call for a strike of Aboriginal station hands. Bindi organizes at Roy Hill Station, demands and is paid wages, and uses the money to hire a truck to collect local workers when the strike breaks out on May 1, 1946. Five hundred people walk from the stations south of Nullagine to Port Hedland. After a confrontation with local police, Bindi leads 86 strikers to Canning Camp on the Shaw River.

One product of the strike is the establishment of Port Hedland's Pindan cooperative settlement to accommodate Aborigines employed in the mining industry. Bindi settles at the cooperative in the 1950s when she is diagnosed as diabetic. She loses a leg in an accident and is fitted with an artificial limb at Perth in October 1959. During her stay in

Evangeline Booth with her father, Sir William Booth.

the capital, she successfully lobbies parliamentarians for a school at Pindan and addresses meetings of the Western Australian branch of the Union of Australian Women on the matter of Aboriginal rights. Daisy Bindi dies at the Native Hospital, Port Hedland, in 1962.

1904   Evangeline Booth, Commander of the Salvation Army in the United States. Evangeline Cora Booth (1865–1950), daughter of Salvation Army founder William Booth, becomes the first woman to serve as commander of the Salvation Army in the United States. She serves in this post until 1934, when she assumes leadership of the Salvation Army worldwide. The Salvation Army is founded in England by William Booth as the Christian Mission in 1865, becoming the Salvation Army in 1878.

1904   First Professional Female Baseball Umpire. Amanda Clement becomes the first woman baseball umpire.

1904   Birth of Japanese Working-Class Writer Sata Ineko. Sata Ineko (1904–),who writes semi-autobiographical works describing the lives of Japanese women and children, is born. Her first short story, "Kyarameru koba kara" ("From the Caramel Factory", 1928), like others which follow, is a depiction of her own work experiences. Ineko is an active participant in Japan's proletarian literature movement, and she joins the outlawed Japan Communist Party in 1932. Through much of her life she experiences poverty, political oppression, and criticism from both the left and the right. Periodically Ineko becomes disenchanted with the Japan Communist Party and either leaves or is expelled. During World War II, leftists accuse her of collaboration with the military government for her participation in writers' tours of the Southeast Asian countries that Japan occupies. A common theme in Ineko's fiction is the effects of complex historical events on essentially apolitical people.

1904   Daisy Bates Conducts Ethnographic Field Work in Western Australia. Australian Daisy May O'Dwyer Bates (1863–1951) studies and assists remote clans of Western Australian Aborigines. Born in Ireland in 1863, she migrates to Australia in 1884. During a short sojourn in north Queensland, she marries (possibly bigamously) Harry (Breaker) Morant. Her marriage to Jack Bates, in New South Wales early in 1885, is certainly bigamous. In 1899, Daisy Bates spends two years on a Trappist Mission to Aborigines in Western Australia and then rejoins her husband on a cattle property, where she studies the kinship structures of local clans and collects Aboriginal vocabularies. In 1904, the Western Australian government engages her to conduct ethnographic fieldwork. She publishes an important paper on marriage laws in 1905 and by 1910 completes the first of her three books. From 1912 she lives almost entirely with Aborigines on a series of isolated camps from which she travels to conferences in a small cart drawn by camels. In 1936, the Australian government provides her with a stipend to prepare her papers for the national collection. From a tent on the Murray River, Bates organizes 99 boxes of material that are transferred to the Commonwealth National Library in 1940. Contemporary anthropologists generally disapprove of her work, and her papers are ignored until the 1980s. She is, however, highly regarded by Aborigines, who call her "Kabbarli," or "wise woman."

DECEMBER 7, 1904 Con Woman Cassie Chadwick Arrested. Con woman Cassie Chadwick is arrested in New York City for impersonating the illegitimate daughter of Andrew Carnegie.

After serving prison time for posing as a wealthy socialite and obtaining lavish lines of credit in San Francisco, Chadwick travels to New York City, where she meets James Dillon, the representative of several Cleveland banks. Chadwick asks Dillon to be her escort, and they travel to Andrew Carnegie's mansion. As Dillon waits, Chadwick enters the house and makes enquiries about a woman she says she proposes to hire; she is told that no such woman has ever been in Mr. Carnegie's employ. Returning to the carriage, Chadwick drops a phoney two-million-dollar promissory note. She dupes Dillon into believing that Andrew Carnegie is her father, and claims to have seven million dollars of similar promissory notes.

Dillon agrees to help Chadwick deposit the notes. Anxious not to embarrass Carnegie, he fails to verify their authenticity. In Cleveland, Chadwick draws heavily on a large line of credit. Bankers vie to extend huge loans. When the promissory notes are examined, bankers find them to be forgeries. Chadwick is arrested on December 7, 1904. Maintaining her innocence, she is sentenced to ten years in prison.

---

1 9 0 5 – 1 9 0 9

1905 Austrian Novelist Bertha von Suttner Wins Nobel Peace Prize. Austrian women's rights activist and novelist Bertha von Suttner (1843–1914) receives the Nobel Peace Prize for her activism against the international arms race. Early in her career, she works in Paris as a secretary to the Swedish dynamite magnate and philanthropist Alfred Nobel. Her friendship with Alfred Nobel contributes to the establishment of the prize, and she is honored herself for a career devoted to the cause of peace and women's rights. Von Suttner heads the Austrian Peace Society and lobbies internationally against the arms race.

1905 Lesbian Author Renee Vivien Publishes *A Woman Appeared to Me.* Renee Vivien (1877–1909), who becomes a leading lesbian writer in early twentieth-century France, publishes her most famous work, a novel entitled *A Woman Appeared to Me.* The novel is based on the events and people in her life between 1899 and 1903. Born Pauline Mary Tarn in England in 1877, Vivien studies in Paris until her family moves to the United States. However, at age twenty-one, Vivien flees to Paris and has her first sexual relationship in 1899 with Natalie Barney, an American heiress who holds a salon in Paris where French and American intellectuals, many of them homosexual, gather. The relationship lasts until 1901 and resumes briefly in 1904, when the two lovers dream of establishing a society of women poets dedicated to Sappho and located on the island of Mytilene (Lesbos). Vivien learns Greek to read Sappho in the original language and eventually translates Sappho's poetry into French. Barney and Vivien are part of the emergence of the early homosexual movement in the late nineteenth century. They articulate a distinctively lesbian self-awareness and share a vision of a society in which women will be free and homosexuality honored, not condemned. Vivien travels extensively during the last years of her life and fills her Parisian apartment with art treasures from the Mediterranean, Orient, and Middle East. Her poetry becomes obsessed with themes of death. Depression, alcoholism, and starvation finally end Vivien's brief life in 1909, after a death-bed conversion to Catholicism.

1905   **Publication of Children's Book** *A Little Princess*. Frances Eliza Hodgson Burnett (1849–1924) publishes *A Little Princess* (1905), a work that later is made into plays and movies. The first movie, starring child actress Shirley Temple, is produced in the 1930s. The second version is released as a feature film in 1994.

1905   **Lucy Parsons, African American Activist, Is Founding Member of Industrial Workers of the World.** Lucy Eldine Gonzales Parsons (1853–1942), African American leader of the Chicago Working Woman's Union, joins Mother Mary Harris Jones and Elizabeth Gurley Flynn as a founding member of the Industrial Workers of the World. Parsons is said to be a stunning woman who is passionate about her loves and hatreds. She also has the reputation for being a commanding, inspirational speaker. For years she travels from coast to coast and speaks in defense of labor causes and free speech.

1905   **Birth of Lillian Hellman, American Playwright.** Lillian Hellman (1905–1984), known as a playwright who wakes up America with her tough-minded dramas about dishonesty, greed, and power, is born in New Orleans to a wealthy German-Jewish family. She attends New York University for three years and then studies journalism at Columbia University as well. In 1934, Hellman is still just a script reader for producer/director Herman Shumlin when she writes her first major hit, *The Children's Hour*, for the stage. This play is an important drama about how a slanderous lie of

lesbianism on the part of a child ruins the lives of two women. After this, Hollywood producer Samuel Goldwyn contracts Hellman to write screenplays for the movies. Hellman adapts many of her stage plays to the screen, including *The Little Foxes* (1936), *Watch on the Rhine* (1940), and *Toys in the Attic* (1959). In 1936, Hollywood, unwilling to deal with the theme of lesbianism, changes the story of *The Children's Hour* to *These Three*, in which the lie concerns a heterosexual love affair. But, in 1961, a remake uses both the original title and theme of Hellman's story. In 1943, she receives the nomination for an Academy Award for best original screenplay for *The North Star*. Hellman also cowrites *The Dark Angel* (1935), and she writes the scripts for *Dead End* (1937), *The Chase* (1966), and *Julia* (1977).

During the McCarthy "witch hunt" against Communists in the early 1950s, Hellman is blacklisted for her refusal to sign movie contracts with restrictive clauses. She is never interested in the seduction of Hollywood and prefers writing for the stage. She has a long-term friendship and love affair with the writer Dashiell Hammett. In 1969 she publishes her memoirs, *An Unfinished Woman*. In her work, Hellman pursues controversial social topics and the truth.

1905   **Elizabeth Gurley Flynn Is Founding Member of Industrial Workers of the World.** At the age of 15, American laborer Elizabeth Gurley Flynn (1890–1964) is a founding member of the Industrial Workers of the World (IWW), whose members are often referred to as "Wobblies." Flynn participates in several historic strikes, including the 1909 strike of New York City waistmakers; the 1912 strikes of Lowell and Lawrence textile mill workers; the 1913 strike of the Paterson, New Jersey, silk workers; the 1916 Mesabi Range miners' strike; and the 1926 Passaic, New Jersey, textile workers' strike. She is also involved in the defense of balladeer Joe Hill and is a pallbearer after his execution. Joe Hill writes his song "Rebel Girl" about Flynn. In 1952 Flynn is tried and convicted under the Smith Act in New York City and then spends 30 months in a West Virginia federal women's prison.

1905   Birth of Maria von Trapp, Austrian Entertainer. Austrian singer Maria von Trapp (1905–1986) is born. Her life story, chronicled in her book *The Trapp Family Singers* (1940), is made into a widely popular Broadway musical and movie, *The Sound of Music,* in 1959 and 1965 respectively.

1905   Mary Calkins Becomes President of American Psychological Association. Mary Whiton Calkins (1863–1930), American psychologist and philosopher, becomes the first woman president of the American Psychological Association. In 1918, she becomes the first woman president of the American Philosophical Association.

1905   Pamela Lyndon Travers, Creator of *Mary Poppins*, Is Born. Pamela Lyndon Travers (1906–), author of works for children, is born in North Queensland, Australia. She publishes *Mary Poppins* in 1934, and *Mary Poppins Comes Back* in 1935. In 1964, *Mary Poppins* is adapted into a feature film starring Julie Andrews by the Walt Disney Company.

OCTOBER 6, 1905   American Tennis Player Helen Wills Moody Is Born. Helen Wills Moody (1905–), a tennis star who challenges restrictions on women players' clothing, is born in Centerville, California. She becomes a great tennis player with a record of eight Wimbledon singles titles, seven U.S. women's singles titles, four French championships, and a gold medal at the 1924 Olympics. From 1923 to 1931, she dominates the U.S. Women's tennis scene, including being ranked number one for several consecutive years. Moody is given the nicknames "Miss Poker Face" and "Queen of the Nets." Her wins at Wimbledon are not surpassed until 1990,

when Martina Navratilova wins her ninth title. Moody's challenge regarding the restrictions in the clothing women tennis players are required to wear contributes to less restricting attire. Moody is also credited for bringing women's tennis to an international level of exposure and acceptance.

1906   Finnish Women Gain the Vote. Women's suffrage is introduced in Finland. Finnish women also win the right to be elected to public office.

1906   Mother Ella Bloor, Political Activist in Chicago's Stock Yard. American activist Mother Ella Reeve Bloor (1862–1951) gets her name from her work with Richard Bloor in the stock yard area of Chicago. Together they gather evidence which Upton Sinclair uses in his expose *The Jungle.* Mother Bloor conducts a number of private investigations. These include an examination of child labor in glass factories in Brighton, New Jersey, in the orphan asylum in Downington, New Jersey, and in mine companies in Johnstown, Pennsylvania.

1906   Birth of Louise Brooks, American Actress of Silent Screen. Louise Brooks (1906–1985), who has a brief but notable career as a silent film star, is born. She grows up in Cherryville, a small town in Kansas, and at age 15 leaves home to pursue a career as a dancer in New York City. In 1925, at age 19, she signs a five-year contract with the Paramount studio. She appears in minor roles in such silent films as *The American Venus* (1926), *Love 'Em and Leave 'Em* (1926), *Rolled Stockings* (1927), and *A Girl in Every Port* (1928).

The turning point in Brooks' career comes in 1928 when German Expressionist director G. W. Pabst hires her to be his "Lulu." Written by German playwright Frank Wedekind, *Lulu* is a synthesis of two plays conceived for the theater: *Pandora's Box* and *The Earth Spirit.* The character of Lulu is simultaneously perverse, childlike, naive, amoral, and sensual. Her eroticism drives men out of their minds in *Lulu* and *Diary of a Lost Girl* (1929). The movies are declared "immoral and inartistic" but eventually become regarded as classic Expressionist films. Brooks' trademark is her black "helmet"—a severe bobbed hairdo with bangs. An unconventional film star, she is also considered "uncooperative" because she goes on strike. Brooks' acting career does not survive the difficult transition from silent to sound pictures. She stars in her last film, *Overland Stage Riders* (1938), with John Wayne. Louise Brooks spends her final years in a small apartment in Rochester, New York, painting and writing her memoirs.

1906   Pioneer Film Animator Claire Parker Is Born. Claire Parker (1906–1981), pioneer film animator, is born in Boston. She studies art at Bryn Mawr College, and in Austria and France. While in Paris, France, Parker studies engraving with Russian-born artist Alexander Alexeieff, and the two eventually marry and move to the United States. In 1932, they build the first model upon which they draw a now-classic film of animation, *Night on Bald Mountain* (1933). They invent a technique of animation known as "pinboard"—a means by which engravings may be brought to life. In this black-and-white technique, the pins are always used as a group, like paint on a brush. Parker is an expert in reading musical scores; she, therefore, is in charge of the relationship between image and music in their films (made before music tracks can be transferred to tape). In 1935 she directs and produces *Rubens,* based on a Parisian art exhibition. From the 1930s to the 1950s, Parker and Alexeieff develop creative advertising films. In homage to her skills, Parker's husband says, "If there had been no Claire Parker, I would have never done animation. I would never have been capable of doing it alone."

1906   Madame C. J. Walker Develops Hair Products for African Americans. African American entrepreneur Sarah Breedlove Walker (1867–1919) opens her business in Denver, Colorado, developing and selling hair care products for black Americans (particularly hair straightener for women and the hot comb). Known as Madame C. J. Walker, she builds a huge mail-order business, establishing an office in Pittsburgh, Pennsylvania, in 1908 and founding laboratories in Indianapolis, Indiana, in 1910. She is believed by some to be the first black woman to become a millionaire.

1906   Marie Curie, First Woman Professor in France. Nobel Prize winner Marie Curie (1867–1934) is appointed to fill her husband, Pierre's, chair at the Sorbonne following his death, becoming the first woman in France to receive professorial rank.

1906   Birth of Yi Nianhua, One of Last to Use Ancient Chinese Writing Style. Yi Nianhua (1906–1989), one of the last writers of *nshu* (literally, "women's writing"), a form of writing practiced exclusively by women in the southern Hunan province in China, is born. Women in this part of China form sworn sisterhoods, writing to each other using the *nshu* script. They also compose wedding songs for each other using this script. Although the practice may be very old, there is virtually no evidence of it prior to the twentieth century.

OCTOBER 23, 1906   Birth of English Swimmer Gertrude Ederle. Gertrude Ederle (1906–), an Olympic swimmer and the first woman to swim across the English Channel, is born. By the age of 17, Ederle sets 18 world distance records. In the 1924 Summer Olympics in Paris, France, she wins a bronze medal in the 100-meter and 400-meter freestyle and a gold as a member of the 400-meter relay team. In August 1926, about one year after her first attempt, she becomes the first woman to swim across the English Channel. Ederle's record time of 14 hours and 39 minutes surpasses by almost two hours the time of the five men who previously swim the Channel. Gertrude Ederle is inducted into the International Swimming Hall of Fame in 1965 and the International Women's Sports Hall of Fame in 1980.

DECEMBER 19, 1906   American Labor Activist Esther Peterson Is Born. Esther Peterson (1906–), an American union organizer and public official, is born. She begins her union work as an instructor for both the Bryn Mawr Summer School for Women Workers and the industrial section of Boston's Young Women's Christian Association from 1932 to 1939. Peterson is an organizer for the American Federation of Teachers (1936), the New England Director of Education for the International Ladies' Garment Workers' Union, and then Director of Education for the Amalgamated Clothing and Textile Workers of America (ACWA). In 1945 she becomes ACWA's legislative representative. In 1948 Peterson begins work with the Swedish Confederation of Trade Unions and its Women's Committee. In 1949 she is a delegate to the founding conference of the International Confederation of Free Trade Unions. President John F. Kennedy appoints Peterson assistant Secretary of Labor and also appoints her head of the federal Women's Bureau and vice chair of the President's Commission on the Status of Women.

1907   Birth of American Actress Barbara Stanwyck. Barbara Stanwyck (1907–1990), who enjoys a 50-year career in film and television, is born Ruby Stevens in a working-class neighborhood in Brooklyn. Her mother dies when Ruby is three, and her father abandons his five children. Ruby is raised by a sister and shuffled from one foster home to another. At 16, she begins performing as a chorus girl in a series of nightclubs and speakeasies and appears in the Ziegfeld Follies. In 1927, she makes her acting debut in the stage play *The Noose* and changes her name to Barbara Stanwyck. In 1928 she marries the Broadway comedian Frank Fay, and the newlyweds

move to Hollywood. Stanwyck's first roles are in B-pictures, until she appears in Frank Capra's *Ladies of Leisure* (1930). Her success and her husband's lack of it (as well as his alcoholism and wife abuse) result in divorce in 1935. The couple adopts a son who remains neglected by both parents throughout his life. In 1937 Stanwyck marries Hollywood leading man Robert Taylor, but they divorce 12 years later.

Stanwyck's screen image is that of a strong, independent woman; she excels in dramas as well as in "screwball" comedies and westerns. Her roles range from reporters to gangster molls, burlesque queens, murderesses, and self-sacrificing mothers. Her most successful films include *Stella Dallas* (1937), *Golden Boy* (1939), *The Lady Eve* (1941), *Meet John Doe* (1941), *Ball of Fire* (1941), *Double Indemnity* (1944), *Sorry, Wrong Number* (1948), *The Furies* (1950), and *Walk on the Wild Side* (1962). Even in her 40s she commands leading roles, but by 50 she is faced with a declining career. She appears on television programs and lands a starring role as the western matriarch in the television series *Big Valley* (1965-69). At 75, she appears in the television mini-series *The Thorn Birds*, which gives her the chance to play an elderly woman assailed by sexual urges. Though herself a staunch conservative, Stanwyck becomes for feminists an icon—the image of the assertive woman. Barbara Stanwyck dies in 1990 from a chronic lung condition.

1907   Edith Head, Hollywood Costume Designer, Is Born. Edith Head (1907–1981), who costumes most of the great stars during her 60-year career, is born. She begins her professional career as an art teacher. She bluffs her way into the wardrobe department at Paramount studios by "borrowing" sketches from schoolmates at the Chouinard Art Institute. Head begins with minor jobs for director Cecil B. De Mille's epic silent films. She lands her first big break on a picture written and produced by Mae West, *She Done Him Wrong* (1933). In addition to dressing Mae West for her first film, Head costumes the sex symbol for her last film, *Sextette* (1978). Head soon becomes the chief costume designer for Paramount. Her "look" for a film often translates into an American fashion sensation: the "Latin Look" for Barbara Stanwyck in *The Lady Eve* (1941); the trend-setting sarong for Dorothy Lamour in *The Jungle Princess* (1936); and the peacock train for Hedy Lamarr in *Samson and Delilah* (1949), among others. She designs clothes for such stars as Audrey Hepburn, Ingrid Bergman, Grace Kelly, Bob Hope, and even Elvis. She even dresses the elephants in *The Greatest Show on Earth* (1952). Head also writes numerous magazine articles, giving fashion advice to the public, and her books include *The Fashion Doctor* (1969) and *How to Dress for Success* (1983). In 1974 the Hollywood Chamber of Commerce awards Head a star on the boulevard, between Alfred Hitchcock and James Cagney. The last film for which Head designs costumes is Steve Martin's *Dead Men Don't Wear Plaid* (1982). During her career Edith Head wins eight Academy Awards, more than any other designer in Hollywood's history.

1907   Astrid Lindgren, Author of *Pippi Longstocking*, Is Born. Astrid Lindgren (1907–), Swedish author of works for children, is born. Her best-known work is *Pippi Longstocking* (1945). Among her many awards are the Hans Christian Andersen Award (1958), the Swedish Academy's Gold Medal (1971), and the Litereris et Artibus Medal from the King of Sweden (1975).

1907   British Author Rumer Godden Is Born. British author Mrs. Lawrence Foster (1907–), who writes works for children and adults using the pseudonym Rumer Godden, is born. Her works include *Black Narcissus* (1939); *Breakfast with the Nikolides* (1941), *The Doll's House* (1947), and *The Fairy Doll*, which is a Carnegie Medal commended book in 1957.

1907   Chinese Radical Qiu Jin Is Killed. Qiu Jin (1875–1907), perhaps the most famous of women radicals in China, is assassinated by the Chinese government. With the support of her mother, Qiu Jin leaves her husband and children and goes to study in Japan. While in Japan, she edits a journal and engages in other political activities. She argues that since men have failed to protect China, women can no longer rely on men. Upon her return to China, she is involved in an unsuccessful uprising and is killed by the government authorities.

1907   Margaret Dreier Robins Becomes President of Chicago WTUL. Margaret Dreier Robins (1869–1945) becomes president of the Chicago Women's Trade Union League (WTUL), a post she holds until 1914. Robins also serves as president of the National WTUL (1907–22). Her other related activities include chair of the Industrial Committee of the Illinois Federation of Women's Clubs (1907–8), and from 1908 to 1917, she serves on the executive board of the Chicago Federation of Labor. She is a member of the American Federation of Labor and the Cook County Central Committee of the Progressive Party. Robins believes that union women make the best organizers and need only a little education to enhance their skills. One of her goals is to establish a training school for organizers. Robins is said to provide an effective bridge between wage-earning women and their middle-class allies.

1907   First Woman to Hold Statewide Public Office in Oklahoma. Kate Barnard (1875–1930), a labor reformer and union organizer, becomes the first woman to win a statewide election in the state of Oklahoma. She works as a teacher, stenographer, and clerk before organizing a union of unemployed men and serving as their delegate to the Oklahoma City Trades Council as well as the State Federation of Labor. Barnard's labor activism begins after she attends the 1904 St. Louis World's Fair and becomes the Matron in Charge of the

Provident Association of Oklahoma City. As a result of these experiences she becomes a champion of labor, working on such issues as wage increases for public employees, protesting the use of convict labor and the use of a blacklist, and regularly posting bond for strikers. This is in addition to her work with the unemployed. Under her leadership, this group of jobless men becomes a politically active union. She also works with a labor-farm coalition, whose goal is to establish a common platform for the constitutional convention of 1906. That same convention creates the office of Commissioner of Charities and Corrections, a position Barnard is elected to in both 1907 and 1910.

1907 **Dr. Jessie Aspinall Practices Medicine in Australia.** Dr. Jessie Strahorn Aspinall (1880–1953) wins the right to practice medicine in Australian hospitals. Born at Forbes, New South Wales, Aspinall studies medicine at University of Sydney. She graduates (M.B., Ch.M) in 1906 and is offered a junior medical residency at the Royal Prince Alfred Hospital. No woman doctor has worked at the hospital before and a shocked board of governors refuses to confirm the appointment. In the ensuing public debate, newspaper editors succumb to a flood of protest meetings and letters from outraged women's groups and support her cause. The hospital board partially concedes. Aspinall's appointment is confirmed for one year only, and members resolve that female residents will be "exempted from attendance on certain cases." However, other hospitals hear the women's message, and in 1907, Aspinall's application for the post of junior house-surgeon at Hobart is accepted. The following year, she returns to Sydney in triumph as resident medical officer and life governor of the Crown Street Women's Hospital. She enters private practice in 1911 but marries mining engineer Ambrose Freeman, accompanying him to Malaya. She bears four children before they return to Sydney in 1922.

Freeman dies eight years later. After her husband's death, Aspinall increases her public engagement, working for the Victoria League, the National Council of Women, and the Young Women's Christian Association. During World War II (1939–45), she assists the Red Cross. In 1941, she gives her house at Bowral to the Red Cross as a convalescent home for ex-servicemen. Jessie Aspinall dies in 1953 and is followed into the medical profession by her youngest daughter.

1907 **Australian Swimmer Annette Kellermann Ushers in Era of Bare Swimwear.** Australian swimmer Annette Marie Sarah Kellermann (1886–1975) emancipates women from neck-to-knee swimwear. When she is arrested on a Boston, Massachusetts, beach for wearing a brief one-piece swimsuit, the subsequent publicity helps change the laws that encase women in neck-to-knee swimwear. Kellermann regards this as her greatest achievement. Born in Sydney, Australia, Kellermann breaks two state records in swimming before moving, in 1902, to Melbourne, where she performs in theater and as an exhibition swimmer and diver. When she leaves Australia in 1905, she holds world records in all women's swimming events. In Europe, Kellermann is promoted as a distance swimmer: she swims the River Thames in England; wins (as the only woman competitor) a seven-mile race in the Seine River in France; and wins a 22-mile challenge down the Danube River. In 1906 Kellermann begins to stage her aquatic act in London, Chicago, Boston, and New York. Kellermann makes six films and works in theaters in Europe, America, and Australia as the "Australian Mermaid" and "Diving Venus." She does her own stunts, which are considered so risky that she cannot get insurance. She publishes two books on health and beauty and a volume of children's stories. During World War II (1939–45), she works with Sister Elizabeth Kenny for the

Australian Red Cross. Annette Kellermann retires to Australia in 1970.

FEBRUARY 25, 1907 **American Playwright Mary Coyle Chase Is Born.** Mary Coyle Chase (1907–), playwright, is born in Denver, Colorado. Her Pulitzer Prize-winning play, *Harvey,* tells the story of an invisible six-foot rabbit and his relationship with the main character, Elwood P. Dowd.

MARCH 1907 **French Feminist Marguerite Durand Establishes Congress of Women's Work.** Marguerite Durand (1864–1936), a prominent Parisian feminist, organizes the Congress of Women's Work to call for equal pay for women. Durand is one of the most influential feminists of *fin de siecle* (turn-of-the-century) France. She belongs to the faction of Republican feminists that consists of mainly Protestant, upper-middle-class women critical of Catholicism. The Republican feminists are a vital force in France in the pre-World War I decades. Durand's greatest accomplishment is the publication of the first daily newspaper written, funded, and edited by women. French law prohibits women from publishing newspapers until the Press Law of 1881. *La Fronde* first appears in 1897, and its title refers to the seventeenth-century rebellion against the monarchy. The newspaper provides unity and leadership at a critical moment in the development of the women's movement. The paper folds in 1905, and Durand then writes for the women's paper *L'Action.* This profeminist paper is one of the few Parisian newspapers to endorse women's suffrage. In March 1907, Durand organizes the Congress of Women's Work to draw attention to such issues as equal pay for women. Equal pay is finally mandated by the Ministry of Labor on July 30, 1946. In 1932 Durand creates the Library of Feminist Documentation, which after her death in 1936 becomes the Biblioteque Marguerite Durand.

MAY 12, 1907 **Birth of American Actress Katharine Hepburn.** Katharine Hepburn (1907–), is born in Hartford, Connecticut. Her father is a physician and her mother a women's rights advocate. The Hepburn household encourages open discussions on such topics as sex, socialism, and politics. Hepburn is an athletic tomboy who also enjoys amateur theatrics. In 1924, she enters the elite women's college Bryn Mawr and joins its college dramatic society. After a brief and unsuccessful marriage, she decides to attempt a career on the stage. Though her parents are not excited about the idea, her mother is secretly pleased that Hepburn chooses a career over marriage.

Hepburn's role in the Broadway play *The Warrior's Husband* attracts the attention of film studios, and in 1932 she moves to Hollywood. Her first movie role in *Bill of Divorcement* proves a success. Hepburn's trademark is her masculine attire and angular, boyish features. She can play aristocrats, working girls, and athletes and appears in dramas and screwball comedies. In 1933 the young actress wins her first Academy Award, for *Morning Glory.* Her other prominent roles include Jo March in *Little Women* (1933), *Alice Adams* (1935), and the aspiring actress in *Stage Door* (1937). Hepburn teams with leading man Cary Grant in the comedies *Bringing Up Baby* (1938), *Holiday* (1938), and *The Philadelphia Story* (1940). From the 1940s through the 1960s, Hepburn is involved in a romantic and acting partnership with Spencer Tracy (who remains married to another woman). Together, they appear in *Woman of the Year* (1942), *Keeper of the Flame* (1942), *Without Love* (1945), *The Sea of Grass* (1947), *State of the Union* (1948), *Adam's Rib* (1949), *Pat and Mike* (1952), *The Desk Set* (1957), and *Guess Who's Coming to Dinner?* (1967).

During the post-World War II "Red Scare" led by Senator Joseph McCarthy, Hepburn joins the Committee for the First Amendment with producer David O.

Selznick, directors John Huston and John Ford, actor Humphrey Bogart, and 300 other Hollywood figures to combat the House Un-American Activities Committee. Fortunately, her career does not suffer, but many others face blacklisting for their liberal political views.

Hepburn avoids the usual fate of aging actresses and has leading roles as she grows older. Her later films include *The African Queen* (1957), *Suddenly Last Summer* (1959), *The Lion in Winter* (1968), and *On Golden Pond* (1981). Hepburn never marries or has children, preferring to commit herself to caring for the aging, alcoholic Tracy until he dies in 1967.

JUNE 14, 1907 **Limited Suffrage Extended to Women in Norway.** Norwegian women gain limited suffrage in parliamentary elections. All women who pay taxes (or whose husbands pay taxes) may vote.

1908 **American Actress Bette Davis Is Born.** One of Hollywood's screen legends, Bette Davis (1908–1989) is born Ruth Elizabeth Davis in Lowell, Massachusetts. Davis' parents divorce when she is ten, and she lives with her mother and younger sister. She later attributes the divorce to her own spirit of rebellion and her distrust of men. She changes her name to "Bette" after Honoré de Balzac's novel, *La Cousine Bette*. In 1927, her mother moves the family to New York City to enroll Bette in drama school. Her success as a stage actress leads to a contract with Universal Studios in Hollywood in 1930. Her first film appearance is with Humphrey Bogart in *The Flirt*. Studio executives doubt her sex appeal, but all agree that Bette has exquisite eyes.

Davis' first great dramatic opportunity and leading role is in the 1934 film adaptation of Somerset Maugham's *Of Human Bondage*. After a series of lackluster roles, she walks out on her Warner Brothers contract and flees to England, where the studio sues her for breach of contract. She is the first star to challenge the studio system, but she loses her case. Nevertheless, she then has a series of screen successes and receives nine Oscar nominations. Davis wins the 1935 Academy Award for *Dangerous* and the 1937 Academy Award for her portrayal of the temptress in *Jezebel*. Her transformed spinster in *Now, Voyager* (1942) and her rich party girl who nobly faces death in *Dark Victory* (1939) become her most memorable roles. Davis weds several times and has two children. After a series of unsuccessful films, Warner Brothers terminates her contract, but Davis makes her screen comeback as the aging actress Margot Channing in *All About Eve* (1950). Her later films typify the lack of options available to aging actresses. She appears with Joan Crawford in the horror film *Whatever Happened to Baby Jane* in 1962 and in *Hush, Hush, Sweet Charlotte* in 1964. She performs in several television features and stars in her last film with another screen legend, Lillian Gish, in *The Whales of August* (1987). Bette Davis dies in 1989 from breast cancer and a series of strokes.

1908 **Birth of Joan Crawford, American Actress.** Joan Crawford (1908–1977), actress in silent and sound films, is born Lucille LeSueur in San Antonio, Texas. Her parents divorce when she is a baby, and her father disappears from her life. Her mother marries a vaudeville theater manager, and young Lucille observes stage acting and dancing. After her mother's second divorce, 13-year-old Lucille takes a job in a department store before pursuing a dancing career. At 15, she wins an amateur dance contest and begins performing in nightclubs. Spotted by a movie executive, Lucille is invited to take a screen test and at 16 moves to Hollywood. She first has small parts, usually dancing the Charleston or Black Bottom. The studio changes her name to Joan Crawford, which she at first detests. With her unique face and strong bone structure, Crawford soon has top billing in such films as *The Taxi Dancer* (1927). Her role as a carefree flapper in *Our Dancing Daughters* (1928) makes Crawford a star and the idol of girls and women throughout the country.

When she begins making sound pictures in the 1930s, Crawford changes her image; her wide red lipstick smear, padded shoulders, and thick eyebrows become her trademark, and again millions of women imitate her style, walk, and speech. By 1936, however, she is a box office failure, until her "comeback" roles in *The Women* (1939) and *A Woman's Face* (1941). Crawford wins the 1945 Academy Award for her performance in *Mildred Pierce.* Middle age brings a series of unfulfilling roles as bitter spinster career women (*The Best of Everything* in 1959) or as monstrous horror film characters (*Whatever Happened to Baby Jane?* in 1962 and *Strait Jacket* in 1964). She marries several times and adopts four children. Crawford dies in 1977.

1908   Publication of Lucy Maud Montgomery's *Anne of Green Gables.* Canadian novelist Lucy Maud Montgomery (1874–1942) writes her best-known novel *Anne of Green Gables,* establishing Anne Shirley, the protagonist, as a central character of childhood. This is followed by several more Anne stories, including *Anne of Avonlea* (1909), *Anne of the Island* (1915), and *Anne of Ingleside* (1939). These perennial classics are read throughout the world by young women and made into films, plays, musicals, television miniseries, and even a ballet.

1908   Bureau of Child Hygiene Established in New York. Sara Josephine Baker (1873–1945), an American physician, founds the Bureau of Child Hygiene in New York City. She works on behalf of public health issues throughout her life. Her accomplishments range from lowering infant mortality rates to designing baby clothes with front openings in order to eliminate suffocation—babies have been strangling in old-style clothes. When Baker refuses a lectureship at New York University because it does not admit women to its graduate programs, the university changes its policy.

1908   Australian Writer Mary Gilmore Publishes Radical Periodicals. Dame Mary Jean Cameron Gilmore (1865–1962), poet, reformer, and one of Australia's best-loved literary figures, begins publishing in radical newspapers and edits the "Women's Page" of the *Australian Worker.* She publishes her first volume of poetry, mainly simple bush lyrics, two years later, in 1910. In 1912 she moves to Sydney and is soon playing a leading role in the literary and political life of New South Wales. As a journalist, Gilmore campaigns for the rights of the dispossessed, particularly Aborigines. She leaves the *Australian Worker* in 1931 and freelances for the next 20 years, working for the communist newspaper *Tribune* beginning in 1952. In addition to her journalism, Gilmore publishes 13 books of verse and four volumes of prose. The themes that dominate her work after 1914 are her hatred of war, her fears for the environment, and her concern for the Aboriginal people. She publishes her last volume of poetry at the age of 89. When Mary Gilmore dies in 1962, she is given a state funeral in Sydney.

1908   Dorothea Mackellar Writes Australia's Best-Known Patriotic Poem. Isobel Marion Dorothea Mackellar (1885–1968), who begins publishing her poems as a very young woman, writes Australia's best-known patriotic poem. She composes "Core of My Heart" at the age of 19 and first publishes it in the *London Spectator* in 1908. She includes it in her first book, *The Closed Door and Other Verses* (1911), as "My Country." The poem becomes enormously popular in Australia in the patriotic atmosphere that accompanies and follows World War I (1914–19); it is set to music and remains a standard inclusion in Australian anthologies. Mackellar writes three novels, two in cooperation with Ruth Bedford, between 1912 and 1914. She is, however, principally a poet and publishes five books of verse by 1925. She also translates little-known Spanish and German poetry into English. Mackellar writes very little after 1926.

1908   Olympic Committee Recognizes Women Athletes. The Olympic Committee gives official recognition to women athletes. American women, however, do not participate until 1920, partly because the Amateur Athletic Union (AAU) in the United States does not sanction women's swimming until 1914. At the previous three Olympics, there are a few brave women who participate "unofficially" in events such as running, tennis, golf, yachting, and archery. After the Interim Games in 1906, women are given official recognition, and events for women's participation continue to be added at every Olympics.

1908   Swedish Women Gain the Vote. Married taxpaying women win local suffrage in Sweden.

1908   Danish Women Extended Suffrage. Women over the age of 25 and wives of taxpayers win local suffrage in Denmark.

JANUARY 28, 1908   First Woman Elected to American Academy of Arts and Letters. Julia Ward Howe (1819–1910) becomes the first woman to be elected to the American Academy of Arts and Letters. Born in New York City, Howe is the author of "The Battle Hymn of the Republic," which becomes the theme song for the Union forces during the Civil War (1861–65). Howe wrote the Hymn in Washington, D.C. in November 1861. It was first published in the *Atlantic Monthly* in February 1862.

1909   Carole Lombard, Actress in "Screwball Comedies," Is Born. Carole Lombard (1909–1942), who enjoys a brief career as a comedic film actress during the 1930s, is born. At age seven, she moves with her family to Hollywood. She studies dramatic acting and becomes ambitious for a film career. At age

12, Lombard has a small role in *The Perfect Crime* and then appears in Mack Sennett comedies performing such standard comedic stunts as pie throwing. Her first starring role is for Fox studios in *Me, Gangster* (1928), and she quickly graduates into female leads. Petite, with golden hair and blue eyes, Lombard combines elegant beauty with wisecracking wit. She is a favorite among directors who cast her in such "zany" comedies as *Man of the World, Ladies Man, Twentieth Century* (1930), *My Man Godfrey* (1936), and the drama *No Man of Her Own.* Lombard marries screen idol Clark Gable, but her marriage and career tragically end in a fatal plane crash in 1942. Lombard is returning from a tour of Indiana, selling war bonds for the U.S. government.

1909   Russian Artist Natalia Sergeyevna Goncharova Founds Rayonnist Movement. Natalia Sergeyevna Goncharova (1881-1962), a Russian painter of international reputation, is the first woman to participate in the modern art Rayonnist movement, which she founds with her husband in Moscow.

1909   Dorothy Jacobs Bellanca, Founding Member of Button Hole Workers Union. At the age of 15, Dorothy Jacobs (later Bellanca) (1894–1946) helps found Local 170 of the Button Hole Workers Union. The local affiliates with the United Garment Workers Union (UGW). However, in 1914, while Jacobs is president, she leads the membership out of the UGW and into the new Amalgamated Clothing Workers Union. In 1915 the 21-year-old Jacobs is elected to the Baltimore Joint Board, and one year later she is elected vice president of the national union. In 1918 she marries August Bellanca and they become an organizing team. In the 1930s Dorothy Bellanca earns the reputation of being the leading organizer and is often called the "Joan of Arc" of her union. She is described as beautiful, articulate, vibrant, and warm. She supposedly has a deep, resonant voice and is an electric speaker. It is said at Bellanca's death that she addresses more meetings, installs more newly organized locals, and speaks to a greater number of workers than any other labor leader. In 1934, Bellanca is reelected to her union's executive board, and from that time until her death she is the union's only woman vice president. In addition to her union work, Bellanca is also a member of the National Women's Trade Union League and the National Consumer's League.

1909   Selma Lagerlöf, First Woman Awarded Nobel Prize in Literature. Selma Lagerlöf (1858–1940) is the first woman to receive the Nobel Prize for Literature, in her native Stockholm, Sweden. Honored for her sagas and legendary narratives, she is also the first woman to become a member of the Swedish Academy in 1914.

1909   French Union for Woman Suffrage Established. Jeanne-Elisabeth Archer Schmahl (1846–1915) founds the French Union for Woman Suffrage.

AUGUST 30, 1909   Birth of Virginia Lee Burton, Author/Illustrator of Children's Books. American author Virginia Lee Burton (1909–1968), who writes and illustrates picture story books for children most often featuring personification of machines or inanimate objects, is born. She trains as a dancer while simultaneously studying art. In 1931 she marries George Demetrios, the sculptor, under whom she studies at the Boston Museum. *Mike Mulligan and His Steam Shovel* (1939), written for Burton's son Mike, is an example of her careful structuring of a story. Mary Anne, a personified machine as protagonist, is established as a great hero in the minds of young children. *Calico: The Wonder Horse* (1941) is the result of her noticing children's intense interest in comics and is a parody of tall tales and westerns. *The Little House* (1942) wins the Caldecott Medal. *Life Story* (1962) is her explanation of life on earth from the beginning, presenting information in dramatic form using a stage as

the focal point throughout but also including detailed, informative drawings to balance the drama with facts. All of her illustrations have a characteristic swirling motion carefully matched to the content of the particular work.

NOVEMBER 22, 1909   "The Uprising of the 20,000" Begins in New York City. "The Uprising of the 20,000" grows from one local to a general strike against several shirtwaist factories in New York City. The parent organization, the International Ladies Garment Workers Union, advises caution. But on November 22, 1909, at a massive meeting of garment workers, the strike of Local 25 becomes a general strike in which workers from 500 shops walk off their jobs. The union expects 3,000 strikers. They get 20,000. The Women's Trade Union League (WTUL) is active in their support of the strike and the strikers. WTUL members walk the picket lines, witness illegal arrests, provide funds for bail, take pictures for publicity, and raise thousands of dollars. Between November 23 and Christmas, 723 women and girls are arrested, and 19 of them are given workhouse sentences. On February 15, 1910, the strike is officially called off even though 1,100 workers are still on strike. Some 339 shops settle with the union. In over 300 shops, workers achieve most of the terms they demand. However, workers at the Triangle Shirtwaist Company return to work without a union agreement. Safety issues such as fire escapes and locked doors are two of the workers' unmet demands. One year later, Triangle is the site of a disastrous fire, and 146 workers, mostly women and girls, lose their lives. Investigation proves that the very issues concerning workers during the strike are directly responsible for those deaths.

1910–1914

1910   Russian Poet Marina Tsvetaeva Publishes First Collection. Marina Tsvetaeva

(1892–1941), who writes Russian poems distinctive for rhythm, originality, and directness, publishes her first collection of poetry. The daughter of a university professor in Moscow, Tsvetaeva travels throughout Europe with her family as a child, studying at the Sorbonne in Paris at the age of 16. She marries Sergei Efron, an army officer who takes part in the resistance to the Bolshevik regime after the Russian Revolution of 1917. Fleeing from the new Soviet Union in 1922, Tsvetaeva and her husband settle first in Prague and then in Paris, living in impoverished exile. While abroad, she publishes poetry establishing her as one of the finest Russian poets of the twentieth century. In the late 1930s, Tsvetaeva, her husband, and their daughter return to the Soviet Union because of World War II, but Efron and the daughter become victims of Stalin's terror. Alone and in despair, Marina Tsvetaeva commits suicide in 1941.

1910   Camp Fire Founded. Charlotte Vetter Gulick (1866–1928), with her husband Luther Halsey Gulick, founds the Camp Fire Girls in Maine. It is the first nonsectarian organization for girls in the United States. The name of the organization is chosen to reflect the origin of the first human communities, the campfire. Camp Fire Girls stresses character development and good mental and physical health. The Camp Fire Law states: "Worship God. Seek Beauty. Give Service. Pursue Knowledge. Be Trustworthy. Hold on to Health. Glorify Work. Be Happy." In 1975, Camp Fire Girls begins admitting boys, and in 1977, Kansas City, Missouri, becomes the headquarters for Camp Fire Boys and Girls. In 1979 the group changes its name to Camp Fire, Inc.

1910   Birth of Mother Teresa. Agnes Bojaxhiu (1910–), later known as Mother Teresa, is born in Albania. From an early age, Agnes knows she will pursue a religious life, and in 1950 founds the Sisters of the Missionaries of Charity. She establishes an orphanage in Cal-

Charlotte Gulick, cofounder of Camp Fire Girls.

cutta, India, and in 1979 is recognized for her work with the Nobel Peace Prize.

1910   Mother's Day First Celebrated. West Virginia becomes the first state to designate a formal Mother's Day. In 1907, two years after her mother dies, West Virginian Anna Jarvis holds a memorial service for her in Grafton, West Virginia, on the second Sunday in May, the day her mother had died. She is so touched by the remembrance that she launches a successful letter-writing campaign to urge legislators to create a formal holiday to honor mothers. By 1911, nearly all the states join West Virginia in celebrating Mother's Day. In 1915, President Woodrow Wilson signs the law making Mother's Day, the second Sunday in May, a national holiday. Ultimately, Jarvis is bitter over the commercialization of the holiday; by the time of her death in 1948, 43 nations declare a Mother's Day holiday.

1910 Union Organizer Fannie Sellins Murdered. Fannie Mooney Sellins (1872–1910) is a widow with four children when she is shot and killed by company men during a miners' strike. Secretary of a garment workers' local labor union, Sellins is also a successful union organizer, and she is loaned to the United Mine Workers of America for its organizing drives in West Virginia. As such, she is imprisoned on a charge of inciting a riot but is paroled by President Woodrow Wilson after serving six months of her sentence. Later, while trying to protect children from the sight of an assassinated miner during a miner's strike in Allegheny County, Pennsylvania, Sellins is bludgeoned, shot, and killed.

1910 Women Gain Suffrage in Washington. Suffrage is granted to women in Washington State, which becomes the 42nd state in 1889. The territorial government of Washington, prior to its becoming a state, provides women with the right to vote in 1883, but the suffrage act is found unconstitutional in 1887.

1910 Yoshioka Yayoi Establishes First Women's Medical School in Japan. Physician, educator, and public official Yoshioka Yayoi (1871–1959) founds Japan's first medical school for women, *Tokyo Joigakko* (later, *Tokyo Joshi Igaku Semmon Gakko*). Serving as the school's first president, she fights for its accreditation, which means that its graduates will automatically become licensed medical doctors; this status is granted in 1920. During her 50-year tenure as president, her school educates more than 7,000 women doctors. Yayoi believes in the "do and learn" principle; her students are even present to learn from her own experiences of childbirth and miscarriage. Much public criticism is leveled against women who engage in "grossly unladylike"

activities like dissecting cadavers, and Yayoi counters these criticisms through the school's paper, *Joikai*. Yayoi also operates a hospital, *Tokyo Shisei Byoin*, and is an active member of government and public organizations. In 1955, she receives the *Fujin Bunka Sho* (Women's Cultural Award), Japan's highest award for women.

1910 Australian Elizabeth Kenny Develops Treatment for Polio Victims. Australian Sister Elizabeth Kenny (1880–1951) invents a new treatment for victims of poliomyelitis. Despite having no training, Kenny is nursing outback (remote rural area) patients whose ailments are diagnosed by telegraph exchange with a doctor, Aeneas McDonnell. Kenny's new treatment for children with infantile paralysis (poliomyelitis) involves hot baths and passive exercise as opposed to the medically accepted patient immobilization. McDonnell's recommendation allows Kenny to enlist in the Australian Army Nursing Service, where she is promoted to the post of Sister. She retains the title when she resumes home nursing, and in 1932, Sister Kenny opens a backyard polio clinic in Townsville. Despite vigorous opposition from the medical profession, her success attracts Queensland government attention, and Kenny Clinics are opened in Townsville and Brisbane, followed by interstate clinics. In 1937, parents of her former patients fund a trip to demonstrate Kenny's method in England. British doctors are as shocked as their Australian counterparts, and on her return, she is condemned by a Royal Commission. Nevertheless, the Queensland government sends her to the Mayo Clinic in Rochester, New York, where Kenny convinces some health authorities that her treatment works. In America she runs courses for doctors and physiotherapists from many parts of the world, and the first Sister Kenny Institute is built in Minneapolis, Minnesota, in 1942. She accepts several honorary degrees, and in 1950, the U.S. Congress grants her free access to the

United States. Elizabeth Kenny retires to Toowoomba, where she dies in 1951. By then her treatment is accepted throughout the world.

1910 Australian Author Mary Grant Bruce Introduces the Billabong Series. Minnie (Mary) Grant Bruce (1878–1958) writes Australia's favorite children's books: the Billabong series. Bruce begins her career as a journalist and also writes patriotic verse but gives up the genre in 1903, the year she forms a women writers' club. From 1898 to 1913, Bruce survives the tough world of Melbourne journalism by writing prolifically about "every subject that I could handle—women's interests, baby welfare, education, agricultural matters, horse-racing, sea-fishing, sport in a dozen forms, theatrical matters—even politics." Success, however, comes after the London publication of one of her children's serials as *A Little Bush Maid* (1910). This grows into the 14-volume "Billabong" series of children's novels. In 1913, Mary Bruce goes to England, where she marries her cousin George Bruce. They remain in Europe until 1939 and only return to Australia when war threatens. George Bruce dies in Victoria in 1948, and Mary Bruce returns to England, where she dies ten years later. In her lifetime Bruce publishes some 40 books, mainly about an idealized Australia. Her talent lies in her ability to reflect contemporary attitudes, and her enormous popularity stems from her depiction of Australians as they wish to see themselves. Nevertheless, the opus is not entirely without depth. There are occasional flashes of feminism, and Bruce's book of legends, *The Stone Axe of Burkamukk* (1922), suggests that, for her time, she is unusually sensitive to Aboriginal culture.

1910 Frances Perkins Joins New York Consumer's League. Frances Perkins (1882–1965) becomes secretary of the New York Consumer's League and works to improve the conditions of undernourished children and sweatshop laborers. Her work with the Consumer's League and the Committee on Safety of the City of New York leads to several new laws protecting workers. She is a strong suffragist, marching in demonstrations and giving speeches on street corners, but throughout her life she opposes the Equal Rights Amendment.

MAY 23, 1910 Margaret Wise Brown, Author of Classic Children's Stories, Is Born. Margaret Wise Brown (1910–1952), often referred to as the laureate of the nursery, is born in Brooklyn, New York. She becomes one of the foremost writers for preschool children. As a student, and later colleague, of Lucy Sprague Mitchell at the Bank Street School, Brown develops her talents as a writer, editor, and collaborator. Influenced by the data collected by Mitchell and her observations at Bank Street, she designs stories that touch on child-like concepts and interests. In 1942 Brown seems to break with Mitchell over the relationship between fantasy and reality in a child's awareness. Brown possesses a flamboyant and seemingly unflappable nature, hiding a sensitive and complex character. Her flights of fancy and eccentric ways are noted by her friends, but she always remains a very private person. She lives through a self-destructive relationship with Michael Strange, the powerful, eccentric, and glamorous former wife of John Barrymore. Leonard Weisgard's illustrations for *Little Island* (1947) win the Caldecott Medal but Brown writes this book under the name of Golden MacDonald. She writes under several pseudonyms, due to both her prolific writing and her humorous attitude towards having a series of differing persona. She is the author of *The Runaway Bunny* (1942) and *Little Fur Family* (1946). In the telling so sparsely of the child's ritual of saying goodnight in *Goodnight Moon* (1947), Brown creates an enduring book. *The Dead Bird* (1958) is one of the earliest and finest examples of a child's encounter with death since the nineteenth century grief-ridden stories. Many of her books are not well-received by reviewers and librarians, who perhaps dismiss her work because it is so simple and unpretentious. However, Brown captures childlike rituals and rites of passage in these books, which remain popular with both children and parents.

DECEMBER 3, 1910 Australian Freda du Faur, First Woman to Climb Mount Cook. Australian mountaineer Emmeline Freda du Faur (1882–1935) becomes the first woman to climb Mount Cook, New Zealand's highest peak. Du Faur is born and educated in Sydney, Australia, where much of her childhood leisure time is devoted to rock climbing in the Ku-ring-gai Chase National Park. During a visit to New Zealand in 1906 she is captivated by the sight of Mount Cook and resolves to be a mountaineer. Her decision is scandalous. She can undertake the necessary physical preparation at the Dupain Institute in Sydney under the supervision of her intimate friend Muriel Cadogan; that is thoroughly acceptable. The scandal arises first because her intended mountain guide is a man, and second because it is understood that mountaineers wear trousers. These difficulties are overcome when du Faur hires a porter to act as chaperone and agrees to undertake all her expeditions in a skirt. The feat is accomplished in the then-record time of six hours. During the next three seasons she climbs many New Zealand mountains. Her achievements include the first ascents of Mount Chudleigh (1911); Mounts Du Faur (named for her), Nazomi, and Dampier (1912); and Mounts Pibrac and Cadogan (both named by her) (1913). On January 4, 1913, she achieves her greatest climb: the first grand traverse of the three peaks of Mount Cook.

1911 Publication of Children's Classic *The Secret Garden*. Frances Eliza Hodgson Burnett (1849–1924) publishes *The Secret Garden*, one of the works for which she is famous. The book is made into a Broadway musical, film, video, and CD-ROM production. Burnett also publishes *A Little Princess* (1905) and *Little Lord Fauntleroy* (1886).

1911 Birth of American Actress Jean Harlow. Actress Jean Harlow (1911–1937), a Hollywood legend as the shapely, wise-cracking, platinum blonde, is born in Kansas City, Missouri. At 16, she runs away from home and marries. On her honeymoon in California, she decides to stay, and her parents move to be near her. While visiting a friend at Fox studios, Harlow is spotted by an executive who sends her to a casting director. She is first placed in two-reeler Hal Roach comedies. After her introduction to Howard Hughes, Harlow receives the leading role in his 1930 film, *Hell's Angels*, and the craze for platinum blondes begins. Critics and audiences alike rave at the petite, shapely, and wise-cracking blonde "bombshell" who combines earthy vulgarity and ribald comedy with glorious beauty. During her seven years on screen, Harlow stars in such popular films as *The Public Enemy* (1931), *Platinum Blonde* (1931), *Red-Headed Woman* (1932), *Blond Bombshell* (1933), *Dinner at Eight* (1933), and *China Seas* (1935). She plays opposite such leading men as Clark Gable, James Cagney, Spencer Tracy, Cary Grant, and Lionel Barrymore.

Harlow's private life is marred by tragedy. From the age of 19, she supports her mother and stepfather, and she has three unsuccessful marriages. She is eager to marry a man who loves her for her mind, not her body, but she cannot escape her screen image. While filming *Saratoga*, Harlow falls fatally ill. Her mother, a Christian Scientist, refuses to have her daughter removed to a hospital until her condition advances beyond salvation. In 1937, at the age of 26, Jean Harlow dies of a cerebral edema.

1911 Campaign Results in First Minimum Wage Law for Women. Elizabeth Glendower Evans (1856–1937) works with Florence Kelley and heads up the campaign in

Massachusetts that results in the first minimum wage law for women passed in the United States. Evans is an active member of the Women's Trade Union League.

1911   Marie Curie Awarded Second Nobel Prize. Nobel Prize winner Marie Curie (1867–1934) becomes the first person to win two Nobel Prizes when she is awarded the prize for chemistry, an honor she earns for the isolation of pure radium. She shares her prior Nobel Prize in physics, awarded in 1903, with her husband and a colleague.

1911   Women Gain the Vote in California. Suffrage is granted to women in California, which becomes the 31st state in 1850.

1911   *Seito*, Japan's First Feminist Publication. *Seito* (*Bluestocking*), Japan's first feminist publication, is published from 1911 to 1916 by *Seitosha* (Bluestocking Society), an organization of upper-middle-class, college-educated women who initially seek to publish women's literature. The first editor, Hiratsuka Raicho (1886-1971), publishes the literature of Japan's foremost feminist writers. Increasingly, both the magazine and the organization shift their focus to women's social concerns. Under the editorship of Ito Noe, the magazine challenges the family system and raises concerns about such issues as prostitution.

1911   Australian Suffragist Vida Goldstein Visits England. At the invitation of the Women's Social and Political Union in England, Australian suffragist Vida Jane Mary Goldstein (1869–1949) visits England, where her speeches draw huge crowds.

1911   Lois Weber, Early Silent Film Director. American film director Lois Weber (1881-1939) works first in New York City and then in Hollywood, California, making her career in silent films directing such stars as Mildred Harris, Billie Dove, and Anna Pavlova. In 1917, she opens her own studio, Lois Weber

Productions. Her work spans the period of early cinema, beginning in 1911. She makes her last film, *White Heat*, in 1934.

MARCH 25, 1911   Triangle Shirtwaist Company Fire. Fire breaks out on the eighth floor of the Triangle Shirtwaist Company in New York City, causing one of the worst industrial accidents of the time. Of the 500 workers crowded into the top three floors, 146 of them, mostly women and children, jump to their deaths, burn to death, or suffocate. Several unsafe conditions contribute to the deaths. Some of the doors are locked to prevent access by union organizers; the fire escapes break under the weight of workers trying to escape; other doors open inwards; fire company ladders only reach to the sixth floor. One year earlier, workers at the Triangle Company are engaged as part of the "Uprising of the 20,000." Two of their demands regard the locked doors and the inadequate fire escapes. Unfortunately, they are not successful in their strike and the Triangle Company refuses to listen to their demands. The appalling disaster galvanizes many women who struggle to improve factory conditions for working women, including Frances Perkins, who becomes Franklin D. Roosevelt's Secretary of Labor; Pauline Newman, an early organizer for the International Ladies Garment Workers' Union; and Leonora O'Reilly, a life-long union activist who is instrumental in passing the first factory inspection law.

MARCH 29, 1911   Passage of Japan's Factory Law of 1911. The Factory Law of 1911, the first Japanese legislation to protect laborers in private industry, establishes a minimum age of 12 for child labor; limits working hours to 12 per day; prohibits night labor for women and children under 16; and establishes guidelines for the compensation of workers injured in accidents. The target of the law is textile manufacturers, who employ 84 percent of women industrial workers. Public outrage is directed against the long hours of women textile workers and working conditions in which tuberculosis frequently develops. Provisions of the legislation are not enforced until 1916, and the ban on night labor and the maximum of a 12-hour work day are not enforced until 1926. Numerous loopholes in the legislation enable factory owners to ignore the law.

1912   Anna Akhmatova, Greatest Russian Woman Poet. Considered the greatest woman poet in Russian literature, Anna Andreyevna Gorenko (1889–1966), who later writes under the pseudonym of Anna Akhmatova, publishes her first poems. In 1910 she marries a fellow poet, Nickolay Gumilyou, by whom she ha a son named Lev, but whom she divorces in 1918. Her numerous poems, published between 1912 and 1923, bring her fame for her honest portrayal of intense human emotions and clarity of expression. Anna Akhmatova is antagonistic toward the Bolshevik regime, which takes over Russia in 1917. Official Soviet critics denounce her poetry, which is only rarely published in Russia after 1923 until the 1960s. Because her son spends years in Siberian prisons after World War II, she knows the anguish caused by totalitarian dictators and expresses this anguish in her verse. After Stalin's death in 1954, the poet and her work are gradually rehabilitated in the Soviet Union. By the time of Akhmatova's death in 1966, she is widely hailed as the greatest woman poet in Russian literature.

1912   French Designer Madeleine Vionnet Opens Fashion House. Madeleine Vionnet (1876–1975) opens her own fashion house and, with the exception of the period of World War I (1914–19), during which she closes her doors, she continues to work under her own name for another 20 years. Her designs, boldly introduced in 1907 to be worn without corsets, are produced from fabric cut diagonally across the grain, that is, on the bias. Fabric cut this way drapes the body, emphasizing the body's natural curves. Vionnet's concern for the liberation of the female body

seems to be paired with a feminist concern for the welfare of working women. In her own atelier she provides her employees with healthful working conditions and generous salaries and benefits.

1912   "Unsinkable Molly Brown" Survives *Titanic* Disaster. Denver socialite Margaret Brown (1867–1932) survives the sinking of the *Titanic* after it strikes an iceberg. Born in Hannibal, Missouri, she marries James Brown, owner of a mine in Colorado. He strikes gold and builds a fabulously extravagant mansion in Denver. Margaret Brown is never accepted by Denver society, although she tries to woo them with lavish parties. She gets her nickname, "Unsinkable Molly Brown," because she is among the 700 survivors of the 2,200 passengers aboard the *Titanic* when it sinks in 1912. A version of her life's story survives in a musical play first staged in 1960 and adapted into a movie, released in 1964.

1912   Suffrage Granted to Women in Oregon. Abigail Duniway (1838?–1915) is finally rewarded for the drive she begins in 1883 to gain the vote for Oregon women, when Oregon voters approve an amendment to the state constitution giving women the vote, five years before suffrage is granted nationwide.

1912   Strike Leader Josephine Casey Institutes "Prayer Pickets." Josephine Casey, an organizer for the Women's Trade Union League, institutes "prayer pickets" during the corset workers' strike in Kalamazoo, Michigan. Often described as one of the more colorful organizers in the International Ladies Garment Workers Union (ILGWU), Josephine Casey is also an active member of the WTUL. In 1912, Casey is sent by the ILGWU to Kalamazoo, Michigan, to lead the strike by corset workers. The strike is precipitated by the Kalamazoo Corset Company when it decides to rid itself of the

Daisy (Margaret) Gordon

union, fires 12 of the most active trade unionists, and refuses to renew its contract with Local 82. When 600 workers walk off their jobs, the company gets an injunction against picketing. Casey then institutes "prayer pickets" outside the company gates, asking workers to get down on their knees and pray. Her arrest garners the union considerable attention and publicity. Casey is also a member of the National Women's Party and frequently speaks out against protective legislation for working women.

1912 Daisy Gordon Is First American Girl Scout. The niece of Juliette Gordon Low, the founder of the American Girl Scouts, Daisy (Margaret) Gordon becomes the first Ameri-

can Girl Scout when she joins the organization in Savannah, Georgia. Technically, Daisy Gordon is a "Girl Guide," as female Scouts are called in England, until Low changes the American organization's name in 1915.

1912 Lillian Baylis Founds Old Vic Theater Company. Lillian Baylis (1874–1937) founds the Old Vic theater company in London, making it a principal center for the performance of Shakespeare's plays. Nineteen years later, in 1931, she founds the Sadler's Wells theater company, which specializes in opera and ballet.

1912 Kansas Women Gain the Vote. Suffrage is granted to women in Kansas.

1912 Suffrage Given to Arizona Women. Women in Arizona are granted the right to vote.

1912 Death of Sarah Decker. Sarah Decker (?–1912), a suffragist and social reformer, is the first president of the Women's Club of Denver, Colorado. In 1898, she is elected vice president of the General Federation of Women's Clubs. Decker serves as president for five years for the Colorado State Board of Charities and Corrections, and she becomes a member of the State Civil Service Commission, acting as the first woman ever to hold an office of this character.

1912 Yosano Akiko, Japanese Feminist, Participates in Written Debate over Motherhood. Yosano Akiko (1878–1942), an advocate for equal rights for women in Japan, participates in a written debate over motherhood in *Seito* magazine. She is a prolific writer who publishes more than 20 volumes of poetry and social commentary ranging from feminist tracts to essays criticizing Japan's foreign aggression. From 1912 to 1919, Akiko is a participant in the *bonsei hogo ronso* (debate over the protection and support of motherhood) that takes place in *Seito* magazine. A central question in the debate is the role that the government should have in determining women's roles and the extent to which the state should support women with children. The debate extends to other issues as well, including emancipating love and marriage from traditional morality, securing women's political rights, combining work and home life, raising women's consciousness, guaranteeing equal access to work and equal earnings, educating children, providing vocational education for women, and improving the lives of middle-aged and older women. Akiko, who is married and the mother of 11 children, advocates a feminism grounded in equal legal, educational, and social rights and responsibilities for women. She envisions a society in which husbands and wives take equal responsibility for their households and each individual receives an education that is practical and supportive of that individual's talents.

1912   Australian Mountaineer Freda du Faur Ascends New Zealand Peaks. Australian mountaineer Freda du Faur (1882–1935) makes the first ascents of three of New Zealand's peaks: Mount Du Faur (later named for her), Mount Nazomi, and Mount Dampier. The next year, she climbs Mounts Pibrac and Cadogan (both named by her).

1912   British Suffragist Emmeline Pankhurst Is Arrested. Emmeline Pankhurst (1857–1928), leader of the British suffrage movement, is arrested for her involvement in the Women's Social and Political Union (WSPU). Pankhurst founds the WSPU of Great Britain in 1903. At first, the WSPU engages in peaceful marches and persuasive tactics to encourage the British government to give women the power to vote. However, by 1909 Pankhurst and her allies are condoning militant measures to acquire women's suffrage. The WSPU begins a campaign of window-breaking and attacks on the meeting places of male politi-

cians. In 1912, Pankhurst is imprisoned and begins a hunger strike. She is quickly released and begins to campaign for women's suffrage again. In 1916, Parliament permits women over 30 to vote, and the age minimum is lowered to 21 in 1928.

1912   The British Women's Relay Swimming Team Wins Olympic Gold. The British women's swimming team is the first women's team ever to win an Olympic gold medal in the 4x100-meter freestyle relay event, in Stockholm, Sweden. This is the first year in which this event is open to women.

JANUARY 12, 1912   Bread and Roses Strike Begins. The Bread and Roses Strike of Lawrence, Massachusetts, gets its name from the workers' desire for something more than the poverty that comes from working in the textile mills. The strike begins when factory owners, who by law have to cut back the workers' hours, force the workers to also take a pay cut. Within days, 20,000 workers in this city of 90,000 are on strike. The strikers, who speak 45 different languages, overcome their language and "old world" political differences to demonstrate strong worker solidarity. One of the most effective strike strategies is the children's exodus from Lawrence to the homes of sympathizers in New York, Philadelphia, and Providence. When the police attack one of these groups, beating children and their striking parents as they try to board a train, it makes the national news. On March 12, 1912, 63 days after it starts, the strike is settled. Thanks to all of the publicity surrounding the police attack on the children, the strikers win an unprecedented ten percent pay hike, the right to overtime pay, and amnesty from arrest.

JANUARY 30, 1912   Pulitzer Prize-Winning American Historian Barbara Tuchman Is Born. Barbara Wertheim Tuchman (1912–), winner of two Pulitzer Prizes, is born in New York City. She receives her first Pulitzer in

British swim team at the International Swimming Hall of Fame in 1912.

1963 for *The Guns of August* (1962), which recounts the early days of World War I (1914–18). In 1972, Tuchman captures her second Pulitzer for *Stilwell and the American Experience in China, 1911–1945* (1971), a work on the career of the U.S. general Joseph W. Stilwell.

MARCH 12, 1912 Juliette Gordon Low Organizes First Girl Scout Troup. Juliette Gordon Low (1860–1927), founder of the Girl Scouts of the U.S.A., organizes the first American group of Girl Scouts in Savannah, Georgia.

APRIL 8, 1912 Birth of Norwegian Skater Sonja Henie. Sonja Henie (1912–1969), champion figure skater, is born in Oslo, Norway. From 1927 to 1940, she takes the figure skating world by storm. She wins ten world championships and six European titles from 1931 to 1940 and wins the gold medal in the 1928, 1932, and 1936 Olympics. She is also acknowledged as the first woman to shorten her skating skirts. She appears in 11 films from 1938 to 1960. In 1943, she stars in the Hollywood film *Wintertime*. Sonja Henie dies on October 12, 1969, in Los Angeles, California.

Juliette Gordon Low, left, with the first group of U.S. Girl Scouts in Savannah, Georgia.

MAY 3, 1912   Author May Sarton Is Born. May Sarton (1912–), poet and novelist, is born in Wondelgem, Belgium.

AUGUST 1, 1912   First Workers' Organization Founded in Japan. The *Yuaikai*, Japan's first workers' organization, is established. The principles with which the organization is founded include developing mutual aid through friendship and cooperation; improving workers' character, increasing their knowledge, and developing their skills; and improving workers' status. The organization does not advocate social reform, such as improving the status of women, apart from their status as workers. Women number fewer than five percent of the membership. In 1916, the Yuaikai begins publishing a magazine for women, *Yuai Fujin* (*The Friendly Lady*), but insufficient support terminates its publication within a year.

1913   Agnes Nestor, First Woman President of International Union. Agnes Nestor (1880–1948) is the first woman to be elected to the position of president of an international union when she becomes president of the International Ladies' Garment Workers' Union (ILGWU). In 1907, she is the first woman to preside over an American Federation of Labor convention. In 1906, Nestor is elected president of the Chicago Women's Trade Union League, a position she holds until her death in 1948. Nestor has the reputation of being a tireless worker, an expert administrator, and a good lobbyist.

1913   Leavitt System for Classifying Stars Becomes Standard. The International Committee on Photographic Magnitudes votes to adopt Henrietta Swan Leavitt's system for their Astrographic Map of the Sky. Leavitt (1868–1921), working at the Harvard Observatory, develops a system that measures the relationship between the brightness of a star and the length of its period of pulsation. Later astronomers use this system to measure the distance between the earth and the stars.

1913   Kewpie Doll Makes Rose O'Neill a Millionaire. Rose O'Neill invents and patents the Kewpie doll. The name, derived from "Cupid," is an appropriate diminutive for the popular toy, which earns its creator more than a million dollars.

1913   American Poet Amy Lowell Champions Modernist Poetry. Amy Lowell (1874–1925), an American poet from New England, is the first woman to lecture on modernist verse in the United States, in Boston. Excited by the "Imagist" poems by H.D. (Hilda Doolittle), Richard Aldington, and Ezra Pound, she begins to correspond with these young poets, who are writing their first modernist works in England. Lowell, with Harriet Monroe of *Poetry* who publishes their work in Chicago, are the American champions of what becomes the modernist movement in literature.

1913   Anna Pavlova Introduces Western Dance in Eastern Countries. Anna Pavlova (1882–1931), the famous Russian ballerina, begins touring internationally, introducing western dance to countries such as Egypt, Japan, China, and India. Her tours include performances in outlying areas as well as in capital cities in order to encourage the reputation and appreciation of classical ballet.

1913   Women in Alaska Gain Vote. Suffrage is granted to women in the territory of Alaska.

1913   Japanese Author Tamura Toshiko Writes Naturalistic Fiction. Tamura Toshiko (1884–1945) becomes a best-selling author of naturalistic fiction that reflects a new women's consciousness in twentieth-century Japan. Her work includes the novels *Miira no kuchibeni* (1913; *Lipstick on a Mummy*), *Onna sakusha* (1913; *Woman Writer*), and *Yamamichi* (1938; *Mountain Road*). In 1938, Toshiko goes to Shanghai, where she edits a women's literary magazine.

1913   Full Suffrage for Norwegian Women. Women gain full suffrage rights in Norway.

JANUARY 4, 1913   Australian Mountaineer Freda du Faur Makes First Grand Traverse of Mount Cook. Australian mountaineer Freda du Faur (1882–1935) achieves her greatest climb when she makes the first grand traverse of the three peaks of Mount Cook. From 1914 du Faur and her companion, Muriel Cadogan, live in England, where du Faur publishes *The Conquest of Mount Cook and Other Climbs* in 1915. She returns to Australia after Cadogan's death in 1929 and dies (suicide) in Sydney in 1935.

DECEMBER 27, 1913   Canadian Author Elizabeth Smart Is Born. Elizabeth Smart, one of Canada's most significant woman authors (1913–1986), is born in Ottawa, Ontario. She begins her writing career at the *Ottawa Journal*, writing society news. During the 1930s, Smart travels extensively and meets George Barker, the British poet, who later becomes the father of her four children. During World War II, she works at the British embassy in Washington, D.C. In 1943 she moves to England, where she works to support herself and her family for the next 20 years by writing advertising copy. She later becomes the literary editor for *Vogue* magazine and *House and Garden*. Smart's first work, *By Grand Central Station, I Sat Down and Wept* (1945), immediately establishes her cult following and is critically hailed as a "masterpiece of poetic prose and a homage to love." Known for its intensity of emotion and unique style, *By Grand Central Station* establishes Smart's popularity as a writer, and this work is republished several times. In 1977, following 32 years of silence, two new works appear: *A Bonus*, a collection of poems; and *The Assumptions of Rogues and Rascals*, a prose poem that also serves as a continuation and commentary on her earlier work. In 1984, *In the Meantime* further establishes her literary reputation.

1914   Mock Parliament Assists Cause of Woman Suffrage in Canada. A Mock Parliament is staged at the Regina Walker Theatre in Winnipeg, Manitoba, Canada, by the Manitoba Political Equality League. Presented the day after Manitoba Premier Roblin rejects the suffrage petition of a women's delegation to the Legislative Assembly, the play is entitled, "How the Vote Was Not Won!" This satire exposes the sanctimonious and contradictory arguments presented by male politicians in order to deny female suffrage. When the curtain rises, the audience views women sitting at desks posing as legislators receiving a delegation of vote-seeking men, who are pushing a wheelbarrow full of petitions. "The Premier" (Nellie McClung) congratulates the men on their appearance but tells them that "man is just made for something better and higher than voting." The crowd roars with recognition at the parody of the premier. This staged performance serves as an important vehicle to shore up public support for women's suffrage and helps to pave the way for the achievement of the vote in 1918.

1914   Kate Gleason, First Woman Member of American Society of Mechanical Engineers. Engineer Kate Gleason (1865–1933) becomes the first woman elected to full membership in the American Society of Mechanical Engineers (ASME). Gleason later becomes the first woman president of a national bank (which becomes a leader in the construction of low-cost housing in the United States) and is elected to the American Society of Civil Engineers in 1927.

1914   Selma Lagerlöf Becomes Member of Swedish Academy. Selma Lagerlöf (1858–1940) is the first woman to become a member of the Swedish Academy. In 1909, she becomes the first woman to receive the Nobel Prize for Literature, in her native Stockholm, Sweden.

1914   Women in Nevada Win Vote. Suffrage is granted to women in Nevada.

1914   Suffrage Granted to Montana Women. Women in Montana gain the right to vote.

1914   Margaret Sanger Establishes Controversial Newsletter on Contraception. Birth control advocate Margaret Sanger (1883–1966) begins a monthly newsletter in the United States, *The Woman Rebel*. The newsletter, setting forth her ideas about the necessity of contraception and birth control, is banned as obscene literature, and Sanger flees the country to avoid being imprisoned. Eventually the charges are dropped, and in 1916 Sanger is able to return to the United States.

1914   Ziegfeld Chorus Girl Marion Davies Meets Publisher William Randolph Hearst. Marion Davies (1897–1961), a convent girl who goes on to perform in the chorus line of the Ziegfeld Follies, is only 17 years old when she attracts the attention of the wealthy and powerful newspaper publisher William Randolph Hearst. He dedicates a sum estimated at seven million dollars to making Davies a star in motion pictures. She is a talented comedienne, yet Hearst forces her into costume dramas which do not suit her. Davies gains significant fame as a hostess at the lavish California estate San Simeon, which Hearst builds for her. Hearst cannot marry her (his first wife refuses to release him), but he lavishes gifts on Davies and aggressively promotes her career. One film, *Show People* (1928), is widely praised as her best performance, but most are unsuccessful. Hearst suffers financial losses in the 1930s which are alleviated by Davies' generosity in selling her property to help him. Orson Welles draws on this well-known romance to create his characters Charles Foster Kane and his wife Susan in his famous film *Citizen Kane* in 1941, and Hearst retaliates by attempting to ruin Welles and suppress the film. After Hearst dies in 1951, Marion Davies, now a wealthy businesswoman, retires from films and marries. She is respected in the Hollywood community as a leading citizen, and her films enjoy a modest critical revival.

JUNE 26, 1914 Birth of Mildred "Babe" Zaharias, American Athlete. Mildred Ella Didrikson Zaharias (1914–1956), all-around athlete and cofounder of the Ladies Professional Golf Association, is born. Nicknamed "Babe," she becomes a star athlete of her high school basketball team, enters nine of the ten track and field events at American Athletic Union (AAU) championships in 1931 and finishes first in seven, and the following year, enters eight events and finishes first in five. These successes place Zaharias on the U.S. track and field team for the 1932 Summer Olympic Games in Los Angeles, California. She wins two gold medals for javelin throw and 80-meter hurdles, and one silver medal in the three events she enters. In 1935, Zaharias takes up golf and becomes one of the most prolific golfers in the sport. Between 1946 and 1948 she wins 17 golf tournaments. Zaharias turns professional in 1948, and the following year, with husband George Zaharias, Fred Corcoran, and Patty Berg, she founds the Ladies Professional Golf Association. "Babe" Zaharias dies on September 27, 1956.

1 9 1 5 – 1 9 1 9

1915 Icelandic Women Gain Suffrage. Icelandic women age 40 and older win the right to vote.

1915 Mother's Day Becomes U.S. Holiday. U.S. President Woodrow Wilson signs the law making Mother's Day, the second Sunday in May, a national holiday. The idea for the holiday is born in 1907, when West Virginian Anna Jarvis (?–1948) holds a memorial service for her mother in Grafton, West Virginia, on the second Sunday in May, the day her mother had died. Jarvis is so touched by the remembrance that she launches a successful letter-writing campaign to urge legislators to create a formal holiday to honor mothers. By 1911, nearly all the states join West Virginia in celebrating Mother's Day.

1915 Author and Illustrator Tasha Tudor Is Born. Tasha Tudor (1915–), an author who illustrates her own works, is born. Her first work, *Pumpkin Moonshine,* is published in 1938. Tudor's illustrated *Mother Goose* appears in 1945.

1915 Birth of Charlotte Zolotow, Author and Editor. Charlotte Zolotow (1915–), children's author and editor, is born. Among her most famous works are *Indian, Indian* (1952), *Mr. Rabbit and the Lovely Present* (1962), and *William's Doll* (1972).

1915 Suffragists March in New York. Members of the National American Woman Suffrage Association, dressed in white and carrying placards with the names of the states they represent, march in support of voting rights for women.

1915 Madame Sul-Te-Wan, One of First African Americans Awarded Contract for Screen Acting. Madame Sul-Te-Wan (1873–1959), also known as Nellie Conley, becomes one of the first African American actresses to receive a motion picture contract as a Hollywood actress. Sul-Te-Wan (she adopts her stage name from her father, Silas Crawford Wan, a Hindu minister) vigorously pursues her acting career by approaching white filmmaker D. W. Griffith for a role in *The Clansman* (1915). Griffith, impressed with Sul-Te-Wan's talent, hires her to appear in this pro-

National American Woman Suffrage Association members from various states march in New York City in support of women's suffrage.

duction but when the film is released, because of its inflammatory portrayal of African Americans, Sul-Te-Wan is held responsible for the protests that erupt and is dismissed from the studio. Vindicating herself of such charges, Sul-Te-Wan is reinstated and manages to land roles in several silent pictures such as *Up From the Depths* (1915), *Intolerance* (1916), *Hoodoo Ann* (1916), *Children Pay* (1916), and *Stage Struck* (1917).

Sul-Te-Wan becomes one of the few actresses, black or white, who makes the transition from the silent to the sound era of filmmaking. Although cast on the screen as a maid in the early phase of her career, she is later raised in status to the role of a voodoo woman in films such as *Heaven on Earth* (1931), *Black Moon* (1934), and *Maid of Salem* (1937).

Referred to as the "grand old lady" of the screen, Sul-Te-Wan continues to act long after most actresses reach their peak. Although Sul-Te-Wan is seldom given screen credit, her career of over 40 years is considered an illustrious one. Sul-Te-Wan dies in 1959.

1915 *Cercles des Fermières* **Unite and Organize Quebecois Rural Women.** The *Cercles des Fermières* (Farm Women Circles) are formed in Chicoutimi, Quebec, reflecting both the common interests of civil and religious authorities regarding the exodus from the land as well as the countryside domestic economy in Quebecois life. Spearheaded by agronomists with the Ministry of Agriculture, the *Cercles des Fermières* are intended to instill in women a desire to stay at home and use homemaking skills to "keep our sons on the land and to stop our daughters from deserting the local parish." These organizations grow quickly, as they speak to the concerns of women absorbed by the responsibilities of domestic and rural work at a time when women have little voice in the governmental or social politics of Quebec. Although they are encouraged by many sectors of society and reinforce a "separate spheres" philosophy, the *Cercles des Fermières* provide opportunities for organization and self-development, open new economic ventures, and validate farm women's work while attempting to professionalize it. The ability to work together towards a common objective lays the groundwork for future women's organizations in Quebec.

1915   Publication of Lillian Gilbreth's *The Psychology of Management*. American industrial engineer Lillian Moller Gilbreth (1878–1972) obtains her Ph.D. in psychology from Brown University and publishes *The Psychology of Management*, a classic in the history of engineering thought and a foundation of modern scientific management theory. The story of her life with her husband and business partner Frank Bunker Gilbreth, with whom she raises 12 children, is dramatized in the film *Cheaper by the Dozen*.

1915   Theda Bara Becomes Seductress "Vamp" of Silent Film Era. Theda Bara (1890–1955) plays a vampire in *A Fool There Was*, telling her man, "Kiss me, my fool,"—and he does. Bara represents a new female film character—the "Vamp." With her waist-length dark hair and darkly kohled eyes, she becomes the first sex goddess of American film. However, Bara's image inspires the damaging myth that women are "femmes fatales" and sexual predators.

1915   Lillian Gish Featured in First Modern Film. Lillian Gish (1896–1993) appears in the first modern feature motion picture, *Birth of a Nation*, by filmmaker D. W. Griffith.

1915   Ruth St. Denis Cofounds First Major American Dance School. Ruth St. Denis (1879–1968) cofounds Denishawn, a dance school in Los Angeles, California, with her husband, Ted Shawn. It is the first major dance school in the United States, and Martha Graham is one of St. Denis' pupils. Denishawn closes in 1932, but St. Denis continues to choreograph and perform until 1955.

1915   Actress Edna Purviance Stars in Chaplin's *The Tramp*. American silent film star Edna Purviance (1894–1958) appears in *The Tramp*. A one-time secretary from San Francisco, Purviance is groomed for stardom by her lover, Charlie Chaplin. Her presence is ubiquitous in Chaplin's early Hollywood films, especially *The Tramp*, released in 1915. She also memorably stars in *A Woman of Paris*, directed by Chaplin in 1923. Her career fades and their relationship ends, but Chaplin keeps her on salary and Purviance appears as an extra in his films.

1915   Women in Denmark Win the Vote. Denmark's constitution is amended to extend suffrage to most women over age 25.

MARCH 11, 1915   Birth of Elinor Marshall Glenn, American Trade Unionist. Elinor Marshall Glenn (1915–), who attains a number of firsts for women and trade unionists in the Los Angeles, California, area, is born. Glenn comes from a union and activist background. Her father is a building tradesman and union painter, and her mother is a suffragette. Glenn attends both New York University and Southwestern Law School. After graduation and as a teacher, she organizes for the American Federation of Teachers in New York. After World War II she serves on the negotiating committee for the State, County, and Municipal Workers of the Congress of Industrial Organizations in Los Angeles. From 1946 to 1953 she is an organizer of the Los Angeles County hospital workers for the United Public Workers. She becomes general manager of the Service Employees International Union (SEIU) Local 434 and continues organizing municipal workers. In 1966 she is part of the historic Los Angeles hospital workers' strike, which leads to the first collective bargaining law for public workers in Los Angeles; she negotiates the first child care provision in a contract with Los Angeles County. In 1970, she negotiates the first contract for public workers in Los Angeles County. Glenn is also the first woman elected to the SEIU international executive board. In 1974, she is elected West Coast vice president of the Coalition of Labor Union Women. Her husband, Haskell Glenn, is also a union organizer.

MAY 17, 1915   American Unionist Olga Madar Is Born. Olga Madar (1915–1996), the first president of the Coalition of Labor Union Women and the first woman elected to the executive board of the United Automobile Workers Union, is born. In 1933, Madar is hired by Chrysler Corporation in Detroit, where she works each summer while attending Eastern Michigan University, earning a B.S. degree in 1938. After working as a therapist and then as a teacher, she joins the Recreation Department of the International United Auto, Aerospace, and Agricultural Implement Workers of America (UAW) in 1944, becoming director of the department three years later. Madar is first elected to the UAW's executive board in 1966, the first woman to reach that position. She is reelected in 1968. She becomes director of the Technical, Office, and Professional Workers Service Department in 1966 and is selected by UAW president Walter Reuther to head the newly established Department of Consumer Affairs of the UAW. Madar is elected vice president of the union in 1970 and 1972. In 1974 she is elected president of the new organization, the Coalition of Labor Union Women. Madar is also a member of the Advisory Committee on Women of the U.S. Department of Labor and a member of the National Women's Political Caucus.

JULY 7, 1915   Birth of Margaret Walker, African American Author. Writer of the best seller *Jubilee*, African American author and poet Margaret Abigail Walker (1915–) is born in Birmingham, Alabama. She moves to New Orleans at age ten.

Walker's first poem is published in 1934 in *Crisis* magazine. At the age of 19, she graduates from Northwestern University with a degree in English. While with the Federal Writers' Project in Chicago, she helps Richard Wright research and edit his masterpiece, *Native Son,* but she receives no credit.

While working on a master's degree at the University of Iowa, Walker finishes her first book of poetry, *For My People* (1942). She wins the Yale Series of Young Poets Award for this work, becoming the first African American to receive the award. In 1943, she marries Firnist James Alexander and they have four children. Walker teaches English at West Virginia State University, Livingstone College, and Jackson State University. She completes her Ph.D. in 1965 at the University of Iowa.

In 1966 Walker publishes *Jubilee,* the story of her family as told to her by her grandmother when Walker was a child. *Jubilee* sells millions of copies and has never been out of print. In 1970 she publishes *Prophets for a New Day,* poetry about the civil rights movement. In 1989 she publishes *This Is My Century: New and Collected Poems,* and in 1990, *How I Wrote Jubilee and Other Essays.*

AUGUST 29, 1915   Birth of Swedish Actress Ingrid Bergman. Actress Ingrid Bergman (1915–1982), a leading lady of Hollywood until her scandalous fall from grace, is born in Stockholm, Sweden. An only child, Bergman is only two when her mother dies, and her father dies ten years later. Raised by an elderly uncle, Bergman is shy and lonely, and she retreats to her fantasy world of make-believe.

Despite her uncle's protests, she is determined to be an actress, and at 18 wins a scholarship to the Royal Dramatic Theatre School. In 1934 she has a small role in a Swedish film and a year later is voted the most promising newcomer on the Swedish screen. Between 1934 and 1939, she makes ten Swedish films. In 1937 she marries Peter Lindstrom, a dentist, who encourages but also controls her acting career. In 1939 Hollywood executives decide to remake her Swedish film *Intermezzo* with Bergman in the English-speaking version. She appears in such American films as *Adam Had Four Sons* (1940); *Notorious* (1940); *Casablanca* (1942); *For Whom the Bell Tolls* (1943); *Gaslight,* for which she wins the 1944 Academy Award; *Spellbound* (1945); and *Joan of Arc* (1948).

Bergman's love affair with the Italian director Roberto Rossellini and the birth of an illegitimate son scandalize the American public. Bergman is called an adulterous and wicked woman and is even denounced on the floor of Congress. Sanctions are demanded against her future films. Bergman is certainly not the first star to have an extramarital affair, but Hollywood and the country become morally conservative and conformist in the post-World War II period. Bergman divorces Lindstrom, remains in Rome, and marries Rossellini. She stars in a series of Rossellini films, none of them critical or financial successes. She makes her Hollywood comeback in 1956, winning her second Academy Award for *Anastasia*. Bergman divorces Rossellini in 1957 and a year later marries millionaire Lars Schmidt. Before her death from cancer on her 67th birthday, Bergman appears in 46 films, 11 stage plays, and five television dramas.

1916   Hollywood Star Betty Grable Is Born. Actress Betty Grable (1916–1973), favorite "pin-up girl" among American soldiers during World War II, is born Ruth Elizabeth Grable in St. Louis, Missouri. Her mother neglects her own acting career for marriage and moth-

erhood, and she pushes Grable into show business. Grable's first job is as a chorus girl in the early sound musicals. Using the name "Frances Dean," she also appears in several short subjects for RKO and Educational Films. As Betty Grable, she appears in a series of "College Co-ed" movies in which she sings and dances. In 1937 she weds the former child actor Jackie Coogan, and the newlyweds star in *College Swing* (1938). They are divorced in 1940. Grable finally lands the role of leading lady in *Down Argentine Way* in 1940, followed by *Moon Over Miami* (1941) and *A Yank in the RAF* (1941).

Grable's popularity soars during World War II. In 1942, she is ranked number eight of the top ten money-making stars. From 1943 until 1951 she ranks number one. Known as "the girl with the million-dollar legs," Grable becomes a favorite "pin-up" among American soldiers. Almost two million copies of her photo in her white bathing suit, looking over her shoulder, are sent out to servicemen. Grable's wartime films include the dance musicals *Sweet Rosie O'Grady* (1943) and *Pin-Up Girl* (1944). In 1943, she marries big band leader Harry James, but the couple divorces in 1964.

With her blond hair and blue eyes, Betty Grable exhibits a wholesome image of "the girl next door." Her post-war films include *The Shocking Miss Pilgrim* (1947), *Mother Wore Tights* (1947), and *How to Marry a Millionaire* (1953). She is not interested in dramatic acting, insisting that she is "strictly a song-and-dance girl." Her popularity steadily declines during the early 1950s, and she begins to perform in nightclubs and on television. Betty Grable's famous leg prints are preserved in cement at Grauman's Chinese Theater in Hollywood.

1916   Molly Wexler Organizes ILGWU Local. Molly Wexler (1896?–?) organizes Local 100 of the International Ladies' Garment Workers' Union (ILGWU) and is elected the first chairlady, as the office is referred to at the time.

1916 Labor Organizer Stella Nowicki Is Born. Stella Nowicki (1916–), a rank and file organizer in the meat packing industry, is born. She leaves home at the age of 17 because of the Great Depression and goes to Chicago, where she spends the next 12 years in the meat packing industry. She becomes a member of the Packinghouse Workers Organizing Committee, and in 1934 she is blacklisted because of her participation in a sit-down strike over unsafe working conditions. Nowicki continues to work in various meat packing jobs under an assumed name. In 1936, she is awarded a scholarship and studies for six weeks at the School for Workers in Industry at the University of Wisconsin in Madison. After completing her studies, she returns to work at Swift Company, where she helps compile *Swift Flashes*, a Congress of Industrial Organizations newsletter. While at Swift, she becomes the education director for Packinghouse District #1 and serves as a member of the grievance committee and the nationwide negotiating team. Nowicki is a committed socialist and a member of the Young Communist League of the Communist Party. In her later years Nowicki becomes active in the women's movement in Gary, Indiana.

1916 Fannia Mary Cohn, First Woman Vice President of Major International Union. Fannia May Cohn (1888–1962) becomes the first woman to serve as a vice president of a major labor union when she is elected vice president of the International Ladies' Garment Workers' Union (ILGWU). Five years later, she founds the Workers Education Bureau of America and helps establish the Brookwood Labor College.

1916 Margaret Higgins Sanger Opens U.S. Birth Control Clinic. American nurse Margaret Sanger (1883–1966) opens one of the country's first birth control clinics in New York City. In 1921 she organizes the first American Birth Control Conference, also in New York City. Sanger devotes her life to educating women about birth control, and in 1953 she is the founder and first president of the International Planned Parenthood Federation.

1916 American Writer and Wit Dorothy Parker Joins *Vogue*. An American writer known for her caustic wit, Dorothy Parker (1893–1967) sells some of her poetry to *Vogue* magazine and also lands a position writing photo captions at the magazine. She writes poetry, short stories, and screenplays for films. In 1931, Parker writes the comic verse "Death and Taxes." She leaves her considerable estate to Martin Luther King, Jr. A self-styled eccentric throughout her life, Parker is an ardent supporter of the rights of the oppressed. She dies in 1967 in New York City.

APRIL 1916 Countess Markiewicz Supports Irish Nationalism During Easter Rebellion. Irish countess Constance Markiewicz (1868–1927) is a prominent supporter of the early twentieth-century Irish nationalist movement against British rule. As head of the Irishwomen's Council, she and many other women supply medical help, courier service, and food for the Irish troops during the Easter Rebellion of Easter Week, 1916. Trained as a sharpshooter, she is second in command at Stephen's Green in Dublin. She surrenders after the fight is lost by the end of the week. Markiewicz is sentenced to execution for her participation in the rebellion, but the British government commutes her sentence to life imprisonment because of her gender. She spends the last ten years of her life in jail or in hiding. Her sister is the poet and suffrage activist Eva Gore-Booth. Markiewicz's commitment to the cause of Irish home rule is inspired by visions of women's rights and their place in the new Irish republic.

JULY 1, 1916 Birth of Olivia deHavilland, British-born Hollywood Actress. Olivia deHavilland (1916-), genteel and accomplished actress in American films, is born in Tokyo, Japan, to British parents. They move Olivia and her sister Joan (Joan Fontaine, also an actress) to California. Young Olivia deHavilland is spotted by famous director Max Reinhardt and cast as Hermia in *A Midsummer Night's Dream*. Her early career as a leading lady is capped by her Oscar-nominated role as the saintly Melanie Wilkes in 1939's Civil War epic *Gone With the Wind*. The actress insists on better parts and willingly accepts suspensions rather than play roles she dislikes. The studio attempts to extend her contract because of those suspensions, but deHavilland takes Warner Brothers to court and wins a landmark victory that substantially reduces the Hollywood studios' power over their stars, limiting contracts to seven years inclusive of suspensions. A cerebral and talented performer, deHavilland draws critical praise for 1948's *The Snake Pit* and an adaptation of Henry James' *Washington Square*, *The Heiress*. She wins Best Actress Academy Awards in 1946 for *To Each His Own* and in 1949 for *The Heiress*. DeHavilland leaves Hollywood for France, where she still resides, and writes a memoir, *Every Frenchman Has One*. She is married to Pierre Galante, editor of *Paris Match,* and makes an occasional film. She is notably paired with Bette Davis in the cult favorite *Hush, Hush, Sweet Charlotte* in 1965.

1917 Germaine Tailleferre Performs with French Music Group *Les Six*. Germaine Tailleferre (1892-1984), a French composer trained at the Paris Conservatory, is the first and only female member of *Les Six*, a group of innovative French musicians which includes Honegger and Poulenc. Their first collective performance takes place in Paris in 1917 and includes Tailleferre's String Quartet. Known initially as *Les Nouveaux Jeunes*, the group

Emma Goldman, left, with Alexandra Kollontai at the Second International Communist Woman's Conference in Moscow in 1921.

acquires the name *Les Six Français*, or *Les Six*, through reviews in 1920.

1917 Emma Goldman Obstructs Selective Service Law. Lithuanian-born American anarchist and staunch pacifist Emma Goldman (1869–1940) is convicted of obstructing the selective service law, fined $10,000, and sentenced to two years in federal prison. Goldman is deported to the USSR in 1919, and publishes *My Disillusionment in Russia* in 1923 before returning to the United States in 1924. In 1931, she publishes her autobiography, *Living My Life*.

1917 Labor Activist Gertrude Barnum Joins U.S. Department of Labor. Labor union activist Gertrude Barnum (1866–1948) joins the U.S. Department of Labor as associate director of Investigative Services.

1917   Rosalie Slaughter Morton, First Woman Professor at Columbia's Medical School. Rosalie Slaughter Morton (1876–1968), an American physician, becomes a professor at the Medical School of Columbia University in New York City, the first woman to hold this title. She is also the first woman to serve as an officer of the American Medical Association. She performs active service as surgeon on the French front during World War I and receives nine decorations from the French, Serbian, and American governments.

1917   Dorothy Parker Cofounds Algonquin Round Table. Journalist, short-story writer, and wit Dorothy Parker (1893–1967) founds, with Robert Benchley and Robert Sherwood, the Algonquin Hotel Round Table luncheon group. The group meets for lunch at the Algonquin Hotel in New York City over many years, and its members are known for their wit and biting criticism.

1917   Suffrage Gained by New York Women. Suffrage is granted to women in New York.

1917   Arkansas Women Allowed to Vote in Primaries. Women are granted the right to vote in the primaries in Arkansas.

1917   Soviet Women Granted Suffrage. Soviet women gain the right to vote.

1917   YWCA Establishes Other Groups. The Young Women's Christian Association (YWCA) fosters the development of other groups to address issues outside its focus on the needs of women. YWCA is a key force in establishing the National Association of Travelers Aid Societies. Other organizations YWCA helps found include the National Federation of Business and Professional Women (1919), the American Council for Nationalities Service (1933), and the United Service Organizations (1941).

Gertrude L. Warren, early 4-H leader.

By the mid-1990s, the World YWCA has non-sectarian associations in more than ninety countries with world membership estimated at some five million (males can join as associate, but not full, members). It is the oldest and largest multiracial women's organization in the world.

1917   Loretta Walsh Enlists in U.S. Navy. Loretta Walsh (1898–?) is the first woman to enlist in the United States Navy. The Navy, short-staffed during the first months after the United States enters World War I, permits women to enlist, but only for duty on U.S. soil. Walsh becomes a yeoman in charge of recruiting for the Naval Coastal Defense Reserve.

1917   Gertrude L. Warren Joins U.S. Government Extension Service To Develop 4-H.

Carrie Chapman Catt, center in white, leads a women's suffrage parade in New York City in 1917.

Three years after the passage of the Smith-Lever Act authorizing the Federal Extension service, Gertrude L. Warren accepts an assignment with that agency in Washington, D.C. In this position, titled "In Charge, Organization of 4-H Club Work," Warren is charged with developing homemaking programs for girls. Her first assignment focuses on girls' canning projects in support of World War I (1914–17) efforts; following the war, she encourages broadening of girls' activities to including clothing, room improvement, foods, and other home economics projects. By the end of 1924, 4-H is recognized across the country, and the 4-H name and emblem are copyrighted, with the use controlled by an act of the U.S. Congress. Warren is instrumental in the establishment of many 4-H programs,

including the annual National 4-H Club Camp, the National 4-H Foundation (now the National 4-H Council), and the National 4-H Center in suburban Washington, D.C., where a building is named in her honor. Among the honors conferred on Warren is the U.S. Department of Agriculture's Superior Service Award (1949).

1917   Carrie Chapman Catt Leads Suffrage Parade. American suffragist Carrie Chapman Catt (1859–1947) leads a group of suffragists in a New York City parade. The march is intended to rally support for women's suffrage. Catt is president of the National American Woman Suffrage Association. The group, with members dressed in white, stages marches in cities and towns across the country in the drive to ratify the constitutional amendment to give women the vote.

FEBRUARY 19, 1917 **Birth of American Author Carson McCullers.** Lula Carson Smith McCullers (1917–1967), who writes novels and stories of female adolescence and rebellion against traditional gender expectations, is born in Columbus, Georgia. As a child, McCullers loves making up stories. She moves to New York City when she is 17 and works at odd jobs, saving money to study at Columbia and New York University. She publishes her first story, "Wunderkind," in 1936 at the age of 19. In 1937 she marries Reeves McCullers; their marriage is a troubled one. In 1940 Carson McCullers publishes *The Heart Is a Lonely Hunter*. Seemingly overnight, she becomes the literary darling of New York. She tries to separate from her husband and begins drinking heavily. In 1941, at age 25, she suffers the first of many cerebral strokes. Despite her illnesses, she continues to write, publishing *The Ballad of the Sad Cafe* (1943) and *The Member of the Wedding* (1946). She adapts *The Ballad of the Sad Cafe* for the Broadway stage. In 1948, distraught over her physical ailments, McCullers attempts suicide and is briefly hospitalized in a psychiatric clinic. In 1953, Reeves McCullers tries to persuade his wife to commit suicide with him, but instead she terminates their relationship. Reeves McCullers commits suicide alone later that year. Carson McCullers continues to publish plays, stories, novels, and children's verses. In 1962, she is confined to a wheelchair and undergoes a mastectomy. On September 29, 1967, she slips into a coma and dies from a massive brain hemorrhage.

MARCH 1917 **Tsarina Alexandra Institutes Policies Triggering the Russian Revolution.** Tsarina Alexandra (1872–1918) institutes policies that bring on the Russian Revolution of March 1917. The following year, she and her entire family are executed by the Bolsheviks. Alix, princess of Hesse-Darmstadt, is born in Germany. In 1894, she marries Tsar Nicholas II of Russia and takes the name of Alexandra. The tsarina, who gives birth to four daughters and a son, dominates her husband. Because their son Alexis suffers from hemophilia, Alexandra comes under the influence of a debauched "holy man" named Rasputin. Her dependence upon Rasputin, who claims to control Alexis' bleeding, is a public scandal. While Nicholas is at the front during World War I, Alexandra takes control of the Russian government in 1915. Her dismissal of competent ministers and appointment of Rasputin's henchmen leads to the collapse of the tsarist regime. In March 1917, the tsar is deposed by a provisional government. After the Bolsheviks take over Russia later that year, Nicholas, Alexandra, and their children are imprisoned. They are executed in July 1918.

APRIL 2, 1917 **Jeannette Rankin, First Woman to Join U.S. House of Representatives.** Elected in 1916 as a Republican from the state of Montana, suffragist and pacifist Jeannette Rankin (1880–1973) takes office as the first female member of the U.S. Congress. She serves as a congresswoman at large from 1917 to 1919 and leaves after one term. She is reelected to the U.S. House of Representatives in 1940, also for one term. During her service, she votes against U.S. participation in World War I (1914–19), and she is the only member of Congress to vote against entering World War II in 1942.

APRIL 5, 1917 **Some British Columbian Women Gain Provincial Vote.** Non-Native, non-Asian women in British Columbia, Canada, obtain the right to vote in provincial elections. British Columbian women begin organizing for the vote soon after the province joins the rest of the country in Confederation (1871). The agitations for woman suffrage apply, in this context, only to non-Native, non-Asian women, since Native and Asian women are excluded from suffrage by other acts of Parliament. Many attempts are made to introduce woman suffrage bills to the legislature during the last decades of the nineteenth century; all are unsuccessful. By the end of the nineteenth century, two women's organizations form that make woman suffrage key planks of their platforms: the Women's Christian Temperance Union and the Local Councils of Women (Victoria and Vancouver). It is not until the 1910s that the campaign for woman suffrage in British Columbia gains momentum. Women argue that their maternal influences should be felt in government as the state becomes increasingly involved in social reform. The reformed-minded Liberal party apparently agrees and adopts woman suffrage into its platform at its convention on May 30, 1913. In 1916, referenda on prohibition and woman suffrage are staged along with the provincial election. Majority voting supports both, and the Liberals win the provincial election. Shortly after the Liberals take office, they put forward a bill granting women suffrage.

MAY 17, 1917 **Birth of Playwright Lorraine Hansberry.** Lorraine Hansberry (1930–1965), African American playwright, is born in Chicago, Illinois. Her first completed work, *A Raisin in the Sun* (1959) wins the New York Drama Critics Circle Award in 1959. Selections from Hansberry's work appear following her death in *To Be Young, Gifted, and Black* (1969).

JUNE 16, 1917 **American Publisher Katharine Graham Is Born.** Katharine Meyer Graham (1917–), publisher of the *Washington Post*, is born in New York. Her mother is a writer and patron of the arts. Her father, a former chairman of the Federal Reserve Board of the United States, owns the *Washington Post*, where Katharine Meyer works for a time as a reporter. She marries Philip Graham in 1940, and he becomes publisher of the *Post* after World War II. The Grahams buy the paper in 1948. In 1963 Phil commits suicide, and Katharine Graham inherits the *Post, News-*

week magazine, and several radio and television stations. She takes control as publisher of the *Post*, overcoming her natural shyness to become a forceful manager. Many say she is a more effective leader than her husband, because she is a good listener and is willing to trust the judgment of her editors. In 1971 she makes the decision to publish the controversial "Pentagon Papers," putting the paper at some risk of litigation. A year later, she personally makes sure that the paper's coverage of the Watergate scandal (a story that the *Post* uncovers first) is tough but fair. In 1974 Graham becomes the first woman member of the board of the Associated Press. Although she credits her own success to "matrimony and patrimony," she is known for her good financial sense, courage, and independence.

JUNE 30, 1917 **Birth of Lena Horne, African American Entertainer.** Lena Horne (1917–), singer, entertainer, and leading African American motion picture actress in the 1940s and 1950s, is born. Horne grows up in Brooklyn, New York, and is recruited to become a screen actress, landing a seven-year contract with Metro-Goldwyn-Mayer (MGM). However, unlike most African American actresses, Horne insists that her contract stipulate that she will not be limited to maids' roles on the screen. Of Horne's most well-known screen appearances, her performances in two musicals with all-African American casts—*Cabin in the Sky* (1943) and *Stormy Weather* (1943)—escalate her to star status.

Horne soon discovers that Hollywood is unwilling or unprepared to locate appropriate screen roles for African American actresses, and in the late 1940s, her contract with MGM is discontinued. Disillusioned with Hollywood and eager to denounce practices she contends are discriminatory, Horne becomes one of the most outspoken African American entertainers. She protests on many fronts: against the restrictive covenants that prevent her from occupying a home in an exclusive residential neighborhood because she is African American; against public accommodations that refuse service to African Americans; and against military companies that invite her to perform for white soldiers, to the exclusion of African American soldiers. On tour, she insists that she and her musicians be allowed to use the front door and front elevators of hotels and to eat in hotel restaurants— all practices African Americans are not permitted in the 1950s. She also insists that blacks be welcomed in her audience.

In 1969, Horne stars in her first dramatic non-singing role in the film *Death of a Gunfighter*. In later years, although Horne is unable to sustain a career as an actress, she continues to garner public appeal while performing on stage and with her recordings.

1918   Charlotte Garrigue Masaryk Encourages Feminism in Czechoslovakia. As the wife of Czechoslovakia's first president, Charlotte Garrigue Masaryk (1850–1923) encourages the growth of feminist ideas among the Czech people. Born into a well-to-do family in Brooklyn, New York, she marries Thomas Masaryk in 1878 and moves to the Habsburg Empire with her husband. The couple adopts the double last name of "Garrigue Masaryk" and has five children. Thomas, a university professor in Vienna and Prague, is active in Czech politics. Although she is American by birth, Charlotte Garrigue Masaryk is closely identified with Czech culture for over 40 years, fostering the appreciation of Czech music, literature, and art. She also encourages the growth of both feminist ideas and the labor movement in Bohemia. When Czechoslovakia is formed in 1918, Thomas Garrigue Masaryk serves as its first president, and Charlotte endears herself to the Czechs as his helpmate. After Charlotte Garrigue Masaryk's death in 1923, her daughter Alice Garrigue Masaryk (1879–1966) carries on her work in the labor movement.

1918   Pauline Newman Becomes President of NWTUL. Long-time worker and organizer for the International Ladies' Garment Workers' Union (ILGWU), Pauline Newman (1891–1986) becomes president of the National Women's Trade Union League (NWTUL), a post she holds until 1923. She previously founds a chapter of NWTUL in Philadelphia, Pennsylvania. Throughout her career, which spans over 75 years, she supports women's involvement in their unions. In some of her many writings, Newman questions the lack of women among the leadership of the labor movement.

1918   Author Madeleine L'Engle Is Born. Madeleine L'Engle (1918–), author of poetry, plays, and works of fiction for children and adults, is born. Her best-known works include *A Wind in the Door* (1973), *A Swiftly Tilting Planet* (1978), and *A Wrinkle in Time* (1962), which wins the 1963 Newbery Medal.

1918   Mary Van Kleeck Directs Industrial Service Section. Mary Van Kleeck (1883–1972), early industrial sociologist and director of industrial studies for the Russell Sage Foundation from 1908 to 1948, is appointed director of the women's industrial service section of the Ordinance Department. She also serves as director of the Woman in Industry Service of the U.S. Department of Labor from 1918 to 1919.

1918   Mabel Edna Gillespie Elected to Executive Committee of Massachusetts AFL. Labor union organizer Mabel Edna Gillespie (1877–1923) becomes the first woman elected to the executive committee of the Massachusetts American Federation of Labor (AFL) and that same year is elected vice president of the group.

1918   Ida Sophia Scudder Establishes Christian Medical College in India. Ida Sophia Scudder (1870–1960), an American physician and medical missionary, founds the Vellore

Christian Medical College and Hospital in Vellore, India. Her purpose is to train Indian women as doctors to serve medical needs where purdah, the seclusion of women from public observation, is practiced.

1918 Birth of Ida Lupino, Multitalented American Film Career Woman. Ida Lupino (1918–), the first woman to make her career in four areas of American film—as an actor, a director, a producer and a writer—is born. After working with Paramount and Warner Brothers, she founds her own production company, Film Makers, with Collier Young. She writes the script for its first production, and when the director dies while on the film, she takes over. She directs, produces, and co-writes each subsequent film. The company is innovative in choosing controversial subjects, such as unmarried mothers and career women, and in fostering new talent.

1918 Michigan Women Gain Vote. Suffrage is granted to women in Michigan.

1918 Suffrage Granted to Women in South Dakota. Suffrage is extended to women in South Dakota.

1918 Oklahoma Women Gain Suffrage. Women in Oklahoma are granted the right to vote.

1918 Women Gain Quasi-Voting Rights in Texas. Women are granted a similar right to that of the right to vote in primary elections within the state of Texas.

1918 Women's Suffrage Resolution Passes in U.S. House. The U.S. House of Representatives passes a resolution to amend the U.S. Constitution providing that "the right of citizens of the United States to vote shall not be denied or abridged by the United States or any state on account of sex." The bill is twice defeated by the Senate, until it finally passes in 1919.

1918 Japanese Imperial Army Forces Women into Sexual Labor. *Karayukisan* (foreign-bound women) and "comfort women" are forced into sexual labor by the Japanese Imperial Army, a practice that continues until 1945. The military ostensibly procures sex for soldiers in order to arouse their fighting spirit, provide a release for their frustrations and fears, and prevent the raping of native women. *Karayukisan* are Japanese women whose impoverished peasant families sell them into prostitution. In addition to servicing Japanese soldiers, *karayukisan* are also sent to brothels throughout Asia to earn foreign currency, which is returned to Japan. By the beginning of World War II, when *karayukisan* begin to infect soldiers with venereal disease, brokers began recruiting young Korean women to serve as "comfort women." By the end of the war, however, the supply of women is enlarged by the indiscriminate kidnapping of Korean women, Philippine women, and women prisoners of war (e.g., Dutch women in Java). Following the Compulsory Draft in 1943, the number of women reaches approximately 200,000, among whom 80,000 are sent to the front lines in Asia. Each woman is made to sexually serve an average of 30–40 soldiers a day, and women who are not submissive are tortured.

1918 Frances Perkins Named to New York State Industrial Commission. Frances Perkins (1882–1965) is appointed to the New York State Industrial Commission, and at $8,000 a year, she is the highest-paid state employee in the nation. Perkins works for several state agencies over the next decade, always pushing for rights for workers and women. When Franklin Roosevelt (1882–1945) becomes President of the United States in 1933, he appoints her Secretary of Labor.

1918 Women Suffrage Granted in Canada. Women gain the right to vote in Canada.

1918 **Women Gain Vote in Germany.** German women are granted suffrage.

1918 **Polish Women Granted Suffrage.** Suffrage is extended to women in Poland.

1918 **Irish Nationalist Constance Markiewicz Elected to Parliament.** Constance Markiewicz, Irish nationalist, becomes the first woman member of the British Parliament, but she never accepts the position. In 1909, Constance Markiewicz founds Na Fianna Eireann, an Irish nationalist version of the Boy Scouts. She becomes more involved with the cause of Irish nationalism, supporting unemployed workers and the unions during the lockouts of 1913. Markiewicz is later beaten on "Bloody Sunday" (August 13, 1913), when armed police attack a gathering of trade unionists. She helps plot the Dublin Easter uprising of 1916, when Irish nationalist militants seize several British-held public buildings. For her role, she is imprisoned, but not executed as are her male associates. While Markiewicz is still in prison, the Irish nationalist party Sinn Fein runs her as its candidate for the British parliament from Dublin. She wins but never serves in the position because she refuses allegiance to the king of England.

1918 **Austrian Women Gain Voting Rights.** Women are granted the vote in Austria.

1918 **Irish Women Granted Suffrage.** Women win the vote in Ireland.

1918 **Some Women Win Vote in Great Britain.** Women age 30 and over who are householders or wives of householders are granted suffrage in Great Britain.

OCTOBER 1918 **Hungarian Pacifist Rosika Schwimmer Named Ambassador to Switzerland.** Rosika Schwimmer (1877–1948), a Hungarian feminist and pacifist, is appointed to serve her country as ambassador to Switzerland—the world's first female ambassador. She serves in this post for a year. Due to polit-

Eva Perón, known as Evita.

ical unrest in Hungary, she emigrates to the United States in the 1930s and in 1948 is nominated for the Nobel Peace Prize.

1919 **Birth of Eva Duarte De Perón.** Eva Duarte De Perón (1919–1952), known as Evita, is born in Los Toldos, Buenos Aires, Argentina. An actress, she is the first wife of Juan Perón, Argentine president, and is a powerful political asset to her husband. Her life story provides the basis for *Evita*, a 1978 Broadway musical by Tim Rice and Andrew Lloyd Webber.

1919 **Delilah Leontium Beasley Writes History of African Americans in California.** Self-taught historian Delilah Leontium Beasley (1867–1934) writes the first history of African Americans in California, *The Negro Trail-Blazers of California*. Beasley reminds readers that seven of the 29 soldiers of the De Anza expedition to California in 1775 are of African descent, and that African Americans play a major role in California's history ever after.

1919   Federated Women's Institutes Founded in Canada. The Federated Women's Institutes help to unite and organize rural Canadian women. Adelaide Hoodless founds the first Women's Institute to foster homecraft and educated motherhood in rural Canada. The motto of the Women's Institutes is "For Home and Country," and their goal is "to promote that knowledge of household science which shall lead to the improvement in the household architecture with special attention to home sanitation, to a better understanding of economics and hygienic value of foods and fuels and to a more scientific care of children." The Women's Institutes of Canada serve to promote a recognition for rural living and the evolution of informed citizens through the study of national and international issues, and to initiate national progress to achieve these goals. This organization spreads slowly, hampered by rural difficulties. Subsequently, the Ontario government offers assistance in organizing Women's Institutes. They offer cash subsidies for hiring lecturers and for hiring demonstrators to teach courses in hygiene, nutrition, cooking, home nursing, and sewing. Within six years, the Women's Institutes membership soars as it meets the needs of rural women and plays a significant role in their education. Women's Institutes improve schools, teach preventive health measures, and promote cultural programs.

1919   Canadian Federation of University Women Established. The Canadian Federation of University Women is founded as a counterpart to and member organization of the International Federation of University Women. Its aim is to emphasize women's roles in social reconstruction and the prevention of war. Perhaps most importantly, it serves as an agent of women's organizations

and networks. In the 1990s it remains as an organization that promotes the involvement of women individually and collectively in professional, economic, and political life while encouraging women scholars and safeguarding the rights of women.

1919   Edith Clarke, First Woman to Earn Master's Degree in Electrical Engineering. Edith Clarke (1883–1959), electric power theorist and mathematician, becomes the first woman to earn a master's degree in electrical engineering when she graduates from Massachusetts Institute of Technology (MIT).

1919   Actress Mary Pickford Cofounds United Artists Studio. Actress Mary Pickford (1893–1979), Douglas Fairbanks, and Charlie Chaplin form their own film studio, United Artists. Pickford becomes star, studio owner, executive producer, and director. In the prime of life, Pickford retreats from her film career. She is the first performer ever to become a millionaire from the craft of acting. Her autobiographical writings include *My Rendevous with Life* (1935) and *Sunshine and Shadow* (1955).

1919   Chinese Author Bing Xin Publishes Poetry and Prose for Chinese Children and Adults. Bing Xin (1902–), the pen name of Xie Wanying, begins to publish her work. She is the first Chinese woman to become a successful writer in the twentieth century, known for both her poetry and prose, and for her work for children as well as for adults. Her subjects include the problems of being a woman and social oppression. Although her reputation suffers during the Cultural Revolution, except for this period (1967–72), she is honored in China throughout her life.

1919   U.S. President Woodrow Wilson Calls Congressional Session to Pass the 19th Amendment. President Woodrow Wilson calls a special session of Congress to pass the 19th Amendment to the U.S. Constitution, stating "the right of citizens of the United States to

Nancy Astor campaigning in the general election of 1931.

vote shall not be denied or abridged by the United States or any state on account of sex." The amendment is passed in the House of Representatives by the necessary two-thirds vote, but it is defeated twice in the Senate. It finally passes both houses of Congress in 1919.

1919   Nancy Astor, First Woman Member of Parliament in Great Britain. Nancy Witcher Langhorne Astor (1879–1964) is elected to take the place of her husband, the wealthy Waldorf Astor, as Member of Parliament (MP) in England after his death. Nancy Astor is born in Danville, Virginia, the daughter of a wealthy tobacco auctioneer. She marries the wealthy Waldorf Astor in 1906, and he is elected to Parliament in 1910. Another woman, Constance Markiewicz (1868–1927),

is elected MP in 1918 (the year British women win the vote and the right to serve in Parliament). But with other members of her party from Ireland, she refuses to meet in England. So when Nancy Astor is introduced into Parliament in 1919, she becomes the first woman to actually serve, and she remains the only woman until 1921. Although elected as a Tory, she refuses throughout her career to vote along party lines. She follows her own instincts and moral sense, supporting issues affecting women and the family and urging strict controls on drinking. She serves in Parliament until 1945.

1919   Some Belgian Women Granted Suffrage. Widows and mothers of male casualties of war gain the vote in Belgium.

1919   Women Gain the Vote in Luxembourg. Suffrage is extended to women in Luxembourg.

1919   Women Gain Suffrage in the Netherlands. Women win the vote in the Netherlands.

1919   Women Win Vote in Sweden. Swedish women gain voting rights.

1919   Establishment of National Federation of Business and Professional Women's Clubs of the U.S.A. The National Federation of Business and Professional Women's Clubs of the U.S.A. is formed as a federation of local groups that promote the full opportunity potential of working women.

1919   German Revolutionary Rosa Luxemburg Is Killed. Rosa Luxemburg, leader of the German Social Democratic Party and the Spartacus Party, is murdered. A German revolutionary in the years preceding World War I, Luxemburg is a Marxist who leads the Social Democratic Party in Germany and helps establish similar parties in Poland and Lithuania. Luxemburg believes that a general strike is the main way for workers to capture power. Her revolutionary activities and writings result in arrest and imprisonment in Poland in 1905-6 and in Germany during 1915-18. In 1919, Luxemburg is arrested for involvement in civil strife and killed by soldiers while in custody.

APRIL 1, 1919   Birth of Thelma Stovall, American Trade Unionist and Public Official. Thelma Loyce Hawkins Stovall (1919–1994),who spends 31 years in public office in Kentucky and 30 years as an active union member, is born. She is first elected as a state legislator in 1949 while she is a floor sweeper at a tobacco factory in Louisville, Kentucky, and a member of the executive board of her local union, Tobacco Workers Union Local #185. She is elected recording secretary and serves in this position for 11 years. This is especially significant since her local, commonly known as "Old Stormy" and known for upheaval, typically elects a new slate of officers each year. Only Stovall is reelected each year. As a public servant and elected official, she is considered a candidate of the people, and trade unionists call her "Madam Labor." Aside from her union activity, Stovall is best known for her action regarding the Equal Rights Amendment (ERA). In 1976 the Kentucky state legislature votes to rescind an earlier legislature's passage of the ERA. In her capacity as acting governor, she vetoes the legislation. The following year, again as acting governor, she calls a special session of the legislature and has them enact legislation putting a cap on property taxes and removing the state sales tax from residential utility bills. She believes these actions are necessary to help working people. Even while in public office, Stovall remains an active union member for 30 years, attending union meetings and conventions and voting in union elections.

APRIL 12, 1919   Beverly Cleary, American Children's Author, Is Born. Beverly Cleary (1919–), creator of Henry Huggins and Ramona Quimby, is born in McMinnville, Oregon.

MAY 10, 1919   American Congresswoman and Governor Ella Tambussi Grasso Is Born. Ella Tambussi Grasso (1919–1981), the first American woman to be elected governor in her own right, without succeeding her husband to the office, is born of Italian immigrants near Hartford, Connecticut. After graduating with distinction from Mount Holyoke College, she takes a master's degree in economics and sociology. She marries Thomas Grasso, a schoolteacher, and goes to work for the Connecticut state government. In 1952 she is elected to the State Assembly as a Democrat, a rare victory in the strongly Republican state. She quickly rises to Secretary of State and works to reform the court system, abolish unnecessary county government, create consumer protection agencies, and ban discrimination in housing. She is active in the national Democratic Party, collaborating on a minority report opposing American involvement in Vietnam. Grasso serves in the U.S. Congress from 1970 to 1974, and then as governor of Connecticut from 1975 to 1980.

AUGUST 22, 1919   **French Swindler Marthe Hanau Buys Financial Magazine.** Marthe Hanau (1890–1935), who achieves notoriety trading four million dollars of fraudulent securities, purchases the *Gazette du Franc et des Nations,* an influential financial magazine; she also establishes *Agence Interpresse,* a wire service supplying financial information to newspapers throughout France. Hanau then creates fraudulent companies that she promotes through these two legitimate mediums. She accepts shares in legitimate companies as secu-

rity. The shares are quickly liquidated. Hanau also invests in real estate, using her own worthless stock as collateral. Although bankers become increasingly suspicious, Marthe Hanau uses influential friends in the French government to blunt any investigation. When investors attempt to withdraw their funds, however, her fraud is exposed. Arrested in December 1928, Hanau has assets totalling 31 million francs. Denying her guilt, Hanau goes on a 22-day hunger strike and becomes a heroine in the press. Released in December 1931, she establishes another newspaper, *Forces.* Hanau is arrested again in 1932, when her own police file, stolen from the desk of the Minister of Finances, appears in the newspaper. Marthe Hanau is discovered dead on July 19, 1935, having taken an overdose of sleeping pills.

Chapter 18

1920 TO 1929

1920 – 1924

1920 Constance Applebee Founds *The Sports-woman*, First Periodical about Women's Sports. Constance M.K. Applebee (1873–1981), director of outdoor sports at Bryn Mawr College and prominent field hockey coach, founds, publishes, and edits *The Sports-woman*, the first periodical that focuses on women's sports, which continues publishing for ten years.

In 1922, Applebee presides at the inaugural meeting of the United States Field Hockey Association (USFHA). She is instrumental in creating international competition by sending teams to England as well as hosting teams from England. Applebee is still coaching at the age of 95.

1920 Mary Anderson, First Head of the Women's Bureau of the Department of Labor. The Women's Bureau of the U.S. Department of Labor is established, and labor activist Mary Anderson (1872–1964) is named its first leader. She continues as director until 1944.

1920 Evangelist Aimee Semple McPherson Launches North American Religious Campaign. Aimee Semple McPherson (1890–1944), one of the greatest evangelistic successes of the early twentieth century, launches a religious campaign in North America, com-

bining evangelism and drama. When she opens her 5,000-seat, $1.25 million Angelus Temple of the Four Square Gospel in Los Angeles, California, "Sister Aimee's" theatrical pulpit techniques make her one of the most publicized religious revivalists in the world. Her ability to attract followers is enhanced by her use of the media and its infatuation with her personal life, particularly her mysterious disappearances, moral and financial scandals, court cases, and marriages. In Western Canada, "Sister Aimee" runs several churches and a bible school. During the Great Depression (1929–39), she discovers the radio as an evangelistic vehicle and soon becomes a well-known radio preacher.

1920 Bronislava Nijinska Choreographs for Diagilev's Ballet Russes. Bronislava Nijinska (1891–1972) is the first woman to choreograph for Russian impresario Sergei Diagilev, in Paris at the Ballet Russes. Trained as a dancer, she performs in Russia and in France before turning to choreography, a profession in which she establishes an international reputation.

1920 Painter Georgia O'Keeffe's Erotic Canvases Bring Her International Acclaim. Internationally renowned artist Georgia O'Keeffe (1887–1986) begins to paint the large, erotic flower canvases for which she is well known. O'Keeffe is also remembered for her symbolic

Board of directors of the National League of Women Voters at the 1920 convention in Chicago. Front row, from left, Maud Wood Park, the organization's first national president, Grace Wilbur Trout, and Carrie Chapman Catt.

still lifes set in the American West, where she paints beginning in the 1940s, and as the subject of over 500 photographs taken by her lifelong companion, photographer Alfred Stieglitz.

1920 Women Gain Full Voting Rights in the United States. The 19th Amendment to the U.S. Constitution, stating "the right of citizens of the United States to vote shall not be denied or abridged by the United States or any state on account of sex," is ratified by the necessary two-thirds, or 36, of the states. Thus, women are guaranteed full suffrage in the United States.

1920 National American Woman Suffrage Association Reorganized as National League of Women Voters. The National American Woman Suffrage Association (NAWSA) has two million members at the time the 19th Amendment to the U.S. Constitution is passed, guaranteeing women the right to vote. Carrie Chapman Catt (1859–1947) reorganizes NAWSA into the National League of Women Voters. Maud Wood Park become the new organization's first president.

1920 Jessie Jack Hooper, First President of Wisconsin League of Women Voters. Jessie Annette Jack Hooper (1865–1935), an American suffragist and pacifist, serves as the first president of the Wisconsin League of Women Voters, in Oshkosh, Wisconsin. She holds this position until 1922, when she resigns to run (unsuccessfully) as Wisconsin's first female Democratic nominee for the U.S. Senate.

1920   First Russian Woman to Be Named People's Artist of the Republic. Maria Nikolaijevna Yermolova (1853–1928), a Russian actress known for her portrayal of active and independent women, is the first woman to receive the title of People's Artist of the Republic, in Moscow. She supports the Russian Revolution of 1917, and in 1922, a studio of the famous Maly Theater in Moscow is named after her, later becoming the well-known Yermolova Theater.

1920   Tilly Devine Runs Australian Prostitution Business. Australian "Madame" Matilda (Tilly) Twiss Devine(1900–1970), known as "Queen of the Loo," operates a profitable prostitution business. Devine is born in England and travels to Sydney, Australia, in 1920 after marrying an Australian soldier during World War I (1914–19). She maintains her independence from her husband's underworld connections by working in the sex industry. Between June 1921 and May 1925 (when she is jailed for two years for slashing a man with a razor), Devine is convicted on 79 prostitution-related charges. By this time, colorful press reports of the "Queen of the Night" make her well-known throughout Australia, and her court appearances attract a packed gallery. Throughout World War II (1939–45) she operates her well-established prostitution business, contributes generously to the war effort, and becomes notorious for her opulent dress and collection of diamond rings. The "Queen of the Loo" divorces her husband in 1943 and remarries two years later. Devine stays in business until 1968, but an enforced payment of £20,000 in back taxes and fines in 1955 encourages her to scale down her opera-

tions. Nevertheless, her exploits continue to entertain the communities within which she operates. Tilly dies in Sydney in 1970, and her life informs Peter Kenna's play *The Slaughter of St. Teresa's Day* (1973).

1920   Kawai Michi Establishes Japanese YWCA. After graduating from Bryn Mawr College in the United States, Kawai Michi returns to Japan; teaches at *Tsuda Eigakujuku* (now Tsuda Women's University), and, with the founder of that school, Tsuda Ume, and others, establishes Japanese branches of the Young Women's Christian Association (YWCA). She becomes the first director-general of the Japanese YWCA and frequently represents it abroad. In this capacity, she develops leadership and vocational programs to prepare university students and young working women for leading democratic lives. In 1921, Michi founds *Keisen Jogakuen* (now Keisen Jogakuen Junior College) and serves as its principal. The school specializes in teaching horticulture. After World War II, she works as a peace activist and serves in the Ministry of Education to help establish Japan's system of two-year junior colleges (in which most of the students are women). Michi writes *Japanese Women Speak* and two autobiographical volumes, *My Lantern* and *Sliding Doors.*

1920   Edith Cowan, First Woman Member of Australian Parliament. Edith Dirksey Brown Cowan (1861–1932) becomes the first woman member of the Australian parliament. She devotes herself to a variety of causes, including state education, care for neglected children and unmarried mothers, day nurseries for working women, and compulsory notification of venereal diseases. The legislative ban on women entering the Western Australian parliament is lifted in 1920, and five women run in the subsequent election. Cowan defeats sitting member Attorney-General T. P. Draper to become Australia's first woman parliamentarian. During the campaign the press repeatedly accuses her of neglecting her family to indulge in politics. After her victory she is surprised, given her acknowledged distaste for housework, to find herself depicted as the member who tidies Parliament House. Her maiden speech is, in part, devoted to refuting allegations that large amounts of taxpayers' money have been spent on the installation of women's toilets in the parliamentary buildings. Cowan uses her term to fight for migrant welfare, infant health centers, and women's rights. The Women's Legal Status Act, which she introduces as a private member's bill, opens the legal profession to women in 1923. However, she fails to win reelection in 1924 and 1927. Edith Cowan devotes the rest of her life to social causes and dies in Perth in 1932.

1920   Nettie Palmer Shapes Twentieth-Century Australian Literature. Janet Gertrude (Nettie) Higgins Palmer (1885–1964) supports other women writers and helps shape twentieth-century Australian literature. She marries novelist Vance Palmer in 1914 and bears two daughters. During World War I she campaigns against censorship and conscription, publishes two volumes of poetry, and writes regular columns for the *Argus*. By the 1920s, Nettie Palmer has emerged as the most important literary critic in Australia. She is committed to the development of a national literature and is the first to publish substantially on Australian woman writers Henry Handle Richardson, Miles Franklin, Katherine Susannah Pritchard, Marjorie Barnard Eldershaw, and Barbara Baynton. As well as fostering the work of younger women, she writes biography and literary criticism, delivers lectures, broadcasts, researches, and reviews, edits, and collects the works of other authors. During the 1930s, Palmer steps up her political involvement. In 1935, she attends the first International Congress of Writers for the Defence of Culture in Paris. She spends time in war-torn Spain in 1936 and plays a powerful role in the Spanish Aid Council and

the anti-fascist movement after her return to Melbourne. Nettie Palmer dies at Hawthorne in 1964.

1920   National Council of Catholic Women Formed. The National Council of Catholic Women (NCCW) is set up as a federation of organizations of Catholic women from the parochial to the national level in order to address church-related and social issues and to foster leadership among Catholic women.

MARCH 28, 1920   *Shin Fujin Kyokai* (New Women's Association) Established in Japan. *Shin Fujin Kyokai* (New Women's Association), Japan's first national women's rights organization, is founded. Its leaders include Hiratsuka Raicho, Ichikawa Fusae, and Oku Mumeo. The organization campaigns for equal opportunity for women and men, with protection for mothers and children. *Josei domei* (*Women's League*) is the organization's magazine. The association's major achievement is persuading the Diet (national legislature) to revoke Article 5 of the 1886 Public Order and Police Law, which prohibits women from attending political meetings.

JUNE 11, 1920   African-American Pianist and Actress Hazel Scott Is Born. Hazel Scott (1920–1981), an African-American concert classical-jazz pianist and screen actress who aggressively opposes racial oppression throughout her career, is born in Port of Spain, Trinidad. A recognized child prodigy, Scott attends the Juilliard School of Music in New York and becomes a classical-jazz pianist. Recruited by motion picture producers, Scott appears in several films as an entertainer seated at a piano. Scott's most controversial appearance is her role in *The Heat's On* (1943). Offended by the studio's request that black actresses wear soiled aprons, Scott refuses, halting production on the picture for three days.

Scott continually takes a public stance against discriminatory practices. She and her husband, U.S. Representative Adam Clayton Powell, Jr., expose and challenge the Daughters of the American Revolution's banning of her performance in Constitution Hall. Scott opposes performing for segregated audiences at major universities and the segregated practices of the National Press Club. She actually sues a restaurant for refusing to serve black patrons. Following the dissolution of her marriage to Powell, she moves to Europe and remarries. Hazel Scott later returns to the United States, where she dies.

JULY 24, 1920 Birth of Bella Abzug, American Feminist and Congresswoman. Feminist Bella Savitzky Abzug (1920–) is born of Russian-Jewish parents in New York City. As a student at Hunter College she protests against fascism during the Spanish Civil War. She marries businessman Martin Abzug in 1944 and takes her law degree from Columbia University the next year. For the next 25 years she practices law as an advocate for civil and human rights. She defends writers accused of un-American activities and civil rights activists in the South, and she campaigns against the Vietnam War. Always an outspoken supporter of women's equality, Abzug is an early member of the National Organization for Women (NOW), a founder of Women Strike for Peace, and a founder of the National Women's Political Caucus. Elected to the U.S. House of Representatives in 1970, "Bellicose Bella" introduces legislation supporting jobs programs, welfare, environmental issues, and the State of Israel. After leaving Congress in 1976, she continues her activism as a writer and speaker. She is the author of *Ms. Abzug Goes to Washington* (1972) and *Gender Gap: Bella Abzug's Guide to Political Power for Women* (1984).

1921 American Union Leader Sara Conboy Appointed to Unemployment Conference. Labor union activist Sara Agnes Conboy (1870–1928) is appointed by President War-

ren G. Harding to the Conference on Unemployment.

1921 Lila Acheson Wallace Cofounds the *Reader's Digest*. Lila Acheson Wallace (1889-1984), an American entrepreneur and art patron, is the cofounder, with her husband, De Witt Wallace, of the *Reader's Digest*, in New York City. The business is instantly successful and by the 1980s subscriptions reach 30 million and the publication is available in 17 languages. Beginning in the 1930s, Wallace becomes a serious art collector, specializing in Impressionist works. She is the first woman to donate a definitive and vast collection of Impressionist art to a major museum, the Metropolitan Museum of Art in New York. She is also the first woman to commit herself to the restoration of Monet's house and gardens at Giverny.

1921 Edith Wharton Wins the Pulitzer Prize. Edith Newbold Wharton (c.1861–1937) wins the Pulitzer Prize for fiction for her novel, *The Age of Innocence.*

1921 Birth of Patricia Wrightson, Australian Author. Patricia Wrightson (1921–), internationally renowned author of works for children, is born in Australia. Wrightson becomes known worldwide following publication of *A Racecourse for Andy* (1968). Her many awards include the Hans Christian Andersen Medal (1986) and Book of the Year Award from the Children's Book Council of Australia.

1921 First American Birth Control Conference. Margaret Sanger (1883–1966) organizes the first American Birth Control Conference in New York City. Sanger devotes her life to educating women about birth control, and in 1953 she is the founder and first president of the International Planned Parenthood Federation.

1921 Women's Socialist Group Established in Japan. Writer, feminist, and anarchist Ito Noe

(1895–1923) helps to establish *Sekirankai* (Red Wave Society), a women's socialist group in Japan. It calls for the abolition of capitalism (which it sees as the source of women's oppression), equal wages, mothers' welfare, and the abolition of prostitution. Two years later, after the birth of her seventh child, Noe and her anarchist lover, Osugi Sakae, are murdered by the military police.

1921   Hani Motoko Founds *Jiyu Gakuen* (Freedom Academy). Hani Motoko (1873–1957) and her husband, Hani Yoshikazu (1880–1955), found Jiyu Gakuen (Freedom Academy) in Japan. Initially, it is an all-girls boarding school striving to cultivate "good wives and wise mothers," who can run a household without depending on servants. Students not only study and pray together, but also live together, doing the cooking and the cleaning. This is a revolutionary curriculum for the daughters of wealthy families. Later, the school adds education for males and higher education divisions.

1921   Women in Hunan Province Gain Vote. Women in the Hunan Province win the right to vote.

1921   Madras Grants Women Vote. Madras is the first Indian province to grant women the vote.

JANUARY 11, 1921   American Economist Juanita Kreps Is Born. Juanita Morris Kreps (1921–), the first woman to hold the office of U.S. Secretary of Commerce and the first woman director of the New York Stock Exchange, is born in a Kentucky coal-mining town. She gets her interest in economics from the high unemployment and resulting social problems there. After finishing her master's degree at Duke University, she marries fellow economist Clifton Kreps and joins the economics faculty at Denison College in the 1940s. In 1973, she becomes Duke University's first woman vice president; the year

before, the first woman public director of the New York Stock Exchange. In 1977 she is sworn in as the first woman U.S. Secretary of Commerce. Kreps maintains an interest in economic issues related to age and retirement, the employment of women, and the treatment of racial minorities. Her expertise in business matters brings her a seat on the boards of major corporations, including United Airlines, J. C. Penney, and Kodak. Her books include *Sex in the Marketplace: American Women at Work* (1972), *Sex, Age and Work: The Changing Composition of the Labor Force* (1975), and *Women and the American Economy* (1976).

FEBRUARY 4, 1921   Birth of American Activist Betty Friedan. Betty Friedan (1921–), author of *The Feminine Mystique* (1963), is born in Peoria, Illinois.

FEBRUARY 15, 1921   Suffrage Monument by Sculptor Adelaide Johnson Unveiled. A monument depicting American suffragists Elizabeth Cady Stanton, Susan B. Anthony, and Lucretia Mott is unveiled in Washington, D.C. In part because of its tremendous weight, the monument is installed in a room known as the crypt directly below the rotunda in the U.S. capitol.

NOVEMBER 24, 1921   Birth of Yochiko Uchida, Japanese American Author. Yochiko Uchida (1921–1992), author of works for young adults, is born in Alameda, California. Uchida is a prolific writer of works for young adults that chronicle the Japanese American experience, especially the forced relocation and incarceration of Japanese Americans during World War II (1939–45). Between 1948 and 1991, Uchida publishes 29 books, 27 of them for young adults. Best-known are *The Best Bad Thing, The Bracelet, New Friends for Susan, Journey to Topaz: A Story of the Japanese-American Evacuation*, and *The Terrible Leak*. For adults, she publishes a memoir, *The Invisible Thread* (1991) and *Desert Exile: The*

Suffrage monument by Adelaide Johnson.

Uprooting of a Japanese American Family (1982).

1922 Margaret Davies, First President of Cooperative Congress in England. Margaret Llewelyn Davies (1861–1944) becomes the first woman president of the Cooperative Congress in England, an organization bringing together cooperative societies representing both men and women workers. In 1886, she joins the local cooperative society. By 1889 she is general secretary of the Women's Cooperative Guild. She uses the platform of the guild to campaign for women's rights, including the right to vote, the right to divorce, and the right to a minimum wage. In 1921, she helps organize the International Women's Cooperative Guild. She writes and edits several books and pamphlets, including *The Women's Co-Operative Guild 1883–1904*

(1904) and *Maternity: Letters from Working Women* (1915). Margaret Davies dies in 1944.

1922 Jingyu Xiang Founds Women's Department in Chinese Communist Party. Feminist revolutionary Jingyu Xiang, instrumental in leading a women's liberation movement in China during the 1920s, establishes the Communist Party women's department in China and becomes its first director. Xiang starts out as a teacher in 1916, promoting education opportunities for girls. Later, she allies herself with the Communists, believing that education and cultural changes are not enough to improve the role women have in China, but that only political upheaval will bring about such social changes. In 1925, Xiang helps found the first nationwide Chinese women's political organization. In 1927, as hostilities between the Communist and Nationalist factions grow, she is arrested by the Nationalists and executed in 1928.

1922 Helena Normanton, First Woman Barrister to Appear at England's High Court of Justice. Helena Florence Normanton (1883–1957), a barrister-at-law, is the first woman to appear at the High Court of Justice in England. She is also the first woman to appear at both the London's Central Criminal Court (1924) and the London Sessions (1926), and the first woman elected to the General Council of the Bar (1945). In 1952, after she retires from the practice of law, Normanton becomes president of the Council of Married Women. She is also active in the International Federation of Business and Professional Women and the International Sorority of Women Lawyers. She writes several scholarly articles and the influential *Everyday Law for Women* (1932). Helena Normanton dies on October 14, 1957.

1922 Birth of Author Eleanor Coerr. Children's author Eleanor Coerr (1922–), who uses the pen name Eleanor Page, is born. Her most famous work is *Sadako and the Thousand Paper Cranes* (1977).

1922   **Birth of American Actress Ava Gardner.** Actress Ava Lavinnia Gardner (1922–1990), who is typecast as the sultry screen goddess, is born, the seventh child of a poor North Carolina tobacco farmer. During the Great Depression, Gardner escapes her surroundings by reading movie magazines and going to the movies. By age 17, she is a dazzling beauty with dark hair, green eyes, a dimpled chin, and a voluptuous figure. She moves to New York City and poses as a model for her brother-in-law. An executive from Metro-Goldwyn-Mayer (MGM) studio spots her photo in a shop window and offers Gardner a seven-year contract as an actress. In Hollywood, Gardner takes voice, dance, and acting lessons, and first appears in small roles. At 19 she marries Mickey Rooney, then the biggest star in Hollywood; they divorce a year later. Her second marriage to band leader Artie Shaw, in 1945, is equally brief.

Gardner's role as a gangster's moll in *The Killers* (1946) wins her *Look* magazine's "Most Promising Newcomer" award. By 1951, she becomes MGM's leading female star. Her affair with married singer Frank Sinatra creates a scandal until the couple weds in 1951. After a tempestuous marriage, they divorce in 1958. Gardner is Ernest Hemingway's favorite actress, and she appears in the screen adaptations of *The Snows of Kilimanjaro* (1952) and *The Sun Also Rises* (1957). By the 1960s, after several unsuccessful films, Gardner retreats from Hollywood and moves to London. She makes a comeback in *Earthquake* (1972) and *The Cassandra Crossing* (1977) and appears in television dramas. Ava Gardner dies at 66 after suffering a series of strokes.

1922   **Polish Actress Pola Negri Invited to Hollywood.** Pola Negri (1894–1987), a Polish actress, is the first European film star to be invited to Hollywood, California, to appear in movies. She has a popular career in silent films, but her heavy accent when speaking English prevents her from playing parts after sound comes to films.

1922   **Australian Activist Emma Miller Posthumously Honored.** A marble bust of Australian activist and suffragist Emma Holmes Miller (1839–1917) is unveiled at the Brisbane Trades Hall. A seamstress by trade, Miller joins the Australian Workers Union and is its first woman organizer in western Queensland. She also becomes involved in parliamentary politics as the first woman member of the Brisbane Workers Political Organization.

FEBRUARY 2, 1922   **American Sylvia Beach Publishes James Joyce's *Ulysses* In Paris.** American-born Sylvia Woodbridge Beach (1887–1962), who opens an English-language bookshop in Paris, France, publishes the first edition of James Joyce's *Ulysses* and devotes much of the next ten years to the novel's clandestine publication and distribution. After World War I (1914–19), Beach opens an English-language bookstore and lending library, called Shakespeare and Company, on Paris' Left Bank. The store is a huge success and attracts eccentric and important expatriate writers of the day, including F. Scott Fitzgerald, Ernest Hemingway, Gertrude Stein, and Beach's idol, James Joyce. Many of these writers leave the United States or Great Britain because their works and lifestyles are not accepted at home. Beach risks prosecution for obscenity by publishing the first edition of *Ulysses* by James Joyce. Modern and difficult in style, the novel is later accepted as one of the most important works of the twentieth century. Shakespeare and Company remains open until World War II (1939–45), when Germans occupying Paris close the shop and arrest Beach. She never reopens, but writes about her experiences in *Shakespeare and Company* (1959).

JUNE 10, 1922   **American Actress and Singer Judy Garland Is Born.** Judy Garland (1922–

1969), who graduates from child star to Hollywood actress and singer, is born Frances Ethel Gumm in Grand Rapids, Minnesota. Her parents are vaudeville performers, and before the age of three, "Baby Frances" makes her own stage debut as a singer. She and her two older sisters tour the country and work in radio, but "Baby" becomes the most famous of the "Gumm Sisters." In 1935 Frances is hired by Metro-Goldwyn-Mayer (MGM) studios and changes her name to Judy Garland. During the 1930s and 1940s, she appears in several films with another child actor, Mickey Rooney, in the Andy Hardy film series. Her most famous role, however, is that of Dorothy in *The Wizard Of Oz* (1939). Famous for her husky but sweet singing voice, Garland appears in such musicals as *For Me and My Gal* (1942), *Meet Me in St. Louis* (1944), and *Easter Parade* (1948). Despite her great talent, she has a fear of performing and a poor self-image which is intensified by the studio's incessant nagging about her weight. Studio employees give the teenaged star drugs to control her weight, and this develops into a lifelong addiction. By 28 Garland is considered a "has-been," and in 1950 MGM releases the actress from her contract due to her drug addiction and frequent absences on film sets. In 1954 she stars in her comeback role for Warner Brothers, *A Star is Born,* and receives an Academy Award for best actress. She spends the last 15 years of her career as a stage entertainer, giving over 1,100 theater, nightclub, and concert performances. Married five times, Garland is the mother of actress/singer Liza Minnelli. Judy Garland dies in London in 1969 from an accidental overdose of sleeping pills.

NOVEMBER 9, 1922   Birth of African American Actress Dorothy Dandridge. Actress Dorothy Dandridge (1922–1965), the first African American to be nominated for an Academy Award as best actress, is born. She and her sister, Vivian, perform together on stage, billed first as the Wonder Kids and later as the Dandridge Sisters. Dorothy Dandridge attempts a solo singing career in nightclubs and pursues small screen roles. By the 1950s, Dandridge becomes an African-American sex symbol, referred to as the "Sepia Beauty of the American Screen." In 1954, her role in *Carmen Jones* escalates her to fame, allowing her to become the first African American to be nominated for an Academy Award as best actress.

Dandridge's screen career begins to merge with her private life. Futile relationships with white men in films such as *The Decks Ran Red* (1958), *Tamango* (1958), and *Malaga* (1962), are mirrored in her private life. Despite her screen success, Dandridge's realization that only limited roles are available to her, coupled with a second failed marriage to white businessman Jack Denison, several lawsuits for unpaid debts, foreclosure on her home, and dwindling finances, force Dandridge into a state of depression. In 1965, she is found dead of an apparent suicide from antidepressants. Dorothy Dandridge has been referred to as the "Black Marilyn Monroe" because of the parallels in their lives.

1923   American Actress Judy Holliday Is Born. Actress Judy Holliday (1923–1965), who typifies the "dumb blonde" in films of the 1940s and 1950s, is born in New York City. She studies piano and ballet, and then acting at Orson Welles' Mercury Theater. Holliday appears in New York nightclubs and lands her first Broadway role in *Kiss Them For Me.* Her success results in the $500 Clarence Derwent Award for best supporting actress. This small fortune enables Holliday to rent a furnished room with her mother while she actively pursues an acting career. Her big break happens when she replaces ailing actress Jean Arthur in the Broadway play *Born Yesterday.* She learns her part in three days and receives rave reviews for her performance as Billie Dawn, the dumb blonde girlfriend of a big-time hood. Billie not only falls in love with her tutor but is transformed into an intelligent, independent woman. In real life, Holliday has an IQ of 172 and reads Proust and Chekov, but throughout her career she is cast as the "dumb blonde." In 1951, she reprises her role as Billie Dawn in the Hollywood film version opposite William Holden and Broderick Crawford. During her seven-year contract with Columbia Pictures, she stars in such comedies as *Adam's Rib* (1949), *It Should Happen To You* (1954), *The Marrying Kind, Bells Are Ringing* (1956), and *The Solid Gold Cadillac* (1956). Judy Holliday dies in 1965.

1923   Lucy Maud Montgomery Is First Canadian Woman Inducted into Royal Society of Arts in England. Novelist Lucy Maud Montgomery (1874–1942), author of the *Anne of Green Gables* stories, is invited to become a member of the prestigious Royal Society of Arts in England, the first Canadian woman so named. In 1935, she is named an Officer of the British Empire.

1923   Helen Wills Moody, Great Women's Tennis Star. From 1923 to 1931, American tennis player Helen Wills Moody (1905–) dominates the U. S. Women's tennis scene, including being ranked number one for several consecutive years. Her record includes eight Wimbledon singles titles, seven U.S. women's singles titles, four French championships, and a gold medal at the 1924 Olympic Games in Paris, France. Moody is given the nicknames "Miss Poker Face" and "Queen of the Nets." Her wins at Wimbledon are not surpassed until 1990, when Martina Navratilova wins her ninth title. Moody's challenge regarding the restrictions in the clothing women have to wear contributes to less restricting attire.

1923   Ida Rosenthal Establishes Maiden Form, First Bra Manufacturer. Ida Cohen Rosenthal (1885–1973) and a partner incorporate the Maiden Form Brassiere Company—the first manufacturer of brassieres. Rosenthal invents the brassiere for customers

of her dress shop. Women like the way their clothes fit when they wear the brassieres, and a new business is born. Gradually, the brassiere makes women's shapes more uniform and helps make possible the manufacture of standard-sized "off the rack" clothing for women. Rosenthal's husband, William, quits his business to join Maiden Form. He is the one who develops standard cup sizes and mass production methods, but it is always Ida who runs the business and controls the money. After William dies in 1958, Ida takes complete responsibility for the company. At the end of the twentieth century, Maidenform, Inc., remains one of the leading manufacturers of women's undergarments in the world.

1923   Deborah Hackett Develops Mining of Rare Australian Minerals. Australian mining entrepreneur Lady Deborah Vernon Hackett (née Drake-Brockman) (1887–1965) begins to investigate the properties of tantalum, a rare mineral found in remote parts of northern Australia. She charters a single-engine plane and spends two years inspecting deposits before travelling to America to secure a contract to supply ore to Fansteel Metallurgical to produce tantalite concentrates. In 1932, during the Great Depression, Hackett floats Tantalite Ltd. on the London stock exchange with the intention of establishing an Australian processing plant. She fails to attract government support, and the associated jobs remain in America. Her faith in tantalum is vindicated when it is used to develop radar in World War II, during which the Commonwealth Government resumes her tantalum and wolfram mines. Deborah marries her third husband, Basil Murphy, in 1936 and as Dr. Buller Murphy (she receives an honorary doctorate of laws from University of Western Australia in 1932), undertakes prodigious work for women's auxiliaries of Melbourne hospitals. After the war, she moves to an orchard property in the Dandenongs and researches and writes *An Attempt to Eat the*

Moon (1958), a book of legends of the Dordenup Aborigines she knows as a child. Deborah Hackett dies in Victoria in 1965.

1923 Women's Legal Status Act Opens Legal Profession to Australian Women. Edith Dirksey Brown Cowan (1861–1932) introduces the Women's Legal Status Act, opening the legal profession to women, during her term as the first woman member of the Australian parliament. Having won her seat in 1920, she fails to win reelection in either 1924 or 1927.

SEPTEMBER 1923 Delilah Leontium Beasley Writes "Activities Among Negroes" Column for Major California Newspaper. Delilah Leontium Beasley (1867–1934) is hired by the Oakland, California, *Tribune* to write a regular column, making her the first African American woman to be published regularly in a major metropolitan newspaper in California. In her column, "Activities Among Negroes," Beasley campaigns against the use in the press of explicitly derogatory words when writing about African Americans.

1924 Helena Normanton, First Woman Barrister to Appear at London's Central Criminal Court. Helena Florence Normanton (1883–1957), a barrister-at-law, is the first woman to appear at the Central Criminal Court in London. She is also the first woman barrister to appear at the High Court of Justice (1922) and at the London Sessions (1926), and first woman elected to the General Council of the Bar (1945).

1924 Florence Rena Sabin, First Woman President of American Association of Anatomists. Medical researcher Florence Rena Sabin (1871–1953) serves as the first female president of the American Association of Anatomists. She is also the first woman elected to the New York Academy of Sciences and the first female member of the Rockefeller Institute.

1924 Yasui Tetsu, First Japanese Woman College President. Yasui Tetsu (1870–1945) becomes the first Japanese woman college president, serving as the president of Tokyo Women's Christian University from 1924 to 1940. During her administration, she emphasizes the development of character and individual responsibility in students.

1924 Creation of Xianglin, Fictional Chinese Character. Xianglin is a fictional character in Lu Xun's short story "New Year's Sacrifice" written in 1924. A poor widow who is coerced into remarriage, her story is told through the eyes of a young narrator from the upper classes. Xianglin repeats the tragic story of her life (her small son is killed by wild animals) to anyone who will listen. Lu Xun often writes about women as emblems of China's weakness.

1924 Birth of Takamine Hideko, Japanese Actress. Takamine Hideko (1924–), a renowned Japanese actress who is first recognized as a child actress, is born. During World War II, her photograph is frequently sent as a gift to Japanese soldiers. Following the war, she maintains her popularity with appearances in the award-winning *Nijushi no hitomi* (1954; *Twenty-four Eyes*) and the critically acclaimed *Na mo naku mazushiku utsukushiku* (1961; *Nameless, Poor, Beautiful*).

1924 Establishment of Women's Suffrage League in Japan. Japanese feminists Ichikawa Fusae (1893–1981) and Yamataki Shigeri (1899–1977) found the *Fusen Kakutoku Domei* (Women's Suffrage League), Japan's major organization of women campaigning for the right to vote. In addition to suffrage, the organization campaigns for consumer rights, leading a drive for lower gas prices in 1927. Increased government suppression of left-wing organizations inhibits the league's activities in the 1930s and leads to its dissolution in 1940.

MARCH 24, 1924 **Birth of Bette Nesmith Graham, Inventor of "Liquid Paper."** Bette Nesmith Graham (1924–1980), a secretary who invented "Liquid Paper," is born in Dallas, Texas. In the 1950s, with no formal training in chemistry and working in her kitchen, Graham experiments with formulations to make an opaque, quick-drying fluid to correct typing errors. She applies for a patent, and offers her invention to IBM, but the company decides not to market her product. Graham begins selling the product locally herself, filling the bottles in her garage with the help of her son. In 1979, she sells "Liquid Paper" to the Gillette Corporation for $47.5 million plus royalties.

AUGUST 13, 1924 **Birth of Monica Clare, Australian Aboriginal Political Activist.** Mona Matilda (Monica) McGowan Clare (1924–1973), an Aboriginal political activist, is born near Goondiwindi, Queensland, Australia, of an Aboriginal father and an English mother. After her mother's death in 1931, she and her brother become wards of the state. They are taken from their father and allocated to white foster parents. After four years, the children are sent to separate training homes and never meet again. Clare is taught domestic skills and sent to work for a succession of white families in suburban Sydney until she turns 18. She then finds factory work and studies secretarial subjects at night school. She becomes politically active and marries building trades union official Les Clare in 1962. Monica Clare begins to work for the union as a clerk, and the travel involved brings her into contact with conditions on a number of Aboriginal reserves. She becomes secretary of the Aboriginal committee of the South Coast Labor Council, from which position she achieves the replacement of transitional Aboriginal housing by homes of Housing Commission standards and access to low-interest loans for residents to buy furniture. After 1967, Clare restructures the committee

as the independent South Coast Illawarra Tribe and successfully campaigns for the establishment of Commonwealth-funded housing cooperatives. She is delegate to several conferences of the Federal Council for the Advancement of Aborigines and Torres Strait Islanders between 1968 and 1972, and she is active on the International Women's Day, May Day, and National Aborigines' Day committees. Monica Clare dies in Sydney in 1973 and her novel, *Karobran,* is published posthumously in 1978.

SEPTEMBER 18, 1924 **Judith Hart, Member of British Parliament, Is Born.** Public official Constance Mary Judith Ridehalgh (1924–) is born in Burnley, Lancashire. She studies at the London School of Economics and marries in 1946. Known professionally as Judith Hart, she is a founder of the Campaign for Nuclear Disarmament and serves in the British Parliament in the 1960s. Hart is a strong voice in Parliament against British colonialism and is accused publicly of having too much sympathy for the Communist Party and the Soviet Union.

DECEMBER 30, 1924 **Birth of Shirley Chisholm, First African American Congresswoman.** Shirley Anita St. Hill Chisholm (1924–), the first African American woman elected to the U.S. Congress, is born in Brooklyn, New York. She grows up in her grandmother's home in Barbados, but returns to New York in her 20s, where she earns a graduate degree in child education, runs a nursery school, marries, and becomes an advisor to the City of New York on daycare centers. In 1964 Chisholm is elected to the state legislature, where she ensures that domestic workers are included in minimum wage laws. In 1968 she is elected to the U.S. House of Representatives, the first African American woman elected to Congress. A Democrat, she is responsible for legislation improving employment, educational opportunities, and living conditions for women, for members of racial minorities, and for people living in inner cities. At times Chisholm is accused of ignoring racial issues in favor of women's and homosexual rights. In 1972 she runs an unsuccessful campaign for the U.S. presidency. Chisholm's campaign raises national discussion about whether the country is—or will ever be—ready for a president who is a woman, or African American. She is the author of the autobiographical *Unbought and Unbossed* (1970) and *The Good Fight* (1973). After leaving Congress, Chisholm teaches at Mount Holyoke College and continues as a public speaker.

1 9 2 5 – 1 9 2 9

1925   **French Fashion Designer Coco Chanel Creates Her Trademark "Little Black Dress."** In the mid-1920s, French fashion entrepreneur Coco Chanel (1883–1971) designs the first "little black dress," austere and unembellished. It comes to embody the "new modern woman," as *Vogue* magazine declares in 1926. Her use of jersey becomes so prolific that she begins to produce it herself in 1935 in her own textile factory. Simple woolen suits with cardigan jackets and plain or pleated skirts become her trademark and maintain their popularity throughout her career. By the mid-1930s, her business becomes so successful that she has more than 3,000 employees in England and France.

      With the commencement of World War II (1939–45) in September of 1939, Chanel goes into retirement. However, by 1956 she refashions her trademark Chanel suit into a tailored suit of trimmed wool, which catapults her back into favor.

1925   **Publication of Anita Loos' *Gentlemen Prefer Blonds*.** American writer Anita Loos (1893–1981) publishes her novel *Gentlemen Prefer Blonds*, which becomes a movie in 1928. The character of Lorelei Lee is a stereotyped caricature of the "dumb blond." The book runs

through 85 editions and is translated into 14 languages, including Chinese. Before her death at age 88, Loos jokes, "Gentlemen may prefer blonds, but they marry brunettes."

1925   **Ethel Leginska, First Woman to Conduct Major American Orchestra.** Ethel Leginska (1886–1970) becomes the first woman to conduct a major American orchestra when she conducts the New York Symphony Orchestra in New York City. Trained as a pianist, Leginska goes on to found the Boston Philharmonic and to compose for both orchestra and opera.

1925   **Florence Rena Sabin's Medical Research into Origin of Red Corpuscles Wins Her Honors.** American medical researcher Florence Rena Sabin (1871–1953) becomes the first female member of the National Academy of Sciences when she is honored for her medical research in the field of histology, during which she determines the origin of red corpuscles.

1925   **Australian Entrepreneur Ma Dalley Runs Successful Scrap Metal Business.** Minnie Mary (Ma) Fimmel Dalley (1880–1965), an Australian entrepreneur who rises from factory hand to City Mayor of Kew, is one of the biggest scrap metal dealers in Australia. In 1905, she is widowed and living in Melbourne, Australia, working in a tea factory by day and sewing oatmeal bags at night. Known as "Ma" Dalley, she begins collecting scrap metal. World War I (1914–19) makes the scrap metal business extremely profitable, and Dalley moves from trading old coppers to dealing in abandoned mining machinery and wrecked ships. By 1925, she is one of the biggest scrap metal dealers in Australia, and she begins to pursue other business interests. She purchases the bankrupt Shepparton Freezing Works for £15,000 and, by 1946, is exporting 20,000 lambs a year to Britain. Dalley pioneers a system of pre-cooling fruit to keep it green until ready for market, manufactures margarine, runs a farm, and acquires city properties. Her employees work a 40-hour week, receive equal pay, and become shareholders in the business. Dalley involves herself in many Melbourne charities ranging from personally handing out food to lending her business skills to the Red Cross. She becomes Justice of the Peace and magistrate in 1935. Dalley is elected to the Kew (Melbourne) City Council in 1948 and appointed to the Order of the British Empire the following year. From 1954 to 1963 she serves as Kew's first woman mayor. Ma Dalley dies at Kew in 1965.

MARCH 25, 1925 Birth of American Author Flannery O'Connor. Flannery O'Connor (1924–1964), American novelist, is born in Savannah, Georgia. Her novels include *Wise Blood* (1952) and *The Violent Bear It Away* (1960). Her short stories are included in many anthologies and collections, including *A Good Man Is Hard To Find and Other Stories* (1955), and *Everything That Rises Must Converge* (1965). A collection of her letters, entitled *The Habit of Being: Letters of Flannery O'Connor,* is published in 1979.

OCTOBER 13, 1925 Birth of Margaret Thatcher, Britain's First Woman Prime Minister. Margaret Thatcher (1925–), who becomes Great Britain's first woman prime minister, is born Margaret Hilda Roberts in Lincolnshire, England. Her interest in conservative politics takes hold early, and in college she is president of the University Conservative Association at Oxford. Her first job after graduation in 1947 is as a research chemist, but she makes her first run for public office in 1949. In 1951 she marries Denis Thatcher and takes up the study of law. Margaret Thatcher wins a seat in Parliament in 1959 and spends the next 20 years working for conservative legislation, especially laws and policies that cut government-subsidized programs in order to strengthen the national economy. In 1975 she is elected leader of the Conserva-

tive Party, the first woman to head a major party in Great Britain, and in 1979 she becomes the first woman prime minister, a post she holds until her resignation in 1990. Thatcher serves the longest term of any twentieth-century prime minister.

1926 Marilyn Monroe, American Sex Symbol, Is Born. Actress Marilyn Monroe (1926–1962) is born Norma Jean Baker in Los Angeles, California. Her childhood is marred by tragedy—her mother's insanity, life in foster homes, rape, and marriage at 16. During World War II she is "discovered" working at an airplane factory by a photographer who puts her picture on the cover of *Yank* magazine. Hired by the film company Twentieth-Century Fox, she is cast in small parts in such films as *Dangerous Years* (1948), *The Asphalt Jungle* (1950), and *All About Eve* (1950). In 1953, she stars in three big-budget color films: *Niagara, Gentlemen Prefer Blondes,* and *How to Marry a Millionaire.* Immediately, Marilyn Monroe becomes an international sensation and sex symbol. On the big screen, her voluptuous figure and girlish whisper represent innocent sexual vulnerability. During the Korean War, she entertains American troops. Her well-publicized marriages to baseball star Joe DiMaggio and playwright Arthur Miller both end in divorce.

Monroe aspires to serious dramatic roles and appears in *Bus Stop* (1956), but she returns to the familiar role of sexy blonde in the box office hit, *The Seven Year Itch* (1956), as well as *The Prince and the Show Girl* (1958) and *Some Like It Hot* (1959). Her career and personal life suffer from her alcohol and drug addiction, as well as the studio's refusal to allow her to deviate from her sex symbol status. In 1962 Monroe completes her last film, *The Misfits* (1962), before dying of an apparent suicide at age 36. Speculations surrounding her suspicious death implicate her involvement with Mafia figures or then-President John F. Kennedy. Despite the sadness of her real-life story, her screen persona becomes an enduring American archetype for female sensuality. More than 30 years after her death, Marilyn Monroe's image continues to be immediately recognizable by millions all over the world.

1926   **British Politician Janet Young Is Born.** Janet Young (1926–), who serves in leadership positions in the British Parliament, is born in Oxford, England. She graduates from Oxford with a degree in philosophy, politics, and economics. Young joins the Oxford City Council in 1957 and is made a life peer in 1971. She takes on serious responsibilities in the House of Lords, including the post of Undersecretary of State for Education. Although Young is the first woman to hold various posts, she is always to some degree in the shadow of her old friend Margaret Thatcher (1925–). When Thatcher becomes leader of the Conservative Party in 1975, Young becomes the party's vice chairman. In 1979 Young becomes Minister of State for Education and Science. She later serves as Leader of the House of Lords and Minister of State for the Foreign and Commonwealth Office. In 1981 she becomes the first minister in charge of the new Management and Personnel Office, responsible for eliminating some 100,000 civil service jobs. In this position, she works to improve job opportunities for women in civil service. In particular, she wants to see more women in top-level positions and to make it easier for new mothers to find part-time work.

1926   **Helena Normanton, First Woman Barrister to Appear at London Sessions.** Helena Florence Normanton (1883–1957), a barrister-at-law, is the first woman to appear at the London Sessions. She is also the first woman barrister to appear at the High Court of Justice (1922) and at the Central Criminal Court (1924), and the first woman elected to the General Council of the Bar (1945).

1926   **Young Women's League Established in Quebec.** Thérèse Casgrain (1896–?), women's rights activist and one of the founding members of the Provincial Suffrage Committee in Quebec, Canada, founds the *Ligue de la Jeunesse Feminine* (Young Women's League) and also establishes a program on Radio Canada called *Femina* to promote women's rights. In 1960, she establishes the League for Human Rights, followed by the Quebec Chapter of the Voice of Women, to protest nuclear threat. In 1966, she founds the *Federation des Femmes du Quebec* in order to bring several organizations together.

1926   **Gossip Columnist Louella Parsons Receives Substantial Salary.** Gossip columnist Louella Parsons (1893–1972) demands the unheard-of salary of $250 per week from publisher William Randolph Hearst. Soon, her column is syndicated to nearly 1,000 papers worldwide. Known as the "hatchet woman," Parsons quickly becomes the most important, powerful, feared—and respected—woman in Hollywood. She also writes for *Photoplay*, the leading fan magazine, and for *Modern Screen*. Parsons' 1944 autobiography, *The Gay Illiterate*, becomes a bestseller. Like her rival, columnist Hedda Hopper, Parsons loses most of her power in Hollywood during the relaxed moral climate of the 1960s.

1926   **Mae West Performs in Her Controversial Play.** American sex symbol Mae West (1893–1980) writes and performs in the stage play *The Constant Sinner*, which is attacked by prudish critics but plays 385 sold-out performances. Finally, the play is raided and West is jailed for ten days. She also writes a play called *The Drag* in which she pleads for "intelligent understanding" of homosexuality. This play sells out to New Jersey audiences, but West is forbidden to bring the play to Broadway.

1926   **American Poet Marianne Moore Becomes First Woman Editor of *The Dial*.** Marianne Moore (1887–1972), an important modernist poet, becomes the first woman to serve as editor of *The Dial* in New York City, a post she holds until 1929. Her works include *Observations* (1924) and *Collected Poems* (1941), for which she wins the Pulitzer Prize. Her generous personality and sharp eye for literary details shape the poetry that is published in this significant periodical, giving the journal an international and lasting influence.

1926　Marion Phillips Organizes Relief for British Miners' Families during Strike. Marion Phillips (1881–1932), a British socialist with a particular concern for women's rights, organizes the Women's Committee for the Relief of Miners' Wives and Children to provide relief for miners' families during the General Strike in 1926 in London, England.

1926　Marie Rambert Founds and Directs Ballet Company in London. Marie Rambert (1888–1982), an English choreographer, dancer, and teacher, is the founder and first director of the Ballet Rambert, in Hammersmith, London. She continues to direct this innovative company until 1966. The Rambert Ballet is known for its classical training combined with the encouragement of new ideas, and it presents a regular London season in addition to going on provincial and continental tours. The company reflects the personality of its founder, for Rambert is known for her inspirational ability and energy. Until her late 70s, Marie Rambert is remarkable for turning sudden cartwheels in unexpected places.

1926　Actress Gloria Swanson Founds Production Company. Gloria Swanson (1899–1983), the first silent movie star to earn $20,000 a week in the 1920s, founds Swanson Productions in Hollywood. This company supports von Stroheim's *Queen Kelly*, in which she plays one of her most powerful roles. Swanson is also remembered for her portrayal of the character Norma Desmond in Billy Wilder's *Sunset Boulevard*.

1926　Kono Taeko, Japanese Novelist, Is Born. Japanese novelist Kono Taeko (1926–), who writes novels exploring the psychological aspects of everyday, human realities, is born.

1926　Carlotta Zambelli, First Dancer Inducted into France's Légion D'Honneur. Carlotta Zambelli (1875–1968), an Italian ballerina who becomes principal dancer at the Paris Opera in 1898, is the first person to enter the Légion D'Honneur for dance, in Paris, France. She is recognized for her brilliant technique and interpretations. She retires as a dancer in 1930 and goes on to serve as director of the Opera Ballet School, a position she holds until 1950.

1926　Indian Women Gain Provincial Vote. Women are granted the vote in provincial elections in India.

APRIL 28, 1926　American Author, Harper Lee, Is Born. Harper Lee (1926–), author of *To Kill a Mockingbird*, is born in Monroeville, Alabama.

AUGUST 1926　First Woman to Swim Across English Channel. Gertrude Ederle (1906–), about one year after her first attempt, becomes the first woman to swim across the English Channel. Her record time of 14 hours and 39 minutes surpasses by almost two hours the time of the five men who previously swim the channel. Ederle is inducted into the International Swimming Hall of Fame in 1965 and the International Women's Sports Hall of Fame in 1980.

NOVEMBER 19, 1926　Birth of Jeane Kirkpatrick, American Political Thinker. Jeane Duane Jordan Kirkpatrick (1926–), a strong anti-Communist voice in American politics, is born in Duncan, Oklahoma. She studies political science in college and does research for the office of intelligence research and for the liberal Fund for the Republic. She goes on to an academic career writing scholarly and popular articles and teaching political science at Georgetown University. She also serves as a consultant to government agencies and Washington think tanks. A major theme of Kirkpatrick's teaching and writing is the threat of Communism. Many academics and politicians think she is too single-minded and even out-of-date in her anti-Communism, but others admire her thinking and clear writing. Two of her books aimed at general readers, *Political Women* (1974) and *The New Presidential Elite: Men and Women in National Politics* (1976), bring her increased exposure and influence. A lifelong Democrat, Kirkpatrick is nonetheless an independent thinker, and a 1979 article in which she criticizes the Carter Administration catches the attention of Ronald Reagan (1911–). In 1981 Kirkpatrick is nominated by President Reagan to be the U.S. permanent representative to the United Nations (UN). In this position, she continues to defy classification as "liberal" or "conservative," as she takes positions supporting El Salvador's military junta, against economic sanctions in South Africa, and condemning Israel without sanctions for an air attack against Iraq. Jeane Kirkpatrick leaves the UN in 1985.

1927   Birth of Josephine Hulett, American Labor Organizer. Josephine Hulett (1927–), a pioneer in the field of organizing domestic workers, is born. She graduates from Philadelphia School of Practical Nursing in 1957, but organizing household workers becomes her career; she organizes in Youngstown, Warren, and Akron, Ohio. Hulett joins the staff of the National Committee on Household Employment in 1969, and in 1969-70 she serves as president of the Youngstown Household Technicians. In 1972 she founds the Ohio Coalition of Household Employees. Hulett also serves on the Afro-American Labor Council and, in 1971, is the first woman to receive its Special Recognition Award. Hulett is also active in the National Association for the Advancement of Colored People, the Urban League, the National Organization for Women's Black Caucus, and the Women in Poverty Task Force.

1927   Barbara Stanwyck Begins Acting Career. Ruby Stevens makes her acting debut in the stage play *The Noose* and changes her name to Barbara Stanwyck (1907–1990). She goes on to become a successful film star, with roles in pictures such as *Stella Dallas* (1937), *Golden Boy* (1939), *The Lady Eve* (1941), *Meet John Doe* (1941), *Ball of Fire* (1941), *Double Indemnity* (1944), *Sorry, Wrong Number* (1948), *The Furies* (1950), and *Walk on the Wild Side* (1962). In her 50s, Stanwyck lands a starring role as the western matriarch in the television series *Big Valley* (1965-69). At 75, she appears in the television mini-series *The Thorn Birds*, which gives her the chance to play an elderly woman assailed by sexual urges.

1927   English Novelist Sarah Grand Elected Mayor of Bath. Sarah Grand (1854–1943), a novelist whose actual name is Frances McFall, is elected Mayor of Bath in England, becoming the first woman to be elected to the office.

1927   Birth of African American Soprano Leontyne Price. Leontyne Price (1927–), the first black American woman to achieve international acclaim in opera, is born. Her rich soprano voice is primarily associated with Verdi's work, but she is also the first woman to sing the leading role in Samuel Barber's *Antony and Cleopatra*, which has its debut as the first opera performed at the new Metropolitan Opera House at Lincoln Center in New York City in 1966. Price retires from the stage in 1985.

1927   Japanese Proletarian Writer Hirabayashi Taiko Publishes Best-Known Story. Hirabayashi Taiko (1905–1972), a Japanese writer active in left-wing political and cultural groups, publishes her best-known work, "Seryoshitsu nite." Along with her anarchist lover,

Taiko is arrested in the general police round-up of radicals following the Tokyo earthquake in 1923. After they are banished from Tokyo, they go to Korea and Manchuria. There, her lover is again arrested and Taiko gives birth to a daughter, who starves to death. This experience becomes the basis of "Seryoshitsu nite" (1927; "At the Charity Clinic"). Another story, "Naguru," (1928, "Beating"), is a story of a woman who is unhappily married and frequently subjected to beatings by her shiftless husband. Taiko becomes a major figure in the Japanese proletarian literature movement, writing about the lives of the poor in rural and urban Japan. Her stories in the 1930s show her hatred of Japan's growing militarism. She does not write during World War II (1939–45) but writes prolifically afterward on a wide range of subjects, including the work of other prominent Japanese women writers.

1927 American Actress Clara Bow, Hollywood's "It" Girl. Clara Bow (1905–1965), born in poverty in Brooklyn, New York, becomes one of the most famous and imitated women in America during her heyday as an actress in silent films. A gifted comedienne, she makes her mark in such films as *Mantrap* (1925), in which she typically plays a clever working-class girl looking for a rich man. Bow's red hair and mobile features make her a vivid presence in Paramount's comedies. Clara Bow is declared by author Elinor Glyn to have the elusive "It": that "quality...which draws all others with its magnetic force." The actress stars in a enormously successful film called *It* in 1927, playing a lingerie salesclerk who plots to win the heart of her boss, the head of the world's largest department store. Bow's life off-screen is one of scandals and mental instability, and her career ends in 1933. She marries former cowboy star Rex Bell, later lieutenant governor of Nevada, and lives in seclusion on his ranch with intermittent stays in sanatoriums. Clara Bow is considered the

personification of F. Scott Fitzgerald's "new woman" of the 1920s, the flapper.

FEBRUARY 19, 1927 Birth of Carson McCullers, American Author. Carson McCullers (1917–67), American novelist, is born in Columbus, Georgia. Her works include *The Heart Is a Lonely Hunter* (1940), *Reflections in a Golden Eye* (1941), *The Member of the Wedding* (1946), *The Ballad of the Sad Café* (1951), and *Clock Without Hands* (1961).

AUGUST 25, 1927 Althea Gibson, African American Tennis and Golf Pro, Is Born. Althea Gibson (1927–), the first African American to break the racial barrier in international tennis during the 1950s, is born in Silver, South Carolina. She works her way up through the tennis ranks of the exclusive black tennis clubs and qualifies to play in the U.S. Ladies Tennis Association (USLTA) tournament. On August 28, 1950, Gibson becomes the first African American to play in a major USLTA tournament. In 1956 she becomes a Grand Slam winner, the first black woman to win the French Open. In 1957, Gibson becomes the first African American woman to win at Wimbledon and a clay court championship, winning again in 1958. Also in 1957, she becomes the first black athlete to win a major U.S. national championship when she plays at Forest Hills. In 1960, Gibson begins playing golf professionally and becomes the first black woman to play in the Ladies Professional Golf Association (LPGA). In 1991, Gibson is the first black woman to receive the Theodore Roosevelt Award of the National Collegiate Athletic Association (NCAA).

DECEMBER 27, 1927 Birth of Anne Armstrong, U.S. Republican Party Leader. Anne Legendre Armstrong (1927–), a leader in the Republican party, is born in New Orleans, Louisiana, into an old Creole family. After attending Vassar College, she serves as a volunteer campaigner and then rises through the ranks of the Republican Party. In 1971 Armstrong becomes cochair of the National Republican Committee, the first woman to hold this office, and supports the Equal Rights Amendment. She is a member of the White House staff from 1972 to 1974, as a counselor to the president with full cabinet status. Armstrong is Ambassador to the Court of St. James in 1976-77, the first woman to hold this important post. Over the next 15 years she holds a number of political and academic posts, and serves on the boards of major international companies, including General Motors and American Express. Intelligent and effective in party politics, Armstrong is cochair of the successful Ronald Reagan-George Bush presidential campaign in 1980. Armstrong is named to the Texas Women's Hall of Fame in 1986 and is awarded the Presidential Medal of Freedom in 1987.

1928 **Publication of Englishwoman Radclyffe Hall's Lesbian Novel,** *The Well of Loneliness.* English author Marguerite Radclyffe Hall (1880-1943) publishes a controversial but bestselling lesbian novel, *The Well of Loneliness,* that narrates the story of Stephen Gordon, a young woman who should have been born a man. The famous sexologist, Havelock Ellis, writes the preface for the novel, which treats lesbianism, or "inversion," with sympathy. Hall sees inversion as an act of God, hence as natural, and she challenges society's view of homosexuality as an abomination. However, she does regard inversion as a type of deformity and pleads for pity as well as equal rights for the lesbian. The book outrages many in English society for its explicit mention of women's intimacy. The Conservative government prosecutes Hall and her publisher. Though banned, the book is published in many languages and becomes a bestseller. Hall is born into a wealthy but troubled English family, and by the time she reaches young adulthood she knows she is a homosexual. She refers to herself as "John" and begins

Elsa Schiaparelli

publishing poems and novels under the name Radclyffe Hall.

1928 **Fashion Designer Elsa Schiaparelli Introduces First Creation.** Italian-born French fashion designer Elsa Schiaparelli (1890–1973) produces her first "invention," a black, short-sleeved sweater knitted with the pattern of a butterfly bow around the neckline. The success of these sweaters emboldens her to experiment further with a quirky illusionism. She is influenced greatly by contemporary art, as she writes in her autobiography *Shocking Life:* "It was the time when abstract Dadaism and Futurism were the talk of the world, the time when chairs looked like tables, and tables like footstools..."

1928 Birth of Shirley Temple, Hollywood's Biggest Child Star. Child actress Shirley Temple (1928–) is born in Santa Monica, California. An exceptionally pretty child, she is famous in her neighborhood for her cuteness. While at dance school, she is spotted by a talent scout. Temple first appears in *Baby Burlesks*—one-reel take-offs on famous motion pictures which star children in adult roles. Temple's salary of $10 per day is higher than that of most adults during the Great Depression. She appears in her first feature film, *Stand Up and Cheer*, in 1934. Her trademarks are her dimples, bright eyes, and curly-top golden hair. After signing a seven-year contract with Fox studio, Temple begins earning $150 per week. In 1934, she receives a special Academy Award for "bringing more happiness to millions of children and millions of grown-ups than any other child of her years in the history of the world."

The Shirley Temple doll sells over 1.5 million copies, and Shirley Temple coloring and comic books, and clothing are mass-marketed. American mothers try to remake their own daughters into carbon copies of Shirley. By 1938, Temple is the number-one money-making star in Hollywood. In her films, she sings and dances and avoids being obnoxiously cute. Her roles include *Curly Top* (1935), *Poor Little Rich Girl* (1936), *Dimples* (1936), *Heidi* (1937), *Rebecca of Sunny Brook Farm* (1938), and *A Little Princess* (1939). By 1939, at age 12, Shirley Temple is a has-been. In 1944, producer David O. Selznick tries to recharge her career as a young adult actress in such films as *Since You Went Away* and *I'll Be Seeing You*. In 1945, Temple marries Air Force Sergeant John Agar and publishes her autobiography, *My Young Life*. *The Bachelor and the Bobby Soxer* (1947) is Temple's last successful film. She has three children with Agar; however, the couple divorces in 1949.

Temple marries media executive Charles Black in 1950 and has two more children. In 1958, she hosts *The Shirley Temple Storybook* on television. She also performs charity and hospital work and makes guest appearances on television variety shows. In 1968, President Nixon appoints Shirley Temple Black as United Nations representative.

1928 Birth of Trinidadian Author Rosa Guy. Rosa Guy (1928–), author and founder of the Harlem Writer's Guild, is born. Guy publishes her first work, *Bird at My Window*, in 1955. Other works include *My Love, My Love, or the Peasant Girl* (1988) and *The Ups and Downs of Carl David III* (1989).

1928 American Economist Mary Williams Dewson Helps First Lady Develop Women's Political Caucuses. Economist Mary Williams Dewson (1872–1962) works with Eleanor Roosevelt, the wife of U.S. President Franklin D. Roosevelt, to develop state women's political caucuses.

1928 Eleanora Sears Wins First Women's Squash Championship. Pioneering American athlete Eleanora Sears (1881–1968) wins the first U.S. women's squash racquets singles championship.

1928 Louise Brooks Stars in *Lulu*. American silent-film actress Louise Brooks (1906–1985) appears in the classic Expressionistic film *Lulu*, directed by G. W. Pabst. *Lulu* is a synthesis of two plays conceived for the theater: *Pandora's Box* and *The Earth Spirit*. The character of Lulu is simultaneously perverse, childlike, naive, amoral, and sensual. The movie is declared "immoral and inartistic."

1928 Actress Carole Lombard Appears in Her First Major Role. Carole Lombard (1909–1942) lands her first starring role for Fox studios in *Me, Gangster*. She quickly graduates into female leads. Petite, with golden hair and blue eyes, Lombard combines elegant beauty with wisecracking wit.

1928 Austrian Singer Lotte Lenya Appears in Premiere of *Three-Penny Opera*. Lotte Lenya

(1898–1981), an Austrian singer of international reputation, plays the part of Jenny, a major character in her husband Kurt Weill's *Three-Penny Opera*, at its premiere in Berlin, Germany. She later stars in the film version of this work. Lenya and Weill leave Germany in 1933 and settle in New York City. Her voice, familiar through her many recordings, recalls the atmosphere of Berlin in the 1920s and 1930s.

1928 **Japanese Poet Yanagihara Byakuren Publishes Autobiographical Novel.** Yanagihara Byakuren (1885–1967), a Japanese poet known for the passionate style of her poems, publishes an autobiographical novel, *Ibara no mi* (*The Fruit of Thorns*).

1928 **Women 21 and Older Granted Vote in Great Britain.** Women at the age of 21 win suffrage in Great Britain. In 1918, Parliament permitted women over 30 to vote.

APRIL 4, 1928 **Maya Angelou, African American Poet and Writer, Is Born.** Maya Angelou (1928–) is born Marguerite Johnson in St. Louis, Missouri. When she is three, her divorced parents send her and her brother, Bailey, alone on a train to Stamps, Arkansas, to live with her paternal grandmother, Annie Henderson, who owns a general store. Stamps is a warm but segregated community. At seven years old, Angelou is taken from Stamps to live with her mother in California, and at age eight, Angelou is raped by her mother's boyfriend. He is later found murdered, and young Maya feels responsible. She returns to Stamps, and for five years, she rarely speaks. Exposed to the world of books, Angelou breaks out of this silence. In 1941, she and Bailey move back to California, where she receives her street education. At age 16, Angelou becomes pregnant with her son, Guy Bailey Johnson. As a single mother, she has many occupations, among them cook, waitress, prostitute, dancer, and the first African American streetcar conductor in San Francisco. In her 20s she

becomes a successful entertainer, and in 1954–55, she travels with the *Porgy and Bess* Touring Company. In the late 1950s and early 1960s, Angelou is an actress, editor, and activist. She works with Martin Luther King, Jr., publishes her first short story, and marries a South African freedom fighter. For three years, she lives in Ghana. In 1981, she accepts a lifetime position as an English professor at Wake Forest University in North Carolina. In 1993 she reads her poem, "On the Pulse of Morning," at President Bill Clinton's inauguration. She publishes several volumes of poetry, including *Just Give Me a Cool Drink of Water 'fore I Die,* and several autobiographical books, including *I Know Why the Caged Bird Sings.* Angelou wins numerous awards and receives many honorary doctorates.

MAY 1928 **Chinese Communist Jingyu Xiang Executed.** Jingyu Xiang (1895–1928), a Chinese feminist revolutionary and a friend of Mao Tse-tung, is arrested and executed by the Nationalists during Xiang Kai Shek's anti-Communist campaign.

1929 **African American Actress Nina Mae McKinney Gets Big Screen Break in *Hallelujah*.** Nina Mae McKinney, an African American screen actress, lands a screen role in King Vidor's *Hallelujah*. This role elevates her from obscurity to stardom and earns her a reputation as the screen's first black sex symbol. *Hallelujah* represents one of the early attempts by a major motion picture studio to produce an all-black cast picture. McKinney portrays a cunning, conniving, and deceitful woman—sexy and irresistible—who leads a black man on the path of self-destruction. Born in Lancaster, South Carolina, McKinney migrates to New York City, where she works as a chorus girl in the stage show *Blackbirds of 1928.* In the 1930s, following *Hallelujah*, McKinney discovers that Hollywood has few roles for talented black actresses. Thus, she is forced to shuttle between the United States and Europe to pursue a stage and acting career, often being billed as the "Black Garbo." McKinney has roles in films such as *Safe in Hell* (1931), *Pie Pie Blackbird* (1932), *Congo Raid* (1935; alternately titled *Sanders of the River*, in which she appears on screen with Paul Robeson), *Reckless* (1935), *St. Louis Gal* (1938), *Gang Smashers* (1938), and *Straight to Heaven* (1939). *Hallelujah* escalates her to fame when she is only 17 years old, but despite her talent, McKinney never again achieves true screen success. In 1949 when she is cast in *Pinky*, McKinney is still being cast as the "rough type," an image that she seems unable to escape.

1929 Rose Markward Knox, First Woman Elected to Board of American Grocery Manufacturers' Association. Rose Markward Knox (1857–1950), head of the Knox Company, is the first woman elected to the board of directors of the American Grocery Manufacturers' Association. She takes over the Knox Company, famous for its gelatin, at the time of her husband's death in 1908 and builds it into a major enterprise, with plants in Johnstown, New York, and Camden, New Jersey.

1929 Gertrude Battles Lane, First Woman Vice President of Crowell Publishing. Gertrude Battles Lane (1874–1941), editor of the *Woman's Home Companion*, becomes the first female vice president of the Crowell Publishing Company in New York City.

1929 Birth of Author, Poet, and Biographer Eloise Greenfield. African American Eloise Greenfield (1929–) is born. She first publishes *Sister* in 1974. *Honey, I Love, and Other Love Poems* follows in 1978. Greenfield receives the Coretta Scott King Award for *Africa Dream* (1978) and the Washington, D.C. Mayor's Art Award in 1983.

1929 Chinese Conductor Xiaoying Zeng Is Born. Xiaoying Zeng (1929–), the first woman to become a conductor in China, is born. She first performs at the age of 14, then goes on to further training both in China and

in Moscow in the 1950s. On her return to China, she soon establishes a national reputation, and in 1977 she becomes principal conductor at the Central Opera Theatre in Beijing.

1929 First Woman Director of Sound Film. Dorothy Arzner (1900–1979) is the first woman to direct a sound film. An experienced editor and director, she is chosen by Paramount to direct its first sound film, *The Wild Party*, in 1929. Arzner begins her film career as a typist at Paramount but moves on to movie editing and in 1925 writes, helps shoot, and edits *Old Ironsides*. She directs 17 feature films and works with many female stars.

1929 Romanian Women Granted Local Suffrage. Women in Romania are extended local suffrage.

1929 Local Voting Rights Won by Greek Women. Women in Greece win local suffrage, but their age requirement is higher than the men's.

1929 Cuneiform Tablets Discovered in Northern Syria. Cuneiform tablets are discovered in the Ras Shamra mound in northern Syria, on the site of the ancient Canaanite capital city of Ugarit. The Ras Shamra texts, as they are now known, show the Canaanite myths and rituals that form the basis of Hebrew biblical stories; highly venerated goddesses appear who have been transformed into monsters, demons, and devils by the Hebrews.

FEBRUARY 9, 1929 Birth of Nelle Pitcock Horlander, American Unionist. Nelle Pitcock Horlander (1929–), who becomes the highest ranking woman in her union in the state of Kentucky, is born. She begins her union career at the age of 20, when she begins working at Southern Bell Telephone Company. She joins the Communications Workers of America Local 3310 in Louisville at the same time. Horlander quickly becomes active in the union and the following year is elected to the position of steward. By 1954 she is elected secretary-treasurer and holds the position of treasurer for 15 years. In 1969, Horlander is elected president and serves for five years before becoming a full-time staff representative for the union. During this time, she negotiates contracts and serves her union as its representative to numerous labor-related organizations and union committees. One of her projects is the campaign to merge the American Federation of Labor and the Congress for Industrial Organizing, at which time she meets and works with Thelma Stovall, another powerful union woman. They become lifelong friends and work together on many union, women's, and political issues. Horlander combines her interests in these areas by being a charter member of Kentucky Women's Advocates, a state vice president of the Coalition of Labor Union Women, and a member of the Gender Fairness Task Force, the Governor's Commission for Full Equality, and the Jefferson County chapter of the National Organization for Women. Horlander is appointed by various Kentucky governors to the Governor's Advisory Council, the Kentucky Commission on Employment of the Handicapped, and the Kentucky Commission on Women.

MAY 16, 1929 **American Poet Adrienne Rich Is Born.** Poet and essayist Adrienne Rich (1929–) is born in Baltimore, Maryland, to Helen Jones and Arnold Rich. Her father, a pathologist, teaches Rich at home and encourages her to write poetry. Rich graduates from Radcliffe College in 1951 and publishes her first volume of poems, *A Change of World*, the same year. The work is selected for the Yale Younger Poets Series. After a book of poems in 1955, the year her first son is born, she does not publish again for eight years. Rich feels strong tensions between her roles as mother, wife, and writer. In 1963 and 1966, she publishes two books of poetry dealing with this theme. In 1980, Rich challenges stereotyped definitions of sexuality in an essay, "Compulsory Heterosexuality and Lesbian Existence." During her career, Rich publishes more than 15 volumes of poems and two collections of essays.

JUNE 8, 1929 **Margaret Bondfield, First Woman Cabinet Minister in Great Britain.** Labor leader Margaret Grace Bondfield (1873–1953), Member of Parliament in England since 1923, becomes Minister of Labour. As the first woman cabinet minister in British history, Bondfield becomes more conservative on unemployment issues. She retires from Parliament in 1938 but continues to work with trade unions. King George V (1865–1936) breaks his customary silence to say in receiving her, "I am pleased to be the one to whom has come the opportunity to receive the first Privy Councillor."

JULY 28, 1929 **Birth of Jacqueline Kennedy Onassis.** Born in Southampton, Long Island, to a wealthy Roman Catholic family, Jacqueline Kennedy Onassis (1929–1994) achieves unparalleled fame as first lady during the Kennedy administration. Her elegance and style captivate the world, symbolizing for Americans their hopes for success and prosperity. In the aftermath of John F. Kennedy's assassination in 1963, Onassis's grace and poise lead the nation in mourning their president. Five years later, in a flurry of criticism and publicity, she is wed to Greek shipping tycoon Aristotle Onassis. The marriage ends with his death seven years later, leaving Onassis and her two children very wealthy. She spends the last twenty years of her life living quietly as a grandmother and editor for several New York publishers. Jacqueline Kennedy Onassis dies of cancer in New York City on May 19, 1994.

OCTOBER 18, 1929 **Judicial Committee of the Privy Council in England Declares Canadian Women "Persons."** The Judicial Committee of the Privy Council (JCPC) in

England, the highest court of appeal on questions related to Canadian law at the time, reverses a 1928 decision of the Canadian Supreme Court and declares women to be "persons" under the 1867 British North America Act (the basis of Canada's constitution). This clears the way for women to be appointed to the Canadian Senate, a non-elected body similar to Britain's House of Lords.

In 1919, the first conference of the Federated Women's Institutes of Canada passes a resolution requesting the Prime Minister to appoint a woman to the Canadian Senate. The Canadian governments of the 1920s (Conservatives under Arthur Meighen and Liberals under William Lyon Mackenzie King) refuse to appoint women to the Senate, stating that women are not eligible under the British North America Act. Five prominent women—Emily Murphy, Nellie McClung, Louisa McKinney, Irene Parlby, and Henrietta Muir Edwards—petition the government to get the Supreme Court of Canada to rule on whether women are included in the phrase "qualified persons" under section 24 of the British North America Act. When the Supreme Court rules that women are not "qualified persons" under this law, the women petition the JCPC in England. Cairine Wilson is appointed the first woman senator in 1930.

Part 5

TAKING HER PLACE
IN SOCIETY 1930 – 1996

$$Chapter\ 19$$

1930 TO 1939

1930 – 1934

1930 **Flora Solomon Hired by British Department Store to Improve Working Conditions.** Flora Solomon (1895–1984) is the first woman hired to improve working conditions at the British department store Marks and Spencer, in London. Born in Russia and educated in Germany, Solomon moves to England with her family in 1914. An ardent socialist, she works at Marks and Spencer until 1948, establishing an innovative Welfare Committee whose program includes canteens, sickness and maternity benefits, health care, and paid holidays.

1930 **Dorothy Eustis Introduces Seeing Eye Dogs to U.S.** Dorothy Harrison Eustis (1886?–1946) introduces the Seeing Eye dog for the blind to the United States. After a brief effort at establishing a school to train guide dogs fails in Nashville, Tennessee, Eustis moves the school to Morristown, New Jersey. Eustis' interest in guide dogs for the blind begins in 1927, when she learns about a school that is training guide dogs in Potsdam, Germany. After visiting the school, Eustis writes an article about it for the *Saturday Evening Post,* and arranges to train a dog for a blind insurance salesman living in the United States.

1930 **Cairine Wilson, First Female Canadian Senator.** Cairine Wilson is appointed the first

woman senator in Canada. This appointment is made possible by the Judicial Committee of the Privy Council (JCPC) in England, the highest court of appeal on questions related to Canadian law at the time. In 1929, the JCPC reverses a 1928 decision of the Canadian Supreme Court and declares women to be "persons" under the 1867 British North America Act (the basis of Canada's constitution). This clears the way for women to be appointed to the Canadian Senate, a non-elected body similar to Britain's House of Lords.

1930 **Jean Harlow Stars in Her First Major Motion Picture.** After her introduction to Howard Hughes, actress Jean Harlow (1911–1937) wins the leading role in his film, *Hell's Angels,* and the craze for platinum blondes begins.

1930 **Birth of Artist and Writer Faith Ringgold.** Faith Ringgold (1930–), African American painter, mixed-media sculptor, artist, and writer, is born. In 1992, she wins both the Coretta Scott King Illustrator Award and the Caldecott Medal for her picture book, *Tar Beach.*

1930 **Japanese Anarchist Takamure Itsue Cofounds Proletarian Women's Art League.** Takamure Itsue (1894–1964), a Japanese historian of women, feminist, and anarchist, joins

Dorothy Eustis, first president of The Seeing Eye.

with several other feminists, including Hirat-suka Raicho (1886–1971), to form the *Musan Fujin Geijutsu Remmei* (Proletarian Women's Art League), a group sympathetic to anarchism. While an unequivocal opponent of capitalism, Itsue is also critical of Marxists, because she thinks that they focus solely on production while ignoring reproduction, the main concern of women. Itsue realizes that reproduction and child care controlled by women can only exist in self-governing, non-hierarchical communities in which women and men are equal producers. For this reason, she advocates anarchism. The second half of Itsue's life is devoted to historical research focused on the development of marriage patterns. For more than three decades, she examines all literary and historical records on courtship and marriage practices to chart the transition from matriarchy to patriarchy in

Japan. She later publishes a pioneering, four-volume work on Japanese women's history, *Josei no rekishi (Women's History)*.

1930 Kubushiro Ochimi Organizes All-Japan Women's Suffrage Conference. Feminist and social activist Kubushiro Ochimi (1882–1972) is a major organizer of the *Zen Nihon Fusen Taikai* (All-Japan Women's Suffrage Conference).

1930 White South African Women Gain Vote. White women in South Africa are granted suffrage.

FEBRUARY 12, 1930 Jennie Kelleher Bowls Perfect 300 Game. Jennie Kelleher of Madison, Wisconsin, is the first woman to bowl a perfect 300 game.

MARCH 26, 1930 Birth of Sandra Day O'Connor, First Woman Justice of the U.S. Supreme Court. Sandra Day O'Connor (1930–), a U.S. Senator from Arizona and the first woman Justice of the U.S. Supreme Court, is born in El Paso, Texas. She grows up on the family's ranch far from the nearest city. There are no schools nearby, so she often stays with her grandmother in El Paso and attends school there. Eventually she goes to Stanford Law School, where she works on the *Stanford Law Review* and marries John O'Connor, another law student. Although she graduates magna cum laude, private law firms will not hire a woman, so O'Connor goes into government and then military service. She steps out of the paid work force for five years to stay home with the couple's three sons, then becomes assistant attorney general for the State of Arizona in 1965. In 1970, she is elected to the state senate and becomes Arizona's first female senate majority leader in 1972. As a senator, O'Connor supports the death penalty and the Equal Rights Amendment. Returning to law in 1975, she serves on her county's Superior Court Bench and then on the Arizona Court of Appeals. In 1981 she is nominated to the U.S. Supreme Court by President Ronald Reagan, who notes her unusual intelligence and fairness. A lifelong moderate or conservative Republican, Sandra Day O'Connor is the first woman to serve on the highest court in the land.

JULY 6, 1930 Aviator Amelia Earhart Sets Speed Record. American aviator Amelia Earhart (1898–1937) sets the woman's speed record in an airplane when she flies 181.18 miles per hour.

JULY 27, 1930 British Politician Shirley Williams Is Born. Shirley Vivien Teresa Brittain Williams (1930–), one of the most prominent women in British government from the 1960s through the mid-1980s, is born in Chelsea, England. Williams' father is a political science professor and politician; her mother is feminist writer Vera Brittain (1893–1970). During college, Williams joins the Labour League of Youth and becomes the first woman to chair the Labour Club. After a year in New York, during which she marries, she returns to England and works as a journalist. She wins a seat in Parliament in 1964 as a Labour candidate and serves there for 15 years. A brilliant political economist and independent thinker, Williams is a strong voice for her country's membership in the European Economic Community, even when her own party opposes it. She becomes a professorial fellow at London's Policy Studies Institute in 1979. In 1981 she helps found the Social Democrat Party and is elected to Parliament again, but she is defeated in 1983. Williams holds several ministerial posts in Parliament, and she works for comprehensive education and restrictions on divorce and abortion. Another interest is new technology and how it will affect employment in the future, the subject of her book *Youth Without Work* (1981). Williams also writes *Politics Is for People* (1981) and *A Job to Live* (1985) and coedits *Ambition and Beyond: The Career Paths of American Politicians* (1993).

Dame Irene Ward

OCTOBER 1, 1930 Gertrude Hickman Thompson, First Woman to Head U.S. Railroad Board of Directors. Gertrude Hickman Thompson (1877–1950) becomes the first woman to serve as head of the board of directors of a U.S. railroad when she is made chair of the board of Magma Arizona Railroad, a position her husband holds until his death three months earlier.

1931 Dame Irene Ward Elected to British Parliament. On her third attempt, Irene Ward (1895?–1980) is elected a member of the British Parliament. She serves in Parliament for 38 of the next 42 years—from 1931 to 1945, and again from 1950 to 1974—making her the longest-serving woman in the House of Commons. While there, she works to promote legislation to protect fishing and shipbuilding interests, nurses, and midwives. Ward is known for her fiery personality. She is one of four women members of Parliament to march on the House of Commons in 1954, seeking equal pay for women. In 1968, Ward is ousted from the chambers of Parliament after continuously shouting "Dictatorship" in protest over new rules on debate procedures. Ward is made Dame Commander of the Order of the British Empire in 1951, and Companion of Honour in 1973.

1931   Ninette de Valois Establishes English Royal Ballet. Ninette de Valois (1898–) founds and serves as the first director of the Royal Ballet in England. She continues to head this company until her retirement in 1963. An Irish dancer of great energy and charm, de Valois is also the founder of the National School of Ballet in Turkey (1947), and the first woman to receive the Erasmus Prize Foundation Award (1974).

1931   Lillian Baylis Founds Sadler's Wells Theater Company. Lillian Baylis (1874– 1937) founds the Sadler's Wells theater company in London, which specializes in opera and ballet. Nineteen years earlier, in 1912, she founded the Old Vic theater company, a principal center for the performance of Shakespeare's plays.

1931   Birth of Isabelita Perón. Maria Estela Martinez de Perón (1931–), known as Isabelita, is born in La Rioja Province, Argentina. In 1961 Isabelita, a dancer, marries Argentinian soldier and president Juan Perón, whose first wife had died in 1952. The two live in Spain until his return to political power in Argentina in 1973, when Isabelita becomes his vice president. When Juan dies in 1974, Isabelita takes over as president, but is ousted in a military takeover in 1976. She is imprisoned on charges of abuse of public property until 1981, when she settles in Madrid, Spain.

1931   Spanish Women Gain Suffrage. Women in Spain over the age of 21 gain the ability to vote and to run for public office.

1931   Educated Women Win Vote in Portugal. Women with at least a secondary education gain the vote in Portugal.

FEBRUARY 18, 1931   Birth of American Author Toni Morrison. Toni Chloe Anthony Morrison (1931–), African American editor, novelist, and teacher, is born in Lorain, Ohio. Her works explore the lives of rural African Americans. Her works include *The Bluest Eye* (1970), *Sula* (1974), *Tar Baby* (1981), and *Beloved* (1987), for which she won the Pulitzer Prize in 1988.

APRIL 1, 1931   Verne "Jackie" Mitchell, First Woman to Play Major League Baseball. Pitcher Verne "Jackie" Mitchell signs a contract to pitch for the Memphis Lookouts of the Southern Association, becoming the first woman to play major league baseball. In an exhibition game against the New York Yankees, she strikes out both Babe Ruth and Lou Gehrig.

JUNE 23, 1931   Lili de Alvarez Plays Tennis at Wimbledon in Shorts. Lili de Alvarez appears on center court in a tennis tournament at Wimbledon wearing shorts, the first woman to don such radical attire in the prestigious tennis event.

1932   Olive Beech Cofounds Beech Aircraft. Olive Anne Mellor Beech (1903–1993) and her husband, Walter Beech, start the Beech Aircraft Corporation. Walter is president, and "O.A." is secretary and treasurer. Business grows slowly; the first year, they don't sell a single plane. In the late 1930s, however, defense contracts flow in. During World War II (1939–45), Beech supplies nearly all of the planes used for training U.S. navigators and bombardiers. When Walter dies in 1950, Olive Anne takes full control, serving as president until 1968, and then as chairman of the board. By the late 1970s, annual sales reach over $240 million. In 1943, the *New York Times* honors Olive Beech as one of the 12 most distinguished women of the year. Later, she is honored by *Fortune* magazine and the Smithsonian Institution for her knowledge and skill.

1932 **Publication of Laura Ingalls Wilder's First Book in *Little House* Series.** At the age of 65, Laura Elizabeth Ingalls Wilder (1867–1957) publishes *The Little House in the Big Woods,* the first of her series of frontier life in America and a Newbery Honor book. These autobiographical stories of her childhood are a fascinating contribution to American women's literature.

1932 **Birth of Chinese Textile Worker and Politician Wu Wenying.** Wu Wenying (1932–), a Chinese textile worker and politician, is born. The first woman to head the largest textile industry in the world, she becomes her government's Minister of the Textile Industry in Beijing, China, in 1983. She leads textile delegations to Germany, Belgium, New Zealand, and Burma in 1985 and to Britain and Bulgaria in 1986.

1932 **German Filmmaker Leni Riefenstahl Forms Production Company.** Leni Riefenstahl (1902–), German filmmaker, forms her own production company and directs and stars in *The Blue Light.* In the film, she portrays a mountain girl who climbs mountains in her bare feet.

1932 **American Theater Director Cheryl Crawford Cofounds Group Theater.** Cheryl Crawford (1902–1986), an American theater director, cofounds (with Harold Churman and Lee Strasberg) the Group Theater in New York, which develops "method" acting. She is also the cofounder (with Eva Le Gallienne and Margaret Webster) of New York City's American Repertory Theater in 1945 and

Miriam Makeba

(with Elia Kazan and Robert Lewis) of the Actors' Studio (also in New York) in 1947.

1932 **Birth of Miriam Makeba, Black South African Singer.** Miriam Makeba (1932–), the first black woman from South Africa to gain an international reputation as a singer, is born. As a girl, she performs in her native country but then gains international attention with her performance in the anti-apartheid film *Come Back Africa* in 1958. In the 1960s, encouraged by Harry Belafonte, Makeba has several record hits in the United States. She takes an active role in the American civil rights movement, then settles in African Guinea in the 1970s. Makeba continues to perform and to voice her political support of black causes.

1932 **Amelia Earhart Receives Award.** Aviator Amelia Earhart (1898–1937) is awarded the

American National Geographic Society Award Medal, presented by President Herbert Hoover. She also receives over 40 other medals and awards.

1932   Claire Parker Creates Innovative Animation Technique. Claire Parker (1906–1981), pioneer American film animator, and her husband, Russian-born artist Alexander Alexeieff, build a model upon which they draw a now-classic film of animation, *Night on Bald Mountain* (1933). They invent a technique of animation known as "pinboard"—a means by which engravings may be brought to life. In this black-and-white technique, the pins are always used as a group, like paint on a brush. Parker is an expert in reading scores; she, therefore, is in charge of the relationship between image and music in their films (made before music tracks can be transferred to tape).

1932   Helene Madison Swims 100 Yards in Under a Minute. Helene Madison of Seattle, Washington, becomes the first woman ever to swim 100 yards in less than one minute.

1932   Establishment of Greater Japan National Defense Women's Association. The *Dai Nippon Kokubo Fujinkai* (Greater Japan National Defense Women's Association) is established by the Japanese Army to mobilize women for World War II–related activities. These activities include: providing labor for the families of men on active duty; performing funerals for the war dead; sponsoring lectures and movies to disseminate military ideas; conducting the savings, frugality, and anti-luxury campaigns; assisting with the annual examination of youths and reservists; sending off and greeting soldiers to and from their barracks; and performing war relief. All married women are automatically members of the association; there are branches in every city, town, and village in Japan. In 1942 the association merges with other organizations under the title *Dai Nippon Fujinkai*, Greater Japan Women's Association.

Jacqueline Cochran

1932   Brazilian Women Win Vote. Women gain suffrage in Brazil.

1932   Women Granted Suffrage in Thailand. Women win the vote in Thailand.

1932   American Aviator Jacqueline Cochran Earns Pilot's License. Jacqueline Cochran (1910–1980) gets her pilot's license. Cochran achieves many firsts as a pioneering aviator.

1932   Discovery of Cave of Famous Prophet Sibyl of Cumae. One of the most famous prophets of the ancient world, Sibyl, writes (or dictates as an oracular spirit to a succession of priestesses) her prophecies in a sacred cave in Cumae, Italy, near Naples. Her prophecies are highly regarded and the written texts—the Sybilline Leaves, or Books—are kept in Rome and consulted on important occasions. It is due to predictions in Sybil's prophecy that the black stone of Cybele is brought to Rome in 204 B.C. Her prophecies are so respected that Jews and Christians both spend centuries rewriting them and adding them to texts to make it seem that Sybil has predicted the coming of the Messiah (and specifically Jesus Christ, in the Christians' case). In 1932 A.D., the original sacred Cumaean cave is discovered. It has a 60-foot-high ceiling and an entrance passageway 375 feet long.

MAY 22, 1932   Amelia Earhart, First Woman to Pilot Across Atlantic Ocean. American aviator Amelia Earhart (1898–1937) is the first woman to fly an airplane across the Atlantic Ocean. When Earhart attempts to fly over the Pacific Ocean in July 1937, her plane is lost in the South Pacific near Howland Island in the Mariannas. She is presumed dead, although days of searching the seas turn up no evidence of her; her navigator, Fred Noonan; or the wreckage of her plane.

AUGUST 24, 1932   Amelia Earhart Sets Woman's Transcontinental Speed Record. American aviator Amelia Earhart (1898–1937) flies from Los Angeles, California, to Newark, New Jersey, setting the woman's nonstop transcontinental speed record.

OCTOBER 27, 1932   Sylvia Plath, American Author and Poet, Is Born. American writer Sylvia Plath (1932–1963) is born in Boston, Massachusetts. Plath's painful experiences during a summer as an editor of a chic women's magazine in New York City are recorded in her novel *The Bell Jar* (1963). She goes on to a stellar but brief career, writing her best verse during the months before her suicide. Her confessional verse is collected in a publication called *Ariel* in 1965. Sylvia Plath dies in 1963 in London, England.

1933   Mae West Launches to Stardom in Movie Debut. Paramount studio asks American sex symbol Mae West (1893–1980) to adapt her successful Broadway play, *Diamond Lil*, to the big screen. The movie version, *She Done Him Wrong*, launches West, as well as her unknown costar, Cary Grant, into stardom.

1933   Gladys Dickason Becomes Active Leader of Amalgamated Clothing Workers of America. Born the daughter of cotton farmers, Gladys Dickason (1903–1971) joins the Amalgamated Clothing Workers of America (ACWA) as an organizer. Dickason is educated at the University of Oklahoma and Columbia University. After completing her Ph.D., she teaches economics at Sweet Briar College and at Hunter College. However, in 1933 Dickason changes careers and becomes an organizer for the ACWA. Two years later she is named the union's director of research, a position she holds until 1954. In 1945 she becomes the ACWA southern regional director and the following year is elected a vice president of ACWA. Also in 1946, she serves as the assistant director for the Southern Organizing Committee for the Congress of Industrial Organizations. In 1946, Dickason is appointed by General Douglas MacArthur to teach Japanese working women the basics of unionism. Dickason is a member of the Industrial Committee of the Cotton Garment Code Authority of the National Recovery Administration, the New York City Board of Education committee to study vocational training, the federal Women's Bureau Labor Advisory Committee, and on the Board of Trustees of Antioch College.

1933   American Economist Mary Williams Dewson Active in Federal Government. Economist Mary Williams Dewson (1872–1962) becomes director of the Women's Division of the Democratic National Party and is named a member of the President's Committee on Economic Security.

1933   Dorothy Day Cofounds the *Catholic Worker*. American writer and activist Dorothy

Day (1897–1980), a convert to Catholicism, cofounds the monthly *Catholic Worker,* which sells for a penny a copy. Influenced by the French priest Peter Maurin, she founds the Catholic Worker Movement, establishing "houses of hospitality" in urban and rural areas for people struggling to subsist during the Great Depression (1929–39). As a pacifist and strong supporter of unionization for farm workers, she advocates the Catholic Church's involvement in labor and antiwar activities. Her autobiography, *The Long Loneliness,* is published in 1952.

1933   Katharine Hepburn Awarded Her First Oscar. American actress Katharine Hepburn (1907–) wins her first Academy Award for best actress for her performance in *Morning Glory.* Her other prominent roles include Jo March in *Little Women* (1933), *Alice Adams* (1935), and the aspiring actress in *Stage Door* (1937).

1933   Edith Head Costumes Sex Symbol Mae West. American costume designer Edith Head (1907–1981) lands her first big break on a picture written and produced by Mae West, *She Done Him Wrong.* In addition to dressing Mae West for her first film, Head costumes the sex symbol for her last film, *Sextette* (1978).

1933   Alicia Markova, "Prima Ballerina" of London's Vic-Wells Ballet. Alicia Markova (1910–), a distinguished English dancer of international reputation, is the first "prima ballerina" of the Vic-Wells Ballet Company, in London, England. She holds this position for two years, partnered by Anton Dolin. With him she founds her own Markova-Dolin Ballet, with which she tours between 1935 and 1938, becoming the first great ballerina to undertake large provincial tours. In 1950 she is a cofounder of the London Festival Ballet. Markova goes on to become director of the Metropolitan Opera Ballet (in 1963), gover-

nor of the Royal Ballet (in 1973), and president of the London Festival Ballet (in 1986).

1933   Australian Louise Dyer's Music Publishing Company Presents First Volumes. Australian Louise Berta Mosson Hanson Smith Dyer (1884–1962), living in Paris, publishes a 12-volume edition of the works of composer Francois Couperin, the first of her *Editions de l'Oiseau-Lyre.* These beautiful books make available early music previously known only in manuscript form. By 1940, Dyer publishes 40 editions of early music; she also publishes works by contemporary Australian women composers Peggy Glanville-Hicks and Margaret Sutherland. Prior to her move to Paris with her husband in 1927, Dyer hosts musical evenings for the social elite in Melbourne, Australia. Her flair and acute ear for talent makes these so successful that she progresses to mounting operatic productions. When the Dyers leave for Europe in 1927, Louise Dyer donates £10,000 to establish a permanent orchestra in Melbourne. Her husband dies in 1938 and Dyer marries Joseph Hanson the following year. By this time she extends her label to gramophone records. Known as *l'Oiseau Lyre* (Lyre Bird), the recording company is the first to record the Monteverdi Vespers, Handel operas, and the complete works of Couperin; it also offers works by Schonberg, Milhaud, and Stravinsky. Her business headquarters moves to Monaco in 1945. Louise Dyer is a key figure in the early music revival as well as a very successful businesswoman. She is appointed Officer of the Legion d'Honneur in 1957 and dies in 1962. Her ashes are brought back to Australia, which she visits frequently during her life in Europe. Dyer bequeaths her Australian estate to the University of Melbourne.

1933   Penelope Lively, Children' Author, Is Born. Penelope Lively (1933–), author of fantasy and science fiction works for children, is born. Her works include *A Stitch in Time* (1976), which wins the Whitbread Award, and *Moon Tiger* (1987) which wins the Booker-McConnell Prize.

1933   Women Win Vote in Turkey. Women are granted suffrage in Turkey.

1933   Pioneer Woman Filmmaker Dorothy Arzner Directs *Christopher Strong.* Dorothy Arzner (1900–1979), who works virtually alone in Hollywood as a woman director in its early days, directs *Christopher Strong* (1933), with Katharine Hepburn in a thinly disguised and highly romanticized portrayal of aviator Amelia Earhart. Arzner was honored for her career by the Directors Guild of America (1975), and she is its first woman member.

MARCH 4, 1933   Frances Perkins Appointed U.S. Secretary of Labor. Frances Perkins (1882–1965), a long-time civil servant in the state of New York, becomes the United States' first woman cabinet member when President Franklin D. Roosevelt appoints her Secretary of Labor. She is reappointed for each of his three additional terms in office. During her tenure, she drafts the Social Security Act and the National Labor Relations Act.

1934   Ingrid Bergman Begins Screen Acting Career. From 1934 to 1939, Swedish actress Ingrid Bergman (1915–1982) makes ten Swedish films. In 1939, Hollywood executives decide to remake her Swedish film *Intermezzo* with Bergman in the English-speaking version. She appears in such American films as *Adam Had Four Sons* (1940); *Notorious* (1940); *Casablanca* (1942); *For Whom the Bell Tolls* (1943); *Gaslight*, for which she wins the 1944 Academy Award; *Spellbound* (1945); and *Joan of Arc* (1948). Bergman's extramarital love affair with the Italian director Roberto Rossellini and the birth of an illegitimate son scandalizes the American public. Bergman divorces her husband, remains in Rome, and marries Rossellini. She stars in a series of Rossellini films, none of them critical or financial successes. She makes her Hollywood come-

Ingrid Bergman

back in 1956, winning her second Academy Award for *Anastasia*. Bergman divorces Rossellini in 1957 and a year later marries millionaire Lars Schmidt. Before her death from cancer on her 67th birthday, Bergman appears in 46 films, 11 stage plays, and five television dramas.

1934   Rose Pesotta Becomes Vice President of the International Ladies' Garment Workers' Union. International Ladies' Garment Workers' Union (ILGWU) organizer Rose Pesotta (1896–?) is elected to an executive board position as a national vice president of the union. However, after three terms she refuses a fourth term, saying, "Ten years in office had made it clear to me that a lone woman vice-president could not adequately represent the women who make up 85% of the International's 305,000 membership."

1934   African American Actress Louise Beavers Receives Movie Contract. Louise Beavers (1902–1962) becomes the first African American actress to receive a starring motion picture contract. Her role as "Delilah" in *Imitation of Life* (1934) escalates her to fame and allows her to become a popular screen domestic servant. The film focuses on the issue of African Americans passing as white but is best known for popularizing the domestic servant stereotype in motion pictures. This portrayal of African American subservience becomes the center of controversy when Sterling Brown, a professor at Howard University, publicly debates Fannie Hurst, the white author of the novel upon which the film is based. Beavers' portrayal in this film establishes her as a dramatic screen actress whose talent rivals that of white screen stars. Some critics even contend that she deserves an Academy Award for her performance.

1934   Evangeline Booth Becomes Commander of Salvation Army Worldwide. Evangeline Cora Booth (1865–1950), daughter of Salvation Army founder William Booth, assumes leadership of the Salvation Army worldwide.

1934   Union Organizer Stella Nowicki Is Blacklisted. Stella Nowicki (1916–), organizer for the Packinghouse Workers union, is blacklisted because of her participation in a sit-down strike over unsafe working conditions. She continues to work in various meat packing jobs under an assumed name.

1934   Eleanor Grinnell Coit Directs American Labor Education Service. Eleanor Grinnell Coit (1894–?) becomes the director of the American Labor Education Service. She establishes residency schools for workers, labor education classes for white collar workers, worker exchange programs with foreign countries, anti-discrimination education, and a study of farm-labor relations.

1934   Bette Davis' First Big Screen Opportunity. American actress Bette Davis (1908–1989) is given her first leading role, in the film adaptation of Somerset Maugham's *Of Human Bondage.*

1934   Actress Mae West Earns Second Largest Salary in U.S. Mae West (1893–1980), who writes and stars in films, earns the largest salary in the United States, second only to publisher William Randolph Hearst.

1934   Child Star Shirley Temple Receives Academy Award. Child actress Shirley Temple (1928–) receives a special Academy Award for "bringing more happiness to millions of children and millions of grown-ups than any other child of her years in the history of the world."

By 1938, Temple is the number-one money-making star in Hollywood. In her films, she sings and dances and avoids being obnoxiously cute. Her roles include *Curly Top* (1935), *Poor Little Rich Girl* (1936), *Dimples* (1936), *Heidi* (1937), *Rebecca of Sunny Brook Farm* (1938), and *A Little Princess* (1939). By 1939, at age 12, Shirley Temple is a has-been. In 1944, producer David O. Selznick tries to recharge her career as a young adult actress in such films as *Since You Went Away* and *I'll Be Seeing You. The Bachelor and the Bobby Soxer* (1947) is Temple's last successful film.

1934   Playwright Lillian Hellman's First Major Success. Playwright Lillian Hellman (1905–1984) writes her first major hit, *The Children's Hour,* for the stage. This play is an important drama about how a slanderous lie of lesbianism on the part of a child ruins the lives of two women. After this, Hollywood producer Samuel Goldwyn contracts Hellman to write screenplays for the movies.

1934   Peggy Guggenheim Founds Modern Art Gallery in Paris. Peggy Guggenheim (1898–1980), an American art collector, founds, with the support of her friend Marcel Duchamp, the Guggenheim-Jeune Art Gallery in Paris, a gallery devoted to modern art. In 1940, she founds the gallery Art of This Century, in New York City.

1934   Diana Wynne Jones, British Children's Author, Is Born. Writer Diana Wynne Jones (1934–), creator of fantasy and science fiction works for children, is born. Jones wins the Guardian Award for *Charmed Life* (1977).

1934   Women in Chile Vote in Municipal Elections. Women gain the vote in municipal elections in Chile.

1934   Women Gain Vote in Cuba. Cuban women are granted suffrage.

JANUARY 27, 1934   Edith Cresson, French Premier, Born. Edith Cresson (1934–) is born to Gabriel and Jacqueline Capion in Boulogne-sur-Seine, France. In addition to French, she learns to speak English and Spanish. Cresson attends the Hautes Etudes Commerciales and later receives a doctorate in demography. She marries Jacques Cresson in 1959 and has three children. Cresson's political career begins when she joins the Convention des Institutions Républicaines and participates in François Mitterand's election campaign. In 1975 she writes *Avec le soleil.* She becomes mayor of Thuré (1977) and Chatellerault (1983). Cresson serves as a member of the European Parliament from 1979 through 1981; Ministers of Agriculture (1981–83), Foreign Trade and Tourism (1983–84), and Industrial Redeployment and Foreign Trade (1984–86). In 1986 she is elected Deputy of Vienne and reelected in 1988. Cresson becomes premier of France in 1991.

MARCH 25, 1934   Birth of Gloria Steinem, Journalist and Women's Rights Activist. Gloria Steinem (1934–) is born in Toledo, Ohio. In the late 1960s and early 1970s, Steinem's feminist interests and journalism career intertwine as she becomes active in the

women's movement. Then in 1972 she helps found *Ms.* magazine and acts as editor in chief and contributor until 1987. Her other accomplishments include helping establish the Women's Action Alliance (1970), National Women's Political Caucus (1971), and Coalition of Labor Union Women (1974). Through her numerous feminist writings, speaking engagements, and affiliations, Steinem comes to be known as a spokeswoman and organizer of the women's movement.

---

1 9 3 5 – 1 9 3 9

1935   Bette Davis Awarded Her First Oscar. American actress Bette Davis (1908–1989) wins the Academy Award for best actress for her performance in *Dangerous.* She repeats this achievement in 1937 for her portrayal of the temptress in *Jezebel.* Her transformed spinster in *Now, Voyager* (1942) and her rich party girl who nobly faces death in *Dark Victory* (1939) become her most memorable roles.

1935   Hallie Flanagan Organizes and Directs Federal Theater Project. Hallie Flanagan (1890–1969) organizes and becomes the first director of the Federal Theater Project, a program of the Works Progress Administration (WPA) during the Great Depression (1929–39). Her project becomes a national network of regional theaters throughout the United States and sponsors stage productions ranging from Shakespeare to vaudeville. Flanagan is also the founder, in 1925, of the Vassar Experimental Theater at Vassar College, where she is a professor from 1925 until 1942. She goes on to serve as Dean and then Professor of Theater at Smith College until 1955.

1935   German Filmmaker Leni Riefenstahl Directs Infamous Nazi Documentary. Leni Riefenstahl (1902–), a German filmmaker, directs *Triumph of the Will,* a film that vividly depicts the charisma of Nazi leader Adolph

Left to right: President Harry S Truman, Mary McLeod Bethune, Madame Vijaya Pandit, ambassador to the U.S. from India, and Dr. Ralph Bunche, former U.S. mediator in Palestine (present-day Israel).

Hitler's personality. With Riefenstahl's other film, *Olympia* (1938), *Triumph of the Will* is widely regarded as a masterpiece of Nazi cinema. She is widely criticized for the film on the grounds that she glorified the Nazi rally at Nuremberg featured in the film. Riefenstahl steadfastly denies any relationship with Hitler and claims not to have understood the Nazis' genocidal plans. Her reputation as a master documentary filmmaker is secure. *Triumph of the Will* is arguably the most effective propaganda film ever made.

1935   Birth of Japanese Writer Kurahashi Yumiko. Japanese author Kurahashi Yumiko (1935–) is born. She is an anti-realist whose literary style is influenced by modern European writers like Franz Kafka.

1935   Motherhood Protection League Established in Japan. Yamataki Shigeri (1899-1977), Yamada Waka, and others form the *Bosei Hogo Remmei* (Motherhood Protection League) in 1935 in Japan. Shigeri continues to work on women's issues during World War II (1939–45) and is active after the war in promoting new rights for women.

1935   National Council of Negro Women Established. The National Council of Negro Women is formed in the United States by Mary McLeod Bethune (1875–1955) as a coalition of national organizations to help improve the status of women in the black community. Bethune becomes the organization's first president. As a noted advocate for African American education, Bethune serves from 1935 to 1944 as Special Advisor on Minority Affairs in the administration of American president Franklin D. Roosevelt. Bethune is the 1935 recipient of the Spingarn Medal, an award given annually to the year's outstanding African American, for her work in education.

1935   American Aviator Jacqueline Cochran First Woman To Fly in Transcontinental Air Race. Pioneer aviator Jacqueline Cochran (1910–1980) is the first woman to fly in the Bendix transcontinental air race across the United States. Cochran achieves many firsts in her lifetime as a pioneering aviator.

APRIL 2, 1935   Mary Hirsch, First Licensed Woman Thoroughbred Trainer. The Jockey Club of the United States licenses Mary Hirsch the first woman trainer of thoroughbred race horses.

1936   Labor Activist Elizabeth Christman Appointed to Commission. President Franklin D. Roosevelt appoints long-time labor union activist Elizabeth Christman to the Commission on Vocational Guidance. Four years later, she becomes a member of the Advisory Committee of the Women's Bureau of the U.S. Department of Labor.

1936   African American Educator Mary McLeod Bethune Heads Division of National Youth Administration. Mary McLeod Bethune (1875–1955) becomes director of the Division of Negro Affairs of the National Youth Administration, becoming the first African American woman to head an American federal agency. Bethune also serves from 1935 to 1944 as Special Advisor on Minority Affairs in the administration of American president Franklin D. Roosevelt.

1936   Margaret Bourke-White Is Staff Photographer at Life Magazine. Margaret Bourke-White (1906–1971) is hired as staff photographer on the new magazine, *Life*. For the next three decades, Bourke-White photographs the human side of news events, including World War II (1939–45), the opening of the concentration camps (where Jews were imprisoned and executed by the Nazis in Germany) following the war, and political unrest in Pakistan, India, and South Africa. She retires from *Life* in 1969.

1936   Birth of Virginia Hamilton, African American Children's Author. Virginia Hamilton (1936–), award-winning African American author of works for children and young adults, is born. In 1967, she publishes her first work, *Zeely*. It becomes the first work in history to win both the National Book Award and the Newbery Medal.

1936   Hedda Hopper Begins Gossip Career on Radio. American gossip columnist Hedda Hopper (1890–1966) gets her start hosting the *Chit Chat Radio Hour*. Hopper begins her own gossip column two years later.

1936   Women's Suffrage Granted to More than Two-thirds of All Countries. Suffrage has been granted to women in more than two-thirds of all countries throughout the world, although women are under legal disabilities in holding public office.

1936   First Lady Eleanor Roosevelt Writes Syndicated Newspaper Column. First lady Eleanor Roosevelt (1884–1962), wife of the 32nd U.S. president, Franklin Delano Roosevelt (1882–1945), begins writing a daily syndicated newspaper column, "My Day," in which she comments on current issues and champions the cause of civil rights. The column often deals with the everyday minutiae of life in the White House and is syndicated to scores of daily newspapers throughout the United States. Eleanor Roosevelt takes full advantage of her access to the president and his appointees to make sure women are represented and considered in policy decisions.

FEBRUARY 21, 1936   Birth of Barbara Jordan, American Congresswoman. U.S. Representative Barbara Jordan (1936–1996) is born in Houston, Texas. Her father is a Baptist minister and her mother a noted orator. She inherits from them her deep, resonant voice and eloquent speech and her strong religious convictions. A gifted student and avid reader, Jordan earns her law degree from Boston University Law School and returns to Houston. In 1962, when she is 26, Jordan is elected president of the Houston Lawyers Association, an African American association of which she is the only female member. She goes on to the Texas State legislature in 1965, and in 1972 she is elected to the U.S. House of Representatives. During her six years in Congress, Jordan sponsors bills providing food stamps, emergency housing, and health programs for the poor. At the Democratic National Convention in 1976, she becomes the first woman and the first African American to deliver the keynote address. Retiring from politics in the late 1970s because of poor health, Jordan holds several academic posts, writes an autobiography, *Barbara Jordan: A Self-Portrait* (1979), and serves on public service committees.

MAY 27, 1936   Sally Stearns, Coxswain of Men's College Crew. Sally Stearns, the first woman coxswain of a men's college varsity crew, leads Rollins College's shell in a race against Marietta College.

JUNE 30, 1936   Novel about the U.S. Civil War, *Gone With the Wind,* is published. American author Margaret Mitchell (1900–1949) publishes her classic novel about the U.S. Civil War, *Gone With the Wind.* It wins the Pulitzer Prize and sells over 25 million copies, and is made into a major feature film in 1939.

1937   Women's Emergency Brigade Essential to Success of General Motors Sit-down Strike. Genora Johnson founds the Women's Emergency Brigade (WEB), days after the start of a sit-down strike by the United Auto Workers (UAW) in Flint, Michigan. While the men sit down in the plant, the women set up the Emergency Brigade to feed the strikers, staff picket lines around the clock, take charge of publicity, run a first-aid station, distribute literature, encourage community support for the strikers, run a day-care center for WEB participants, establish a welfare committee and a speaker's bureau, and visit wives who oppose the strike.

On the night of the "Battle of Bulls Run," Genora Johnson takes the microphone and calls for the women of the city to come down and join their men on the picket line. Thousands push their way through the police lines and join the strikers. The police are routed, the strike is saved, and membership in the UAW skyrockets. The Flint WEB starts with 50 women, soon grows to 350, and becomes the model for similar brigades in other auto cities.

1937   Bette Davis Wins Second Oscar. American actress Bette Davis (1908–1989) wins her second Academy Award for best actress for her portrayal of the temptress in *Jezebel.* Her first Academy Award is for her 1935 performance in *Dangerous.*

1937   Publication of Zora Neale Hurston's *Their Eyes Were Watching God.* Zora Neale Hurston (1903–1960) publishes her best-known novel, *Their Eyes Were Watching God.* Born in Eatonville, Florida, Hurston is the first woman successfully to combine careers as a cultural anthropologist and an accomplished writer of fiction. She graduates from Barnard College in New York City in 1928 and goes on to do important research into black folklore in the American South as well as in Haiti and Jamaica. She also establishes her reputation during the 1930s with fiction chronicling rural black life. In addition to *Their Eyes Were Watching God*, she also publishes *Mules and Men* (1935) and *Tell My Horse* (1938). She dies in poverty at Fort Pierce, Florida, after having worked for several years as a domestic servant. Her achievements are rediscovered in the 1980s.

1937   Anne O'Hare McCormick Wins Pulitzer Prize for Coverage of Italian Fascism. Anne O'Hare McCormick (1881–1954) receives the Pulitzer Prize for distinguished correspondence, the first woman to be so honored. She is given the prize for her international reporting on the rise of Italian Fascism for the *New York Times*. McCormick also becomes in 1936 the first woman to sit on this newspaper's editorial board. She dies in New York in 1954.

1937   Nadia Boulanger, First Woman to Conduct London Orchestra. In London, Nadia Boulanger (1887–1979) becomes the first woman to conduct a symphony orchestra. A French composer, teacher, and conductor, she is also the first woman to conduct regular subscription concerts with the Boston Symphony Orchestra (in 1938) and with the New York Philharmonic (in 1939), and the first woman to conduct the Hallé Orchestra (in 1963).

1937   American Lyricist Dorothy Fields Wins Academy Award. Lyricist Dorothy Fields (1904–1974), daughter of well-known vaudevillian Lew Fields, wins the Academy Award for songwriting, becoming the first woman to win the Oscar in this category. She is honored for her lyrics to Jerome Kern's tune "The Way You Look Tonight," featured in the 1936 movie *Swing Time* with Ginger Rogers and Fred Astaire.

1937   Margaret Rudkin Establishes Pepperidge Farm. Margaret Fogarty Rudkin (1897–1967) establishes Pepperidge Farm Products, which she develops into a multimillion-dollar business. The firm takes its

Margaret Rudkin, founder of Pepperidge Farm.

name from the Rudkin family estate in Connecticut, which they call Pepperidge Farm. Following a doctor's advice for the treatment of her children's asthma, Rudkin starts baking bread with fresh ingredients and no chemical additives. After much trial and error, she devises a recipe that pleases her family, and she begins selling the bread to her local grocer. Because of the expensive ingredients she uses, her bread costs more than other bread, but demand quickly grows. The idea of a wealthy society woman selling homemade bread appeals to journalists, and the small business receives free publicity. In 1940, Rudkin sells more than 50,000 loaves. In 1960, the Rudkins sell the company to the Campbell Soup Company for some $28 million. Rudkin still runs Pepperidge Farm as a director until 1962, when her son takes over. Her cookbook, *The Margaret Rudkin Pepperidge Farm Cookbook* (1963), becomes a bestseller.

1937 **Women in Philippines Gain Vote.** Women's suffrage is legalized in the Philippines.

JULY 29, 1937 **Amelia Earhart Presumed Lost at Sea.** American aviator Amelia Earhart (1898–1937) attempts to fly over the Pacific Ocean, but her plane is lost in the South Pacific near Howland Island in the Mariannas. She is presumed dead, although days of searching the seas turn up no evidence of her; her navigator, Fred Noonan; or the wreckage of her plane.

SEPTEMBER 4, 1937 **First U.S. Women's Bicycling Championship.** The National Amateur Bicycling Association holds its first U.S. women's bicycling championship in Buffalo, New York. Doris Kopsky of Belleville, New Jersey, wins the one-mile race in 4 minutes, 22.4 seconds.

1938 **American Golfer Patty Berg Named Outstanding Female Athlete of the Year.** Patty Berg (1918–) is voted Outstanding Female Athlete of the Year by the Associated Press after winning the 1938 U.S. Women National Amateur Golf Tournament, along with nine other victories in 13 tournament entries. Berg is the first woman golfer to earn over $100,000. In 1940 Berg turns professional, with the Wilson Company as her corporate sponsor. In 1948, she is part of the group—with Babe and George Zaharias and George Corcoran—that founds the Ladies Professional Golf Association (LPGA). Berg is inducted into the LPGA Hall of Fame in 1951. Her low scores in 1953, 1955, and 1956 earn her the Vare Trophy.

1938 **American Aviator Jacqueline Cochran Sets Transcontinental Record.** Pioneer aviator Jacqueline Cochran (1910–1980) sets a transcontinental record when she flies across the United States in 10 hours and 28 minutes.

1938 **Sylvia Porter Begins Writing Weekly Financial Newspaper Column.** Sylvia Feldman Porter (1918–1991) takes on a weekly column for the *New York Post,* initially called "Financial Post Marks," explaining investment news and terms for the common reader, but without revealing that the columnist is a woman. The column is so successful that its title is changed to "S.F. Porter Says," and finally, in 1942, the *Post* reveals the full name and gender of its most important financial writer. The column is syndicated in papers across the country. In 1975 she publishes *Sylvia Porter's Money Book,* offering advice for managing money.

1938 **Establishment of Philadelphia Girls Rowing Club.** The Philadelphia Girls Rowing Club is formed, creating much interest and bringing support to the sport of women's rowing. Its program becomes one of the best in the United States.

1938 **Nadia Boulanger Conducts Boston Symphony.** French composer, teacher, and conductor Nadia Boulanger (1887–1979) becomes the first woman to conduct regular subscription concerts with the Boston Symphony Orchestra.

1938 **Leni Riefenstahl Directs Documentary on Olympic Games in Berlin.** Leni Riefenstahl (1902–), a German filmmaker, directs *Olympia,* a documentary about the 1936 Olympic Games in Berlin, Germany. The film is given its premiere on Adolph Hitler's birthday. Although Riefenstahl is acknowledged as a skilled filmmaker, her career is tainted by her association with Hitler and Nazism, based on the perspective of *Olympia* and *Triumph of the Will,* a 1935 documentary depicting the charisma of Nazi leader Adolph Hitler.

Edith Clara Summerskill

German actress and filmmaker Leni Riefenstahl.

1938 American Author Judy Blume Is Born. Judy Blume (1938–), American author of works for children and young adults, is born. Works include *Are You There God? It's Me, Margaret* (1970).

JANUARY 11, 1938 Frances Moulton, First Woman to Serve as U.S. Bank President. Frances Estelle Mason Moulton becomes the first woman to serve as president of a U.S. bank when she is elected president of the Limerick National Bank in Limerick, Maine, to fill the vacancy caused by the death of her father.

MARCH 7, 1938 Birth of Janet Guthrie, American Race Car Driver. Race car driver Janet Guthrie (1938–) is born in Iowa City, Iowa. Before she starts racing, flying is her passion, and at age 13 she flies her first plane,

making her first parachute jump three years later. By age 17, she earns her pilot's license. Guthrie starts racing stock cars in 1961 and wins several awards and races. By 1971, she achieves nine straight finishes in the top endurance events in the United States. In 1973, Guthrie wins the NAR racing championship. In 1976, she becomes the first woman to race in NASCAR's (National Association for Stock Car Auto Racing) Winston Cup. She finishes in 15th place, winning $3,555. In 1977, Guthrie becomes the first woman to qualify for the Indianapolis 500. She fails to finish the race because her car breaks down, but on May 29, 1978, she tries again and becomes the first woman to complete this race, finishing eighth.

APRIL 12, 1938 Edith Summerskill Elected to British Parliament. Edith Clara Summerskill (1901–1980), a physician, is elected to Parlia-

Hattie McDaniel, right, with fellow actress Louise Beavers.

ment in England as a Labour candidate. Her primary concerns as Member of Parliament are clean food, preventive medicine, abortion and birth control, equal pay for women, and equal rights for married women. As parliamentary secretary to the Ministry of Food, she is responsible for a 1949 bill on the pasteurization of milk, which she considers her "finest hour." President of the Married Women's Association, Summerskill works to enact the Married Woman's Property Act (1964) and the Matrimonial Homes Act (1967). She goes to the House of Lords as a life peeress in 1961 and is appointed Companion of Honour in 1966. In addition to her legislative work, she is the author of *Babies without Tears* (1941), *The Ignoble Art* (1956), *Letters to My Daughter* (1957), and the autobiographical *A Woman's*

World (1967). Edith Summerskill dies at her home on February 4, 1980.

1939 **Hattie McDaniel, First African American to Receive an Academy Award.** Hattie McDaniel (1895–1952) wins the Academy Award for best supporting actress for her role as "Mammy" in *Gone With the Wind*. McDaniel is the first African American to receive an Academy Award. She is one of Hollywood's screen legends, playing domestic servants in the 1930s and 1940s. McDaniel's career, including appearances in some 300 pictures, begins to decline in the late 1940s. She appears on television in the *Amos 'n Andy Show* and the *Eddie Cantor Show*. She stars as "Beulah" on radio and television. Her deteriorating health, dissolving marriage, and inability to bear children contribute to the depression McDaniel suffers. Finally, losing her battle against breast cancer, Hattie McDaniel dies at the age of 57 on December 26, 1952.

1939   Ethel Waters Becomes One of the First African American Women to Star on Broadway. Singer and actress Ethel Waters (1896–1977) becomes one of the first African American women to star on Broadway, in *Mamba's Daughters.* When her roles in *Cabin in the Sky* and *The Member of the Wedding* are made into motion pictures, Waters is catapulted into everlasting fame. For her role in *Pinky* (1949), a film that focuses on the issue of African Americans passing as white, she receives an Oscar nomination for best supporting actress.

1939   Publication of Virginia Lee Burton's *Mike Mulligan and His Steam Shovel.* American author Virginia Lee Burton (1909–1968) writes and illustrates the classic children's book *Mike Mulligan and His Steam Shovel.* Written for her son Mike, it is an example of her careful structuring of a story. Mary Anne, a personified machine as protagonist, is established as a great hero in the minds of young children.

1939   Judy Garland in Role of *Wizard of Oz's* **Dorothy.** American singer-actress Judy Garland (1922–1969) appears as Dorothy in *The Wizard of Oz,* her most famous role. During the 1930s and 1940s, Garland appears in several films with another child actor, Mickey Rooney, in the Andy Hardy film series. Known for her husky but sweet singing voice, Garland appears in such musicals as *For Me and My Gal* (1942), *Meet Me in St. Louis* (1944), and *Easter Parade* (1948).

1939   Myra Hess Organizes Alternative Concerts in London during the Blitz. Myra Hess (1890–1965), an English pianist, is the first person to organize alternative music performances when the London concert halls are closed down during World War II (1939–

Nadia Boulanger confers with members of the Philadelphia Orchestra.

45). She organizes a series of daily lunchtime concerts performed at the National Gallery. She herself performs at many of these, and in 1941 she is created Dame of the British Empire in recognition of her services as a public benefactor.

1939   African American Opera Singer Marian Anderson Performs at Lincoln Memorial. The Daughters of the American Revolution (DAR) refuse to allow African American opera singer Marian Anderson (1902–1993) to perform a concert in Philadelphia's Constitution Hall, claiming that the date has been previously booked. This action causes then-first lady Eleanor Roosevelt to resign her membership in the DAR and to assist Anderson in performing an open-air concert on Easter Sunday at the Lincoln Memorial in Washington, D.C. More than 75,000 people attend the concert, where Anderson performs the U.S. National Anthem and *Ave Maria*, among other works. Her repertoire includes both spirituals and opera. President Franklin Roosevelt later invites Anderson to perform for King George VI of England at the White House, making her the first African American artist to sing there. In 1961, Anderson sings at the inauguration of President John F. Kennedy, and in 1963, she wins the Presiden-

tial Medal of Freedom. In April 1993, Marian Anderson dies one month after suffering a stroke.

1939 Nadia Boulanger Conducts New York Philharmonic. Nadia Boulanger (1887–1979), a French composer, teacher, and conductor, becomes the first woman to conduct regular subscription concerts with the New York Philharmonic. On March 10 the same year, she becomes the first woman to conduct the Philadelphia Orchestra.

Chapter 20

1940 TO 1949

1940 – 1944

c. 1940 Japanese Women Not Deployed for War-Related Jobs. The Japanese military government declines to mobilize women in compulsory labor outside the home during World War II (1939–45). Japan's labor needs during the war are fulfilled primarily by redeploying male workers from nonessential industries. This labor force is augmented by five million, mostly unmarried, women; three million students; one million older men; hundreds of thousands of conscripted Chinese and Koreans (both women and men); and (in the last year of the war) more than two million men deferred from military service. Unmarried women work as they have before the war, primarily wherever non-skilled, low-paid, light labor is needed. Women are not brought into positions of production-line or management responsibility. Pay scales, as is the case before the war, are discriminatory— based on age, sex, and experience, rather than job performance. The military government exhorts married women to remain at home and care for their children.

c. 1940 Doris Day Becomes an American Favorite. After a successful career as a band singer, Cincinnati native Doris Day (1924–) becomes a favorite American film star from the 1940s through the 1960s because of her vivacity and her many talents. She proves her-

self to be a dramatic actress of substance in the film *Love Me or Leave Me* (1955) with Jimmy Cagney, playing singer Ruth Etting. Her comedies with Rock Hudson in the 1960s saddle Day with the image of a "perpetual virgin," which severely restricts her career. She retires from films and works as an animal rights activist in California.

1940 Actress Betty Grable Gets First Starring Role. American song-and-dance actress Betty Grable (1916–1973) lands the role of leading lady in *Down Argentine Way*. Grable's popularity soars during World War II. Known as "the girl with the million-dollar legs," Grable becomes a favorite "pin-up" among American soldiers. Almost two million copies of her photo in her white bathing suit, looking over her shoulder, are sent out to servicemen. Grable's wartime films include the dance musicals *Sweet Rosie O'Grady* (1943) and *Pin-Up Girl* (1944).

1940 Anne Bauchens Wins Academy Award For Film Editing. Anne Bauchens (1881–1967), a pioneering American film editor since 1918, becomes the first woman to receive an Academy Award for film editing when she wins for her work on *North West Mounted Police*. Director Cecil B. De Mille is so impressed with her work on his films that he refuses to work with any other editor—

every one of his films from 1919 to 1956 is cut by Bauchens.

1940   Grandma Moses Has First Solo Exhibition at Age 80. Anna Mary Moses (1860–1961), known as "Grandma Moses" and remembered for her detailed primitive paintings of American rural life, has her first solo exhibition at the age of 80, in New York City. Her work is discovered by a collector in 1938 and included in an exhibition at the Museum of Modern Art in 1939. Moses begins painting at about age 75.

1940   Cofounder of Halas and Batchelor Cartoon Films. Joy Batchelor (1914–) is the cofounder, with her husband, the Hungarian animator John Halas, of Halas and Batchelor Cartoon Films. This company, an innovator in the production of animated cinema, produces and directs cartoons for cinema, television, and commercials as well as for promotional, scientific, and instructional films.

1940   Neighborhood Associations Established In Japan for War Effort Support. The *tonari-gumi* (neighborhood association) system is established by the Japanese government to provide for local control and mobilize households for support of the war effort. Units of 10-20 contiguous households, populated mostly by women, children, and the elderly, are organized as the lowest level of the national government. The neighborhood associations are used to promote reverence for the emperor, provide air raid protection, distribute government directives, deliver supplies, provide public welfare and relief, and supervise campaigns to prevent the waste of resources.

1940   Frances Payne Bolton Joins U.S. Congress. Frances Payne Bingham Bolton (1885–1977) begins a decades-long career as a Republican in the U.S. House of Representatives. Bolton is from a wealthy family, the granddaughter of a former U.S. senator, and

lives part of her adult life as a volunteer and socialite. Like most of her female contemporaries in Congress, Bolton is first elected to fill a vacancy left by the death of her husband. She quickly makes the position her own and works to further causes important to her, especially increased training and respect for nurses. The Bolton Bill establishes the Cadet Nurse Corps, providing well-trained nurses during World War II (1939–45). During the 1950s, her son Oliver is elected to Congress, and they become the only mother-son team in the House. Independent thinkers both, they often cast opposing votes. In 1966, she introduces a bill to eliminate gender-specific language in regulations commissioning nurses for the Army and Navy; this bill reduces (but does not stop) discrimination against male nurses in the military. Bolton calls for women to be drafted equally with men, explaining that "women's place includes defending the home." She does not like attention drawn to her own gender and insists on the title "Congressman Bolton."

1940   Mother Ella Bloor Publishes Autobiography. American political activist and labor organizer Mother Ella Reeve Bloor (1862–1951) writes her autobiography, *We Are Many*, covering the period 1870–1940. In 1906 she works with Richard Bloor in Chicago's stock yards to gather evidence used by Upton Sinclair in his expose *The Jungle*. In 1909 she joins the Women's Suffrage Association and becomes chair of the Department of Working Women. During World War I she works with Elizabeth Gurley Flynn and other pacifists; together they found the Workers Defense Union. Her union-organizing efforts take her to Schenectady, New York, and an Electrical Workers Union strike; New York City for the United Cloth and Cap Makers Union strike; Passaic, New Jersey, and North Carolina for textile workers' strikes; and Pennsylvania and Colorado for strikes by miners.

MAY 2, 1940   Belle Martell Officiates Boxing Match. Belle Martell of Van Nuys, California, is the first woman boxing referee. She officiates her first card, eight bouts in San Bernardino, California.

JUNE 10, 1940 **Margaret Chase Smith Joins U.S. House of Representatives.** Upon the death of her husband, Margaret Chase Smith (1897–1995) takes over his seat in the U.S. House of Representatives. She goes on to serve nine years in the House and 23 years in the U.S. Senate, and she unsuccessfully attempts to win the Republican party nomination as presidential candidate in 1964.

JUNE 19, 1940 **American Cartoonist Dale Messick Publishes "Brenda Starr."** After four years of trying to sell her work, Dale Messick publishes her first "Brenda Starr" comic strip in the Chicago *Tribune,* becoming the first woman to create and publish a syndicated comic strip. While trying to find a publisher for her cartoons, she changes her name from Dalia to Dale to conceal the fact that she is a woman. "Brenda Starr" is also notable as the first comic strip to feature a woman.

JUNE 23, 1940 **Birth of Wilma Rudolph, Champion African American Runner.** Wilma Rudolph (1940–1994), who overcomes childhood polio to become a successful high school basketball player and track star, is born. In 1956, Rudolph qualifies to compete in the Summer Olympic Games in Melbourne, Australia, where she helps her team win a bronze medal.

In 1960, just prior to the Olympic Games in Rome, Italy, Rudolph sets a world record and wins the American Athletic Union (AAU) championships in 100- and 200-meter events. At the 1960 Olympics, she becomes the first woman to win three gold medals in the same Olympic Games. Among the many awards she wins are the Associated Press Female Athlete of the Year award in 1960–61 and the James E. Sullivan Award in 1961. Rudolph is inducted into the National Track and Field Hall of Fame in 1974; into the

Wilma Rudolph

International Women's Sport Hall of Fame in 1980; and in 1983, into the U.S. Olympic Hall of Fame. Wilma Rudolph dies of brain cancer on November 12, 1994.

1941 **Psychiatrist Karen Horney Establishes Two Psychoanalysis Organizations.** Karen Horney (1885–1952) founds two organizations in New York City: the Association for the Advancement of Psychoanalysis, and the American Institute of Psychoanalysis. Horney is born in Hamburg, Germany, becoming a psychoanalyst and establishing her reputation at the Berlin Psychoanalytic Institute in the 1920s. She is the first woman actively to challenge Freudian ideas about female psychology, calling into question his theories of the Oedipal complex and penis envy. In 1932, Horney moves to the United States and settles in New York. The Karen Horney Clinic in New York

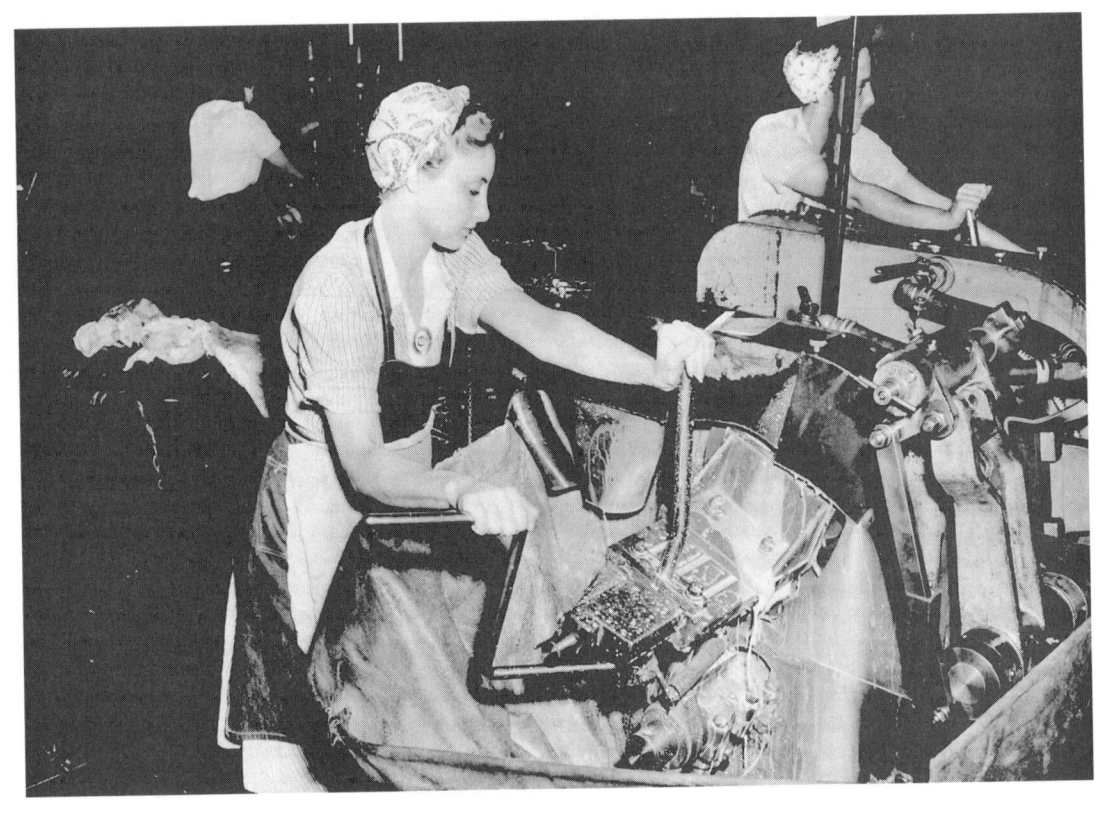

Woman worker operating a grinding machine at a bayonet factory.

City, named after this distinguished teacher, therapist, and writer, opens shortly after her death, in 1952.

1941 American Marianne Moore Awarded Pulitzer Prize for Poetry. Marianne Moore (1887–1972), an important modernist poet, wins the Pulitzer Prize for her *Collected Poems.* Moore was born in Kirkwood, Missouri, and educated in Pennsylvania at Bryn Mawr College, the Metzger Institute, and Carlisle Commercial College. She edited *The Dial*, a magazine, from 1926 to 1929, when it ceased publication.

1941 War-Time Japanese Film *Chocolate and Soldiers* Debuts. The Japanese film, *Chokoreto to heitai* (*Chocolate and Soldiers*), directed by

Sado Take, is produced. It tells the story of a family caught in World War II and the mother's (played by actress Sawamura Sadako) stoic struggle to survive. In addition to the theme that the woman must fulfill her obligations of wife and mother and accept her fate without question, there is the secondary theme that a woman alone cannot be entrusted to care for her family, but needs the assistance of older males in the family, as well as the solicitous support of the community. Sadako's portrayal represents the classic Japanese woman's way of coping with war and loss.

JUNE 1941 Soviet Women Fully Participate in Armed Forces. As with most nations during World War II (1939–45), industry in the Soviet Union is largely staffed by women because the men are all drafted into the military. Unlike other nations, however, women are also assigned a combat role in the Soviet armed forces. More than 800,000 women serve in the armed forces, comprising 8 percent of its total strength. Fighting behind enemy lines, the partisan movement employs 27,000 female fighters, with women comprising 10–25 percent of some units. Women fight at the front as artillery personnel, pilots, infantry, engineers, naval personnel, and snipers. Many are highly decorated. Although a low portion of the total number of women in the Soviet armed forces fight in the front lines, the integration of female combat units is unique among all combatant states.

JULY 3, 1941 Eleanor Dudley, National Intercollegiate Golf Champion. Eleanor Dudley wins the first women's national intercollegiate golf championship, sponsored by Ohio State University in Columbus, Ohio.

OCTOBER 25, 1941 American Novelist Anne Tyler Is Born. Anne Tyler (1941–), American novelist, is born in Minneapolis, Minnesota. Tyler grows up in Raleigh, North Carolina, and writes about life there and in Baltimore, Maryland. She publishes her first work, *If Morning Ever Comes*, in 1964. Other works include *Morgan's Passing* (1980), *Dinner at the Homesick Restaurant* (1982), and *The Accidental Tourist* (1985).

1942 *New York Post* Reveals Gender of Popular Financial Column's Author. The *New York Post* reveals that the author of its most popular financial column is a woman, Sylvia Porter. Since the early 1930s, financial reporter Sylvia Porter publishes anonymously because her editors believe investors will not respect a woman's advice. When her column becomes wildly popular, the *New York Post* decides to capitalize on her gender and puts her photo and byline on the column.

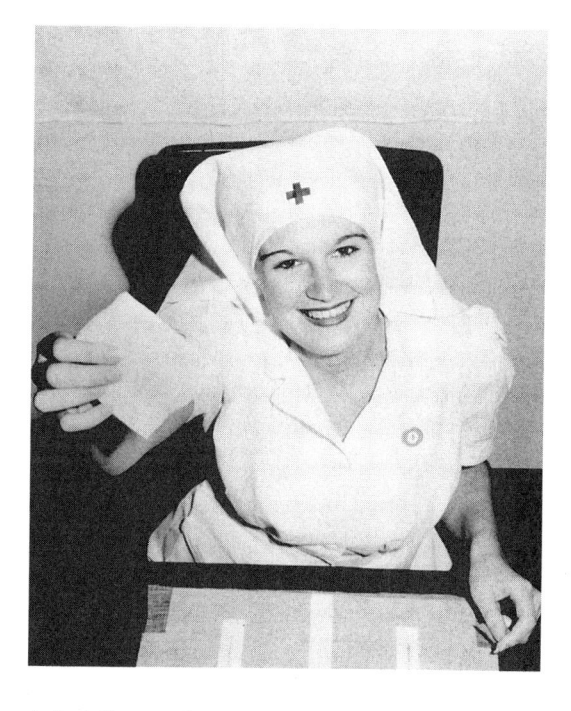

A Red Cross volunteer in Douglas County, Nebraska displays the three-millionth gauze square produced by the volunteers in her unit.

1942 American Women Work in Factories to Support War Effort. American women take jobs in factories that are formerly held exclusively by men. When thousands of young men enlist in the military when the United States enters World War II (1939–45) following the December 1941 bombing of Pearl Harbor, American women contribute to the war effort by filling the factory posts left vacant.

1942 Red Cross Volunteers Provide Vital Manpower. Volunteers worldwide support the Red Cross by helping to prepare medical supplies—for example, volunteers cut and fold gauze into bandages to be sent to military hospitals near combat zones.

1942 Ellen Glasgow Wins Pulitzer Prize. Virginia author Ellen Anderson Gholson Glasgow (1873–1945) receives the Pulitzer Prize for her nineteenth novel, *In This Our Life*. A prolific and successful writer, Glasgow often shocks readers of her time with her portrayals of strong, independent women.

1942   Women Worldwide Adjust to Wartime Rationing. Staples such as sugar, eggs, bread, and flour, are rationed in those countries involved in World War II. In addition, families are trained to respond to various war readiness drills, and are encouraged to participate in drives to sell war bonds and to salvage critical materials such as metal and rubber. In the cities of England, most families send their children to live with relatives in rural areas, or in Canada, to escape the German bombing raids.

1942   Elizabeth Hawes Serves as UAW International Representative. Elizabeth Hawes becomes the first woman to serve as an International Representative in the Education Department of the United Auto Workers (UAW) union. It is her job to deal with the problems of women in the union. She travels to locals all around the country and encourages women to help themselves deal with such issues as equal pay and seniority rights. She also finds that while women engage in strikes, they learn how to get "things all the time by sheer mass pressure." After touring the country for the UAW, Hawes concludes that women workers are not getting equality with men, but she does acknowledge that some advances are made by and for women workers during World War II.

1942   African American Poet Margaret Walker Wins Award. Margaret Abigail Walker (1915–) wins the Yale Series of Young Poets Award for her first book of poetry, *For My People,* becoming the first African American to receive the award.

1942   Virginia Lee Burton's *The Little House* Awarded Caldecott Medal. American Virginia Lee Burton (1909–1968) wins the Caldecott Medal for *The Little House,* a children's picture book in which a house experiences the

Mildred Helen McAfee

changing seasons in the country, the advancements in architecture and transportation, and the ensuing urbanization of the area.

1942   Mildred McAfee, First Director of WAVES. Mildred Helen McAfee (1900–) becomes the first director of the newly formed Women Accepted for Volunteer Emergency Service (the WAVES), a naval reserve program for women, in 1942. McAfee serves as president of Wellesley College from 1936 until 1942 when she is called into military service. She returns to Wellesley after World War II to resume her presidency, from 1945 to 1949.

1943   Anne Loughlin, First Woman President of General Council of the Trades Union Congress. Anne Loughlin (1894–1979), an English union organizer who goes to work in a clothing factory at the age of 12, is the first woman to serve as president of the General

Council of the Trades Union Congress, the same year she is made a Dame of the British Empire. In 1948, Loughlin is elected general secretary of the Tailors and Garment Workers Union, the first woman in England to become head of a mixed union.

1943 Lena Horne Becomes a Hollywood Star. African American actress Lena Horne (1917–) is escalated to star status by her performances in two musicals with all-African American casts— *Cabin in the Sky* and *Stormy Weather.*

1943 African American Actress Hazel Scott Halts Film Production. Offended by her film studio's request that African American actresses wear soiled aprons in the film *The Heat's On,* actress Hazel Scott (1920–1981) refuses, halting production on the picture for three days.

1943 Maya Deren, Successful Independent Filmmaker. Maya Deren (1922–1961) is the first woman to succeed as an independent filmmaker. Her major works include *Meshes of the Afternoon* (1943) and *Ritual in Transfigured Time* (1946). A measure of her achievement is that she is the first person to receive an award from the John Simon Guggenheim Memorial Foundation, in 1946.

1943 American Aviator Jacqueline Cochran Flies a Bomber Across the Atlantic Ocean. Pioneer aviator Jacqueline Cochran (1910–1980) is the first woman to pilot a bomber across the Atlantic Ocean, from the United States to England. Cochran also becomes a director of the Women Auxiliary Service Pilots in the U.S. Air Force the same year.

1943 Oveta Culp Hobby Organizes the Women's Army Auxiliary Corps. Texan Oveta Culp Hobby (1905–1995) organizes and directs the Women's Army Auxiliary Corps. As Colonel of the Women's Army Auxiliary Corps (WAACS), Hobby retains her position in the corps when it changes to the Women's Army Corps (WACS) in 1943.

JANUARY 6, 1943 Clare Boothe Luce Joins U.S. Congress. Clare Boothe Luce (1903–1987) is elected to the U.S. House of Representatives as a Republican from Connecticut. There she fights for racial equality in the military and in the workplace, and becomes a strong anti-Communist.

APRIL 27, 1943 Judy Johnson, First Woman to Ride in Steeplechase Race at Major U.S. Track. An English woman, Judy Johnson, rides Lone Gallant to a tenth place finish in a field of 11 horses in a steeplechase event at the Pimlico Racetrack at Baltimore, Maryland, the first woman steeplechase jockey racing at a major American racetrack.

JUNE 7, 1943 Nikki Giovanni, African American Poet, Is Born. African American poet Nikki Giovanni (1943–) is born Yolande Cornelia Giovanni, Jr., in Knoxville, Tennessee. Her first volume of poetry is entitled *Black Feeling, Black Talk.* She is strongly involved with the Black Power movement, which works to gain power and equality for African Americans in the 1960s. During the 1960s, Giovanni organizes the first Black Arts Festival in Cincinnati, Ohio. In 1968, she moves to New York City where she lives for the next 10 years, recording albums, writing books of poetry and essays (*Spin a Soft Black Song, Cotton Candy on a Rainy Day, Ego Tripping* among them), and giving speeches.

Giovanni receives much criticism, including threats on her life in 1984, because she refuses to take part in the boycott of South Africa. In 1989, she accepts a permanent position as Professor of English at Virginia Polytechnic. In 1994 she publishes *Racism 101,* a book of essays.

JUNE 15, 1943 Bolton Bill Signed into Law. The Bolton Bill, introduced by U.S. Representative Frances Payne Bolton (1885–1977)

Oveta Culp Hobby is sworn in as director of the Women's Army Auxiliary Corps.

of Ohio, is signed into law. The bill provides federal funds to train nurses and to establish a uniformed nurses' reserve. The bill ultimately provides over 120,000 trained military nurses for American forces during World War II (1939–45).

1944   Ingrid Bergman Receives First Oscar. Swedish actress Ingrid Bergman (1915–1982) wins her first Academy Award for best actress for her performance in the film noir classic, *Gaslight*. In 1956, Bergman receives her second Academy Award for her role in *Anastasia*.

1944   Swimmer Ann Curtis Receives James E. Sullivan Award. Ann Curtis, a champion swimmer, is the first woman to receive the prestigious James E. Sullivan Award from the

Amateur Athletic Union (AAU), honoring the outstanding amateur athlete of the year.

1944   Women's Professional Golf Association Formed. Hope Seignious, Betty Hicks, and Ellen Griffin found and incorporate the Women's Professional Golf Association (WPGA).

1944   Women Granted Suffrage in France. French women win the vote.

FEBRUARY 9, 1944   Birth of Alice Walker, African American Writer. African American poet and novelist Alice Walker (1944–) is born in Eatonton, Georgia, the youngest of eight children in her sharecropper family. In 1952, at the age of eight, she is accidentally shot with a BB gun by her brother and loses the sight in her right eye. For six years, Walker does not raise her head; she feels ugly and withdraws into the world of books.

On less than 20 dollars a week, Walker's mother buys her daughter three important gifts: a sewing machine for independence, a suitcase for travel, and a typewriter for writing. After graduating as valedictorian in her high school class, Walker is offered a scholarship to Spelman College in Georgia. She later transfers to Sarah Lawrence College in New York, where she graduates in 1965. In 1967, Walker moves to Mississippi with her husband, a civil rights attorney. Her first book, *Once: Poems,* is published in 1968. In 1969, her daughter Rebecca is born.

Walker's first marriage ends in 1978, and she moves to California with her partner, Robert Allen. Together they establish Wild Trees Press in 1984. Walker publishes many books, including *The Color Purple* (1982), which wins the Pulitzer Prize in 1983 and is made into a successful movie. Her other works include *The Temple of My Familiar* (1989) and *Possessing the Secret of Joy* (1992). In 1993, Walker coauthors a book on female genital mutilation in Africa.

JUNE 1944   American Journalist Martha Gellhorn Covers D-Day Invasion. Martha Gellhorn (1908–) is the only woman journalist to go ashore with the troops during the D-Day invasion of Normandy, France, during World War II. Gellhorn first becomes a war correspondent in 1937 during the Spanish Civil War, when she joins her lover, writer Ernest Hemingway, in Madrid, Spain. Her dispatches from Spain are published in *Collier's* magazine. Primarily a novelist, she returns to war correspondence during World War II in 1943 when she goes to London, leaving Hemingway, to whom she has been married since 1940, and all but forcing him to join her in her courageous endeavor. She covers both the Italian and North African campaigns before he

arrives in London, and she delivers the final blow to his fragile ego (and to the marriage) by going ashore in the D-Day invasion while he is forced to watch from a landing craft. Journalists are ordered to stay away from the beach at Normandy, but Gellhorn hides in the bathroom of a hospital ship and finds an opportunity to sneak ashore with stretcher bearers. In 1966 she returns to war correspondence a third time, writing a series of articles from Vietnam for the British publication *The Guardian.* Her shocking articles on the war's effect on Vietnamese civilians are among the first written by a western correspondent that challenge the American involvement in the Vietnam War.

NOVEMBER 1, 1944   Appalachian Author Lee Marshall Smith Is Born. Author Lee Marshall Smith (1944–), who captures the voices and stories of Appalachia, is born in Grundy, Virginia. Her roots run deep in the Appalachian mountains: four generations of her family hail from Grundy. As a child, she absorbs the dialects, voices, and stories of her home in the coal mining region of the Virginia-Kentucky border. Eventually, many of her novels will be set in rural Appalachia. Smith attends Hollins College in Virginia (1961–63), where she becomes a go-go dancer for an all-girl rock band called "The Virginia Woolfs." She publishes her first book, *The Last Day the Dogbushes Bloomed,* in 1968. Early in her career, she works as a reporter for various newspapers and teaches English. After her second and third novels (1971–73), Smith encounters an emotional dry spell. In 1980, she publishes *Black Mountain Breakdown* and then two of her best works in the 1980s: *Oral History* (1983); and *Fair and Tender Ladies* (1986). In 1992 she publishes *The Devil's Dream* (1992). Smith is a professor of fiction writing at Duke University, the University of North Carolina, and North Carolina State University.

1 9 4 5 – 1 9 4 9

1945   Indonesian Women Gain Suffrage.
Women are granted the constitutional right to
vote in Indonesia, although they do not actually
vote until the first general election in 1955.

**1945   Eleanor Roosevelt Appointed Delegate
to the United Nations.** Eleanor Roosevelt
(1884–1962) becomes the first person to represent the United States at the United
Nations. She takes up the post in 1946 and
serves until 1951. In 1961, she is reappointed
delegate to the U.N., and serves until her
death. From 1947 to 1951, Roosevelt chairs
the U.N. Human Rights Commission.

**1945   Barbara Castle Elected to British Par-
liament.** English journalist Barbara Betts
Castle (1910–) is elected a Member of the
British Parliament, where she serves in the
House of Commons for over 34 years. During the 1970s, she sponsors and pushes
through Parliament the Equal Pay Act, banning gender discrimination in the workplace.
She holds several cabinet positions, including
Minister of Overseas Development, Minister
of Transport, and Secretary of State for
Social Services. She becomes a member of
the European Parliament in 1979, serving as
vice chairman of the Socialist Group. A
skilled writer, Castle publishes a study of
British feminists Sylvia and Christabel
Pankhurst (1987), two controversial volumes
of *The Castle Diaries* in 1980 and 1984, and
Fighting All the Way in 1993.

**1945   Helena Normanton, First Woman
Member of England's General Council of the
Bar.** Helena Florence Normanton (1883–
1957), a barrister-at-law, is the first woman
elected to the General Council of the Bar in
England. She is also the first woman barrister
to appear at the High Court of Justice (1922),
at the Central Criminal Court (1924), and at
the London Sessions (1926). In 1952, after
she retires from the practice of law, she

becomes president of the Council of Married
Women. She is also active in the International
Federation of Business and Professional
Women and the International Sorority of
Women Lawyers. She writes several scholarly
articles and the influential *Everyday Law for
Women* (1932). Helena Normanton dies on
October 14, 1957.

1945   Actress Joan Crawford Awarded Oscar.
American actress Joan Crawford (1908–1977)
wins the Academy Award for best actress for
her performance in *Mildred Pierce*.

**1945   Cheryl Crawford Cofounds the Ameri-
can Repertory Theater.** Cheryl Crawford
(1902–1986), an American theater director,
cofounds (with Eva Le Gallienne and Margaret Webster) the American Repertory Theater
in New York City; two years later, with Elia
Kazan and Robert Lewis, she establishes the
Actors' Studio, also in New York.

**1945   Founding of Japan League of Women
Voters.** Japanese feminist, suffragist, and politician Ichikawa Fusae (1893–1981) establishes
the *Nihon Fujin Yukensha Domei* (Japan
League of Women Voters).

**1945   Margery Hurst Establishes Brook Street
Bureau in England.** English entrepreneur
Margery Berney Hurst (1913–1989) opens her
own business, the Brook Street Bureau of
Mayfair, Ltd., at the end of World War II
(1939–45). The Brook Street Bureau provides
businesses with temporary secretaries. Hurst is
very selective in choosing the secretaries who
work for her and the companies she sends
them to. By 1965 she is a millionaire, and her
company has over 200 branches in Great Britain, the United States, Hong Kong, and Australia. Hurst establishes the Society for
International Secretaries in London, and it
spreads to the United States and Australia. A
strong spokeswoman for women's rights, she
also campaigns for greater cooperation
between businesses in Great Britain and the

Margery Berney Hurst

United States. In 1970 Hurst is elected one of the first woman members of Lloyd's of London. Her autobiographies, *No Glass Slipper* and *Walking Up Brook Street*, are published in 1967 and 1988 respectively. She is awarded the Order of the British Empire in 1976, the year she retires as managing director of Brook Street Bureau. Margery Hurst dies on February 11, 1989.

1945   **Women Win Vote in Italy.** Italian women gain suffrage.

1945   **Japanese Women Gain Vote.** Women are extended voting rights in Japan.

1945   **Hungarian Women Extended Suffrage.** Women in Hungary gain voting rights.

1945   **Vote Given to Women in Yugoslavia.** Women are granted suffrage in Yugoslavia.

1945   **Local Suffrage for Women in Venezuela.** Women gain local suffrage in Venezuela.

AUGUST 15, 1945   **Future Bangladesh Prime Minister Is Born.** Khaleda Begum Zia (1945–) is born to Iskanter and Begum Taiyaba Majumdar on August 15, 1945, in Dinajpur, Bangladesh. She marries Ziaur Rahman and has two children. Zia becomes a member of the Bangladesh Nationalist Party. In 1991 Zia is elected prime minister of her country.

1946   **Agatha Barbara Elected to Maltese Parliament.** Agatha Barbara (1923–) is the first woman elected to the parliament of Malta. She subsequently serves two terms as minister of education, and one as minister of labor, culture, and welfare. Barbara is elected the first woman president of that country on February 16, 1982.

1946   **Gladys Dickason Teaches Trade Union Basics to Japanese Women.** Labor organizer Gladys Dickason (1903–1971) is appointed by General Douglas MacArthur to teach Japanese working women the basics of unionism following World War II (1939–45).

1946   **Actress Ava Gardner on Edge of Hollywood Stardom.** American actress Ava Gardner (1922–1990) wins *Look* magazine's "Most Promising Newcomer" award for her role as a gangster's moll in *The Killers.* By 1951, she becomes Metro-Goldwyn-Mayer's leading female star.

1946   **Marguerite de Angeli Publishes First Modern Children's Book About Racial Prejudice.** Marguerite Lofft de Angeli (1889–1987) writes *Bright April,* considered the first modern children's book about a black child and racial prejudice. De Angeli wins the Newbery Medal for *The Door in the Wall* (1949), set in thirteenth-century England. Another historical novel, *Black Fox of Lorne* (1956), is a Newbery Honor book. Her *Book of Nursery and Mother Goose Rhymes* (1954), containing lavish illustrations, is a Caldecott Honor book. The

ROSIE THE RIVETER, SYMBOL FOR AMERICAN WOMAN DEFENSE WORKERS DURING WORLD WAR II

1946 Rosie the Riveter became the symbol for all women defense workers in the United States during World War II (1939–45). She was originally drawn by Norman Rockwell for the cover of the Saturday Evening Post. Rosie was depicted as a young war worker, muscular, but pert, rose-cheeked and with a rivet gun slung across her lap. Her foot was firmly planted on a copy of *Mein Kampf*, symbolizing her participation in helping to stamp out fascism. At the same time there is a powder puff and a mirror sticking out of a pocket in her coveralls. Women war workers were most often union members. They belonged to the Auto Workers, the Steel Workers, and the Rubber Workers unions, and many more that were crucial to the war effort. In many instances, in spite of union membership, the women were subjected to different wages and separate seniority lists for men and for women. Nevertheless, these women supported the no-strike agreements in effect during the war. But in a true union spirit they found that collective action and the pressure of numbers often was enough to bring about necessary changes. "Rosie the Riveter" was also a song about a defense worker named Rosie and her boyfriend named Charlie. Rosie the Riveter became the subject of a 1981 documentary film in which five "Rosies" tell their story of war work and what happened to all the "Rosies" at the end of the war.

Lapeer City Branch Library Board renames its library in her honor on August 22, 1981. She is named Distinguished Daughter of Pennsylvania in 1958.

1946 Billie Holliday, First Female Jazz Singer to Perform Solo at New York Town Hall. Billie Holiday (1915–1959), an African American performer known internationally both for her music and for her tempestuous life, performs at Town Hall in New York City, becoming the first female jazz singer to give a solo performance there.

1946 Kitamura Sayo, Founder of Japanese Dancing Religion. Kitamura Sayo (1900–1967) founds the Japanese religious movement popularly known as *odoru shukyo* (dancing religion). After experiencing personal troubles, she claims, in 1944, to have heard a divine voice. After World War II (1939–45), she declares herself to be the only daughter and the shrine of the sun goddess, Amaterasu o Mikami. Sayo begins preaching and faith healing. She is particularly sought to purify Japanese society of the defilement she associates with the war. Sayo is known for being particularly eloquent and skillful in using everyday imagery to gain followers and prepare them for the divine age to come. Her words and deeds are recorded in *Seisho* (*Book of Life* or *Bible*). Since her followers express their divine bliss in freestyle dancing, the movement comes to be known as the dancing religion.

1946 **Limited Suffrage Granted to Women in El Salvador.** Women win the vote in El Salvador, but with a higher age requirement than for men.

1946 **Some Algerian Women Gain Vote.** Women with French Civil Status win voting rights in Algeria.

1946 **Mary Ritter Beard Publishes** *Women As a Force in History*. American historian and activist Mary Ritter Beard (1876–1958) publishes her influential study of women's role in history, entitled *Women As A Force in History*. A lifelong activist and historian, she publishes extensively, both alone and in collaboration with her husband, Charles Austin Beard.

SEPTEMBER 1, 1946 **First U.S. Women's Open Golf Tournament.** Patty Berg defeats Betty Jameson in the final round to win the first U.S. Women's Open golf tournament.

1947 **Venezuelan Women Given Vote.** Women win the full vote in Venezuela.

1947 **Publication of Early Childhood Classic** *Goodnight Moon*. Prolific American children's author Margaret Wise Brown (1910–1952) publishes the popular classic *Goodnight Moon*. Wise Brown captures childlike rituals and rites of passage in her books, which remain popular with both children and parents.

1947 **Mildred "Babe" Didrikson Zaharias, First American to Win British Women's Golf Championship.** Mildred "Babe" Didrikson Zaharias (1914–1956), an American golfer

Mary Beard

and champion athlete, wins the British Ladies' Amateur Golf Championship.

1947 **Cheryl Crawford Cofounds the Actors' Studio.** Cheryl Crawford (1902–1986), an American theater director, cofounds (with Elia Kazan and Robert Lewis) the Actors' Studio in New York City.

1947 **Establishment of Turkey's National School of Ballet.** Ninette de Valois (1898–) founds the National School of Ballet in Turkey.

1947 **Japanese Women Obtain Equal Access to Educational Opportunities.** The educational reform of 1947, enacted during the American occupation of Japan following World War II (1939–45), establishes for the first time coeducation and equal access to educational opportunities for women in Japan.

1947 **Japan's New Constitution Guarantees Equal Rights to Women.** When World War II ends in 1945, Japan begins to rebuild its government. The 1947 constitution guarantees equal rights to women and makes individuals, rather than the family, the primary legal entity. In the field of family law, husbands and wives are recognized as equal partners in marriage, with equal financial responsibility and authority over the children. The same grounds for divorce are applicable to husband and wife. Equitable property settlements and custody arrangements are provided by law. Women are recognized as legal persons, capable of holding property and entering into legal agreements. In these provisions, the constitution of 1947 overturns the Meiji Civil Code of 1898, which denies women legal status.

1947 **Labor Standards Law Enacted in Japan.** The Labor Standards Law of 1947, enacted during the American occupation of Japan following World War II (1939–45), is the basis of regulating minimum protection for industrial workers in Japan. The wide-ranging law establishes guidelines for minimum wages, minimum hours of work, rest and holidays, apprentice training, safety and health standards, and special standards for the employment of women and children. This legislation continues the tradition of protective legislation for women industrial workers in Japan.

1947 **Educational Reform Enacted in Japan.** The Educational Reform of 1947, enacted during the American occupation following World War II (1939–45), establishes coeducation and equal access to educational opportunities in Japan.

1947 **Dorothy Fuldheim Is TV News Anchor.** Dorothy Fuldheim, a newscaster in Cleveland, Ohio, becomes the first female television news anchor. Fuldheim receives the assignment at

Dorothy Fuldheim

WEWS-TV, the first station in the region between New York and Chicago, Illinois, to go on the air. At first, the beer company that sponsors the newscast is reluctant to back a newscast anchored by a woman, but the station stands by her and the beer company relents. Fuldheim remains at the anchor desk for 18 years. During her career she interviews such notables as Adolf Hitler, Jimmy Carter, and Queen Farida of Egypt. By 1979, at age 86, she is still anchoring the early newscast in Cleveland, earning the distinction of being on the job longer than any other television broadcaster, male or female.

1947 **Mexican Women Granted Municipal Vote.** Women obtain the vote in municipal elections in Mexico.

1947 Women Win Vote in Bulgaria. Bulgarian women are granted suffrage.

1947 Women Gain Vote in Argentina. Suffrage is extended to women in Argentina.

1947 Women Win Suffrage in China. Chinese women gain voting rights.

AUGUST 16, 1947 First African American Woman Senator Is Born. Carol Elizabeth Moseley (1947–) is born in Chicago, Illinois, to Joseph and Edna Moseley. She receives her bachelor's degree in political science from the University of Illinois, Chicago. In 1972 the University of Chicago Law School confers a law degree on Moseley. During the mid-1970s, Moseley serves as an assistant attorney in the U.S. Attorney's Office. Moseley marries Michael Braun and they have one child before divorcing. Mayor of Chicago Harold Washington names Moseley his floor leader in the legislature in 1983. In 1988 Moseley is elected the Cook County recorder of Deeds. She cochairs Illinois senator Paul Simon's 1990 reelection campaign. In 1992 Moseley runs for the U.S. Senate from the State of Illinois. On November 3, 1992, she is elected the first African American woman senator in the United States.

OCTOBER 23, 1947 United States Women's Curling Association Founded. Curling is a game played by two teams of four players each. The teams slide a large stone with a handle across a stretch of ice toward a target. By the mid-1940s, curling is popular with women in the United States, and the United States Women's Curling Association is founded with headquarters at Omaha, Nebraska. The association sponsors competitions, publishes rules and regulations, and promotes the sport of curling for women.

OCTOBER 26, 1947 Birth of Hillary Rodham Clinton. Hillary Rodham Clinton (1947–) is born in Park Ridge, Illinois. She attends Wellesley College and Yale Law School and becomes a nationally recognized activist on education and children's issues, a mother, and a trusted political adviser to her husband, President Bill Clinton. Hillary Clinton chairs an Arkansas state commission on education, serves on dozens of corporate and civic boards, and makes a career as one of America's leading attorneys. Within a week of her husband's inauguration, Clinton is appointed chair of a high-level task force charged with producing a health-care reform plan. Clinton's outspoken activism is often the target of sharp criticism from the media and her husband's political opponents, particularly during the 1992 presidential campaign and subsequent Whitewater investigations.

1948 Anne Loughlin, First Woman in England to Head Mixed Union. Anne Loughlin (1894–1979), an English union organizer, is elected general secretary of the Tailors and Garment Workers Union, the first woman in England to become head of a mixed union.

1948 Women Win Vote in Romania. Romanian women gain suffrage.

1948 Dutch Athlete Fanny Blankers-Koen Wins Four Olympic Gold Medals. At the Summer Olympic Games in London, England, Dutch athlete Fanny Blankers-Koen (1918–) becomes the first and only woman to win four gold medals in track and field in a single Olympics (100-meter, 200-meter, 80-meter hurdles, and anchor of the 4x100-meter relay). Also this year, she is named Female Athlete of the Year by the Associated Press. By the end of her career, Blankers-Koen has set 13 world records, earned five European golds, and won 58 Dutch national track and field titles. In 1980, Blankers-Koen is elected into the International Women's Sports Hall of Fame.

A NEW CONSTITUTION IN JAPAN

1947 Japan's constitution, which overturned the Meiji Constitution of 1897, was promulgated. As Japan was under the United States' military occupation at the time, the constitution reflected U.S. assumptions about the means necessary to bring about democracy, equality, and individual freedom. The 1947 constitution was a conscious attempt to overturn the foundations of feudalism and militarism which were perceived to have resulted from the Meiji Constitution. With respect to women's issues, U.S. occupation officers, primarily under the direction of Lieutenant Ethel B. Weed, sought guidance from the Japanese women's rights activists who had been active before the war. Together, they formulated provisions in the constitution that established adult female suffrage; prohibited arranged marriages; imposed equal access to divorce for men and women; provided equal inheritance rights; enabled women to be the legal guardians of their own children and property; provided a standard of equal pay for equal work; and instituted coeducation from elementary school through the university. Most revolutionary, the constitution included an equal rights provision for women. It must be noted, however, that while the constitution, in many respects, brought about theoretical equality, social practices have continued to be discriminatory to women in Japan.

1948 Soprano Joan Cross Establishes Opera School in London. Joan Cross (1900–), English soprano and opera producer, founds and serves as first director (until 1964) of the Opera School in London. The school is renamed the National School of Opera in 1955. Cross is also known as the first woman to sing the central female roles in a number of Benjamin Brittain's works, including Ellen in *Peter Grimes* (1945), Mrs. Billows in *Albert Herring* (1947), Elizabeth in *Gloriana* (1953), and Mrs. Grose in *Turn of the Screw* (1954). Cross is a founding member of the English Opera Group.

1948 Lina Wertmuller Gains Warner Brothers Directing Contract. Lina Wertmuller gains an exclusive directing contract with Warner Brothers. In 1976, Wertmuller is nominated for an Academy Award, the first woman ever to be nominated in the category of best director.

1948 Golda Meir, Israeli Ambassador to Soviet Union. One of the original signers of the 1948 proclamation declaring Israel's independence, Golda Mabovich Meir (1898–1978) serves as ambassador from Israel to the Soviet Union from 1948 to 1949.

1948 Indian Co-operative Union Founded. Kamaldevi Chattopadhyay (1903–), an Indian reform leader and sponsor of the crafts movement, is the founder of the Indian Co-operative Union. This group is devoted to helping refugees participate in commercial enterprise after the partition of India. (In August 1947, India and Pakistan become two separate and independent nations. Pakistan becomes a predominantly Muslim nation, and its borders are established from territory that was formerly part of India. This is known as "partition.") In 1952, Chattopadhyay helps to found the World Crafts Council.

1948 Women Win Vote in Israel. The democratic nation of Israel is founded and women are given voting rights.

1948 Women Granted Suffrage in South Korea. Women win the vote in South Korea.

DECEMBER 10, 1948 Universal Declaration of Human Rights Passes in United Nations' General Assembly. As a United States delegate to the United Nations, former first lady Eleanor Roosevelt (1884–1962) lobbies for and essentially writes the Universal Declaration of Human Rights. When the declaration is passed in the General Assembly, delegates from around the world give her a standing ovation.

1949 Mildred "Babe" Didrikson Zaharias Cofounds LPGA. Mildred Ella Didrikson Zaharias (1914–1956), nicknamed "Babe," founds the Ladies Professional Golf Association (LPGA) with her husband George Zaharias, Fred Corcoran, and Patty Berg. Zaharias begins to play golf in 1935, and between 1946 and 1948, wins 17 golf tournaments. Zaharias turns professional in 1948.

1949 African American Actress Ethel Waters Receives Oscar Nomination. Ethel Waters (1896–1977), an African American actress and singer whose acting career originates in the theater, receives an Oscar nomination for best supporting actress for her role in *Pinky*, a film that focuses on the issue of African Americans passing as white.

1949 Children's Author Marguerite de Angeli Awarded Newbery Medal. American children's book author Marguerite Lofft de Angeli (1889–1987) wins the Newbery Medal for *The Door in the Wall*. Set in thirteenth-century England, it tells the story of young Robin, a handicapped protagonist, who learns to value his own inner strengths in spite of his crooked leg. Another historical novel, *Black Fox of Lorne* (1956), is a Newbery Honor book. In 1968 Marguerite de Angeli is honored with the Regina Medal for the body of her work.

1949 French Writer Simone De Beauvoir Publishes *Le deuxième sex*. Simone De Beauvoir (1908–1986), French novelist and feminist, publishes her landmark work, *Le deuxième sex,* a study of women in society. The phrase "women's liberation" is used for the first time in this work, which is translated and published as *The Second Sex* in English in 1953.

1949 Puppeteer Shirley Dinsdale, First Woman to Receive Emmy. Shirley Dinsdale (1928–) becomes the first woman to win an Emmy award for work on television. She is recognized as "most outstanding television personality" for her work on her puppet show *Judy Splinters.*

1949 Japan's Family Court System Established. The family court (*katei saibansho*) system of Japan, which has jurisdiction over domestic and juvenile cases, is established. Family court probation officers play an important role in both domestic and juvenile cases; they are trained in psychology, education, and sociology, as well as specific training for their position. There are two separate procedures for domestic cases, depending on the nature of the case. Cases concerning relationships between parents and children (e.g., adoption, depriving a parent of parental rights) are handled by a determination procedure, in which the judge makes the final decision. Cases concerning marital relationships (e.g., divorce, custodial rights of divorced parents, inheritance from spouse's estate) can be handled by the determination procedure, but are more commonly handled by a conciliation process. The conciliation process includes a judge as well as part-time commissioners, "citizens of learning and good sense." While these commissioners can be either male or female, they reflect prevailing social assumptions, which might be counter to the interests of women in domestic disputes.

1949 Women Win Vote in Chile. Women gain suffrage in Chile.

MAY 29, 1949 Wilson Sporting Goods Sponsors Ladies Professional Golf Association. Wilson Sporting Goods agrees to sponsor the formation of the Ladies Professional Golf Association (LPGA). The group becomes an officially chartered organization in 1950.

OCTOBER 12, 1949 Eugenie Moore Anderson Becomes U.S. Ambassador. Eugenie Moore Anderson (1909–) of Red Wing, Minnesota, is the first woman to serve as a U.S. ambassador. She is appointed ambassador to Denmark by President Harry S Truman. The swearing-in ceremony takes place in the office of secretary of state Dean Acheson on October 28, 1949. Anderson holds the post until 1953. In 1962, she is appointed ambassador to Bulgaria.

1 9 5 0 – 1 9 5 4

1950 Suffragist Susan B. Anthony Elected to American Hall of Fame. Social reformer and suffragist Susan B. Anthony (1820–1906) is elected to the American Hall of Fame. On July 29, 1979, the U.S. government issues a one-dollar Susan B. Anthony coin, making her the first U.S. woman to have her likeness on a coin in general circulation.

1950 Women Over 21 Gain Vote in India. Women over the age of 21 win the vote in India.

1950 Women Gain Full Suffrage in El Salvador. Women win full suffrage in El Salvador; in 1946 women can vote, but the age requirement is higher than for men.

1950 Florence Chadwick Swims Both Ways across English Channel. American Florence Chadwick is the first woman to swim both ways across the English Channel. She swims from France to England in 1950, setting a new record of 13 hours and 20 minutes; and the next year, she swims from England to France, completing her round trip.

1950 Women Gain Suffrage in Haiti. Women in Haiti win the right to vote.

AUGUST 28, 1950 African American Althea Gibson Plays in Major Tennis Tournament. Althea Gibson (1927–) becomes the first African American to play in a major U.S. Ladies Tennis Association (USLTA) tournament. She continues to break racial barriers in international tennis during the 1950s, winning the French Open and at Wimbledon.

SEPTEMBER 15, 1950 War Correspondent Marguerite Higgins Joins U.S. Marine Amphibious Landing at Inchon, Korea. War correspondent Marguerite Higgins (1920–1966) is in the fifth wave of U.S. Marines who land at Inchon, Korea. She becomes a war correspondent for the *New York Herald Tribune* during World War II (1939–45) in Europe. When war breaks out in Korea in 1950, Higgins is refused accreditation at first because of her gender. Higgins is awarded a 1951 Pulitzer Prize for her account of the battle at Inchon.

1951 Armi Ratia Cofounds Finnish Textile Design Firm. Armi Ratia (1912–1979), a Finnish designer, is cofounder with her husband of Marimekko, a textile design firm for which she becomes the first managing director. A very successful international business, Marimekko is exporting to over 20 countries by 1970. In 1968, Ratia becomes the first Finnish woman to be awarded the American Neiman Marcus Award in recognition for her art and business success.

Marguerite Higgins

1951   Charlotte Whitton, Canada's First Woman Mayor. An early crusader for the rights of women and children, Charlotte Whitton (1896–?) becomes Canada's first female mayor and is reelected to this position four times. She continues as an alderman until her retirement in 1972. Whitton is best recalled for being Ottawa's flamboyant and outspoken mayor during 1950s and 1960s. The highlights of these years are the many verbal battles and one physical battle with her male colleagues.

1951   Adrienne Rich Publishes First Poems. American poet Adrienne Rich (1929–) graduates from Radcliffe College and publishes her first volume of poems, *A Change of World*, which is selected for the Yale Younger Poets Series. After a book of poems in 1955, the

year her first son is born, she does not publish again for eight years.

1951   Marguerite Higgins Wins Pulitzer Prize for Korean Battle Coverage. War correspondent Marguerite Higgins (1920–1966) is the first woman awarded a Pulitzer Prize for overseas reporting. She wins the Pulitzer for her account of the battle at Inchon, Korea; she accompanies the U.S. Marine amphibious landing there on September 15, 1950.

1952   National Federation of Regional Women's Organizations Established in Japan. Yamataki Shigeri (1899–1977) founds *Chifuren* (National Federation of Regional Women's Organizations) and serves as its president. The objectives of the organization include elevating the status of women and promoting social welfare. The organization is particularly active in consumer protection issues. With the backing of Chifuren, Shigeri is elected to the House of Councillors (the upper house of Japan's national legislature) in 1962 and 1965.

1952   Educated Lebanese Women Win Vote. Women who have completed elementary school in Lebanon gain the vote.

1952   Women Granted Suffrage in Greece. Women gain equal suffrage rights in Greece.

1952   First Randle Women's International Team Trophy in Riflery. Sponsored by the National Rifle Association, the first match is held for the Randle Women's International Team Trophy, which goes to the winning ten-woman team in a small-bore rifle match. The American women's team wins for the first 13 years before the British triumph in 1965.

JANUARY 15, 1952   Women Curlers Compete in New York. The St. Andrew Golf Club hosts the first bonspiel for women curlers in the New York area. A bonspiel is a competition between two curling clubs; curling is a team sport played by sliding a large stone with a handle on an ice "court" toward a target.

FEBRUARY 7, 1952 **Molecular Biologist Rosalind Franklin Makes Significant Contribution to Discovery of DNA Structure.** British molecular biologist Rosalind Franklin (1920–1958) records the existence of a form of deoxyribonucleic acid, commonly known as DNA, which transmits genetic information. Her colleague, Maurice Wilkins, shares Franklin's research (without her knowledge or consent) with Francis Crick and James Watson, who are undertaking similar research at Cambridge University. In April 1953, Crick and Watson announce the discovery of the structure of DNA. In their article in *Nature*, Crick and Watson do not reveal the role played by Franklin. In 1962, Crick, Watson, and Wilkins are awarded the Nobel Prize. Rosalind Franklin, educated at St. Paul's Girl's School and Newnham College, Cambridge, begins her career at the British Coal Utilization Research Association. She is introduced to X-ray crystallography at the Laboratoire Central de l'État in Paris and applies X-ray crystallography to the search for the structure of DNA. Franklin's research contributes to today's understanding of DNA, but her recognition is obscured by personal antipathy, and deepened by a discredited and self-serving account of events published in James Watson's *The Double Helix.* Rosalind Franklin dies of cancer in London on April 16, 1958.

AUGUST 28, 1952 **Birth of American Poet Laureate Rita Dove.** Rita Dove (1952–), appointed American poet laureate on October 1, 1993, is born in Akron, Ohio. At the time of her appointment, she is the youngest person and the first African American to serve as the nation's poet laureate. In 1987, her book-length poetry collection, *Thomas and Beulah,* wins the Pulitzer Prize.

1953 **Publication of English-Language Version of Simone De Beauvoir's Landmark**

Marilyn Monroe during the filming of *The Seven-Year Itch.*

Work. *The Second Sex,* an English-language version of *Le deuxième sex* (1949) by Simone De Beauvoir (1908–1986) is published. It is a study of women in society, and introduces the phrase "women's liberation."

1953 **Marilyn Monroe, Leading Sex Symbol of the 1950s.** Marilyn Monroe (1926–1962) stars in three big budget color feature films: *Niagara, Gentlemen Prefer Blondes,* and *How to Marry a Millionaire.* Immediately, Marilyn Monroe becomes an international sensation and sex symbol. On the big screen, her voluptuous figure and girlish whisper represent innocent sexual vulnerability. More than 30 years after her tragic and premature death, her image continues to be immediately recognizable by millions all over the world.

1953   Active Unionist Odessa Komer Joins UAW. Odessa Komer (1925–) becomes a member of United Automobile Workers (UAW) Union Local 228 when she goes to work as an assembler at Ford Motor Company in Michigan. Soon after joining the union, she becomes active and is elected to numerous union positions. These include executive board (1956–58), District Committee (1958–65), delegate to the Ford Council and Sub Council 5 (1961–67), and delegate to the 1964 and 1966 constitutional conventions. She also serves on the By Laws Committee and is the education chair. In each instance, Komer is the first woman to hold the position. In 1974 she is elected to the national office of vice president of the union and also becomes head of the Women's Department for the national union. Komer holds those positions until she retires in 1992.

1953   Joan Maud Littlewood Founds England's Theatre Workshop. Joan Maud Littlewood (1914–), an English director, is the founder and first manager of the Theatre Workshop in Stratford, England. A graduate of the Royal Academy of Dramatic Art in London, Littlewood founds precursors of the Theatre Workshop in Manchester with her husband, the singer and writer Ewan McColl: the Theatre Union, followed by the Theatre of Action. Littlewood encourages experimental drama and becomes one of the most influential stage directors working in England after World War II.

1953   Planned Parenthood Founded by Margaret Sanger. Margaret Sanger (1883–1966), who devotes her life to educating women about birth control, founds the International Planned Parenthood Federation. She is also Planned Parenthood's first president.

1953   Mexican Women Granted Suffrage. Women gain full voting rights in Mexico; in 1947 they can vote in municipal elections.

1953   American Aviator Jacqueline Cochran Breaks the Sound Barrier. Pioneer aviator Jacqueline Cochran (1910–1980), flying an F-86 Saber jet at 760 miles per hour over the Rogers Dry Lake near Edwards Air Force Base in California, breaks the sound barrier. Cochran achieves many firsts in her lifetime as a pioneering aviator.

FEBRUARY 15, 1953   Tenley Albright Wins World Figure Skating Championship. Tenley Albright is the first American woman to win the world figure skating championship.

MARCH 3, 1953   Clare Boothe Luce Named American Ambassador to Italy. President Dwight Eisenhower appoints former Republican Congresswoman Clare Boothe Luce (1903–1987) Ambassador to Italy, where she oversees peaceful settlements of longstanding territorial disputes. She is the first American woman to hold a diplomatic post at this level. She receives many honors at home and abroad, including the Hammarskjold Medal in 1966 and the Medal of Freedom in 1983.

MARCH 11, 1953   Oveta Culp Hobby Appointed First American Secretary of Health, Education, and Welfare. Texan Oveta Culp Hobby (1905–1995) is appointed by President Dwight D. Eisenhower to be the first Secretary of Health, Education and Welfare in a U.S. cabinet, a position she holds until 1955. A Texas lawyer and newspaperwoman, Hobby works for the War Department and helps in the education of a women's army corps. Appointed colonel of the Women's Army Auxiliary Corps (WAACS), Hobby retains her position in the corps when it changes to the Women's Army Corps (WACS) in 1943.

JUNE 1953   Coronation of Elizabeth II. After the death of her father, King George VI of England, Elizabeth Alexandra Mary Windsor (1926–) assumes the British throne amidst worldwide celebration.

Oveta Culp Hobby, with President Dwight Eisenhower, right, is sworn in as Secretary of Health, Education, and Welfare.

JUNE 21, 1953   Benazir Bhutto, Future Prime Minister of Pakistan, Is Born. Benazir Bhutto (1953–) is born to Zulfikar Ali and Busrat Bhutto in Pakistan. She is educated at Radcliffe College in the United States and Oxford University in England. In 1987 she marries Asif Ali Zardari and they have two children. Bhutto becomes prime minister of Pakistan in 1988, and she writes her autobiography, *Daughter of Destiny,* in 1989.

SEPTEMBER 7, 1953   Maureen Connolly Wins the Grand Slam of Tennis. Maureen Connolly (1934–1969) of the United States wins the Australian, French, American, and British tennis titles to become the first woman to win tennis' Grand Slam.

1954   African American Actress Dorothy Dandridge Nominated for Academy Award. Dorothy Dandridge (1922–1965), dubbed the "Black Marilyn Monroe," is the first African American to be nominated for an Academy Award as best actress in *Carmen Jones.* Dandridge's screen career begins to merge with her private life. Futile relationships with white men in films such as *The Decks Ran Red* (1958), *Tamango* (1958), and *Malaga* (1962) are mirrored in her private life. Despite her screen success, Dandridge's realization that only limited roles are available to her, coupled with a difficult personal life and dwindling finances, force her into a state of depression. In 1965, Dorothy Dandridge is found dead of an apparent suicide from antidepressants.

1954   Laura Ingalls Wilder Award Established. The Laura Ingalls Wilder Award is established by the Children's Services Division of the American Library Association. The award, named in honor of children's author Laura Ingalls Wilder (1867–1957), is to be given every five years to an author who, over a period of years, makes a substantial and lasting contribution to literature for children. Wilder is known for her autobiographical *Little House* series of life on the American frontier.

1954   Sono Ayako, Popular Japanese Writer of Post-World War II Era. Japanese writer Sono Ayako (1931–) comes to public attention while she is still a university student. She gains prominence with the story "Enrai no kyakuta-chi" (1954; "Guests from Across the Sea"), which describes U.S. military occupation forces. Ayako is recognized as an eloquent narrator who analyzes Japanese society from the perspective of an intellectual, Catholic woman.

1954   Publication of *Ladies of Courage* Profiling American Women in Politics. Eleanor Roosevelt (1894–1962) and Lorena Hickok publish a tribute to American women in politics, *Ladies of Courage.* The work also provides advice for women on strategies to use in pursuing a political career.

1954   First Oral Contraceptive Trials on Humans Begin in Massachusetts. Katherine Dexter McCormick, the second woman to graduate from Massachusetts Institute of Technology (1904), funds a research project to test oral contraceptives on human volunteers. Dr. Gregory Pincus, working at the Worcester Foundation for Experimental Biology in Shrewsbury, Massachusetts, tests his oral contraceptive on women volunteers.

APRIL 15, 1954   American Contraception Advocate Margaret Sanger Addresses Diet, Japanese Parliament. Margaret Sanger (1883–1966), who devotes her life to educating women about birth control, in the first address by a woman ever made to the Diet, the Japanese parliament, urges Japanese women to use birth control. Sanger founds the International Planned Parenthood Federation in 1953.

---

1 9 5 5 – 1 9 5 9

1955   Mary Quant Opens "Bazaar" in Chelsea. Mary Quant (1934–) and two partners open a shop, "Bazaar," in the Chelsea area of London, England, to sell their own clothing designs. The shop becomes popular—within less than a decade, it expands into a multi-million-dollar enterprise—and Mary Quant's influence over young women's fashions soon spreads worldwide.

1955   Australian Joan Sutherland, First to Sing Part of Jennifer in Opera *The Midsummer Marriage*. Joan Sutherland (1926–), the famous Australian coloratura soprano, is the first person to sing the part of Jennifer in Michael Tippett's opera *The Midsummer Marriage,* at Covent Garden in London. Trained in Australia and at the Royal College of Music and Opera School in London, Sutherland quickly establishes an international reputation. She is known particularly for her interpretations of Donizetti's Lucia and Bellini's Norma. She is made a Dame of the British Empire in 1979.

1955   Italian Entrepreneur Giuliana Benetton Founds Knitwear Company. Giuliana Benetton (1938?–) is founder and first president of Benetton, the world's largest knitwear company. She locates the business in Treviso, Italy, the town near Venice where she grows up. By 1986, the company has 4,000 outlets in 54 countries, having become the world's largest manufacturer of knitwear and greatest consumer of virgin wool.

1955   Marian Anderson, First African American Woman Soloist to Sing at Metropolitan Opera. Opera singer Marian Anderson (1902–1993) becomes the first African American woman soloist to sing on the stage of the Metropolitan Opera House in New York City. Her debut role at the Met is as Ulrica in *Un Ballo in Maschera* (*The Masked Ball*). Born in Philadelphia, Pennsylvania, Anderson begins singing at age six in her church choir. Her solo career is launched when she is selected over 300 singers in a contest, giving her the opportunity to sing with the New York Philharmonic Orchestra. Although the famous conductor Arturo Toscanini is widely quoted praising Anderson's voice as one "heard once in a hundred years," she is forced to perform in segregated concert halls. In 1939, the Daughters of the American Revolution (DAR) refuse to allow Anderson to perform a concert in Philadelphia's Constitution Hall, claiming that the date has been previously booked. This action causes then-First Lady Eleanor Roosevelt to resign her membership in the DAR and to assist Anderson in performing an open-air concert on Easter Sunday at the Lincoln Memorial in Washington, D.C. More than 75,000 people attend the concert, where Anderson performs the U.S. National Anthem and *Ave Maria,* among other works.

1955   Women Win Vote in Nicaragua. Women gain voting rights in Nicaragua.

1955   Indonesian Women Gain Vote. Women in Indonesia vote for the first time, ten years after they win suffrage.

MAY 18, 1955   Mary McLeod Bethune Dies. African American educator Mary McLeod Bethune (1875–1955) dies at the age of 80. As a noted advocate for African American education, Bethune serves from 1935 to 1944 as

Fashion designer Coco Chanel.

Special Advisor on Minority Affairs in the administration of American president Franklin D. Roosevelt. Bethune is the 1935 recipient of the Spingarn Medal, an award given annually to the year's outstanding African American, for her work in education.

SEPTEMBER 7, 1955   Women Granted Suffrage in Peru. Women win the vote in Peru.

DECEMBER 1, 1955   Bus Boycott in Montgomery, Alabama. On the first day of the trial of civil rights pioneer Rosa Parks, African Americans in Montgomery, Alabama, launch a boycott of the city bus system. Parks refuses to give up her seat to a white passenger on a Montgomery bus, and is arrested.

1956   French Designer Coco Chanel Presents Updated Suit. French fashion designer Coco

Chanel (1883–1971), after 15 years of retirement, refashions her trademark Chanel suit into a tailored two-piece, collarless suit of trimmed wool, which catapults her back into favor.

1956 Ingrid Bergman Receives Second Academy Award. Swedish actress Ingrid Bergman (1915–1982) wins a second Academy Award for her role in *Anastasia*. She receives her first Academy Award in 1944 for her performance in *Gaslight*. Before her death from cancer on her 67th birthday, Bergman appears in 46 films, 11 stage plays, and five television dramas.

1956 Althea Gibson, First Black Tennis Player to Win French Open. Althea Gibson (1927–) becomes the first black woman to win the French Open Tennis Tournament. In 1957 she becomes the first African American woman to win at Wimbledon. In 1950 she breaks a racial barrier by playing in a major U.S. Ladies Tennis Association tournament.

1956 College Rodeo Nationals Include Woman's Event. The College Rodeo Nationals feature a women's event for the first time; the barrel race is won by Kathleen Younger of Colorado A&M.

1956 American Actress Grace Kelly Marries Prince Rainier III of Monaco. Grace Patricia Kelly (1929–1982), an actress who appeared in *High Noon* (1952), *Rear Window* (1954), *The Country Girl* (1954), *To Catch a Thief* (1955), and *High Society* (1956), marries Prince Rainier III of Monaco and retires from acting.

1956 Women Gain Full Voting Rights in Pakistan. Women win full suffrage in Pakistan.

1956 Women Granted Full Vote in Senegal. Women gain full suffrage in Senegal.

FEBRUARY 2, 1956 Tenley Albright Wins Olympic Gold Medal in Figure Skating. At

Tenley Albright

the Winter Olympic Games in Cortina, Italy, Tenley Albright of Newton, Massachusetts is the first American woman to win the gold medal in figure skating. Albright, a pre-medical student, goes on to become a physician.

1957 Women Extended Suffrage in Ghana. Women are granted the right to vote in Ghana.

1957 Women Win Vote in Colombia. Women are extended suffrage in Colombia.

1957 Sarah Caldwell Establishes Boston Opera Company. Sarah Caldwell (1928–) founds the Opera Company of Boston. Caldwell is born in Maryville, Missouri, and attends the New England Conservatory of Music. She teaches at the Berkshire Music Center from 1948 to 1952, heads the Opera

Workshop Department at Boston University from 1952 to 1960, and in 1983, becomes artistic director of the New Opera Company of Israel.

1957   Althea Gibson, First Black Tennis Player to Win at Wimbledon. Althea Gibson (1927–) becomes the first African American woman to win at Wimbledon, site in England of the prestigious tennis tournament. She is also the first black to win a clay court championship.

1957   Eirlys Roberts Founds Consumer's Association in England. Eirlys Rhiwen Cadwalader Roberts establishes the nonprofit Consumer's Association in Great Britain. Her first career is in journalism, but she serves in military intelligence during World War II (1939–45). Roberts is part of the United Nations Mission to Albania just after the war and then serves ten years in the Information Division of the Treasury. In 1957 she leaves government service to found the Consumer's Association. The association, with Roberts as editor, begins publishing *Which?* magazine in 1961. Written to help consumers make sensible choices about their purchases, the magazine gives extensive information about products and rates them for efficacy and safety. By the time Roberts steps down as editor in 1977, the circulation of *Which?* is over seven million. During the 1970s Roberts also serves as director of the Bureau of European Consumer Organizations, is a member of the Royal Commission on the Press, and chairs the Research Institute for Consumer Affairs. Roberts receives the Order of the British Empire in 1971, and Companion of the Order of the British Empire in 1977.

1957   Prostitution Made Illegal in Japan. Feminists in Japan are finally successful in their lobbying to have the government make prostitution illegal.

1957   Women Win Vote in Lebanon. Women are extended suffrage in Lebanon; in 1952, only women who have completed elementary school are allowed to vote.

1957   Ethel Andrus Founds American Association of Retired Persons. Ethel Andrus (1884–1967), former teacher, is founder and first president of the American Association of Retired Persons (AARP). By the 1990s, AARP becomes a powerful lobbying group on issues of importance to retired Americans. Andrus was also the founder in 1947 and first president of the National Retired Teachers Association (NRTA), work which led to her founding of the larger association eleven years later.

JANUARY 2, 1957   Patricia McCormick Competes in Bullfight. In San Cuidad Juarez, Mexico, Patricia McCormick enters the arena as America's first woman bullfighter.

1958   Soprano Kirsten Flagstad Directs Norwegian State Opera. Kirsten Malfrid Flagstad (1895–1962), a Norwegian soprano known primarily for her Wagnerian roles, is the first person to serve as director of the Norwegian State Opera in Oslo, from 1958 until 1960. She is also the first woman to sing the demanding roles of Sieglinde, Isolde, and Brunnhilde at the Metropolitan Opera in New York City in the year in which she makes her debut there, 1935–36.

1958   Marion E. Kenworthy Becomes President of American Psychoanalytic Association. American psychiatrist Marion E. Kenworthy (1891–1980) becomes the first woman president of the American Psychoanalytic Association. In 1930, Kenworthy became the first woman professor of psychiatry at Columbia University.

1958   Maria-Teresa de Filippis Races in European Grand Prix. An Italian, Maria-Teresa de

Iolanda Balas

Judith Hart in 1964, at her desk as minister of Social Security.

Filippis, is the first woman to compete in a modern European Grand Prix auto race.

OCTOBER 18, 1958　Iolanda Balas Clears Six Feet in High Jump. The first woman to clear six feet in the high jump is Romanian Iolanda Balas.

1959　Judith Hart Elected to British Parliament. A founder of the Campaign for Nuclear Disarmament, Judith Hart (1924–) is elected to Parliament as a Labour candidate. During the 1960s she holds several ministerial posts, including Minister of Social Security and Minister of State for Overseas Development. Hart also is charged with supervising Great Britain's youth and regional development programs.

1959　Margaret Thatcher Elected to Parliament in Great Britain. After several years of legal practice, Margaret Thatcher (1925–) wins a seat in the British Parliament. During the next 20 years she works for conservative legislation, especially laws and policies seeking to strengthen the national economy by cutting government-subsidized programs.

1959　Florence Ellinwood Allen, Early Woman Judge, Retires. Florence Ellinwood Allen (1884–1966), Ohio judge and feminist, retires. Allen becomes the first woman judge to sit on a general court (1920) when she wins the office of common appeals court judge over nine male opponents. In 1922, Allen becomes the first woman elected to the Ohio Supreme Court, and in 1932 the first woman on the

Indira Gandhi

U.S. Court of Appeals. She receives her law degree from New York University in 1913, and in 1960, they honor her with the Gallatin Award for outstanding alumna.

1959   Shirley Muldowney, Pro Drag Racer. Shirley Muldowney (1942–) begins drag racing professionally. She is the first woman to qualify for the top competition in hot rod racing. In 1975 she qualifies to compete for the supercharged, nitro-burning, unlimited AA-fuel dragster category. In 1977, 1980, and 1982, Muldowney wins the National Hot Rod Association world championship.

1959   Barbie Doll Debuts. The Barbie Doll is introduced by American toy manufacturer,

Mattel. Barbie is created by Ruth Handler, who also develops the first breast prosthesis for mastectomy patients.

1959   Publication of History of American Women's Movement. Eleanor Flexner, noted American historian, publishes *Century of Struggle,* detailing the history of the women's movement in the United States. Mabel Newcomer publishes a *Century of Higher Education for Women* the same year. Her study indicates that since 1920, women's participation in higher education in the United States had been declining.

1959   Japanese Author Ariyoshi Sawako Publishes First Long Novel. Ariyoshi Sawako

(1931–1984), one of Japan's most popular writers after World War II (1939–45), publishes her first long novel, *Kinokawa* (*The River Ki*). A student of traditional Japanese drama, Sawako's early works deal with clashes between the traditional world of the Japanese arts and the contemporary culture. She then goes on to write a series of multi-generational historical novels in which women are the protagonists. *Kinokawa* (1959; *The River Ki*), her first long novel, is a story of four generations of women in rural Japan. *Hanaoka Seishu no Tsuma* (1966; *The Doctor's Wife*) is a fictionalized history of the eighteenth-century surgeon Hanaoka Seishu and his devoted wife. In these novels, Sawako shows a concern with women's place in the family and society. Her heroines demonstrate Japanese women-centered values. From the mid-1960s, Sawako writes novels addressing specific contemporary social problems, including racial prejudice, pollution, and care for the elderly.

1959   **Women Win Vote in Morocco.** Women gain suffrage in Morocco.

FEBRUARY 2, 1959   **Indira Gandhi Elected President of the Congress Party in India.** Indira Gandhi (1917–1984), daughter of Indian prime minister Jawaharlal Nehru, is elected president of the Congress Party in India.

APRIL 28, 1959   **Senate Confirms Appointment of Claire Boothe Luce Ambassador to Brazil.** Journalist, politician, and diplomat Claire Boothe Luce is confirmed by the U.S. senate as ambassador to Brazil. She resigns less than one week later, on May 1, because of continuing vocal opposition to her service in the post, led by Senator Wayne Morse.

1960 – 1964

1960 **British Diplomat Barbara Salt Appointed Minister to Israel.** When she is made a minister in the British Embassy in Israel, Dame Barbara Salt (1904–1975) becomes the first woman to hold the post of minister in the British Foreign Service. She is first transferred to Israel in 1957, and she handles important negotiations during a crisis with Iran in 1958. Salt would have become Ambassador to Israel in 1963, but illness leads to the amputation of both her legs, and she is unable to accept the job. Not long after, however, Salt is mobile and hard at work, serving on Civil Service boards, preparing publications, delivering addresses, and participating in financial negotiations with Israel, Romania, and the Soviet Union. She retires from public life in 1973 to take up historical research on World War II. Barbara Salt dies on December 28, 1975.

1960 **Runner Wilma Rudolph Wins Three Gold Medals at Olympics.** At the Summer Olympic Games in Rome, Italy, African American runner Wilma Rudolph (1940–1994) becomes the first woman to win three gold medals—in the 100-meter, 200-meter, and a relay—in the same Olympic Games. She is the first woman in 30 years to be invited to the Millrose Games, a premiere indoor track event, where she wins the 60-yard dash.

Among the many awards she wins are the Associated Press Female Athlete of the Year award in 1960–61 and the James E. Sullivan Award in 1961. Rudolph is inducted into the National Track and Field Hall of Fame in 1974; into the International Women's Sport Hall of Fame in 1980; and in 1983, into the U.S. Olympic Hall of Fame. Wilma Rudolph dies of brain cancer on November 12, 1994.

1960 **Black Tennis Champion Althea Gibson Turns to Pro Golf.** African American tennis champion Althea Gibson (1927–) begins playing golf professionally and becomes the first African American woman to play in the Ladies Professional Golf Association (LPGA). In 1991 Gibson becomes the first African American woman to receive the Theodore Roosevelt Award of the National Collegiate Athletic Association (NCAA).

1960 **Photographer Diane Arbus At Peak of Career.** Photographer Diane Arbus (1923–1971) rebels against her upper-class upbringing in New York City to photograph social poses and people of the less-privileged segments of American society. Her work achieves critical and popular acclaim through the 1960s.

1960 **American Historian Margaret Leech Wins Second Pulitzer Prize.** Margaret Leech (1893–1974) wins the Pulitzer Prize for history for her work about U.S. president William McKinley, entitled *In the Days of McKinley*. She is the first woman to win the history prize twice. Her first Pulitzer Prize for history was awarded in 1942 for *Reveille in Washington*, a work on the U.S. Civil War.

1960   English Actress Margaret Rutherford Portrays Agatha Christie's Miss Marple. British actress Margaret Rutherford (1892–1972) becomes internationally famous playing English murder novelist Agatha Christie's Miss Marple in films and television broadcasts during the 1960s. In 1963, Rutherford wins an Oscar for *The VIPs*. Rutherford is remembered for her portrayal of this apparently innocent and naive elderly lady who is, in fact, clever and sophisticated. Margaret Rutherford dies in England in 1972.

1960   Birth-Control Pill Approved by U.S. Food & Drug Association. Developed in the 1950s, the first oral contraceptive is approved for distribution to consumers in May 1960. The G. D. Searle Company of Chicago is the first company to market the pill, calling its brand Enovid. By 1964, six brands are available for prescriptive use by women. Its nearly 100 percent effectiveness in preventing pregnancy, affordable price, minimal health risks, and reversible effects make the pill an appealing choice of contraception for women.

JANUARY 1960   Soviet Newspaper Reports on Women in the Workforce. A Soviet newspaper, *Izvestia*, reports that women make up 45% of the labor force, but represent a higher percentage of professionals. Of all Soviet medical personnel, 85% are women.

JANUARY 24, 1960   Ecclesiastical Council of the Catholic Church Issues Restrictions on Women. Pope John XXIII convenes an ecclesiastical council in Rome to consider a number of issues. Sacraments (baptism, holy communion, marriage) are denied to women in Rome with bare arms or who wear men's clothing.

MARCH 6, 1960   Switzerland's Parliament Grants Women Voting Rights in Municipal Elections. Women in Switzerland win the right to vote in municipal elections only. It will be more than ten years before Swiss women win the right to vote in all elections.

JULY 26, 1960   Sirimavo Bandaranaike Becomes Prime Minister of Ceylon. Sirimavo Bandaranaike (1916–) is sworn in as prime minister of Ceylon (after 1972, Sri Lanka), the first woman to head a modern parliamentary government. She leads the socialist Sri Lanka Freedom Party, founded by her husband, S.W.R.D. Bandaranaike, in an overwhelming victory. She loses the office in 1965, but is returned to office in the election of 1970. After a period of unrest, and an attempted overthrow of her government, she is defeated in 1977.

SEPTEMBER 25, 1960   Emily Post, Etiquette Expert, Dies. Emily Price Post (1873?–1960) dies after a lifelong career promoting good manners. She publishes *Etiquette* in 1922, and establishes herself as the authoritative expert on the subject of social behavior.

NOVEMBER 1960   First All-Female Race for U.S. Senate. Margaret Chase Smith (1897–1995), representative to the U.S. Congress from Maine, and Lucia Marie Cormier, a six-term member of the Maine House of Representatives, compete in the first all-female election for a U.S. senate seat. Smith is the winner, and goes on to serve 23 years in the U.S. Senate.

1961   Harper Lee Wins Pulitzer Prize for *To Kill a Mockingbird*. American author Harper Lee (1926–) wins the Pulitzer Prize for her novel *To Kill a Mockingbird*, about Southern white lawyer Atticus Finch who defends black Americans in Alabama. She is the first woman to win the Pulitzer Prize since 1942.

1961   Janet Graeme Travell Appointed White House Physician. Janet Graeme Travell

Janet Graeme Travell, President John F. Kennedy's physician.

(1901–), physician to John F. Kennedy since his 1955 spinal surgery, is appointed White House physician, the first woman to hold the post.

1961   Eleanor Roosevelt Reappointed Delegate to the United Nations. Eleanor Roosevelt (1884–1962) is reappointed delegate to the U.N., and serves until her death. In 1945, she becomes the first person to represent the United States at the United Nations, taking up the post in 1946 and serving until 1951. From 1947 to 1951, Roosevelt chairs the U.N. Human Rights Commission.

1961   Aviator Jerrie M. Cobb Passes Astronaut Tests. Jerrie M. Cobb is the first of 14 women to qualify to become an astronaut.

1961   Opera Star Marian Anderson Sings at Presidential Inauguration. African American opera singer Marian Anderson (1902–1993) performs at the inauguration of President John F. Kennedy. In 1963, she wins the Presidential Medal of Freedom.

1961   Women in Paraguay Given Vote. Paraguay becomes the last republic in the Americas to grant women the vote.

1961   Publication of British Consumer Magazine *Which?* Eirlys Roberts, founder of the nonprofit Consumer's Association in Great Britain, begins publishing *Which?* magazine; she continues as editor until 1977. The magazine, written to help consumers make sensible choices about their purchases, gives extensive information about products and rates them for efficacy and safety. By the time Roberts steps down as editor, the circulation of *Which?* is over seven million.

JULY 29, 1961   American Runner Wilma Rudolph Sets Record. Wilma Rudolph (1940–1994) sets a women's record in the 100-meter dash, with a time of 0:11:2. Among the many awards she wins are the Associated Press Female Athlete of the Year award in 1960–61 and the James E. Sullivan Award in 1961. In 1980, Rudolph is named to the Women's Sports Hall of Fame.

DECEMBER 1961   Esther Peterson Heads U.S. Women's Bureau. Labor activist Esther Peterson heads the first U.S. Women's Bureau. As assistant secretary of the Department of Labor, Peterson has responsibility for the Bureau of Labor Standards and the Bureau of Employees' Compensation.

DECEMBER 14, 1961   Establishment of President's Commission on the Status of Women. The President's Commission on the Status of Women, under the administration of U.S. President John F. Kennedy, is established by Executive Order 10980, and headed by former first lady Eleanor Roosevelt (1884–1962). The commission successfully pushes for the passage of the Equal Pay Act (1963), the first federal law requiring equal compensation for men and women in federal jobs.

DECEMBER 28, 1961   Edith Wilson Dies. Edith Wilson (1872?–1961), widow of president Woodrow Wilson, dies at the age of 89. Mrs. Wilson, with her husband's advisors, oversees much of the workings of the presidency after Woodrow Wilson's collapse and debilitating stroke leaves him bedridden from October 1919 until he leaves office in March 1921.

1962   Death of American Sex Symbol Marilyn Monroe. American actress Marilyn Monroe

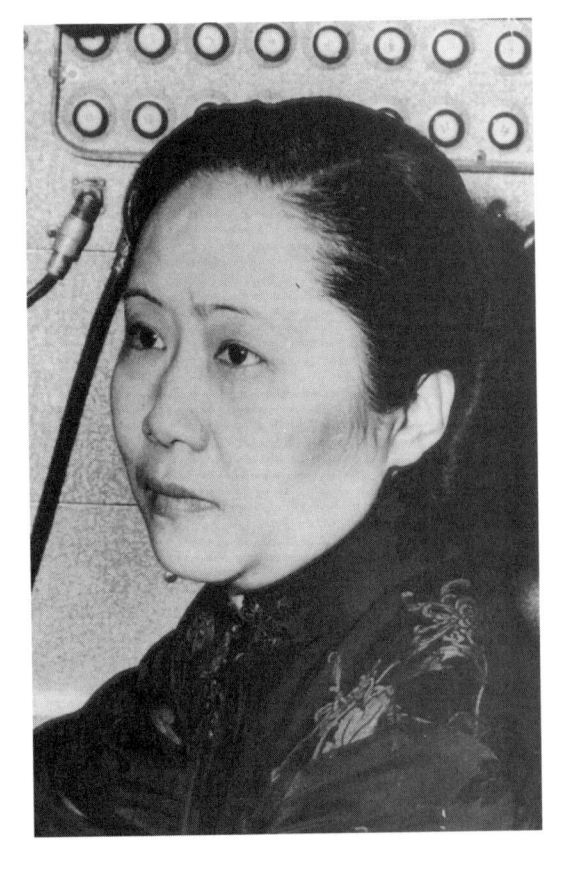

Chien-Shiung Wu

(1926–1962) completes her last film, *The Misfits* (1962), before dying of an apparent suicide at age 36. Speculations surrounding her suspicious death implicate her involvement with Mafia figures or then-President John F. Kennedy. Despite the sadness of her real-life story, her screen persona becomes an enduring American archetype for female sensuality. More than 30 years after her death, her image continues to be immediately recognizable by millions all over the world.

1962   Physicist Chien-Shiung Wu Is Woman of the Year. Chinese-born physicist Chien-Shiung Wu (1912–) receives the American Association of University Women's Woman of the Year Award. Wu works for most of her career in the United States, where she is on the faculty of Columbia University.

1962   Gertrude Elion Discovers Imuram. Gertrude Elion discovers Imuram, a drug that helps prevent the patient from rejecting the transplanted organ in kidney transplant procedures. Elion patents a total of 45 drug treatments during her career, many with her collaborator, Dr. George Hitchings.

1962   National Women's Rowing Association Established. The National Women's Rowing Association is formed.

1962   Ballerina Margot Fonteyn Begins Dancing Partnership with Rudolf Nureyev. England's beloved prima ballerina Margot Fonteyn (1919–) begins a decade of dancing as Russian ballet dancer Rudolf Nureyev's partner.

1962   Shirley Clarke Cofounds New York Film-makers' Co-operative. Shirley Clarke (1925–), an American filmmaker, cofounds with Jonas Mekas the New York Film-makers' Co-operative. She becomes the first person to shoot a film in Harlem with her second film, *The Cool World*, in 1963.

1962   Feminist Yamataki Shigeri Elected to Japan's Legislature. Yamataki Shigeri (1899–1977), with the backing of *Chifuren*, a feminist organization she founds, is elected to the House of Councillors (the upper house of Japan's national legislature). She is elected again in 1965.

AUGUST 3, 1962   Eugenie Moore Anderson Appointed Ambassador to Bulgaria. Eugenie Moore Anderson (1909–) of Red Wing, Minnesota, is the first woman to serve as a U.S. ambassador to Bulgaria, becoming the first woman ambassador to represent the United States in a communist nation. In 1949, Anderson was appointed ambassador to Denmark by president Harry S Truman.

1963   Helen Bryant Establishes Afro-American Total Theater Arts Foundation. Helen Bryant (1939–1983) founds and serves as first president of the Afro-American Total Theater Arts Foundation. Five years later, she founds the Richard Allen Center of Culture and Art. Both are in New York City.

1963   First Girl Participates in Small-Fry Baseball League in New Jersey. Nancy Lotsey joins the New Jersey Small-Fry League and becomes its first girl player. Due in part to her pitching and batting skills, Lotsey's team wins the championship.

1963   U.S. Women's Tennis Team Wins First Federation Cup. The International Lawn Tennis Federation inaugurates the Federation Cup, an international team competition. The U.S. women's team wins the first Federation Cup, beating the Australian team, 2-1, at London, England.

1963   American Feminist Betty Friedan Publishes *The Feminine Mystique*. Betty Goldstein Friedan (1921–) publishes *The Feminine Mystique*, in which she analyzes the role of women in American society. The work becomes a best-seller.

1963   Publication of Sylvia Plath's *The Bell Jar*. American writer Sylvia Plath (1932–1963) publishes her novel *The Bell Jar*. The novel features her account of her painful experiences during a summer as an editor of a chic women's magazine in New York City. Plath commits suicide in London, England, the same year.

1963   Iranian Women Win Vote. Iranian women gain suffrage.

1963   Women Gain Vote in Kenya. Women are granted the right to vote in Kenya.

1963   Women Granted Suffrage in Libya. Women win the vote in Libya.

Barbara Tuchman

Cosmonaut Valentina Tereshkova

1963 **American Historian Barbara Tuchman Wins Pulitzer Prize.** Author and historian Barbara Wertheim Tuchman (1912–1989) is the first woman to receive the Pulitzer Prize for general non-fiction for *The Guns of August.* In 1979, Tuchman is elected the first female president of the American Academy and Institute of Arts and Letters

MAY 28, 1963 **Equal Pay Act Passed in U.S.** The Equal Pay Act is passed by the U.S. Congress. It is the first federal law requiring equal compensation for men and women in federal jobs. Bills to achieve the goal of equal compensation regardless of gender had been first submitted to Congress in 1943.

JUNE 16–19, 1963 **Cosmonaut Valentina Tereshkova Orbits the Earth.** Valentina Tereshkova (1937–) orbits the earth 45 times,

becoming the first woman (and the tenth person) to do so. She is the solo pilot on the Vostock 6 space capsule, and travels 1,242,800 miles during her orbital journey. She joins the cosmonaut program of the Soviet Union in 1962.

JULY 1963 **Marguerite Higgins Becomes War Correspondent in Vietnam.** Although married and the mother of two young children, veteran reporter Marguerite Higgins (1920–1966) returns to war correspondence in Vietnam. She previously covers World War II and Korea. Strongly anti-Communist, Higgins takes the stance that the United States can and should win the war in Vietnam, an opinion which is hotly debated within the Press Corps in Saigon. Her 1965 book *Our Vietnam Nightmare* insists that the United States will be successful in Vietnam unless American public opinion in the 1960s turns against the war. In late 1965, Higgins returns from Vietnam desperately ill with a tropical illness. She dies in January 1966, never to know that her prophecy of the war's end will come true.

JULY 2, 1963 **Newsday Publisher Alicia Patterson Dies.** Alicia Patterson (1906–1963), founder, publisher, and editor of *Newsday,* a newspaper published in New York City, dies. Patterson founded *Newsday* in 1940.

AUGUST 5, 1963 **Katharine Graham Becomes President of Washington Post Company.** Upon the death of her husband, Philip Graham, Katharine Graham (1917–) takes over as president of the Washington Post Company, which she co-owns with him. The company owns the *Washington Post, Newsweek* magazine, and several radio and television stations. Her strong leadership leads to her becoming in 1974 the first woman named to the board of the Associated Press.

OCTOBER 11, 1963 **Report Issued by President's Commission on the Status of Women.** Entitled *American Women,* the report prepared by the (U.S.) President's Commission on the Status of Women documents sex discrimination in nearly all corners of American society, and urges the U.S. Supreme Court to clarify legal status of women under the Constitution.

NOVEMBER 1963 **Sarah Tilghman Hughes Swears in President Lyndon Baines Johnson.** Sarah Tilghman Hughes (1896–1985) swears Lyndon Baines Johnson in as president of the United States following the assassination of president John F. Kennedy. She is the first woman to conduct the swearing-in ceremony.

DECEMBER 10, 1963 **Maria Goeppert-Mayer Wins Nobel Prize for Physics.** Maria Gertrude Goeppert-Mayer (1906–1972) wins the Nobel Prize for physics, the first American woman and only the second woman in history to win the prize. (The first was Marie Curie in 1903.) Her prize, shared with Eugene Paul Wigner and Hans Jensen, recognizes research on the shell structure of the nucleus of atoms.

1964 **Ukrainian Artist Sonia Delaunay Has Retrospective at Louvre.** Sonia Terk Delaunay (1885-1979) becomes the only woman artist to enjoy during her lifetime a retrospective exhibition at the Louvre Museum in Paris, France. Delaunay is born in Gradizhsk in the Russian Ukraine and grows up in St. Petersburg. She studies drawing at the University at Karlsruhe, Germany, and moves to Paris in 1905, where she has her first solo show three years later. Influenced by the Fauvist movement, Delaunay works with dazzling colors and juxtaposes dark outlines with exotic patterning in a manner which is likened to that of Paul Gauguin and Henri Matisse.

In 1909, Delaunay begins to experiment in the mediums of embroidery, appliqué, and collage, utilizing both textiles and paper to produce decorative and utilitarian objects from book covers to lampshades. Her husband, artist Robert Delaunay, whom she marries in 1910, has ideas on color and light that greatly influence her work during the early years of their marriage. Together, the two found the art movement known as Orphism; in 1918, they design sets and costumes for Russian impresario Serge Diaghilev. Delaunay produces paintings, book illustrations and covers, posters, and theatrical costumes. She also devises what becomes known as "simultaneous" dresses, creating garments that juxtapose contrasting colors and forms and use contrasting fabrics.

During the first half of the 1920s, she establishes her own printing workshop to produce "simultaneous" textiles, each run printed (usually on silk) with squares, triangles, and stripes in a range of four colors.

After the Great Depression (1929–39), Sonia Delaunay returns to painting virtually full-time. She continues to design furnishing

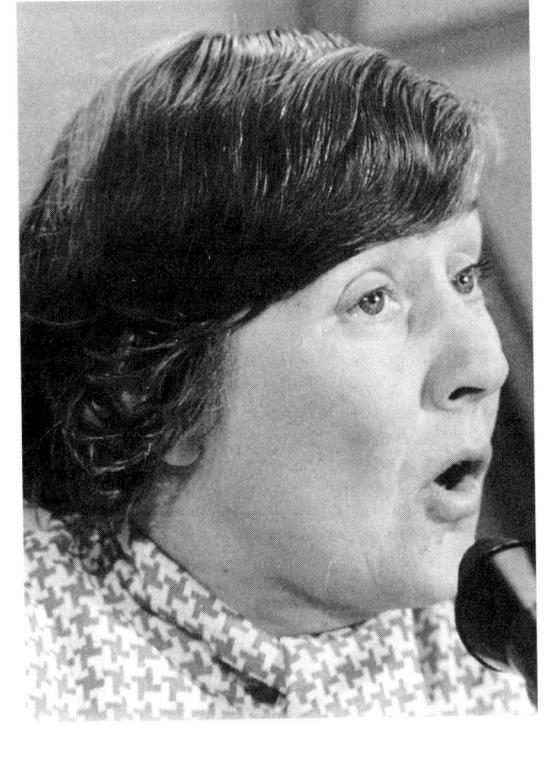

Shirley Williams

brilliant political economist and independent thinker, she is a strong voice for her country's membership in the European Economic Community, even when her own party opposes it. In 1981 she helps found the Social Democrat Party and is elected to Parliament again, but she is defeated in 1983. Williams holds several ministerial posts in Parliament, and works for comprehensive education and restrictions on divorce and abortion. Another interest is new technology and how it will affect employment in the future, the subject of her book *Youth Without Work* (1981). Williams also writes *Politics Is for People* (1981) and *A Job to Live* (1985) and coedits *Ambition and Beyond: The Career Paths of American Politicians* (1993).

1964   Phyllis Schlafly Publishes *A Choice Not an Echo. A Choice Not an Echo* is written and self-published by conservative American Phyllis Schlafly (1924–). The work is designed to support Republican presidential nominee, Barry Goldwater, and becomes known as one of the "top ten conservative books of all time."

1964   National Women's Rowing Championship Held. The first national championship regatta for women's rowing is held.

1964   Donna Mae Mins Wins Sports Car Club of America Championship. Donna Mae Mins becomes the first woman to win a Sports Car Club of America (SCCA) championship, beating out 31 men in the Class II production category for imported two-seaters.

1964   Poet Nikki Giovanni Founds Black Arts Festival. African American poet Nikki Giovanni (1943–) organizes the first Black Arts Festival in Cincinnati, Ohio.

1964   American Swimmer Donna de Varona Wins Olympic Gold Medal. Donna de Varona (1947–), an American swimmer, is the first woman to win an Olympic gold medal in the 400-meter individual medley

textiles and theatrical sets and costumes into the 1960s. Sonia Delaunay dies in 1979.

1964   British Chemist Dorothy Crowfoot Hodgkin Wins Nobel Prize in Chemistry. Dorothy Crowfoot Hodgkin (1910–), British crystallographer, wins the Nobel Prize for Chemistry, becoming the second woman to be so honored (Marie Curie was the first in 1911). Hodgkin was honored for her discoveries of molecular structures of such substances as vitamin B12, insulin, and penicillin.

1964   Shirley Williams Elected to British Parliament. Shirley Vivien Teresa Brittain Williams (1930–) wins a seat in British Parliament in 1964 as a Labour candidate and serves there for 15 years. Williams is one of the most prominent woman in British government in the period from 1960 to the mid-1980s. A event at the Summer Olympics in Tokyo, Japan. This is the first year in which this event is open to women.

1964   Ariane Mnouchkine Establishes Parisian Théatre du Soleil. French theater director Ariane Mnouchkine (1939–), founds the famous innovative collective Théatre du Soleil in Paris, France. The group explores mime as well as the dramatic heritage of other theatrical traditions (Chinese, Greek, commedia dell'arte, for example). The company continues to present exciting theatrical productions and remains organized on egalitarian principles.

1964   Civil Rights Act Prohibits Job Discrimination. The Civil Rights Act prohibits job discrimination on the basis of sex or race and establishes the Equal Employment Opportunity Commission (EEOC). The EEOC is the agency that addresses charges of discrimination in the workplace.

1964   Woman Win Vote in Sudan. Woman gain voting rights in the Sudan.

APRIL 17, 1964   Aviator Geraldine Mock Flies Solo Around the World. German-born Geraldine Mock (1925–) becomes the first woman to fly solo around the world. Known as Jerrie, Mock takes off in a single-engine plane from Port Columbus, Ohio, on March 19, 1964, makes 21 stops, and logs 22,858.8 miles before completing the flight.

MAY 2, 1964   Nancy Astor, First Woman Member of British Parliament, Dies. Nancy Witcher Langhorne Astor (1879–1964) is elected Member of Parliament (MP) in England in 1919, replacing her husband after his death. She remains the only woman until 1921, and serves in Parliament until 1945.

JULY 8, 1964   Dr. Mary Calderone Founds the Sex Information and Education Council of the United States. American physician Dr. Mary Steichen Calderone (1904–), in support of her efforts to promote sex education in schools, founds the Sex Information and Education Council of the United States (SIECUS). SIECUS provides advice and publications on sex education for teachers, physicians, counselors, religious groups, and schools. From 1953 to 1964, Calderone is medical director of Planned Parenthood Federation of America.

JULY 13–18, 1964   Margaret Chase Smith Attempts to Win Presidential Nomination. Margaret Chase Smith (1897–1995) makes an unsuccessful bid to become the Republican party nominee for U.S. president. Smith receives 27 delegate votes at the Republican convention in San Francisco, more than any other candidate except the winner of the nomination, Senator Barry Goldwater of Arizona. Upon the death of her husband, Smith begins her career in politics by taking over his seat in the U.S. House of Representatives. She goes on to serve nine years in the House and 23 years in the U.S. Senate.

1965 – 1969

C. 1965   American Artist Judy Chicago Cofounds Feminist Studio Workshop. Judy Chicago (1939–), an American artist who takes her surname from the name of the city where she grows up, cofounds the Feminist Studio Workshop in Los Angeles, California, in the mid-1960s. The studio later becomes the Women's Building, an organization and place devoted to fostering women's art.

1965   Aileen Hernandez Becomes Sole Woman U.S. Equal Employment Opportunity Commissioner. The Equal Employment Opportunity Commissioners, including Aileen Hernandez, the only woman, are appointed to oversee enforcement of the Civil Rights Act. Franklin D. Roosevelt Jr. is chair of the commission.

1965 Mary Two-Axe Early Helps Reclaim Native Canadian Women's Rights. Mary Two-Axe Early mounts a campaign on her own behalf against the Indian Act clauses that deprive Indian women of their status upon marriage to non-status men. Early, a widow, is a Mohawk Indian from Caughnawaga reserve in Quebec. She is barred from the home she inherits on the reserve because her late husband is not a status Indian. Clause 12 (1)(b) of the Indian Act gives Indian status to wives and children of Indian men, but denied it to Indian women marrying non-status men. The children of the latter are classified as non-status as well. As early as 1968, Mohawk wives of non-status husbands organize under Mary's leadership a group called Indian Rights for Indian Women. This begins a new stage of Native women's involvement in the fight for equality. Despite these protest movements, the Canadian government is unresponsive, fearful of provoking the hostility of Indian band leaders. In 1981, the government gives permission to individual Indian bands to request that subsection 12 (1)(b) not apply to them, but the majority of Indian bands endorse the status quo. Finally in 1985, a law repeals the offending clause of the Indian Act, although the reintegration of women into the reserves remains a tedious and difficult process.

1965 Patricia Roberts Harris, First African American Woman Ambassador. Patricia Roberts Harris (1924–1985) is appointed U.S. Ambassador to Luxembourg, becoming the first African American woman ambassador. She serves as a delegate to the United Nations, as a member of the executive board of the NAACP (National Association for the Advancement of Colored People) and the Legal Defense Fund, and as a member of the National Commission on the Causes and Prevention of Violence.

1965 Helen Taussig Is First Woman To Head the American Heart Association. Helen

Helen Brooke Taussig

Brooke Taussig (1898–1986), American pediatrician, becomes the first woman to head the American Heart Association. Taussig is known for her research on congenital heart disease.

1965 American Folksinger Joan Baez Establishes Institute for the Study of Non-Violence. Joan Baez (1941–), an American folksinger and political activist, founds the Institute for the Study of Non-Violence in Carmel, California. Baez is also the cofounder of Humanitas, the International Human Rights Commission, in 1979.

1965 Establishment of Twyla Tharp Dance Company. Innovative American choreographer Twyla Tharp (1942–), who studies at Pomona

College, the American Ballet Theater School, and Barnard College, is the founder of the Twyla Tharp Dance Company in New York City. She creates dances not only for her own troupe but for other companies and is known as one of the most original contemporary choreographers.

1965   Maria Callas, First to Sing Title Role in Glanville-Hicks' *Sappho*. American-born Greek opera diva Maria Callas (1923–1977) sings the title role in Peggy Glanville-Hicks' *Sappho* in San Francisco, California, becoming the first woman to sing the role. Callas is ranked as one of the greatest dramatic sopranos in the twentieth century.

1965   American Photographer Dorothea Lange Exhibits Work at Museum of Modern Art. The work of American photographer Dorothea Lange (1895–1965) is featured in a one-person show at the Museum of Modern Art in New York City. She is the first woman photographer to have such an exhibition. Known for her documentary work during the Great Depression (1929–39), Lange is particularly remembered for her famous picture "The Migrant Mother." With her husband Paul Taylor, she publishes a book, *An American Exodus: A Record of Human Erosion* (1939).

1965   Women in Afghanistan Win Vote. Women in Afghanistan are granted suffrage.

JANUARY 1965   Patsy Mink Become Hawaii's Representative to Congress. Patsy Mink (1927–) takes the oath of office for her first of six consecutive terms as a Representative to the U.S. Congress from Hawaii. She is the first Asian American woman to serve in Congress, and the first woman to represent Hawaii there. Mink, of Japanese descent, runs unsuccessfully for the U.S. presidency in 1972, and for governor of Hawaii in 1986, also unsuccessfully. In 1990, Mink returns to Congress to serve the remainder of Representative Daniel Akaka's term. (Akaka is appointed to the senate seat left vacant by the sudden death of Senator Spark Matsunaga.)

MAY 14, 1965   Frances Perkins, First Woman Presidential Cabinet Member, Dies. Frances Perkins (1882–1965), a long-time civil servant from New York, dies. Perkins is the United States' first woman cabinet member when President Franklin D. Roosevelt appoints her Secretary of Labor in 1933. She is reappointed for each of his three additional terms in office. During her tenure, she drafts the Social Security Act and the National Labor Relations Act.

NOVEMBER 1965   "Jane Crow and The Law" Published in *George Washington Law Review*. Dr. Pauli Marry and Mary O. Eastwood publish an article entitled "Jane Crow and The Law." Their work, published in the *George Washington Law Review*, is an examination of women's legal status under the U.S. Constitution.

NOVEMBER 4, 1965   American Journalist Dickey Chapelle Dies in Combat in Vietnam. Georgette (Dickey) Chapelle (1918–1965) is killed by a land mine in Vietnam, the first woman war correspondent to die in combat. An American journalist, Chapelle begins her career as a war correspondent in the South Pacific during World War II (1939–45). Fearless and passionately patriotic, she loves the thrill of battle, calling herself an "interpreter of violence." During the Hungarian Revolution in 1956, she is captured by the Russians and held prisoner for nearly two months. She hates Communism and comes to Vietnam as a freelance journalist in 1961 with a distinct bias. For four years she travels to and from South Vietnam, writing articles for *National Geographic* and *National Observer,* and making speeches in defense of American involvement in the Vietnam war whenever she is in the United States. On November 4, 1965, Chapelle joins a U.S. Marine combat patrol in the jungles near Chu Lai, Vietnam. When a

Patsy Mink

land mine detonates, Chapelle is struck by shrapnel in the throat and dies almost instantly.

NOVEMBER 4, 1965   Margaret Laneive "Lee" Breedlove Sets Women's Land Speed Record. At the Bonneville Salt Flats in Utah, Margaret Laneive "Lee" Breedlove sets a women's land speed record at 308.65 miles per hour.

1966   British Designer Mary Quant Creates New Fashion Look. Mary Quant (1934–) is credited with making the mini-skirt a fashion staple during the 1960s, along with high vinyl boots and the "wet look." Her colorful and innovative clothes are recognized and

sought after around the world. Quant is born in London, England, and pressed by her parents to train for a teaching career, studies art at Goldsmith's College, University of London, working toward an art teacher's diploma. In 1955, unsuccessful in her attempt to obtain the teacher's diploma, Quant and two partners start their own clothing shop, "Bazaar," in the Chelsea area of London. Within less than a decade, it expands into a multi-million-dollar enterprise in Europe and the United States.

Bazaar originally sells merchandise obtained from a range of manufacturers, but Quant grows dissatisfied with the designs available and begins to produce her own, the

Mary Quant displays her Order of the British Empire.

most recognizable of which include the mini-skirt and hotpants, whose popularity peaks in the late 1960s and early 1970s. The business grows quickly, until the designs are being mass-produced and widely distributed. For her part in making London an international center of fashion, Quant becomes in 1966 the first woman fashion designer to be made Officer of the Order of the British Empire. The same year she publishes her autobiography, *Quant by Quant*.

By the 1970s Quant's designs become more conventional. She is still influential, but no longer radical. She eventually turns to a new career, creating a successful line of cosmetics. A collection of bed and bath linens also bear her name. In 1984 she publishes another book, *Color by Quant*. Mary Quant is named to the Hall of Fame of the British Fashion Council in 1990.

1966   Publication of Margaret Walker's Best-seller, *Jubilee*. African American author Margaret Walker publishes *Jubilee*, the story of her family as told to her by her grandmother when Walker is a child. *Jubilee* sells millions of copies and has never been out of print.

1966   Mary Wells Lawrence Cofounds Top Advertising Agency. Mary Georgene Berg Wells Lawrence (1928–) and two colleagues found the advertising firm of Wells, Rich, Greene, Inc. in New York City. One of their first contracts is a complete restyling of Braniff Airlines. Wells persuades Braniff president Harding Lawrence to paint his airplanes bright colors. The two later marry. Wells Lawrence becomes chief executive officer and chair of the board of the agency in 1971. By 1973 the firm is ranked 13th in billings of nearly 700 firms ranked by *Advertising Age*, and Wells Lawrence is said to be the highest-paid woman executive in the United States. She retires in 1990.

1966   Dorothy "Dottie" Jones Begins Career as UAW Union Activist. Dorothy "Dottie" Jones begins her 30-year career as a union activist as a rank-and-file member of the United Auto Workers (UAW) Union Local 372 when she goes to work at the Chrysler Trenton Engine Plant. In 1982 she is appointed assistant director of the Walter P. Reuther Senior Center in Detroit, Michigan. In 1984 she joins the UAW Women's Department. The following year, UAW vice president Odessa Komer appoints Jones assistant director of the Women's Department. Her appointment by the governor to the Michigan Women's Commission leads to her election as President of the National Association of Commissions for Women. Jones is also an active member of the National Association for the Advancement of Colored People (NAACP). She is also involved with the Coalition of Black Trade Unionists, the National Council of Negro Women, and the A. Philip Randolph Insti-

White House Fellows of 1966. Jane Cahill Pfeiffer is at center.

tute. In 1985, Jones is selected as one of the 25 outstanding black women of Michigan. She is also presented with the Outstanding Leadership Award by the University of Michigan and the Feminist Achievement Award by the Michigan State chapter of the National Organization for Women.

1966   Jane Cahill Pfeiffer, First Woman White House Fellow. President Lyndon Johnson appoints Jane Cahill Pfeiffer to serve as the first woman White House fellow. Pfeiffer takes a leave of absence from her position with IBM, where she is in charge of the company's space tracking system located on the island of Bermuda. During her White House fellowship, she works with Robert Wood, undersecretary of the department of housing and urban

development, to streamline the housing and home finance agency.

1966   California Unionist Elinor Marshall Glenn Negotiates Child Care Provision. American trade unionist Elinor Marshall Glenn (1915–) negotiates the first child care provision in a contract with Los Angeles County, California. In 1970, she negotiates the first contract for public workers in Los Angeles County.

1966   U.S. Representative Frances Payne Bolton Works for Rights of Military Nurses. U.S. Representative Frances Payne Bolton (1885–1977) introduces a bill in Congress to eliminate gender-specific language in regulations commissioning nurses for the Army and Navy.

Constance Baker Motley with President Lyndon B. Johnson.

This bill reduces (but does not stop) discrimination against male nurses in the military. She calls for women to be drafted equally with men, explaining that "women's place includes defending the home." She does not like attention drawn to her own gender and insists on the title "Congressman Bolton."

1966   Constance Baker Motley Appointed U.S. District Court Judge. Constance Baker Motley (1921–) is the first African American woman appointed judge of the U.S. District Court for the Southern Division of New York. A civil rights lawyer who works to eliminate state-enforced segregation in the South, Motley successfully argues nine civil rights cases before the U.S. Supreme Court. Her most famous case involves desegregation, James Meredith against the University of Mississippi. She is also the first black woman elected to the New York State Senate, and the first to serve as Manhattan borough president.

APRIL 19, 1966   Roberta Gibb Bingay, First Woman to Run in Boston Marathon. Roberta Gibb Bingay finishes ahead of more than half the 415 men in the Boston Marathon, wearing a hooded sweatshirt to disguise her appearance because women are not allowed to run in the race. The next year Katherine Switzer will run in the Boston Marathon, registered as K. Switzer, and will be apprehended by a race official.

APRIL 22, 1966   The U.S. Equal Employment Opportunity Commission Approves Sex-

Segregated "Help Wanted" Advertisements. The Equal Employment Opportunity Commission (EEOC) issues guidelines for "Help Wanted" classified advertising that approves dividing the ads according to gender of the prospective applicants. Eight months later, on December 19, 1966, five National Organization for Women (NOW) officers and 35 members petition the EEOC to hold hearings to amend the regulations permitting segregation of classified advertising by sex.

JUNE 29–29, 1966 National Organization for Women Founded. The National Organization for Women (NOW) is founded by Betty Friedan (1921–) and 27 associates who are frustrated by the failure of the Equal Employment Opportunity Commission to enforce the Civil Rights Act. Each of the 28 founding members contributes five dollars to help fund the organizing effort. The organizing conference is held October 29–30, when elections are held. The officers are Betty Friedan, president; Kay Clarenbach, chair of the board; Aileen Hernandez, executive vice president; Richard Graham, vice president; and Caroline Davis, secretary-treasurer. NOW is devoted to promoting full participation in society for women and advocates for adequate child care for working mothers, abortion rights, and the Equal Rights Amendment to the U.S. Constitution.

SEPTEMBER 6, 1966 Birth Control Advocate Margaret Sanger Dies. Margaret Sanger (1883–1966), who devotes her life to educating women about birth control, dies in Tucson, Arizona, a few days before her 88th birthday. In February 1953, Sanger founded the International Planned Parenthood Federation.

1967 Muriel Siebert Buys a Seat on the New York Stock Exchange. American Muriel Siebert (1932–) is the first woman to own a seat on the New York Stock Exchange. The seat cost $445,000, plus an initiation fee of more than $7,500.

FEBRUARY 1, 1967 Establishment of Royal Commission on the Status of Women in Canada. The Royal Commission on the Status of Women, which helps to determine the agenda of second-wave Canadian feminists, is created largely due to the efforts of Laura Sabia. Sabia, who earlier calls together representatives of some 30 national women's organizations to discuss their common concerns, spearheads a call for a royal commission on women's status. After being ignored by the Pearson government, Sabia threatens to march two million women on Ottawa. This ultimatum leads to the establishment of a royal commission whose mandate is "to inquire and report upon the status of women in Canada and to recommend what steps might be taken by the Federal government to ensure women equal opportunities with men in all aspects of society." Led by Florence Bird (the first woman to head a royal commission), the commission examines 469 briefs and 1,000 letters, and holds public hearings in 14 cities in all ten provinces and territories. The commission reports its findings and 167 recommendations in 1970, published in a single inexpensive volume which becomes a bestseller. Four governing principles are made apparent: (a) women should be free to choose whether or not they work outside the home; (b) care of children is a responsibility shared by mother, father, and society; (c) society has a responsibility for women because of pregnancy and childbirth—special maternity treatment is always necessary; and (d) in certain areas women will require special treatment to overcome the adverse effects of discrimination.

These guiding principles become the agenda of many second-wave Canadian feminists during the 1970s.

FEBRUARY 10, 1967 National Organization for Women Formally Incorporated. The National Organization for Women (NOW), is incorporated in Washington, D.C., and establishes headquarters at 1629 K Street, NW, Suite 500. Now was founded June 28–29, 1966, and held its first convention October 28–29, 1966.

FEBRUARY 22–23, 1967 NOW (National Organization for Women) Creates Chapter Structure, Task Forces, and Standing Committees. NOW creates the structure for establishing chapters at its National Board Meeting in Chicago, Illinois. The National Board also creates Task Forces as follows: Equal Opportunity of Employment; Legal and Political Rights; Education; Women in Poverty; The Family; Women and Religion. The Standing Committees are: Legal; Finance; Membership; Public Relations; Special Committee for Constitutional Protection (to evaluate need for the Equal Rights Amendment to the U.S. Constitution); Employment; Legal and Political Rights; Family; Education; Women and Religion; Image of Women; and Poverty.

MARCH 13, 1967 U.S. Senator Eugene McCarthy Introduces the Equal Rights Amendment. Senator Eugene McCarthy, with 37 co-sponsors, introduces S. 3567, the Equal Rights Amendment, in the U.S. senate.

APRIL 1967 Katherine Switzer Runs in the Boston Marathon. Katherine Switzer runs in the Boston Marathon, registered as "K. Switzer" since the race is closed to women. Published photographs of an official trying to tear her number off her back create an outcry of public opinion. A male runner, whom Switzer later married and divorced, blocks the official from completing the task. Switzer competes officially in this race when it is finally opened to women in 1972. (In 1966, Roberta Bingay was the first woman to run the race without her gender being discovered.)

MAY 9, 1967 American Journalist Philippa Schuyler Dies Covering Vietnam War. Philippa Schuyler (1932–1967), an African Amer-

ican journalist covering the Vietnam War for the Manchester, New Hampshire, *Union Leader*, is killed at Da Nang, Vietnam, in a helicopter accident. She is considered a combat casualty.

OCTOBER 13, 1967 U.S. Executive Order Prohibits Sex Discrimination in Government. The NOW (National Organization for Women) counts a victory in the passage of Presidential Executive Order 11246. This order, issued by President Lyndon Baines Johnson, prohibits sex discrimination in employment by the federal government and by contractors doing business with the federal government.

1968 Finnish Designer Armi Ratia Given American Neiman Marcus Award. Armi Ratia (1912–1979), a Finnish designer and cofounder with her husband of Marimekko, a textile design firm, becomes the first Finnish woman to be awarded the American Neiman Marcus Award in recognition for her art and business success.

1968 *The Lion in Winter* Is Screen Version of Eleanor of Aquitaine's Life. The film *The Lion in Winter* tells the story of the life of Eleanor of Aquitaine and stars Katharine Hepburn in an Academy Award-winning performance. Eleanor of Aquitaine (1122–1204), the lively and headstrong daughter of William X, the duke of Aquitaine (1122–1204) is the most influential woman of the twelfth century, ruling successively as queen of France and England.

1968 Janice Lee York Romary Carries U.S. Flag in Olympic Games Opening Ceremony. Janice Lee York Romary of San Mateo, California, is the first woman to carry the U.S. flag in the opening ceremonies of the Olympic Games.

1968 Former Child Star Shirley Temple Black Named U.S. Representative to UN. U.S. President Richard M. Nixon appoints former

Shirley Temple Black and President Gerald R. Ford, right. Black is Chief of Protocol for Ford's administration.

child actress Shirley Temple (1928–) as U.S. representative to the United Nations.

1968 Venita Walker VanCaspel Becomes Member of Pacific Stock Exchange. Venita Walker VanCaspel (1922–) is the first female member of the Pacific Stock Exchange in San Francisco, California.

1968 Japanese Novelist Oba Minako Publishes *Sanbiki no kani*. Oba Minako (1930–), a Japanese novelist, publishes *Sanbiki no kani* (*Three Crabs*). Having lived with her family in Alaska for a decade, Minako often writes on themes of loneliness. Her novel *Sanbiki no kani,* which depicts the sad aspects of living overseas, wins the Akutagawa Prize.

JANUARY 15, 1968 The Jeanette Rankin Brigade Demonstrates Against the Vietnam War

at the Opening of the U.S. Congress. A coalition of women numbering over 5,000 converges on Washington, D.C. to demonstrate on the opening day of the U.S. Congress against the United States' involvement in the Vietnam War. Jeanette Rankin (1880–1973), the honorary leader of the demonstrators, is the first woman elected to U.S. House of Representatives. She is elected as a Republican to represent Montana, where women are given the right to vote in state elections prior to 1920, when national suffrage is won. In 1917, she is the only member of Congress to vote against U.S. entry into World War I, and in 1941, the only member of Congress to vote against entry into World War II.

FEBRUARY 3, 1968 U.S. Equal Employment Opportunity Commission Rules That Gender Is Not A Requirement To Be A Flight

Attendant. This ruling allows male flight attendants to be hired. Since 1966, airlines have been fighting in court to have the Equal Employment Opportunity Commission (EEOC) rule that sex is a Bona Fide Occupational Qualification (BFOQ) for flight attendants (at that time, they were known as stewardesses). Flight attendants launch similar legal complaints against the airlines' policy that they quit if they get married, pregnant, or when they reach the age of 32–35.

1969 **British Actress Glenda Jackson Wins Academy Award.** Glenda Jackson (1936–), a versatile English actress known internationally for her film roles, wins the first of two Academy Awards for best actress for *Women in Love.* She wins the second Oscar in 1973 for the comedy *A Touch of Class.* In 1971 she wins a British Academy Award for *Sunday Bloody Sunday* and an Emmy Award for the title role in the television series *Elizabeth R.*

1969 **American Feminist Kate Millett Publishes *Sexual Politics.*** Originally written as a doctoral thesis, Kate Millett publishes her analysis of the history and extent of sexism in American society, titled *Sexual Politics: A Surprising Examination of Society's Most Arbitrary Folly.* It becomes a best-seller.

1969 **American Sharon Sites Sails from Japan to California.** American Sharon Sites sails her 25-foot sloop 5,000 miles from Yokohama, Japan, to San Diego, California, in 74 days, becoming the first woman to sail solo across the Pacific Ocean.

1969 **Cyclist Audrey McElmury Wins World Road Racing Championship.** Cyclist Audrey McElmury wins the women's world road racing championship in Bruno, Czechoslovakia. With her victory, McElmury becomes the first American, man or woman, to win a world road racing title.

Golda Meir

JANUARY 3, 1969 **Shirley Chisholm, First African American Woman to Join U.S. Congress.** Shirley Chisholm (1924–), a Democrat from Brooklyn, New York, takes her seat in the U.S. House of Representatives. Chisholm is the first African American woman elected to Congress. She is responsible for legislation improving employment, educational opportunities, and living conditions for women, members of racial minorities, and for people living in inner cities. In 1972 she runs an unsuccessful campaign for the presidency.

FEBRUARY 7, 1969 **Jockey Diane Crump Rides at Parimutuel Track.** Diane Crump becomes the first American woman jockey to ride at a parimutuel track; she rides her first mount to a tenth-place finish at a Hialeah, Florida, race track.

FEBRUARY 22, 1969   Barbara Jo Rubin Wins Thoroughbred Horse Race. Barbara Jo Rubin rides Cohesion to victory at the Charles Town, West Virginia, track to become the first woman jockey to win a race at a U.S. thoroughbred track.

MARCH 17, 1969   Golda Meir Becomes Prime Minister of Israel. Golda Mabovich Meir (1898–1978), born in the Ukraine and raised in the United States, becomes Israel's fourth Prime Minister. Meir begins her political activity in the United States as a member of the Labor Zionist Party. She commits herself to the establishment of a Jewish homeland by moving to Palestine in 1921. By 1929 she is an elected delegate to the World Zionist Congress, and she helps smuggle Jews into Palestine during World War II. As one of the original signers of the 1948 proclamation declaring Israel's independence, Meir is appointed Israel's minister to Moscow. From 1953 to 1966, she serves on the Israeli delegation to the United Nations General Assembly. Meir is made prime minister in 1969 after an eight-month retirement from politics. During her time in office, tensions with neighboring Arab states are high and she loses political support. Meir resigns on April 10, 1974.

Chapter 23

1970 TO 1979

1970 – 1974

1970 Farm Workers' Representative Dolores Huerta Negotiates First Contract with Grape Growers. Dolores Huerta (1930–), cofounder with Cesar Chavez of the National Farm Workers Association, negotiates a contract with the Delano, California, grape growers. For the first time, table grapes are shipped with the union label. In 1974, the union is reorganized as the United Farm Workers and is affiliated with the AFL-CIO. Chavez becomes president and Huerta is elected the union's first vice president.

1970 Elinor Marshall Glenn Negotiates First LA Public Workers' Contract. Trade unionist Elinor Marshall Glenn (1915–) negotiates the first contract for public workers in Los Angeles County, California. Glenn is also the first woman elected to the Service Employees International Union (SEIU) international executive board. In 1974, she is elected West Coast vice president of the Coalition of Labor Union Women. Her husband, Haskell Glenn, is also a union organizer.

1970 Australian Feminist Germaine Greer Publishes *The Female Eunuch*. Australian author and lecturer Germaine Greer (1939–) publishes *The Female Eunuch*. The work, which depicts marriage as slavery for women and alleges that women's sexuality is distorted by a male-dominated society, enjoys great success.

1970 Chinese Journalist Sally Aw Sian Chairs International Press Institute. Sally Aw Sian (1931–), a Chinese journalist, is the first woman to chair the International Press Institute, a position she holds in Hong Kong until 1971. She is also the founder and first chair of the Chinese Language Press Institute.

JANUARY 14, 1970 United Airlines Discontinues Men-Only Executive Flights. United Airlines lifts the ban on women passengers on its men-only executive flights between New York City and Chicago, Illinois.

MAY 2, 1970 Jockey Diane Crump Rides in the Kentucky Derby. Diane Crump(1949–), an experienced jockey, becomes the first woman to ride in the Kentucky Derby.

MAY 11, 1970 Canadian House of Commons Adjourns Under Pressure by Abortion Rights Activists. In Ottawa, Ontario, Canada, women protesters chain themselves to seats in the public galleries of Canada's House of Commons to protest the country's restrictions on abortion.

JUNE 1, 1970 Maggie Kuhn Founds Gray Panthers. Margaret (Maggie) E. Kuhn (1905–1995), community activist throughout her life, founds the Gray Panthers. This organization, the first of its kind in the United States, devotes its energies to fighting ageism (prejudice and discrimination against older people) and to bringing attention to the needs of the elderly in America.

JUNE 13, 1970   Chi Cheng Runs 100 Yards in Ten Seconds. Chi Cheng of Taiwan is the first woman to run 100 yards in ten seconds flat.

AUGUST 10, 1970   Equal Rights Amendment to the U.S. Constitution Passes One House of Congress. The Equal Rights Amendment (ERA) passes in the U.S. House of Representatives by a vote of 350 to 15.

AUGUST 15, 1970   Pat Palinkas, First Woman to Play Professional Football. After she signs with the Orlando Panthers in the Atlantic Coast Professional Football League, Pat Palinkas becomes the first woman to play in a professional football game. She holds the ball for the point-after-touchdown kicks.

AUGUST 26, 1970   National Women's Strike for Equality Staged on 50th Anniversary of 19th Amendment. Fifty years after the U.S. Congress passed the 19th Amendment to the Constitution guaranteeing women the right to vote, women across the United States protest their lack of economic and social progress. Headed by feminist Betty Friedan (1921–), the Women's Strike for Equality holds rallies and demonstrations in 90 cities and towns in 42 states. An estimated 50,000 women march down Fifth Avenue in New York City.

SEPTEMBER 23, 1970   Virginia Slims Tennis Tournament, First Professional Tournament for Women, Is Organized. Tennis player Billie Jean King (1943–); Gladys Heldman, publisher of *World Tennis* magazine; and eight other players organize the Virginia Slims Tennis Tournament in Houston, Texas, the first tournament for women professional tennis players held separate from male players.

NOVEMBER 3, 1970   Bella Abzug Elected to U.S. Congress. Bella Abzug (1920–), a founder of the National Women's Political Caucus, is elected to the U.S. House of Representatives. During her six years in Congress, "Bellicose Bella" introduces legislation supporting jobs programs, welfare, environmental issues, and the State of Israel. Her flamboyant and effective style brings national attention to women's issues and abilities. After leaving Congress in 1976, she continues her activism as a writer and speaker. She is the author of *Ms. Abzug Goes to Washington* (1972) and *Gender Gap: Bella Abzug's Guide to Political Power for Women* (1984).

DECEMBER 14, 1970   National Press Club in Washington, D.C., Admits Women. The National Press Club, with membership closed to women since its founding, votes to admit women members for the first time.

1971   Josephine Hulett Honored by Afro-American Labor Council. Labor union organizer Josephine Hulett (1927–) becomes the first woman to receive the Afro-American Labor Council's Special Recognition Award.

1971   Hannah Weinstein Founds Third World Cinema. Hannah Weinstein (1911–1984), an American film producer and civil rights and peace activist, founds the Third World Cinema in New York City. This association, with 40 percent of its stock owned by the East Harlem Community Organization, encourages films that involve blacks and women in all aspects of production. Among the motion pictures Weinstein makes with this group are *Claudine* (1972), *Greased Lightning* (1976), and *Stir Crazy* (1980).

1971   Anne Armstrong, First Woman to Cochair National Republican Committee. Anne Legendre Armstrong (1927–) becomes cochair of the National Republican Committee, the first woman to hold this office, and supports the Equal Rights Amendment. She joins the White House staff during the second term of President Richard Nixon from 1972 to 1974, as a counselor to the president with full cabinet status. Armstrong is Ambassador to the Court of St. James's in 1976–77, the first woman to hold this important post.

1971 Erin Pizzey Establishes Chiswick Women's Aid Society in London. Erin Pizzey (1939–), a leader in the feminist campaign against domestic violence, founds the Chiswick Women's Aid Society in Chiswick, London. She attracts much publicity for her cause and in 1979 becomes director of Chiswick Family Rescue. She writes both fiction and nonfiction on the subject of family violence.

1971 Swiss Women Granted Suffrage. Women in Switzerland win the vote.

1971 Title "Mrs." Required for Vote in New Jersey. Merna Ellentuck of Roosevelt, New Jersey, is forbidden to vote without putting "Mrs." before her name.

1971 Tennis Player Billie Jean King Wins $100,000 in Single Season. American tennis star Billie Jean King (1943–) is the first female athlete in any sport to earn more than $100,000 in a single season.

MARCH 1, 1971 American Lyricist Dorothy Fields Elected to Songwriters' Hall of Fame. Lyricist Dorothy Fields (1904–1974), daughter of well-known vaudevillian Lew Fields, is elected to the Songwriters' Hall of Fame, one of ten songwriters and the only woman in the first group elected to the Songwriters' Hall of Fame. Among her hundreds of songs are such hits as "On the Sunny Side of the Street," "Exactly Like You," "I Won't Dance," and "Don't Blame Me." She becomes the first woman to win an Oscar for songwriting when she is honored for her lyrics to Jerome Kern's tune "The Way You Look Tonight" in 1937.

The song is featured in the 1936 movie *Swing Time* with Ginger Rogers and Fred Astaire.

MAY 27, 1971 Girls in New York Compete on Boys' Teams. A New York State Education Department Law goes into effect permitting girls to compete as members of boys' teams in noncontact sports.

JUNE 30, 1971 Jockey Mary Bacon Posts 100th Victory. Jockey Mary Bacon is the first woman jockey to ride 100 winners, posting her 100th victory at the Thistledown Race Track in Cleveland, Ohio, aboard California Lassie.

JULY 10, 1971 National Women's Political Caucus Formed. At a conference attended by more than 2,000 women, the National Women's Political Caucus is founded. The goal of the Caucus is to support women interested in running for political office, to advocate for more women candidates within the major political parties, and to organize women at the local, state, and national levels to become more politically active. Among the founding members are Bella Abzug (1920–), Gloria Steinem (1934–), Shirley Chisholm (1924–), and Betty Friedan (1921–).

JULY 16, 1971 Jeanne Holm, First Woman U.S. Air Force General. Jeanne Marjorie Holm (1921–) becomes the first female Air Force general on July 16, 1971, in Washington, D.C. She serves at the Pentagon in Washington as Director of Women in the Air Force from 1965 until 1972. In 1973, she becomes the first Major General, the highest rank achieved by any woman in the American armed forces. After her retirement in 1974, she founds Women in Government and serves as this organization's first chairperson.

JULY 26, 1971 Photographer Diane Arbus Dies. Diane Arbus (1923–1971), photographer of the underprivileged, commits suicide. Her work is acclaimed through the 1960s, but she becomes increasingly withdrawn and depressed toward the end of the decade.

AUGUST 27, 1971 Photographer Margaret Bourke-White Dies. Margaret Bourke-White (1906–1971) dies of Parkinson's disease. In 1929, she begins her career as a photojournalist when she is hired by *Fortune* magazine.

1972 Shirley Chisholm Runs for U.S. President. Shirley Chisholm (1924–), a Democrat from Brooklyn, New York, becomes the first African American woman to run for president. Although her campaign is unsuccessful, it raises national discussion about whether the country is—or ever will be—ready for a president who is a woman, or African American.

1972 Sandra Day O'Connor, Arizona's First Woman Senate Majority Leader. Sandra Day O'Connor (1930–) becomes Arizona's first female senate majority leader. As an Arizona state senator, she supports the death penalty and the Equal Rights Amendment. Returning to law in 1975, she serves on her county's Superior Court Bench and then on the Arizona Court of Appeals. In 1981, O'Connor is nominated to the U.S. Supreme Court by President Ronald Reagan, who notes her unusual intelligence and fairness.

1972 Russian Gymnast Olga Korbut Performs Award-Winning Feats at Olympics. Olga Korbut (1955–), a Russian gymnast, demonstrates in competition a backwards somersault on uneven parallel bars during the Olympic Games in Munich, Germany. She is also the first and only female to do a backflip on the balance beam during these games, at which she wins three gold medals.

1972 African American Dancer Judith Jamison Joins Board of National Endowment for the Arts. Judith Jamison (1943–), an African American dancer, is the first woman elected to the board of the National Endowment for the Arts. She is also the first black woman and the

first black artist to serve in this capacity. Jamison is recognized for her wide experience in dance in the United States, Europe, and Africa.

1972 Equal Rights Amendment Passed by U.S. Congress. The Equal Rights Amendment (ERA) is passed by both houses of the U.S. Congress and is signed by President Richard Nixon. The amendment expires in 1982, without being ratified by the required two-thirds of the states; it is three states short of full ratification.

1972 Women Refused Voter's Registration for Using "Ms." Title. Nancy Allyn of California and Donna Brogan of Georgia are refused permission to register to vote if they use "Ms." as their title.

JANUARY 1972 First Issue of *Ms.* Magazine Sells Out. The first issue of the feminist magazine *Ms.* is published as a thirty-page insert of the December 1971 issue of *New York* magazine, founded by Clay Felker and Gloria Steinem (1934–) in 1968. *Ms.* is published as its own periodical in January 1972, and within just over a week's time, the 300,000-copy run of the magazine is sold out. Founding editor Gloria Steinem describes *Ms.* as a magazine created by women and for women. Steinem is the publication's editor in chief and former *Look* editor Patricia Carbine is the publisher.

FEBRUARY 20, 1972 Juanita Kreps, First Woman Director of the NYSE. Juanita Morris Kreps (1921–) becomes the first woman public director of the New York Stock Exchange (NYSE).

MARCH 2, 1972 Women Journalists Enter Men's Dressing Rooms in New York. The New York State Athletic Commission decides to allow women journalists into dressing rooms at men's boxing and wrestling matches.

MARCH 19, 1972 First Women's Collegiate Basketball Championship. The Association for Intercollegiate Athletics for Women (AIAW) holds its first women's collegiate basketball championship, and Immaculate College defeats West Chester State, 52–48.

MARCH 22, 1972   Equal Rights Amendment Passes the Senate. The U.S. Senate passes the Equal Rights Amendment to the U.S. Constitution by a vote of 84 to 8, sending it to President Richard M. Nixon for his signature.

APRIL 17, 1972   Nina Kuscsik Wins First Women's Boston Marathon. In the 76th annual Boston Marathon, Nina Kuscsik of Long Island, New York, wins the first women's competition with a time of 3 hours, 8 minutes, 58 seconds.

JUNE 1972   Bernice Gera Umpires Professional Baseball Game. American umpire Bernice Gera becomes the first woman to umpire a professional baseball game. She takes the field in a game between minor league teams, the Auburn Phillies and the Geneva Rangers.

JUNE 23, 1972   Title IX Becomes Law. President Richard Nixon signs into law Title IX of the Higher Education Act banning sex bias in athletics and other activities at all educational institutions receiving federal assistance.

NOVEMBER 8, 1972   Pat Schroeder Wins Seat in U.S. Congress. Pat Schroeder (1940–) begins her long career in politics. She is the first woman to represent Colorado, entering Congress at a time when few women hold such office. She immediately becomes an outspoken proponent of military spending cuts and other reforms, calling on the military to end harassment against female officers and homosexuals. Schroeder works for legislation protecting families as well, contributing largely to the passage of the Family and Medical Leave Act. Although she considers a presidential run in 1988, Schroeder finds that her gender overshadows her achievements, forcing her to back out of the race. Schroeder contin-

ues to serve as a representative of Colorado, a position she has maintained continuously.

DECEMBER 18, 1972   Anne Armstrong Named Counselor to U.S. President. At the start of the second term of President Richard Nixon, women's groups protest his failure to appoint women to important positions. Nixon counters by naming Anne Armstrong (1927–) counselor to the president, with full cabinet status. Armstrong soon founds the first White House Office of Women's Programs.

1973   Judith Hart Publishes Book on Britain's Responsibilities to Third World. Former member of British Parliament Judith Hart (1924–) publishes her ideas on Great Britain's responsibilities to Third World nations in *Aid and Liberation: A Socialist Study of Aid Policies.* Throughout the 1970s, Hart involves herself in negotiations between the European Community and various Third World countries, including Zambia and Rhodesia (now Zimbabwe). She is strongly opposed to British involvement in the European Economic Community (EEC).

1973   Juanita Kreps, First Woman Vice President at Duke. Juanita Morris Kreps (1921–) becomes Duke University's first woman vice president. The year before she becomes the first woman public director of the New York Stock Exchange, and in 1977 she is sworn in as the first woman U.S. Secretary of Commerce.

1973   First National Conference of Black Women in Canada. The members of the Canadian Women's Negro Association call together the first National Conference of Black Women. This conference is to "provide a network of solidarity for Black Women in Canada and to be a united voice in the defense and extension of human rights and liberties for Blacks in Canada." This important milestone underscores the need for solidarity among black women but also across racial lines.

1973 Women of Jordan Win Vote. Women gain the right to vote in Jordan.

1973 Establishment of National Right to Life Committee. The National Right to Life Committee is formed as a pro-life organization opposing abortion, euthanasia, and infanticide.

1973 Marcia Frederick Wins World Gymnastics Title. Marcia Frederick becomes the first American woman to win a world gymnastics title, taking the gold in the uneven parallel bars.

1973 Lynne Cox Sets World Record for Swimming English Channel. Lynne Cox swims the English Channel in 9 hours, 36 minutes, setting a new world record for women and men.

1973 *Fear of Flying* Becomes Bestseller. American writer and poet Erica Jong's (1942–) first novel is revolutionary in its explicit and honest portrayal of a woman's flight from marital ennui. Housewives, students, and career women alike embrace the novel for its intelligent, realistic depiction of female sexuality and independence.

JANUARY 3, 1973 Barbara Jordan Joins U.S. Congress. Elected as a Democrat from Texas to the U.S. House of Representatives, Barbara Jordan (1936–1996) takes office as the first African American congresswoman from the South.

JANUARY 21, 1973 Supreme Court Protects Abortion Rights with *Roe v. Wade*. In 1969 Sarah Weddington and Linda Coffee challenge Texas District Attorney Henry Wade over the constitutionality of state abortion statutes that prevent Jane Roe (Norma McCorvey) from terminating a pregnancy. At that time, all abortions in the state are banned except in cases where a woman's life is endangered by a pregnancy. In Georgia, abortion laws are also challenged in the case of *Doe v. Bolton*. In both cases, the Supreme Court decides that in the first trimester of a pregnancy women have the right to choose an abortion. From that point on, pro-life and pro-choice movements wage political, legal, and religious battles over abortion rights and funding issues.

FEBRUARY 1973 Movement to Canonize Australian Mary Helen McKillop Introduced. The movement for beatification and canonization of Australian Mother Mary Helen McKillop (1842–1909) is formally introduced. McKillop spends her lifetime establishing schools, convents, and charitable institutions throughout Australia and Asia. She is beatified in January 1995 and is expected to become Australia's first saint.

FEBRUARY 1973 First Women's World Invitational Swim Meet. The first Women's World Invitational Swim Meet is held at East Los Angeles College in California.

MARCH 1, 1973 Robyn Smith Wins Stakes Horse Race. Robyn Smith becomes the first woman jockey to win a stakes race when she rides North Sea to victory in the $27,450 Paumanauk Handicap at Aqueduct Raceway, Queens, New York.

APRIL 26, 1973 Crystal Lee Jordan Sutton Becomes Member of Textile Workers Union of America. Crystal Lee Jordan Sutton, subject of the 1979 film *Norma Rae,* joins the Textile Workers Union of America, and a month later, on May 30, is fired from her job at J. P. Stevens Company. When she goes to her worktable, she makes the sign that is the inspiration for a dramatic scene in *Norma Rae.* She pulls out a sheet of cardboard, and with a black marker, letters on it UNION. She then climbs on top of the table and slowly begins to turn, holding the sign high so coworkers can see it. Later that night, she is jailed and union organizers have to bail her out. Jordan is also the subject of the *Ms.* magazine ERA-TV documentary *Woman Alive!* The J. P. Stevens workers vote to be represented by the Textile Workers Union of America on August 28, 1974.

JULY 19, 1973 U.S. Tennis Association Announces Men and Women Will Win Equal Prize Money. The United States Tennis Association announces that the U.S. Open tennis championships will award equal prize money to women and men.

AUGUST 26, 1973 Mary Boitano Wins the Dipsea Race. Mary Boitano wins the 6.8-mile Dipsea Race in Marin County, California, the first time a female runner wins the race in its 68-year history.

1974 Carla Anderson Hills Named U.S. Assistant Attorney General. Carla Anderson Hills (1934–) is appointed Assistant Attorney General in the Civil Division of the U.S. Department of Justice, the first woman to hold this position. The next year President Gerald R. Ford appoints her U.S. Secretary of Housing and Urban Development (HUD), making her only the third woman in the country to hold a cabinet post. Criticism that a woman cannot be tough enough to direct the agency is soon quieted as Hills earns a reputation for efficient, no-nonsense administration. After stepping down in 1977, she returns to private law practice, and creates a controversy by lobbying her HUD successor on behalf of one of her law clients. Hills serves on the boards of several industrial corporations, including Standard Oil, American Airlines, IBM, and Corning Glass Works. In 1989, Hills is named U.S. trade representative, charged with steering U.S. trade policies with important European, Canadian, and Japanese markets.

1974 Coalition of Labor Union Women Is Organized. A non-partisan organization within the trade union movement, the Coalition of Labor Union Women (CLUW) is formed to articulate the concerns of working women. CLUW works to promote affirmative action in the workplace, strengthen the role of women in their unions, organize unorganized working women, and increase the involvement of women in the political and legislative process. CLUW and its chapters play a major role in ending discrimination against women and minorities—in hiring, promotion, classification, pay, and other aspects of employment—and expand women's roles in all job-related activities. Since the beginning of CLUW's push to make women more active in union affairs at all levels, women are elevated to top positions in local unions and state and local central bodies, and to the presidency and other leadership positions of international unions as well as the executive council of the AFL-CIO.

1974 Olga Madar Becomes First President of Coalition of Labor Union Women. Olga Madar, former member of the United Automobile Workers (UAW) union executive board, is elected president of a new organization, the Coalition of Labor Union Women.

1974 Dolores Huerta Becomes Vice President of United Farm Workers Union. Dolores Huerta, an activist in the cause of migrant workers, is elected vice president of the new United Farm Workers (UFW) union, an affiliate of the AFL-CIO. Her longtime collaborator, Cesar Chavez, is elected president.

1974 First Women's Rowing World Championships Held. The first world championships for women's rowing are held.

1974 Ella Tambussi Grasso Elected Governor of Connecticut. Ella Tambussi Grasso (1919–1981) is elected governor of Connecticut, becoming the first woman in the United States to be elected governor in her own right (other women are elected to finish out the terms of their dead husbands). In 1978, Grasso becomes the first woman governor to be reelected. After the discovery in 1980 that she has terminal cancer, she continues to run the state from her hospital bed for as long as she can. She resigns from office on New Year's Eve, 1980, and dies on February 5, 1981.

1974 Katharine Graham, First Woman Board Member of Associated Press. Katharine Graham (1917–), publisher of the *Washington Post*, becomes the first woman member of the board of the Associated Press. Although she credits her own success to "matrimony and patrimony" (both her husband and her father own the *Post* before her) she is known during her entire career for good financial sense, courage, and independence.

1974 Julia Miller Phillips Produces Oscar-winning Movie *The Sting*. Julia Miller Phillips (1944–) is the first woman to win an Academy Award as a producer. She is honored for *The Sting*, which also wins an Oscar for best movie. Phillips writes a popular book on life in Hollywood, *You'll Never Eat Lunch in This Town Again* (1990).

1974 Golda Meir Resigns as Israeli Prime Minister. Golda Mabovich Meir (1898–1978) resigns as prime minister of Israel, an office to which she is elected in 1969. During her time in office, tensions with neighboring Arab states are high and she loses political support.

1974 Barbara Rainey Named First Woman Pilot by U.S. Navy. Barbara Rainey (1948–1982) becomes the first woman to serve as a pilot in the U. S. Navy. Rainey's promising career as a naval pilot ends with her sudden death in 1982 from unspecified causes while on active duty.

MAY 16, 1974 **Martha Peterson, First Woman Elected to Exxon Board.** On May 16, 1974, Martha Peterson, president of Barnard College and a dean of Columbia University, becomes the first woman to serve on the board of directors of Exxon Corporation, the largest U.S. oil company.

Barbara Rainey

JUNE 12, 1974 **Girls Can Play Little League Baseball.** Little League baseball announces that its teams will be open to girls.

JULY 1974 **Isabel Perón Becomes President of Argentina.** Isabel Perón (1931–) of Argentina becomes the world's first female president when she takes over the office on the death of her husband, Juan Perón. She holds this position until she is ousted during a political coup on March 24, 1976.

NOVEMBER 13, 1974 **Plutonium Plant Worker Karen Silkwood Dies under Mysterious Circumstances.** Karen Gay Silkwood (1946–1974) dies under mysterious circumstances three months after giving testimony to the Atomic Energy Commission about health and safety violations at the plutonium plant where she works. Silkwood is a member of the Oil, Chemical, and Atomic Workers Local 5-

283 in Crescent, Oklahoma, and works at the Kerr-McGee Metallography Laboratory beginning in 1972. The plant tests plutonium pellets. Silkwood becomes aware of serious health and safety violations and begins working with her union to document the violations, providing testimony to the Atomic Energy Commission in August 1974. During the course of her employment and toward the end of her undercover investigation, Silkwood becomes seriously contaminated in the plant several times, to the point that on November 7, 1974, Kerr-McGee inspectors find her apartment and personal belongings so "hot" that everything has to be packed and buried in a nuclear waste dump. A few days later, Silkwood leaves a union meeting in Crescent to meet a newspaper reporter and a union official in Oklahoma City. Witnesses report seeing her with a folder containing numerous papers and documents that Silkwood claims are the proof of Kerr-McGee's violations. On the way to that meeting she is killed in an automobile accident of suspicious and unexplained origin. In 1984, the story of Karen Silkwood is documented in the movie *Silkwood*, which stars Meryl Streep in the title role.

Margaret Thatcher

1 9 7 5 – 1 9 7 9

1975 Margaret Thatcher Elected Leader of British Conservative Party. Margaret Thatcher (1925–) is elected leader of the Conservative Party, the first woman to head a major party in Great Britain.

1975 Janet Young, Vice Chairman of British Conservative Party. When Margaret Thatcher (1925–) becomes leader of the Conservative Party in England, Janet Young (1926–) becomes the party's vice chairman.

1975 Chinese Engineer Zhengying Qian First Woman Minister of Water Conservation. Zhengying Qian (1923–), one of China's first female engineers, is the first

woman to become Minister of Water Conservation, in Beijing. In 1982 her authority is broadened, and she becomes the first woman in her country to serve as Minister of Water Conservation and Power.

1975 Pioneer Filmmaker Dorothy Arzner Honored by Directors Guild. Dorothy Arzner (1900–1979) is honored for her career by the Directors Guild of America. Arzner is the first woman member of the Directors Guild.

1975 Diana Nyad Swims around Manhattan. Diana Nyad swims around Manhattan Island in 7 hours, 57 minutes, breaking a record set by Bryon Somers almost 50 years before.

MARCH 10, 1975 Carla Anderson Hills Named U.S. Secretary of Housing and Urban Development. President Gerald Ford appoints Carla Anderson Hills (1934–) the U.S. Secretary of Housing and Urban Development (HUD). She is the first woman to hold this post, and only the third woman cabinet member in the nation's history.

1976   Women's Rowing Becomes Olympic Sport. Women's rowing becomes an Olympic sport at the summer Olympic Games in Montreal, Quebec, Canada.

1976   Susan R. Estrich, First Woman President of *Harvard Law Review*. Susan R. Estrich (1952–) becomes the first female president of the *Harvard Law Review*. She goes on to become the first woman to manage a major U.S. presidential campaign when she heads Michael Dukakis' Democratic campaign for the presidency in 1987.

1976   Congressional Medal of Honor Reinstated for Mary Edwards Walker, M.D. U.S. Senate Resolution 569 reinstates the Congressional Medal of Honor awarded in 1865 to Mary Edwards Walker, M.D. (1832–1919), for her work during the Civil War (1861–65). Walker's medal, and those of 910 other recipients, are taken away in a bureaucratic review in 1917. In reinstating Walker's medal, the citation declares her "a woman one hundred years ahead of her time [who] pursued many occupations including teaching, lecturing, and writing on women's rights, and campaigning for women's suffrage and other progressive reforms; ... the only woman in the history of the United States to have ever received the Nation's highest award for valor...."

1976   Sarah Caldwell Conducts Metropolitan Opera. Sarah Caldwell (1928–) conducts a performance of Verdi's *La Traviata* starring soprano Beverly Sills, becoming the first woman to conduct the Metropolitan Opera. Known as an innovative and independent conductor, Caldwell founds the Opera Company of Boston in 1957. In 1983, she becomes artistic director of the New Opera Company of Israel.

1976   Portuguese Women Win Political Rights. Women of Portugal gain full political rights.

1976   Chantal Akerman, Belgian Filmmaker, Gains Acclaim for Film. Belgian filmmaker Chantal Akerman (1950–), who explicitly denies the label of "feminist" filmmaker, gains critical acclaim for her film *Jeanne Dielman, 23 Quai du Commerce, 1080 Bruxelles*. Her films deal with the lives of women in a distinctively analytical and intimate manner, and her subject matter ranges from a documentary on a theater group (*Un jour Pina a demandé*, 1983) to a musical (a rare commercial success), *The Golden Eighties*, in 1986. Her remarkable career begins in the INSAS film school of Brussels and the Université Internationale du Théâtre in Paris, and her reputation is built in the art house circuit and film festivals. A significant theme in her work is the mother-daughter relationship, central to the film *News from Home* (1976) which features a mother's letters to a faraway daughter in New York City, doubtless inspired by Akerman's sojourn in the East Village of New York City when she works at a pornography theater as a ticket seller.

1976   Golfer Judy Rankin Wins More than $100,000 in Single Season. Judy Rankin is the first professional female golfer to win more than $100,000 in a single season.

FEBRUARY 19, 1976   Anne Armstrong Sworn in as U.S. Ambassador to Court of St. James's. President Gerald Ford affirms his commitment to appointing qualified women to important and prestigious posts by naming Anne Armstrong (1927–) as U.S. Ambassador to the Court of St. James's. She serves as head of the embassy in London until 1977.

MARCH 24, 1976   Isabel Perón Unseated as Argentinian President. Isabel Perón (1931–) is ousted as president of Argentina during a political coup. She becomes the world's first

Barbara Jordan at the 1976 Democratic National Convention.

female president when she takes over the office on the death of her husband, Juan Perón.

MARCH 28, 1976 Krystyna Choynowski-Liskiewicz Sails Around World Alone. Krystyna Choynowski-Liskiewicz of Poland is the first woman to sail around the world solo.

JULY 12, 1976 Barbara Jordan Delivers Keynote Address at Democratic Convention. Congresswoman Barbara Jordan's reputation as one of the twentieth century's great orators is sustained by her keynote address to the 1976 Democratic National Convention. Jordan is the first woman and the first African American to deliver the keynote address.

SEPTEMBER 1976 Barbara Walters, First Woman TV News Anchorwoman. Barbara

Walters (1931–) becomes the first female network television news anchorwoman when she joins Harry Reasoner as coanchor of the *ABC Evening News.*

1977 Phyllis Schlafly Campaigns Effectively Against Modern Feminist Issues. Phyllis Schlafly (1924–) argues against modern feminism in her book *The Power of the Positive Woman* and works against the Equal Rights Amendment to the U.S. Constitution. Her "Stop ERA" campaign, with its warnings that the amendment will pave the way for homosexual weddings, is largely responsible for the amendment's failure to pass. That same year, she is selected as one of the ten most admired women in the world by readers of *Good Housekeeping* magazine. Schlafly is founder and president of the Eagle Forum, a national conservative, pro-family organization.

1977 American Physiologist Rosalyn Yalow Wins Lasker Award. Rosalyn Sussman Yalow (1921–) becomes the first woman to win the Albert Lasker Basic Medical Research Award. The same year, she also shares the Nobel Prize for physiology or medicine with Roger Guillemin and Andrew Schalley. Yalow's research centers on techniques for measuring hormones and enzymes in the blood.

1977 Chinese Physicist Xide Xie Founds Modern Physics Institute. Xide Xie (1921–), a Chinese physicist of international reputation, is the founder of the Modern Physics Institute in Shanghai. With a doctorate in her field from MIT, she spends her career at Fudan University and at the Institute of Technical Physics, both in Shanghai.

1977 U.S. Labor Historian Barbara Mayer Wertheimer Publishes Book on Working Women in America. Labor organizer Barbara Mayer Wertheimer publishes her most famous work, *We Were There: The Story of Working Women in America.* Wertheimer begins her career as an organizer for the Amalgamated

Clothing Workers of America. She soon moves up to associate director and then to acting director of education. In 1961 Wertheimer becomes a writer and consultant for the American Labor Service, and in 1966 she is named senior extension associate for Cornell University's School of Industrial and Labor Relations. From 1972 to 1973 she conducts a study of obstacles to female participation in unions. In 1973, Wertheimer is named Director of Trade Union Women's Studies for Cornell University's New York State School of Industrial and Labor Relations.

1977   Jan Todd Lifts More than 1,000 Pounds in Three Lifts. Weightlifter Jan Todd bench presses 176 1/4 pounds, dead lifts 441 pounds, and lifts 424 1/4 pounds from a squat to become the first woman ever to lift more than 1,000 pounds in three power lifts.

JANUARY 21, 1977   Patricia Roberts Harris, First Woman to Hold Two U.S. Cabinet Posts. U.S. President Jimmy Carter appoints Patricia Roberts Harris (1924–1985) Secretary of Housing and Urban Development, making her the first African American woman to hold a cabinet post. Two years later, Harris becomes U.S. Secretary of Health, Education, and Welfare.

JANUARY 23, 1977   Juanita Kreps Sworn in as U.S. Secretary of Commerce. Appointed by President Jimmy Carter, economist Juanita Kreps (1921–) becomes the first woman to serve as U.S. Secretary of Commerce, and only the fifth woman to hold a cabinet post. She resigns in 1979.

MARCH 1977   Betty Cook Wins Offshore Motorboat Race. At age 50, Betty Cook becomes the first woman to win a major offshore motorboat race when she wins the Bushmills Grand Prix off Newport Beach, California.

Toshiko Akiyoshi

SEPTEMBER 29, 1977   Eva Shain Officiates Heavyweight Championship Fight. Eva Shain is the first woman to officiate a heavyweight championship fight; the match is between Muhammad Ali and Ernie Shavers.

c. 1978   Underground Feminist Periodical Appears in Russia. Three issues of an underground feminist periodical entitled *Women and Russia: An Almanac to Women about Women* appear in St. Petersburg (then Leningrad). It reports on the problems of Russian women and reveals that they do not enjoy equality with men in the communist system. Such criticism cannot be condoned by the repressive

Soviet regime. As a consequence, the editor-in-chief Tatyana Mamonova (1943–) and three other women involved in the publication are expelled from the Soviet Union. Articles from *Women and Russia* appear in English abroad.

1978   Jazz Musician Toshiko Akiyoshi Receives Honor. Toshiko Akiyoshi (1929–), leader of the 17-piece Toshiko Akiyoshi Jazz Orchestra, becomes the first woman in jazz history to win *Down Beat* magazine's "Best Big Jazz Band" award. Akiyoshi's music combines the traditional American big band music made popular during the 1930s and 1940s with an international flair. In 1982, Akiyoshi's career is the subject of a documentary, *Jazz Is My Native Language,* describing the effects of her Asian ethnicity (she was born in China to Japanese parents) on her uniquely American style of music.

1978   Circle of Stone Depicting Moon-Goddess Coyolxauhqui Unearthed in Mexico City. In an archaeological find as important as that of the Aztec Calendar Stone in 1790, a ten-ton circle of stone showing the dismemberment of the Aztec moon-goddess Coyolxauhqui is unearthed in 1978 during construction work in Mexico City. The archaeologists present are so moved by the discovery that they sing a hymn to the goddess, who has been buried for over 500 years but resurfaces in one piece. Further excavations reveal one of the greatest Aztec religious centers in Mexico, surrounding the stone. Coyolxauhqui is the daughter of the great mother-goddess of the Aztecs, Coatlicue. She is killed either by her siblings, in one version, during an attempt to murder their mother (a plot in which Coyolxauhqui participates), or, in another version, by the sun-god so that Coyolxauhqui won't warn their mother of the murderous plot. In either event, Coyolxauhqui's head is set in the night sky to become the moon.

Janet Guthrie, after finishing the Indianapolis 500.

MAY 28, 1978   Janet Guthrie, First Woman to Complete Indianapolis 500. American race car driver Janet Guthrie (1938–) races in the Indianapolis 500, finishing in eighth place and becoming the first woman to complete the race. In 1977 she is the first woman to qualify for this race, but her car breaks down so she fails to finish it.

SEPTEMBER 25, 1978   Major League Baseball Cannot Bar Women Sportswriters from Locker Rooms. In a suit brought by *Sports Illustrated* reporter Melissa Ludtke, U.S. District Court Judge Constance Baker Motley rules that major league baseball cannot legally bar a woman sportswriter from the locker room after a game.

OCTOBER 2, 1978   Beverly Johnson Scales Peak El Capitan. Beverly Johnson of Wyo-

Mother Teresa

ming becomes the first woman to scale El Capitan in Yosemite National Park.

DECEMBER 9, 1978 **Women's Professional Basketball League Holds First Game.** The first game of the Women's Professional Basketball League takes place between the Chicago Hustle and the Milwaukee Does.

1979 **Nobel Peace Prize Awarded to Mother Teresa.** Mother Teresa, born Agnes Bojaxhiu (1910–) in Albania, is recognized for her work at the orphanage she established in Calcutta, India. With Lucinda Vardey Mother Teresa publishes *A Simple Path* in 1995 describing her work and her philosophy. The work is in part a response to journalist Christopher Hitchens attack on Mother Teresa's anti-abortion and anti-contraception attitudes, which he outlines in his 1995 work, *The*

Missionary Position: Mother Teresa in Theory and in Practice.

1979 **American Folksinger Joan Baez, Cofounder of Humanitas.** Joan Baez (1941–), an American folksinger and political activist, cofounds Humanitas, the International Human Rights Commission.

1979 **American Soprano Beverly Sills Named Director of New York City Opera.** Soprano Beverly Sills (1929–) is the first female opera singer to be appointed director of the New York City Opera. She joins this company as a performer in 1955 and creates an international reputation, although she does not make her debut at the rival Metropolitan Opera until 1975.

1979 **Boys Town Admits Girls.** Boys Town, a private institution for homeless, abused, neglected, and disabled children of every race and religion, admits girls for the first time since its founding in 1917. Established in 1917 in Omaha, Nebraska, by Edward J. Flanagan, as of the mid-1990s more than 8,500 children receive care at Boys Town annually.

APRIL 1979 **Beverly Kelley Commands U.S. Coast Guard Vessel.** Beverly Gwinn Kelley (1952–) is the first woman to command a U.S. Coast Guard vessel at sea. Through July, 1981, Kelley commands a Coast Guard patrol boat off the coast of Hawaii.

MAY 4, 1979 **Margaret Thatcher, Great Britain's First Woman Prime Minister.** Margaret Thatcher (1925–) becomes Great Britain's first woman prime minister. She fosters stringent economic policies, cutting public spending programs and reducing the national money supply. Her tough economic positions, and her equally tough military stands with the then-Soviet Union over Afghanistan and with Argentina over the Falkland Islands, earn her the title "The Iron Lady." She resigns as prime

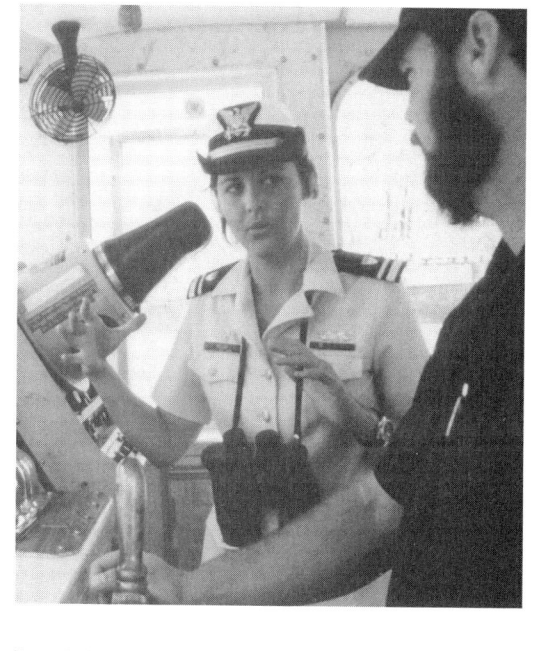

Beverly Kelley

minister in 1990, having served the longest term of any twentieth-century prime minister.

JULY 21, 1979   National Women's Hall of Fame Dedicated. The National Women's Hall of Fame is dedicated at Seneca Falls, New York, site of the First Women's Rights Convention. Twenty women, selected in

1973, are inducted, namely: Jane Addams (1860–1935), Marian Anderson (1902–1993), Susan B. Anthony (1820–1906), Clara Barton (1821–1912), Mary McLeod Bethune (1875–1955), Elizabeth Blackwell (1821–1910), Pearl S. Buck (1892–1973), Rachel Carson (1907–1964), Mary Cassatt (1845–1926), Emily Dickinson (1830–1886), Amelia Earhart (1898–1937), Alice Hamilton (1869–1970), Helen Hayes (1900–), Helen Brooke Taussig (1898–1986), and Harriet Tubman. The 1976 honorees are Abigail Adams (1744–1818), Margaret Mead (1901–1978), and Mildred "Babe" Didrikson Zaharias (1914–1956).

JULY 29, 1979   Susan B. Anthony One-Dollar Coin Issued by U.S. Government. The U.S. government issues a one-dollar coin featuring a likeness of suffragist and social reformer Susan B. Anthony (1820–1906), making her the first U.S. woman to have her likeness on a coin in general circulation.

AUGUST 30, 1979   Ann Meyers Signs a Contract to Play in National Basketball Association. Ann Meyers becomes the first woman to sign a contract to play in the National Basketball Association (NBA), signing a one-year contract with the Indiana Pacers.

Chapter 24

1980 TO 1989

1 9 8 0 – 1 9 8 4

c. 1980 Aduke Alakija, First Black African Woman Director of Mobil Oil. Aduke Alakija (1921–), a Nigerian lawyer, is the first black African woman to hold the position of director of Mobil Oil Company. Educated in England, Alakija works throughout her life for social issues and women's rights.

1980 Vigdís Finnbogadóttir Becomes President of Iceland. Vigdís Finnbogadóttir (1930–) becomes first woman president of Iceland. Born in Reykjavík, Iceland's capital, she receives part of her education in France. From 1962 to 1972, she teaches French and works as a cultural hostess for the Icelandic Tourist Bureau during the summer. She is persuaded to run for president, and wins a narrow victory over three men. She is reelected in 1984, when she is unopposed, and again in 1988. Married in 1954 and divorced in 1963, Finnbogadóttir adopts a baby daughter in 1972, one of the first adoptions by a single person in Iceland.

1980 Adrienne Rich Writes Essay on Sexuality. American poet and essayist Adrienne Rich (1929–) challenges stereotyped definitions of sexuality in an essay, "Compulsory Heterosexuality and Lesbian Existence." During her career, Rich publishes more than 15 volumes of poems and two collections of essays.

1980 Women's Rights National Historical Park Created in Seneca Falls. The U.S. Congress passes an act to create the Women's Rights National Historical Park to preserve the setting of the First Women's Rights Convention in Seneca Falls, New York, in 1848. Women's Rights National Historical Park includes Declaration Park, with a granite water wall engraved with the text of the "Declaration of Sentiments" adopted during the 1848 convention. The remaining portions of the Wesleyan Chapel where the meeting took place are preserved, and the Elizabeth Cady Stanton House is restored. In the nearby town of Waterloo, New York, the M'Clintock House, owned by Quakers Jane and Richard Hunt and rented by Quaker abolitionists Mary Ann and Thomas M'Clintock, still stands; the convention planners met here on July 16, 1848, to draft "The Declaration of Sentiments." The Women's Rights National Historical Park is administered by the National Park Service.

JANUARY 26, 1980 American Runner Mary Decker Sets Record. Mary Decker (1958–) runs a mile in under 4½ minutes, the first woman to do so.

FEBRUARY 1980 Joyce D. Miller, First Woman Elected to AFL-CIO Executive Council. American unionist Joyce D. Miller (1928–) is the first woman to be elected to the

Andrea Hollen

executive council of the AFL-CIO, a major organization representing labor unions. A life-long union leader, Miller devotes her attention particularly to social services and women's concerns.

APRIL 14, 1980   Jeanne Sauvé, Canada's First Woman Speaker of the House. Jeanne Sauvé (1922–) becomes the first woman Speaker of the House of Commons in Canada, where her extensive reforms are generally acclaimed. Four years later, she is sworn in as Governor General of Canada on May 14, 1984—the first woman ever to hold the post.

MAY 28, 1980   West Point Military Academy Graduates First Women. The U.S. Military Academy at West Point graduates its first class to include women. The top, or "distin-guished" cadets graduate in order of overall performance. Andrea Hollen, a distinguished

cadet, is the first woman cadet in the class of 1980 to receive her diploma. Of the 62 female cadets who graduate, 61 participate in the May 28 ceremony. The 63rd cadet, along with a dozen male cadets, graduates on June 26, 1980. All receive commissions as second lieu-tenants in the U. S. Army upon graduation from the Academy.

JUNE 1980   Kateri Tekakwitha, First Native American Beatified by the Roman Catholic Church. Mohawk Indian Kateri Tekakwitha (1656–1680), who converts to Catholicism and becomes a well-known mystic, is declared Blessed by the Roman Catholic Church, becoming the first Native American to be beatified.

JUNE 1980   Females Can Caddy in U.S. Open. For the first time, the Professional Golf Asso-ciation (PGA) allows female caddies in the U.S. Open at the Baltusrol Golf Club in Springfield, New Jersey. Pamela Shuttleworth of Santa Monica, California, caddies for PGA player Jim Dent.

1981   Jie Zhang's Book *Leaden Winds* Offi-cially Declared Most Popular Novel in China. Jie Zhang (1937–), a Chinese author, pub-lishes her novel, *Leaden Winds.* In doing so, she becomes the first woman to write a book officially declared the most popular novel in China, a designation accorded to the work the year it is published. In 1987, a collection of her short stories appears in English transla-tion, *As Long as Nothing Happens, Nothing Will.*

1981   Maya Lin Designs Vietnam Veterans Memorial. Maya Lin (1959–), Chinese American artist and sculptor, wins the compe-tition to design the Vietnam Veterans War Memorial when her design is chosen from among the 1,420 entries submitted. Her design features a black granite wall inscribed with the names of the nearly 58,000 American service personnel who died fighting the Vietnam War. Other important public installations designed by Lin are the *The Women's Table* at Yale University (1993), and *Eclipsed Time* (1994), a 16-by-30 foot glass and steel clock gracing the ceiling of the Long Island Railroad/Pennsylvania Station terminal in New York City.

1981   Declaration of Women's History Week in U.S. The U.S. Congress passes a Joint Resolution declaring the first Women's History Week in the United States.

1981   Actress Melina Mercouri Is Greek Minister of Culture and Sciences. Greek film actress Melina Mercouri (1923–) assumes the post of minister of culture and sciences in the government of Greece. She launches an unsuccessful campaign to have Greek artifacts returned from Britain. She leaves this post in 1989.

1981   Publication of *The Book of Goddesses and Heroines*. Patricia Monaghan first publishes her widely researched work, *The Book of Goddesses and Heroines,* in 1981, one of the first works of its kind and scope to appear. Nine years later she revises and enlarges it for a second edition.

1981   Gro Harlem Brundtland, Norwegian Prime Minister. Gro Harlem Brundtland (1939–) becomes prime minister of Norway in 1981. Born to Gudmund and Inga Harlem in Oslo, Norway, Brundtland earns degrees from Oslo University and Harvard University. She marries Arne Olav Brundtland and they have four children. In 1974 she becomes Norway's Minister of the Environment and is associated with a program to create nature reserves. Her support for more liberal abortion laws focuses attention on the absence of women in Norwegian politics.

JANUARY 29, 1981   Jeanne Kirkpatrick Becomes Permanent U.S. Representative to the United Nations. Nominated U.S. permanent representative to the United Nations by President Ronald Reagan, Jeane Jordan Kirkpatrick (1926–) becomes the Republican president's first Democratic appointee. On January 29, her nomination is confirmed by unanimous vote of the U.S. Senate. In this position, she continues to defy classification as liberal or conservative, as she takes positions supporting El Salvador's military junta, against economic sanctions in South Africa, and condemning Israel without sanctions for an air attack against Iraq. Kirkpatrick leaves the United Nations in 1985.

MARCH 26, 1981   Social Democrat Party Founded in Great Britain. Believing that the Labour Party has become too leftist and too heavily influenced by trade unions, politician Shirley Williams (1930–) and three others found the more centrist Social Democrat Party in Great Britain. It is the first major new party in Great Britain in 80 years. It lasts only ten years but sees several of its members, including Williams, elected to Parliament.

APRIL 4, 1981   Sue Brown Coxes Oxford University Crew. Sue Brown from Oxford University in England becomes the first woman to cox against Cambridge in the 152-year history of the Oxford-Cambridge race. Brown coxes the Oxford crew to an eight-length victory over Cambridge.

APRIL 27, 1981   North American Soccer League Hires Betty Ellis to Officiate. Betty Ellis is hired as the first female soccer game official by the North American Soccer League.

JULY 29, 1981   Lady Diana Spencer Marries Britain's Prince of Wales. Attended by a congregation of 2,500 and a worldwide TV audience of 750 million, the famed royal wedding of Prince Charles of England, first in line to the British throne, and Lady Diana Spencer (1961–) transpires under the dome of St. Paul's Cathedral. Two million spectators—whose behavior is monitored by 4,000 police-

Sandra Day O'Connor is sworn in as first woman justice on the U.S. Supreme Court.

men and 2,228 soldiers—jam the processional route, cheering, shouting, and waving flags and banners. Eleven months later, the couple's first son, Prince William, is born, followed two years later by a second son, Harry. In the fifteen years that follow the wedding, rumors of marital breakdown prove to be fact, and the world continues to follow each twist in the sordid divorce proceedings.

AUGUST 1981 **Tonia Schlegel Wins All-American Soap Box Derby.** Thirteen-year-old Tonia Schlegel of Hamilton, Ohio, is the first girl to win the All-American Soap Box Derby held annually in Akron, Ohio.

SEPTEMBER 25, 1981 **Sandra Day O'Connor Becomes First Woman Justice of U.S. Supreme Court.** Sandra Day O'Connor (1930–) is sworn in as U.S. Supreme Court Justice. Nominated by President Ronald Reagan, she is the first woman to serve on the highest court in the land.

NOVEMBER 1981 **Janet Young Appointed Minister of Great Britain's Management and Personnel Office.** When Baroness Janet Young (1926–) is appointed minister in charge of Great Britain's new Management

and Personnel Office, she is given just over two years to reduce the number of civil servants from 732,000 people to 630,000. While working toward this goal, she also attempts to get more women into top-level positions, to create part-time jobs for new mothers, and to increase the ethnic and racial diversity of the civil service.

NOVEMBER 21, 1981 **National Collegiate Athletic Association Sponsors First Women's Championships.** The first women's championships sponsored by the National Collegiate Athletic Association (NCAA) are held; prior to 1981, all NCAA championships are men's events. Women's events this year include: National Collegiate Division II Women's Cross Country Championships, hosted by Southeast Missouri State University, Cape Girardeau, Missouri; National Collegiate Division III Women's Cross Country Championships, hosted by Carthage College, Kenosha, Wisconsin; National Collegiate Division II Field Hockey Championship, hosted by Pfeiffer College, Misenheimer, North Carolina; National Collegiate Division III Field Hockey Championship, hosted by Westfield State College, Westfield, Massachusetts; and National Collegiate Division I Field Hockey Championship, hosted by University of Connecticut, Storrs, Connecticut.

NOVEMBER 23, 1981 **Women's Collegiate Cross Country Running.** The first National Collegiate Division I Women's Cross Country Championships are hosted by Wichita State University, Wichita, Kansas.

DECEMBER 18–19, 1981 **Women's Collegiate Volleyball.** The first National Collegiate Division II Women's Volleyball Championship is hosted by University of California, Riverside; Division III Championship is hosted by Maryville College, Maryville, Tennessee; and Division I Championship is hosted by University of California, Los Angeles.

President Agatha Barbara of Malta with Chinese President Li Ziannina in 1985.

1982   Chinese Actress Ruifang Zhang Leads Delegation to Manila Film Festival. Ruifang Zhang (1918–), a nationally known Chinese film actress, heads the Chinese delegation to the First Manila Film Festival in the Philippines. In recognition of her illustrious career in cinema, Zhang is elected vice chair of the Shanghai Branch of the Chinese Communist Party in 1985.

1982   American Geneticist Barbara McClintock Wins Nobel Prize. Barbara McClintock (1902–1992) wins the Nobel Prize for her work with maize, or Indian corn. The Nobel Committee, in describing her discovery of so-called jumping genes, ranks it as "one of the two great discoveries of our time in genetics." McClintock is the first American woman to win the Nobel Prize in a scientific category by herself (previous winners had shared the honor). McClintock first presents her findings on dissociator, or "jumping," genes in 1951. Ironically, her gender and eccentric personality combine to prevent her from achieving recognition in academia throughout her career.

FEBRUARY 16, 1982   Agatha Barbara, First Woman President of Malta. Agatha Barbara (1923–), a prominent politician in Malta, is elected the first woman president of that country on February 16, 1982. In 1946, while Malta is still under British rule, Barbara is the first woman elected to Parliament. She serves two terms as minister of education, and one as minister of labor, culture, and welfare.

MARCH 11–13, 1982 Women's Collegiate Swimming and Diving. Northeast Missouri State University, Kirksville, Missouri, hosts the first National Collegiate Division II Women's Swimming and Diving Championships. In Division III, Swimming and Diving Championships are hosted by University of Massachusetts, Boston. The University of Florida, Gainesville, hosts the Division I Championships.

MARCH 18–20, 1982 Women's Collegiate Basketball. In Springfield, Massachusetts, the first National Collegiate Division II Women's Basketball Championship is hosted by American International and Springfield Colleges. In Division III, the first Championship is hosted by Elizabethtown College, Elizabethtown, Pennsylvania.

MARCH 25–27, 1982 Women's Collegiate Fencing. The first National Collegiate Women's Fencing Championships are held at San Jose State University, San Jose, California.

MARCH 25–27, 1982 Women's Collegiate Gymnastics. The first National Collegiate Division II Women's Gymnastics Championships are hosted by Springfield College, Springfield, Massachusetts; Division I Gymnastics Championships are hosted by University of Utah, Salt Lake City.

MARCH 26–28, 1982 Women's Collegiate Basketball. The National Collegiate Athletic Association (NCAA) holds the first National Collegiate Division I Women's Basketball Championship, hosted by Old Dominion University, Norfolk, Virginia.

MAY 1982 Milka Planinc Becomes Premier of Yugoslavia. Milka Planinc (1924–) is born in Croatia. She graduates from the Higher Administration in School in Zagreb and becomes party instructor of Zagreb City. In 1957 she serves as the political secretary of Treönjevka People's Assembly. Planinc is

head of the Zagreb secretariat for education and culture in 1961. From 1963 to 1965 she serves as Republican Secretary for Education of Croatia. Throughout the 1970s Planinc works with Yugoslavian president Josip Tito to suppress Croatian nationalism. In May 1982 Planinc becomes president of the Coordination Commission of the Federal Executive Council. She serves until 1986.

MAY 16–23, 1982 Women's Collegiate Tennis. The first National Collegiate Division I Women's Tennis Championships ever held are hosted by University of Utah, Salt Lake City. In Division II, the championships are hosted by Southern Illinois University, Edwardsville, Illinois; and in Division III, they are hosted by Millsaps College, Jackson, Mississippi.

MAY 22–23, 1982 Women's Collegiate Lacrosse. The first National Collegiate Women's Lacrosse Championship is hosted by Widener College, Chester, Pennsylvania.

MAY 25–29, 1982 Women's Collegiate Outdoor Track. The first National Collegiate Division II Women's Outdoor Track Championships are hosted by California State University, Sacramento; in Division III, by North Central College, Naperville, Illinois; in Division I, Brigham Young University, Provo, Utah.

MAY 25–29, 1982 Women's Collegiate Golf. The first National Collegiate Women's Golf Championships are hosted by Stanford University, Stanford, California.

MAY 27–30, 1982 Women's Collegiate Softball. The first National Collegiate Division I Women's Softball Championship is hosted by Creighton University, Omaha, Nebraska; Division II Championship, by Sacred Heart University, Bridgeport, Connecticut; Division III Championship, by Trenton State College, Trenton, New Jersey.

1983   African American Writer Alice Walker Awarded Pulitzer Prize. Alice Walker (1944–) wins the Pulitzer Prize for her novel *The Color Purple* (1982). The story is later adapted into a major motion picture. In 1993, she coauthors a book on female genital mutilation in Africa.

1983   Ellen Taaffe Zwilich Awarded Pulitzer Prize for Music. Composer Ellen Taaffe Zwilich (1939–) is the first woman to win a Pulitzer Prize for music. She is honored for her *Symphony no. 1, Three Movements for Orchestra,* a composition commissioned by the American Composers Orchestra.

1983   Sarah Caldwell Directs Israeli Opera. Conductor Sarah Caldwell (1928–) becomes artistic director of the New Opera Company of Israel.

1983   Glenda Jackson, First Woman Director of United British Artists. English actress Glenda Jackson (1936–) becomes the first woman to serve as a director of United British Artists. She is also one of the cofounders of the Women's Playhouse Trust. Jackson makes her film debut in 1963 in *This Sporting Life* and also joins the Royal Shakespeare Company. She wins two Academy Awards for best actress: in 1969 for *Women in Love;* and in 1973 for the comedy *A Touch of Class.* In 1971, Jackson wins a British Academy Award for *Sunday Bloody Sunday* and an Emmy Award for the title role in the television series *Elizabeth R.*

1983   Publication of *The Woman's Encyclopedia of Myths and Secrets.* Barbara G. Walker publishes her work, *The Woman's Encyclopedia of Myths and Secrets,* containing an alphabetical listing of many of the world's goddesses, rituals, and other subjects related to or affecting women. Walker also writes a companion volume entitled *The Woman's Dictionary of Symbols and Sacred Objects.*

1983   Barbra Streisand Writes, Directs, Produces, and Stars in *Yentl.* Barbra Streisand (1942–) is the first woman to write, direct, produce, and star in a Hollywood movie. Her film *Yentl* explores the restrictions placed on girls and women in Orthodox Jewish society. Born in New York City in 1942, Barbra Streisand overcomes professional obstacles to become one of the most famous entertainers in America. She is a singing sensation, a smash on Broadway, and takes Hollywood by storm in *Funny Girl* (1968). Her 1991 venture, *The Prince of Tides,* which she directs, stars in, and coproduces, earns her five Academy Award nominations, including best picture. Streisand continues to perform as an actress and singer, but is most likely to be seen supporting charitable causes, such as AIDS and breast cancer research, and at political fund-raisers.

1983   Madonna Debuts on Pop Charts and MTV. Madonna (1958–) releases a self-titled first album, and its songs "Holiday" and "Burning Up" become hits after their videos receive frequent air play by MTV. By the late 1980s, Madonna will be well on her way to reaching pop icon status after having had sixteen consecutive Top 5 hits and using her keen marketing ability to sell her continually-reinvented image to captivated fans around the globe.

1983   Gloria Steinem's *Outrageous Acts and Everyday Rebellions* Published. Gloria Steinem (1934–) compiles her twenty years of work as a journalist and feminist into the bestseller *Outrageous Acts and Everyday Rebellions.* The book contains selections of her writings on a range of topics including politics, pornography, her mother, and Marilyn Monroe. In the book, Steinem also chronicles her development as a feminist.

JANUARY 1983   Elizabeth Dole Appointed Secretary of Transportation. The seventh woman to hold a cabinet position, Elizabeth

Dole (1936–) is appointed secretary of transportation by President Ronald Reagan. Dole is responsible for enacting auto manufacturing rules, requiring that all new automobiles have air bags or automatic safety belts and rear, eye-level brake lights. She also improves security in airports and hires more federal marshals. After holding the office longer than any of her predecessors, Elizabeth Dole resigns from the position in 1987 to help her husband, Senator Robert Dole, in his presidential bid. She later goes on to become Secretary of Labor under President George Bush and president of the American Red Cross.

JUNE 18–24, 1983 Astronaut Sally Ride Is First American Woman in Space. Sally Kristen Ride (1951–) flies on a six-day flight of the space shuttle *Challenger*. Having been selected to become an astronaut in 1978, she is the first American woman to travel in space. While a student at Stanford University, Ride also achieves national ranking as a tennis player, but elects to pursue her interests in physics and space exploration rather than a career in professional tennis.

MAY 14, 1984 Jeanne Sauvé, Canada's First Woman Governor General. Jeanne Sauvé (1922–) is sworn in as Governor General of Canada, the first woman ever to hold the post. Sauvé is born at Prud'homme, Saskatchewan. She is educated at the University of Ottawa and is the national president of the Young Catholic's Student Group (1942-47). Following her marriage in 1948, Sauvé begins a distinguished career as a freelance journalist and broadcaster in Montreal. She is elected as a liberal Member of Parliament from Montreal in 1972, and her government tenure is highlighted by a series of ministerial portfolios. On April 14, 1980, Sauvé becomes the first woman Speaker of the House of Commons where her extensive reforms are generally acclaimed.

JULY 19, 1984 Geraldine Ferraro Nominated as Vice-Presidential Candidate. The first woman ever to be nominated for such an office, Geraldine Ferraro (1935–) accepts Walter Mondale's invitation to the ticket with the knowledge that their campaign will not be easy. A former lawyer and Congresswoman, Ferraro is not prepared for the criticism and personal attacks that follow her nomination. The campaign is not able to recover from the media blitz, in which Ferraro is accused of such debaucheries as tax fraud and involvement in organized crime. The Mondale/Ferraro ticket loses in a landslide to incumbent Ronald Reagan.

OCTOBER 31, 1984 Assassination of Indira Gandhi, Prime Minister of India. Indira Gandhi (1917–1984), the four-term prime minister who presides over India from the 1960s to the early 1980s, is assassinated. Gandhi is the daughter of Jawaharlal Nehru (1899-1964), the first prime minister of independent India. In 1955, Gandhi becomes a member of the Working Committee of the ruling Congress party. By 1959, she becomes president of that political party, and she is made prime minister in 1966 as a moderate within the Congress party. Gandhi is instrumental in guiding the modernization of India, assisting in the creation of Bangladesh and establishing India as a non-aligned nation. Gandhi becomes embroiled in a Sikh separatist movement in the early 1980s and is assassinated by her Sikh security guards.

1 9 8 5 – 1 9 8 9

1985 Senda Berenson, Creator of Women's Basketball, Inducted into Hall of Fame. Senda Berenson (1868–1954), who develops the rules of women's basketball, is inducted into the Naismith Basketball Hall of Fame.

1985 Gail Reals, First American Woman Brigadier General. Gail Reals (1937–) is the

Gail Reals

first woman promoted to the rank of brigadier general in direct competition with men, in 1985. Reals enjoys a distinguished career in the U. S. Marine Corps between 1956 and her retirement in 1990.

1985   Death of Ruth Gordon, American Actress Who Achieves Cult Status. Ruth Gordon (1896–1985), an American actress whose stage and film career spans 70 years, dies. Early in her career, Gordon is told by the American Academy of Dramatic Arts that she is too short, too ugly, and too talentless to be an actress. Years later, she receives an Academy Award for Special Achievement. Her secret to success, she says, is "I never face facts." Born a seaman's daughter in Quincy, Massachusetts, Gordon attends drama school in New York City and makes her Broadway debut in 1918. One critic writes, "Anyone who looks like that must get off the stage." However, bad reviews soon turn to good, and Gordon even performs with the prestigious Old Vic Company in England. With her husband, Garson Kanin, she cowrites the screenplays for the Spencer Tracy-Katherine Hepburn films *Adam's Rib* (1949) and *Pat and Mike* (1952). She receives three Oscar nominations for screenwriting. In her old age, Gordon becomes a cult figure as an actress in the films *Rosemary's Baby* (1968) and *Harold and Maude* (1972). At 87, she appears in *Maxie* (1985) and insists on doing her own stunt work. For this film, she rides a motorcycle for the first time in her life. At the time of her death in 1985, she is working on a new play.

1985   Margaret Atwood's *The Handmaid's Tale* Published. In *The Handmaid's Tale* Canadian author and feminist Margaret Eleanor Atwood (1939–) unfolds a vision of the future in which dictatorial rule by Fundamentalist Christians and environmental pollution that has disrupted most women's reproductive capabilities have created a hostile living environment for women. Women are either Handmaids, the official breeders for society, or men's chattel.   Atwood's first book to be set in the future is dominated by the themes of feminism evident in her earlier works. *The Handmaid's Tale* receives mixed reviews from critics. The book is adapted to film in 1990.

DECEMBER 14, 1985   Wilma P. Mankiller Becomes Chief of Cherokee Nation. Wilma P. Mankiller is sworn in as the first woman to serve as tribal chief of the Cherokee nation. Between 1985 and her retirement in 1994, Mankiller increases the tribe's membership from 55,000 to 156,000 and adds three health centers and nine children's programs to the facilities on Cherokee land.

1986   **International Olympic Committee Appoints Anita DeFrantz to Lifetime Membership.** The International Olympic Committee (IOC) appoints former Olympic rower Anita DeFrantz to lifetime membership in the IOC. DeFrantz becomes the only American woman, and one of only five women, on the 91-member committee.

1986   **Oprah Winfrey Reaches National Audience.** After achieving success with her talk show in the Chicago television market, Oprah Winfrey (1954–) takes her sympathetic dialogue to the nation with the syndication of *The Oprah Winfrey Show*. With a daily viewership of 17,000,000 people, Winfrey becomes one of the most famous women in television. In addition to taking over production of *The Oprah Winfrey Show,* Winfrey brings to the screen productions that convey important social and spiritual messages that might otherwise be lost in the Hollywood shuffle. One of the highest-paid professionals in show business today, Oprah Winfrey has achieved both popular and critical acclaim.

1986   **Corazon Aquino Becomes President of Philippines.** Corazon Aquino's world is shattered in August 1983 when her husband Benigno Aquino is murdered as he begins a challenge to Philippine president Ferdinand Marcos. By 1984, Corazon Aquino is the most influential figure in the opposition to the Marcos regime. In her campaign to unseat Marcos in the 1986 elections, Aquino grows in strength and confidence, and when Marcos realizes that she is capable of winning, he attempts to rig the election. Although Marcos declares himself the winner, he is never recognized by Filipinos, who respond to his declaration by rioting and protesting outside the Malacanang Palace. Within a month, Marcos flees to Hawaii and Corazon Aquino assumes the presidency. Among her first actions are the release of 441 political prisoners and the forced retirement of 22 generals loyal to Marcos. At a March 2, 1986, outdoor mass before

Painting of the astronauts who perished in the explosion of the space shuttle *Challenger,* January 28, 1986.

a crowd of one million, Aquino says that the writ of habeas corpus, the right of a prisoner to appear before a judge, is again the law of the land. She also abolishes the government's power to imprison people at will, a decree that Marcos had imposed in 1981.

JANUARY 28, 1986   **American Space Shuttle *Challenger* Explodes on Take-Off.** The space shuttle *Challenger* explodes 73 seconds after taking off, killing all seven crew members. Two women—Judith Resnick and Christa McAuliffe, the first civilian teacher in space— are among those who perish.

MAY 1, 1986   **Ann Bancroft at North Pole.** Ann Bancroft becomes the first woman to the top of the world when she and her five male companions reach the North Pole by dogsled.

1987   Susan R. Estrich, First Female to Manage Major U.S. Presidential Campaign. When she heads Michael Dukakis' Democratic campaign for the U.S. presidency, Susan R. Estrich (1952–) becomes the first woman to manage a major presidential campaign.

1987   Declaration of Women's History Month in U.S. The U.S. Congress passes a Joint Resolution declaring March as National Women's History Month in the United States.

1987   Establishment of Operation Rescue. The right-to-life group Operation Rescue is formed as an interfaith coalition to persuade women from undergoing fetus abortion procedures. The group is best known for the publicity generated through its sit-ins and blockades at abortion clinics.

1987   Gayle Sierens Does Play-by-Play for NFL Game. Gayle Sierens is the first woman broadcaster to do play-by-play commentary for a National Football League (NFL) game, Kansas City vs. Seattle.

1987   Publication of *The Firebrand*, Kassandra's Version of the Trojan War. Marion Zimmer Bradley publishes her novel, *The Firebrand*, which tells the story of the Trojan War (c.1180 B.C.) from the point of view of Kassandra (or Cassandra). Kassandra is a Trojan priestess of Apollo to whom the god gives the gift of prophecy.

1987   Publication of *The Queen of Swords*. In 1987 Judy Grahn publishes the book *The Queen of Swords*, a modern-day retelling of the ancient Sumerian myth of the descent of Inanna, Queen of Heaven and Earth, to the underworld and her eventual return to the upper realm.

FEBRUARY 4, 1987   National Women in Sports Day. The first National Women in Sports Day is celebrated in Washington, D.C.

Wilma P. Mankiller

1988   Julie Croteau Plays Baseball on Men's Collegiate Team. Julie Croteau takes the field for NCAA Division III St. Mary's College of Maryland as the first woman to play on a men's collegiate baseball team.

1988   Record Number of Bowlers Compete in Women's International Bowling Congress Championship. The Women's International Bowling Congress (WIBC) Championship tournament in Reno/Carson City, Nevada, breaks all participation records, with 77,735 bowlers competing.

1988   Benazir Bhutto, Prime Minister of Pakistan. The first woman to head a Muslim nation, Benazir Bhutto (1953–), becomes prime minister of Pakistan. She serves until 1990.

AUGUST 1, 1988 Phyllis Holmes Becomes President of National Association of Intercollegiate Athletics. Phyllis Holmes begins her term as president of the National Association of Intercollegiate Athletics (NAIA), the first woman to serve as president of any national coed sports organization.

SEPTEMBER 1988 Barbara Harris Elected Bishop of Worldwide Anglican Communion. The Reverend Barbara Harris is elected the first woman bishop of the Worldwide Anglican Communion, a 454-year-old organization.

1989 Carla Anderson Hills Appointed U.S. Trade Representative. Carla Anderson Hills (1934–) is named U.S. trade representative, charged with steering U.S. trade policies with important European, Canadian, and Japanese markets. In 1975 Hills becomes the first woman to fill the position of U.S. Secretary of Housing and Urban Development.

1989 Lori Norwood Wins World Modern Pentathlon. Lori Norwood becomes the first American woman to win the individual title at the World Modern Pentathlon Championships.

1989 Goddess Worship in the Ancient World Illuminated. In 1989 Marija Gimbutas publishes her work, *The Language of the Goddess,* which examines archaeological evidence for the worship of the Goddess throughout the ancient world.

APRIL 5, 1989 Aung San Suu Kyi Under House Arrest in Myanmar. Aung San Suu Kyi (1946–), whose father Aung San was assassinated the year after her birth, is placed

Aung San Suu Kyi

under house arrest in response to her political campaign to restore democracy to her country. Her father, Aung San, was a leader in the fight for independence from the British Empire. Aung San Suu Kyi, herself a leader of the National League for Democracy, leaves her English husband, Michale Aris, and her two sons in England to return to Burma in 1988. She remains under house arrest in her home in Yangon (formerly Rangoon) for 2,190 days until her release on July 10, 1995. While detained, Suu Kyi becomes the eighth woman to be awarded the Nobel Peace Prize, in 1991.

Chapter 25
1990 TO 1996

1 9 9 0 – 1 9 9 4

1990   Margaret Thatcher Resigns as Prime Minister of Great Britain. Margaret Thatcher (1925–), elected as Great Britain's first woman prime minister in 1979, resigns. She serves the longest term of any prime minister in the twentieth century. Also in 1990, she releases the first volume of her autobiography, *The Downing Street Years.*

1990   Margaret Booth Given Lifetime Achievement Award by American Cinema Editors. In Hollywood, California, Margaret Booth (1898–), a pioneering American film editor, is the first woman to receive a Lifetime Achievement Award from the American Cinema Editors. She is honored for a career of creative film editing work that begins in 1916. Booth is remembered for such films as *The Barretts of Wimpole Street* (1934), *The Way We Were* (1973), and *Annie* (1982).

1990   Violeta Chamorro Becomes President of Nicaragua. Violeta Chamorro (1929–) is born in Rivas, Nicaragua. She attends the Roman Catholic High School for Girls in San Antonio, Texas, and Blackstone College in Southside, Virginia. Chamorro marries Pedro Joaquín Chamorro Cardenal in 1950 and has four children. Pedro Cardenal publishes the newspaper *La Prensa*, which is critical of the Somoza government in Nicaragua. His politi-

cal views make him unpopular, and on January 10, 1978, Cardenal is assassinated. After the death of her husband, Violeta Chamorro becomes publisher of *La Prensa* and uses the paper to oppose the Sandinista government. In September 1989 Chamorro becomes the leader of the opposition party, Unión Nacional Opositora. Chamorro is elected president of Nicaragua in February 1990.

JUNE 1990   Bernadette Locke Coaches Men's College Basketball. Bernadette Locke becomes the first woman to coach a major college men's sport when she accepts the position of assistant coach on the University of Kentucky men's basketball team.

NOVEMBER 1990   Mary Robinson Elected President of Ireland. Mary Robinson, an international lawyer, activist, and Catholic, wins election as the first woman president of Ireland. This victory is notable in that it comes in a period in Irish history of controversy over abortion and women's rights. Robinson promotes legislation that enables women to serve on juries and gives 18-year olds the right to vote.

DECEMBER 1990   Juli Inkster Wins Spalding Invitational Pro-Am Golf Tournament. Juli Inkster of Los Altos, California, becomes the first woman to win the only professional golf tournament in the world in which women and men compete head-to-head. Juli pars the 18th hole of the Spalding Invitational Pro-Am at Pebble Beach for a one-stroke victory over Professional Golf Association tour member Mark Brooks.

1991   Jo Ann Fairbanks Referees International Soccer Event. Jo Ann Fairbanks serves as a lineswoman in the women's qualifying rounds for the North and Central American and Caribbean regional soccer tournament in Haiti, becoming the first U.S. female referee at an international soccer event.

1991   Betsy Gotbaum Is New York City Parks Commissioner. New York City's first woman parks commissioner, Betsy Gotbaum, oversees 26,300 acres, approximately 13 percent of New York. It includes recreation centers, playgrounds, and shoreline.

1991   *Buffalo Woman Comes Singing* Details Spiritual Quest. Brooke Medicine Eagle publishes a book in 1991 entitled *Buffalo Woman Comes Singing*, detailing her spiritual quest.

1991   Bush Appoints Antonia Novello Surgeon General. Antonia Novello (1944–) is born in Fajardo, Puerto Rico. Novello and her brother are raised by their schoolteacher mother after their parents divorce. Novello receives her bachelor of science and masters degrees from the University of Puerto Rico. In 1970 Novello begins her internship and residency in pediatrics at the University of Michigan Medical Center in Ann Arbor. The Pediatrics Department at the University of Michigan awards Novello the Intern of the Year award in 1971. She serves as a fellow in pediatric nephrology at the University of Michigan's medical center in 1973 and 1974. Novello leaves Michigan and joins the staff of the Georgetown University Hospital in Washington, D.C., as a pediatric nephrology fellow in 1974. In 1978 and 1979 she serves as a project officer at the National Institute of Health's National Institute of Arthritis,

Metabolism and Digestive Diseases. Johns Hopkins University grants Novello a masters degree in public health in 1982. Novello works at various positions at the NIH until 1989, including deputy director of the National Institute of Child Health and Human Development. During this time, Novello also serves as a clinical professor of pediatrics at Georgetown University Hospital. In 1989 President George Bush appoints Novello to the post of surgeon general. She is the first woman and the first Hispanic to hold this position. One of Novello's particular concerns while surgeon general is restricting alcohol advertising aimed at children and teenagers.

JANUARY 1991   Judy Sweet Elected President of NCAA. The National Collegiate Athletic Association (NCAA) elects Judy Sweet as its first female president.

FEBRUARY 1991   Tonya Harding Lands Triple Axel Figure Skating Jump. Tonya Harding becomes the first American woman to land a triple axel in figure skating competition.

APRIL 1991   Bernadine Healy, First Woman Head of National Institutes of Health. President George Bush appoints Bernadine Healy, M.D. (1944–), a cardiovascular researcher, to direct the National Institutes of Health. Healy is the first woman to head the biomedical research facility, which employs 3,200 of America's most prominent medical researchers. Prior to assuming the directorship of NIH, Healy was Chief of the Cleveland Clinic Foundation's Research Institute.

MAY 1991   Barbara Hedges Named Athletic Director for University of Washington. Barbara Hedges is named athletic director for the University of Washington—the first female athletic director of a National Collegiate Athletic Association (NCAA) Division I school that includes football.

Bernadine Healy, M.D.

MAY 2, 1991 Boys Town Elects Sarah Williamson Mayor. Sarah Williamson, (1975–) is elected the first female mayor of Boys Town, a 75-year-old institution in Omaha, Nebraska. Founded in 1917, Boys Town serves 8,500 homeless, abused, neglected, and disabled children of all races and religions each year. Originally founded as a home for boys, Boys Town began admitting girls in 1979.

JUNE 8, 1991 Julie Krone Rides in Belmont Stakes. Julie Krone becomes the first female jockey to ride in the 123-year-old Belmont Stakes, the third leg of horse racing's Triple Crown.

JULY 15, 1991 Sandra Ortiz-Del Valle Officiates Men's Professional Basketball Game.

Sandra Ortiz-Del Valle officiates the United States Basketball League (USBL) game between the New Haven Skyhawks and the Philadelphia Spirit, making her the first woman to officiate a men's professional basketball game.

JULY 31, 1991 U.S. Senate Approves Combat Positions for Women Pilots. The U.S. Senate votes in favor of allowing women pilots in the military to serve on combat missions.

SEPTEMBER 6, 1991 Comic-strip Character, Blondie, Takes a Job Outside the Home. In the comic strip *Blondie,* the title character takes a job outside the home after more than 60 years of homemaking and child-rearing. During her first week on the job, she has to take her children to work with her because their sitter is ill, she experiences sexual harassment, suffers physical problems from hours of sitting at a computer terminal, and learns that her salary is only 60% of that earned by men in her office.

OCTOBER 1991 Susan Faludi Publishes *Backlash.* Susan Faludi, American author, publishes *Backlash, The Undeclared War on American Women,* documenting the backlash against the feminist movement. The book became a best-seller.

OCTOBER 2, 1991 American Jockey Julie Krone Ranks in Top Three in New York. Julie Krone (1964–) ranks third among jockeys in New York State. Krone's winnings total over $37 million, more than any other woman jockey's.

OCTOBER 8, 1991 Allegations of Sexual Harassment Force Reopening of U.S. Senate Hearings on Supreme Court Nominee. Pressured by women and the media, the U.S. Senate is forced to reopen hearings on the candidacy of Clarence Thomas, who is nominated to serve on the U.S. Supreme Court to replace Justice Thurgood Marshall, who

NOW "March for Women's Lives," 1992.

announces his retirement in June. Anita Hill, former Thomas staff member, gives graphic testimony of Thomas's sexual comments over the next few days. Thomas is confirmed by a vote of 52 to 48 in the Senate.

NOVEMBER 11, 1991 Memorial to U.S. Women Who Died in Vietnam Is Approved. A memorial to the more than 10,000 women who died, the majority of whom are nurses, during the U.S. involvement in Vietnam, clears the third and final federal commission authorized to review memorials. The model is designed by Santa Fe, New Mexico, artist Glenna Goodacre.

DECEMBER 1991 U.S. Women's Soccer Team Wins First World Championship. The U.S. women's soccer team defeats Norway to claim the first women's world soccer championship.

1992 Publication of *The Feminist Companion to Mythology.* Carolyne Larrington publishes a collection of essays by various women scholars (including herself) on the subject of world mythologies from a feminist perspective, called *The Feminist Companion to Mythology.* Larrington creates the book because, in her words, "Women need to know the myths which have determined both how we see ourselves and how society regards us."

1992 "Year of the Women" Political Elections Occur. In the United States, more women than ever before enter the political arena as office seekers. Between the Democratic and Republican parties, 18 women run for Senate, 154 for the House of Representatives, 6 for governor, and 3 for lieutenant governor. This record number of female political candidates contributes to 1992 being labeled the "Year of the Women."

1992   Hanna Suchocka Elected Prime Minister of Poland. Hanna Suchocka (1946–) is born in Pleszewa, Poland. She graduates from Poznan University in 1968 and becomes a jurist and member of the law faculty at the university later that year. Suchocka serves as advisor to the Solidarity Trade Union from 1980 through 1981. In 1992 she becomes Poland's first woman prime minister.

JANUARY 10–12, 1992   National Organization for Women Celebrates 25th Anniversary. The eighth president of the National Organization for Women (NOW), Patricia Ireland, presides over the organization's Silver Anniversary celebration in Washington, D.C. The concurrent Annual Conference features the Global Feminist Conference, with delegates from 45 countries. The final event is a performance by the Women's Philharmonic conducted by JoAn Falletta, the first-ever women's concert at the Kennedy Center for the Performing Arts.

APRIL 5, 1992   National Organization for Women Organizes March on Washington. An estimated 750,000 women, men, and children march in Washington, D.C. in support of the "pro-choice" position on abortion.

MAY 1992   Betty Boothroyd Becomes Speaker of Britain's House of Commons. The House of Commons chooses Betty Boothroyd by a vote of 372 to 238 as the first woman speaker in its 615-year history. At the time, there are 59 women among the 651 members of the House of Commons.

JULY 5, 1992   Muriel Siebert Is Veuve Clicquot Business Woman of the Year. Muriel Siebert, first woman to own a seat on the New York Stock Exchange, is Veuve Clicquot Business Woman of the Year. The international award was established by Madame Nicole-Barbe Clicquot, a widow who took over her husband's winery in 1805 and ran it

International political activist Irene Natividad.

successfully for over 60 years. Siebert is only the thirteenth woman to receive the award.

JULY 13, 1992   Global Forum of Women Held in Dublin, Ireland. Organized by Asian American political activist Irene Natividad, the four-day Global Forum of Women attracts women political leaders from 53 countries to Dublin, Ireland. Speakers include Mary Robinson, president of Ireland; Vigdís Finnbogadóttir, president of Iceland, Bella Abzug, former U.S. representative to Congress, and Jingqing Ciar, Tiananmen Square student leader.

DECEMBER 25, 1992   Christine Janin Celebrates Achievement on the Summit of Anoncagua. Christine Janin is the first woman to climb the highest peak on each of the world's continents. She completes this series of climbs on Christmas Day, 1992, when she reaches the summit of Aconcagua, a volcanic mountain in the Andes of western Argentina.

1993 Jockey Julie Krone, First Woman to Win Triple Crown. Julie Krone (1964–), an American jockey, wins the Belmont Stakes in New York, riding the horse Colonial Affair. In doing so, she becomes the first woman to win a Triple Crown horse racing event. (The Triple Crown consists of three prestigious horse races: the Kentucky Derby, the Belmont Stakes, and the Preakness.)

1993 Takako Doi Is Speaker of Lower House of the Diet, Japan's Parliament. Takako Doi is the first woman to serve as speaker of the lower house of the Diet, the parliament in Japan. She vows to take an activist role.

1993 Artist Rachel Whiteread Wins Turner Prize. British artist Rachel Whiteread becomes the first woman to win Britain's coveted Turner Prize, drawing international attention to her work, and to the work of women artists.

1993 *The Women's Table* Installed at Yale University. Chinese American artist and sculptor Maya Lin (1959–) designs and installs *The Women's Table* at Yale University. The sculpture and water table, dedicated to women at Yale through the institution's history, consists of a granite table with a series of numbers spiraling out from its center. The numbers represent the number of women students at Yale for each year since its founding in the early 1700s. Since most of the numbers are zeros, the work graphically illustrates women's historical exclusion from Yale.

1993 Toni Morrison Awarded Nobel Peace Prize in Literature. In recognition of her contributions as a novelist, African American author Toni Morrison (1931–) receives the Nobel Prize in Literature. Her writing, in novels such as The Bluest Eye (1969) and Sula

(1973), is honored for its realism, vision, and vivid dialogue and narration. Prior awards won by Morrison include the 1977 National Book Critics Circle Award for Song of Solomon (1977) and the 1988 Pulitzer Prize in fiction for Beloved (1987).

1993 Joycelyn Elders Appointed U.S. Surgeon General. Ignoring a rash of conservative criticism, President Clinton appoints African American Joycelyn Elders (1933–) surgeon general. Elders, respected for her work as a pediatric endocrinologist, becomes well known for her outspoken views on abortion, sex education, and drug legalization. Controversy surrounding her ideology eventually leads her to resign from the position.

JANUARY 1993 Hillary Rodham Clinton to Chair Committee on Health Care Reform. Within a week of his inauguration, U.S. President Clinton announces that his wife, Hillary Rodham Clinton (1947–), will take the unpaid position as chair of a high-level task force charged with producing a health-care reform plan.

JANUARY 20, 1993 Maya Angelou Reads Poem at Presidential Inauguration. African American poet Maya Angelou (1928–) reads her poem, "On the Pulse of Morning," at President Bill Clinton's inauguration. She publishes several volumes of poetry, including *Just Give Me a Cool Drink of Water 'fore I Diiie* (1971), and several autobiographical books, including *I Know Why the Caged Bird Sings* (1970).

MARCH 12, 1993 Janet Reno Sworn in as Attorney General of United States. Janet Reno (1938–) takes the oath to become the seventy-eighth attorney general of the United States, the first woman ever to achieve this position. Her work as a state prosecutor in Florida demonstrates her commitment to the public's welfare, most notably in her efforts for children's rights and prisoner rehabilitation programs. As attorney general, Reno is forthright in her politics, making changes in the nation's crime policy and responding openly to the press and the American people.

AUGUST 3, 1993 Ruth Bader Ginsburg Appointed to Supreme Court. Praised for her commitment to the details of the law, her incisive questioning of lawyers arguing before her, and her talent for winning over colleagues with dispassionate and well-reasoned arguments, Ruth Bader Ginsburg (1933–) is confirmed by the Senate for a position on the Supreme Court in a vote of 96 to 3. She becomes the 107th Supreme Court Justice, its second female jurist, and the first justice to be named by a Democratic president since Lyndon B. Johnson's administration.

OCTOBER 1993 Kim Campbell Is Prime Minister in Canada. Kim Campbell becomes Canada's first woman prime minister, succeeding Brian Mulroney. Earlier in 1993, Campbell becomes Canada's first woman defence minister.

1994 Faiza Mohammed al-Kharafi Heads University in Kuwait. Faiza Mohammed al-Kharafi, the first woman to head a university in the Arab world, says her priority is expansion of higher education in her country.

MAY 19, 1994 Death of Jacqueline Kennedy Onassis. The United States mourns the loss of its most beloved first lady, Jacqueline Kennedy Onassis (1929–1994), who dies in her home in New York City from a strain of cancer known as non-Hodgkin's lymphoma. Onassis is laid to rest at the side of her first husband, John Fitzgerald Kennedy, at Arlington National Cemetery in Washington, D.C.

JULY 1, 1994 Judith Rodin Becomes President of the University of Pennsylvania. Research psychologist Judith Rodin, Ph.D., becomes the first woman to run an Ivy League school when she takes over the presidency of the University of Pennsylvania in Philadelphia.

NOVEMBER 12, 1994 American Runner Wilma Rudolph Dies. Wilma Rudolph (1940–1994), winner of three gold medals at the 1960 Olympic Games, dies of a brain tumor. Rudolph retired from competition in 1964.

DECEMBER 1994 Joycelyn Elders Resigns from Surgeon General Post. Following a tumultuous year as surgeon general, Joycelyn Elders (1933–) resigns from the post. After suggesting in a speech that masturbation be taught in schools as an alternative to sexual relations, Elders is besieged with criticism from conservatives and moderates alike. President Clinton, under pressure from the press and a Republican Congress, urges Elders to resign from the position.

---

1 9 9 5 – 1 9 9 6

1995 Former British Prime Minister Margaret Thatcher Publishes Second Volume of Autobiography. Margaret Thatcher (1925–), Great Britain's first woman prime minister (1979–90), releases the second volume of her autobiography, *The Path to Power*, in which she delivers a particularly stinging rebuke to her successor and former protégé, Prime Minister John Major. The first volume, *The Downing Street Years*, is published in 1990, the year she resigns as prime minister.

1995 Sakhile Nyoni Is Botswana's First Woman Pilot. Captain Sakhile Nyoni flies dignitaries, politicians, and businesspeople on domestic flights in Botswana. Nyoni is the country's first woman pilot.

JANUARY 1995 Australian Mother Mary Helen McKillop Beatified by Roman Catholic Church. Mother Mary Helen McKillop (1842–1909) is beatified by the Roman Catholic Church and is expected to become Aus-

Cadet Rebecca E. Marier and General Gordon R. Sullivan at U.S. Military Academy at West Point commencement.

tralia's first saint. The cause for her beatification and canonization is formally introduced on February 1, 1973.

JUNE 1995 **Rebecca E. Marier, First Female Valedictorian at West Point.** Cadet Rebecca E. Marier (1973–) of Metairie, Louisiana, is the first woman to graduate at the top of her class at the U.S. Military Academy at West Point. Cadet Marier ranks highest in the class of 1995 overall in academics, military, and physical training. Marier receives the Richard Mason Award, presented to the cadet with highest class standing who has been accepted to medical school. Marier plans to attend Harvard Medical School in Cambridge, Massachusetts.

AUGUST 9, 1995 **American Bar Association Elects Roberta Cooper Ramo President.** Roberta Cooper Ramo, an attorney from Albuquerque, New Mexico, becomes the first woman to hold the office of president of the American Bar Association. Ramo assumes the leadership post in the 117-year-old ABA at its annual meeting in Chicago, Illinois. At a news conference, Ramo states that, as president of the ABA, she hopes to promote education of school children about the Constitution, to continue financial support for the Legal Services Corporation which provides legal advice and services for the poor, and to combat domestic violence.

SEPTEMBER 4–15, 1995 **International Women's Conference Draws Thousands to Beijing, China.** An estimated 30,000 women attend the United Nations' Fourth World Conference on Women: Action for Equality, Development, & Peace in Beijing. Among the attendants are delegates from the 185 Member States of the United Nations, representatives from 2,500 non-governmental organizations, and 3,500 media representatives. The conference, held every five years since 1975, provides a forum in which women can communicate about their rights, roles, and status in various societies, and individual, national, and world issues.

1996 **Japanese Shinto Has the Sun-Goddess Amaterasu.** In the present-day world, Japanese Shinto is the only religion with a large number of followers that has a female supreme deity—Amaterasu, the sun-goddess. She is considered the ruler of all gods and goddesses, guardian of the Japanese people, and symbol of Japanese cultural unity. Her emblem, the rising sun, appears on Japan's flag.

1996 **Pele, the Volcano Goddess.** When volcanoes threaten to erupt on Hawaii, people still make offerings to the fire-goddess Pele. Believed to reside in the volcanoes (especially her favorite, Kilauea), Pele is one of the few

Roberta Cooper Ramo

January 17, 1996   Texas Democrat Barbara Jordan, Former American Congresswoman, Dies. Barbara Jordan, a Democrat who represented Texas in the U.S. Congress, dies in Austin, Texas after a long battle with neuromuscular disease. Jordan left her archives to Texas Southern University.

JANUARY 20, 1996   German Leni Fischer Elected President of Council of Europe's Parliamentary Assembly. The Council of Europe's Parliamentary Assembly choose German Minister of Parliament (MP) Leni Fischer as its new President. Fischer is the first woman ever to hold the post.

MAY 22, 1996   Women Military Officers Press for More Combat Roles. Women military officers in the North Atlantic Treaty Organization (NATO) press for wider roles in combat for women. They point to the service of women during the Persian Gulf War (1990–91), when five of the nations participating—United States, United Kingdom, Canada, Norway, and Denmark—assigned women to duty in the combat zone. Although these female military personnel were not technically assigned to combat, they ferried fuel, food, and troops into combat areas, maintained equipment, and provided communications and intelligence information.

goddesses in the world who continues to be worshipped by her people.

AND LEGENDS

African

NANA BUKULU, CREATOR OF THE UNIVERSE TO THE FON PEOPLE OF DAHOMEY IN NORTHWEST AFRICA: Nana Bukulu was the creator of the universe, according to the Fon people of Dahomey in northwest Africa. Her daughter, Mawu, created the earth and the human beings who live on it. First, Mawu used clay mixed with water to make the people, but after awhile she began to run short of materials so she resorted to using the bodies of those who had died, which is why some people look like their ancestors.

OSHUN, GODDESS OF THE NIGER RIVER IN AFRICA: A goddess of the Niger River in Africa, Oshun was brought across the Atlantic to become one of the four supreme deities of the Macumba religion in Brazil. Shown wearing jewels, holding a mirror, and waving a fan, Oshun is the goddess of love, beauty, and flirtation.

Asia Minor

MEDEA, MAGICAL WIFE OF JASON: Medea was the daughter of King Aeëtes of Colchis in present-day Asia Minor. The Greek hero Jason came to Colchis with his Argonauts in search of the fabled Golden Fleece. They planned to steal it and carry it back to Iolcus in

Greece. The goddesses Hera and Athena decided to help Jason win the fleece by persuading Aphrodite, the goddess of love and beauty, to make Medea fall madly in love with Jason.

When Jason landed at Colchis, he boldly demanded that Aeëtes yield the fleece. The king replied that if Jason could yoke two fire-breathing bulls, plough the field of Ares, and sow it with magic serpents' teeth, he would gladly give him the fleece. Jason had no idea how to perform these stupendous feats. However, at this moment, Aphrodite's son, Eros, drove one of his magic arrows into Medea's heart, and she fell hopelessly in love with Jason.

Through the intermediary of her maid, Medea engineered a meeting with Jason. She offered to help him win the fleece if he promised to make her his wife and take her back to Greece with him. Jason swore he would be faithful, so she gave him a magic ointment that would protect him from the fire-breathing bulls. When Jason miraculously accomplished all of the tasks, Aeëtes reneged on his promise and plotted to kill Jason and burn his ship. Medea, having learned of her father's plan, led Jason and his Argonauts to the fleece. It was hanging from an oak tree which was guarded by an immense dragon. Medea drugged the monster, Jason stole the fleece, and they all fled to their waiting ship.

In order to escape their pursuers, they had to kill Medea's half-brother, Apsyrtes. The couple fled to the magic island of Medea's aunt, the sorceress Circe. Circe purified them of their blood guilt with a ritual, and Jason and Medea were married.

Medea used her magic to help the Argonauts pass all the supernatural dangers that lay between them and Iolcus. However, before arriving, they discovered the ruler of Iolcus, Pelias, had killed Jason's parents and brother in his absence. Medea dissuaded the Argonauts from launching into a hasty war. She used her magic to convince King Pelias that the goddess Artemis would restore his youth if he would allow his daughters to cut him into pieces and boil his limbs in a giant cauldron on the roof of the palace. When the Argonauts saw the blaze of the fire under the cauldron, they rushed into Iolcus.

Medea and Jason proceeded to Corinth, whose vacant throne belonged to Medea's family. The Corinthians accepted Jason as their king, and he reigned for ten happy years. Then, for a number of reasons, Jason decided to divorce Medea and marry a Theban princess. Medea pretended to acquiesce and sent Jason's intended a beautiful robe as a wedding present. However, once the princess donned the robe, it burst into flames and consumed everyone in the palace except Jason, who escaped by leaping out of a window.

Medea fled Corinth in a chariot drawn by winged serpents. Her children by Jason were stoned to death by the enraged Corinthians. However, the dramatist Euripides (who some say was bribed by the Corinthians, who are ashamed of this ending) claimed that Medea killed two of her own children and set fire to the palace, killing the rest.

Medea fled to Thebes, then Athens, where she married King Ageus. However, when she tried to poison his long-lost son, Theseus, Medea was forced to flee again. Finally she returned to Colchis. She never

died, but became an immortal and reigned in the Elysian Fields.

Egyptian

ATUM ARISES FROM EMPTINESS IN EGYPTIAN CREATION MYTH: In one ancient Egyptian creation myth, Atum ("the Complete One") was called "The Great He-She." Atum, later identified with the sun god Ra, had arisen from the primordial ocean of emptiness called Nun. Atum created the gods Shu (male) and Tefnut (female) by spitting. Shu and Tefnut mated, and Geb and Nut were born, locked in a close embrace. Their father, Shu, separated them, lifting Nut (female) above him to form the arch of the sky. Geb (male) lay beneath to form the earth. Nut is often found in Egyptian representations with her body painted blue and encrusted with stars, arching over the flat plain of her brother, the earth.

EGYPTIAN GODDESS CALLED "MOTHER OF THE GODS:" Neith, the oldest of Egypt's pre-dynastic goddesses, came from the ancient city of Sais in Egypt's western delta. She wore the red crown of Lower Egypt and carried a bow and crossed arrows. Her titles included "Great Goddess" and "Mother of the Gods."

In dynastic Egypt, Neith became a domestic goddess. Her arrows came to be represented by a symbol that scholars believe to be a shuttle, connecting her name to the Egyptian word "ntt," "to weave." In the seventeenth century B.C., the Pharaoh Psammetichus I, who originated from Sais, exalted her to the rank of a state deity. The historian Herodotus describes her new temples, obelisks, and sacred lakes at Sais.

In the Osiris myth, during the epic trial of Set and Horus, the tribunal of gods twice turned to her for guidance and twice ignored her advice.

FIRST DIVINE COUPLE, TEFNUT AND SHU: Tefnut and her twin brother Shu were the first divine couple. Their status as both brother and sister and as mates mirrored the ancient Egyptian royal custom of a brother-Pharaoh marrying his sister-Queen. Tefnut and Shu were said to share one soul. She was the personification of the life-giving dew and moisture. When Shu lifted their daughter over their sun to create the sky (Nut) and the earth (Geb), Shu's tears fell to the earth and created incense-bearing plants. Tefnut was depicted as a lioness, or with the head of a lion, wearing the solar disk. She was also considered a protectress of the god Osiris.

EGYPTIAN GODDESS NUT FORMED DAYTIME

SKY: Nut is represented in Egyptian illustrations as a woman's body arching over the earth. Her body is sometimes painted blue and bespangled with stars. She was born locked in an embrace with her brother/husband Geb (the earth). Her father, Shu, separated the two by pulling Nut away from the earth, forming the daytime sky. At night, Nut descended again to Geb, creating darkness. When storms occurred during the day, it was supposed that Nut had slipped down among the mountains that supported her.

Nut was a primordial mother goddess, her many children including the important Egyptian gods Osiris, Horus, Set, Isis, and Nephthys. Nut and Geb were also the parents of the sun and the moon. Sometimes Nut is represented as a great cow with the sun and the moon for eyes. The hieroglyph for her name represents both a waterpot and a womb. Every day the sun was born from her womb and sailed along the waters of her heavenly belly. The dawn was associated with the blood she shed in giving birth to the sun.

She became associated with another goddess, Khepri, a winged protectress of the dead, who were thought to be the myriad stars lodged in her nighttime body. Her figure is painted on the inner lid of coffins so that the soul of the deceased will rise to join the blessed dead in the sky.

ISIS: Isis, daughter of Geb (earth) and Nut (sky), was the sister and wife of the god Osiris. She helped her brother civilize humanity by instituting marriage and teaching women corn-grinding, flax-spinning, and weaving. Others say she herself taught Osiris the art of agriculture.

Isis was the Great Enchantress and mistress of magic arts and medicine. When Osiris was murdered and cast into the Nile in a sealed coffin by his scheming brother Set, Isis cut off half her hair and began an epic journey to find her husband's body. Everywhere she wandered, she asked the people if they had seen the coffin. She discovered it had floated to Byblos in Phoenicia, where a gigantic tamarisk tree had grown up around it. The king of Byblos had cut down the tree and used it as a pillar in his palace.

Isis travelled to Byblos, where the king's wife had just given birth to a son. The queen was attracted to Isis and made her the child's nursemaid. Isis tried to bestow the child with immortality, but was surprised by the queen as she was holding the baby in a sacred fire. The queen's cries broke the magic spell.

Isis now revealed her identity to the royal couple. The king gave her the pillar, which she cut away to reveal her husband's coffin. Isis grieved violently as she sailed back to Egypt. She used her magical powers to conceive a son by her dead husband. When she arrived, she hid in the Delta marshes, but Set discovered the coffin while hunting by moonlight and had his dead brother's body torn into 14 parts and scattered throughout the kingdom.

Isis again began to search for her husband's body. After she had found all the pieces, she remodeled her husband's body and anointed it with precious oils. Egyptians believed that the fate of the body after death was intimately related to the fate of the soul after death. By restoring Osiris' body, Isis restored him to eternal life as king of the dead.

This part of the myth represents the foundation of the Egyptian rite of embalmment.

Set was furious at Isis' defiance and cast her into prison. She escaped, returned to her hiding place in the swamps, and gave birth to Horus, Osiris' heir. Without any means of support, she had to beg to support herself and her son. While she was gone, Set stole into the marshes in the form of a poisonous snake and bit Horus. Isis returned to find her child half-dead. The embodiment of innocence was dying from the poison of evil.

Thoth, the boatman of the sun-god Ra, heard Isis' lamentations. He stopped Ra's boat and called on the sun god's power to cast a spell: until the poison left Horus' body, no rain would fall, no food would grow, no temples would be opened and eternal darkness would reign. Ra's power expelled the poison. Thoth charged the human marsh-dwellers and fisherman to care for the baby Horus. Ra and Osiris would watch over him and Isis would spread his cult. Thus, Horus became the son of the sun—one of the Pharaoh's titles. Horus was the archetype for the Pharonic rulers of ancient Egypt. The sun god charged human beings to love, respect, and protect the Pharaoh.

The cunning Isis wanted to obtain some of the sun's power for her child. From Horus' saliva she fashioned a deadly viper and laid it in the path of Ra. When he was bitten, he was unable to cure himself because he had not created this being. Isis offered to cure him with her magic, but only if he gave her his secret name, which she could transmit to her son. This secret name communicated Ra's power to Horus (and his earthly counterpart, the Pharaoh). This trinity—divine father, mother, and son—is an archetype alive today in the Christian trinity (Father, Son, and Holy Ghost).

Horus grew up in the care of human beings but was often visited by his magical mother. She instructed him in warfare and imbued him with the desire to wreak vengeance on Set when he came of age. When he reached manhood, Horus was joined by other deities in an epic war on Set. When this war dragged on and on, Set invoked a tribunal of the gods which lasted more than 80 years. Set claimed he should rule because he was older and stronger. Horus insisted he was the rightful heir of Osiris and had justice on his side.

The trial dragged on and on, involving the entire Egyptian pantheon. Finally, Isis bribed her way into the courtroom. With her sorcery, she changed herself into a beautiful maiden and attracted the attention of Set. In this disguise, she regaled the amorous Set with her sad story: a greedy uncle was trying to deprive her fatherless son of all his cattle. She tricked Set into saying this was unjust, then changed herself into a bird and flew above the court crying out that he had condemned himself.

Still, the gods decreed that Set and Horus should face each other in mortal combat. They changed themselves into hippopotamuses for the battle. Isis, knowing this was a form advantageous to Set, cast a magical harpoon into the water trying to catch him. First she accidentally injured Horus. Then she snagged Set, but released him when he appealed to her in the name of their common parents, Geb and Nut. Horus, enraged at his mother's weakness, sprang out of the water and cut off his mother's head. Thoth later replaced it with the head of a cow. This exemplifies Isis' identification with the ancient mother goddess, Hathor, who was always represented as a divine cow.

Isis was revered as a faithful wife, mourner, divine protector of children, and magical healer. She and her sister Nephthys are often represented as birds watching over either end of coffins or the lids of funerary jars. She is also represented as a woman with a throne on her head. In statues, she is often shown suckling the infant Horus.

HATHOR DEPICTED AS NURTURING COW:
Hathor, the daughter of Ra and Nut, is one of

the few Egyptian gods always represented full-face instead of profile. She was thought of as a divine, life-giving cow. Normally she was the goddess of music, dancing, joy, and motherhood. She presided over women's toilet and was considered a kind of midwife and protectress of pregnant women. However, she was also known as "The Eye of Ra," which Ra sent to subdue rebellious subjects. In this role, she assumed the form of a bloodthirsty lioness-deity, Sekhmet. Having tasted blood, she could not be appeased. In order to pacify his destructive daughter, Ra covered the fields with a red-colored beer. Hathor, thinking it was blood, lapped it up, became drunk and became her gentle self again.

The identities of Isis and Hathor came to be merged. Hathor came to be regarded as the divine nurse of Horus (and by extension, the Pharaoh). She is often pictured as an immense, starry cow suckling an infant king. As the cult of Osiris grew, she also began to be pictured as a divine cow suckling the dead king or other dead souls. Dead men were called "Osiris" while dead women were called "Hathor."

As the goddess of music and dancing, Hathor is also associated with the musical instrument called the sistrum.

SESHAT, THE CELESTIAL LIBRARIAN: Seshat, called "Lady of Books," was the celestial librarian and patroness of arithmetic, architecture, and history. Seshat was often portrayed with the Pharaoh, measuring the dimensions of royal temples and tombs when they were being planned. She wrote down the king's name on the leaves of the Tree of Life and marked the years of his life on a notched palm branch. Seshat appears as a woman wearing a flower or star, dressed in a leopard skin and holding a pen and scribe's ink palette.

VULTURE-GODDESS NEKHEBET: Nekhebet was a vulture-goddess whose city, Nekheb, stood across the Nile from Nekhen (Hierakonpolis), and whose patron deity was the fal-con-god Horus. The two cities were the prehistoric capital of Upper Egypt. After the country became unified, Nekhebet remained attached to the south as a protective deity.

As time went on, she became absorbed into the solar mythology of Lower Egypt, becoming known as the daughter and right eye of Ra. She was the wife of Hapi (a name for the Nile), who opened the flood gates allowing the river to flow out of the divine ocean. She is often represented as a woman or a white vulture wearing the white crown of Upper Egypt. Nekhebet is also depicted spreading her wings above the Pharaoh and holding his royal whisk in her talons.

COBRA-GODDESS UDJAT: Udjat, also known as Edjo or Buto, was an Egyptian cobra-goddess from the Delta marshes. The *uraeus* or cobra seen on the headdress of the Pharaoh is a representation of Udjat. She is represented with her hood open, ready to spit poison on the Pharaoh's enemies or to burn them with her fiery gaze.

In the solar mythologies, the *uraeus* was originally the right eye of the sun god Ra. He placed it in a position of honor on his brow. Therefore, Udjat is also associated with the burning heat of the sun. She was represented as a woman wearing either the *uraeus* or the red crown of Lower Egypt. This emblem linked her with the enchantress Isis, and her temple was known for its famous oracle.

Babylonian

BABYLONIAN GODDESS TIAMAT CREATED THE UNIVERSE FROM HER OWN BODY: The Babylonian goddess Tiamat, Goddess-Mother (Tia-Mat), created the universe from her own formless body, the same formless body that later became Tehom, The Deep, in the Hebrew myths of creation found in Genesis 1:2 of the Hebrew Bible. Later Babylonian myths show Tiamat being divided by her son Marduk after a long and complicated battle at the end of which Marduk kills Tiamat and separates her into two parts, the upper and lower waters. The Greek word for Tiamat, Diameter (Dia-Mater, or Meter), comes from this understanding of Tiamat divided into two halves, as a diameter bisects a whole circle.

English

ROOT OF THE ENGLISH WORD "MENSTRUA-TION:" The English word "menstruation" comes from Mens, the name of the Roman goddess of the "right moment."

Finnish

CREATION MYTH FROM FINLAND: A Finnish creation myth tells of Luonnotar, "daughter of nature," floating in the heavens for eons before finally becoming lonely and throwing herself down into the sea. She then floated there for another seven centuries until one day a duck appeared, looking for a place to build her nest. The duck saw Luonnotar's knee break through the water, built her nest on it, and laid her eggs there. After three days, Luonnotar's leg cramped and twitched, the eggs fell into the sea, and the universe was created: The lower part of the eggshells became the earth; the upper part, the sky; the yolks became the sun; and the whites, the moon. Luonnotar then shaped the earth into peninsulas and islands with her hands.

Germanic

HELL, THE CHRISTIAN PLACE OF ETERNAL PUNISHMENT: The word for the Christian place of eternal punishment, Hell, came from the name of the Germanic goddess, Hel, Queen of the Underworld. Hel's place, however, was not a place of punishment but rather a sacred cave (or oven) of fiery death and rebirth.

Cronus and Rhea

Greek

GAEA, OR MOTHER EARTH: In the Olympic creation myth, Gaea, or Mother Earth, emerged from Chaos and bore her son, the sky-god Uranus. He showered her with rain and she bore flowers, trees, birds, and animals. As the rain collected in the low places, lakes and seas came into being.

Earth's first children were hundred-handed giants and one-eyed Cyclopes. When the Cyclopes rebelled against Uranus, he flung them into the Underworld. Thereupon, Mother Earth persuaded the giants, the Titans, to attack Uranus. When drops of his blood fell upon Mother Earth, she bore the Three Erinnyes or Furies, who avenge crimes of patricide and perjury.

ATHENA: The goddess Athena (Roman: Minerva) invented the flute, the trumpet, the earthenware pot, the plough, the rake, the ox-yoke, the horse-bridle, the chariot, and the ship. She taught mortals about numbers, cooking, weaving, and spinning. Although she was a war-like goddess, she preferred settling dis-

Athena (Minerva)

3000 B.C. The goddess-worshipping Libyans may have carried Athena's cult there from Lower Egypt. Cretan culture spread her worship to prehistoric Greece.

When the Hellenic peoples immigrated into Greece, they fused the gods and goddesses of the indigenous peoples with their own Olympic pantheon. It was said that Zeus tried to seduce his mother's sister, the Titaness Metis, who presided over wisdom and knowledge. Although Metis tried to escape by turning herself into many different forms, each time Zeus changed his form to match and finally caught her. Mother Earth declared that Metis' child would be a girl, but if she bore another, it would be a son who would depose Zeus, even as Zeus had deposed Cronos and Cronos had deposed *his* father, Uranus. To protect himself, the wily Zeus swallowed the pregnant Metis whole. However, one day Zeus' head began to ache as if it would burst open. He summoned the divine smith Hephaestus. Hephaestus broke a hole in Zeus' skull and Athena sprang forth, fully armed, shouting her war cry.

Athena was renowned as the protectress of Athens, but before the advent of the Hellenic peoples, she was also worshipped at sacred temples in Argos, Sparta, Troy, Smyrna, Epidaurus, Troezen, and Pheneus. The Athenians worshipped a monumental statue of Athena that was housed in the Acropolis, whose shattered ruins are visible today. Her cult was maintained by priestesses, and the city's most important festivals involved processions and sacrifices to Athena.

Despite Athena's central position in the life of Athens, in classical times (700–400 B.C.), Athenian women were among the most secluded and constrained in the entire ancient world. They had many fewer freedoms and legal rights than their contemporaries across the Mediterranean in Egypt. For example, although Athena was the goddess of crafts, and despite the fact that women manufactured

putes. She was merciful: whenever the Greek judges' votes in a criminal trial were tied, Athena's vote was cast to liberate the accused.

The Pelasgian peoples of ancient Greece traced the goddess Athena's origins to Lake Tritonis in Libya, where she was called Neith. She was raised by three goat-skin-clad Libyan nymphs. Athena's costume, the goatskin aegis, resembled the costume of Libyan virgins.

Archaeologists say that pottery remains show a Libyan immigration into Crete around

The Fates

beautiful earthenware in nearby Crete, Athenian women were forbidden this occupation.

THE FATES: The ancient Greeks believed that the white-clad Fates—Clotho, Lachesis, and Atropos—controlled the length of both mortals' and immortals' lives. Clotho spun each life as a linen thread, Lachesis measured it on her rod, and Atropos cut the thread with her shears. While some thought Zeus could intervene with the Fates' spinning to change the fate of individuals, others insisted that Zeus himself was subject to their power. Their white robes indicated that they were manifes-

tations of the Moon goddess, and linen thread was sacred to the Egyptian Moon goddess, Isis.

APHRODITE: Legend says that Aphrodite (Roman: Venus) was born from sea foam and rode to shore on a scallop shell. Wherever she stepped, grass and flowers sprang from the soil. When she arrived in Paphos on Cyprus, the four Seasons adorned her. The three Fates assigned her only one duty, to make love. She wore a magic girdle (a kind of decorative belt) that made everyone fall in love with its wearer. When she travelled through the air, she was accompanied by doves and sparrows.

Zeus made Aphrodite marry the lame and ugly Hephaestus, god of smiths. However, her lover was Ares, the drunken, quarrelsome god of war, who fathered her children Phobus, Deimus, and Harmonia. When Hephaestus heard about their liaison, he hammered out a gossamer-fine bronze hunting net that he attached to Aphrodite's bed and told her he was going to be out of town for a few days. Aphrodite wasted no time calling Ares to her bed. They became entangled in the bed, and Hephaestus summoned all the gods to witness his dishonor and demanded that Zeus return the marriage gifts. Zeus refused, and in the end, Ares promised to pay the equivalent of the marriage gifts if Hephaestus let him go. Aphrodite promptly returned to Paphos, where she bathed in the sea, magically renewing her virginity.

Aphrodite later slept with Hermes and bore him Hermaphroditus, who was both male and female. To Poseidon she bore Rhodus and Herophilus. To Dionysus, Aphrodite bore Priapus, whom Hera made monstrously ugly. Zeus, in an attempt to protect himself from Aphrodite's irresistible magic girdle, made her fall in love with a mortal, King Anchises, to whom she bore the hero Aeneas.

Aphrodite fell in love with a mortal one more time, the handsome Adonis. Ares, growing jealous, turned himself into a boar and gored Adonis to death when he was out hunting. Horrified that her lover would now be the property of the Persephone, Queen of Hades, Aphrodite appealed to Zeus to allow Adonis to spend at least half of the year with her. While Adonis was in Tartarus, the world was engulfed in winter. When he returned to Aphrodite's side, spring returned. Adonis is the Greek name for the Syrian vegetation god Tammus.

At Paphos every spring, Aphrodite's priestesses would bathe in the sea and miraculously have their virginity renewed. Aphrodite's principal place of worship was at Paphos in Cyprus. Christians later converted her Cyprian temple into a shrine for the Virgin Mary, but people continued, even to modern times, to hail Mary in this shrine as "All-holy Aphrodite." Aphrodite was worshipped throughout the ancient world under many titles, including Melaenis ("the black one"), Scotia ("dark one"), Androphonos ("man slayer"), and Epitymbria ("of the tombs"). She was worshipped in Syria and Palestine as Ishtar, or Ashtaroth.

HERA, WIFE OF ZEUS: Hera was originally the pre-Hellenic Great Goddess. She was known as the Great Mother Goddess of the early Aegeans, and mother to all the Greek gods and goddesses. Hera was demoted by the patriarchal Greeks to a subordinate and shrewish wife. Her forced marriage to her faithless brother, Zeus, however, was full of jealousy and conflict, symbolizing the strife between earlier matriarchal cults and the patriarchal ones that overthrew them. Samos and Argos were her most sacred cities in ancient Greece, but the Arcadians also claimed her. The Hellenic peoples adopted Hera into their pantheon by making her Zeus' sister; she was forced to marry Zeus after he ravished her. At their wedding, Mother Earth gave Hera the tree of golden apples that was guarded by the Hesperides on Mount Atlas. She bore Zeus the deities Ares (god of war),

Hephaestus (god of smiths), and Hebe (who became the cup-bearer to the gods).

Zeus and Hera were always fighting and always on opposite sides of human quarrels. When he was really angry at her, Zeus did not hesitate to hurl a thunderbolt at her or even flog her. He was notoriously unfaithful to her, seducing any nymph or human female who took his fancy. Jealous Hera would subject these unfortunates to all kinds of trials and tribulations.

Hera once led a conspiracy in which the other gods helped her tie Zeus up. When he broke free, he hung her up in the sky with a golden bracelet on each wrist and an anvil on each ankle.

RHEA, MOTHER OF ZEUS: In Greek myth, the goddess Rhea, another name for the ancient Great Mother goddess also known as Hera, married her brother, the Titan Cronus, and gave birth to most of the gods and goddesses of the Olympic pantheon. Since Cronus was warned that one of his own sons would eventually depose him, he devoured each of his wife Rhea's children as she gave birth. In this way she lost the goddesses Hestia, Demeter, Hera, and the gods Hades and Poseidon. When Rhea bore Zeus, she gave him to Mother Earth to hide in the caves of the Mediterranean island of Crete. Rhea wrapped a stone in swaddling clothes and gave it to Cronus to swallow. When Zeus was old enough, Rhea made him cupbearer to Cronus. She gave her husband a honeyed drink which forced him to vomit up all her children he had swallowed.

After the defeat of Cronus by her children, Rhea forbade Zeus to marry because of his lustful nature. Enraged, he threatened to rape her. She turned herself into a menacing serpent, to no avail. Zeus turned himself into a male serpent and violated her.

Some scholars believe that the many myths of goddess rape surrounding Zeus and other male gods symbolize the victory of patriarchal religions and social systems over ancient matrilocal or matrilineal traditions. It is thought that as power and influence passed into the hands of male kings, the power and prestige of goddesses was also attenuated in myth and ritual.

ARTEMIS, MAIDEN OF THE SILVER BOW: Artemis and Apollo were born of the union of Zeus and Leto, a daughter of the Titans. Artemis was a virginal hunting goddess and was goddess of the moon. She carried a silver bow and arrows. Artemis absorbed many of the attributes of the Roman goddess, Diana, until eventually the two became synonymous. Apollo, her brother, was god of the sun. She, like her brother, had the power both to send plagues and to heal. Because her mother bore her with hardly any pain, Artemis was considered the patron goddess of childbirth and protectress of children. Her chariot was pulled by four sacred deer. She frequented mountains and lived for the hunt.

The mortal hunter Actaeon stumbled upon Artemis and her attendants as she was bathing in a stream. He dared to stay and watch. When she discovered his presence, she changed him into a stag, and his own hounds chased him until he fell, at which time they tore him to pieces.

The bloody rites of the prehistoric Taurian Artemis included human sacrifice. The Spartans worshipped Artemis with ritual floggings. Artemis was worshipped each year in Attica at the city of Brauron. It is known that the ritual included races and the participation of two young girls dressed as she-bears. This ritual, called the Arkteia (playing the she-bear), recalled Artemis' anger at Callisto, who had been seduced by Zeus. Artemis (or some say Hera) changed Callisto into a bear, and Artemis would have hunted her to death, but Zeus caught her up into heaven and set her image in the stars as a constellation. In her ancient incarnation as "Lady of the Wild Things," Artemis also received annual sacri-

fices of wild animals, birds, and plants that were the totems of various Greek clans. The olive was her sacred tree.

HESTIA, GODDESS OF THE HEARTH: Mild and honorable Hestia (whose name means "hearth"), a daughter of Rhea, refused marriage to both Poseidon and Apollo, swearing by Zeus's head to remain a maiden forever. For having avoided another war among the gods, Zeus gave Hestia the first victim at every public sacrifice. She was the charitable goddess of the hearth in private homes. She protected suppliants and invented the art of building houses.

Since the hearth was both the center of domestic activity and a sacred altar in every home, Hestia represented personal security, happiness, and the sacred duty of hospitality. Before every meal, small offerings were made at the family hearth. In Athens, a new baby was carried around the hearth a few times shortly after birth in a ritual called *amphidromia*. A new bride was led from her father's hearth to the hearth in her new home.

Many Greek states maintained a public hearth at a kind of town hall as a symbol of civic unity. Foreign ambassadors were invited to dine at the city's public *hestia*. At Athens this temple, called a *prytaneion*, included a statue of Hestia.

DEMETER, HARVEST GODDESS: The gentle goddess Demeter ("barley-mother"), goddess of grain and the harvest, had no husband. Despite that, her priestesses initiated brides and bridegrooms in sexual intercourse. In one of his many extramarital liaisons, Zeus fathered the beautiful Core by Demeter.

Once, a mortal dared to invade Demeter's sacred grove and cut the holy trees. When the goddess, appearing in disguise, ordered him to stop, he threatened her with his axe. She revealed herself and condemned him to suffer the pangs of a terrible hunger, no matter how much he might eat.

Hades, god of the underworld, fell in love with Demeter's daughter Core. With the tacit connivance of Zeus, he carried her off one day to his domain, called Tartarus.

Demeter, distraught with grief, wandered all over the world searching for Core. After ten days, she arrived in disguise at the Mycenaen city of Eleusis where the Queen invited her to become wet-nurse to her infant son. Demeter decided to make the child an immortal. She held him over a fire to purge away his mortality but was discovered by the Queen, who cried out, breaking the spell. (This part of the myth strongly recalls the search of the Egyptian goddess Isis for her lost husband Osiris.)

Now that Demeter's identity was revealed, one of the Queen's sons reported having recently seen a chariot drawn by black horses dash down into an enormous cavern that had suddenly opened in the earth. The chariot-driver was holding a shrieking girl.

Demeter was so angry that she determined not to return to Olympus, but wandered the earth, forbidding the trees to carry fruit or plants to grow. Although Zeus tried to reconcile with her, she swore that the earth would remain barren until Core had been returned to her.

Zeus decreed that Core could return to her mother, if in all this time she had not eaten anything in Tartarus. Unfortunately, Core had eaten seven tiny pomegranate seeds. Demeter still insisted that nothing would be allowed to grow while Core dwelt in the underworld. Finally, a compromise was reached. Core would spend three months each year as Persephone (Roman: Proserpina), Queen of Tartarus. The remaining nine months she would spend with Demeter. Each winter, when Core descended to Tartarus, the trees lost their leaves, the cold winds blew, and the earth lost its fertility. In spring, when she reascended to her mother's side, Demeter awakened everything to life again.

Hecate

To reward the royal family of Eleusis, Demeter taught their son the art of agriculture and gave him seed corn and planting tools. She instructed them in her sacred rituals, the ecstatic Eleusinian Mysteries.

HECATE, GODDESS OF WITCHES: Hecate lived in Tartarus and was the close companion of Queen Persephone. Originally a Great Goddess, Hecate had the bodies and heads of three animals: lion, dog, and mare. These were pre-historic totemic symbols related to the calendar and seasons. Zeus respected Hecate so much that he let her keep her ancient power of bestowing or withholding from mortals any gift that they desired.

Although Hecate had been part of the Triple-Goddess of the ancient Greek peoples, the Hellenes emphasized her destructive powers and transferred her creative ones to other deities. During the Middle Ages (900–1300 A.D.), Hecate was reduced by Hellenistic peoples to a goddess of black magic rituals.

CASSIOPEIA, MOTHER OF ANDROMEDA:

Cassiopeia had boasted that both she and her daughter, Andromeda, were more beautiful than the Nereids (sea nymphs). The Nereids complained to Poseidon, god of the sea, who sent both a plague and a terrible sea monster to terrorize them. Andromeda's father, King Cephus, was told by an oracle that the only way to appease Poseidon was to chain his daughter, clad only in her jewels, to a rock and sacrifice her to the sea monster. This Cephus reluctantly did.

Perseus, returning from his encounter with the Gorgon Medusa, saw Andromeda's desperate situation. Alighting near her parents, he won their agreement that, if he could save her, she would be his wife. Perseus beheaded the monster with the magic sickle, but when he came to claim his bride, a previous suitor summoned by Cassiopeia brought an army to oppose Perseus. Perseus was outnumbered and had to pull Medusa's head from its sack and turn 200 of his attackers into stone.

As a punishment to the faithless Cassiopeia, Zeus tied her in a basket and set the image in the stars in such a way that sometimes the basket was upside down. He also placed Andromeda's image in the stars, as a reward for her devotion to Perseus.

PENELOPE, WIFE OF ODYSSEUS, BECAME MODEL OF THE CHASTE NOBLEWOMAN:

Penelope was the daughter of the sea-nymph Periboea and Icarius, the younger brother of Tyndareus, King of Sparta. When she was born, she was called Arnaea, and her father ordered her flung into the sea. However, a flock of purple-striped ducks buoyed her up, fed her, and brought her safely to shore. Her

Penelope

father and mother relented and changed her name to "Penelope," which means "duck."

Odysseus (known as Ulysses to the Romans), ruler of the Greek City of Ithaca, begged King Tyndareus to help him win his niece, Penelope, for his wife. Tyndareus rigged a foot race of suitors for Penelope's hand, and Odysseus won. Her father begged Odysseus to remain in Sparta with his bride (an example of the matrilocal tradition of the early Greek peoples), but Odysseus refused. As Odysseus tried to drive away with his bride, Icarius followed them and begged Penelope to stay. Impatiently, Odysseus told her to either step down from the chariot and stay with her father, or come with him. Penelope's only response was to draw down her veil. Her father admitted defeat and raised an image to the goddess of modesty on that spot.

Odysseus was called to help Menelaus fight the Trojan War. When it was over, due to Zeus's curse, he spent ten years being blown around the Mediterranean by tempests, unable to return to Ithaca. Most people assumed he was dead.

Penelope was besieged by 112 suitors whom she was obliged to house and feed. They demanded that she remarry. Her husband would be the next ruler of Ithaca. These wicked suitors had agreed among themselves to kill Odysseus' son, Telemachus, when he returned from Sparta.

Penelope had declared at first that Odysseus must still be alive because his homecoming had been foretold by an oracle. As time passed, she gave the excuse that she had to finish weaving the shroud of her elderly father-in-law before she made her decision. She made this project last three years by painstakingly unraveling at night most of what she had woven during the day.

Odysseus finally returned to Ithaca, magically disguised as a beggar by the goddess Athena. He visited the hall where the suitors were feasting to size them up. When the suitors treated him rudely, Penelope was scandalized and sent for this beggar to see if he had any news of her husband. Odysseus managed to maintain his disguise and told her he had recently encountered Odysseus, who would soon return.

The next day, Penelope announced that she would accept any suitor who could accomplish one of Odysseus' famous feats of skill: namely, string his mighty bow and shoot an arrow through 12 axe-rings at a single shot. None of the suitors could even bend the bow to string it. When all had given up, Odysseus seized the bow and strung it easily. He swiftly shot the arrow through the 12 axe-rings. To add to the suitors' amazement, he threw off his beggar disguise and proceeded to slaughter the lightly-armed suitors.

When the massacre was finished, Odysseus asked his old nurse if any of the women of the house had slept with the suitors. She told him that 12 of the women had lost

their honor. Odysseus made those 12 clean the hall of all the suitors' blood, and then hanged them outside the palace, all in a row.

Although Penelope was now reunited with her long-lost husband, her tribulations were not over. In order to make peace with the suitors' enraged families, Odysseus accepted a tribunal's decree of ten years of banishment. At first, their son Telemachus ruled over Ithaca. Then, an oracle predicted Odysseus would be killed by his own son. In despair over this horrible prophecy, Telemachus abdicated and left Ithaca. Penelope then ruled the kingdom until Odysseus returned.

However, the prophecy eventually came true. Telegonus, Odysseus' son by the sorceress Circe, came in search of his father. He was blown off course by a tempest and didn't realize he had arrived at Ithaca. Telegonus killed Odysseus during a raid on the town, learning too late of his father's identity.

After a year of banishment, Telegonus returned to Ithaca and married Penelope. Telemachus married Circe, uniting both branches of the family.

CIRCE INFLUENCED ODYSSEUS: The goddess Circe ruled over the Island of Dawn. She was the sister of the Colchian King Aeëtes and Medea's aunt. She would invite any men who wandered onto her island by mistake to a sumptuous feast, at which she would drug them and then turn them into wild beasts. She turned the Greek hero Odysseus' shipmates into a herd of swine. When Odysseus heard of it, he set off with his sword to fight her. Before he got there, he was intercepted by Hermes, who offered him a charm against Circe's magic. Her drugs and charms did not work on Odysseus, and he threatened to kill her. She pleaded for mercy, swore an oath not to harm him ever again, and changed his crew back into human beings. Thereafter she invited him to share her bed. She sent him on a trip to Tartarus to consult the seer Teiresias for advice on how to overcome the curse that had kept Odysseus wandering for ten years, unable to return home. She also warned him against the hypnotic song of the Sirens and many other perils. Circe's son by Odysseus, Telegonus, would accidentally kill his father and thereafter marry Odysseus' wife, Penelope. Circe herself would marry Odysseus' son, Telemachus.

CASSANDRA FORETOLD THE SECRET OF THE TROJAN HORSE:

Cassandra, daughter of King Priam and Queen Hecuba of Troy, fell asleep one day in the temple of Apollo. The god appeared to her and promised to teach her the art of prophecy if she would sleep with him. Cassandra agreed, but after accepting his gift, refused her part of the bargain. Apollo begged her to give him one kiss. When she did, he spat in her mouth, which ensured that no one would ever believe what she prophesied.

When Troy was at the height of its influence, wealth, and power, Cassandra predicted that its end was near. Priam had her locked up in a pyramidal building and ordered her keeper to inform him of all her prophetic utterances.

When the Trojans wheeled the Greeks' Trojan Horse into their city, Cassandra predicted that it contained armed men. But a so-called deserter from the Greek camp swore to King Priam that it had been left to placate the goddess Athena, and that it had been prophesied that, if the Trojans took the horse into their city, they would be invincible. No one believed Cassandra.

After the fall of Troy, the Greek leader Agamemnon claimed Cassandra as his prize and took her home with him. His adulterous wife, Clytaemnestra, took pains to be well informed before the couple arrived. When Clytaemnestra welcomed them with open arms, Cassandra remained outside the palace in a trance, claiming that she could see blood running all over the palace. Agamemnon didn't believe her. After dispatching her hus-

band in his bath, Clytaemnestra beheaded Cassandra with one swing of her axe.

THE MANY MYTHS OF LEDA AND ZEUS:

The myth of Leda and Zeus appears in many forms. In one, Zeus fell in love with the moon-goddess Nemesis and tried to ravish her. Nemesis turned herself into a fish and fled; he pursued her as a beaver. She leaped ashore and turned herself into a wild animal; he turned himself into a bigger, faster animal. This continued through many changes until at last she took the form of a wild goose. Zeus became a swan and captured her. Nemesis flew to Sparta to lay her divinely impregnated egg. Queen Leda found the hyacinth-colored egg lying in a marsh. When it hatched, there was a beautiful girl inside, whom she called "Helen" ("moon-goddess"). Others say the divine egg fell to earth from the moon.

Another version of the myth says that Zeus, in the form of a swan, raped Queen Leda herself, who bore the magic egg. When it hatched, both Helen and her son Polydeuces were inside. Leda's other children, Clytaemnestra and Castor, were King Tyndareus' children.

THE WEDDING OF THETIS:

Thetis (also called Tethys) was one of the original Titans created by Mother Earth. Her name was derived from the Greek word *ithenai*, "to order." She was a manifestation of the moon-goddess as ruler of the sea.

When Hera bore the sickly Hephaestus, she dropped him from Olympus into the sea, where Thetis sheltered him in an underwater grotto. He rewarded her kindness by setting up his smithy and making her beautiful jewelry and useful objects. When Hera saw Thetis wearing a beautiful brooch, she pestered her to find out where she had obtained it. When Thetis hesitatingly admitted that it was the work of Hephaestus, Hera swiftly took him back to Olympus.

It was prophesied that any son born to Thetis would be greater than his father. So, although both Zeus and Poseidon desired her, they decided it would be safer to marry her to a mortal. Hera chose the chaste hero Peleus to be Thetis' husband. All the Olympians were invited to attend their wedding.

It was at Thetis' wedding that the goddess Eris, who had not been invited, wickedly threw down the golden apple engraved with the inscription "To the Fairest!" which became the subject of such jealous dispute between Hera, Aphrodite, and Athena.

Thetis had seven sons by Peleus, who became ruler of Iolcus. Since she wanted her sons to be immortal, she set them in the fire to burn away their mortal parts, then covered them with divine ambrosia to bring them back to immortal life. In this way she managed to send her first six sons to Olympus. However, Peleus snatched her seventh son from her before she could complete the treatment. She missed covering his right ankle-bone, leaving him invulnerable except for this one spot. Since this son had never placed his lips to her breast, she called him "Achilles" ("no lips"). Enraged by Peleus' interference, Thetis returned to the sea. In another version, Thetis made her son almost immortal by dipping him into the River Styx while holding him by the right heel, which was therefore left vulnerable.

Achilles became one of the Greeks' greatest heroes during the Trojan War. It was prophesied that they could not win the war without him. Thetis also made many prophecies about this conflict which came true. For example, she predicted that the first to land at Troy would be the first to die. Thetis even brought Achilles a suit of armor forged by Hephaestus to protect him. Even so, Achilles was eventually killed by Paris, whose divinely guided arrow struck Achilles in the right heel, his one vulnerable spot.

After his death, Thetis decided to let Agamemnon award the arms of Achilles to the most courageous Greek left alive. Agamemnon chose the Greek warrior Odysseus.

The 50 Nereids were mermaid attendants of the beautiful sea-goddess Thetis, who rode a harnessed dolphin. When Achilles died at Troy, the Nereids accompanied Thetis there for 17 days and nights of mourning.

PARIS, ATHENA, AND THE GOLDEN APPLE:

Paris was born to King Priam and Queen Hecuba of Troy. Shortly after his birth it was prophesied that he would be the ruin of Troy, so he was given to a shepherd to be exposed on Mount Ida. The shepherd, returning five days later, was amazed to see the infant being suckled by a she-bear and took the infant home with him and raised him as his own son. One day, Paris' true parentage would be discovered and King Priam would take him back.

Although Paris grew up herding cattle, his noble birth was betrayed by his intelligence, strength, and beauty. He attracted the attention of the gods, and Zeus commanded him to decide which of the three goddesses, Hera, Athena, or Aphrodite, was the most beautiful. He was given a golden apple to be awarded to the goddess of his choice. At first, Paris claimed it was an impossible task. He wanted to divide the apple into three, but Zeus would not allow it. The goddesses agreed to abide by his decision and even disrobed for his inspection. He examined them one at a time, and each one offered him a bribe. Hera offered to make him the lord of all Asia and the richest man in the world. Athena offered to make him victorious in all his battles and the handsomest and wisest man in the world. But Aphrodite offered to win him Helen of Sparta, the most beautiful woman in the world, for his mistress. Paris immediately awarded her the golden apple.

By this contest, Paris won the enmity of Athena and Hera, and became entangled with the beautiful Helen. In the legend of *The Iliad*, these connections would lead to the disastrous Trojan War and the total defeat of the previously powerful and glorious kingdom of Troy.

THE WEAVER ARACHNE BECAME A SPIDER:

Arachne, a mortal princess, claimed that she was so skillful at weaving that not even Athena could compete with her. Athena assumed the form of an old woman and visited Arachne, who boasted of her skill, denied that the goddess had taught her, and dared Athena to compete with her. Athena dropped her magical disguise, and although Arachne turned pale, she maintained her challenge. Athena wove a marvelous tapestry recounting tales of the gods' displeasure with mortals. Impudent Arachne filled her loom with scenes of the gods' failings and errors, including Zeus' many infidelities. Finally, Athena struck Arachne's web with her shuttle and it fell to pieces. Then Athena touched Arachne on the forehead, at which Arachne suddenly became aware of the enormity of her impiety. She was so ashamed she hanged herself in despair. Athena pitied her and turned her into a spider and the rope into the spider's thread.

THE ORACLE AT DELPHI:

The Greeks believed that their gods could speak to them by the intermediary of oracles, priests or priestesses who entered into a trance or read the entrails of animals to discover the gods' will. The most influential of these oracles were women.

The most famous oracle, the Delphic oracle, was established in Greece by the ancient Cretans, who attained a high level of civilization before the Hellenes settled there. The first prophetess, Daphnis, was said to have been appointed by the goddess Mother Earth herself. Seated on a tripod, carrying the Cretan sceptre (*labrys* or double axe), she would achieve her trance state by inhaling the fumes that arose from the legendary Python, who lived in the bottom of a great chasm.

Eventually, the shrine became Apollo's, who was said to have slain the Python and established his own worship on the site. While a priestess still inhaled the fumes and entered into a trance, her ecstatic mutterings were

Medusa

interpreted by a priest who translated them into poetic speech. The priestesses were regarded as Apollo's brides and were sworn to celibacy. After one was seduced by a votary, the chief oracle was required to be at least 50 years old.

At Patrae, Demeter's priestesses prophesied from a mirror lowered into a sacred well by a rope. The priestesses of Mother Earth at Aegeira drank bull's blood, thought to be poisonous to humans. At Dodona, the priestesses of Zeus listened to the cooing of doves, the rustling of oak leaves, or the clanking of bronze pots suspended from branches to receive the word of the gods.

MEDUSA, THE GORGON:

Originally the serpent-goddess of the Libyan Amazons representing female wisdom, Medusa was demonized in later Greek mythology, which transformed her into a Gorgon who had serpents for hair. According to the myth, Medusa had offended Athena, who turned her into a hideous monster with serpents for hair, huge teeth, and a protruding tongue. Anyone who gazed upon her turned into stone. Athena and Hermes helped the hero Perseus slay Medusa. Athena gave him a highly-polished shield and

Amazons

instructed him not to look directly at Medusa, but only at her reflection. Hermes gave him a pair of winged sandals, a helmet of invisibility, a sickle to cut off the Gorgon's head, and a magic sack in which to hold it. Perseus discovered Medusa in the Land of the Hyperboreans among the rain-worn statues of men and animals turned into stone by her gaze. With Athena's help, he gazed into his shield and cut off Medusa's head with the sickle. The winged horse, Pegasus, sprang out of Medusa's body. Perseus donned the helmet of invisibility and escaped.

AMAZONS: The Amazons are recalled in Greek legend as a tribe of warrior women who held sway over much of North Africa, Anatolia, and the Black Sea. The word "Amazon" is most often thought to be derived from the Greek words *a mazon,* which mean "without breasts." Legend has it that the Amazons cut

off one breast to allow them to handle their weapons in battle. The historian and poet Robert Graves suggests that "amazon" can be traced to an Armenian word meaning "moon-women." The priestesses of the moon-goddess on the shores of the Black Sea and in Libya all bore weapons.

The Amazons were said to have lived in the mountainous country around the river Thermodon near the south shore of the Black Sea. They were said to have been the first to tame horses and to have founded several cities, all leading centers of goddess-worship. According to the legend, the Amazons were children of the god of war, Ares, and the nymph Harmonia. They were devoted to the worship of the chaste huntress goddess, Artemis, whose symbol was the moon. They did not marry, but performed a group ritual marriage with the youth of a neighboring people once a year. As soon as an Amazon knew she was pregnant, she returned home. Daughters became Amazons and sons were sent back to the male tribe. It was even rumored that the Amazons killed or disabled male children to prevent them from becoming warriors.

Their queen, Lysippe, decreed that men must perform all household tasks while women fought and governed. They were famous cavalry women and carried bronze bows and short shields shaped like a half moon. Their clothes were supposed to be made from the skins of wild beasts. Their capital was called Themiscyra and their empire at one time extended west to the borders of Grecian Thrace and south to Phyrgia. Three other Amazonian queens, Marpesia, Lampado, and Hippo, founded the cities of Ephesus, Smyrna, Cyrene, and Myrine in Asia Minor. The temple of Ephesian Artemis was included in the list of the seven wonders of the ancient world.

The Amazon queen Penthesileia fought in the Trojan War, driving Achilles from the field several times before he finally killed her and fell in love with her dead body.

One of Hercules' legendary labors was to capture the girdle (a kind of decorative belt) of the Amazon queen Hippolyta. There are many versions of this legend, but they all agree that Hercules killed Hippolyta and made off with the girdle and her weapons.

In the legendary history of Athens, their hero Theseus took part in Hercules' expedition against the Amazons. He abducted another Amazon queen, Antiope, and carried her back to Athens. The Amazons pursued him to the doors of the city, even sacrificing to Ares on the Aeriopagus, a sacred precinct of the city. After months of terrible fighting, the Athenians repulsed the Amazons, whose power was broken forever.

Depictions of Athenians battling Amazons were recorded by ancient historians on the throne of Zeus at Olympia, at Athens on the central wall of the Painted Colonnade, and on the shield of the monumental image of the goddess Athena.

The legends of the Libyan Amazons say that they once inhabited the fruitful island of Hespera in Lake Tritonis. They founded a city called Chersonesus and even attacked the Atlantians' fabled capital, Cerne. Their queen, Myrine, captured Cerne at the head of 30,000 cavalry and 3,000 infantry, all armed with bows and arrows. She lost her territory to another warring tribe and emigrated across North Africa to Arabia. Legend has it that it was Myrine who built the city of Mitylene on the island of Lesbos. Myrine was finally killed by the King of Thrace, and her army retreated to Libya.

CLYTAEMNESTRA MURDERED AGAMEMNON: The central crime of the tragic history of the House of Atreus is Clytaemnestra's murder of her husband, Agamemnon, King of Mycenae, on his return from the Trojan War. Clytaemnestra was subsequently murdered by her children to avenge their father's death. These two murders expressed the struggle between the old matriarchy and the conquering patriarchy in the Greek city-states.

Agamemnon had forced Clytaemnestra, a princess of Sparta, to marry him and killed her child by her previous husband. On the eve of the Trojan War, Agamemnon sacrificed their daughter, Iphigeneia, in response to an oracle's prediction that this sacrifice would give the Greeks a favorable wind to take their ships to Troy. Right after the sacrifice, the promised wind sprang up and Agamemnon sailed for Troy. He was gone ten years, during which time Clytaemnestra took a lover, the pretender to the Mycenean throne, Aegisthus.

Wishing to be forewarned of Agamemnon's return, Clytaemnestra arranged for a string of beacon fires to be lighted on the tops of mountains all the way from Troy to Mycenae as soon as the Greeks were victorious. When at long last the beacons were lit, Clytaemnestra and Aegisthus made their preparations.

When Agamemnon finally arrived home with his captive, the Trojan princess Cassandra, the queen warmly welcomed him. Cassandra, a prophetess, went into a trance and said she saw blood running everywhere. Agamemnon ignored her and followed Clytaemnestra, who had prepared a warm bath for him in a silver tub. Just as Agamemnon stepped out of the bath, she threw a net she had woven around him and Aegisthus ran a double-edged sword through him. After a pitched battle, Aegisthus' allies massacred all of Agamemnon's followers. Clytaemnestra ran outside and beheaded Cassandra with one swing of her axe.

Far from being repentant, Clytaemnestra declared the day an annual festival day. Her young son, Orestes, was spirited away to prevent his murder by Aegisthus, and Agamemnon's body was thrown into the river instead of being properly buried.

Clytaemnestra's daughter, Elektra, nursed an implacable hatred for the murderous royal couple. She often sent messages to Orestes, urging him to avenge his father's death. After seven years, Orestes consulted the Delphic oracle. The priestess advised him that he must avenge his father's death and kill his mother. The priestess warned him he would suffer the harassment of the Furies (Erinnyes) and offered him refuge at Delphi when the deed was accomplished.

Orestes returned to Mycenae and was eagerly welcomed by Elektra. They gained access to Clytaemnestra by claiming that he was a messenger bringing her the news of Orestes' death. Delighted, Clytaemnestra summoned Aegisthus to hear the good news. Orestes struck him down, then beheaded his mother, despite her appeals for mercy. Another version of the legend says that Orestes invoked a tribunal to try his mother for her crime, and the tribunal condemned Clytaemnestra to death.

The greatest poets of classical Greece, Aeschylus, Eurpides, and Sophocles, drew from this legend. In fact, the story of the fall of the House of Atreus has inspired playwrights and poets of all ages.

IPHIGENEIA, CHIEF PRIESTESS AT TAURUS: In one version of the classic Greek myth, Iphigeneia, daughter of Agamemnon and Clytaemnestra, was sacrificed at sea by her father in return for favorable winds. In another version, she was rescued from being sacrificed by her father by Artemis, who installed her as chief priestess of Artemis' temple in Taurus. Both versions may have been created to cover up Iphigeneia's actual role as chief or high priestess of Artemis at Taurus and the practice there of sacrificing all strangers to the goddess and nailing their heads to crosses. The Taurians were a savage people who worshipped Artemis with human sacrifice. All strangers and even sailors shipwrecked in that country were sacrificed to the Taurian Artemis. According to some versions of the myth, Iphigeneia hated

human sacrifice but piously obeyed the goddess.

Her brother Orestes, hounded by the Furies for having killed his mother, Clytaemnestra, appealed to the Delphic oracle for relief. He was instructed to steal the image of Taurian Artemis. Orestes did not know that his sister had survived the sacrifice and was now the Chief Priestess. When Orestes tried to approach Taurus, he was captured and handed over to the temple for sacrifice. However, on conversing in Greek with Iphigeneia, he discovered her true identity. She helped Orestes steal the image and fled with him in his ship.

There are different versions of the end of this legend. Some say Iphigeneia and Orestes installed the image in Sparta, or at Brauron near Athens (where a great festival to Artemis was held annually), or perhaps somewhere in Italy. In Sparta, legend says that the image continued to require human sacrifice until the time of Lycurgus, the great lawgiver of Sparta. He replaced that practice with ritual flogging of young men until the image was satiated with human blood.

ORPHEUS CHARMED WITH MUSIC: Orpheus was the son of a Thracian king and the muse Calliope, although some say Apollo was his father. He was an enchanting musician and poet who could tame wild beasts and move rocks and trees with his music. He married Eurydice, originally the goddess of the Underworld whose sacred animal was the serpent; her marriage in Greek mythology to Orpheus was considered a demotion. One day, while Eurydice was out walking, Aristaeus tried to rape her. As she fled, she was bitten by a serpent and died. Orpheus descended to Tartarus and charmed all its guardians and terrors with his music. He prevailed upon Hades to restore Eurydice to the upper world, on one condition. Hades decreed that Orpheus must not look behind him until Eurydice was back under the light of the sun. Eurydice followed Orpheus back up the passage, guided by the sound of his lyre. Just as she reached the mouth of the passage, he turned around to look at her and she was lost to him forever. Orpheus decided he would never touch another woman.

Orpheus did not honor the god Dionysus (Roman: Bacchus) and taught men other mysteries. He preached that Apollo was the greatest of all gods and encouraged men to live without women as he did. Dionysus sent his ecstatic female followers, the Maenads (Roman: Bacchantes), to destroy Orpheus. They tore him to pieces and threw his head into a river where it floated down to the sea, still singing. Orpheus' head and lyre drifted to the island of Lesbos (a center of lyric music) where it prophesied day and night, until Apollo, seeing his own oracles being neglected, ordered it to stop.

THE GREATER AND LESSER ELEUSINIAN MYSTERIES:

Eleusis, a city of the Kingdom of Mycenae, was the site of two great religious festivals. The Greater Mysteries were celebrated in honor of both Demeter and her daughter Core (or Persephone). The Lesser Mysteries were a preparation for the Greater Mysteries and were held in honor of Core alone.

All the participants in the mysteries were sworn to secrecy, so little is known about what actually happened during the ecstatic rites. During the Greater Mysteries, it seems that the initiates symbolically reenacted Demeter's love affair with the Titan Iasius (or perhaps Zeus). The mystagogues who presided over the festival then entered the sanctuary with joyous shouts, carrying a winnowing-fan that held the child Iacchus, the fruit of this ritual marriage. On the sixth day of the mysteries, a riotous hymn celebrating Iacchus was sung during a torchlight procession from Demeter's temple.

All Greek men and women, free or slaves, were eligible for initiation. Men dominated the administration of the festival, but the chief priest was assisted by two priestesses. The chief priestess of Demeter, who, like her counterpart in Athens, came from one of Eleusis' aristocratic families, played a leading role in the ritual. She held her position for life, and public records at Eleusis were dated by the name of the priestess and the year of her tenure.

The Lesser Mysteries were said to have been founded by Demeter to purify Hercules and ready him for participation in the Greater Mysteries. They celebrated the god Dionysus and involved the ritual washing and sacrifice of a sow. After their purification, initiates had to wait a full year before participating in the Greater Mysteries.

Greek/Roman

THE FURIES: Called the Three Furies by the Romans and the Erinys (Erinnyes) by the Greeks, these goddesses lived in Tartarus. The Furies—Tisiphone, Alecto, and Megaera—heard the complaints of mortals against children who were disrespectful to parents or hosts who offended guests. They punished crimes by hounding their victims relentlessly. They had snakes for hair, dogs' heads, coal-black bodies, bats' wings, and blood-shot eyes. They carried scourges and tormented their victims to death. Because they were afraid to mention these goddesses by name, people referred euphemistically to them as "The Eumenides" ("kindly ones" or "the well-meaning one"). The Erinys personified guilt and shame, and they later came to represent men's hidden fear of women.

Hebrew

THE GODDESS ANAT: The goddess Anat (or Anath), from whose name comes the word "anathema" (cursed or hated), was the supreme deity of the Ugaritic pantheon who was worshipped by Canaanites, Amorites,

The Furies

Syrians, Egyptians, and Hebrews. A complex goddess with four distinct aspects—warrior, mother, virgin, and wanton—Anat had tremendous energy and power. She occupied the Jerusalem temple, with her god-consort El, for centuries, and although she was demonized by later Hebrews and Christians, many of her myths and rituals were appropriated by them to become part of even their most important dramas, such as Passover and the Passion narrative of Jesus Christ.

THE PATRIARCHAL HEBREWS: The patriarchal Hebrews promoted their religion as a male monotheistic one, and indeed they succeeded in destroying the female divine to a tragic extent. But that female force continued to make itself known in various forms, including Hokkma (wisdom), Torah (law), and Shekinah (spirit, or soul). Though dismissed as "simply metaphor" by some, these three figures are all definitely feminine and all appear as independent, articulate beings in Hebrew scriptures and legends.

Inuit

INUIT SEA-GODDESS, SEDNA, RULED THE SEA: One of the names for the Inuit sea-goddess is Sedna, who, according to the story, was a beautiful woman who was tricked into marriage by a sea bird. Her father, Anguta, rescued her in a kayak, but when the bird-people created a storm in revenge, Anguta threw Sedna overboard to try to save his own life. Sedna clung to the side of the kayak, and Anguta cut her fingers off. She then threw her arms over the side of the boat, and her father cut them off, too, and knocked one of her eyes out with his paddle before she sank to the bottom of the sea. There Sedna lived as ruler of the sea; her amputated fingers and arms became the fish and sea creatures, and she decided how many of them she would allow the Inuit people to kill for food. If the people offended her, she would punish them with starvation and storms until a shaman made the journey to her land under the sea and made things right with her again.

Japanese

WOMEN HELD POSITIONS OF POWER: According to the earliest historical chronicles of Japan, which have been thought to combine mythology with verifiable history, women held positions of power in the family, religion, and government. Within the primitive familial bands, women were valued for their fertility. Because goddesses played a central role in the Shinto religion, women, often imperial princesses, occupied positions of authority as the high priestesses in major shrines. Queens of the Yamatai, the most powerful of the tribal bands, were said to have brought order to the land and engaged in diplomacy with the rulers to the west on the mainland of Asia.

WOMEN SHAMANS: It is thought that ancient Japanese folk religion was a combination of both north Asian and Pacific-Southeast Asian elements. As in other cultures, women's procreative powers were worshipped and gave them a special status in agricultural rites, especially for rice planting. Women shamans, called Miko, mediated between humanity and the gods through ecstatic trances. The Shinto goddess Amatseru Omikami was considered the ancestress of the imperial family, and she was worshipped in the emperor's residence until the tenth century A.D. At the start of each new reign, an imperial princess was designated to serve the high priestess at the Ise Temple. Children were selected to serve for years at local shrines. Eventually, though, due to the influence of ideas from the Asian mainland, women shamans became passive vessels for divine possession. Their revelations would be induced and interpreted by men. Shamanistic customs were banned in 1873 in an effort

to purify the Shinto religion. However, in today's climate of religious freedom, some women have resumed shamanistic practices.

Native American

THE NATIVE AMERICAN NAVAJO CREATION MYTH: The Native American Navajo creation myth tells of Atse Estsan, the first woman, who was born in the First World and gradually made her way to the surface of the Fifth World, where human beings of the present time live. Atse Estsan brought the people of the Third World with her, and together they created this current world. Eventually, Atse Estsan retired to the eastern sky, leaving the goddess Estsanattehi, the wife of the sun, on the Fifth World to help her people.

UTI HIATA, THE PAWNEE NAME FOR "MOTHER CORN:" Uti Hiata is the Pawnee name for "Mother Corn," one of the most important divine beings of the Native American Plains tribes. Daughter of H'Uraru, the sacred Mother Earth, Uti Hiata brought the Plains people up to earth from the underworld and taught them the ways of life, magic, agriculture, and religious ritual.

NOKOMIS FED CREATURES WHO LIVED ON HER LAND: Nokomis, meaning "grandmother," was the Algonquin name for the Iroquois goddess known as Eithinoha ("Our mother"). Nokomis fed the creatures who lived on her land, including humans, from her own body, signifying the understanding that life continues by consuming other life.

Roman

"GENIUS" AND "JUNO" WERE SPIRITS GIVING LIFE AND SEXUAL CREATIVITY: In ancient Rome, every man was considered to have a "genius"—the spirit that gave him life and sexual creativity—and every woman had a similar female spirit, called a "juno," named after the Roman Great Mother goddess. Later language development kept the male soul-word, "genius," but dropped the female equivalent.

JULIUS CAESAR DESCENDED FROM VENUS:

Julius Caesar composed a eulogy for his aunt, Julia, which traced her family lines from ancient kings (the Marcii Reges). He added that the lineage of his own family, the Julii, could be traced to the goddess Venus.

MINERVA, ORIGINAL ROMAN GODDESS OF ARTS AND CRAFTS, AND OF THE MIND:

Though later assimilated by the Greek goddess of wisdom and war, Athena, and so coming to be synonymous with her, Minerva was originally the Roman goddess of arts and crafts, and of the mind (or intellect). She was believed to have invented music as well. The Roman goddess of war, and of all conflicts, was Bellona, from whose name the Latin word for war, bellum, was taken.

SABINE WOMEN REGAINED FERTILITY: Leg-

end held that Rome was founded by Romulus, a prince who had been exposed at birth, but was suckled by a wolf and then raised by shepherds. When he established Rome on the Palatine hills near the Tiber River, he opened his town to outcasts and fugitives from neighboring communities. Romulus wanted to provide respectable wives for his community and tried to negotiate with his neighbors, the Sabine people. They rejected his request, telling him that he ought to find female runaways and outcasts to be wives for his men. Angered, Romulus resorted to cunning. He announced a huge sacrifice to the god Poseidon that he knew would draw people from all over the region to Rome. Once everyone had gathered and the sacrifice was about to begin, he gave a signal. His men descended on the crowd, abducting 30 women. According to legend, the women accepted their fate and quickly

began having children. When the fathers of the women finally tried to attack Rome to liberate their daughters, the women ran between the opposing forces holding their children in their arms and negotiated peace.

Ancient Roman legend recounts that after a time, the Sabine women no longer conceived children. They went to pray in a sacred grove, where the goddess Lucina's voice informed them that they had to be impregnated by the sacred goat. An Etruscan augur understood the goddess' words. He sacrificed a goat and made the women submit to beatings with strips of the hide. Thereafter they were all able to conceive. At the Lupercalia, Roman wives who wished to conceive allowed themselves to be beaten by the *Luperci*, young men dressed in goat skins.

VERGINIA'S DEATH PROVOKED UPRISING:

Roman legend says that a commissioner in the early Republic of Rome lusted after the young Verginia, a Roman citizen who was betrothed to another. He used his power to have her declared a slave so that he could get possession of her. When Verginia's father found himself powerless to prevent this calamity, he took her to the marketplace and killed her in public, crying that this was the only way he could make her free. This provoked a popular uprising that reasserted the liberties of the people.

Slavic

BABA YAGA, THE SLAVIC WITCH-GODDESS:

The Slavic witch-goddess, Baba Yaga, was believed to live in the last sheaf of grain harvested each year, showing her basis in the ancient birth-and-death goddess who died each winter (harvest-time) and was reborn in the spring. Demoted to a frightening hag in the later folktales, Baba Yaga still gave gifts (though often in a terrifying manner) of life and death to those who sought her out, depending on the deepest needs of the moment.

Documents

OF HISTORY

LETTERS OF ABIGAIL AND JOHN ADAMS, 1776. *While John Adams was attending the Continental Congress in Philadelphia, which wrote and ratified the constitution for the fledgling United States of America, he and his wife Abigail exchanged these letters. Many have commented on the irony that, while passing a revolutionary document on the rights of man, John Adams would not take seriously his wife's plea for the status of women in the new republic.*

31 March, 1776 *(to John Adams from Abigail)* in the new code of laws which I suppose it will be necessary for you to make, I desire you would remember the ladies and be more generous and favorable to them than your ancestors. Do not put such unlimited power into the hands of the husbands. Remember, all men would be tyrants if they could. If particular care and attention is not paid to the ladies, we are determined to foment a rebellion, and will not hold ourselves bound by any laws in which we have no voice or representation.

That your sex are naturally tyrannical is a truth so thoroughly established as to admit of no dispute; but such of you as wish to be happy willingly give up the harsh title of master for the more tender and endearing one of friend. Why, then, not put it out of the power of the vicious and the lawless to use us with cruelty and indignity with impu-

nity. Men of sense in all ages abhor those customs which treat us only as the vassals of your sex.

14 April, 1776 *(John Adams's reply to Abigail)* As to your extraordinary code of laws, I cannot but laugh. We have been told that our struggle has loosened the bonds of government everywhere; that children and apprentices were disobedient; that schools and colleges were grown turbulent; that Indians slighted their guardians, and Negroes grew insolent to their master. But your letter was the first intimation that another tribe, more numerous and powerful than all the rest, were grown discontented.

7 May, 1776 *(Abigail Adams's response)* I cannot say that I think you are very generous to the ladies; for, whilst you are proclaiming peace and good-will to men, emancipating all nations, you insist upon retaining an absolute power over wives. But you must remember that arbitrary power is like most other things which are very hard, very liable to be broken; and, notwithstanding all your wise laws and maxims, we have it in our power, not only to free ourselves, but to subdue our masters, and, without violence, throw both your natural and legal authority at our feet;—"Charm by accepting, but submitting sway, Yet have our humor most when we obey."

A VINDICATION OF THE RIGHTS OF WOMAN, 1792.

The following are excerpts from A Vindication of the Rights of Woman *by Mary Wollstonecraft.*

Men complain, and with reason, of the follies and caprices of our sex, when they do not keenly satirize our headstrong passions and groveling vices. Behold, I should answer, the natural effect of ignorance! The mind will ever be unstable that has only prejudices to rest on, and the current will run with destructive fury when there are no barriers to break its force. Women are told from their infancy, and taught by the example of their mothers, that a little knowledge of human weakness, justly termed cunning, softness of temper, *outward* obedience, and a scrupulous attention to a puerile kind of propriety, will obtain for them the protection of man; and should they be beautiful, everything else is needless, for, at least, twenty years of their lives. . . .

How grossly do they insult us who thus advise us only to render ourselves gentle, domestic brutes! For instance, the winning softness so warmly, and frequently, recommended, that governs by obeying. What childish expressions and how insignificant is the being—can it be an immortal one? who will condescend to govern by such sinister methods! . . .

I may be accused of arrogance; still I must declare what I firmly believe, that all the writers who have written on the subject of female education and manners from Rousseau to Dr. Gregory,* have contributed to render women more artificial, weak characters, than they would otherwise have been; and, consequently, more useless members of society. I might have expressed this conviction in a lower key; but I am afraid it would have been the whine of affectation, and not the faithful expression of my feelings, of the clear result, which experience and reflection have led me to draw. . . .[I]n the works of the authors I have just alluded to. . .my objection extends to the whole purport of those books, which tend, in my opinion, to degrade one half of the human species, and render women pleasing at the expense of every solid virtue.

Though, to reason on Rousseau's ground, if man did attain a degree of perfection of mind when his body arrived at maturity, it might be proper, in order to make a man and his wife *one*, that she should rely entirely on his understanding; and the graceful ivy, clasping the oak that supported it, would form a whole in which strength and beauty would be equally conspicuous. But, alas! husbands, as well as their helpmates, are often only overgrown children; nay, thanks to early debauchery, scarcely men in their outward form—and if the blind lead the blind, one need not come from heaven to tell us the consequence. . . .

Rousseau declares that a woman should never, for a moment, feel herself independent, that she should be governed by fear to exercise her *natural* cunning, and made a coquettish slave in order to render her a more alluring object of desire, a *sweeter* companion to man, whenever he chooses to relax himself. He carries the arguments, which he pretends to draw from the indications of nature, still further, and insinuates that truth and fortitude, the corner stones of all human virtue, should be cultivated with certain restrictions, because, with respect to the female character, obedience is the grand lesson which ought to be impressed with unrelenting rigour.

What nonsense! when will a great man arise with sufficient strength of mind to puff away the fumes which pride and sensuality have thus spread over the subject! If women are by nature inferior to men, their virtues is a relative idea; consequently, their conduct should be founded on the same principles, and have the same aim.

Connected with man as daughters, wives, and mothers, their moral character may be estimated by their manner of fulfilling those simple duties; but the end, the grand end of their exertions should be to unfold their own faculties and acquire the dignity of conscious virtue. They may try to render their road pleasant; but ought never to forget, in common with man, that life yields not the felicity which can satisfy an immortal soul. I do not mean to insinuate that either sex should be so lost in abstract reflections or distant views, as to forget the affections and duties that lie before them, and are, in truth, the means appointed to produce the fruit of life; on the contrary, I would warmly recommend them, even while I assert, that they afford most satisfaction when they are considered in their true, sober light.

Probably the prevailing opinion, that woman was created for man, may have taken its rise from Moses's poetical story; yet, as very few, it is presumed, who have bestowed any serious thought on the subject, ever supposed that Eve was, literally speaking, one of Adam's ribs, the deduction must be allowed to fall to the ground; or, only be so far admitted as it proves that man, from the remotest antiquity, found it convenient to exert his strength to subjugate his companion, and his invention to show that she ought to have her neck bent under the yoke, because the whole creation was only created for his convenience or please. . . .

Youth is the season for love in both sexes; but in those days of thoughtless enjoyment provision should be made for the more important years of life, when reflection takes place of sensation. But Rousseau, and most of the male writers who have followed his steps have warmly inculcated that the whole tendency of female education ought to be directed to one point:—to render them pleasing.

Let me reason with the supporters of this opinion who have any knowledge of human nature, do they imagine that marriage can eradicate the habitude of life? The woman who has only been taught to please will soon find that her charms are oblique sunbeams, and that they cannot have much effect on her husband's heart when they are seen every day, when the summer is passed and gone. Will she then have sufficient native energy

to look into herself for comfort, and cultivate her dormant faculties? or, is it not more rational to expect that she will try to please other men; and, in the emotions raised by the expectation of new conquests, endeavour to forget the mortification her love or pride has received? When the husband ceases to be a lover—and the time will inevitably come, her desire of pleasing will then grow languid, or become spring of bitterness; and love, perhaps, the most evanescent of all passions, gives place to jealous or vanity.

I now speak of women who are restrained by principle or prejudice; such women, though they would shrink from an intrigue with real abhorrence, yet, nevertheless, wish to be convinced by the homage of gallantry that they are cruelly neglected by their husbands; or, days and weeks are spent in dreaming of the happiness enjoyed by congenial souls til their health is undermined and their spirits broken by discontent. How then can the great art of pleasing be such a necessary study? it is only useful to mistress; the chaste wife, and serious mother, should only consider her power to please as the polish of her virtues, and the affection of her husband as one of the comforts that render her task less difficult and her life happier. But, whether she be loved or neglected, her first wish should be to make herself respectable, and not to rely for all her happiness on a being subject to like infirmities with herself. . . .

If all the faculties of woman's mind are only to be cultivated as they respect her dependence on man; if, when a husband be obtained, she have arrived at her goal, and meanly proud rests satisfied with such a paltry crown, let her grovel contentedly, scarcely raised by her employments above the animal kingdom; but, if, struggling for the prize of her high calling, she look beyond the present scene, let her cultivate her understanding without stopping to consider what character the husband may have whom she is denied to marry. Let her only determine, without being too anxious about present happiness, to acquire the qualities that ennoble a rational being, and a rough inelegant husband may shock her taste without destroying her peace of mind. She will not model her soul to suit the frailties of her companion, but to bear with them: his character may be a trial, but not an impediment to virtue. . . .

That a proper education; or, to speak with more precision, a well stored mind, would enable a woman to support a single life with dignity, I grant; but that she should avoid cultivating her taste, lest her husband should occasionally shock it, is quitting a substance for a shadow. To say the truth, I do not know of what use is an improved taste, if the individual be not rendered more independent of the casualties of life; if new sources of enjoyment, only dependent on the solitary operations of the mind, are not opened. . . .

Gentleness of manners, forebearance and long-suffering, are such amiable God-like qualities. . . .but what a different aspect it assumes when [gentleness] is the submissive demeanour of dependence, the support of weakness that loves, because it wants protection; and is forbearing, because it must silently endure injuries; smiling under the lash at which it dar not snarl. . . .

How women are to exist in that state where there is to be neither marrying or giving in marriage, we are not told. For though moralists have agreed that the tenor of life seems to prove that *man* is prepared by various circumstances for a future state, they constantly concur in advising *woman* only to provide for the present. Gentleness, docility, and a spaniel-like affection are, on this ground, consistently recommended as the cardinal virtues of the sex; and, disregarding the arbitrary economy of nature, one writer has declared that it is masculine for a woman to be melancholy. She was created to be the toy of man, his rattle, and it must jingle in his ears whenever, dismissing reason, he chooses to be amused. . . .

If . . . [women] be really capable of acting like rational creatures, let them not be treated like slaves; or, like the brutes who are dependent on the reason of man, when they associate with him;

but cultivate their minds, give them the salutary, sublime curb of principle, and let them attain conscious dignity by feeling themselves only dependent on God. Teach them, in common with man, to submit to necessity, instead of giving, to render them more pleasing, a sex to morals. . . .

These may be termed Utopian dreams. Thanks to that Being who impressed them on my soul, and gave me sufficient strength of mind to dare to exert my own reason, till, becoming dependent only on him for the support of my virtue, I view, with indignation, the mistaken notions that enslave my sex.

I love man as my fellow; but his scepter, real, or usurped, extends not to me, unless the reason of an individual demands my homage; and even then the submission is to reason, and not to man. In fact, the conduct of an accountable being must be regulated by the operations of its own reason; or on what foundation rests the throne of God?

It appears to me necessary to dwell on these obvious truths, because females have been insulated, as it were; and, while they have been stripped of the virtues that should clothe humanity, they have been decked with artificial graces that enable them to exercise a short-lived tyranny. Love, in their bosoms, taking place of every nobler passion, their sole ambition is to be fair, to raise emotion instead of inspiring respect; and this ignoble desire, like the servility in absolute monarchies, destroys all strength of character. Liberty is the mother of virtue, and if women be, by their very constitution, slaves, and not allowed to breathe the sharp invigorating air of freedom, they must every languish like exotics, and be reckoned beautiful flaws in nature. . . .

And if it be granted that woman was not created merely to gratify the appetite of man, or to be the upper servant, who provides his meals and takes care of his linen, it must follow, that the first care of those mothers or fathers, who really attend to the education of females, should be, if not to strengthen the body, at least, not to destroy the constitution by mistaken notions of beauty and female excellence. . . .

To preserve personal beauty, woman's glory! the limbs and faculties are cramped with worse than Chinese bands, and the sedentary life which they are condemned to live, whilst boys frolic in the open air, weakens the muscles and relaxes the nerves. As for Rousseau's remarks . . . that they have naturally, that is from their birth, independent of education, a fondness for dolls, dressing, and talking—they are so puerile as not to merit a serious refutation. . . .

I have, probably, had an opportunity of observing more girls in their infancy than J. J. Rousseau—I can recollect my own feelings, and I have looked steadily around me; yet, so far from coinciding with him in opinion respecting the first dawn of the female character, I will venture to affirm, that a girl, whose spirits have not been damped by inactivity, or innocence tainted by false shame, will always be a romp, and the doll will never excite attention unless confinement allows her no alternative. Girls and boys, in short, would plan harmlessly together, if the distinction of sex was not inculcated long before nature makes any difference. I will go further, and affirm, as an indisputable fact, that most of the women, in the circle of my observation, who have acted like rational creatures, or shown any vigour of intellect, have accidentally been allowed to run wild. . . .

A wild wish has just flown from my heart to my head, and I will not stifle it though it may excite a horse-laugh. I do earnestly wish to see the distinction of sex confounded in society, unless where love animates the behaviour. For this distinction is, I am firmly persuaded, the foundation of the weakness of character ascribed to woman; is the cause why the understand is neglected, whilst accomplishments are acquired with sedulous care: and the same cause accounts for their preferring the graceful before the heroic virtues. . . .

Women have seldom sufficient serious employment to silence their feelings; a round of little cares, or vain pursuits frittering away all strength of mind and organs, they become naturally only objects of sense. In short, the whole tenor of female education (the education of society) tends to render the best disposed romantic and inconstant; and the remainder vain and mean. In the present state of society this evil can scarcely be remedied, I am afraid, in the slightest degree; should a more laudable ambition ever gain ground they may be brought nearer to nature and reason, and become more virtuous and useful as they grow more respectable. . . .

We respect to virtue, to use the word in a comprehensive sense, I have seen most in low life. Many poor women maintain their children by the sweat of their brow, and keep together families that the vices of the fathers would have scattered abroad; but gentlewomen are too indolent to be actively virtuous, and are softened rather than refined by civilization. Indeed, the good sense which I have met with, among the poor women who have had few advantages of education, and yet have acted heroically, strongly confirmed me in the opinion that trifling employments have rendered woman a trifler. Man, taking her body, the mind is left to rust; so that while physical love enervates man, as being his favourite recreation, he will endeavour to enslave woman: —are, who can tell, how many generations may be necessary to give virour to the virtue and talents of the freed posterity of abject slaves?

DECLARATION OF SENTIMENTS, JULY 19, 1848. *Three hundred people, mostly women, came to Seneca Falls, New York to attend the July 19-20 Women's Rights Convention, the first of its kind. Following is the "Declaration of Sentiments" that paraphrased the Declaration of Independence and asserted that "all men and women are created equal."*

When, in the course of human events, it becomes necessary for one portion of the family of man to assume among the people of the earth a position different from that which they have hitherto occupied, but one to which the laws of nature and of nature's God entitle them, a decent respect to the opinions of mankind requires that they should declare the causes that impel them to such a course.

We hold these truths to be self-evident: that all men and women are created equal; that they are endowed by their Creator with certain inalienable rights; that among these are life, liberty, and the pursuit of happiness; that to secure these rights governments are instituted, deriving their just powers from the consent of the governed. Whenever any form of government becomes destructive of these ends, it is the right of those who suffer from it to refuse allegiance to it, and to insist upon the institution of a new government, laying its foundation on such principles, and organizing its powers in such form, as to them shall seem most likely to effect their safety and happiness. Prudence indeed, will dictate that governments long established should not be changed for light and transient causes; and accordingly all experience hath shown that mankind are more disposed to suffer, while evils are sufferable, than to right themselves by abolishing the forms to which they were accustomed. But when a long train of abuses and usurpations, pursuing invariably the same object evinces a design to reduce them under absolute despotism, it is their duty to throw off such government, and to provide new guards for their future security. Such has been the patient sufferance of the women under this government, and such is now the necessity which constrains them to demand the equal station to which they are entitled.

The history of mankind is a history of repeated injuries and usurpations on the part of man toward woman, having in direct object the establishment of an absolute tyranny over her. To prove this, let facts be submitted to a candid world.

He has never permitted her to exercise her inalienable right to the elective franchise.

He has compelled her to submit to laws, in the formation of which she had no voice.

He has withheld from her rights which are given to the most ignorant and degraded men—both natives and foreigners.

Having deprived her of this first right of a citizen, the elective franchise, thereby leaving her without representation in the halls of legislation, he has oppressed her on all sides.

He has made her, if married, in the eye of the law, civilly dead.

He has taken from her all right in property, even to the wages she earns.

He has made her, morally, an irresponsible being, as she can commit many crimes with impunity, provided they are done in the presence of her husband. In the covenant of marriage, she is compelled to promise obedience to her husband, he becoming, to all intents and purposes, her master—the law giving him power to deprive her of her liberty, and to administer chastisement.

He has so framed the laws of divorce, as to what shall be the proper causes, and in case of separation, to whom the guardianship of the children shall be given, as to be wholly regardless of the happiness of women—the law, in all cases, going upon a false supposition of the supremacy of man, and giving all power into his hands.

After depriving her of all rights as a married woman, if single, and the owner of property, he has taxed her to support a government which recognizes her only when her property can be made profitable to it.

He has monopolized nearly all the profitable employments, and from those she is permitted to follow, she receives but a scanty remuneration. He closes against her all the avenues to wealth and distinction which he considers most honorable to himself. As a teacher of theology, medicine, or law, she is not known.

He has denied her the facilities for obtaining a thorough education, all colleges being closed against her.

He allows her in Church, as well as State, but a subordinate position, claiming Apostolic authority for her exclusion from the ministry, and, with some exceptions, from any public participation in the affairs of the Church.

He has created a false public sentiment by giving to the world a different code of morals for men and women, by which moral delinquencies which exclude women from society, are not only tolerated, but deemed of little account in man.

He has usurped the prerogative of Hehovah himself, claiming it as his right to assign for her a sphere of action, when that belongs to her conscience and to her God.

He has endeavored, in every way that he could, to destroy her confidence in her own powers, to lessen her self-respect, and to make her willing to lead a dependent and abject life.

Now, in view of this entire disfranchisement of one-half the people of this country, their social and religious degradation—in view of the unjust laws above mentioned, and because women do feel themselves aggrieved, oppressed, and fraudulently deprived of their most sacred rights, we insist that they have immediate admission to all the rights and privileges which belong to them as citizens of the United States.

In entering upon the great work before us, we anticipate no small amount of misconception, misrepresentation, and ridicule; but we shall use every instrumentality within our power to effect our object. We shall employ agents, circulate tracts, petition the State and National legislatures, and endeavor to enlist the pulpit and the press in our behalf. We hope this Convention will be followed by a series of Conventions embracing every part of the country.

SOJOURNER TRUTH'S ADDRESS, 1851.

Sojourner Truth addressed an Ohio convention of women's rights. Frances D. Gage was president of the convention, and published her recollection of Truth's historic speech.

The leaders of the movement trembled on seeing a tall, gaunt black woman in a gray dress and white turban, surmounted with an uncouth sunbonnet, march deliberately into the church, walk with the air of a queen up the aisle, and take her seat upon the pulpit steps. A buzz of disapprobation was heard all over the house, and there fell on the listening ear, "An abolition affair!" "Woman's rights and niggers!" "I told you so!" "Go it, darkey!"

I chanced on that occasion to wear my first laurels in public life as president of the meeting. At my request order was restored, and the business of the Convention went on. Morning, afternoon, and evening exercises came and went. . . . Again and again, timorous and trembling ones came to me and said, with earnestness, "Don't let her speak, Mrs. Gage, it will ruin us. Every newspaper in the land will have our cause mixed up with abolition and niggers, and we shall be utterly denounced." My only answer was, "We shall see when the time comes."

The second day the work waxed warm. Methodist, Baptist, Episcopal, Presbyterian, and Universalist ministers came in to hear and discuss the resolutions presented. One claimed superior rights and privileges for man, on the ground of "superior intellect"; another, because of the "manhood of Christ; if God had desired the equality of woman, He would have given some token of His will through the birth, life, and death of the Saviour." Another gave us a theological view of the "sin of our first mother."

There were very few women in those days who dared to "speak in meeting"; and the august teachers of the people were seemingly getting the better of us, while the boys in the galleries, and the sneerers among the pews, were hugely enjoying the discomfiture, as they supposed, of the "strong-minded." . . . When, slowly from her seat in the corner rose Sojourner Truth, who, til now, had scarcely lifted her head. "Don't let her speak!" gasped half a dozen in my ear. She moved slowly and solemnly to the front, laid her old bonnet at her feet, and turned her great speaking eyes to me. There was a hissing sound of disapprobation above and below. I rose and announced "Sojourner Truth," and begged the audience to keep silence for a few moments.

The tumult subsided at once, and every eye was fixed on this almost Amazon form, which stood nearly six feet high, head erect, and eyes piercing the upper air like one in a dream. At her first word there was a profound hush. She spoke in deep tones, which, though not loud, reached every ear in the house, and away through the throng at the doors and windows.

"Wall, chilern, whar dar is so much racket dar must be somethin' out o'kilter. I tink dat 'twixt de niggers of de Souf and de womin at de Norf, all talkin' 'bout rights, de white men will be in a fix pretty soon. But what's all dis here talkin' 'bout?

"Dat man ober dar say dat womin needs to be helped into carriages, and lifted ober ditches, and to hab de best place everywhar. Nobody eber helps me into carriages, or ober mud-pubbles, or gibs me any best place!" And raising herself to her full height, and her voice to a pitch like rolling thunder, she asked. "And a'n't I a woman? Look at me! Look at my arm! (and she bared her right arm to the shoulder, showing her tremendous muscular power). I have ploughed, and planted, and gathered into barns, and no man could head me! And a'n't I a woman? I could work as much and eat as much as a man—when I could get it— and bear de lash as well! And a'n't I a woman? I have borne thirteen chilern, and seen 'em mos' all sold off to slavery, and when I cried out with my mother's grief, none but Jesus heard me! And a'n't I a woman?

"Den dey talks 'bout dis ting in de head; what dis dey call it?" "Intellect," whispered some one near. "Dat's it, honey. What's dat got to do wid womin's rights or nigger's rights? If my cup won't hold but a pint, and yourn holds a quart, wouldn't ye be mean not to let me have my little half-measure full?" And she pointed her significant finger, and sent a keen glance at the minister who had made the argument. The cheering was long and loud.

"Den dat little man in black dar, he say women can't have as much rights as men, 'cause Christ wan't a woman! Whar did your Christ come from?" Rolling thunder couldn't have stilled that crowd, as did those deep, wonderful tones, as she stood there with outstretched arms and eyes of fire. Raising her voice still louder, she repeated, "Whar did your Christ come from? From God and a woman! Man had nothin' to do wid Him." Oh, what a rebuke that was to that little man.

Turning again to another objector, she took up the defense of Mother Eve. I can not follow her through it all. It was pointed, and witty, and solemn; eliciting at almost every sentence deafening applause; and she ended by asserting: "If de fust woman God ever made was strong enough to turn de world upside down all alone, dese women togedder (and she glanced her eye over the platform) ought to be able to turn it back, and get it right side up again! And now dey is asking to do it, de men better let 'em." Long-continued cheering greeted this." 'Bleeged to ye for hearin' on me, and now ole Sojourner han't got nothin' more to say."

Amid roars of applause, she returned to her corner, leaving more than one of us with streaming eyes, and hearts beating with gratitude. She had taken us up in her strong arms and carried us safely over the slough of difficulty, turning the whole tide in our favor. I have never in my life seen anything like the magical influence that subdued the mobbish spirit of the day, and turned the sneers and jeers of an excited crowd into notes of respect and admiration. Hundreds rushed up to shake hands with her, and congratulate the glorious old mother, and bid her Godspeed on her mission of "testifyin' agin concerning the wickedness of this 'ere people."

ELIZABETH CADY STANTON'S ADDRESS TO THE NEW YORK STATE LEGISLATURE, 1860.

In 1854, a proposed law of women's property had been defeated in New York. Six years later, Susan B. Anthony and Elizabeth Cady Stanton collaborated on many speeches and writings to promote the passage of this historic legislation. The following are excerpts from Stanton's address on the event of the passage of the Married Women's Property Act.

You who have read the history of nations, from Moses down to our last election, where have you ever seen one class looking after the interests of another? Any of you can readily see the defects in other governments, and pronounce sentence against those who have sacrificed the masses to themselves; but when we come to our own case, we are blinded by custom and self-interest. Some of you who have no capital can see the injustice which the laborer suffers; some of you who have no slaves, can see the cruelty of his oppression; but who of you appreciate the galling humiliation, the refinements of degradation, to which women (the mothers, wives, sisters, and daughters of freemen) are subject, in this the last half of the nineteenth century? How many of you have ever read even the laws concerning them that now disgrace your statute-books? In cruelty and tyranny, they are not surpassed by any slaveholding code in the Southern States; in fact they are worse, but just so far as woman, from her social position refinement, and education, is on a more equal ground with the oppressor.

Allow me just here to call the attention of that party now so much interested in the slave of the Carolinas, to the similarity in his condition and that of the mothers, wives, and daughters of the Empire State. The negro has no name. He is Cuffy Douglas or Cuffy Brooks, just whose Cuffy he may chance to be. The woman has no name. She is Mrs. Richard Roe or Mrs. John Doe, just whose Mrs. she may chance to be. Cuffy has no right to his earnings; he can not buy or sell, or lay up anything that he can call his own. Mrs. Roe has no right to her earnings; she can neither buy nor sell, make contracts, nor lay up anything that she can call her own. Cuffy has no right to his children; they can be sold from him at any time. Mrs. Roe has no right to her children; they may be bound out to cancel a father's debts of honor. The unborn child, even, by the last will of the father, may be placed under the guardianship of a stranger and a foreigner. Cuffy has no legal existence; he is subject to restraint and moderate chastisement. Mrs. Roe has no legal existence; she has not the best right to her own person. The husband has the power to restrain, and administer moderate chastisement.

Blackstone [author of *Commentaries on the Laws of England*] declares that the husband and wife are one, and learned commentators have decided that that one is the husband. In all civil codes, you will find them classified as one. Certain rights and immunities, such and such privileges are to be secured to white male citizens. What have women and negroes to do with rights? What know they of government, war, or glory?

The prejudice against color, of which we hear so much, is no stronger than that against sex. It is produced by the same cause, and manifested very much in the same way. The negro's skin and the woman's sex are both *prima facie* evidence that they were intended to be in subjection to the white Saxon man. The few social privileges which the man gives the woman, he makes up to the negro in civil rights. The woman may sit at the same table and eat with the white man; the free negro may hold property and vote. The woman may sit in the same pew with the white man in church; the free negro may enter the pulpit and preach. Now, with the black man's right to suffrage, the right unquestioned, even by Paul, to minister at the altar, it is evident that the prejudice against sex is more deeply rooted and more unreasonably maintained than that against color. . . .

Just imagine an inhabitant of another planet entertaining himself some pleasant evening in searching over our great national compact, our Declaration of Independence, our Constitutions, or some of our statute-books; what would he think of those "women and negroes" that must be so fenced in, so guarded against? Why, he would certainly suppose we were monsters, like those fabulous giants or Brobdingnagians of olden times, so dangerous to civilized man, from our size, ferocity, and power. Then let him take up our poets, from Pope down to Dana; let him listen to our Fourth of July toasts, and some of the sentimental adulations of social life, and no logic could convince him that this creature of the law, and this angel of the family altar, could be one and the same being. Man is in such a labyrinth of contradictions with his marital and property rights; he is so befogged on the whole question of maidens, wives, and mothers, that from pure benevolence we should relieve him from this troublesome branch of legislation. We should vote, and make laws for ourselves. Do not be alarmed, dear ladies! You need spend no time reading Grotius, Coke, Puffendorf, Blackstone, Bentham, Kent, and Story to find out what you need. We may safely trust the shrewd selfishness of the white man, and consent to live under the same broad code where he has no comfortably ensconced himself. Any legislation that will do for man, we may abide by most cheerfully. . . .

Now do not think, gentlemen, we wish you to do a great many troublesome things for us. We do not ask our legislators to spend a whole session in fixing up a code of laws to satisfy a class of most unreasonable women. We ask no more than the poor devils in the Scripture asked, "Let us alone." In mercy, let us take care of ourselves, our property, our children, and our homes. True, we are not so strong, so wise, so crafty as you are, but if any kind friend leaves us a little money, or we can be great industry earn fifty cents a day, we would rather buy bread and clothes for our children than cigars and champagne for our legal protectors. There has been a great deal written and said

about protection. We, as a class, are tired of one kind of protection, that which leaves us everything to do, to dar, and to suffer, and strips us of all means for its accomplishment. We would not tax man to take care of us. No, the Great Father has endowed all his creatures with the necessary powers for self-support, self-defense, and protection. We do not ask man to represent us; it is hard enough in times like these for man to carry backbone enough to represent himself. So long as the mass of men spend most of their time on the fence, not knowing which way to jump, they are surely in no condition to tell us where we had better stand. In pity for man, we would no longer hang like a mill-stone round his neck. Undo what man did for us in the dark ages, and strike out all special legislation for us; strike the words "white male"; from all your constitutions, and then, with fair sailing, let us sink or swim, live or die, survive or perish together.

MARRIED WOMEN'S PROPERTY ACT, NEW YORK, 1860. *This statute became law one month after Elizabeth Cady Stanton addressed the New York State legislature. For the first time, women had the right to keep their own earnings, equal power as joint guardians of their own children, and property rights as widows; all significant advances for the legal status of women.*

The People of the State of New York, represented in Senate and Assembly, do enact as follows (excerpted):

Section I. The property, both real and personal, which any married woman now owns, as her sole and separate property; that which comes to her by descent, devise, bequest, gift or grant; that which she acquires by her trade, business, labor, or services, carried on or performed on her sole or separate account; that which a woman married in this State owns at the time of her marriage, and the rents, issues and proceeds of all such property, shall notwithstanding her marriage, be and remain her sole and separate property, and may be used, collected, and invested by her in her own name, and shall not be subject to the interference or control of her husband, or liable for his debts, except such debts as may have been contracted for the support of herself or her children, but her as his agent.

2. A married woman may bargain, sell, assign, and transfer her separate personal property, and carry on any trade or business, and perform any labor or services on her sole and separate account, and the earnings of any married woman from her trade, business, labor, or services shall be her sole and separate property, and may be used or invested by her in her own name.

3. Any married woman possessed of real estate as her separate property may bargain, sell and convey such property, and enter into any contract in reference to the same; but no such conveyance or contract shall be valid without the assent, in writing, of her husband, except as hereinafter provided. . . .

7. Any married woman may, while married, sue and be sued in all matters having relation to her property, which may be her sole and separate property, or which may hereafter come to her by descent, devise, bequest, or the give of any person except her husband, in the same manner as if she were sole. And any married woman may bring and maintain an action in her own name, for damages against any person or body corporate, for any injury to her person or character, the same as if she were sole; and the money received upon the settlement of any such action, or recovered upon a judgment, shall be her sole and separate property.

8. No bargain or contract made by any married women, in respect to her sole and separate property . . . shall be binding upon her husband, or render him or his property in any way liable therefor.

9. Every married woman is hereby constituted and declared to be the joint guardian of her children, with her husband, with equal powers,

rights, and duties in regard to them, with the husband.

10. At the decease of husband or wife, leaving no more child or children, the survivor shall hold, possess, and enjoy life estate in one-third of all the real estate of which the husband or wife died seized.

11. At the decease of the husband or wife integrate, leaving minor children or children, the survivor shall hold, possess and enjoy all the real estate of which the husband or wife died seized, and all the rents, issues, and profits thereof during the minority of the youngest child, and one-third thereof during his or her natural life.

SOJOURNER TRUTH'S SPEECH "KEEP THE THING GOING WHILE THINGS ARE STIRRING," 1867. *In the contentious post-Civil War period, the Fourteenth Amendment to the Constitution gave blacks the vote, but omitted any reference to women. The amendment's second section introduced the world "male" into the Constitution for the first time. While women's rights organizations had been strong supporters of enfranchisement for the negro, they were shocked and dismayed by the turn of events. In 1867, Sojourner Truth made this stand for the rights of black women.*

My friends, I am rejoiced that you are glad, but I don't know how you will feel when I get through. I come from another field—the country of the slave. They have got their liberty—so much good luck to have slavery partly destroyed; not entirely. I want it root and branch destroyed. Then we will all be free indeed. I feel that if I have to answer for the deeds done in my body just as much as a man, I have a right to have just as much as a man. There is a great stir about colored men getting their rights, but not a word about the colored women; and if colored men get their rights, and not colored women theirs, you see the colored men will be masters over the women, and it will be just as bad as it was before. So I am for keeping the thing going while things are stirring; because if we wait til it is still, it will take a great while to get it going again. White women are a great deal smarter, and know more than colored women, while colored women do not know scarcely anything. They go out washing, which is about as high as a colored woman gets, and their men go about idle, strutting up and down; and when the women come home, they ask for their money and take it all, and then scold because there is no food. I want you to consider on that, chil'n. I call you chil'n; you are somebody's chil'n, and I am old enough to be mother of all that is here. I want women to have their rights. In the courts women have no right, no voice; nobody speaks for them. I wish woman to have her voice there among the pettifoggers. If it is not a fit place for women, it is unfit for men to be there.

I am above eighty years old; it is about time for me to be going. I have been forty years a slave and forty years free, and would be here forty years more to have equal rights for all. I suppose I am kept here because something remains for me to do; I suppose I am yet to help to break the chain. I have done a great deal of work; as much as a man, but did not get so much pay. I used to work in the field and bind grain, keeping up with the cradler; but men doing no more, got twice as much pay; so with the German women. They work in the field and do as much work, but do not get the pay. We do as much, we eat as much, we want as much. I suppose I am about the only colored woman that goes about to speak for the rights of the colored women. I want to keep the thing stirring, now that the ice is cracked. What we want is a little money. You men know that you get as much again as women when you write, or for what you do. When we get our rights we shall not have to come to you for money, for then we shall have money enough in our own pockets; and may be you will ask us for money. But help us now until we get it. It is a good consolation to know that when we have got this battle once fought we shall not be coming to you any more. You have been having our rights so long, that you think, like a slave-holder, that you own us. I know that it is hard for one who has held the

reins for so long to give up; it cuts like a knife. It will feel all the better when it closes up again. I have been in Washington about three years, seeing about these colored people. Now colored men have the right to vote. There ought to be equal rights now more than ever, since colored people have got their freedom. I am going to talk several times while I am here; so now I will do a little singing. I have not heard any singing since I came here.

THE FOURTEENTH AMENDMENT TO THE U.S. CONSTITUTION, 1868.

The Fourteenth Amendment was both a triumph and a defeat for women's activists. Many women activists had been intimately involved with the abolitionist movement and celebrated the protection of the rights of black people. However, in Section 2, Congress explicitly defined electors as male. This represented an awful setback to the cause of women's suffrage.

Section 2. Representatives shall be apportioned among the several States according to their respective numbers, counting the whole number of persons in each State, excluding Indians not taxed. But when the right to vote at any election for the choice of electors for President and Vice-President of the United States, Representatives in Congress, the Executive and Judicial officers of a State, or the members of the Legislature thereof, is denied to any of the *male* inhabitants of such State, being twenty-one years of age, and citizens of the United States, or in any way abridged, except for participation in rebellion, or other crime, the basis of representation therein shall be reduced in the proportion which the number of such *male* citizens shall bear to the whole number of male citizens twenty-one years of age in such State.

SUSAN B. ANTHONY VOTES, NOVEMBER 5, 1872.

The following letter to Elizabeth Cady Stanton described Anthony's experience when she cast her vote in Rochester, New York, in the election of 1872. Since 1868, about 150 women had defied the laws that denied them suffrage, confronting election officials and casting illegal ballots. Anthony's protest and the trial that followed created the most publicity of all these attempts.

DEAR MRS. STANTON: Well, I have been and gone and done it! positively voted the Republic ticket—straight—this A.M. at seven o'clock, and *swore my vote in, at that;* was registered on Friday and fifteen other women followed suit in this ward, then in sundry other wards some twenty or thirty women *tried* to *register,* but all save two were refused. All my three sisters voted—Rhoda De Garmo, too. Amy Post was rejected, and she will immediately bring action against the registrars; then another woman who was registered, but vote refused, will bring action for that—similar to the Washington action. Hon. Henry R. Selden will be our counsel; he has read up the law and all of our arguments, and is satisfied that we are right, and ditto Judge Samuel Selden, his elder brother. So we are in for a fine agitation in Rochester on this question. . . .

How I wish you were here to write up the funny things said and done. Rhoda De Garmo told them she wouldn't swear nor affirm, "but would tell them the truth," and they accepted that. When the Democrats said that my vote should *not* go in the box, one Republican said to the other, "What do you say, Marsh?" "I say put it in." "So do I," said Jones; "and we'll fight it out on this line if it takes all winter." Mary Hallowell was just here. She and Sarah Willis tried to register, but were refused; also Mrs. Mann, the Unitarian minister's wife, and Mary Curtis, sister of Caharine Stebbins. Not a jeer, not a word, not a look disrespectful has met a single woman.

If only now *all the Woman Suffrage women* would work to *this* end of *enforcing the existing Constitutional supremacy of National law* over the State law, what strides we might make this very winter! But I'm awfully tired; for five days I have been on the constant run, but to splendid purpose; so all right. I hope you voted too.

Affectionately, SUSAN B. ANTHONY.

ACCOUNT OF THE TRIAL OF SUSAN B. ANTHONY FOR ILLEGAL VOTING, NOVEMBER 1872.

In her trial for having illegally cast a vote in the 1872 election, Judge Hunt denied Susan B. Anthony the right to testify in her own defense. He ruled that the Fourteenth Amendment was inapplicable and instructed the jury to find a verdict of guilty. He rejected a request for a new trial. The following is the transcript of the end of one of the most infamous trials in the history of the suffrage movement.

. . . JUDGE HUNT—(Ordering the defendant to stand up), "Has the prisoner anything to say why sentence shall not be pronounced?"

MISS ANTHONY—Yes, your honor, I have many things to say; for in your ordered verdict of guilty, you have trampled under foot every vital principle of our government. My natural rights, my civil rights, my political rights, my judicial rights, are all alike ignored. Robbed of the fundamental privilege of citizenship, I am degraded from the status of a citizen to that of a subject; and not only myself individually, but all of my sex, are, by your honor's verdict, doomed to political subjection under this, so-called, form of government.

JUDGE HUNT—The Court cannot listen to a rehearsal of arguments the prisoner's counsel has already consumed three hours in presenting.

MISS ANTHONY—May it please your honor, I am not arguing the question, but simply stating the reasons why sentence cannot, in justice, be pronounced against me. Your denial of my citizen's right to vote, is the denial of my right of consent as one of the governed, the denial of my right of representation as one of the taxed, the denial of my right to a trial by a jury of my peers as an offender against law, therefore, the denial of my sacred rights to life, liberty, property and—

JUDGE HUNT—The Court cannot allow the prisoner to go on.

MISS ANTHONY—But your honor will not deny me this one and only poor privilege of protest against this high-handed outrage upon my citizen's rights. May it please the Court to remember that since the day of my arrest last November, this is the first time that either myself or any person of my disfranchised class has been allowed a word of defense before judge or jury—

JUDGE HUNT—The prisoner must sit down—the Court cannot allow it.

MISS ANTHONY—All my prosecutors, from the 8th ward corner grocery politician, who entered the complaint, to the United States Marshal, Commissioner, District Attorney, District Judge, your honor on the bench, not one if my peer, but each and all are my political sovereigns; and had your honor submitted my case to the jury, as was clearly your duty, even then I should have had just cause of protest, for not one of those men was my peer; but, native or foreign born, white or black, rich or poor, educated or ignorant, awake or asleep, sober or drunk, each and every man of them was my political superior; hence, in no sense, my peer. Even under such circumstances, a commoner of England, tried before a jury of Lords, would have far less cause to complain than should I, a woman, tried before a jury of men. Even my counsel, the Hon. Henry R. Selden, who has argued my cause so ably, so earnestly, so unanswerably before your honor, is my political sovereign. Precisely as no disfranchised person is entitled to sit upon a jury, and no woman is entitled to the franchise, so, none but a regularly admitted lawyer is allowed to practice in the courts, and no woman can gain admission to the bar—hence, jury, judge, counsel, must all be the superior class.

JUDGE HUNT—The Court must insist—the prisoner has been tried according to the established forms of law.

MISS ANTHONY—Yes, your honor, but by forms of law all made by men, interpreted by men, administered by men, in favor of men, and against women; and hence, your honor's ordered verdict of guilty, against a Untied States citizen for the exercise of *"that citizen's right to vote,"* simply because that citizen was a woman and not a man . . . As . . . the slaves who got their freedom must take it over, or under, or through the unjust forms of law, precisely so, now, must women, to get their right to a voice in this government, take it; and I have taken mine, and mean to take it at every possible opportunity.

JUDGE HUNT—The Court orders the prisoner to sit down. It will not allow another word.

MISS ANTHONY—When I was brought before your honor for trial, I hoped for a broad and liberal interpretation of the Constitution and its recent amendments, that should declare all United States citizens under its protecting aegis—that should declare equality of rights the national guarantee to all persons born or naturalized in the United States. But failing to get this justice—failing, even, to get a trial by a jury *not* of my peers—I ask not leniency at your hands—but rather the full rigors of the law.

JUDGE HUNT—The Court must insist —

(Here the prisoner sat down)

JUDGE HUNT—The prisoner will stand up.

(Here Miss Anthony rose again.)

The sentence of the Court is that you pay a fine of one hundred dollars and the costs of the prosecution.

MISS ANTHONY—May it please your honor, I shall never pay a dollar of your unjust penalty. All the stock in trade I possess is a $10,000 debt, incurred by publishing my paper—*The Revolution*—four years ago, the sole object of which was to educate all women to do precisely as I have done, rebel against your man-made, unjust, unconstitutional forms of law, that tax, fine, imprison and hang women, while they deny them the right of representation in the government;

and I shall work on with might and main to pay every dollar of that honest debt, but not a penny shall go to this unjust claim. And I shall earnestly and persistently continue to urge all women to the practical recognition of the old revolutionary maxim, that "Resistance to tyranny is obedience to God."

JUDGE HUNT—Madam, the Court will not order you committed until the fine is paid.

THE ORIGIN OF THE FAMILY, PRIVATE PROPERTY, AND THE STATE BY FRIEDRICH ENGELS, 1884.

Friedrich Engels (1820-1895) was co-author with Karl Marx of the Communist Manifesto. The Origin of the Family, Private Property and the State *explained the oppression of women in Marxist terms. The ideas of Engels were based on the work of the American anthropologist Lewis H. Morgan, who dared to posit that many prehistoric societies were actually matriarchal.*

These excerpts from Chapter II, "The Family," illustrate some of Engels' ideas about how private property and exclusion of women from the work force (social production) created monogamous marriage and the oppression of women. These ideas greatly influenced many of the early feminists of the 1800s.

The overthrow of mother-right* was the world historical defeat of the female sex. The man took command in the home also; the woman was degraded and reduced to servitude, she became the slave of his lust and a mere instrument for the production of children. This degraded position of the woman, especially conspicuous among the Greeks of the heroic and still more of the classical age, has gradually been palliated and glozed over, and sometimes clothed in a milder form; in no sense has it been abolished.

The establishment of the exclusive supremacy of the man shows its effects first in the patriarchal family, which now emerges as an intermediate form. . . .

Its essential features are the incorporation of unfree persons, and paternal power; hence the perfect type of this form of family is the Roman. The original meaning of the word "family" (*familia*) is not that compound of sentimentality and domestic strife which forms the ideal of the present-day philistine; among the Romans it did not at first even refer to the married pair and their children, but only to the slaves. *Famulus* means domestic slave, and *familia* is the total number of slaves belonging to one man. . . . The term was invented by the Romans to denote a new social organism, whose head ruled over wife and children and a number of slaves, and was invested under Roman paternal power with rights of life and death over them all. . . .

Such a form of family shows the transition of the pairing family** to monogamy. In order to make certain of the wife's fidelity and therefore of the paternity of the children, she is delivered over unconditionally into the power of the husband; if he kills her, he is only exercising his rights. . . .

(The monogamous family) . . . develops out of the pairing family . . . its decisive victory is one of the signs that civilization is beginning. It is based on the supremacy of the man, the express purpose being to produce children of undisputed paternity; such paternity is demanded because these children are later to come into their father's property as his natural heirs. It is distinguished from pairing marriage by the much greater strength of the marriage tie, which can no longer be dissolved at either partner's wish. As a rule, it is now only the man who can dissolve it, and put away his wife. The right of conjugal infidelity also remains secured to him at any rate by custom. . . .

We meet this new form of the family in all its severity among the Greeks. While the position of the goddess in their mythology, as Marx points out, brings before us an earlier period when the position of women was freer and more respected, in the heroic age we find the woman already being humiliated by the domination of the man and by competition from girl slaves. The legitimate wife was expected to put up with all this, but herself to remain strictly chaste and faithful.

In the heroic age a Greek woman is, indeed, more respected than in the period of civilization, but to her husband she is after all nothing but the mother of his legitimate children and heirs, his chief housekeeper and the supervisor of his female slaves, whom he can and does take as concubines if he so fancies. It is the existence of slavery side by side with monogamy, the presence of young, beautiful slaves belonging unreservedly to the *man*, that stamps monogamy from the very beginning with its specific character of monogamy *for the woman only*, but not for the man. And that is the character it still has today. . . .

Girls (in Athens) only learned spinning, weaving, and sewing, and at most a little reading and writing. They lived more or less behind locked doors and had no company except other women. The women's apartments formed a separate part of the house, on the upper floor or at the back, where men, especially strangers, could not easily enter, and to which the women retired when men visited the house. They never went out without being accompanied by a female slave; indoors there were kept under regular guard.

. . . In Euripides a woman is called an *oikourema*, a thing (the word is neuter) for looking after the house, and, apart from her business of bearing children, that was all she was for the Athenian—his chief female domestic servant. The man had his athletics and his public business, from which women were barred; in addition, he often had female slaves at his disposal and during the most flourishing days of Athens an extensive system of prostitution which the state at least favored. It was precisely through this system of prostitution that the only Greek women of personality were able to develop, and to acquire that intellectual and artistic culture by which they stand out as high above the general level of classical womanhood as the Spartan women by their qualities of character. But that a woman had to be a hetaira*** before she could be a woman is the worst condemnation of the Athenian family.

This Athenian family became in time the accepted model for domestic relations, not only among the Ionians, but to an increasing extent among all the Greeks of the mainland and colonies also. But, in spite of locks and guards, Greek women found plenty of opportunity for deceiving their husbands. . . .

This is the origin of monogamy as far as we can trace it back among the most civilized and highly developed people of antiquity. It was not in any way the fruit of individual sex-love, with which it had nothing whatever to do; marriages remained as before marriages of convenience. It was the first form of the family to be based, not on natural, but on economic conditions on the victory of private property over primitive, natural communal property. The Greeks themselves put the matter quite frankly: the sole exclusive aims of monogamous marriage were to make the man supreme in the family, and to propagate, as the future heirs to his wealth, children indisputably his own. Otherwise, marriage was a burden, a duty which had to be performed, whether one liked it or not, to gods, state, and one's ancestors. In Athens the law exacted from the man not only marriage but also the performance of a minimum of so-called conjugal duties.

Thus when monogamous marriage first makes its appearance in history, it is not as the reconciliation of man and woman, still less as the highest form of such a reconciliation. Quite the contrary. Monogamous marriage comes on the scene as the subjugation of the one sex by the other; it announces a struggle between the sexes unknown throughout the whole previous prehistoric period. In an old unpublished manuscript, written by Marx and myself in 1846, I find the words: "The first division of labor is that between man and woman for the propagation of children." And today I can add: The first class opposition that appears in history coincides with the development of the antagonism between man and woman in monogamous marriage, and the first class oppression coincides with that of the female sex by the male. Monogamous marriage was a great historical step forward; nevertheless, together with slavery and private wealth, it opens the period that has lasted until today in which every step forward is also relatively a step backward, in which prosperity and development for some is won through the misery and frustration of others. It is the cellular form of civilized society, in which the nature of the oppositions and contradictions fully active in that society can be already studied. . . .

Nowadays there are two ways of concluding a bourgeois marriage. In Catholic countries the parents, as before, procure a suitable wife for their young bourgeois son, and the consequence is, of course, the fullest development of the contradiction inherent in monogamy: the husband abandons himself to hetaerism and the wife to adultery. Probably the only reason why the Catholic Church abolished divorce was because it had convinced itself that there is no more a cure for adultery than there is for death. In Protestant countries, on the other hand, the rule is that the son of a bourgeois family is allowed to choose a wife from his own class with more or less freedom; hence there may be a certain element of love in the marriage, as, indeed, in accordance with Protestant hypocrisy, is always assumed, for decency's sake. Here the husband's hetaerism is a more sleepy kind of business, and adultery by the wife is less the rule. But sine, in every kind of marriage, people remain what they were before, and since the bourgeois of Protestant countries are mostly philistines, all that this Protestant monogamy achieves, taking the average of the best cases, is a conjugal partnership of leaden boredom, known as "domestic bliss.". . . .

In both cases, however, the marriage is conditioned by the class position of the parties and is to that extent always a marriage of convenience. In both cases this marriage of convenience turns often enough into crassest prostitution, sometimes of both partners, but far more commonly of the women, who only differs from the ordinary courtesan in that she does not let out her body on piece-work as a wage-worker, but sells it once

and for all into slavery. And of all marriages of convenience Fourier's words hold true: "As in grammar two negatives make an affirmative, so in matrimonial morality two prostitutions pass for a virtue." Sex-love in the relationship with a woman becomes, and can only become, the real rule among the oppressed classes, which means today among the proletariat—whether this relation is officially sanctioned or not. But here all the foundations of typical monogamy are cleared away. Here there is no property, for the preservation and inheritance of which monogamy and male supremacy were established; hence there is no incentive to make this male supremacy effective. What is more, there are no mans of making it so. Bourgeois law, which protects this supremacy, exists only for the possessing class and their dealings with the proletarians. The law costs money and, on account of the worker's poverty, it has no validity for his relation to his wife. Here quite other personal and social conditions decide. And now that large-scale industry has taken the wife out of the home onto the labor market and into the factory, and make her often the breadwinner of the family, no basis for any kind of male supremacy is left in the proletarian household—except, perhaps, for something of the brutality towards women that has spread since the introduction of monogamy. The proletarian family is therefore no longer monogamous in the strict sense, even where there is passionate love and firmest loyalty on both sides, and maybe all the blessings of religious and civil authority. Here, therefore, the eternal attendants of monogamy, hetaerism and adultery, play only an almost vanishing part. The wife has in fact regained the right to dissolve the marriage, and if two people cannot get on with one another, they prefer to separate. In short, proletarian marriage is monogamous in the etymological sense of the word, but not at all in its historical sense.

. . . In the old communistic household, which comprised many couples and their children, the task entrusted to the women of managing the household was as much a public and socially necessary industry as the procuring of food by the men. With the patriarchal family, and still more with the single monogamous family, a change came. Household management lost its public character. It no longer concerned society. It became a *private service*; the wife became the head servant, excluded from all participation in social production. Not until the coming of modern large-scale industry was the road to social production opened to her again—and then only to the proletarian wife. But it was opened in such a manner that, if she carries out her duties in the private service of her family, she remains excluded from public production and unable to earn; and if she wants to take part in public production and earn independently, she cannot carry out family duties. And the wife's position in the factory is the position of women in all branches of business, right up to medicine and the law. The modern individual family is founded on the open or concealed domestic slavery of the wife, and modern society is a mass composed of these individual families as its molecules.

In the great majority of cases today, at least in the possessing classes, the husband is obliged to earn a living and support his family, and that in itself gives him a position of supremacy, without any need for special legal titles and privileges. Within the family he is the bourgeois and the wife represents the proletariat. In the industrial world, the specific character of the economic oppression burdening the proletariat is visible in all its sharpness only when all special legal privileges of the capitalist class have been abolished and complete legal equality of both classes established. The democratic republic does not do away with the opposition of the two classes; on the contrary, it provides the clear field on which the fight can be fought out. And in the same way, the peculiar character of the supremacy of the husband over the wife in the modern family, the necessity of creating real social equality between them, and the way to do it, will only be seen in the clear light of day when both possess legally complete equality of rights. Then it will be plain that the

first condition for the liberation of the wife is to bring the whole female sex back into public industry, and that this in turn demands the abolition of the monogamous family as the economic unit of society. . . .

We are now approaching a social revolution in which the economic foundations of monogamy as they have existed hitherto will disappear just as surely as those of its complement—prostitution. Monogamy arose from the concentration of considerable wealth in the hands of a single individual—a man—and from the need to bequeath this wealth to the children of that man and of no other. For this purpose, the monogamy of the woman was required, not that of the man, so this monogamy of the woman did not in any way interfere with open or concealed polygamy on the part of the man. But by transforming by far the greater portion, at any rate, of permanent, heritable wealth—the means of production—into social property, the coming social revolution will reduce to a minimum all this anxiety about bequeathing and inheriting.

. . . Full freedom of marriage can therefore only be generally established when the abolition of capitalist production and of the property relations created by it has removed all the accompanying economic considerations which still exert such a powerful influence on the choice of a marriage partner. For then there is no other motive left except mutual inclination.

And as sexual love is by its nature exclusive—although at present this exclusiveness is fully realized only in the woman—the marriage based on sexual love is by its nature individual marriage . . . If now the economic considerations also disappear which made women put up with the habitual infidelity of their husbands—concern for their own means of existence, and still more for their children's future—then, according to all previous experience, the equality of woman thereby achieved will tend infinitely more to make men really monogamous than to make women polyandrous.

But what will quite certainly disappear from monogamy are all the features stamped upon it through its origin in property relations; these are, in the first place, supremacy of the man, and secondly, indissolubility. The supremacy of the man in marriage is the simple consequence of his economic supremacy, and with the abolition of the latter will disappear of itself. The indissolubility of marriage is partly a consequence of the economic situation in which monogamy arose, partly tradition from the period when the connection between this economic situation and monogamy was not yet fully understood and was carried to extremes under a religious form. . . .

What we can now conjecture about the way in which sexual relations will be ordered after the impending overthrow of capitalist production is mainly of a negative character, limited for the most part to what will disappear. But what will there be new? That will be answered when a new generation has grown up: a generation of men who never in their lives have known what it is to buy a woman's surrender with money or any other social instrument of power; a generation of women who have never known what it is to give themselves to a man from any other considerations than real love, or to refuse to give themselves to their lover from fear of the economic consequences. When these people are in the world, they will care precious little what anybody today thinks they ought to do; they will make their own practice and their corresponding public opinion about the practice of each individual— and that will be the end of it.

*Mother-right, according to Engels, was the "reckoning of descent in the female line."

**In the pairing family, one man lives with one woman. Polygamy and infidelity are permitted the man, but adultery by the woman is strictly forbidden. The marriage is easily dissolved and the children belong to the mother alone.

***A courtesan, usually a slave.

ELIZABETH CADY STANTON, "SOLITUDE OF SELF," 1892.

At 76, Elizabeth Cady Stanton gave the following speech at her last public appearance in 1892. Although Stanton continued to send speeches to be read by Susan B. Anthony, many consider this to be her masterpiece.

The point I wish plainly to bring before you on this occasion is the individuality of each human soul—our Protestant idea, the right of individual conscience and judgment—our republican idea, individual citizenship. In discussing the rights of woman, we are to consider, first, what belongs to her as an individual, in a world of her own, the arbiter of her own destiny, an imaginary Robinson Crusoe with her woman Friday on a solitary island. Her rights under such circumstances are to use all her faculties for her own safety and happiness. . . .

It is only the incidental relations of life, such as mother, wife, sister, daughter, which may involve some special duties and training. In the usual discussion in regard to woman's sphere . . . her rights and duties as an individual, as a citizen, as a woman (are uniformly subordinated) to the necessities of these incidental relations, some of which a large class of women may never assume. In discussing the sphere of man we do not decide his rights as an individual, as a citizen, as a man, by his duties as a father, a husband, a brother, or a son, relations some of which he may never fill. Moreover, he would be better fitted for these very relations, and whatever special work he might choose to do to earn his bread, by the complete development of all his faculties as an individual.

Just so with woman. The education that will fit her to discharge the duties in the largest sphere of human usefulness, will best fit her for whatever special work she may be compelled to do.

The isolation of every human soul and the necessity of self-dependence must give each individual the right to choose his own surroundings. The strongest reason for giving woman all the opportunities for higher education, for the full development of her faculties, her forces of mind and body; for giving her the most enlarged freedom of thought and action; a complete emancipation from all forms of bondage, of custom, dependence, superstition; from all the crippling influences of fear; is the solitude and personal responsibility of her own individual life. The strongest reason why we ask for woman a voice in the government under which she lives; in the religion she is asked to believe; equality in social life, where she is the chief factor; a place in the trades and professions, where she may earn her bread, is because of her birthright to self-sovereignty; because, as an individual, she must rely on herself. No matter how much women prefer to lean, to be protected and supported, nor how much men desire to have them do so, they must make the voyage of life along, and for safety in an emergency they must know something of the laws of navigation. . . .

Nothing strengthens the judgment and quickens the conscience like individual responsibility. Nothing adds such dignity to character as the recognition of one's self-sovereignty; the right to an equal place, everywhere conceded; a place earned by personal merit, not an artificial attainment by inheritance, wealth, family, and position. Seeing, then, that the responsibilities of life rest equally on man and woman, that their destiny is the same, they need the same preparation for time and eternity. The talk of sheltering woman from the fierce storms of life is the sheerest mockery, for they beat on her from every point of the compass, just as they do on man, and with more fatal results, for he has been trained to protect himself, to resist, to conquer.

Whatever the theories may be of woman's dependence on man, in the supreme moments of her life he can not bear her burdens. . . . We may have many friends, love, kindness, sympathy and charity to smooth our pathway in everyday life, but in the tragedies and triumphs of human experience each mortal stands alone.

But when all artificial trammels are removed, and women are recognized as individuals, responsible for their own environments, thoroughly educated for all positions in life they may be called to fill; with all the resources in themselves that liberal thought and broad culture can give; guided by their own conscience and judgment; trained to self-protection by a healthy development of the muscular system and skill in the use of weapons of defense, and stimulated to self-support by a knowledge of the business world and the pleasure that pecuniary independence must ever give; when women are trained in this way they will, in a measure, be fitted for those years of solitude that come to all, whether prepared or otherwise.

HELEN L. SUMNER, HISTORY OF WOMEN IN INDUSTRY IN THE UNITED STATES, 1911.

Congress authorized a study about the history, occupations, numbers and other vital statistics of female workers in response to the social upheavals and rise of labor unionism between 1870 and 1910. In 1908, work began on this monumental study, called Women and Child Wage-Earners in the United States. *When the report was finally finished, in 1911, its 19 volumes laid the groundwork for the establishment of the Women's Bureau of the United States Department of Labor in 1920.*

Following is an excerpt from the "Introduction and Summary" of Volume IX, History of Women in Industry in the United States, *written by Helen L. Sumner.*

The history of women in industry in the United States is the story of a great industrial readjustment, which has not only carried woman's work from the home to the factory, but has changed its economic character from unpaid production for home consumption to gainful employment in the manufacture of articles for sale. Women have always worked, and their work has probably always been quite as important a factor in the total economy of society as it is to-day. But during the nineteenth century a transformation occurred in their economic position and in the character and conditions of their work. Their unpaid services have been transformed into paid services, their work has been removed from the home to the factory and workshop, their range of possible employment has been increased and at the same time their monopoly of their traditional occupations has been destroyed. The individuality of their work has been lost in a standardized product.

The story of woman's work in gainful employments is a story of constant changes or shiftings of work and workshop, accompanied by long hours, low wages, insanitary conditions, overwork, and the want on the part of the woman of training, skill, and vital interest in her work. It is a story of monotonous machine labor, of division and subdivision of tasks until the woman, like the traditional tailor who is called the ninth part of a man, is merely a fraction, and that rarely as much even as a tenth part, of an artisan. It is a story, moreover, of underbidding, of strike breaking, of the lowering of standards for men breadwinners.

In certain industries and certain localities women's unions have raised the standard of wages. The opening of industrial schools and business colleges, too, though affecting almost exclusively the occupations entered by the daughters of middle-class families who have only recently begun to pass form home work to the industrial field, has at least enabled these few girls to keep from further swelling the vast numbers of the unskilled. The evil of long hours and in certain cases other conditions which lead to overstrain, such as the constant standing of saleswomen, have been made the subject of legislation. The decrease of strain due to shorter hours has, however, been in part nullified by increased speed of machinery and other devices designed to obtain the greatest possible amount of labor from each woman. Nevertheless, the history of woman's work in this country shows that legislation has been the only force which has improved the working conditions of any large number of women wage-earners. Aside form the little improvement that has been effected in the lot of working women, the most surprising fact brought out in this study is the long period of time through which large numbers of women have worked under conditions which have involved not only great hardships to themselves but shocking waste to the community.

Changes in occupations of women. The transfer of women from nonwage-earning home work to gainful occupations is evident to the most superficial observer, and it is well known that most of this transfer has been effected since the beginning of the nineteenth century. In 1870 it was found that 14.7 per cent of the female population 16 years of age and over were breadwinners, and by 1900 the percentage was 20.6 per cent. During the period for which statistics exist, moreover, the movement toward the increased employment of women in gainful pursuits was clear and distinct in all sections of the country and was even more marked among the native-born than among the foreign born. It must be borne in mind, however, that even in colonial days there were many women who worked for wages, especially at spinning, weaving, the sewing trades, and domestic service. Many women, too, carried on business on their own account in the textile and sewing trades and also in such industries as the making of blackberry brandy. The wage labor of women is as old as the country itself and has merely increased in importance. The amount, however, of unremunerated home work performed by women must still be considerably larger than the amount of gainful labor, for even in 1900 only about one-fifth of the women 16 years of age and over were breadwinners.

Along with the decrease in the importance of unremunerated home labor and the increase in the importance of wage labor has gone a considerable amount of shifting of occupations. Under the old domestic system the work of the woman was to spin, to do a large part of the weaving, to sew, to knit; in general, to make most of the clothing worn by the family, to embroider tapestry in the days and regions where there was time for art, to cook, to brew ale and wine, to clean, and to perform the other duties of the domestic servant. These things women have always done. But machines have now come in to aid in all these industries—machines which in some cases have brought in their train men operatives and in other cases have enormously increased the productive power of the individual and have made it necessary for many women, who under the old regime, like Priscilla, would have calmly sat by the window spinning, to hunt other work. One kind of spinning is now done by men only. Men tailors make every year thousands of women's suits. Men dressmakers and even milliners are common. Men make our bred and brew our ale and do much of the work of the steam laundry where our clothes are washed. Recently, too, men have learned to clean our houses by the vacuum process.

Before the introduction of spinning machinery and the sewing machine the supply of female labor appears never to have been excessive. But the spinning jenny threw out of employment thousands of "spinsters," who were obliged to resort to sewing as the only other occupation to which they were in any way trained. This accounts for the terrible pressure in the clothing trades during the early decades of the nineteenth century. Later on, before any readjustment of women's work had been effected, the sewing machine as introduced, which enormously increased the pressure of competition among women workers. Shortly after the substitution of machinery for the spinning wheel the women of certain localities in Massachusetts found an outlet in binding shoes—an opportunity opened to them by the division of labor and by the development of the ready-made trade. But when the sewing machine was introduced this field, at least for a time, was again contracted. Under this pressure, combined with the rapid development of wholesale industry and division of labor, women have been pressed into other industries, almost invariably in the first instance into the least skilled and most poorly paid occupations. This has gone on until there is now scarcely an industry which does not employ women. Thus

woman's sphere has expanded, and its former boundaries can now be determined only by observing the degree of popular condemnation which follows their employment in particular industries.

The attitude of the public toward the employment of women has, indeed, made their progress into gainful occupations slow and difficult, and has greatly aggravated the adjustment pains which the industrial revolution has forced upon woman as compared with those of man, whose traditional sphere is bounded only by the humanly possible. This attitude has, moreover, been an important factor in determining the woman's choice of occupations. . . .

The scarcity of labor supply in particular places or at particular times has often been responsible for the use of women's work. Thus during the early years of the Republic the employment of women in manufacturing industries was doubtless greatly accelerated by the scarcity and high price of other labor. This, too, was doubtless largely responsible for the fact that, in the early years of the cotton industry, a larger proportion of women was employed in the cotton mills of Massachusetts and New Hampshire than in those of Rhode Island, New Jersey, and Pennsylvania. One of the remedies frequently suggested in the thirties and forties for the evils under which working women suffered was that "the excess of spinsters" should be transported to the places where "there is a deficiency of women."

The Civil War was another force which not only drove into gainful occupations a large number of women, but compelled many changes in their employments. In 1869 it was estimated that there were 25,000 working women in Boston who had been forced by the war to earn their living. The war, too, caused a large number of cotton factories to shut down, and thousands of women thus thrown out of employment were obliged to seek other occupations.

Similar to war in its influence, and in some ways more direful, has been the influence of industrial depressions. The industrial depression which began in 1837, for example, temporarily destroyed the newly-arisen wholesale clothing manufacture, and caused untold hardships to the tailoresses and seamstresses of New York and Philadelphia. These women turned, naturally, to any occupation in which it was possible for them to engage. Industrial depressions, too, like war, have taken away from thousands of women the support of the men upon whom they were dependent and have forced them to snatch at any occupation which promised them a pittance.

Expansion of woman's sphere. As a result of these factors and forces and in many cases of others less general in their operation, woman's sphere of employment has been greatly expanded during the past hundred years. . . .

It is evident that, on the whole, there has been a certain expansion of woman's sphere—a decrease in the proportion employed in certain traditional occupations, such as "servants and waitresses," "seamstresses," and "textile workers," but an increase in the proportion employed in most other industries, many of them not originally considered as within woman's domain. There has been, for instance, an increase in the proportion of women engaged as "bookkeepers and accountants," as "saleswomen," as "stenographers and typewriters," and in "other manufacturing and mechanical pursuits," and this movement has affected, roughly speaking, all elements according to nativity or conjugal condition, of the population of working women. . . .

Home and factory work. In general, it may be said that during the past century the amount of home work of women for pay has steadily decreased and the amount of factory work has steadily increased. . . . Home workers have become sweat-shop workers and sweat-shop workers are gradually becoming factory workers. So long ago as now to be almost forgotten a similar transformation took place in the textile industries. Indeed,

this is the general tendency of the employment of both men and women in manufacturing industries. Independent domestic production has practically become a thing of the past. But the history of woman's work shows that their wage labor under the domestic system has often been under worse conditions than their wage labor under the factory system. The hours of home workers have been longer, their wages lower, and the sanitary conditions surrounding them more unwholesome than has generally been the case with factory workers. The movement away from home work can hardly, then, be regretted.

General conditions of life and labor. The conditions under which the working women of this county have toiled have long made them the object of commiseration. Mathew Carey devoted a large part of the last years of his life, from 1828 to 1839, to agitation in their behalf. Again and again he pointed out in newspaper articles, pamphlets, and speeches that the wages of working women in New York, Philadelphia, Baltimore and Boston were utterly insufficient for their support; that their food and lodging were miserably poor and unwholesome; and that the hours they were obliged to work were almost beyond human endurance. . . .

In 1845 an investigation of "female labor" in New York, used as the basis of a series of articles in the New York Tribune, developed "a most deplorable degree of servitude, privation, and misery among this helpless and dependent class of people," including "hundreds and thousands" of shoe binders, type rubbers, artificial-flower makers, match-box makers, straw braiders, etc., who "drudge away, heart-broken, in want, disease, and wretchedness." . . .

Again in 1869 the working women of Boston, in a petition to the Massachusetts legislature . . . asserted that they were insufficiently paid, scantily clothed, poorly fed, and badly lodged, that their physical health, if not already undermined by long hours and bad conditions at work, was rapidly becoming so, and that their moral natures were being undermined by lack of proper society and by their inability to attend church on account of the want of proper clothing and the necessity, being constantly occupied throughout the week, "to bring up the arrears of our household duties by working on the Lord's Day." . . .

Wages and unemployment. The low wages paid to women and the inequality of men's and women's wages have always been the chief causes of complaint. . . .

The average wages paid to women in New York in 1863, taking all the trades together, were said to have been about $2 a week and in many instances only 20 cents a day, while the hours ranged from 11 to 16 a day. The price of board, which before the war had been about $1.50 a week, had been raised by 1864 to from $2.50 to $3.

During the war period, indeed, . . . the wages of women increased less, on the whole, than the wages of men, while their cost of living increased out of all proportion to their wages. This fact was recognized, at least, by the labor papers of that period. "While the wages of workingmen have been increased more than 100 per cent," said the Daily Evening Voice, in commenting upon the report for 1864 of the New York Working Women's Protective Union, "and complaint is still made that this is not sufficient to cover the increased cost of food and fuel, the average rate of wages for female labor has not been raised more than 20 per cent since the war was inaugurated; and yet the poor widow is obliged to pay as much for a loaf of bread or a pail of coal as the woman who has a husband or a stalwart son to assist her. In many trades the rate of wages has been lowered during the year, until it has become a mere pittance, while in other occupations the prices paid to females are generally insufficient to main them comfortably." . . .

One of the causes of complaint of the organized working women of Boston in 1869 was "the present fragmentary nature, the insufficiency, and great precariousness of the poor working women's labors," which "render it impossible for them to procure the common necessaries of existence, or make any provision for sickness and old age." . . .

That working women should receive the same pay as men for the same work has long been the desire of trade-unionists. Though not expressly states, it was implied in the resolution of the National Trades' Union in 1835, which complained that "the extreme low prices given for female labor, afford scarcely sufficient to satisfy the necessary wants of life, and create a destructive competition with the male laborer." . . . A generation later the National Labor Union, moreover, repeatedly passed resolutions expressing sympathy for the "sewing women and daughters of toil," urging them to unite in trade-unions, and demanding for them "equal pay for equal work." . . .

Again in 1868 the president of the National Labor Union, in his opening address to the congress, referred to "the extent to which female labor is introduced into many trades" as "a serious question," and stated that "the effect of introducing female labor is to undermine prices, that character of labor being usually employed, unjustly to the women, at a lower rate than is paid for male labor on the same kind of work." . . .

Scope and sources of the report. In this report on the history of women in industry, wage-earning occupation alone are considered. The unremunerated home work of women . . . is necessarily neglected. Women engaged in professions, in independent business, and in agriculture, too, are considered only in relation to the wage-earning women in industry. . . .

The character and conditions of woman's work within recent years have been fully described in reports, books, magazines, and newspapers which can be easily obtained, but the history of the formative period of woman's work has long been buried away in rare old books and papers, many of them until recently unknown even to close students of the labor question. The history of the wage labor of woman during and shortly after this formative period, moreover, is not only comparatively unknown, but furnishes the only positive basis for any historical interpretation of women in industry.

LETTERS FROM WOMEN WHO WENT TO JAIL FOR SUFFRAGE, 1917. *In January 1917, picketing for suffrage began outside the White House. Over the next two years, more than a thousand women took turns as "silent sentinels" holding banners at the entrance to the White House every day, no matter what the weather, and in spite of the entry of the United States into World War I.*

At first, bystanders sometimes attacked the picketers and tore up their banners. In June 1917, after weeks of unrest, the police arrested the women for obstructing traffic. The following are excerpts of reports from two women who were imprisoned during these protests.

. . . When Mrs. Gould and Miss Younger asked Florida women to go to Washington to help, I volunteered. I am seventy-three, but except for my lame foot I was well. . . .

I picketed three times with these splendid women, carrying a purple, white and gold suffrage flag. The third time we spent the night in the House of Detention because we refused to give bail. . . .

They ran through that "trial" rapidly the next day. We did not answer them or pay any attention. We knew, of course, that we would all be convicted and sentenced for months, just as the hundred and more other women who had done this thing for suffrage. . . .

It was about half past seven at night when we got to Occoquan workhouse. A woman was standing behind a desk when we were brought into this office, and there were six men also in the room. Mrs. Lewis, who spoke for all of us, refused to talk to the woman—who, I learned, was Mrs. Herndon—and said she must speak to Mr. Whittaker, the superintendent of the place.

"You'll sit here all night then," said Mrs. Herndon. I saw men beginning to come up on the porch through the window. But I didn't think anything about it. Mrs. Herndon called my name, but I did not answer. "You had better answer or it will the worse for you," said one man. "I'll take you and handle you, and you'll be sorry you made me," said another. The police woman who came with us begged us to answer to our names. We could see she was afraid.

Suddenly the door literally burst open and Whittaker rushed in like a tornado; some men followed him. We could see the crowds of them on the porch. They were not in uniform. They looked as much like tramps as anything. They seemed to come in—and in—and in. One had a face that made me think of an orang-outang. Mrs. Lewis stood up—we had been sitting and lying on the floor; we were so tired—but she hardly began to speak, saying we demanded to be treated as political prisoners when Whittaker said:

"You shut up! I have men here glad to handle you. Seize her!" I just saw men spring toward her and some one screamed, "They have taken Mrs. Lewis," when a man sprang at me, and caught me by the shoulder. I am used to being careful of my bad foot and I remember saying, "I'll come with you; don't drag me; I have a lame foot." But I was jerked down the steps and away into the dark. I didn't have my feet on the ground; I guess that saved me. I heard Mrs. Cosu, who was being dragged after me, call, "Be careful of your foot."

It was very black. The other building as we came to it, was low and dark. I only remember the American flag flying above because it caught the light from a window in a wing. We were rushed into a large room that we found opened on a long hall with brick dungeons on each side. "Punishment cells" is what they call them. They are dungeons. Mine was filthy; it had no window save a little slit at the top and no furniture but a sheet-iron bed and an open toilet flushed from outside the cell.

In the hall outside was a man called Captain Reems. He had on a uniform and was brandishing a stick as thick as my fist and shouting as we were shoved into the corridor. "Damn you, get in here!" I saw Dorothy Day brought in. She is a very slight girl. The two men were twisting her arms above her head. Then suddenly they lifted her up and banged her down over the arm of an iron bench—twice. As they ran me past she was lying there with her arms out, and I heard one of the men yell, "The _____ suffrager! My mother ain't no suffrager. I'll put you through _____."

At the end of the corridor they pushed me through a door. I lost my balance and fell on the iron bed. Mrs. Cosu struck the wall. Then they threw in two mats and two dirty blankets. There was no light but from the corridor. The door was barred from top to bottom. The walls were brick cemented over. It was bitter cold. Mrs. Cosu would not let me lie on the floor. She put me on the couch and stretched out on the floor. We had only lain there a few minutes trying to get our breath when Mrs. Lewis, doubled over and handled like a sack of something, was literally thrown in by two men. Her head struck the iron bed and she fell.

We thought she was dead. She didn't move. We were crying over her as we lifted her to the bed and stretched her out, when we heard Miss Burns call: "Where is Mrs. Lewis?"

Mrs. Cosu called out, "They've just thrown her in here." We were roughly told by the guard not to dare to speak again, or we would be put in straight-jackets. We were so terrified we kept very still. Mrs. Lewis was not unconscious; she was only stunned. But Mrs. Cosu was desperately ill as the night wore on. She had a bad heart attack, and then vomiting. We called and called. We asked them to send our doctor because we

thought she was dying; there was a woman guard and a man in the corridor, but they paid no attention. A cold wind blew in on us from the outside, and we all lay there shivering and only half conscious until early morning. . . .

I was released on the sixth day, and passed the dispensary as I came out. There were a group of my friends, Mrs. Brannan and Mrs. Morey and several others. They had on coarse striped dresses and big grotesque heavy shoes. I burst into tears as they led me away, my term having expired. I didn't want to desert them like that, but I had done all I could.

Alice Paul is in the psychopathic ward. She dreaded forcible feeding frightfully, and I hate to think how she must be feeling. I had a nervous time of it, gasping a long time afterward, and my stomach rejecting during the process. I spent a bad restless night, but otherwise I am alright. The poor souls who fed me got liberally besprinkled during the process. I heard myself making the most hideous sounds, like an animal in pain, and thought how dreadful it was of me to make such horrible sounds. . . . One feels so forsaken when one lies prone and people shove a pipe down one's stomach. . . .

We still get no mail; we are "insubordinate." It's strange, isn't it: if you ask for food fit to eat, as we did, you are "insubordinate"; and if you refuse food you are "insubordinate." Amusing. I am really all right. If this continues very long I perhaps won't be. I am interested to see how long our so-called "splendid American men" will stand for this form of discipline. . . .

All the officers here know we are making this hunger strike that women fighting for liberty may be considered political prisoners; we have told them. God knows we don't want other women ever to have to do this over again.

AN APPEAL FOR WOMAN SUFFRAGE BY PRESIDENT WOODROW WILSON, JANUARY 10, 1918. *President Woodrow Wilson appeared* *before the Senate to belatedly appeal for the passage of the Nineteenth Amendment to the Constitution of the United States. The amendment guaranteeing a woman's right to vote had already been passed by the House of Representatives. Formerly an enemy of the women's rights movement, Wilson changed his stance in response to 70 years of increasing activism, the fear of rising Bolshevism overseas, and the pressure of World War I.*

The Senate failed to pass the amendment by only two votes. However, in 1919, Congress finally approved the Nineteenth Amendment.

The unusual circumstances of a world war in which we stand and are judged in the view not only of our own people and our own consciences but also in the view of all nations and peoples will, I hope, justify in your thought, as it does in mine, the message I have come to bring you. I regard the concurrence of the Senate in the constitutional amendment proposing the extension of the suffrage to women as vitally essential to the successful prosecution of the great war of humanity in which we are engaged. I have come to urge upon you the considerations which have led me to that conclusion. . . .

This is a peoples' war and the peoples' thinking constitutes its atmosphere and morale, not the predilections of the drawing room or the political considerations of the caucus. If we be indeed democrats and wish to lead the world to democracy, we can ask other people to accept in proof of our sincerity and our ability to lead them whither they wish to be led nothing less persuasive and convincing than our actions. . . . They are looking to the great, powerful, famous Democracy of the West to lead them to the new day for which they have so long waited; and they think, in the logical simplicity, that democracy means that women shall play their part in affairs alongside men and upon an equal footing with them. If we reject measures like this,. . . . they will cease to believe in us; they will cease to follow or to trust us. They have seen their own Governments accept this interpretation of democracy,—seen old Governments like that of Great Britain, which did not profess to be democratic, promise readily and as of course this justice to women, though they had before refused it, the strange revelations of this war having made many things new and plain, to governments as well as to peoples.

Are we alone to refuse to learn the lesson? Are we alone to ask and take the utmost that our women can give,—service and sacrifice of every kind,—and still say we do not see what title that gives them to stand by our sides in the guidance of the affairs of their nation and ours? We have made partners of the women in this war; shall we admit them only to a partnership of suffering and sacrifice and toil and not to a partnership of privilege and right?. . . .

. . . I tell you plainly, as the commander in chief of our armies and of the gallant men in our fleets, as the present spokesman of this people in our dealings with the men and women throughout the world who are now our partners, as the responsible head of a great government . . . I tell you plainly that this measure which I urge upon you is vital to the winning of the war and to energies alike of preparation and of battle.

And not to the winning of the war only. It is vital to the right solution of the great problems which we must settle, and settle immediately, when the war is over. We shall need then a vision of affairs, which is theirs, and, as we have never needed them before, the sympathy and insight and clear moral instinct of the women of the world. The problems of that time will strike to the roots of many things that we have not hitherto questioned, and I for one believe that our safety in those questioning days, as well as our comprehension of matters that touch society to the quick, will depend upon the direct and authoritative participation of women in our counsels. We shall need their moral sense to preserve what is right and fine and worthy in our system of life as well as to discover just what it is that ought to be purified and reformed. Without their counselings we shall be only half wise.

That is my case. This is my appeal. Many may deny its validity, if they choose, but no one can brush aside or answer the arguments upon which it is based. The executive tasks of this war rest upon me. I ask that you lighten them and place in my hands instruments, spiritual instruments, which I do not now possess, which I sorely need, and which I have daily to apologize for not being able to employ.

NINETEENTH AMENDMENT TO THE U.S. CONSTITUTION, AUGUST 26, 1920.

By August 26, 1920, the Nineteenth Amendment had been ratified by the states and became part of the Constitution of the United States.

The right of citizens of the United States to vote shall not be denied or abridged by the United States or by any State on account of sex.

Congress shall have power to enforce this Article by appropriate legislation.

AMERICAN BIRTH CONTROL LEAGUE, PRINCIPLES AND AIMS, 1921.

The first national organization to promote birth control in the United States was formed in 1915 by a group of New York women inspired by the arrest of Margaret and William Sanger, who had defied the laws against distributing birth control literature. Called the National Birth Control League, it had by 1917 helped form 20 birth control leagues around the country to fight laws against contraception. However, by 1921, that organization had dissolved due to differences among birth control advocates.

In 1921, Margaret Sanger formed the American Birth Control League. By 1926 it claimed more than 37,000 members and state affiliates in Illinois, Ohio, California, Michigan, and Texas. The following excerpts were published in 1921, in the league's newsletter, Birth Control Review.

The complex problems now confronting America as the result of the practice of reckless procreation are fast threatening to grow beyond human control.

Everywhere we see poverty and large families going hand in hand. Those least fit to carry on the race are increasing most rapidly. People who cannot support their own offspring are encouraged by Church and State to produce large families. Many of the children thus begotten are diseased or feeble-minded; many become criminals. The burden of supporting these unwanted types has to be borne by the healthy elements of the nation. Funds that should be used to raise the standard of our civilization are diverted to the maintenance of those who should never have been born.

In addition to this grave evil we witness the appalling waste of women's health and women's lives by too frequent pregnancies. These unwanted pregnancies often provoke the crime of abortion, or alternatively multiply the number of child workers and lower the standard of living . . .

We hold that children should be

1. Conceived in love;

2. Born of the mother's conscious desire;

3. And only begotten under conditions which render possible the heritage of health.

Therefore we hold that every woman must possess the power and freedom to prevent conception except when these conditions can be satisfied . . .

Instead of being a blind and haphazard consequence of uncontrolled instinct, motherhood must be made the responsible and self-directed means of human expression and regeneration.

These purposes, which are of fundamental importance to the whole of our nation and to the future of mankind, can only be attained in the means of Birth Control. That, therefore, is the first object to which the efforts of this League will be directed.

Aims of the American Birth Control League are to enlighten and educate all sections of the American public in the various aspects of the dangers of uncontrolled procreation and the imperative necessity of a world program of Birth Control.

The League aims to correlate the findings of scientists, statisticians, investigators and social agencies in all fields. To make this possible, it is necessary to organize various departments:

Research: To collect the findings of scientists, concerning the relation of reckless breeding to delinquency, defect and dependence.

Investigation: To derive from these scientifically ascertained facts and figures, conclusions which may aid all public health and social agencies in the study of problems of maternal and infant mortality, child-labor, mental and physical defects and delinquence in relation to the practice of reckless parentage.

Hygienic and phsyiological instruction by the Medical profession to mothers and potential mothers in harmless and reliable methods of Birth Control in answer to their requests for such knowledge.

Sterilization of the insane and feeble-minded and the encouragement of this operation upon those afflicted with inherited or transmissible diseases, with the understanding that sterilization does not deprive the individual of his or her sex expression, but merely renders him incapable of producing children.

Educational: The program of education includes: The enlightenment of the public at large, mainly through the education of leaders of thought and opinion—teachers, ministers, editors and writers—to the moral and scientific soundness of the principles of Birth Control and the imperative necessity of its adoption as the basis of national and racial progress.

Political and Legislative: To enlist the support and co-operation of legal advisors, statesmen and legislators in effecting the removal of state and federal statutes which encourage dysgenic breeding, increase the sum total of disease, misery and poverty and prevent the establishment of a policy of national health and strength.

Organization: To send into the various States of the Union field workers to enlist the support and arouse the interest of the masses, to the importance of Birth Control so that laws may be changed and the establishment of clinics made possible in every State.

International: This department aims to co-operate with similar organizations in other countries to study Birth Control in its relations to the world population problem, food supplies, national and racial conflicts, and to urge upon all international bodies organized to promote world peace, the consideration of these aspects of international amity. . . .

EQUAL RIGHTS AMENDMENT, 1923. *The following proposed amendment to the Constituiton of the United States was introduced into Congress in 1923. It was the first of many attempts to enshrine the rights of women in the constitution of the nation. It was nicknamed "the Lucretia Mott" amendment after the president of the first, short-lived American Equal Rights Association (1866-1869).*

The proposed Equal Rights Amendment split the women's movement into opposing camps. Supporters insisted on enshrining the equal rights of women in the document that forms the well-spring of our nation's laws. Opponents feared passage would enable legislatures to undo hard-won labor law protection for women. This split among women, as well as opposition by male legislators, was to prove the downfall of all equal rights legislation throughout the 20th century.

The Lucretia Mott amendment (1923):

"Men and women shall have equal rights throughout the United States and every place subject to its jurisdiction."

PRESIDENT'S COMMISSION ON THE STATUS OF WOMEN, 1963.

In 1961, amid the violent atmosphere of the black civil rights struggle, President Kennedy agreed to a federal study of the status of women in the United States. In that year, he established the President's Commission on the Status of Women to investigate the "prejudice and outmoded customs that act as barriers to the full realization of women's basic rights" and to make recommendations in the areas of employment practice, social security and tax law, labor laws, and services such as child care.

In 1963 the commission issued its report which, while not going as far as militant feminists had hoped, still reflected a major shift in attitude toward the rights of women at the national level. The following are excerpts from the recommendations of the President's Commission.

Means of acquiring or continuing education must be available to every adult at whatever point he or she broke off traditional formal schooling. The structure of adult education must be drastically revised. It must provide practicable and accessible opportunities, developed with regard for the needs of women, to complete elementary and secondary school and to continue education beyond high school. Vocational training . . . should be included at all of these educational levels. Where needed and appropriate, financial support should be provided by local, State, and Federal governments and by private groups and foundations. . . .

. . . Public and private agencies should join in strengthening counseling resources. . . . Institutions offering counseling education should provide both course content and ample supervised experience in the counseling of females as well as males, adults as well as adolescents.

The education of girls and women for their responsibilities in home and community should be thoroughly re-examined with a view to discovering more effective approaches. . . .

Home and Community: For the benefit of children, mothers, and society, child-care services should be available for children of families at all economic levels. . . .

Tax deductions for child-care expenses of working mothers should be kept commensurate with the median income of couples when both husband and wife are engaged in substantial employment. The present limitation on their joint income, above which deductions are not allowable, should be raised. Additional deductions, of lesser amounts, should be allowed for children beyond the first. The 11-year age limit for child-care deductions should be raised. . . .

Community programs under public and private auspices should make comprehensive provisions for health and rehabilitation services, including easily accessible maternal and child health services, accompanies by education to encourage their use.

Volunteers' services should be made more effective . . . through tapping the large reservoir of additional potential among youth, retired people, members of minority groups, and women not now in volunteer activities.

Women in Employment: Equal opportunity for women in hiring, training, and promotion should be the governing principle in private employment. An Executive order should state this principle and advance its application to work done under Federal contracts. . . .

Many able women, including highly trained professionals, who are not free for full-time employment, can work part time. The Civil Service Commission and the Bureau of the Budget should facilitate the imaginative and prudent use of such personnel throughout the Government service.

Labor Standards: The federal Fair Labor Standards Act, including premium pay for overtime, should be extended to employment subject to Federal jurisdiction but now uncovered, such as work in hotels, motels, restaurants, and laundries, in additional retail establishments, in agriculture, and in nonprofit organizations.

State legislation, applicable to both men and women, should be enacted, or strengthened and extended to all types of employment to provide minimum-wage levels approximating the minimum under federal law and to require premium pay at the rate of at least time and a half for overtime. . . .

. . . The best way to discourage excessive hours for all workers is by broad and effective minimum wage coverage, both federal and state. . . .

Until such time as this goal is attained, State legislation limiting maximum hours of work for women should be maintained, strengthened, and expanded. . . .

State laws should establish the principle of equal pay for comparable work.

State laws should protect the right of all workers to join unions of their own choosing and to bargain collectively.

Security of Basic Income: A widow's benefit under the Federal old-age insurance system should be equal to the amount that her husband would have received at the same age had he lived. This objective should be approached as rapidly as may be financially feasible.

The coverage of the unemployment-insurance system should be extended. Small establishments and nonprofit organizations should be covered now through Federal action, and State and local government employees through State action. Practicable means of covering at least some household workers and agricultural workers should be actively explored.

Paid maternity leave or comparable insurance benefits should be provided for women workers' employers, unions, and governments should explore the best means of accomplishing this purpose.

Women Under the Law: Early and definitive court pronouncement, particularly by the United States Supreme Court, is urgently needed with regard to the validity under the 5th and 14th amendments of laws and official practices discriminating against women, to the end that the principle of equality become firmly established in constitutional doctrine. . . .

The United States should assert leadership, particularly in the United Nations, in securing equality of rights for women . . . and should demonstrate its sincere concern for women's equal rights by becoming a party to appropriate conventions.

Appropriate action, including enactment of legislation where necessary, should be taken to achieve equal jury service in the States.

State legislatures, and other groups concerned with the improvement of State statutes affecting family law and personal and property rights of married women . . . should move to eliminate laws which impose legal disabilities on women.

Women as Citizens: Women should be encouraged to seek elective and appointive posts at local, State, and National levels and in all three branches of government.

Public office should be held according to ability, experience, and effort, without special preferences or discriminations based on sex. Increasing consideration should continually be given to the appointment of women of demonstrated ability and political sensitivity to policy-making positions.

Continuing Leadership: To further the objectives proposed in this report, an Executive order should:

1. Designate a Cabinet officer to be responsible for assuring that the resources and activities of the Federal Government bearing upon the Commission's recommendations are directed to carrying them out, and for making periodic progress reports to the President.

2. Designate the heads of other agencies involved in those activities to serve, under the chairmanship of the designated Cabinet officer, as an interdepartmental committee to assure proper coordination and action.

3. Establish a citizens committee, advisory to the interdepartmental committee and with its secretariat from the designated Cabinet officer, to meet periodically to evaluate progress made, provide counsel, and serve as a means for suggesting and stimulating action.

U.S. EQUAL PAY ACT, 1963. *The 1963 Equal Pay Act was the first federal law against sex discrimination covering all workers subject to the Fair Labor Standards Act of 1938: executive, administrative, and professional employees, as well as agricultural and domestic workers. The Department of Labor is charged with enforcement.*

No employer having employees subject to any provisions of this section shall discriminate within any establishment in which such employees are employed, between employees on the basis of sex by paying wages to employees in such establishment at a rate less than the rate at which he pays wages to employees of the opposite sex in such establishment for equal work on jobs the performance of which requires equal skill, effort, and responsibility, and which are performed under similar working conditions, except where such payment is made pursuant to . . . a differential based on any other factor other than sex. . . .

CIVIL RIGHTS ACT, TITLE VII, 1964. *Having been born in the pressure cooker of the Nineteenth century abolition movement, the cause of women's rights found itself allied again with a movement to secure rights for America's minority populations. In*

1964 the Congress passed the Civil Rights Act, which extended important protections to racial minorities and women.

Title VII and Job Discrimination: Sec. 703 Discrimination Because of Race, Color, Religion, Sex, or National Origin

(a) It shall be an unlawful employment practice for an employer—

(1) to fail or refuse to hire or discharge any individual, or otherwise to discriminate against any individual with respect to his compensation, terms, conditions, or privileges of employment, because of such individual's race, color, religion, sex, or national origin; or

(2) to limit, segregate, or classify his employees in any way which would deprive or tend to deprive any individual of employment opportunities or otherwise adversely affect his status as an employee, because of such individual's race, color, religion, sex, or national origin.

(b) It shall be an unlawful employment practice for an employment agency to fail or refuse to refer for employment, or otherwise to discriminate against, any individual because of his race, color, religion, sex, or national origin, or to classify or refer for employment any individual on the basis of his race, color, religion, sex, or national origin.

(c) It shall be an unlawful employment practice for a labor organization—

(1) to exclude or to expel from its membership, or otherwise to discriminate against, any individual because of his race, color, religion, sex, or national origin;

(2) to limit, segregate, or classify its membership, or to classify or fail or refuse to refer for employment any individual, in any way which would deprive or tend to deprive any individual of employment opportunities, or would limit such employment opportunities or otherwise adversely

affect his status as an employee or as an applicant for employment, because of such individual's race, color, religion, sex, or national origin; or

(3) to cause or attempt to cause an employer to discriminate against an individual in violation of this section. . . .

NATIONAL ORGANIZATION FOR WOMEN, 1967.

Women who had taken part in the federal Citizens' Advisory Council on the Status of Women and other commissions studying women's rights banded together in 1966 to form the National Organization for Women (NOW) to fight for an end to sex discrimination. NOW went on to become the largest and best-known women's rights organization. It began with 300 members in 1967. By 1974, its 700 chapters in the U.S. and nine other countries reported approximately 48,000 members.

Following is the statement of objectives agreed upon at NOW's first national conference, held in November 1967.

WE DEMAND:

I. That the U.S. Congress immediately pass the Equal Rights Amendment to the Constitution and that such then be immediately ratified by the several States.

II. That equal employment opportunity be guaranteed to all women, as well as men . . .

III. That women be protected by law to ensure their rights to return to their jobs within a reasonable time after child-birth without loss of seniority or other accrued benefits, and be paid maternity leave as a form of social security and/or employee benefit.

IV. Immediate revision of tax laws to permit the deduction of home and child-care expenses for working parents.

V. That child-care facilities be established by law on the same basis as parks, libraries, and public schools, adequate to the needs of children from the pre-school years through adolescence, as a community resource to be used by all citizens from all income levels.

VI. That the right of women to be educated to their full potential equally with men be secured by Federal and State legislation . . .

VII. The right of women in poverty to secure job training, housing, and family allowances on equal terms with men, but without prejudice to a parent's right to remain at home to care for his or her children; revision of welfare legislation and poverty programs which deny women dignity, privacy, and self-respect.

VIII. The right of women to control their own reproductive lives by removing from the penal codes laws limiting access to contraceptive information and devices, and by repealing penal laws governing abortion.

REDSTOCKINGS MANIFESTO, 1969.

The Redstockings were a group of New York activists who sought to effect a change in women's attitudes by using untried methods to raise consciousness about the importance of the women's movement. They defined the concept of "sisterhood" in their 1969 "Redstockings Manifesto."

VI. We identify with all women. We define our best interest as that of the poorest, most brutally exploited woman.

We repudiate all economic, racial, educational or status privileges that divide us from other women. We are determined to recognize and eliminate any prejudices we may hold against other women.

We are committed to achieving internal democracy. We will do whatever is necessary to ensure that every woman in our movement has an equal chance to participate, assume responsibility, and develop her political potential.

VII. We call on all our sisters to unite with us in struggle.

We call on all men to give up their male privileges and support women's liberation in the interest of our humanity and their own.

In fighting for our liberation we will always take the side of women against their oppressors. We will not ask what is "revolutionary" or "reformist," only what is good for women.

The time for individual skirmishes has passed. This time we are going all the way.

WOMEN'S NATIONAL ABORTION COALITION, 1971.

The following announcement of a Women's National Abortion Conference came at a time of increasing activism in the women's movement in the United States. In 1969, the Redstockings held a public meeting at which twelve women described their own experiences with abortion to a large audience. After many mass demonstrations and lobbying, the Women's National Abortion Coalition was formed to unite the efforts of many different groups towards the goal of legalization of abortion.

. . . We believe that the most democratic way we could launch a national campaign for the repeal of all abortion laws would be to move quickly to hold a national women's conference on abortion. We want to gather the growing numbers of women who are eager to get involved—Black, Chicana, Latina, Asian, Puerto Rican and Native American women, campus women, gay women, high school students, housewives, professional, welfare and working women, young women and older women, women from churches, political organizations, trade unions, the military and communities across the country—and together decide on a course of action that can best win the repeal of all abortion laws with no forced sterilization. We will also be concerned with the repeal of restrictive contraception laws that exist in 30 states.

At a national conference we can both share information and experiences and discuss proposals for action. Women from New Haven, for example,

have already suggested holding a massive demonstration in Washington in October demanding that the Supreme Court recognize the rights of women and declare all existing abortion legislation unconstitutional. Such a demonstration would coincide with Supreme Court hearings on whether a woman's constitutional right to privacy applies to abortion. The outcome of this decision will have national significance. Others are discussing the possibility of working for a constitutional amendment or other federal legislation that would wipe out all state abortion laws.

We are calling this conference for July 16, 17 & 18, 1971, in New York City. This date has special symbolic significance, since it is the anniversary of the historic 1848 Seneca Falls Convention, where our sisters of the last century met and organized the first women's rights movement. Our actions can be as historic as theirs . . .

OFCC GUIDELINES, OFFICE OF FEDERAL CONTRACT COMPLIANCE, 1973.

In 1973, the Office of Federal Contract Compliance issued new guidelines requiring federal contractors to take corrective or "affirmative" action to end sex discrimination. The following excerpt illustrates the wide-ranging scope of these regulations.

(a) Written personnel policies relating to this subject area must expressly indicate that there shall be no discrimination against employees on account of sex. If the employer deals with a bargaining representative for its employees and there is an agreement on conditions of employment, such agreement shall not be inconsistent with these guidelines.

(b) All employees regardless of sex shall be given an equal opportunity to qualify for any job except where sex is a bona fide occupational qualification.

(c) The employer shall not make any distinction based upon sex in employment opportunities, wages, hours or other conditions of employment.

Nor shall the employer make any distinction based upon sex in the granting of fringe benefits, including medical, hospital, accident, life insurance, pension and retirement benefits, profit sharing and bonus plans, credit union benefits, leave and other terms and conditions of employment . . .

(d) Any distinction between married and unmarried persons of one sex that is not made between married and unmarried persons of the opposite sex shall be considered to be a distinction made on the basis of sex. Similarly, an employer shall not deny employment to women with young children unless it has the same exclusionary policies for men.

(e) An employer shall not make available benefits for the wives and families of male employees where the same benefits are not made available to female employees and their husbands and families; nor shall an employer make available benefits to the husbands and families of female employees which are not made available to male employees and their wives and families.

(f) The employer's policies and practices must assure comparable physical facilities including recreational facilities and other employee services to both sexes. The employer shall not refuse to hire men or women, or deny men or women a particular job because there are no restrooms or associated facilities.

(g) An employer shall not deny a female employee the right to any job that she is qualified to perform in reliance upon a State "protective" law. For example, such laws include those which prohibit women from performing certain types of occupations (e.g., a bartender); from working at jobs requiring more than a certain number of hours; and from working at jobs that require lifting or carrying more than designated weights. Such legislation has been found to result in restricting employment opportunities for men and/or women. Accordingly, it cannot be used as basis for denying employment or for establishing sex as a bona fide occupational qualification for the job.

(h)(1) Women shall not be rejected for employment, suspended from employment, or required to take leave involuntarily solely on account of the condition of pregnancy . . .

PROCLAMATION 4252, INTERNATIONAL WOMEN'S YEAR, JANUARY 30, 1975. *This presidential proclamation, issued by Richard M. Nixon, officially designated the United States observance of 1975 as International Women's Year as proclaimed on December 18, 1972 by the United Nations General Assembly.*

By the President of the United States: A Proclamation: There is a growing awareness today of the significant contributions that American women have made to our country's development, its culture, and its social and economic life. Women have enriched our society as homemakers and mothers and our community life through dedicated service as volunteers. Their entry into the labor force in increasing numbers has strengthened and expanded our economy. Despite these important contributions, women continue to face inequities as they seek a broader role in the life of our Nation.

In recent years, we have made significant progress toward remedying this situation, not only by striking down barriers to the employment and advancement of women in Government, but by ending discriminatory practices in other fields through legislation, Executive order, and judicial decree. Even when legal equality is achieved, however, traditional discriminatory attitudes, beliefs and practices may persist, preventing women from enjoying the full and equal rights that they deserve.

This Administration is committed to providing an opportunity for women to participate on an equal basis with men in our national life. We support the Equal Rights Amendment, we are moving vigorously to ensure full equal employment opportunity for women in the Federal service, and we are enforcing the law requiring similar efforts in business and institutions which receive Federal contracts or assistance.

The United Nations General Assembly, by adoption of Resolution 3010 of December 18, 1972, designated 1975 as International Women's Year. This resolution offers an exceptional opportunity to intensify the national effort already underway in the United States to further advance the status of women.

In observing International Women's Year, we should emphasize the role of women in the economy, their accomplishments in the professions, in Government, in the arts and humanities, and in their roles as wives and mothers.

The Congress approved the Equal Rights Amendment to the Constitution in 1972. It would be a fitting tribute to American's women to complete the ratification of this amendment by 1975.

Let us begin now to work together, men and women, to make 1975 an outstanding year for women in the United States, and lend our support to the advancement of women around the world.

NOW, THEREFORE, I, RICHARD NIXON, President of the United States of America, do hereby designate the year 1975 as International Women's Year in the United States. I call upon the Congress and the people of the United States, interested groups and organizations, officials of the Federal Government and of State and local governments, officials of the Federal Government and of State and local governments, educational institutions, and all others who can be of help, to begin now to provide for the observance of International Women's Year with practical and constructive measures for the advancement of the status of women, and also to cooperate with the activities of the status of women, and also to cooperate with the activities and observances to be arranged under the auspices of the United Nations.

IN WITNESS WHEREOF, I have hereunto set my hand this thirtieth day of January in the year of our Lord nineteen hundred seventy-four, and of the Independence of the United States of America the one hundred ninety-eighth.

PROCLAMATION 4903, WOMEN'S HISTORY WEEK, FEBRUARY 26, 1982. *This presidential procalamation, issued by Ronald Reagan, officially designated the first week in March—in 1982, the week of March 7—as Women's History Week in the United States.*

By the President of the United States: A Proclamation. American women of every race, creed and ethnic background helped found and build our Nation in countless recorded and unrecorded ways. As pioneers, teachers, mothers, homemakers, soldiers, nurses and laborers women played and continue to play a vital role in American economic, cultural and social life. In science, business, medicine, law, the arts and the home, women have made significant contributions to the growth and development of our land. Their diverse service is among American's most precious gifts.

As leaders in public affairs, American women not only worked to secure their own rights of suffrage and equal opportunity but also were principal advocates in the abolitionist, temperance, mental health reform, industrial labor and social reform movements, as well as the modern civil rights movement. Their dedication and commitment heightened awareness of our society's needs and accelerated our common efforts to meet those needs.

As volunteers, women have provided invaluable service and leadership in American charitable, philanthropic and cultural endeavors. And, as mothers and homemakers, they remain instrumental in preserving the cornerstone of our Nation's strength—the family.

In 1981, the Congress by joint resolution (P.L. 97-28, August 4, 1981) designated the week beginning March 7, 1982, as "Women's History Week" and asked the President to issue a proclamation to commemorate and encourage the study, observance and celebration of the vital role of women in American history. In formally acknowledging the achievements of women, we honor a vital part of our common heritage.

NOW, THEREFORE, I, RONALD REAGAN, President of the United States of America, do hereby proclaim the week beginning March 7, 1982, as Women's History Week. Recognizing that the many contributions of American women have at times been overlooked in the annals of American history, I encourage all citizens to observe this important week by participating in appropriate ceremonies and activities planned by individuals, governmental agencies, and private institutions and associations throughout the country.

IN WITNESS WHEREOF, I have hereunto set my hand this 26th. day of February in the year of our Lord nineteen hundred and eighty-two, and of the Independence of the United States of America the two hundred and sixth.

RONALD REAGAN

PROCLAMATION 5619, WOMEN'S HISTORY MONTH, MARCH 16, 1987. *This presidential proclamation, issued by Ronald Reagan, officially designated the month of March as Women's History Month in the United States.*

By the President of the United States: A Proclamation: From earliest times, women have helped shape our Nation. Historians today stress all that women have meant to our national life, but the rest of us too should remember, with pride and gratitude, the achievements of women throughout American history.

Those achievements span the wide range of human endeavor. They have not been attained without the quiet courage and sacrifice of millions of women, some famed, most not. Women have established themselves in business and the professions, and today women outnumber men as undergraduates at our colleges and universities. Women have fought for moral and social reform and have taken part in and led many great social and political movements of our land. Women have founded many of our philanthropic, cultural, educational, and charitable institutions. Women have served our Nation with valor and distinction during wartime, nursing the wounded, piloting airplanes, performing vital jobs in defense plants. Women have forged a place for themselves in public life, serving on the Supreme Court, in the Congress, and in Cabinet posts; becoming Ambassadors; and holding Federal Executive posts that affect the lives of every citizen.

Most importantly, as women take part in the world of work, they also continue to embrace and nurture the family as they have always done. All Americans can be truly grateful for the role of women as the heart of the family and for their every accomplishment today and throughout our history.

The Congress, by Senate Joint Resolution 20, has designated the month of March 1987 as "Women's History Month" and authorized and requested the President to issue a proclamation in observance of this event.

NOW, THEREFORE, I, RONALD REAGAN, President of the United States of America, do hereby proclaim March 1987 as Women's History Month. I call upon all Americans to mark this month with appropriate observances to honor the achievements of American women.

IN WITNESS WHEREOF, I have hereunto set my hand this sixteenth day of March, in the year of our Lord nineteen hundred and eighty-seven, and of the Independence of the United States of America the two hundred and eleventh.

RONALD REAGAN

GENERAL BIBLIOGRAPHY

A

Anderson, Bonnie S. and Judith P. Zinsser. *A History of Their Own.* New York: Harper and Row, 1988.

Attwater, Donald. *The Penguin Dictionary of Saints.* Harmondsworth, Eng.: Penguin, 1983.

B

Beard, Mary. *Woman as Force in History.* New York: Macmillan, 1946.

Bluestone, Nathalie Harris. *Woman and the Ideal Society.* Oxford: Oxford Univeristy Press, 1987.

Boulding, Elise. *Women in the Twentieth Century World.* New York: Sage, 1977.

Brown, Peter. *The Body and Society: Men, Women, and Sexual Renunciation in Early Christianity.* New York: Columbia University Press, 1988.

————. *The Cult of the Saints.* Chicago: Peter Smith, 1981.

C

Cleverdon, Catherine L. *The Woman Suffrage Movement in Canada: The Start of Liberation, 1900–1920.* Toronto: University of Toronto Press, 1974.

D

DuBois, Ellen Carol, ed. *Elizabeth Cary Stanton, Susan B. Anthony: Correspondence, Writings, Speeches.* New York: Schocken, 1981.

E

Evans, Sara. *Born for Liberty: A History of Women in America.* New York: The Free Press, 1989.

F

Foley, Helen P., ed. *Reflections of Women in Antiquity.* New York: Gordon and Breach, 1981.

Fraser, Antonia. *Mary Queen of Scots.* New York: Delacorte, 1969.

————. *The Warrior Queens.* New York: Vintage Books, 1990.

————. *The Weaker Vessel.* New York: Vintage Books, 1985.

G

Guttmann, Allen. *Women's Sports: A History.* New York: Columbia University Press, 1991.

H

Hafkin, Nancy J. and Edna G. Bay, eds. *Women in Africa: Studies in Social and Economic Change.* Stanford, CA: Stanford Univesity Press, 1976.

Harris, Ann Sutherland and Linda Nochlin. *Women Artists: 1550–1950.* New York: Alfred A. Knopf, 1989.

Hiley, Michael. *Victorian Working Women.* Boston: David R. Godine, 1979.

Hine, Darlene Clark, Elsa Barkley Brown, and Rosalyn Terborg-Penn, eds. *Black Women in America: An Historical Encyclopedia.* (Brooklyn, NY: Carlson Publishing Inc., 1993.

J

James, Edward T., ed. *Notable American Women: A Biographical Dictionary.* Cambridge, MA: Belknap, 1971.

Just, Roger. *Women in Athenian Law and Life.* London, Eng.: Routledge, 1989.

K

Kenneally, James J. *The History of American Catholic Women.* New York: Crossroad, 1990.

Kerber, Linda K., Alice Kessler-Harris, and Kathry Kish Sklar. *U.S. History as Women's History: New Feminist Essays.* Chapel Hill: University of North Carolina Press, 1995.

——— and J. D. Mathews, eds. *Women's America: Refocusing the Past.* New York: Oxford University Press, 1982.

King, Margaret L. *Women of the Renaissance.* Chicago: University of Chicago Press, 1991.

Kraditor, Ailees S. *The Ideas of the Woman Suffrage Movement, 1890–1920.* New York: Norton, 1981.

L

Lacey, W.K. *The Family in Classical Greece.* Ithace, NY: Cornell University Press, 1968.

Lefkowitz, Mary R. *Women in Greek Myth.* London, Eng.: Duckworth, 1986.

——— and Maureen B. Fant. *Women's Life in Greece and Rome.* Baltimore, MD: Johns Hopkins University Press, 1982.

Lerner, Gerda. *The Creation of Feminist Consciousness: From the Middle Ages to 1870.* New York: Oxford University Press, 1993.

M

MacKenzie, Midge, ed. *Shoulder to Shoulder.* New York: Knopf, 1975.

Mandel, William M. *Soviet Women.* New York: Anchor Press, 1975.

O

Ogilvie, Marilyn Bailey. *Women in Science.* Cambridge, MA: MIT Press, 1991.

O'Neill, Lois Decker. *The Women's Book of World Records and Achievements.* Garden City, NY: Anchor Press, 1979.

Orleck, Annelise. *Common Sense and a Little Fire: Women and Working-Class Politics in the United States, 1900–1965.* Chapel Hill: University of North Carolina Press, 1995.

P

Pantal, Pauline Schmitt, ed. *A History of Women in the West: vols. I–IV.* Cambridge, MA:

Belknap, 1992.

Power, Eileen. *Medieval Women.* Cambridge, MA: Cambridge University Press, 1975.

R

Read, Phyllis J. and Bernard L. Witlieb. *The Book of Women's Firsts.* New York: Random House, 1992.

Reeves, Minou. *Female Warriors of Allah: Woman and the Islamic Revolution.* New York: E.P. Dutton, 1989.

S

Smith, Jessie Carney. *Notable Black American Women.* Detroit: Gale Research, 1992.

T

Trager, James. *The Women's Chronology: A Year-by-Year Record, from Prehistory to the Present.* New York: Henry Holt, 1994.

Trofimenkoff, Susan Mann and Alison Prentice, eds. *The Neglected Majority: Esays in Canadian Women's History.* Toronto: McClelland, 1977.

V

Vare, Ethlie Ann and Greg Ptacek. *Mothers of Invention: From the Bra to the Bomb, Forgotten Women and Their Unforgettable Ideas.* New York: Quill, 1987.

INDEX OF WOMEN

A

Abbott, Berenice 279
Aberdeen, Lady 269
Abutsu, Ni 77–78
Abzug, Bella 339, 432, 433, 462
Adams, Abigail 445
Adams, Hannah 133, 143
Adams, Harriet Stratemeyer 266
Addams, Jane 245, 445
Adelaide, Empress 64
Aethelflaed 62
Agnesi, Maria 125
Agrippina (the Elder) 34, 36, 37, 40
Agrippina the Younger 39, 41, 42, 43
Ahhotep, Queen 11
Akazome, Emon 63
Akerman, Chantal 440
Akhmatova, Anna 310
Akiko, Yosano 311
Akiyoshi, Toshiko 443
Alakija, Aduke 446
Albright, Tenley 402, 406
Alcott, Louisa May 174, 214
Alexandra, Tsarina 326
al-Kharafi, Faiza Mohammed 464
Al-Lat 55
Allen, Florence Ellinwood 408
Allyn, Nancy 434
Al-Uzza 55
Amalasuntha 52
Amaterasu o Mikami 16, 17, 26, 465
Amatseru Omikami 488
Amazons 483–484
Amenouzume no Mikoto 17
Ana 27
Anat 486–487
Anderson, Elizabeth Garrett 217, 229, 235

Anderson, Eugenie Moore 398, 415
Anderson, Marian 379, 405, 413, 445
Anderson, Mary 230, 335
Andromeda 478
Angelou, Maya 355, 463
Anguissola, Sofonisba 95
Anna Amalia (of Brunswick) 133
Anne, Queen 123
Anthony, Susan B. 160, 165, 194, 198, 200, 206, 210, 218, 221, 222, 224, 232, 241, 257, 262, 267, 399, 445
Aphrodite 26, 35, 467, 474–475
Applebee, Constance 233, 335
Aquino, Corazon 455
Arachne 482
Arakida, Reijo 127
Arbus, Diane 411, 433
Ariyoshi, Sawako 409
Arlington, Lizzie 279
Armstrong, Anne 352, 432, 435, 440
Arzner, Dorothy 356, 369, 439
Asherah 15
Aspasia 24
Aspinall, Jessie 299
Astell, Mary 119
Astor, Nancy 243, 332, 419
Athena 51, 472–474, 481, 482
Atropos 474
Atse Estsan 488
Atum 468
Atwood, Margaret 454
Auclert, Hubertine 191, 239
Audouard, Olympe 217
August, Rebecca Beck 245
Augusta, Sophia Frederica. See Catherine the Great, Empress
Aung, San Auu Kyi 457
Austen, Jane 139

Austin, Harriet N. 199
Aw Sian, Sally 431
Ayako, Sono 404

B

Baba Yaga 489
Bache, Sarah Franklin 142
Bacon, Delia 158, 205
Bacon, Mary 433
Badb 27
Baez, Joan 420, 444
Bagley, Sarah 178, 187
Bagnold, Enid 259
Bagshaw, Elizabeth 247
Bai, Laskshmi 205
Baker, Norma Jean. See Monroe, Marilyn
Baker, Sara Josephine 233, 302
Balas, Iolanda 408
Balthild, Saint 56
Ban, Zhao 42
Bancroft, Ann 455
Bandaranaike, Sirimavo 412
Bannerman, Helen 280
Bara, Theda 261, 319
Barbapiccola, Guiseppa Eleanora 127
Barbara, Agatha 391, 450
Barnard, Kate 298
Barnes, Juliana 86
Barnett, Ida B. Wells 275
Barney, Natalie 232, 293
Barnum, Gertrude 288, 323
Barry, Leonora 257
Barton, Clara 445
Bassi, Laura 139
Bast 14
Batchelor, Joy 382

INDEX BY DAY AND MONTH

JANUARY

January 1, 1752	Birth of Elizabeth "Betsy" Griscom Ross in Philadelphia, Pennsylvania.
January 2, 1957	Patricia McCormick competes in bullfight.
January 3, 1793	Birth of suffragist Lucretia Coffin Mott.
January 3, 1969	Shirley Chisholm is first African American woman to join U.S. Congress.
January 3, 1973	Barbara Jordan joins U.S. Congress.
January 4, 1896	Suffrage granted to women in Utah.
January 4, 1913	Australian Freda du Faur makes first grand traverse of Mount Cook.
January 5, 1835	Birth of Olympia Brown, first woman minister.
January 5, 1885	Birth of Isabella McCorkindale, Australian temperance campaigner and feminist.
January 6, 1759	Wedding of Martha and George Washington.
January 6, 1943	Clare Boothe Luce joins U.S. Congress.
January 7, 1894	Jean Crook Devanny, Australian novelist and political activist, is born.
January 7, 1903	Birth of American author Zora Neale Hurston.
January 8, 1816	French mathematician Sophie Germain wins prestigious award.
January 8, 1870	The *Woman's Journal* premiers.
January 10–12, 1992	National Organization for Women celebrates 25th anniversary.
January 11, 1851	Taiping Rebellion in China.
January 11, 1921	American economist Juanita Kreps is born.
January 11, 1938	Frances Moulton becomes first woman to serve as U.S. bank president.
January 12, 1912	Bread and Roses strike begins.
January 14, 1970	United Airlines discontinues men-only executive flights.
January 15, 1952	Women curlers compete in New York.
January 15, 1968	The Jeanette Rankin Brigade demonstrates against the Vietnam War at the opening of the U.S. Congress.

January 17, 1996	Texas Democrat Barbara Jordan, former American congresswoman, dies.
January 18, 1212	Queen Tamara of Georgia dies.
January 18, 1777	Mary Katherine Goddard, printer, is commissioned to print Declaration of Independence.
January 19, 1856	African American slave Biddy Mason wins freedom in lawsuit.
January 20, 1479	Queen Isabella begins to create a united Spain with her husband Ferdinand of Aragon.
January 20, 1993	Maya Angelou reads poem at presidential inauguration.
January 20, 1996	German Leni Fischer elected president of Council of Europe's Parliamentary Assembly.
January 21, 1973	Supreme Court protects abortion rights with Roe v. Wade.
January 21, 1977	Patricia Roberts Harris becomes first woman to hold two U.S. Cabinet posts.
January 23, 1977	Juanita Kreps sworn in as U.S. secretary of commerce.
January 24, 1960	Ecclesiastical Council of the Catholic Church issues restrictions on women.
January 26, 1980	American runner Mary Decker sets record.
January 27, 1934	Edith Cresson, French premier, born.
January 28, 1908	First woman elected to American Academy of Arts and Letters.
January 28, 1986	American space shuttle Challenger explodes on take-off.
January 29, 1499	Catherine von Bora, future wife of Martin Luther, is born.
January 29, 1981	Jeane Kirkpatrick becomes permanent U.S. representative to the United Nations.
January 30, 1912	Pulitzer Prize-winning American historian Barbara Tuchman is born.

F E B R U A R Y

February 1, 1793	Society of Revolutionary Republican Women founded in Paris.
February 1, 1967	Establishment of Royal Commission on the Status of Women in Canada.
February 2, 1745	Birth of Hannah More, British religious writer.
February 2, 1922	American Sylvia Beach publishes James Joyce's *Ulysses* in Paris.
February 2, 1956	Tenley Albright wins Olympic Gold Medal in figure skating.
February 2, 1959	Indira Gandhi elected president of the Congress Party in India.
February 3, 1968	U.S. Equal Employment Opportunity Commission rules that gender is not a requirement to be a flight attendant.
February 4, 1921	Birth of American activist Betty Friedan.
February 4, 1987	National Women in Sports Day.
February 6, 1808	Revolutionary War veteran Anna Maria Lane granted pension.

February 7, 1867	Birth of Laura Ingalls Wilder, author of *Little House* series of books about life on American frontier.
February 7, 1952	Molecular biologist Rosalind Franklin makes significant contribution to discovery of DNA structure.
February 7, 1969	Jockey Diane Crump rides at parimutuel track.
February 8, 1587	Mary Stuart, forced to flee Scotland for England, is executed.
February 9, 1929	Birth of Nelle Pitcock Horlander, American unionist.
February 9, 1944	Birth of Alice Walker, African American writer.
February 10, 1967	National Organization for Women formally incorporated.
February 11, 1802	Lydia Maria Child, American author and abolitionist, is born.
February 12, 1930	Jennie Kelleher bowls perfect 300 game.
February 15, 1820	Birth of Susan B. Anthony, American social reformer and suffragist.
February 15, 1921	Suffrage monument by sculptor Adelaide Johnson unveiled.
February 15, 1953	Tenley Albright wins World Figure Skating championship.
February 16, 1982	Agatha Barbara becomes first woman president of Malta.
February 17, 1848	Birth of Louisa Lawson, founder of Australia's first feminist paper.
February 18, 1872	Mary Williams Dewson, American economist, is born.
February 18, 1931	Birth of American author Toni Morrison.
February 19, 1917	Birth of American author Carson McCullers.
February 19, 1976	Anne Armstrong sworn in as U.S. Ambassador to Court of St. James's.
February 20, 1972	Juanita Kreps becomes first woman director of the NYSE.
February 21, 1856	National Dress Reform Association established.
February 21, 1936	Birth of Barbara Jordan, American congresswoman.
February 22–23, 1967	NOW (National Organization for Women) creates chapter structure, task forces, and standing committees.
February 22, 1833	American author Rebecca Sophia Clarke (Sophie May) is born.
February 22, 1848	Revolution of 1848 breaks out in Paris.
February 22, 1969	Barbara Jo Rubin wins thoroughbred horse race.
February 23, 1787	Educator Emma Hart Willard is born.
February 23, 1890	Birth of Lotte Lyell, Australia's first woman film star.
February 25, 1907	American Playwright Mary Coyle Chase is born.
February 27, 1869	Birth of Alice Hamilton, authority on industrial diseases.
February 28, 1856	Birth of Elizabeth Glendower Evans, American labor organizer and reformer.
February 28, 1884	Birth of Emma Callaghan, Australian Aboriginal nurse and civil rights activist.

M A R C H

March 1, 1971	American lyricist Dorothy Fields elected to Songwriters' Hall of Fame.
March 1, 1973	Robyn Smith wins stakes horse race.
March 2, 1972	Women journalists enter men's dressing rooms in New York.
March 3, 1953	Clare Boothe Luce named American ambassador to Italy.
March 4, 1877	Birth of Mabel Edna Gillespie, American labor activist.
March 4, 1933	Frances Perkins appointed U.S. secretary of labor.
March 6, 1960	Switzerland's Parliament grants women voting rights in municipal elections.
March 6, 1052	Death of Emma, influential wife and mother of English kings.
March 7, 1938	Birth of Janet Guthrie, American race car driver.
March 8, 1702	Anne becomes Queen of England.
March 8, 1902	Louise Beavers, African American actress, is born.
March 10, 1975	Carla Anderson Hills named U.S. secretary of housing and urban development.
March 11–13, 1981	Women's collegiate swimming and diving.
March 11, 1915	Birth of Elinor Marshall Glenn, American trade unionist.
March 11, 1953	Oveta Culp Hobby appointed first U.S secretary of health, education, and welfare.
March 12, 1912	Juliette Gordon Low organizes first Girl Scout troup.
March 12, 1993	Janet Reno sworn in as attorney general of United States.
March 13, 1967	U.S. Senator Eugene McCarthy introduces the Equal Rights Amendment.
March 14, 1868	Birth of Emily Murphy, Canadian advocate of women's legal and property rights.
March 14, 1889	Marguerite de Angeli, award-winning American author/illustrator of children's books, is born.
March 17, 1969	Golda Meir becomes prime minister of Israel.
March 18–20, 1982	Women's collegiate basketball.
March 18, 1871	Paris Commune, revolutionary government of Paris, is formed.
March 19, 1868	American athlete Senda Berenson is born.
March 19, 1972	First women's collegiate basketball championship.
March 22, 1972	Equal Rights Amendment passes the Senate.
March 24, 1924	Birth of Bette Nesmith Graham, inventor of "Liquid Paper."
March 24, 1976	Isabel Perón unseated as Argentinian president.
March 25–27, 1982	Women's collegiate fencing.
March 25–27, 1982	Women's collegiate gymnastics.
March 25, 1347	St. Catherine of Siena, Italian mystic and author, is born.

March 25, 1911	Triangle Shirtwaist Company fire.
March 25, 1925	Birth of American author Flannery O'Connor.
March 25, 1934	Birth of Gloria Steinem, journalist and women's rights activist.
March 26–28, 1982	Women's collegiate basketball.
March 26, 1930	Birth of Sandra Day O'Connor, first woman justice of the U.S. Supreme Court.
March 26, 1981	Social Democrat Party founded in Great Britain.
March 28, 1515	Birth of Teresa of Ávila, Spanish nun and mystic.
March 28, 1920	*Shin Fujin Kyokai* (New Women's Association) established in Japan.
March 28, 1976	Krystyna Choynowski-Liskiewicz sails around world alone.
March 29, 1874	First lady Lou Henry Hoover is born.
March 29, 1911	Passage of Japan's Factory Law of 1911.

A P R I L

April 1, 1204	Eleanor of Aquitaine dies at 83.
April 1, 1872	Birth of Alessandra Kollontai, prominent woman in early Soviet Union.
April 1, 1919	Birth of Thelma Stovall, American trade unionist and public official.
April 1, 1931	Verne "Jackie" Mitchell, first woman to play major league baseball.
April 2, 1917	Jeannette Rankin, first woman to join U.S. House of Representatives.
April 2, 1935	Mary Hirsch, first licensed woman thoroughbred trainer.
April 3, 1200	Queen Cunegunde becomes a saint through her supposed celibacy.
April 3, 1870	Birth of Sara Conboy, American union leader.
April 4, 1896	First intercollegiate women's basketball game played.
April 4, 1928	Maya Angelou, African American poet and writer, is born.
April 4, 1981	Sue Brown coxes Oxford University crew.
April 5, 1888	Birth of Fannia Mary Cohn, union organizer, leader, and educator.
April 5, 1917	Some British Columbian women gain provincial vote.
April 5, 1989	Aung San Suu Kyi under house arrest in Myanmar.
April 5, 1992	National Organization for Women organizes march on Washington.
April 8, 1912	Birth of Norwegian skater Sonja Henie.
April 10, 1882	Frances Perkins, American public official, is born.
April 10, 1903	Birth of Clare Boothe Luce, American writer and public official.
April 12, 1861	Emma Edmonds enlists in Union Army, becomes successful spy.
April 12, 1919	Beverly Cleary, American children's author, is born.
April 12, 1938	Edith Summerskill elected to British Parliament.
April 13, 1892	Gladys Moncrieff, popular Australian actress, is born.
April 14, 1980	Jeanne Sauvé is Canada's first woman speaker of the house.

M A Y

May 9, 1967	American journalist Philippa Schuyler dies covering Vietnam War.
May 10, 1919	American congresswoman and governor Ella Tambussi Grasso is born.
May 11, 1970	Canadian House of Commons adjourns under pressure by abortion rights activists.
May 12, 1907	Birth of American actress Katharine Hepburn.
May 14, 1965	Frances Perkins, first woman presidential cabinet member, dies.
May 14, 1984	Jeanne Sauvé sworn in as Canada's first woman governor general.
May 16–23, 1982	Women's collegiate tennis.
May 16, 1929	American poet Adrienne Rich is born.
May 16, 1974	Martha Peterson is first woman elected to Exxon board.
May 17, 1718	Birth of Maria Agnesi, Italian mathematician.
May 17, 1915	American unionist Olga Madar is born.
May 17, 1917	Birth of playwright Lorraine Hansberry.
May 18, 1955	Mary McLeod Bethune dies.
May 19, 1536	Henry VIII has his wife Anne Boleyn beheaded.
May 19, 1861	Birth of Australian soprano Nellie Melba.
May 19, 1879	Nancy Astor, first woman member of parliament in Great Britain, is born.
May 19, 1994	Death of Jacqueline Kennedy Onassis.
May 20, 1782	Deborah Sampson Gannett enlists in the U.S. army.
May 22–23, 1982	Women's collegiate lacrosse.
May 22, 1932	Amelia Earhart is first woman to pilot across Atlantic Ocean.
May 22, 1996	Women military officers press for more combat roles.
May 23, 1826	Frances Fuller Victor, who helps to define the American West, is born.
May 23, 1910	Margaret Wise Brown, author of classic children's stories, is born.
May 25–29, 1982	Women's collegiate golf.
May 25–29, 1982	Women's collegiate outdoor track.
May 26, 1689	Mary Wortley Montagu, literary correspondent, is born.
May 27–30, 1982	Women's collegiate softball.
May 27, 1936	Sally Stearns, coxswain of men's college crew.
May 27, 1971	Girls in New York compete on boys' teams.
May 28, 1963	Equal Pay Act passed in U.S.
May 28, 1978	Janet Guthrie, first woman to complete Indianapolis 500.
May 28, 1980	West Point Military Academy graduates first women.
May 29, 1677	Treaty of Middle Plantation is endorsed.
May 29, 1851	African American orator Sojourner Truth gives speech on discrimination.
May 29, 1949	Wilson Sporting Goods sponsors Ladies Professional Golf Association.
May 30, 1431	Joan of Arc, savior of France, is burned at the stake.

J U N E

June 1, 1310	Marguerite Porete, author of *The Mirror of Simple Souls*, executed for heresy.
June 1, 1660	Mary Barrett Dyer executed for her Quaker beliefs.
June 1, 1880	Birth of Jeannette Rankin, first woman elected to U.S. house of representatives.
June 1, 1970	Maggie Kuhn founds Gray Panthers.
June 4, 1811	Harriet Beecher Stowe, author of *Uncle Tom's Cabin*, is born.
June 4, 1857	Laskshmi Bai of India renounces alliance to British crown.
June 4, 1873	Birth of Constance Applebee, founder of first periodical about women's sports.
June 7, 1943	Nikki Giovanni, African American poet, is born.
June 8, 1929	Margaret Bondfield, first woman cabinet minister in Great Britain.
June 8, 1991	Julie Krone rides in Belmont Stakes.
June 10, 1895	African American actress Hattie McDaniel is born.
June 10, 1922	American actress and singer Judy Garland is born.
June 10, 1940	Margaret Chase Smith joins U.S. house of representatives.
June 11, 1920	African American pianist and actress Hazel Scott is born.
June 12, 1974	Girls can play Little League Baseball.
June 12, 918	Death of Aethelflaed, who repels Viking forces and helps unify England.
June 13, 1970	Chi Cheng runs 100 yards in ten seconds.
June 14, 1907	Limited suffrage extended to women in Norway.
June 15, 1215	The Magna Carta signed at Runnymede, England.
June 15, 1943	Bolton Bill signed into law.
June 16–19, 1963	Cosmonaut Valentina Tereshkova orbits the earth.
June 16, 1917	American publisher Katharine Graham is born.
June 17, 1782	Last regular execution for witchcraft in Western Europe.
June 18, 1900	American author Laura Zametkin Hobson is born.
June 18–24, 1983	Astronaut Sally Ride is first American woman in space.
June 19, 1656	New England authorities execute Anne Hibbins as a witch.
June 19, 1940	American cartoonist Dale Messick publishes "Brenda Starr."
June 21, 1953	Benazir Bhutto, future prime minister of Pakistan, is born.
June 22, 1813	Laura Secord provides vital information to British Army.
June 22, 1876	Birth of French fashion designer Madeleine Vionnet, originator of bias cut.
June 23, 1931	Lili de Alvarez plays tennis at Wimbledon in shorts.
June 23, 1940	Birth of Wilma Rudolph, champion African American runner.
June 23, 1972	Title IX becomes law.

June 25, 1291	Death of Eleanor of Provence, queen of England.
June 26, 1839	Birth of Emma Miller, Australian suffragist.
June 26, 1881	American rural educator Jessie Field Shambaugh is born.
June 26, 1914	Birth of Mildred "Babe" Didrikson Zaharias, American athlete.
June 29, 1966	National Organization for Women (NOW) founded.
June 30, 1917	Birth of Lena Horne, African American entertainer.
June 30, 1936	Novel about the U.S. Civil War, *Gone With the Wind,* is published.
June 30, 1971	Jockey Mary Bacon posts 100th victory.

J U L Y

July 1, 1553	Lady Jane Grey serves as queen of England for nine days.
July 1, 1793	Charlotte Corday assassinates Jacobin leader Jean Paul Marat.
July 1, 1916	Birth of Olivia deHavilland, British-born Hollywood actress.
July 1, 1994	Judith Rodin becomes president of the University of Pennsylvania.
July 2, 1898	Lizzie Arlington is first American woman to sign baseball contract.
July 2, 1963	Newsday publisher Alicia Patterson dies.
July 3, 1941	Eleanor Dudley is national intercollegiate golf champion.
July 5, 1992	Muriel Siebert is Veuve Clicquot Business Woman of the Year.
July 6, 1930	Aviator Amelia Earhart sets speed record.
July 7, 1915	Birth of Margaret Walker, African American author.
July 8, 1775	Mary Draper Ingles abducted by Shawnees.
July 8, 1964	Dr. Mary Calderone founds the Sex Information and Education Council of the United States.
July 10, 1706	Virginia witchcraft trial takes place in Lynnhaven River.
July 10, 1804	Birth of Emma Smith, active in Mormon Church.
July 10, 1971	National Women's Political Caucus formed.
July 12, 1976	Barbara Jordan delivers keynote address at Democratic Convention.
July 13–18, 1964	Margaret Chase Smith attempts to win presidential nomination.
July 13, 1992	Global Forum of Women held in Dublin, Ireland.
July 15, 1991	Sandra Ortiz-Del Valle officiates men's professional basketball game.
July 16, 1971	Jeanne Holm, first woman U.S. Air Force general.
July 18, 1804	Elizabeth Gould, English artist of Australian fauna, is born.
July 19, 1848	Women's Rights Convention in Seneca Falls, New York.
July 19, 1973	U.S. Tennis Association announces men and women will win equal prize money.
July 19, 1984	Geraldine Ferraro nominated as vice-presidential candidate.
July 21, 1979	National Women's Hall of Fame dedicated.

July 24, 1898	Birth of American aviator Amelia Earhart, first woman to fly across Atlantic Ocean.
July 24, 1920	Birth of Bella Abzug, American feminist and congresswoman.
July 26, 1960	Sirimavo Bandaranaike becomes prime minister of Ceylon (present-day Sri Lanka).
July 26, 1971	Photographer Diane Arbus dies.
July 27, 1775	Second Continental Congress authorizes army medical department with female nurses and matrons.
July 27, 1828	Ranavalona I of Madagascar launches coup d'etat, unleashing mass genocide.
July 27, 1930	British politician Shirley Williams is born.
July 28, 1609	Dutch artist Judith Leyster is born.
July 28, 1866	Birth of Beatrix Potter, English writer and illustrator for children.
July 28, 1929	Birth of Jacqueline Kennedy Onassis.
July 29, 1600	Anna Pappenheimer and her family executed for witchcraft.
July 29, 1937	Amelia Earhart presumed lost at sea.
July 29, 1961	American runner Wilma Rudolph sets record.
July 29, 1979	Susan B. Anthony one-dollar coin issued by U.S. government.
July 29, 1981	Lady Diana Spencer marries Britain's Prince of Wales.
July 30, 1848	Birth of Ellis Rowan, painter of Australian flora and fauna.
July 31, 1991	U.S. Senate approves combat positions for women pilots.

A U G U S T

August 1, 1912	First workers' organization founded in Japan.
August 1, 1988	Phyllis Holmes becomes president of National Association of Intercollegiate Athletics.
August 3, 1962	Eugenie Moore Anderson appointed ambassador to Bulgaria.
August 3, 1993	Ruth Bader Ginsburg appointed to Supreme Court.
August 5, 1963	Katharine Graham becomes president of Washington Post Company.
August 6, 1833	Saint-Simonian Claire Démar commits suicide.
August 8, 1810	Birth of Mary Gove Nichols, American reformer for women's health.
August 9, 1995	American Bar Association elects Roberta Cooper Ramo president.
August 10, 1858	Birth of Anna J. Cooper, African American educator and feminist.
August 10, 1970	Equal Rights Amendment to the U.S. Constitution passes one house of Congress.
August 13, 1818	Women's rights advocate Lucy Stone is born.
August 13, 1924	Birth of Monica Clare, Australian aboriginal political activist.

August 15, 1945	Future Bangladesh Prime Minister Khaleda Begum is born.
August 15, 1970	Pat Palinkas, first woman to play professional football.
August 16, 1947	First African American woman senator Carol Moseley Braun is born.
August 17, 1837	Birth of Charlotte L. Forten-Grimké.
August 19, 1858	English writer Edith Nesbit is born.
August 19, 1883	Birth of Gabrielle (Coco) Chanel, French fashion designer.
August 22, 1919	French swindler Marthe Hanau buys financial magazine.
August 24, 1932	Amelia Earhart sets woman's transcontinental speed record.
August 25, 1847	Birth of Elizabeth Flynn Rodgers, first woman member of Knights of Labor.
August 25, 1927	Althea Gibson, African American tennis and golf pro, is born.
August 26, 1970	National Women's Strike for Equality staged on 50th anniversary of Nineteenth Amendment.
August 26, 1973	Mary Boitano wins the Dipsea Race.
August 27, 1971	Photographer Margaret Bourke-White dies.
August 28, 1950	African American Althea Gibson plays in major tennis tournament.
August 28, 1952	Birth of American poet laureate Rita Dove.
August 29, 1915	Birth of Swedish actress Ingrid Bergman.
August 30, 1909	Birth of Virginia Lee Burton, author/illustrator of children's books.
August 30, 1979	Ann Meyers signs a contract to play in National Basketball Association.

SEPTEMBER

September 1, 1804	French author George Sand is born.
September 1, 1946	First U.S. Women's Open Golf Tournament.
September 3, 1849	Birth of Maine author Sarah Orne Jewett.
September 4–15,1995	International Women's Conference draws thousands to Beijing, China.
September 4, 1937	First U.S. Women's Bicycling Championship.
September 6, 1800	Birth of Catharine Beecher, promoter of the teaching profession in America.
September 6, 1839	French socialist Louise-Léonier Rouzade is born.
September 6, 1966	Birth control advocate Margaret Sanger dies.
September 6, 1991	Comic-strip character, Blondie, takes a job outside the home.
September 7, 1903	Margaret Dorothea Landon, American author, is born.
September 7, 1953	Maureen Connolly wins the grand slam of tennis.
September 7, 1955	Women granted suffrage in Peru.
September 10, 1740	Birth of Mary Willing Byrd, manager of Westover Plantation.
September 10, 1886	American writer Hilda Doolittle, known as H.D., is born.

September 10, 1890   Elsa Schiaparelli, French fashion designer, is born in Italy.

September 12, 1590   Maria de Zayas, popular Spanish novelist, is born.

September 14, 1883   Margaret Higgins Sanger, founder of Planned Parenthood, is born.

September 15, 1950   War correspondent Marguerite Higgins joins U.S. Marine amphibious landing at Inchon, Korea.

September 18, 1924   Judith Hart, member of British Parliament, is born.

September 23, 1970   Virginia Slims Tennis Tournament, first professional tournament for women, is organized.

September 24, 1825   Birth of Frances E. W. Harper, African American literary figure, abolitionist, and feminist.

September 25, 1960   Emily Post, etiquette expert, dies.

September 25, 1978   Major league baseball cannot bar women sportswriters from locker rooms.

September 25, 1981   Sandra Day O'Connor becomes first woman justice of U.S. Supreme Court.

September 26, 1875   Mary Dreier, supporter of New York Women's Trade Union League, is born.

September 27, 1760   School for African American children opens in colonial Virginia.

September 28, 1881   Birth of Eleanora Sears, American sportswoman.

September 29, 1977   Eva Shain officiates heavyweight championship fight.

O C T O B E R

October 1, 1847   Comet named after woman for first time.

October 1, 1847   English radical and theosophist Annie Besant is born.

October 1, 1930   Gertrude Hickman Thompson, first woman to head U.S. Railroad board of directors.

October 2, 1978   Beverly Johnson scales peak, El Capitan.

October 2, 1991   American jockey Julie Krone ranks in top three in New York.

October 3, 1771   Christiana Campbell's Williamsburg Tavern serves famous patrons.

October 3, 1836   Cornerstone of first building of Mount Holyoke Seminary is laid.

October 5, 1789   Women's march on Versailles changes course of French Revolution.

October 6, 1565   Marie de Gournay, the French "Minerva," is born.

October 6, 1905   American tennis player Helen Wills Moody is born.

October 8, 1991   Allegations of sexual harassment force reopening of U.S. Senate hearings on Supreme Court nominee.

October 9, 1890   Birth of American evangelist Aimee Semple McPherson.

October 11, 1884   Eleanor Roosevelt, who revolutionizes role of the political wife, is born.

October 11, 1963   Report issued by President's Commission on the Status of Women.

October 12, 1537	Jane Seymour bears male heir for King Henry VIII.
October 12, 1850	Opening lectures at Female Medical College of Pennsylvania.
October 12, 1949	Eugenie Moore Anderson becomes U.S. Ambassador.
October 13, 1925	Birth of Margaret Thatcher, Britain's first woman prime minister.
October 13, 1967	U.S. Executive Order prohibits sex discrimination in government.
October 14, 1879	Birth of Australian author Stella Miles Franklin.
October 16, 1793	Queen Marie Antoinette guillotined in France.
October 18, 1881	Canadian doctor Elizabeth Bagshaw, birth control advocate, is born.
October 18, 1929	Judicial committee of the privy council in England declares Canadian women "persons."
October 18, 1958	Iolanda Balas clears six feet in high jump.
October 23, 1906	Birth of English swimmer Gertrude Ederle.
October 23, 1947	United States Women's Curling Association founded.
October 25, 1771	Death of Catherine Kaidyee Blaikley, Williamsburg midwife.
October 25, 1941	American novelist Anne Tyler is born.
October 26, 1947	Birth of Hillary Rodham Clinton.
October 27, 1932	Sylvia Plath, American author and poet, is born.
October 28, 1599	Birth of Sister de L'Incarnation, religious educator in Quebec.
October 31, 1517	Protestant Reformation begins, but does not immediately change attitudes toward women.
October 31, 1825	Catherine Spence, "The Grand Old Woman of Australia," is born.
October 31, 1896	Birth of Ethel Waters, African American singer and actress.
October 31, 1984	Assassination of Indira Gandhi, prime minister of India.

NOVEMBER

November 1, 1215	Fourth lateran council decrees marriage a sacrament.
November 1, 1944	Appalachian author Lee Marshall Smith is born.
November 1, 990	Birth of Gisela, German queen.
November 3, 1793	French feminist Olympe de Gouges executed for treason.
November 3, 1970	Bella Abzug elected to U.S. Congress.
November 4, 1965	American journalist Dickey Chapelle dies in combat in Vietnam.
November 4, 1965	Margaret Laneive "Lee" Breedlove sets women's land speed record.
November 7, 1845	*The Voice of Industry* becomes vehicle for mill workers to express dissatisfaction.
November 8, 1972	Pat Schroeder wins seat in U.S. Congress.
November 9, 1922	Birth of African American actress Dorothy Dandridge.
November 11, 1991	Memorial to U.S. women who died in Vietnam is approved.

November 12, 1815	Birth of Elizabeth Cady Stanton, American reformer and suffragist.
November 12, 1994	American runner Wilma Rudolph dies.
November 13, 1974	Plutonium plant worker Karen Silkwood dies under mysterious circumstances.
November 14, 1777	Ann Neill advertises opening of her general store in Virginia.
November 16, 1776	Margaret "Molly" Corbin takes wounded husband's place in battle.
November 19, 1926	Birth of Jeane Kirkpatrick, American political thinker.
November 21, 1981	National Collegiate Athletic Association sponsors first women's championships.
November 22, 1909	"The Uprising of the 20,000" begins in New York City.
November 23, 1981	Women's collegiate cross country running.
November 24, 1849	Birth of children's author Frances Hodgson Burnett.
November 24, 1921	Birth of Yochiko Uchida, Japanese American author.
November 26, 1832	American surgeon Mary Edwards Walker is born.
November 29, 1832	American author Louisa May Alcott is born.
November 30, 1485	Renaissance poet Veronica Gambara, who presides over flourishing court, is born.
November 30, 1874	Birth of Canadian novelist Lucy Maud Montgomery, creator of *Anne of Green Gables* stories.

D E C E M B E R

December 1, 1955	Bus boycott in Montgomery, Alabama.
December 2, 1855	Eliza Clark Garrett's will establishes Garrett Biblical Institute.
December 3, 1910	Australian Freda du Faur, first woman to climb Mount Cook.
December 4, 1791	Birth of Jane Franklin, founder of Scientific Institutions in Australia.
December 7, 1904	Con woman Cassie Chadwick arrested.
December 8, 1573	Sophia Brahe assists in calculation of lunar eclipse.
December 9, 1978	Women's Professional Basketball League holds first game.
December 10, 1830	Birth of American poet Emily Dickinson.
December 10, 1948	Universal Declaration of Human Rights passes in United Nations' General Assembly.
December 10, 1963	Maria Goeppert-Mayer wins Nobel Prize for Physics.
December 11, 1542	Mary, future queen of Scots, is born.
December 14, 1897	Birth of Margaret Chase Smith, U.S. congresswoman.
December 14, 1961	Establishment of President's Commission on the Status of Women.
December 14, 1970	National Press Club in Washington, D.C., admits women.
December 14, 1985	Wilma P. Mankiller becomes chief of Cherokee Nation.

December 16, 1775	Birth of Jane Austen, English novelist.
December 16, 1901	American anthropologist Margaret Mead is born.
December 18–19, 1981	Women's collegiate volleyball.
December 18, 1972	Anne Armstrong named counselor to U.S. president.
December 19, 1906	American labor activist Esther Peterson is born.
December 22, 1789	American missionary Ann Hasseltine Judson is born.
December 23, 1523	Katherine Shütz marries priest, becomes Lutheran reformer.
December 25, 1870	Birth of Helena Rubinstein, creator of modern cosmetics industry.
December 25, 1992	Christine Janin celebrates achievement on the Summit of Anoncagua.
December 27, 1913	Canadian author Elizabeth Smart is born.
December 27, 1927	Birth of Anne Armstrong, U.S. Republican Party leader.
December 28, 1961	Edith Wilson dies.
December 30, 1607	Native American Pocahontas saves life of colonist John Smith.
December 30, 1805	Birth of Marie d'Agoult, great French author known as Daniel Stern.
December 30, 1924	Birth of Shirley Chisholm, first African American congresswoman.
December 31, 1885	Muriel Heagney, Australian advocate of equal pay for women, is born.

SUBJECT INDEX